TENNESSEE
CIVIL WAR
MONUMENTS

TENNESSEE
CIVIL WAR MONUMENTS

An Illustrated Field Guide

TIMOTHY S. SEDORE

Indiana University Press

This book is a publication of

Indiana University Press
Office of Scholarly Publishing
Herman B Wells Library 350
1320 East 10th Street
Bloomington, Indiana 47405 USA

iupress.indiana.edu

Manufactured in the United States of America

Library of Congress Cataloging-in-Publication Data

Names: Sedore, Timothy S. (Timothy Stephen), author.
Title: Tennessee Civil War monuments : an illustrated field guide / Timothy S. Sedore.
Description: Bloomington, Indiana : Indiana University Press,
    [2020] | Includes bibliographical references and index.
Identifiers: LCCN 2019020824 (print) | LCCN 2019021899 (ebook) | ISBN 9780253045614
    (ebook) | ISBN 9780253045645 (alk. paper) | ISBN 9780253045607 (alk. paper)
Subjects: LCSH: Tennessee—History—Civil War, 1861-1865—Monuments—Guidebooks.
    | Confederate States of America—Monuments—Guidebooks. | Monuments—
    Tennessee—Guidebooks. | Monuments—Southern States—Guidebooks. |
    Soldiers' monuments—Tennessee—Guidebooks. | Soldiers' monuments—
    Southern States—Guidebooks. | War memorials—Tennessee—Guidebooks. |
    War memorials—Southern States—Guidebooks. | United States—History—Civil
    War, 1861-1865—Monuments—Guidebooks. | Collective memory—Tennessee.
Classification: LCC F437 (ebook) | LCC F437 .S43 2020 (print) | DDC 973.7/6—dc23
LC record available at https://lccn.loc.gov/2019020824

1 2 3 4 5   25 24 23 22 21 20

Pages ii and iii: Union common soldier, monument to the 77th Pennsylvania
Volunteer Infantry on the Shiloh battlefield (Chapter 1 [1.10.4]), erected 1902.

Pages xviii and 1: The Confederate common soldier at Gallatin,
Tennessee (Chapter 4 [4.23.1]), erected 1903.

Dedicated to my wife and fellow traveler,
Patricia
Faith, hope, love.

Dedicated to my parents,
Michael and Annie M. Sedore,
from the North and from the South, respectively,
who formed a union that lasted fifty-six years.

In memory of Michael Sedore's service,
US Army Air Force, 1941–1945.

Contents

List of Maps   viii
Preface   x
Acknowledgments   xiv
List of Abbreviations   xvii

Introduction   2

1. Shiloh National Military Park: "Witness and Testimony"   38

2. Chattanooga, Including Chickamauga and Chattanooga
   National Military Park: "Nov. 25, 1863 5 P.M."   144

3. East Tennessee: The "Loyal and True"   228

   Sullivan County   231
   Washington County   233
   Greene County   236
   Unicoi County   244
   Cocke County   246
   Claiborne County   247
   Hamblen County   248
   Knox County, Including Knoxville   251
   Monroe County   263
   Polk County   263
   Bradley County   264
   Bledsoe County   270

4. Middle Tennessee: "Valorous Gray, Glorious Blue"   272

   Cumberland County   275
   Van Buren County   276
   Warren County   276
   Smith County   279
   DeKalb County   279
   Grundy County   282
   Franklin County   283
   Lincoln County   287
   Wayne County   291
   Moore County   291
   Coffee County   292

Bedford County   300
Cannon County   304
Marshall County   307
Giles County   309
Maury County   314
Williamson County, Including the Franklin Battlefield   318
Rutherford County, Including Murfreesboro and
    Stones River National Battlefield   337
Wilson County   348
Trousdale County   351
Macon County   353
Davidson County   353
Sumner County   368
Robertson County   370
Montgomery County   370
Stewart County, Including Fort Donelson National Military Park   373
Dickson County   377

5. West Tennessee: "History Is an Impartial Witness"   378
Benton County   381
Henry County   381
Weakley County   384
Obion County   386
Dyer County   388
Gibson County   393
Lake County   397
Tipton County   398
Henderson County   401
Decatur County   403
Madison County   404
Haywood County   409
Hardin County   410
Hardeman County   411
Shelby County, Including Memphis   414
McNairy County   423
Chester County   424

6. Conclusion   427

Selected Sources   434
Index   438

Maps

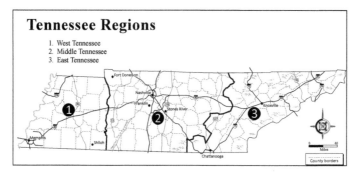

Map 1. Regions of Tennessee

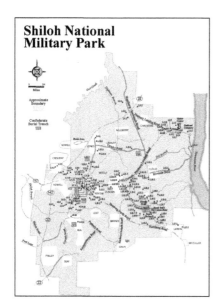

Map 2. The Shiloh Battlefield

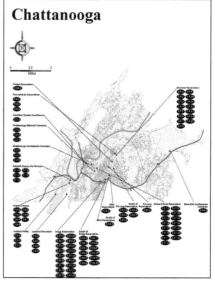

Map 3. Chattanooga and Hamilton County

Map 4.
East Tennessee

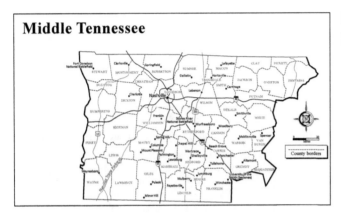

Map 5.
Middle Tennessee

Map 6. West Tennessee

Preface

FIVE SUMMERS OF TRAVEL across the Tennessee landscape led to the field research for this book—the words, images, and settings of some four hundred outdoor Civil War battlefield monuments, courthouse and town monuments, and cemetery and city monuments, including obelisks, statues, arches, shafts, reliefs, stelae, columns, and pyramids.

Five summers may seem like a long time for a project of this scale; I recognize that I might have done this work more quickly or efficiently. However, as a full-time professor in New York—some six hundred miles from Bristol, Tennessee, and one thousand miles from Memphis—I did not have the leisure to linger in Tennessee and complete this task in one or two visits. I took a more measured approach. Between each summer's venture, I examined the texts of these monuments one by one, on a day-to-day basis. The interpretation of the monuments was written by hand—free hand—from successive drafts, during the fall, winter, and spring of the intervening academic years, as time permitted. Much of the work was done while commuting via the Long Island Railroad and New York City subway to my office and teaching position. I took into consideration the rhetoric and aesthetics of inscription, adornment, materials, statuary, images, iconography, setting, location, and other contextual elements. My goal was to posit a critical analysis of a heretofore uncollected canon of multifarious verbal, imagistic, and iconographic American rhetoric.

I systematically covered the Tennessee landscape: I walked the ground where each monument stands; I examined the monuments' texts in person—in situ. I then wrote this book in order to understand the Civil War monument as a text—words, images, and context. The idea of monuments as texts may suggest to readers that the medium of monumentation is bloodless, abstract. For my part, the experience I had with the words and images of Civil War monumentation on the sites on which they were erected brought me as close to the events of the war and the wartime generation as a mortal human in the twenty-first century can obtain.

In fact, the dynamics of American Civil War monuments resonate with life in the twenty-first century in ways that should not be surprising. In a sense, the conflicts that led to the war are still incendiary, like an explosive device left over from a previous war that remains undetonated. Of course the military conflict is over, and the war changed many things. It was not fought in vain. It formally ended slavery. It freed many. It did not resolve all of the issues that led to it, however, and it came at a cost that is still being paid. The war resulted in an estimated 618,000 deaths. Men were killed, disabled, or died of disease on a regular basis. It was a disaster on the scale of the world wars of the twentieth century. Indeed, parallels to the American Civil War may be discerned from a letter written by the French novelist Francois Maurial to the artist Jacque Emile Blanche in July 1918, just months before the end of World War I. The same words might have been written in Richmond or New York in 1865: "We are all in the same boat," he observed, "it is an era organized for death, and those who escape it for reasons of age or infirmity can no longer bring order to their lives nor peace to their thoughts."

The monument archive presented here may seem static, the medium of monumentation may seem inert, but it is not. The monuments in this book are trans-liminal: they cross horizons between life and death, as well as between the past and the present.

By coincidence, I completed the field research for this book on August 9, 2017, just one day before violence erupted near the statue of Confederate general Robert E. Lee in Charlottesville, Virginia. White nationalists in Charlottesville protested the city's plan to remove the statue; counterdemonstrators opposed them. The event descended into violence, resulting in the death of a counter-demonstrator and two state troopers. Four Confederate statues had already been removed from public sites in New Orleans, Louisiana, in May 2017. Four Confederate statues were removed from public sites in Baltimore, Maryland, later that month. Also in August 2017, administrators at Bronx Community College, the City University of New York, arranged to remove busts of Robert E. Lee and Thomas J. "Stonewall" Jackson from the Hall of Fame. In December, city officials arranged for the statues of Jefferson Davis and Nathan Bedford Forrest to be removed in Memphis.

I do not know what the future holds for this medium of commemoration, but this monumentation archive is current and accurate as of 2018—153 years after the war's end. Monuments seem staid and stable, but the conflict they commemorate still inflames public feelings. We should wish that the dead could rest, that their graves would be undisturbed, but this may not be the case. Looking forward, how future generations judge this subject will, of course, be their privilege and responsibility. Looking back, as I note in other books I have written on this subject, I cannot claim to know how readers whose ancestors were slaves read monuments, nor can I claim to speak for those whose ances-tors fought for the Confederacy or put up monuments and statuary. However, I can testify that indifference to the Civil War monument seemed to prevail when I did this research in Virginia, Tennessee, and Mississippi. In the years that were required to personally visit these sites, I attracted scant notice or curiosity from local residents, no matter how long it took to photograph a monument, transcribe an inscription, or study it on site. I note this only to point out that I was as much unnoticed as the monuments themselves were. They attracted no more attention than the landscaping, the architecture of ad-jacent buildings, or the hundreds of other war memorials at the sites I studied. I never saw any members of the United Daughters of the Confederacy (UDC) or Sons of Confederate Veterans (SCV) at any cemeteries I researched, nor did I see more than perhaps a score of visitors.

Ultimately, it may not matter what the monument makers were trying to express. Many courthouse monuments were erected to commemorate veterans' service, in the same way that monuments were erected to commemorate the servicemen and servicewomen of World War I, World War II, the Korean War, the Vietnam War, and the Gulf wars. It should also be noted that many Confederate cemetery monuments are decidedly focused on mourning rather than politics, much as many veterans' monuments of other American wars are. Politics is one thing; commemoration another. "Rest in peace, Thy Warfare is over" is a common benediction. However, the war the soldiers served in is still controversial.

Union general Ulysses S. Grant justly declared that "the war is over" at Appomattox in 1865. He exhibited a generosity that might not have been expected from the victor of a bloody conflict when he declared that "the rebels"— the enemy—"are our countrymen again." The military conflict was indeed over, and, politically speaking, the country was reunited, the sacrifices were not in vain. However, the war continues to have a grip on the American soul. Civil War monuments symbolize all the drama associated with life, death, race, violence, passion, prejudice, incompetence, genius, sublime sacrifice, profound callousness, and all the complexity of military and political maneuvers. The war exploded unexpectedly, it raged longer than most could imagine, and it subsided into quiescence, but the ashes can still be stirred into conflagration.

Timothy S. Sedore
Pennsylvania

Acknowledgments

THE AUTHOR GRATEFULLY ACKNOWLEDGES the support, in the form of grants, of the Research Foundation of The City University of New York during the course of this project. In addition, a sabbatical leave to work on this project was granted by Bronx Community College, CUNY. I am especially grateful to my colleagues in the English Department at BCC for their initial support of my sabbatical leave for this project.

The editor at Indiana University Press, Ashley Runyon, deserves special mention for her support, as does John Coski, of the American Civil War Museum in Richmond, Virginia. Sylvia Rodrigue, editor at Southern Illinois University Press, was notably supportive and encouraging for the first book of this type, on Virginia monuments, and my colleagues, June Hadden Hobbs and Elizabethada Wright, encouraged this work at an early stage.

I take additional pleasure in acknowledging the assistance of the following institutions, groups, and individuals. At Andrew Johnson National Historic Site, Tony Greer. At Chickamauga and Chattanooga National Military Park, James Ogden, Anton Heinlein, and Jim Hyatt. At Fort Donelson National Battlefield, Doug Richardson. At Shiloh National Military Park: Timothy Arnold, Ashley Berry, Joe Davis, Amanda Martin, Chris Mekow, Heather Smedley, and Stacy Allen. At Stones River National Battlefield: Amanda Magera, Jim Lewis, and Gib Backlund. At Oaklands Historic House Museum, Murfreesboro, Raina van Setter.

Regarding the Davis Bridge battlefield and the courthouse monument at Bolivar, Herbert Wood; at Nashville Fort Negley Visitors Center and Park, Tracy Harris and Krista Castillo; regarding the McGavock Cemetery, Franklin, Timothy Burgess; regarding the Mississippi monument on the Shiloh battlefield, Kim Sessums; regarding Mt. Olivet Cemetery, Barbara Buchanan Parsons, President, Tennessee Division of the UDC; at Paris, Julie Wilson of the Paris Chapter 2521 of the UDC; at Manchester, Johnnie Turner of the Capt. Calvin C. Brewer Chapter No. 2505; at Trousdale Place, Gallatin, Andrea Hassell Koons, Clark Chapter No. 13, UDC; at the McClung Museum of Natural History and Culture, University of Tennessee, Knoxville, Joan Lynsky Marke; at the Knox County Public Library System, Steve Cotham.

I extend thanks to Joe Edgette and Richard Sauers for their invitations to give several papers on this subject at successive conferences of the panels they chair: the Death in American Culture panel of the Mid-Atlantic Popular & American Culture Association (MAPACA) and the Cemeteries and Gravemarkers Area of the Popular Culture Association (PCA). I extend thanks to attendees and fellow panelists at these sessions. Some of the ideas presented in this book were also presented at Civil War Round Tables, including the New York Civil War Round Table, the North Shore Civil Round Table, the Richmond Civil War Round Table, the Shenandoah Valley Civil War Round Table, the Civil War Round Table of Eastern Pennsylvania, and the Bucks County Civil War Round Table.

In the quest to describe, photograph, document, and reflect upon four hundred monuments in Tennessee, many Tennesseans offered directions, sometimes at crucial crossroads, sometimes to obscure sites, with failing light at the end of a day's travels. Of particular note: Danny Cheshier of Bolivar; Robin Jackson of Chapel Hill; Carol Price of Woodbury; Janet Rose of Pulaski; and Officer Perry of the Covington Police Department.

As I noted in my book on Mississippi's Civil War monuments, I would be remiss if I did not acknowledge that many persons made this book possible by erecting, dedicating, and conserving the archive of public monuments presented here. That archive, in turn, is an acknowledgement of the service and sacrifice of the wartime generation.

As part of the research that led to this book, I visited the cities, towns, and farms where the wartime generation lived. I often found myself walking where the wartime generation walked or marched or fought. I visited their graves, and I read the correspondence and memoirs they left behind. The wartime generation had all the frailty and failings that afflict every generation. However, I also admired many of them for their strength of character, courage, sacrifice, and integrity. In the time it took to write this book, I came to know some of them as well as I do my students or even members of my family. Above all individuals or institutions, it was my spouse, Patricia Radecki, who set an example of fortitude by traveling the American landscape with me over the course of the several years and several thousand miles required to do the fieldwork for this book. Patricia was also a pivotal source of moral support during the writing. The challenge of doing this work deepened the bond between us—to her credit—and, in fact, she made this book possible.

Abbreviations

BR   Business route
CR   County route
GAR   Grand Army of the Republic
CSA   Confederate States of America
SCV   Sons of Confederate Veterans
UDC   United Daughters of the Confederacy
TR   Tennessee state route
VI   Volunteer Infantry
Vol.   Volunteer

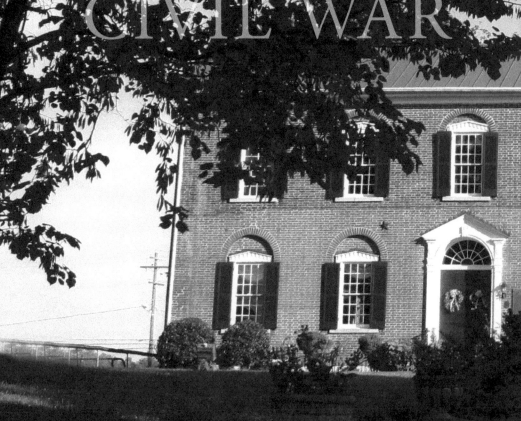

TENN
CIVIL WAR

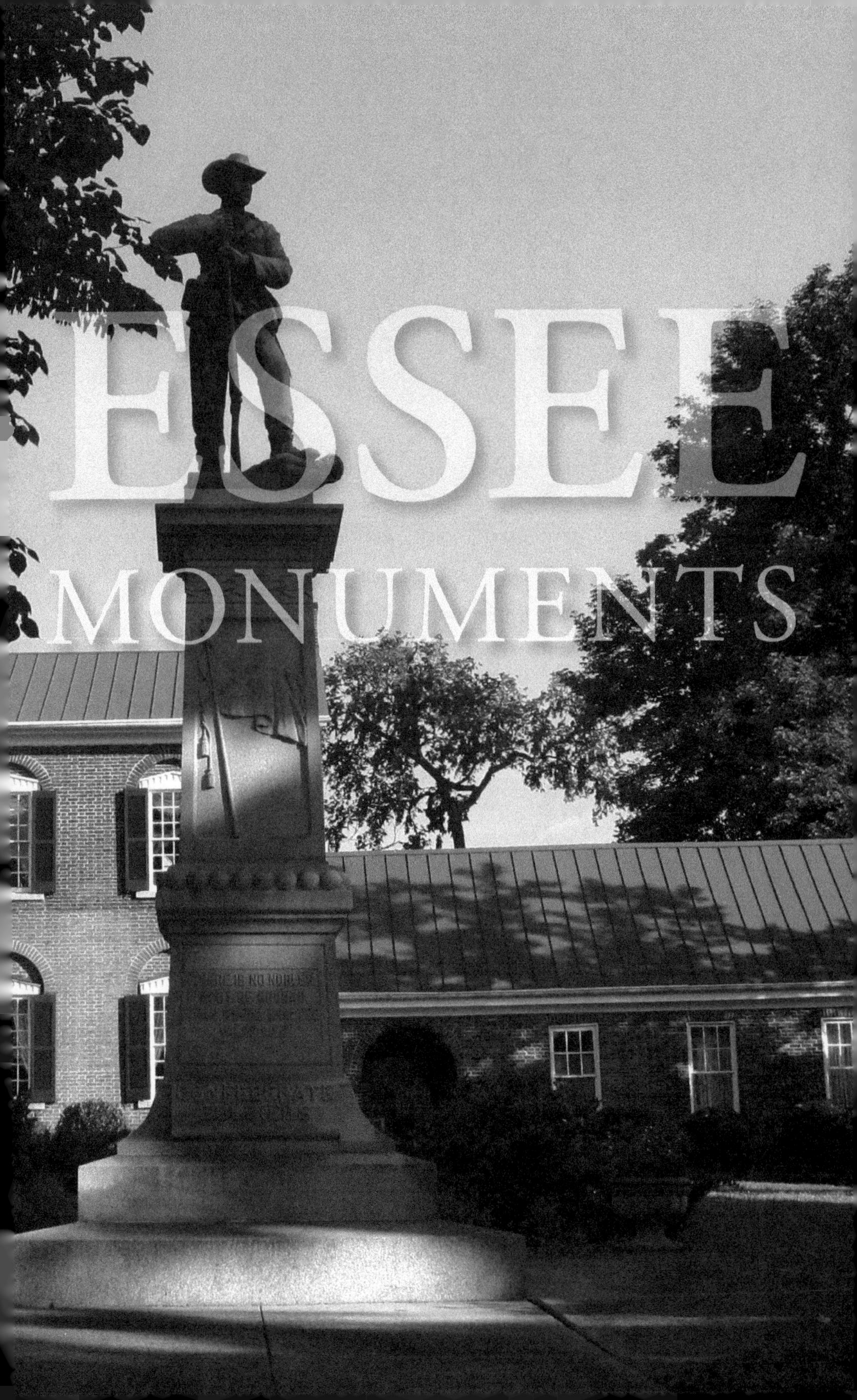
ESSE
MONUMENTS

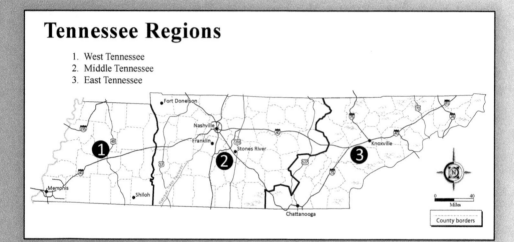

Tennessee Regions

1. West Tennessee
2. Middle Tennessee
3. East Tennessee

INTRODUCTION

THIS BOOK is a commentary and field guide to American Civil War monuments at outdoor locations in Tennessee.[1] By monuments I refer to the array of bronze or granite or marble commemorations erected by local or Northern and Southern state governments, and women's or veterans' or sons of veterans' groups. Several hundred monuments stand in this state: obelisks, statues, shafts, reliefs, stelae, columns, and pyramids have been erected. They range from Bristol on the Virginia state line to the Shiloh battlefield, and from Chattanooga to Memphis, on the Mississippi River.

The commemoration movement in Tennessee began in 1863, with the Hazen monument erected by Union soldiers on the Stones River battlefield just a few months after that engagement. It peaked around 1913, during the semicentennial of the war, but it continues to this day. This genre of public discourse is distinctive, and the sentiments, causes, and allegiances that are espoused on monuments vary. At this writing, some four hundred monuments stand at battlefields, county courthouses, the state capitol in Nashville, roadside locations, and local and national cemeteries.

They offer, to this writer, a vexing subject. Civil War monuments vary in form, features, and details; they also present striking paradoxes. They are at once intimate and aloof—formed of cold stone yet invested with a rhetoric of life emotions. They are fixed in marble, bronze, or granite, but they are dynamic in ideology, interpretation, and evocation. They posit a distinct way of understanding the past. At Chattanooga, for example, the stout, solid granite Illinois state regiment monuments that are ranged across Missionary Ridge and Lookout Mountain make one set of claims: Illinois's regimental monuments are grim, seemingly laconic in their lack of detail, but their message is one of triumph. The Confederate monuments at courthouse locations across the state offer a provocative counterwitness—the typical sculpture of the Confederate soldier appears to be vigilant, unyielding, ostensibly indomitable.

One of New York's tributes to its regiments that fought at Chattanooga stands today along Interstate 24, exit 175, in Lookout Valley. The monument intrudes on the interstate with a kind of fanfare, even panache. Others are irreconcilably solemn and majestic: The enormous obelisk at the Confederate cemetery in Chattanooga was erected in what is today an active, dynamic community, the Chattanooga campus of the University of Tennessee. The monument, dedicated on May 10, 1877, has a three-word inscription of simple, majestic insufficiency: "Our Confederate Dead."

This book is not a history. It does not purport to offer a survey of the spectrum of political or ideological polemics associated with the war's commemoration. It is this: a detailed overview of significant features on the Civil War landscape. As such it is a reference guide to a hitherto uncollected text: a series of some four hundred interconnected multimedia sites—verbal and visual rhetoric—affording the reader an opportunity to see how the Tennessee Civil War landscape unfolds as a series of testimonies that form a collective narrative.

Connection

I have been studying this subject for some years. I have done so for at least three reasons. First, in my professional training in literature—English, rhetoric—I trust that words mean something. Words mediate. "In the beginning was the word" is the way the gospel of John begins. Words serve to mediate between the past and present. Civil War monuments—with five words inscribed on this plaque at this field, twenty-five words on that plaque at that field—bring order to the landscape; they give a particular meaning and context to it.

Second, as a runner virtually all my adult life, I have long been someone who takes the measure of the American landscape on a daily, practical basis: this hill, the rise and fall of the landscape. So, too, when I look at the Civil War landscape of the Stones River, of the Shiloh, Franklin, Nashville, or Chattanooga battlefields, I think on how "they"—the generation that fought the war—were here, how they looked out on this ground, this stream, this hillock, that range of mountains or that river or stream or valley, and how monuments sharpen this vision.

Third, I was born just after World War II—"the war." I was part of something in which I did not participate but in which many people around me did. The generation before me spoke of the war, lived through the war, and took the war's reality for granted; I did not and could not. They spoke of the war with an ease and familiarity that I could not grasp. Although I knew the wartime generation well, I did not know much about what was, for most of them, the central, defining conflict of their lifetime.

In a similar way, the American Civil War made this nation what it is today, but it occurred before twentieth and twenty-first century denizens could live and know it. The war defines us, but it defies understanding. Its cause is debated, its course was unpredictable, and its ramifications continue to unfold, but Civil War monuments tell us how the generation that lived through the war—and their descendants—want us to remember it.

Tennessee

Tennessee was the last state to secede from the Union, doing so on June 8, 1861. It was the first state to be readmitted to the Union, on July 24, 1866.

Tennessee sent 186,000 soldiers to the Confederate States Army (CSA). Some 31,000 Tennesseans joined the Union Army, more soldiers—many of them African American—than the other Confederate states together.

For all the attention paid to the Civil War—some fifty thousand books, essentially one published book per day since the war ended—the western theatre of the war has been overlooked. It is true that the war began in the east—in Virginia—and effectively ended there. Further, the largest battles were fought in the east: twenty-six major actions and hundreds of smaller engagements took place in Virginia.

However, the campaigns in Tennessee, though of less notoriety, are arguably more important strategically—and thus of greater importance in history—than those in the eastern theater of the war. Historian Richard M. McMurry contends that although the Battle of Gettysburg is significant and the war began and ended in Virginia, the western states—and Tennessee in particular—is where the course of the war was decided. "At these points," he concludes, "and at hundreds of others on the great battlefields of the West, the war was won and lost."[2]

In retrospect it might seem obvious that Tennessee would be fatally vulnerable to riverine invasion. Federal forces effectively penetrated the heart of the state by dint of the Cumberland, Tennessee, and Mississippi Rivers. The first setback occurred when Confederate forces were defeated at Mills Springs, Kentucky, on January 19, 1862, and were compelled to retreat to Middle Tennessee. Naval and army forces under Flag Officer Andrew H. Foote and Brig. Gen. Ulysses S. Grant, respectively, seized Fort Henry on the Tennessee River on February 6. Union forces then turned on Fort Donelson, overlooking the Cumberland River, and forced its surrender on February 16. Union troops entered Nashville on February 23.

By March, Southern forces under the command of General Albert Sydney Johnston had withdrawn entirely from the state and were based in Corinth, Mississippi. A Confederate counteroffensive at Shiloh, on the Tennessee River on April 6–7, was bitterly contested across two days of fighting but was unavailing, and Johnston was killed in action.

Southern forces would not give up, however. Lt. Gen. Braxton Bragg led the Army of Mississippi north later that summer. Acting in concert with Confederate forces under Lt. Gen. Edmund Kirby Smith, the two armies penetrated central Kentucky. It was arguably the strategic high point of Confederate fortunes in the west. But after the battle of Perryville on October 8, 1862—a tactical victory, but a strategic reverse—the Southern forces withdrew to Tennessee, where they fought again with their Union counterparts at Stones River, near Murfreesboro, on December 31–January 2, 1863. Union troops under Maj. Gen. William S. Rosecrans advanced from Nashville; Bragg's army, now the Army of Tennessee, advanced against them. Heavy casualties resulted, but no victory was won by Bragg, and the Confederate army ceded the ground and withdrew to winter quarters centered around Tullahoma and Shelbyville in Middle Tennessee.

Active campaigning resumed in June 1863. Rosecrans, by dint of deft maneuvers, forced Bragg's army south toward Chattanooga, giving control of Middle Tennessee to the Union Army of the Cumberland. The Union Army entered Chattanooga on July 7—a climax to the Tullahoma Campaign of June 23–June 30. A reversal was in the offing, however: defeat of the Union Army at the Battle of Chickamauga, September 18–20, its withdrawal to Chattanooga, and a siege of that city undertaken by the Confederate Army that nearly surrounded and crippled its Union counterparts.

It was not enough. The dramatic breaking of the siege during the battle of Chattanooga, November 23–27, compelled Confederate forces to withdraw from the state again, leading to the campaign for Atlanta, its loss, the March to the Sea, and the Carolinas campaign.

By conventional scenarios, the defeat at Chattanooga should have been the end of the military campaign in Tennessee—apart from multifarious cavalry or partisan actions. However, Confederate Lt. Gen. John B. Hood led the Army of Tennessee back into the state after the loss of Atlanta in September 1864. The army was staggered by its casualties in a frontal assault on Union troops at the battle of Franklin on November 30, 1864, but continued north to Nashville, where it was defeated and routed and nearly destroyed at the Battle of Nashville on December 15–16. Formal campaigning in the state ended with the army's withdrawal, harassed but not destroyed, into Alabama.

With that legacy to commemorate, various private, federal, state, and local agencies and committees took a hand. Scores of battlefield monuments were erected on the fields of Chickamauga and Chattanooga National Military Park and Antietam National Military Park after they were established in 1890, as well as at Shiloh National Military Park after its establishment in 1894. Stones River National Battlefield would follow in 1927; Fort Donelson National Military Park in 1928. In addition, Fort Pillow was placed on the National Register of Historic Places in 1973 and was established as a state park, and Parker's Crossroads National Battlefield Park was dedicated in 2006.

Many battlefields remain unmarked or unprotected. The site of Fort Sanders was long ago given over to residential development near the University of Tennessee campus. Fort Henry has been submerged by the waters of what is now Kentucky Lake since the 1930s. Efforts to establish a national park on the Franklin battlefield were unsuccessful, but McGavock Confederate Cemetery was established in 1866, a Confederate memorial park now stands on Winstead Hill, and the 112-acre Eastern Flank Battlefield Park, formerly the Country Club of Franklin, was developed through a public/private partnership as one of the largest recent battlefield reclamations in the nation.

However, the legacy of the war in public space continues to center on the monuments to the war and the legacy they proclaim. The movement retains a dynamic quality. Whether or not these monuments—such as the Forrest monument in Memphis—should stand at all, they continue to attract attention. The state of Mississippi's monument at Shiloh erected in October 2015, however, manifests the continuing interest, even passion, for mediating the landscape with monumentation. Mississippian Kim Sessums's proposal for the monument, "Why a Mississippi Monument at Shiloh?" includes the following observations: "Monuments, by their very nature, are often history made visible whether they commemorate specific individuals or people groups, or whether they commemorate significant events in history. The best of such monuments lead us as visitors on a path to better comprehend the past and somehow apply that knowledge and wisdom to our present."

Sessums concludes: "Should monuments not be designed so as to draw the viewer in for a closer look and consideration? Should they be instructive to a point but not quenching intellectual, spiritual, and emotional curiosity? Should they not exist so that we all might, as T. S. Eliot once wrote, 'Kneel where prayer has been valid'? Surely any War Memorial is a sacred challenge."

Comparison

The author's work in this area includes a book-length survey of Virginia's Confederate monuments, some four hundred in number.[3] That book led, almost inevitably, to an interest in how the monument movement worked itself out in Tennessee, another scene of extensive warfare—second only to Virginia in engagements and casualties—but a theater of war in which resident loyalties were much more deeply divided.

Confederate monuments in the two states have striking contrasts. In Virginia, for example, statues of generals Robert E. Lee, Thomas J. "Stonewall" Jackson, and J. E. B. Stuart preside over the landscape in grand equestrian form at Richmond. In addition, equestrian statues of Lee and Jackson are at Charlottesville, and a third equestrian statue of Jackson stands on the Manassas battlefield, but no such adulation attends the memory and reputation of Tennessee generals.

Jefferson Davis has a statue in Memphis, as does Nathan Bedford Forrest's gravesite, and some solid, reputable officers are commemorated, such as A. P. Stewart (Chattanooga), Edmund Kirby Smith (Sewanee), Robert Hatton (Lebanon), and Patrick R. Cleburne (Wartrace). Granite stelae for Hiram B.

Grandbury, John C. Carter, John Adams, Otto Strahl, and Patrick R. Cleburne stand on Winstead Hill of the Franklin battlefield.

But the senior military leadership of the Army of Tennessee—Albert S. Johnston, Braxton Bragg, John B. Hood—who suffered repeated defeats at the hands of the Union Army, are not given the tribute of a statue. They are acknowledged, they are respected, but they are not idolized.

In Tennessee, the common soldier holds sway. Confederate monuments have the towns, and they vastly outnumber Union monuments there. On two of the major Tennessee battlefields—Shiloh and Chattanooga—the Union soldier dominates. There are no statues of Union generals Ulysses S. Grant, George H. Thomas, William T. Sherman, or Philip S. Sheridan. Union monuments are virtually absent from the Franklin battlefield—there is one exception—but they are heavily concentrated on the battlefields of Chattanooga, with 83 monuments. At Shiloh there are no fewer than 130. In fact, there are more Union monuments than Confederate monuments in Tennessee. Indeed, there are almost as many Illinois monuments (regimental and statewide tributes, 85) as there are Tennessee Confederate monuments statewide (96). The message is clear: the Union Army won the ground; they defeated their Confederate opponents.

The idea that history is told by the victors is, arguably, not true, however. There's a way of looking at this that can lead one to conclude that the North won the military victory but not the political conflict—that in the end the political victory was won by the South. The South defeated? Militarily, yes. The testimony is self-evident on the stout, rounded, granite state monuments from Illinois; the tall, imposing, limestone Indiana monuments at Shiloh; lofty shafts surmounted by flag-waving common soldier statues from Iowa at Shiloh and Chattanooga; and the collective host of monuments from Ohio, Pennsylvania, New York, New Jersey, Massachusetts, Kansas, Connecticut, Michigan, Minnesota, Wisconsin, Missouri, and the US Regulars.

Those statistics and generalizations, however, are deceiving. Statues of Confederate soldiers still stand in towns as small as Mulberry, Tennessee, population seventeen hundred, and as large as cities like Knoxville, Nashville, and Murfreesboro.

The celebrated common soldier is not a contradiction in terms. A statue of Sam Davis, a Confederate soldier who was hanged as a spy by Union soldiers, stands on the state capitol grounds at Nashville. Davis has another statue in Centennial Park in Nashville, a third statue at the courthouse at Pulaski, Tennessee, and a fourth monument at Minor Hill, where he was captured by Union soldiers. The place where he was tried for espionage is marked (fifth) as is the place where he was executed (sixth). Finally, an obelisk (seventh) stands over his gravesite at his home in Smyrna, which is now a state-owned museum.

Statues of Confederate soldiers still stand as sentinels in the towns and, to a lesser extent, on Tennessee battlefields. In a sense, the Union soldier retains a pervasive presence and kind of control of the battlefield, especially at Chattanooga and Shiloh, as well as the national cemeteries at Ft. Donelson, Knoxville, Nashville, Stones River, Chattanooga, and Memphis, but from a monumentation perspective the state is still in the hands of those who seceded.

Is it true, as Robert Penn Warren writes in his *The Legacy of the Civil War*, that "at the moment when Lee handed Grant his sword was the Confederacy born; or to state matters another way, in the moment of death the Confederacy entered upon its immortality"? To judge by Tennessee's monuments, yes. The decisiveness and impact of the Union military victory was arguably vitiated by tacit agreement. Through their monuments, state and local governments articulate a voice of dissent or justification and retain a power and cultural influence that federal troops in war or postwar occupation could not—would not—overcome or mitigate. A culture of defiance persists to this day. A subcurrent of sectional tension survived the war after all.

The Women

Who made this movement into a cultural phenomenon? The veterans themselves—often with the support of federal, state, and local governments—took the initiative, especially with Northern monuments erected in Tennessee, but women were crucial to the movement's vigor and success in commemorating the dead and honoring veterans in the South.

Just as the South as a whole was defined and redefined by the war, the women of the monument movement in the South were defined and redefined. Local groups such as the Ladies' Memorial Association (LMA) and, beginning in 1894, chapters of the United Daughters of the Confederacy (UDC) took the initiative in organizing committees and identifying, collecting, burying, remembering, and commemorating the dead, as well as honoring or supporting veterans in their old age. These women's groups were not powerless. Pre-suffrage Southern women did not have the vote, but they initiated and sustained the fund-raising for most monument projects—often for decades until completion—and they facilitated the cleanup of cemeteries, set dates for decorating graves, and collected and distributed flowers. In fact, as William A. Blair observes in his *Cities of the Dead*,[4] women's groups "eventually controlled virtually all aspects of the process: conception, financing, monument design, and dedication ceremonies." The women of the postwar era knew the common soldier not as a warrior but as a husband, brother, cousin, father, grandfather, friend, or neighbor. A close reading of LMA- or UDC-sponsored monument inscriptions suggests that sentiment for the living—veterans—and remembrance of the Confederate dead are dominant themes. In many ways, the matter was personal, not political. Both sides confronted death on an unprecedented scale in US history. Unlike the North, the South had no victory to provide any measure of solace or consolation for the losses suffered by individual families. Instead, defeat defined the legacy they bore. A full examination of the ways in which Southern women interpreted that legacy is beyond the scope of this book, but the monuments they erected merit political consideration: after all, many if not most monuments sponsored by women stand in public spaces—in city-owned cemeteries and public squares. As personal and intimate as the losses were, these were social organizations that sought and won a place to position an interpretation of the meaning of the war in prominent public spaces.

Northern and Southern monuments consistently fail to reckon with the emancipationist legacy of the war. War department constraints on political or social consequences of the war did not preclude Union monuments from claiming victory, however. Contrary to the triumphalism of many Union monuments at courthouse sites across the North and on Southern battlefields, there is a subtext of tragedy discernible in many Southern monuments. UDC monuments often sentimentalize the cause, they celebrate the veterans, they justify the deeds of the dead in wartime. But historian Drew Gilpin Faust, in her *Mothers of Invention: Women of the Slaveholding South in the American Civil War*, reflecting on historian C. Vann Woodward's assertion that Southerners have had to live with a distinctive "burden of southern history," observes that Southern women derived an intimate knowledge of evil and tragedy from the defeat they experienced in the war and its aftermath. This legacy has "persisted into our time," she writes, "leaving southerners little basis for the American delusion that there is nothing whatever that is beyond their power to accomplish."[5] They even drew upon the wave of French sculpture after that country's humiliating defeat in the Franco-Prussian War. "Glory to the defeated"—*Gloria Victis*—was a theme in French commemoration. Faust concludes: "Invented from necessity and born of disappointment and desperation, southern female assertiveness grew from different roots than that of their northern sisters. . . . The appeal, the character, and the extent of southern feminism has been shaped by women's sense of their own limitations. Southern women, like their men, had learned to think of success as elusive; their own experience made it difficult for them to identify with the confidence of Susan B. Anthony's much quoted rallying cry, 'Failure is impossible.'"[6]

Inscriptions: The Common Soldier

There are approximately seventy-one statues of soldiers in Tennessee. Writer John Winberry observes that "if the South has a symbol, it is the statue of the

Confederate soldier which stands in the county seat. . . . Hands resting on the barrel of his grounded rifle, knapsack and blanket roll on his back, he stares in stony silence to the north whence came the invading Yankee armies."

They do not all "stare in stony silence to the north." That is a myth: although the Mount Olivet statue in Knoxville faces north, the Franklin statue faces south, the Davis statue in Memphis faces east, and the Chattanooga Cemetery obelisk faces west, to cite but a few examples. There is another myth that should be disabused about Tennessee. Among the statues, forty-four are of Confederate soldiers, but there are twenty-seven statues of Union soldiers.[7]

Some of the Union inscriptions are sentimental, even jocular. The Fort Hill Cemetery monument in Cleveland "Perpetuate[s] the Memory of the Boys in Blue in the War of 1861–65." But they are not always so unprovocative. The Knoxville National Cemetery monument takes note that "Tennessee Furnished For The Union Army 31092 Men," among whom there were "6776 Casualties." It gives tribute to "Tennessee Men / Who Laid Down their Lives a Voluntary / Sacrifice on / Freedom's Altar." Many Union monuments in Tennessee seem to stress "mere" reconciliation between North and South. In fact, they celebrate victory. The monument to the 79th New York VI in the Fort Sanders neighborhood in Knoxville, for example, makes it clear that preservation of the Union—their raison d'etre—was achieved. On the front of the monument is a relief of a Union and Confederate soldier, shaking hands, with an unfurled US flag waving behind them. "We Shall As Brothers Stand," it declares, "One Heart, One Soul For Our Free Land."

The Peace Monument on Lookout Mountain, Tennessee, erected by the state of New York in 1910, offers the words of President (and former Union soldier) William McKinley in proclaiming "Reunited—One Country Again and One Country Forever." The North won a great military and political victory in making that claim. But Civil War monuments are tangible physical reminders of a conflict that still defies final reckoning. The builders of Southern monuments evince a great deal of interest in that final reckoning, and they evince a very different perspective. To cite but a few examples, the town square monument on Main Street in Mount Pleasant takes a positive stance, confident that history will venerate their soldiers. It is "Erected in Memory of Our Confederate Soldiers," it declares. They are "In Our Perpetual Remembrance [and] History Has Enshrined Them Immortal."

The Altamont cemetery monument in Grundy County is less optimistic, however, citing a kind of prophecy attributed to Maj. Gen. Patrick R. Cleburne:

"SURRENDER MEANS THAT THE HISTORY OF / THIS HEROIC STRUGGLE WILL BE WRITTEN BY THE ENEMY, THAT OUR YOUTH WILL BE TRAINED / BY NORTHERN SCHOOL TEACHERS, LEARN FROM / NORTHERN SCHOOL BOOKS THEIR VERSION OF

The Lynchburg, Moore County, courthouse tablet, erected in 1927, is "In Loving Memory Confederate Soldiers" and exhorts its viewers to "Preserve The Truth In History." According to the Confederate monument at Union City, Obion County, the common soldier did nothing less than to "Preserve . . . Anglo-Saxon Civilization To The South." The testimony ascribed to the Mulberry town square common soldier, unveiled in 1908, is equally clear: "We Kept the Southland's Faith: [We] Fell at the Post of Duty." The 1996 Smithville Courthouse Monument is "Dedicated To The Memory of All Dekalb Countians Who Served the Confederacy," proclaiming that "They Sacrificed Much for the Cause of an Independent South."

The common soldier who presides over these monuments was, in many ways, a role model. Historian Gaines M. Foster observes that

> In a fund-raising speech for the statue to the private soldier on Libby Hill in Richmond, [the Reverend] Moses Hoge maintained that [monuments] served as a form of history for people who did not read, particularly young schoolboys and workingmen. "Books are occasionally opened," he added, "monuments are seen every day, and the lesson of that lofty figure which is to tower over Libby Hill [is to] 'Live nobly; there is a reward for patriotic duty; republics are not ungrateful.'" Stephen D. Lee agreed that monuments were erected not only to remember the dead but more "for the sake of the living, that in this busy industrial age these stones to the Confederate soldier may stand like great interrogation marks to the soul of each beholder. Are you also ready to die for your country? Is your life worthy to be remembered along with theirs?"

To all appearances, the individual soldier was heralded, not because of his social status, or for the strategy and tactics of officers, or the oratory and influence of politicians, but as one who transcended events and mortal flesh. It might be said that the soldier/sculpture on the pedestal surmounts a veritable mount of Calvary on the county square.

That depiction is consonant with historian Richard Slotkin's description of violence in America as a sort of Eucharist. Violence, Slotkin contends, is used as a tool of transcendence, a "regeneration through violence," as he puts it in the title of his book. Slotkin calls attention to Henry David Thoreau's interpretation of the violence of eighteenth-century captivity narratives as a perversion of the Eucharist. In doing so, Slotkin writes that such violence serves to "link the present dweller in the land to the reality of that bloody revelation of wilderness by means of a sacrament. . . . It is a Eucharist, with real rather than figurative flesh and blood, a revision of the Eden myth in which the eating of the apple of knowledge is a sacrament rather than a sin."[8]

The sacrifice of 618,000 lives to the purported causes of the Civil War cannot be overlooked as another more gruesome perversion of this American Eucharist. In that sense, one could find in the common soldier a central figure in a veritable cult of the dead. In his essay "The Religion of the Lost Cause," historian Charles Reagan Wilson observes that a "southern civil religion emerged because defeat in the Civil War . . . created the spiritual and psychological need for southerners to reaffirm their identity, an identity which came to have outright religious dimensions. Each Lost Cause ritual and organization was tangible evidence that southerners had made a religion out of their history. As with all ritualistic repetition of archetypal actions, southerners in their institutionalized Lost Cause religion were trying symbolically to overcome history."

Are they messianic figures? They seem to be, although neither of the two traditional definitions quite applies to the common soldier. Statue depictions give no impression that the figure is either a charismatic leader or a figure that is capable of resurrection. In general the soldier looks like a workman, ready to go about his business, making his way in the world with his trade. The state of Minnesota's statue of a soldier on the Shiloh battlefield is prototypical. He looks like a young, skilled ironworker. He holds no weapon and in fact looks like a civilian, an apprentice blacksmith or metalworker, save for the fact that his weapons of war are at hand: two light artillery pieces flank the monument.

In general, the pose of the common soldier on a pedestal is neither aloof nor abstract. Many of them look relaxed, unmartial, unheroic—at ease: part-time professionals, citizen-soldiers. They have "an aura of dignity and endurance," historian Gaines M. Foster observes, "but otherwise they hardly seem . . . suited for a war memorial."

The testimony of the men themselves is instructive. The body of Col. Jason D. Webb, 51st Alabama Infantry, is interred at Confederate Memorial Cemetery, Winchester. He has as his epitaph the assertion that he was "A Soldier of the Cross." The inscription on the Jesse Walling Monument on Main Street in McMinnville, a granite plaque set—uniquely—between two buildings, reads in part, "I ENLISTED / IN THE LORD'S / CAUSE WHEN YOUNG. / LATER / I ENLISTED / IN THE / CONFEDERATE / CAUSE AND / WAS WOUNDED / AT / MURFREESBORO."

The remains of Confederate Brig. Gen. Francis A. Shoup—soldier, a postwar Episcopal rector, and professor of math—are at Sewanee cemetery. Shoup's tomb displays two crosses: the Christian cross and the crossed cannons of the artillery.

One could certainly unfold a discussion around the theme of the cause of the Confederacy and the religious affiliation claimed by these men, but to judge

State of Minnesota, Common Soldier, Shiloh Battlefield

by this admittedly anecdotal testimony, they follow a cause, but they do not claim to lead one.

The monument makers are more apt to articulate what the cause was. The 1904 Lewisburg courthouse common soldier is given tribute for service "In Defense / Of the Sovereign Rights of the States."

The 1937 Shelbyville courthouse column is dedicated to "SOLDIERS FROM BEDFORD / COUNTY WHO FOUGHT FOR THE / CONFEDERACY IN THE WAR / BETWEEN THE STATES, 1861–1865." On their 1995 courthouse shaft at Savannah, Hardin County, the Sons of Confederate Veterans declare "SACRED IS THE MEMORY OF THE / MEN AND WOMEN OF HARDIN / COUNTY FOR THE[IR] SACRIFICES . . . IN DEFENDING THE HOMELAND[.]"

The statues of soldiers of the cause seem vigilant enough: they appear to be watchful and alert, sometimes pensive, even wistful, but they do not look particularly military or militant. They are unmartial, unbellicose, practical—ordinary. They are manifestly prosaic. True, they are uplifted; they stand on pedestals, but they do not transcend mortality. The state of Wisconsin's statue of a common soldier on the Shiloh battlefield is depicted as one in his death throes, and the state of Illinois's common soldier, at Memphis National Cemetery, reposes in death, lying atop a sarcophagus.

The Smithsonian Inventory of Outdoor Sculpture offers a revealing verbal sketch of the Mulberry town square common soldier. He is "slightly smaller than life-sized and youthful looking." He wears a uniform that includes a hip-length coat, baggy trousers, a brimmed hat, and a belt buckle with CSA on it.

Mulberry Town Square Common Soldier, Confederate

His left hand rests on a canteen and knife handle. He has the strap of a bag over his proper left shoulder and across his body. He has a sash or blanket draped over his right shoulder. A tree stump, symbolizing the brevity of life (a common feature of statue monumentation), is located immediately behind and to the side of his left foot.

Who is he? He is remembered as one "of the 300 / Confederate / Unconquered Soldiers / Who Went Out / From Mulberry." He faces north, ready to move, but his destination is likened to that of an apostle, one who is sent, not that of a leader. He and his fellows are led, but they also chose to be led. Resurrection was not within the capabilities of the common soldier, but the heroic ideal associated with him endures, and his presence is still part of public life. The conflict, in that sense, was not resolved. Instead, it evolves. It changes form. He might otherwise be said to be in constant tension, much as a bridge is in constant tension, and stands only so long as the tension is sustained. He is defined and redefined with every generation.

History and Periodization

Civil War monuments are often classified by the year they were erected. The categories are deceptively neat, but the years 1861 to 1889 have been called the

Bereavement and Funereal Era, those from 1890 to 1920 the Reconciliation, or Celebration era, and those from 1920 to the present the Commemorative Era.[9]

The monument movement began early. The Hazen monument on the Stones River battlefield was erected in 1863, only a few months after the battle.[10] A white stone and plaster column was dedicated in Union City on October 21, 1869, at a cemetery containing the graves of twenty-nine unknown Confederate dead. The first courthouse monument may be at Bolivar, where an obelisk dedicated to the Confederate dead of Hardeman County was erected on the courthouse square in 1873. The movement drew upon the neoclassical revival of the nineteenth century.[11] It was common practice in Greek city-states to use stone slabs and bronze plaques to display public records, including laws, decrees, treaties, religious notices, and war memorials.[12] The use of ancient Greek and Roman styles—such as columns, arches, and stelae—was pervasive. In addition, Egyptian Revival obelisks, for example, were erected across Tennessee, from Greeneville to Memphis, most notably perhaps by the state of Indiana, which placed twenty-two inscribed obelisks on the Shiloh battlefield—each sixteen feet high and weighing 7.5 tons.

In the Bereavement and Funereal Era, 1861–89, the need to retrieve, identify, and bury the dead occasioned memorials in a style that nineteenth-century Americans admired and emulated.[13] They were designed to commemorate and eulogize the dead and exhort the living and were thus quite in line with platonic precedents. Many of the monuments of the period are mournful but dignified, affectionate but not effusive. The soldiers' monuments in particular give cogent, affecting tribute to the recently departed: the Hazen's Brigade monument, for example, in "Memory of its Soldiers Who Fell at Stone River," or the "gallant dead of Maj Genl Wheeler's Cavalry Corps," who fell at the battle of Farmington (1874). The declaration on the granite obelisk at Chattanooga Confederate cemetery is striking in its terseness: "Confederate Dead" comprises the entire inscription. There are also remembrances of "Our Fallen Heroes" at Columbia (1882) and of "Our Boys" at Trenton, but in general they convey a funereal aspiration that memory will prevail over the passing of time.

Monuments of the Reconciliation, or Celebration Era, 1890–1920, are apt to be more sentimental than the preceding generation. Frequently they make claims of either injustice or self-justification. At Jackson's courthouse monument, the inscription beneath the common soldier statue intimates that overwhelming odds were the cause of the Union victory: "FEDERAL RECORDS SHOW THEY HAD / FROM FIRST TO LAST TWO MILLION SIX HUN- / DRED THOUSAND MEN IN SERVICE; WHILE THE / CONFEDERATES ALL TOLD HAD BUT LITTLE / OVER SIX HUNDRED THOUSAND."

These common soldier monuments often express unabashed affection. They can be celebratory. The inscription on the marble shaft at Mount Olivet

Cemetery in Nashville praises the "Valor, Devotion, and Sacrifice Unto Death of Confederate Soldiers of Tennessee." The monument, unveiled May 16, 1892, goes on to suggest that nature itself is in accord with this affection: "THE WINDS OF HEAVEN KISSING ITS SIDES, / HYMN AN EVERLASTING REQUIEM / IN MEMORY OF THE UNRETURNING BRAVE."

Knoxville's Confederate dead—including those from the ill-fated, arguably ill-conceived charge at Fort Sanders—are commemorated by the local Ladies' Memorial Association who, on May 19, 1892, dedicated a monument that praised the "heroic courage and the unshaken constancy / of more than 1600 soldiers of the South, / who in the great war between the states, / 1861 to 1865, / Were Inspired / By the holiness of a patriotic and impersonal love / And in the mountain passes of Tennessee, / whether on stricken field or in hospital ward, / Gave ungrudgingly their lives / To their Country."

By comparison, the proliferation of battlefield monuments of this time can seem perfunctory, but they represent the peak of influence of the Civil War generation in the monument movement. The years 1894 to 1899 have been regarded as the golden age of battlefield preservation. Federal legislation established national battlefield parks at Antietam, Chattanooga, and Chickamauga in 1890, Shiloh and Gettysburg in 1895, and Vicksburg in 1899. The Commemorative Era, from 1920 to the present, marks the final phase of the movement. In the 1920s and 1930s, many monuments nostalgically commemorated what was thought to be a simpler time. Historical interpretation was the prevailing theme: patriotic tributes or religious rationales were less common.

Some large-scale commemorations were established: the national parks at Fort Donelson in 1927 and Stones River in 1928—although these came after the peak of battlefield development and did not benefit from that movement's proliferation of monuments. A battlefield tribute to both sides, Union and Confederate, was erected at Nashville and unveiled November 11, 1927, as the Peace Monument. An obelisk erected in 1931 at Erwin, Unicoi County, gives tribute to Confederate soldiers. Both monuments, however, include tributes to World War I soldiers as well. The last twentieth-century statue of a Confederate soldier was unveiled June 3, 1933, in Fort Donelson National Military Park, and bears a more than passing resemblance to an American enlisted man of World War I.

The monuments of the next few decades were modest in scale; the inscriptions were less strident and more spare—a trend that would continue into the 1940s, although World War II interrupted construction from 1941 to 1949. At Russellville, a campsite of the Army of Tennessee is noted with a stone marker and bronze plaque erected June 3, 1928. A UDC monument at Johnson City, an inscribed boulder dedicated October 8, 1931, marks the site of a "training

Camp of Confederate Regiments from the South on their way by rail to Virginia to join General Lee."

Many monuments of the 1950s and early 1960s were characterized by centennial apologetics and reconciliation.[14] In Springfield, the Elmwood Cemetery Tablet (1958) is a modest commemoration, while the Island Number 10 battlefield monument (1956) near Tiptonville offers a copious narrative of a battlefield long submerged under the Mississippi River.

A perhaps surprisingly conciliatory statement—Forrest's farewell speech to his troops in 1865—was posted at the Beech Grove Confederate Cemetery in 1954. A centennial-era monument to Jefferson Davis was erected in Memphis in 1964, granite tributes to Texas Confederates were erected at Shiloh and Fort Donelson in 1964, and a bronze tablet to Michigan's Civil War soldiers at Stones River was posted in 1966. They were few in number but rich in praise and acknowledgement: "Texas Remembers" is an especially memorable paean.

There was a lull thereafter. The passing of the centennial and the height of the Vietnam War conflict and Civil Rights Movement were all factors in giving pause to the monumentation movement. The state of Missouri's 1971 monument at Shiloh and the UDC's courthouse monument at Decaturville, erected in 1978, are exceptions. With the rise or revival of chapters of the Sons of Confederate Veterans in the 1970s and 1980s, another generation of monuments was emplaced. Many were erected at sites that had been previously overlooked: a partial list includes courthouse sites at Spencer (1988), Smithville (1996), Jones Chapel (1996), Crossville (2001), Charlotte (2001), Winchester (2003), and Altamont (2004) and commemorative sites at Alexandria (1999) and Wartrace (2011), as well as several erected circa 2000 at Winstead Hill, on the Franklin battlefield. The inscriptions on these monuments were didactic and instructive, designed to offer a historical perspective as well as strike an emotional chord. Erected in a style of what might be described as a retro design harkening back to fiftieth-year commemorations, they lacked the statuary, rich decoration, and lofty scale of earlier monuments. They were, in short, less expensive, but they often compensated with expansive lists of battles or narratives, or rosters of units, and they gave unqualified praise to the wartime generation. They were provocative but nostalgic, celebratory but somehow defiant of unspecified or unexpressed injustices.

At Smithville in DeKalb County, the courthouse monument dated 1996 is prototypical in its praise: "THIS MONUMENT IS DEDICATED / TO THE MEMORY OF ALL / DEKALB COUNTIANS WHO / SERVED THE CONFEDERACY. / THEIR COURAGE AND / PATRIOTISM TO THE STATE OF / TENNESSEE IS AN EXAMPLE / TO ALL GENERATIONS."

With the coming of the twenty-first century, more monuments have been erected. An expansive Confederate Plaza in Dyer County is notable for its enormous hilltop battle flag, which is conspicuously visible from the four-lane highway, US 51. Advances in technology have lessened the cost of some materials and aided in bringing to bear new technology and new media—for example, the song "Dixie" that can be heard at the press of a button at Tullahoma's Confederate cemetery.

Although monuments such as the Nathan B. Forrest shrine in Memphis have a contentious and controversial place on the landscape, the monumentation movement continues. The state of Mississippi sponsored an impressive monument dedicated on the Shiloh battlefield in 2015, sculpted by Kim Sessums, depicting three Mississippians advancing under fire toward Union lines.

Design and Materials

Typical postwar monuments or markers are made of bronze or white bronze (zinc), marble or granite, and pink Tennessee marble, a crystalline limestone quarried in east Tennessee. Iron, copper, limestone, and aluminum as well as common fieldstone were also used. The monuments fall under one of these types:

- An obelisk: a tall, slender four-sided stone pillar tapering toward a peaked top.
- A slab, tablet, or pillar, sometimes called a stele: an upright stone or plaque set on a stone base.
- A statue: set on a stone pedestal, plinth, or base, sometimes with a shaft or dado that displays an inscription; the whole is surmounted by a sculpture of a soldier, usually standing at parade rest.
- A plaque or tablet of bronze, marble or granite on a wall. (This book includes two anomalous examples at Murphreesboro and McMinnville.)
- A shaft or column, sometimes surmounted by a soldier.
- A tablet, cast in iron, one of many posted on the Chattanooga and Shiloh battlefields displaying rosters, narratives or unit positions (addressed in chap. 6).

Ceremonies

Dedication ceremonies for local monuments were momentous events in the lives of communities. Monuments were long anticipated. The fund-raising process often took decades to complete. Media, in the form of newspapers and magazines, advertised the approaching date of dedication ceremonies, reported their occurrence, and published proceedings and speeches in the aftermath.

An obelisk, this one a tribute to Confederate soldiers at Chattanooga dedicated May 10, 1877. A granite base and obelisk.

A relief: a granite shaft with a sculptured portrait of a common soldier in high relief across the front, this to the 48th Ohio VI at Shiloh.

A granite stele: the John Hunt Morgan tablet, erected 1903, on Main Street at the Greene County courthouse. An upright stone, slab, tablet, or plaque set on a granite base. A less expensive, less artful, more text-oriented form of expression.

A courthouse soldier standing on Main Street at the Greene County courthouse, Greeneville, dedicated July 3, 1909: a private soldier, in bronze, standing at parade rest surmounting a granite shaft and base.

The Franklin statue and column, dedicated May 16, 1907: granite plinth, base, dado, and column surmounted by the sculpted figure of a Confederate private soldier.

Arches stand at entryways to the national cemeteries in Chattanooga and Madison, and at Silverdale Confederate Cemetery, Chattanooga.

They reported several days of festivities, successive arrivals of dignitaries, parades, dinners, and ceremonies of dedication.

At Mount Pleasant, for example, the festivities of September 27, 1907, began at the train station. The *Confederate Veteran* reported: "Thousands of hearts beat 'double-quick' when the Fayetteville band emerged from the train to the strains of 'Dixie' . . . while the Leonidas Polk Bivouac, in full uniform of gray and carrying the banner on which the portrait of their warrior bishop had been painted . . . fell into line of march . . . These, with numerous decorated vehicles, including a brilliant float containing thirteen beautiful girls . . . formed a process which wound through the streets of Mt. Pleasant to the Public Square, where the monument stands."

Announcements followed, then a general welcome, a pastoral invocation, and a poem, "Remembering," by Mrs. Octavia Zollicoffer. After "Prof. James A. Bostick's remarks," all were invited to "partake of the feast spread for them in the Cumberland Presbyterian church." The "delightful function began with a choicely worded toast by Miss Matt Dobbins, who passed the loving cup to the old soldiers assembled . . . the twelve, or fewer, surviving members of the Bigby Grays."

The unveiling of the monument took place that afternoon. The climax of the occasion took place with solemnity and a sudden uproar: "While the band played softly the ribbons were drawn by the thirteen maidens who had personified on the float the thirteen Confederate States. A shout went up when the parting drapery revealed the stately column surmounted by Darricoat's statue of a Confederate soldier."

Some flavor of the speeches, in turn, is indicated by the report published in *Confederate Veteran* for the monument at Franklin on November 30, 1899. Sponsored by the Franklin Chapter No 14, United Daughters of the Confederacy (which is still extant at this writing), the sheathed monument was climactically unveiled by two little girls, Susie Winstead and Leah Cowan. The Reverend J. H. McNeilly, a wartime chaplain who was present at the battle of Franklin, gave an opening prayer, saying in part, that God "didst not give victory to our arm [but] we bow in absolute submission to thy will. Thou knowest what is best. But we praise and bless thee for the characters which were purified by the war, and for the example of those who didst not measure duty by success, who preferred death to dishonor, and who showed to all the world how they valued the rights and liberties thou didst give their land."

George Washington Gordon, a US congressman and Confederate brigadier general, gave the address, calling the battle of Franklin "one of the most dramatic and sanguinary conflicts recorded in the annals of warfare" and comparing it to "the bloody battles of the world, from Marathon to Waterloo, from Waterloo to Balaklava, and from Balaklava to Gettysburg." He took exception to denigrating accusations about the status of Confederate veterans, declaring that "we were and are no more traitors and rebels than George Washington and his contemporaries. If they had failed, they too would have been called rebels and traitors; but as they succeeded, they have been honored and exalted as heroes and patriots. This is the difference between the accidents of success and failure."

On the Union side, at Chattanooga, Dan Sickles seemed to be more conciliatory. Sickles, a notorious New York lawyer and politician as well as a Union major general, did not fight in Tennessee, but he was wounded and lost a leg at the Battle of Gettysburg. The state of New York deployed fourteen regiments of infantry and two batteries at Chattanooga, and the state sponsored a prominent monument at Lookout Mountain. Sickles chaired the monument commission and spoke at the dedication ceremonies on November 15, 1910. He chose his words carefully, stating that the monument was not erected "to celebrate a victory." Neither was it "a monument to glory over old adversaries." It was, instead, a "great memorial—a great historical memorial—to peace and reconciliation. This monument says to the South: Let us embrace you as brethren once more. Let us live together as brothers forevermore."

Sentiment and reconciliation prevailed at the ceremonies for the state of New Jersey's monument on Orchard Knob in Chattanooga. The remarks given by Edward C. Stokes on November 23, 1896, dwelled less on the cause for which New Jerseyans fought than on their youth at the time.

> We speak of them reverently. We speak of them lovingly. They were our fathers; our husbands; our brothers; our sons; aye, the great majority of them were our sons. We sometimes call them "our boys," and we do so with strict regard to accuracy and truth. They were, indeed, boys. Of the veterans who are here at this hour, all of them enlisted at the early age of seventeen and eighteen years, and the commander of that regiment that fought upon yonder spot, to-day present in the person of General Mindil, was but twenty years old when thirty-three years ago he led these boys on the field of action.

In that same spirit of reconciliation, it was not unusual for former Confederate soldiers to offer a testimony or tribute at seeing a Union monument erected. The dedication of the state of Ohio's monument at the Cravens House occasioned these remarks from Joseph B. Cumming on October 17, 1917: "I take pleasure as a Confederate soldier in feeling that this monument is erected, albeit unconsciously and unintentionally, also to the memory of brave Confederates. . . . This monument stands not more for the glory of battle than for the beatitude of peace. Glory perennial as the great river that flows at our feet, peace everlasting as the Mountain that towers above it."

Slavery

There is no explicit mention of slavery in Tennessee monuments. There is a great deal of attention paid to rights, including states' rights; to service and honor; and to justification, courage and sacrifice, but in the twenty-thousand-word text that comprises the liturgy of Tennessee monument rhetoric, the word "slavery" never occurs.[15]

The subject is not avoided entirely; it is, arguably, an implicit subtextual element. The tribute to the United States Colored Troops (USCT) at the national cemetery in Nashville is a conspicuous exception for leaving no doubt of the cause being fought for, although even here the word "slavery" is not ventured (and, it should be noted, many USCT troops were freedmen). Some Southerners, as historian Sarah Driggs observes, including many African Americans, see in Confederate "monuments an affront, a reminder if not a celebration of the days of slavery and white supremacy." Historian Kirk Savage makes a convincing case that a racial hierarchy was implicit and that this tension persists to this day. Savage avers that the "history of slavery and its violent end was told in public space—specifically in the sculptural monuments that increasingly came to dominate public space in nineteenth century America."

There is justice in Savage's assertions. In his book *The Cause Lost: Myths and Realities of the Confederacy*, historian William C. Davis concludes that it "is impossible to point to any other local issue but slavery and say that Southerners would have seceded and fought over it." However, he pointedly adds that "if slavery is the reason secession came, that does not mean that it is the reason 1 million Southern men subsequently fought. In fact, study reveals that the two had absolutely nothing in common." He concludes that "probably 90 percent of the men who wore the gray had never owned a slave and had no personal interest at all either in slavery or in the shadow issue of state rights. The widespread Northern myth that the Confederates went to the battlefield to perpetuate slavery is just that, a myth. Their letters and diaries, in the tens of thousands, reveal again and again that they fought and died because their Southern homeland was invaded and their natural instinct was to protect home and hearth."

To judge by these monuments, the war was about slavery, but not solely about slavery. The war was about states' rights, but not solely about states' rights. Slavery was present and tolerated; racism persisted and persists. The truth, as this writer sees it, is more frightening: the generation that fought the war was composed of decent, flawed people, capable of greatness and profound misjudgments. Those misjudgments included a tolerance of a host of inequities that included slavery, but that tolerance exacted a toll in blood.

However one interprets the meaning of the war, and the moral culpability that surrounds its participants, it is evident that the dead—Union and Confederate—are still at work. The physical presence of these monuments to their deeds and their remains is a part of the American landscape and ongoing narrative. Monuments cannot last forever, but, undisturbed, they will last for eons. The sphinx of Giza, Egypt—of limestone in an admittedly favorable dry desert climate—is five thousand years old. Nature, if unaided, will take a long time to weather most Civil War monuments into physical oblivion.

On the other hand, although they are in public space, many, perhaps most, monuments are easily overlooked. Once a monument was erected and the ceremonies were over, little public mention was made of it thereafter. Monuments took their place in the community, as it were, and, barring accident, dislocation, relocation, or repair, many of them remain a part of their community to this day. For all I could tell, it was with genuine, affecting curiosity and unawareness a few years ago when an African American man working on a maintenance job on the county courthouse grounds asked this writer, "What *is* this?" pointing at a Confederate courthouse monument as I photographed it one summer day.

In crucial ways, that question is still unanswered. The issue of what the monumentation stands for is an ongoing, evolving, contemporary discussion with direct relevance to contemporary conceptions of the nation's core beliefs and history. Calls to drop Confederate emblems from public space have been vociferous since the summer of 2015.[16] Responding to protests, the University of Mississippi lowered the state flag that flies on the campus.[17] Contention over the state flag of Mississippi, with its emblem of the Confederate battle flag, continues at this writing.[18] Controversy continues over outdoor public Confederate monumentation in New Orleans, Louisiana; Baltimore, Maryland; Charlottesville and Richmond, Virginia; at Stone Mountain, Georgia, and—most notably for this project—the Nathan Bedford Forrest gravesite and statue in Memphis. Forrest's abilities as a military tactician are uncontested. However, his legacy is inextricably tied to the wealth he gained in the antebellum slave trade, his position as Imperial Wizard of the original Ku Klux Klan, and the extent of his responsibility for the massacre at Fort Pillow. Agitation to remove his remains and the equestrian statue over his grave from the site in Memphis culminated in the monument's removal, by night, in 2017.

Monuments offer a very public, constant, muted testimony. As a daily presence, they may not seem to merit a second glance. As a collected text under scrutiny, the four hundred Tennessee monuments tantalize as artifacts and testimonies.

In an earlier study of the Winchester National and Stonewall Confederate cemeteries across the street from one another in Winchester, Virginia, I took note of the paradox and irony of the opposing testimonies of those sites. Tennessee may be a larger conundrum, a challenge to Lincoln's notion of a house or nation divided not being able to stand. Tennessee, to judge by these monuments, is a house divided. It is, in an important sense, in a state of perpetual disequilibrium (to borrow a phrase from microeconomics). At some level the issue of union versus states' rights and secession as just causes remain in tension. Slavery is still an issue. It remains the country's original sin, the effects of which are still rippling across the American landscape.

Looked at collectively, the presence of these opposing testimonies on the Tennessee landscape serves to remind visitors that the American Civil War was not just a sectional conflict, a contention over issues of law, an argument over the right to secede, or, for that matter, an issue of slavery. It came to be, as historian Charles Reagan Wilson describes it, "a holy war, on both sides."

The phrase merits attention. In the Gettysburg Address, Wilson avers that Lincoln "converted the Union into a near-mystical icon worthy of worship" and extended "America's fundamental mission of embodying freedom and renewing religious meanings tied up with the nation."[19] Reconciling that transcendent perspective on both sides with the violence that inspired it is something even Lincoln would not address and which continues to defy summary judgment or definitive understanding. The "mission" that Wilson refers to goes beyond the way the war is commonly perceived.

Too often, historian Harry S. Stout observes, "we have preferred a violent but glamorized and romantic Civil War. Military histories," he continues, "have focused on strategies and tactics and the sheer drama of battles in action. Political histories have focused—especially in the present—on slavery and emancipation, accounting the evil so complete and pervasive as to justify even murder."[20]

The mystery of the origins or validity of the reasons for the conflict are not addressed.[21] Historian James McPherson argues in his *Battle Cry of Freedom* that the "greatest danger to American survival at mid-century . . . was neither class tension nor ethnic division[, but] sectional conflict between North and South over the future of slavery." That facet is never explicitly addressed in Tennessee's monument rhetoric.

Can these monuments offer avenues of inquiry to a final judgment on the war? Perhaps. They certainly have had their place in the discourse on the meaning of the war. But although they have symbolic import, the nature of that import is elusive.

They are, for example, not particularly religious—not explicitly. That may seem surprising, but the facts are clear. A granite cross, erected by the United

Daughters of the Confederacy in 1950 at the Confederate Memorial Cemetery in Winchester, Franklin County, is the only cross on any Civil War monument in Tennessee. The 1873 courthouse shaft and urn at Bolivar gives tribute to Hardeman County's "Sons Fallen in the Service of the Confederate States." Its makers express the "Hope of a Joyful Resurrection," but this is a general hope—the only one of its kind in Tennessee—and even here no special hope or blessing is conveyed to the Confederate dead for the cause for which they fought.

One might expect more. The motto of the Confederacy, Deo Vindice ("God Will Judge"), occurs twice—on the monument to Maj. Gen. A. P. Stewart, erected in 2010, at Beech Grove Confederate Cemetery, and at Charlotte, at the Dickson County courthouse erected in 2001—but even these expressions are modest, arguably a mere evincing of the ideal that the civil government will act with God as ultimate judge. Nor are they as political as one might imagine. In fact, by deliberate and stated policy in the case of the national battlefield parks, they were intended to be apolitical.

These inscriptions stand in almost consummate contrast to the fiery, arguably seditious rhetoric of many dedication speeches. This is from George Washington Gordon's address at Franklin, Tennessee, October 28, 1895:

> No. We did not want war and we did not inaugurate it. All we asked was to be let alone. But the North, which had become more populous and powerful than the South, determined to preserve her commercial interests, hence the war. If the people of the North had believed that they could have been happier and richer without the South than with her, what rational ground would they then have to expend six billions of money and sacrifice a half million of lives to keep the South in the Union? . . . I have deemed it appropriate to say thus much (though it is little of what could be said) in vindication of the cause for which we fought and our comrades died from the charge of treason and rebellion that we hear and read from day to day. If the charge were not constantly uttered and reiterated, published and re-published, I should not have thought it expedient to make any vindication on this solemn and sacred occasion.

Much ink was spilled; many voices were lifted. To try to engage with the whole of this rhetoric within the span of this short introduction would be to do an injustice to its breadth. To describe it in broad terms is to do an injustice to the various currents of emotion or conviction that have flowed since the war's end: to mention reconciliation, grievance, grieving, defiance, sedition, prejudice, denial, justification, and triumphalism is to address only a few.

Great was the effort to vindicate or celebrate the cause of the Confederacy, grieve the losses, or commemorate the triumph of the Union. Of the South, historian Charles Reagan Wilson, for example, describes "a ritualistic structure of activities that represented a religious commemoration and celebration of the Confederacy," in particular the ways in which "Southern ministers and other rhetoricians portrayed Robert E. Lee, Stonewall Jackson, Jefferson Davis, and many other wartime heroes as religious saints and martyrs."[22]

Was the American Civil War about the restoration of the Union? Yes. Slavery? Yes. Did the soldiers fight for "cause and comrades" as historian James McPherson contends? Yes.

In general, pragmatism prevails among Union monuments in the South, reflecting war department oversight and the evolving understanding of war as a science. Most Union battlefield monuments emphasize the role of the common soldier: what he did, when, at what peril, and at what cost. At Shiloh and Chattanooga, the Illinois unit monument inscriptions are written after the manner of after-action reports. Broadly speaking, Union battlefield monuments emphasize the deeds that were done. Confederate monuments in towns and cities emphasize the cause soldiers fought for and the sacrifice they offered.

What they do not say is as important as what they do say. Let one illustration—one facet—suffice.

In recent years, several historians have given consideration to the irony of the fact that so many Northerners and Southerners held the Bible to be sacred or inerrant but could not agree on its meaning in reconciling the moral and ethical issue of slavery. Both sides broadly—though not exclusively—cited the Bible as the basis for their strikingly divergent positions on the matter. In this light, historian Harry S. Stout elaborates on the meaning of the holy war to which Wilson refers, averring that the war's meaning took on a "mythic transcendence not unlike the significance of the Eucharist for Christian believers." He writes:

> For the Civil War to achieve its messianic destiny and inculcate an ongoing civil religion, it required a blood sacrifice that appeared total. While the term "baptism in blood" did not originate in the Civil War, it enjoyed a prominence in the war rhetoric of both the Union and the Confederacy that had no precedent. . . . For the unbeliever, both blood sacrifices seem irrational. But for the true believer, blood saved. Just as Christians believe that "without the shedding of blood there can be no remission for sins," so Americans in the North and the South came to believe that their bloodletting contained a profound religious meaning for their collective life as nations.

On this subject Stout adds, intriguingly, that a great national civil American religion was given birth by the travail of the war. As he puts it, "The incarnation of a national American civil religion may have been the final great legacy of the Civil War. How could a people of such diversity, who had more than adequately demonstrated their capacity to live at war possibly come together in peace without some functioning civil religion? And how does any real religion come into being without the shedding of blood?"

The fact that the issue came to entail blood sacrifices was meaningful but tragic, of course. Tragic, too, was the nature of the outcome. Historian Mark A. Noll observes that the "North—forced to fight on unfriendly terrain that it had helped to create—lost the exegetical war. The South certainly lost the shooting war. But constructive orthodox theology was the major loser when American believers allowed bullets instead of hermeneutical self-consciousness to determine what the Bible said about slavery." No person or group was able to come to the fore to stop the bloodletting. In consequence, Noll notes, the "Book that made the nation [nearly destroyed] the nation; the nation that had taken to the Book was rescued not by the Book but by the force of arms."[23]

In this regard, the monumentation of Tennessee could be said to represent a kind of ongoing irresolution, because, in an important sense, as historian Daniel Aaron concludes in his survey of postwar rhetoric, the war could never quite be confronted by either the North or South. He writes:

> The War was not so much unfelt as unfaced. Northern writers found it easier and more reassuring to portray it as an exalted example of national redemption than as a grisly historical moment when the political system broke down and the nation took a "moral holiday." . . . Eventually . . . both sides [agreed that each was] "right" as well as sincere and gallant and neither wholly to blame, [and] the War became a reason for national [self-con]gratulation rather than a subject for reflective soul-searching. By this time Whitman's "real" War lay buried underneath reams of special pleading and irrelevant minutiae.[24]

Here are the "minutiae": the remains of soldiers at national cemeteries at Nashville, Chattanooga, Shiloh, Memphis, Knoxville, Fort Donelson, and Stones River, or the Confederate cemeteries at Franklin, Murfreesboro, Knoxville, Chattanooga, Memphis, and other sites too numerous to mention or otherwise unknown. These form a kind of unconsummatable sacrament. Whatever animus, hostility, or fraternization occurred between the two sides during or after the war, these are, in death, bonded by their common confrontation of the principle, defining conflicts of their era. Sympathy and reconciliation may have prevailed after the war, but those sentiments were fostered too late for these men to benefit. Their bond is in the mysterious, binding ties of conflict, its enmities and friendships. In many cases, the remains of these men still lie where they fought. In that sense, the conflict of 1861–65, has not ended.[25]

Parameters and Method

Included in this study are outdoor Civil War courthouse and town monuments, cemetery and city monuments, and battlefield monuments: obelisks, statues, shafts, reliefs, stelae, columns, and pyramids. I was as descriptive and comprehensive with inscriptions and architectural features as space permitted. Where any text from inscriptions was omitted, ellipses [. . .] have been inserted. Due diligence was done to document every site, but this study may have inadvertently overlooked monuments. Corrections or additions are welcome.

This book is organized geographically. It moves sequentially, site to site, across the Shiloh battlefield in chapter 1, to Chattanooga and Hamilton County in chapter 2, from northeast Tennessee at Bristol to the outskirts of Chattanooga in chapter 3, from south to north in Middle Tennessee in chapter 4, and across the Mississippi River Valley, including the city of Memphis in chapter 5. I examined these monuments and the sites where they are placed as a collected text, albeit a widely dispersed series of four hundred distinctive texts at particular, specific locations. Assembling a comprehensive roster of texts/monuments could only be accomplished by researching a wide range of sources, including the Smithsonian Institution Research Information System, Ralph Widener's still useful *Confederate Monuments: Enduring Symbols of the South and the War Between the States*, and the 1964 centennial-era booklet *Directory of Civil War Monuments and Memorials in Tennessee*.

It was also incumbent on this writer to travel to each site in this book—every courthouse or cemetery or battlefield, including every monument on the Shiloh and Chattanooga battlefields—notwithstanding the time, research, logistics, driving, and weather vagaries involved. Much of the search was successful to the extent of being able to read the subtext of the landscape—the higher ground where a cemetery or fort might be, the logic of the terrain that would dictate the path of an old road or railroad cut or where a battle might have been fought. It also afforded me the opportunity of seeing rural Tennessee as an enormous, intriguing landscape—what F. Scott Fitzgerald justly romanticizes as the "vast obscurity beyond the city, where the dark fields of the republic roll on under the night."

This book is focused on a distinct genre of Civil War commemoration. I did not include monuments that list Civil War soldiers or veterans as part of a larger tribute or recognition of veterans of other wars. The distinction might seem arbitrary: some overlap occurred with the monuments at Erwin and Nashville, for example, which give tribute to soldiers of World War I and the American

Civil War, vis-à-vis the monuments at Elizabethton. I made some deliberate exclusions, such as the excellent series of state or federally sponsored historical wayside markers or plaques, Tennessee Civil War Trails wayside markers, and the Civil War Trust's wayside battlefield narratives, though a discussion of their import is offered in chapter 6.

I did not include war memorials that "merely" give Civil War recognition. I excluded markers for headquarters locations—for example, Grant at Savannah, Bragg at Murfreesboro or Chattanooga. I excluded wayside tablets, narratives, position markers, or rosters on tablets, such as those erected on the battlefields at Chattanooga, Shiloh, Fort Donelson, and Stones River. I excluded parodies and a few monuments located on private property. I did not include war memorials that recognized the Civil War among tributes to the service of soldiers, such as the VFW monument at the Hancock County Courthouse in Sneedville, surmounted by what appears to be a generic common soldier.

Because I examined Civil War monuments as a distinct genre, I did not include wayside tablets, some two thousand in number, which are found across the state. I made allowances for such anomalies as the Michigan and Indiana tablets at Stones River (4.18.10) and Beech Gap (4.11.18), respectively. I included the Beech Gap tablet because it resembles the larger granite state unit monuments at Shiloh and Chattanooga, and I included the Stones River tablet as a monument because its language and evident intention was to serve as a state monument.

The largest deliberate exclusion is tombstones, a study that would run to volumes and is moreover a different genre. However, I admit to some arbitrariness: I made exceptions for the Nathan Bedford Forrest grave and equestrian statue, which, until its removal in 2017, served as a provocative kind of public shrine at Memphis, as well as some contextual or thematic examples, such as the graves of Sam Davis at Smyrna, Brig. Gen. Francis A. Shoup at the Sewanee Cemetery, S. A. Cunningham at Willow Mount Cemetery in Shelbyville, and Brig. Gen. Robert Hatton at Cedar Grove Cemetery in Lebanon.

Notes

1. I will use "American Civil War" and "Civil War" to describe the events of 1861–65, although the War Between the States or other descriptions may be more accurate or preferred, and the official term for the conflict is the War of the Rebellion, a description that reflects Northern interpretations. "Civil War" is rarely used on Confederate monuments, but the description reflects common contemporary usage. I will also use the term "Confederate monuments" broadly, although some monument inscriptions deliberately avoid the use of the word "Confederate." Similarly, the phrase "Confederate soldiers" is one I will use broadly; however, many monuments identify their soldiers by state, with no reference to their status as Confederate soldiers. "Casualty" will be defined as a person wounded, killed, or taken prisoner.

2. McMurry writes: "Those who would understand the military history of the Civil War—the campaigns and battles that sealed the fate of the Confederacy and preserved the Union—must look elsewhere than to southern Pennsylvania. They must go to the Peach Orchard—at Shiloh, not Gettysburg; to the railroad cut—at Atlanta, not Gettysburg; to Missionary Ridge, not Cemetery Ridge; to the Carter House, not the Codori House." ("The Pennsylvania Gambit and the Gettysburg Splash," in *The Gettysburg Nobody Knows*, ed. Gabor S. Borritt [New York: Oxford University Press, 1997], 202.)

3. Timothy S. Sedore, *An Illustrated Guide to Virginia's Confederate Monuments* (Champaign-Urbana: Southern Illinois University Press, 2011).

4. William Blair, *Cities of the Dead: Contesting the Memory of the Civil War in the South, 1865–1914* (Chapel Hill: University of North Carolina Press, 2004), 82.

5. Drew Gilpin Faust, *Mothers of Invention: Women of the Slaveholding South in the American Civil War* (Chapel Hill: University of North Carolina Press, 1996), 255.

6. Faust, 256–57.

7. The number is approximate. Some sculptures in bas or high relief are close kin to statues but are not included in this count. Other examples not included are mail-order or store-bought reproductions.

8. Richard Slotkin, *Regeneration through Violence: The Mythology of the American Frontier, 1600–1860* (Middletown, CT: Wesleyan University Press, 1973), 523.

9. Susan Soderburg, *Lest We Forget: A Guide to Civil War Monuments in Maryland* (Shippensburg, PA: White Mane, 1995), xiv–xvi. The use of stone markers is older, of course.

10. A marble shaft was erected to Francis S. Bartow at Manassas on September 4, 1861, only a few months after the war's first major battle. The shaft was placed on the site where Bartow was killed at the head of his brigade. (Union troops destroyed the monument when the Confederates retreated, but a vestige remains to this day.)

11. B. F. Cook, *Greek Inscriptions: Reading the Past* (Berkeley: University of California Press, 1987), 5.

12. Biblical references testify to similar practices. The Old Testament book of Proverbs enjoins hearers or readers of the text to respect the meaning of deeds and property and thus, by extension, to "remove not the ancient landmarks, which thy fathers have set" (22:28). The New Testament book of 1 Peter 2:4–6, borrowing from Isaiah 28:16, refers to Jesus Christ as "a cornerstone chosen and precious, and whoever believes in him will not be put to shame."

13. In his book *Lincoln at Gettysburg*, historian Garry Wills observes that a principal contrast in the Gettysburg Address "is between life and death. Plato says that the twin tasks of the Epitaphios are to extol the dead and to exhort the living . . . to 'laud the dead and lead survivors.' The Funeral Oration has two major sections—*epainesis*, or praise for the fallen, and *paranesis*, or advice for the living" (59).

14. In his *Judgment and Grace in Dixie*, Wilson declares,

> In the 1950s and 1960s, Confederate symbolism reemerged in the segregationist Lost Cause, a popular movement in response to the civil rights movement. Spokesmen for the Lost Cause organizations, and especially ministers in them, had rarely discussed racial issues in the post-Civil War era. Perhaps they simply did not have to do so because the Southern white consensus on racial supremacy was so great. In any

event, to earlier generations the Lost Cause symbols had taught complex lessons, including spiritual lessons of human limitation, suffering, the heroic sacrifices of the Confederates, and finally their tragic defeat. But in the 1950s, the Confederate symbols took on a harsher racial meaning. Segregationists used the symbols of the Lost Cause, and they became explicitly, almost exclusively identified with white supremacy in a new way. (25)

15. In the course of my research, I found that the only overt use of the word "slavery" on a Civil War monument of any kind—Northern or Southern—is in Boston's Common and Public Garden, on the Soldiers & Sailors Monument. Erected in 1779, the obelisk inscription reads, in part, that the destruction of slavery was one of the laudable outcomes of the war. "To The Men Of Boston" it says, "WHO DIED FOR THEIR COUNTRY ON LAND AND SEA / IN THE WAR WHICH KEPT THE UNION WHOLE / DESTROYED SLAVERY AND MAINTAINED THE CONSTITUTION."

16. Campbell Robertson, Monica Davey, and Julie Bosman, "Calls to Drop Confederate Emblems Spread Nationwide," *New York Times*, June 24, 2015, https://www.nytimes.com/2015/06/24/us/south-carolina-nikki-haley-confederate-flag.html.

17. Daniel Victor, "University of Mississippi Lowers State Flag with Confederate Symbol," *New York Times*, October 26, 2015, https://www.nytimes.com/2015/10/27/us/university-mississippi-lowers-state-flag-confederate-emblem.html.

18. Campbell Robertson, "Mississippi Flag, a Rebel Holdout, Is in a New Fight," *New York Times*, November 7, 2015, https://www.nytimes.com/2015/11/08/us/mississippi-flag-a-rebel-holdout-is-in-a-new-fight.html.

19. Charles Reagan Wilson, "'Religion and the American Civil War in Comparative Perspective," in *Religion and the American Civil War*, ed. Randall M. Miller, Harry S. Stout, and Charles Reagan Wilson (New York: Oxford University Press, 1998), 396–97.

20. Harry S. Stout, *Upon the Altar of the Nation: A Moral History of the Civil War* (New York: Penguin, 2006), 459.

21. Daniel Aaron observes that the American Civil War has given rise to voluminous commentary and research on its causes, so much so that it "has probably inspired more miscellaneous commentary—histories, biographies, memoirs, fiction, poetry—than all of America's other wars put together. It is, indeed, the war whose course has been most minutely traced and whose causes and consequences have been most exhaustively debated.

22. Charles Reagan Wilson, *Baptized in Blood: The Religion of the Lost Cause 1865–1920* (Athens: University of Georgia Press, 1980), 25.

23. Mark A. Noll, *The Civil War as a Theological Crisis* (Chapel Hill: University of North Carolina Press, 2006), 8. Noll justly, if sardonically, concludes that for "the history of theology in America, the great tragedy of the Civil War is that the most persuasive theologians were the Rev. Drs. William Tecumseh Sherman and Ulysses S. Grant" (66). He might well have added the name of Union general Philip Sheridan, whose name is still notorious in Virginia for his scorched earth policy in the Shenandoah Valley Campaign of 1864.

24. Daniel Aaron, *The Unwritten War: American Writers and the Civil War* (New York: Alfred A. Knopf, 1973), 328. Whitman's "real War" is a reference to the following passage from *Prose Works*: "Future years will never know the seething hell and the black infernal background of countless minor scenes and interiors, (not the official surface courteousness of the Generals, not the few great battles) of the Secession war; and it is best they should not—the real war will never get in the books."

25. Several historians have taken note of the war as a continuing conflict. John C. Waugh writes that the "Civil War has been a twice-fought affair—the war itself lasting four years, and the writing about the war, which is likely to never end" (Waugh in McWhiney, 7). Thomas Beer concludes that the war "ceased physically in 1865[, yet] its political end may be reasonably expected about the year 3000" (quoted in Aaron, 1973). And David Goldsmith goes further, although it is hard to credit him statistically. In his *Still Fighting the Civil War,* he ventures the judgment "that there is a war going on here." He continues,

> It is an ancient conflict, as war and time go in this country. The Civil War is like a ghost that has not yet made its peace and roams the land seeking solace, retribution, or vindication. It continues to exist, an event without temporal boundaries, an interminable struggle that has generated perhaps as many casualties since its alleged end in 1865 as during the four preceding years when armies clashed on the battlefield. For the society that became the South after 1865—and, truly, one could not speak of a distinct South before that time—the Civil War and the Reconstruction that followed shaped the form it takes today (1).

Shiloh National Military Park

N

0   1/4
Miles

Approximate
Boundary

Confederate
Burial Trench

Owl Creek

Tilghman Branch

Hamburg, Savannah Road

22

1.3.1

1.3.2

1.4.2

1.2.2

MULBERRY

CHALMERS

Pittsburg Landing Road

Visitor
Center

1.2.9
1.2.10
1.2.11
1.2.3
1.2.14
1.2.4
1.2.8
1.2.5
1.2.13
1.2.12
1.2.1
1.2.6
1.2.7

National
Cemetery
1.1.1

Picnic Area

SOWELL

JONES

1.4.1

CAVALRY

Cavalry Road

1.23.4

1.22.2

1.22.1

Dill Branch

1.21.2

Tennessee River

CRESCENT

1.23.3

1.23.2

1.23.1

1.23.5

1.23.6

1.22.3

1.22.4

1.13.1

CLOUD

Riverside Drive

1.21.1

1.20.2

1.5.1

1.5.2

1.6.3

1.6.4

1.6.2

1.6.1

1.6.5

WOOLF

1.7.20

1.12.7

1.12.6

1.12.9

1.12.8

1.17.3

Corinth, Pittsburg Landing Road

1.12.11

1.16.1

1.20.1

1.15.5

1.15.4

1.15.3

1.13.1

142

HOWELL

1.7.13

1.7.21

1.7.6

1.7.5

1.7.1

1.7.2

1.7.3

1.7.11

1.7.16

1.7.12

1.7.22

1.7.18

1.7.14

1.7.17

1.7.15

1.11.3

1.12.1

1.12.4

1.12.2

1.12.3

1.14.11

1.14.12

1.14.10

1.15.2

1.15.1

1.19.4

1.19.3

1.19.9

1.19.2

1.19.5

1.19.1

1.19.6

142

1.7.19

1.7.4

1.7.10

1.7.3

1.7.9

1.7.8

REVIEW

DUNCAN

1.14.3

1.14.4

WICKER

Bloody
Pond

1.19.8

1.19.7

1.8.2

1.8.1

1.8.11

Shiloh
Church

1.10.3

1.10.2

1.10.4

Sunken Road

Hamburg-Purdy Road

Sarah Bell's
Old Cotton Field

1.18.2

1.18.6

LOST

1.8.4

1.8.3

1.8.5

1.8.6

1.8.7

1.8.10

1.8.8

1.8.9

1.10.1

1.14.5

1.14.6

1.14.7

1.14.8

1.14.9

Peach
Orchard

1.18.3

1.18.5

1.18.4

1.18.1

Shiloh Branch

1.8.14

BARNES

Eastern Corinth Road

1.16.2

1.17.1

1.17.2

Hamburg Road

LARKIN

1.8.12

1.8.13

REA

Peabody Road

22

Corinth Road

Reconnoitering Road

SPAIN

1.9.1

MCCULLER

Pratt Lane

FRALEY

SEAY

22

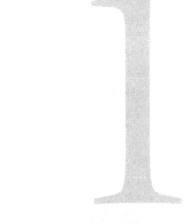

SHILOH
NATIONAL MILITARY PARK
"WITNESS AND TESTIMONY"

ACH CIVIL WAR BATTLEFIELD has a complexity of its own, but Ulysses S. Grant famously observed that the Battle of Shiloh has a particular mystery to it, that it "has been perhaps less understood, or, to state the case more accurately, more persistently misunderstood, than any other engagement . . . during the entire rebellion." The ground on which the Battle of Shiloh was fought retains much of the rural character and topography it had on April 6–7, 1862, when the area was the setting for an early war cataclysm that led to 25,000 casualties among the 80,000 participants, and that presaged the 618,000 deaths that the war would visit on the country. The park was established by act of Congress in 1894, in part as a means of ensuring that the unrecovered dead would be undisturbed. Today the grounds cover over five thousand acres: the War Department erected 651 informative and descriptive wayside iron tablets and road signs, and superintended the grounds until 1933, when oversight was transferred to the National Park Service. A host of monuments now stand on the battlefield. Most of these are Union monuments, and most are to individual state units: forty-one monuments from Illinois, thirty-four from Ohio, twelve from Iowa, twenty from Indiana, and one each from Pennsylvania, Minnesota, and Michigan. By Park Commission stipulations, no Union monuments were erected to individual officers. Only one is to an individual soldier, Pvt. J. D. Putnam of the 14th Wisconsin, and only one is to a Confederate officer, Joseph Wheeler, colonel of the 19th Alabama Cavalry at Shiloh.

Several salient points should be noted. First, the Park Commission retained—and retains—final say on the wording and placement of the monuments. No cause, no victory, no defeat is mentioned. There are no overt apologetics or politics. "Witness and Testimony" predominate: this is the message of Shiloh's small unit monumentation. The inscriptions were approved for accuracy, tone, and content, and in keeping with mandates to display inscriptions as veritable after-action reports. Justly so, David W. Reed, Shiloh Park Commission's first historian, insisted that small unit monument inscriptions, such as regiments or batteries, be factual and historically accurate. Reed also mandated that inscriptions be without praise or criticism. The result may seem abstract: tactical maneuvers are summarized; who was in command is noted; casualties are reported; and small unit action—regiments or batteries—is emphasized. It was evidently intended to be objective, as well as to do honor to the common soldier. There are no equestrian monuments at Shiloh—unlike

Gettysburg, for example—and there is nothing like the hosts of monuments to officers that are displayed at Vicksburg. Intentionally or not, Reed, a soldier in the 12th Iowa who fought at Shiloh, had a central role in leaving a legacy emphasizing deeds done by the Union soldier at Shiloh.

Second, these are not landscape portraits; nevertheless, the monuments have a still-life artistry element to them. Each small-unit Shiloh monument offers a cryptic witness. Collectively, they offer a time-and-place narrative flow across the battlefield. The layout of this chapter, therefore, follows that narrative flow. This chapter cannot substitute for the histories of the battle that have been written, but it enables the reader to follow the course of the action by dint of what each unit reported at each site—on the ground, on foot—as they were in 1862, at least as they testified afterward. The entries in this book also detail where individual regiments or batteries came from, their service before and after Shiloh, when they mustered out, and their losses while in service. The successive ranks of unit monuments—from south of Shiloh Church to the Sunken Road east toward the river and north to the Last Line of Defense—are manifest evidence of the tumult and shifting fortunes that occurred here.

Third, it is not possible to do a faithful study of the landscape of the battlefield and ignore the monumentation, but, ironically, the inscriptions on the unit monuments were a neglected resource among historians. Some redress has occurred in recent decades. Historian Timothy Smith observes that Edward Cunningham used the battlefield's terrain and the array of tablets and monuments in his study, as have Stacy Allen and James Gentsch. In fact, a multivolume text could be devoted to these monuments, one that would take into account the military and larger thematic elements of this array. A philosopher-historian who is a student of the landscape could take the matter to a deeper level. On the one hand, the monuments of Shiloh can seem repetitive—there are so many, they are so similar. On the other hand, one may think of the monuments themselves as jewels of a sort. They are relatively large and blunt as stones, of course, but they are affixed to the landscape as precisely and permanently as mortal hands can make them. The stones were shaped by artisans: each is utterly distinctive; and they have enormous symbolism and value as a testimony of blood, sweat, fear, and trauma.

Fourth, the inscriptions, in turn, are comparable to musical lyrics. They may not be poetic; even as prose they can seem mechanical, laconic, or formulaic. However, as with the most memorable musical lyrics, the words are precisely chosen. And just as lyrics are integrated within the flow of melodic phrasing, so the inscriptions at Shiloh are integrated into the terrain of the battlefield. Shiloh's monument inscriptions are set into place on a unique liturgical landscape in the same way that lyrics are emplaced within the framework

State of Iowa, Column and Statue, with adjacent obelisks of the 17th, 51st, and 58th Indiana Infantry nearby

of musical scores—this place, this ground for these words. Their poetry is in their consonance with the landscape.

Having said all this, I should note that monuments are not equally accessible. The Beaux-Arts style of the Iowa state monument attracts particular notice. Its location near the park headquarters and visitors center brings professional and amateur photographers. It is also a place for family photos, and small children to clamber—at some hazard—on the monument. The column is lofty, and the base is spacious: granite steps allow visitors easy access to the base of the monument itself—technically, the base is termed a stylobate or temple floor. Open communion is invited, as it were. The inscription, including the Gettysburg Address, is simple but lofty, like the monument itself. The bronze wreath, the statue of a female in the act of writing an inscription, and surmounting eagle in the act of taking wing, are collectively visually dramatic. In some sense, history lives in the dynamics of the Iowa monument: the whole of the shrine looks as if it were still in the act of being completed, and the visitor takes on a role or place in the present tense dynamic.

The three Indiana obelisks standing in a row nearby do not garner nearly the same notice, and with good reason. Obelisks are common architectural forms of the time, but there is an arch, abstract quality to them. In fact, they are derived from a religious rhetoric that was intended to be otherworldly. Their Egyptian Revival features seem reserved. With their sharpened points directed upward, intended to represent veritable shafts of light—stretching toward the gods, as the Egyptians would have it—they are, in short, aloof: they defy ordinary, common interaction.

No Southern state participated initially in the monument movement at Shiloh. Early twentieth-century initiatives to fund monuments among the state legislatures of Texas, Georgia, and Florida were not successful. However, privately funded monuments were erected to the 2nd Tennessee Infantry in 1905 and the Crescent Regiment (Louisiana) in 1915. The United Daughters of the Confederacy (UDC) also stepped in. The largest dedication ceremony in the commemorative history of Shiloh took place on May 17, 1917, when the UDC unveiled its monument, "Victory Defeated by Death and Night," before an estimated crowd of fifteen thousand people. The UDC of Alabama erected a monument to its soldiers in 1907, and the Arkansas UDC did likewise in 1910.

In 1964, during the centennial of the war, the State of Texas erected a granite stele. Thereafter, the border states of Missouri and Kentucky erected monuments, in 1971 and 1974, respectively. Further redress has occurred. The State of Tennessee erected a monument in Woolf Field in 2005, and the State of Mississippi dedicated a monument at Rhea Springs in 2015.

Mass Graves

Federal troops held the field in the aftermath of the battle and interred the Union and Confederate dead. General P. G. T. Beauregard requested permission from General Grant for a mounted party to return to Shiloh to bury the Confederate dead. Grant refused, writing in response that "owing to the warmth of the weather I deemed it advisable to have all the dead of both parties buried immediately . . . now it is accomplished."

An unknown number of dead of both armies remain on the battlefield, unmarked or unidentified. The Union dead were removed to a new national cemetery in 1869. However, most of the Confederate dead at Shiloh have never been disinterred. They remain on the field in several large mass graves and

Mass graves site stele near Rhea Springs, with UDC stele

Illinois Stele: Typical Unit Monument for Illinois, one of forty-one erected by the state; this one, to the 58th Ill VI

many smaller individual plots. In contrast, one thousand dead were reinterred from the Antietam battlefield in 1872 to Washington Confederate Cemetery in Hagerstown, and some three thousand dead were exhumed from Gettysburg and reinterred at Hollywood Cemetery in Richmond in 1872–73.

Five sites—"Trenches Interring Confederate Dead"—are known, marked, and commemorated, but at least six mass graves remain unmarked and anonymous. The known sites were originally marked with a concrete wall twelve inches high with ten-inch cannonballs placed at intervals along the edge.

The United Daughters of the Confederacy later took a hand by sponsoring the placement of granite stelae of Mount Airy granite at each of the five known sites. Two were erected, then dedicated May 17, 1917, the same year as the UDC monument to the Confederate soldier; the UDC would go on to sponsor three more in 1935.

Illinois

The most common monument at Shiloh is from Illinois. The Illinois state legislature approved funding for monumentation at Shiloh on June 7, 1897. The legislation provided for one central monument as well as one monument for each regiment of infantry, each battery, and one, collectively, for Illinois cavalry. The regimental and artillery monuments are standardized and virtually identical: each is a granite stele, typically sixty-nine inches tall, seventy-four inches wide, and thirty-six inches deep, on a base ninety-two inches wide, nineteen inches high, and fifty-two inches deep, with bronze plaques on the reverse side. The monuments cost $470 each. The standard monument is an inscribed granite stele with a bronze plaque on the reverse.

The state dedicated its monuments on the site of the Illinois State Memorial, on May 17–18, 1904, with Cornelius Cadle, chairman of the Shiloh Park Commission, accepting the monuments on behalf of the federal government. Among the speakers was former Confederate Brig. Gen. Basil W. Duke, who fought at Shiloh. Of the importance of the occasion, Duke said, "When a people renders such honors to the heroic dead it honors itself. The national care bestowed on this historic spot is as much a potent lesson to the future as a sacred duty to the past, for it commemorates the virtues without which nations can not survive. May those who fell here never be forgotten, and may these monuments erected to their memory remain as enduring admonitions to the youth of succeeding generations, to love and serve their country equally as well."

Indiana

Indiana has no central monument, but the state sponsored the erection of inscribed obelisks to nineteen infantry regiments, two batteries of artillery, and one regiment of cavalry. John R. Lowe, a native Indianan who served with the 11th Indiana at Shiloh, was the designer of the prototype: each obelisk stands sixteen feet, six inches, surmounting a base eight feet, two inches square; the whole weighs some thirteen thousand pounds. The Muldoon Granite Company of Louisville, Kentucky, executed the design in oolitic Indiana limestone. The dedication ceremonies took place on April 6–7, 1903, the forty-first anniversary of the battle.

Indiana Obelisk: standard unit monument, one of twenty-four erected by the state; this one, for the 23rd Indiana VI

Iowa

The State of Iowa dedicated eleven regimental markers and the Iowa State Monument on November 23, 1906. Iowa Governor Albert B. Cummins made the presentation at the ceremonies; the memorials were accepted for the park by Commissioner Cornelius Cadle. The state's Beaux-Arts central monument stands along "Grant's Last Line," near the park's visitors center, and is one of the most prominent on the battlefield. The eleven unit monuments are of Vermont granite, of one type, approved by Iowa's Shiloh Battlefield Commission, designed by the firm of Shenan and Flavin: decorated stelae surmounting a base of bronze and Vermont Barre granite—standing nine feet, four inches high on a base ten feet, one inch wide.

Ohio

Dedication ceremonies for thirty-four Ohio regimental monuments took place on June 6, 1902. The presentation of the monuments was made by Judge David F. Pugh of Ohio, a veteran of the 46th Ohio VI; acceptance on behalf of the War Department was made by Commission Chairman Cadle at Shiloh. The state erected no central monument. Unlike the other states with multiple monuments, the Ohio unit monuments are of various designs. The medium is light Barre granite, all built by the Hughes Granite and Marble Company, Clyde, Ohio. There is uncertainty about the designer of the Ohio monuments, but it is believed to be a man named Loester, who may have been an employee of the Hughes Company.

US Army Regulars

Since states provided most of the monuments at Shiloh, the role of US Army Regulars at Shiloh might well have been overlooked; however, the federal government intervened, providing $5,750 for three monuments to be erected, one each for artillery, cavalry, and infantry. The decision on placement was made by David W. Reed; Reed also wrote the inscriptions. The monuments were carved in Barre granite by the Hodges Granite Company of St. Louis: obelisks surmounting a two-tiered base, each displays a prominent "U.S." in raised relief. The obelisks were dedicated December 9, 1910.

Background: The Battle

The fall of Fort Henry and Fort Donelson in February 1862 were major setbacks to Confederate ambitions. Confederate Gen. Albert S. Johnston was compelled to yield Kentucky and much of West and Middle Tennessee to Union forces. From Corinth, Mississippi, a railroad crossroads, Johnston staged a counter-offensive with the Confederate Army of the Mississippi against the Union

Iowa Stele: Standard Unit Monument, one of twelve erected by the state, this one for the 2nd Iowa VI

Ohio: Unit Monument, the 48th VI, one of thirty-four erected by the state, of various types

US Infantry, Regulars, Obelisk, Standard, one of three

Army of the Tennessee on April 6, 1862, commanded by Maj. Gen. Ulysses S. Grant. Johnston's ambition was to defeat the Federals at Pittsburg Landing before they could unite with the Army of the Ohio, which was en route, under the command of Maj. Gen. Don Carlos Buell.

The Confederates took the Union forces by surprise on the morning of April 6; they gave ground. Thousands of Union soldiers took flight, but others rallied or gave ground stubbornly. Although driven hard, the Union forces did not break, and Grant kept his nerve and stayed in the fight. Johnston was mortally wounded; General P. G. T. Beauregard succeeded him. Eventually the Union troops established a defense line covering Pittsburg Landing ("Grant's Last Line of Defense"), anchored with artillery and augmented by arriving elements of the Army of the Ohio. Fighting continued until after dusk, but the Union soldiers withstood the onslaught.

By next morning, April 7, most of Buell's troops were in place. The combined Union forces, about forty thousand men, outnumbered the Confederates, who by now mustered fewer than thirty thousand. The Southerners, under Beauregard, were unaware of the disparity and launched a counterattack in response to an advance by elements of Buell's army at 6:00 am. At first, the attack was successful, but Union resistance solidified and drove the Confederates back. Beauregard ordered a counterattack, which stopped the Union advance but progressed no further. Beauregard, recognizing that his army could not win and had sustained over ten thousand casualties, yielded the ground to the Federals and withdrew his army to Corinth. Grant's army earned the victory— they held the field—but they did not pursue closely.

The Union forces—the combined Army of the Tennessee and Army of the Ohio—sustained some 13,000 casualties among their aggregate of 65,000, including 1,754 dead. The Confederate Army of the Mississippi, nearly 45,000 men, had over 10,000 casualties, including 1,728 dead. Total casualties are said to have been 23,746.

National Cemetery

1.1.1 Subject: 9th Illinois VI, Stele
Location: Section G   N 35 08 00 07 / W 88 19 09 36
Dedicated: May 17–18, 1904
Media: Bronze, granite
Monument is a decorated stele surmounting a base.

Inscription

U.S. / 9TH ILLINOIS INFANTRY / VOLUNTEERS / U.S.A.

APRIL 6, 1862 / PRESENT FOR DUTY 578 / KILLED AND DIED OF WOUNDS 103 / WOUNDED 263. / TOTAL KILLED AND WOUNDED, 366

Shiloh National Cemetery, 9th Illinois VI, Stele

The ten-acre tract of Shiloh National Cemetery was established in 1866. The dead were taken from 156 locations on the battlefield, as well as 565 sites along the Tennessee River. Headboards of wood for each grave were replaced in 1876–77 by granite stones. The cemetery inters the remains of 3,584 Union soldiers, 2,359 of them unknown. This is the only unit monument in the cemetery: the 9th Illinois monument stands on a bluff overlooking the river and Pittsburg Landing. Among Union regiments, the 9th had the highest casualties of any regiment at Shiloh and was given two monuments on the field: here at the cemetery where its dead are buried, and another monument near Shiloh Church (1.18.4 [numbers refer to labels in chapter]).

Grant's Last Line of Defense

Union cavalry saw limited service at the Battle of Shiloh, mostly as pickets, guards, orderlies, or couriers. Terrain did not suit the use of cavalry, but the legislation for Shiloh monuments stipulated that all units on the field during the battle would be commemorated, regardless of the extent of their service. In addition, some units of infantry or artillery arrived too late to the battlefield to see combat; others were detailed to guard supply lines. All units from Ohio, Illinois, and Indiana were deemed worthy of monuments regardless of the extent of their service. Their monuments were also placed here, on the margin of the Union Army's Last Line of Defense.

1.2.1 Subject: Battery H, Illinois Vol. Artillery
Location: N 35 08 01 35 / W 88 19 18 24
Dedicated: May 17–18, 1904
Media: Bronze, granite
Monument is a decorated stele surmounting a base.

Inscription

ILLINOIS / BATTERY "H" / 1 REGIMENT LT. ARTILLERY / UNASSIGNED / ARMY OF THE TENNESSEE

. . . COMMANDED BY / CAPT. AXEL SILFERSPARRE. / THIS BATTERY CONSISTING OF FOUR 20 POUNDERS, ARRIVED / AT THE LANDING APRIL 5, 1862. DURING SUNDAY THE GUNS / WERE BROUGHT BY HAND TO THIS POSITION AND DID GOOD / SERVICE IN RESISTING THE AFTERNOON ATTACK UPON THIS / LINE. THE BATTERY HAD 6 MEN MISSING.

Battery H was organized at Chicago, mustered in February 20, 1862. Mustered out June 14, 1865.

1.2.2 Subject: Illinois Vol. Cavalry, Shaft
Location: N 35 08 03 48 / W 88 19 23 54
Dedicated: May 17–18, 1904
Media: Bronze, granite
Monument is a hexagon surmounting a base.

Inscriptions

ILLINOIS / "THE NATURE OF / THE BATTLE WAS / SUCH THAT CAVALRY / COULD NOT BE USED / IN FRONT. I THERE / FORE FORMED OURS / INTO LINE IN REAR." / GRANT. / ARMY OF THE / TENNESSEE

TO / 1ST BATTALION, / 4TH CAVALRY, / MCCLERNAND'S / 1ST DIVISION *[IN RESERVE]*

HER / COMPANIES A & B, / 2ND CAVALRY, CAPT. THOS. J. LARRISON. / THESE COMPANIES WERE / ACTING AS DIVISION HEAD / QUARTERS GUARD AND ESCORT / AND WERE NOT ACTIVELY / ENGAGED IN THE BATTLE OF / APRIL 6TH AND 7TH, 1862. / W. H. L. WALLLACE / (2ND) DIVISION

CAVALRY / 3D BATTALION, 11TH CAVALRY, *[IN RESERVE]*

2ND & 3D BATTALIONS, / 4TH CAVALRY, *[NOT ACTIVELY ENGAGED]*

SHILOH / *[1ST & 2ND BATTALIONS, / 11TH CAVALRY]*

3 MEN / WERE KILLED AND 3 WOUNDED. / PRENTISS' / (6TH) DIVISION

Standing ten feet high and ten feet in diameter, the distinctive Illinois cavalry monument, erected at a stated cost of $2,596, was designed by Richard Bock, who also designed Illinois's state monument. Shaped in the form of a hexagon, the monument was likened by Bock to a hitching post.

Illinois Vol. Cavalry, Shaft

1.2.3 Subject: 2nd Indiana Vol. Cavalry, Obelisk
Location: N 35 09 03 75 / W 88 19 24 36
Dedicated: April 6–7, 1903
Medium: Limestone
Monument is a decorated obelisk surmounting a base.

Inscriptions

2D / REGIMENT, / CAVALRY. / COMMANDED BY / LIEUT. COL. EDWARD M. MCCOOK

4TH DIVISION—GEN. NELSON—/ ARMY OF THE OHIO. / INDIANA.

ARRIVED OPPOSITE PITTSBURG LANDING / ON SUNDAY EVENING, APRIL 6TH, 1862, WITH / GEN. NELSON'S DIVISION. WAS ORDERED TO REMAIN / THERE UNTIL IN THE AFTERNOON OF / THE 7TH, WHEN IT / CROSSED THE RIVER TO THE BATTLEFIELD. CASUALTIES, / WOUNDED 2 MEN; MISSING 1 MAN; TOTAL 3.

The regiment was present on the battlefield but did not see combat. The 41st Indiana (2nd Indiana Cavalry) organized at Indianapolis in September 1861, the first complete cavalry regiment raised in the state. Shiloh. Corinth. Pea Ridge. Tuscumbia. Perryville. Talbot's Station. Atlanta. Raid through Alabama. Mustered out July 22, 1865. Loss by death, 131.

1.2.4 Subject: State of Iowa, Column and Statue, Female
Location: N 35 09 02 63 / W 88 19 28 04
Dedicated: November 23, 1906
Media: Bronze, granite
Monument is an eagle surmounting a column and base, with the figure of a woman inscribing a tribute along the plinth.

Inscriptions
[Front]
E PLURIBUS UNUM

[Eagle clutching shield and ribbon at top of monument]
THIS MONUMENT IS ERECTED / BY THE STATE OF IOWA

IN COMMEMORATION / OF THE LOYALTY, PATRIOTISM
AND BRAVERY OF HER SONS / WHO, ON THIS BATTLEFIELD
OF SHILOH / ON THE 6TH AND 7TH / DAYS OF APRIL / A.D. MDCCCLXII
FOUGHT TO PERPETUATE THE SACRED / UNION OF THE STATES.
IOWA

[Sculpted figure of a female with pen in hand inscribing the following words]
BRAVE OF THE BRAVE, THE TWICE FIVE THOUSAND MEN
WHO ALL THAT DAY STOOD IN THE BATTLE'S SHOCK,
FAME HOLDS THEM DEAR, AND WITH IMMORTAL PEN
INSCRIBES THEIR NAMES ON THE ENDURING ROCK

REGIMENTS ENGAGED.

[Roster]

"THE WORLD / WILL LITTLE NOTE
NOR LONG REMEMBER / WHAT WE SAY HERE,
BUT IT CAN NEVER FORGET / WHAT THEY DID HERE".
[Inscribed on bronze wreath of oak and laurel]
IOWA / IN / MEMORY OF SHILOH

From a Beaux-Arts design by native Iowan Frederick Triebel, the Iowa monument stands seventy-five feet high, with a Corinthian column surmounted by a bronze eagle clutching a shield bearing the emblem of the United States. At its base, the figure of a woman is ascending the steps and inscribing the deeds of Iowa's soldiers on the pages of history. Triebel's wife, Santina Triebel, was the model for the figure.

This state monument and the Iowa regimental monuments are of Barre granite and cost $8,051. Iowa's monuments were dedicated on November 23, 1906. The Shiloh event was the last in a series of war memorials dedicated during the course of a tour by the Iowa delegation of state monuments at Chattanooga, Chickamauga, Vicksburg, and Andersonville.

State of Iowa: The figure of a woman inscribing "Brave of the brave"

- The excerpt beginning "The World Will Little Note" is taken from the Gettysburg Address. "E Pluribus Unum" is taken from the national motto of the United States and is translated from the Latin as "From many, one."

1.2.5 Subject: 17th Indiana VI, Obelisk
Location: N 35 09 02 22 / W 88 19 28 48
Dedicated: April 6–7, 1903
Medium: Limestone
Monument is a decorated obelisk surmounting a base.

Inscription

17TH / REGIMENT / INFANTRY, / COMMANDED BY / COL. JOHN T. WILDER. / 15TH BRIGADE—GEN. HASCALL— / 6TH DIVISION—GEN. WOOD— / ARMY OF THE OHIO. / INDIANA

. . . THIS REGIMENT ARRIVED ON THE BATTLEFIELD AT 12 / O'CLOCK ON THE NIGHT OF APRIL 7, 1862, TOO LATE / TO PARTICIPATE IN THE BATTLE. . . .

Organized at Indianapolis, mustered on June 12, 1861. West Virginia. Shiloh. Chickamauga. Chattanooga. Atlanta. Wilson's Raid. Mustered out August 8, 1865. Regiment lost 237 men killed, mortally wounded, or by disease.

1.2.6 Subject: 51st Indiana VI, Obelisk
Location: N 35 09 02 22 / W 88 19 29 08
Dedicated: April 6–7, 1903
Medium: Limestone
Monument is a decorated obelisk surmounting a base.

Inscription

51ST / REGIMENT / INFANTRY / COMMANDED BY / COL. ABEL D. STREIGHT, / 20TH BRIGADE—GEN. GARFIELD / 6TH DIVISION—GEN. WOOD / ARMY OF THE OHIO. / INDIANA.

. . . THIS REGIMENT WAS DETAILED . . . TO GUARD / AND BRING UP THE BRIGADE TRAIN . . . AND WAS NOT ENGAGED AT SHILOH.

Organized at Indianapolis, mustered in December 14, 1861. Perryville. Stones River. Regiment captured, Galesville, May 3, 1863; exchanged November 1863. Franklin. Nashville. Mustered out December 13, 1865. Regiment lost 264 men killed, mortally wounded, or by disease.

1.2.7 Subject: 58th Indiana VI, Obelisk
Location: N 35 09 02 31 / W 88 19 29 58
Dedicated: April 6–7, 1903
Medium: Limestone
Monument is a decorated obelisk surmounting a base.

Inscription

58TH / REGIMENT / INFANTRY, / COMMANDED BY / COL. HENRY M. CARR, / 15TH BRIGADE—COL. M. S. HASCALL— / 6TH DIVISION—GEN. WOOD— / ARMY OF THE OHIO. / INDIANA.

. . . THIS REGIMENT / ARRIVED ON THE BATTLEFIELD APRIL 7, 1862, / TOO LATE TO PARTICIPATE IN THE BATTLE.

Organized at Princeton and Indianapolis, December 22, 1861. Corinth. Stones River. Tullahoma. Chickamauga. Chattanooga. Atlanta. March to the Sea. Carolinas Campaign. Grand Review. Mustered out July 25, 1865. Lost 258 officers or enlisted men killed, mortally wounded, or by disease.

1.2.8 Subject: Illinois Vol. Siege Artillery, 2nd Regt., Stele
Location: N 35 09 01 90 / W 88 19 30 82
Dedicated: May 17–18, 1904
Media: Bronze, granite
Monument is a decorated stele surmounting a base.

Inscription
ILLINOIS / SIEGE GUNS / 2D REGIMENT—ARTILLERY / UNASSIGNED / ARMY OF THE TENNESSEE

BATTERY "B". / COMMANDED BY / CAPT. RELLY MADISON. / THIS BATTERY OF SIEGE GUNS WAS THE NUCLEUS / AROUND WHICH WAS RALLIED THE LINE / THAT SUCCESSFULLY RESISTED THE ATTACK OF SUNDAY EVENING, APRIL 6, 1862. / THERE WERE NO CASUALTIES.

Organized at Springfield, June 20, 1861. Mustered out July 15, 1865. Lost thirty enlisted men killed, mortally wounded, or by disease.

Illinois Vol. Siege Artillery, 2nd Regt., Stele

1.2.9 Subject: Battery A, 1st Vol. Ohio Light Artillery, Stele
Location: N 35 09 03 27 / W 88 19 33 34
Dedicated: June 6, 1902
Medium: Granite
Monument is a decorated shaft surmounting a base.

Inscriptions

OHIO

[Relief of two crossed ramrods, two olive wreaths; inscription framed with cannonball reliefs]

BATTERY A / 1ST LIGHT ARTILLERY / COMMANDED BY / CAPT. W. F. GOODSPEED / MCCOOK'S (2D) DIVISION / ARMY OF THE OHIO

[Two flanking cannon barrels]

THIS BATTERY ARRIVED ON THE FIELD ABOUT 2 PM, APRIL 7, / 1862, TOO LATE TO BE ENGAGED.

1.2.10 Subject: 65th Ohio VI, Stele
Location: N 35 09 03 27 / W 88 19 33 98
Dedicated: June 6, 1902
Medium: Granite
Monument is a decorated shaft surmounting a base.

Inscriptions

OHIO

[Two reliefs of crossed rifles, knapsack, blanket roll, and canteen]

65TH INFANTRY / COMMANDED BY / CHARLES G. HARKER / GARFIELD'S (20TH) BRIGADE / WOOD'S (6TH) DIVISION / ARMY OF THE OHIO

THIS REGIMENT ARRIVED ON THE FIELD AT 1.30 PM, APRIL / 7, 1862, ADVANCED TO THE FRONT, NEAR SHILOH CHURCH, BETWEEN / 3 AND 4 PM, TOO LATE TO BE ENGAGED.

Organized at Mansfield, November 1861. Shiloh. Corinth. Perryville. Stones River. Tullahoma. Chickamauga. Chattanooga. Atlanta. Franklin. Nashville. Mustered out November 30, 1865. Lost 257 officers and enlisted men killed, mortally wounded, or by disease.

1.2.11 Subject: 5th Ohio Vol. Cavalry, Stele
Location: N 35 09 03 30 / W 88 19 34 66
Dedicated: June 6, 1902
Medium: Granite
Monument is a decorated shaft surmounting a base.

Inscription

OHIO

[Relief of three olive wreaths and one central torch]

1 2 3 / BATTALIONS / 5TH CAVALRY / COMMANDED BY / COL. WM. H. H. TAYLOR /
1ST AND 2D BATTALIONS, HURLBUTS (4TH) DIVISION / 3D BATTALION, L. WALLACE'S
(3D) DIVISION / ARMY OF THE TENNESSEE

1ST AND 2D BATTALIONS WERE IN RESERVE, APRIL 6, 1862. . . .

Shiloh. Corinth. Central Mississippi Campaign. Lexington. Salem Cemetery.
Chattanooga. Atlanta. March to the Sea. Carolinas Campaign. Mustered out
October 30, 1865. Lost 170 officers or enlisted men killed, mortally wounded,
or by disease.

1.2.12 Subject: 56th Ohio VI, Stele
Location: N 35 09 03 38 / W 88 19 35 20
Dedicated: June 6, 1902
Medium: Granite
Monument is a decorated shaft surmounting a base.

Inscription
[Inscription framed by two Ionic columns in relief]

OHIO / 56TH INFANTRY, / COMMANDED BY / COL. PETER KINNEY, / WITTLESEY'S
(3D) BRIGADE, / L. WALLACE'S (3D) DIVISION, / ARMY OF THE / TENNESSEE.

THIS REGIMENT WAS LEFT TO GUARD / STORES AT CRUMP'S LANDING.

Organized at Camp Morrow, Portsmouth; mustered in December 12, 1861.
Shiloh. Corinth. Vicksburg. Red River Campaign. Mustered out April 25, 1866.
Lost 216 officers or enlisted men killed, mortally wounded, or by disease.

1.2.13 Subject: 64th Ohio VI, Stele
Location: N 35 09 03 52 / W 88 19 35 90
Dedicated: June 6, 1902
Medium: Granite
Monument is a decorated stele surmounting a base.

Inscriptions

OHIO / 64TH INFANTRY, / COMMANDED BY / COL. JOHN FERGUSON, / GARFIELD'S (20TH) BRIGADE, / WOOD'S (6TH) DIVISION, / ARMY OF THE OHIO.

THIS REGIMENT ARRIVED ON THE FIELD AT 2 PM, APRIL 7, / 1862, TOO LATE TO BE ENGAGED.

Organized at Camp Buckingham, Mansfield, mustered in November 9, 1861. Shiloh. Corinth. Perryville. Stones River. Tullahoma. Chickamauga. Atlanta. Franklin. Nashville. Mustered out December 3, 1865. Lost 274 officers or enlisted men killed, mortally wounded, or by disease.

1.2.14 Subject: 68th Ohio VI, Stele
Location: N 35 09 03 58 / W 88 19 36 44
Dedicated: June 6, 1902
Medium: Granite

Inscription

68TH / INFANTRY / OHIO / COMMANDED BY / COL. SAMUEL H. / STEEDMAN / THAYER'S / (2D) BRIGADE, / L. WALLACE'S / (3D) DIVISION, / ARMY / OF THE / TENNESSEE

THIS REGIMENT / WAS LEFT TO GUARD / STORES AT CRUMP'S / LANDING.

Organized at Camp Latta, Napoleon, by December 1861. Fort Donelson. Shiloh. Corinth. Central Mississippi Campaign. Vicksburg. Meridian. Atlanta. Carolinas Campaign. Grand Review. Mustered out July 10, 1865. Lost 300 officers or enlisted men killed, mortally wounded, or by disease.

1.3.1 Subject: US Cavalry, Shaft
Location: N 35 09 25 41 / W 88 20 19 94
Dedicated: December 9, 1910
Medium: Granite
Monument is an obelisk surmounting a base.

Inscription

U.S. / 2ND U.S. CAVALRY COMPANY "C" / 4TH U.S. CAVALRY COMPANY "I" / LIEUT.
JAMES POWELL COMMANDING. / 2ND. DIV. (W. H. L. WALLACE) / ARMY OF THE
TENNESSEE

[Relief of laurel wreath, crossed swords surmounting shield]

THESE COMPANIES WERE ENGAGED ALL DAY APRIL 6, 1862, IN / FRONT OF THEIR
CAMP, AS SKIRMISHERS ON THE RIGHT OF THE / UNION ARMY. / CASUALTIES: 1
KILLED, 5 WOUNDED, TOTAL 6.

Co. "C": Forts Henry and Donelson. Shiloh. Corinth. Central Mississippi.
Joined regiment at Falmouth, May 1863. Co. "I," 4th Cavalry (formerly 1st
Cavalry): Wilson's Creek. Fort Donelson. Shiloh. Corinth. Perryville. Stones
River. Tullahoma. Chickamauga. Sparta. Kilpatrick's Raid. Nashville. Wilson's
Raid. Combined losses 171 officers or enlisted men killed, mortally wounded,
or by disease.

1.3.2 Subject: 66th Illinois VI, Shaft
Location: N 35 09 17 19 / W 88 20 20 38
Dedicated: May 17–18, 1904
Media: Bronze, granite
Monument is a decorated stele surmounting a base.

Inscriptions

ILLINOIS / 14TH MISSOURI / AFTERWARDS DESIGNATED / 66TH ILLINOIS INFANTRY
/ 2ND BRIGADE—MCARTHUR / 2ND DIVISION—W. H. L. WALLACE / ARMY OF THE
TENNESSEE

... COMMANDED BY COL. B. S. COMPTON. / THIS REGIMENT KNOWN AS BIRGES
SHARP SHOOTERS ARMED / WITH DEER RIFLES WAS DETACHED FROM ITS BRIGADE
AT / 9.30 A.M. APRIL 6TH 1862 AND ORDERED TO GUARD SNAKE / CREEK BRIDGE[.]
IT WAS SOON ORDERED BACK TO THIS PLACE / AND WAS ENGAGED HERE AND IN
FIELD BEYOND THE CREEK. / ON MONDAY A PART OF THE COMMAND WAS ENGAGED
IN / FRONT OF 3D DIVISION. / *[LOST]* 2 MEN KILLED AND 6 MEN / WOUNDED—
TOTAL, 8

Organized at Benton Barracks, October 1861. Mustered in as 14th Missouri
VI, November 23, 1861; as 66th Illinois VI, November 20, 1862. Fort Donelson.
Shiloh. Corinth. Iuka. Atlanta. Carolinas Campaign. Grand Review. Mustered
out July 7, 1865. Lost 227 officers or enlisted men killed, mortally wounded,
or by disease.

9th Indiana Vol. Artillery, Shaft

West of TN 22, West of Woolf Field

1.4.1 Subject: 9th Battery, Indiana Vol. Artillery, Obelisk
Location: N 35 09 14 16 / W 88 20 18 58
Dedicated: April 6–7, 1903
Medium: Limestone
Monument is a decorated obelisk surmounting a base.

Inscription

9TH / BATTERY, / THOMPSON'S / (NOT BRIGADED) / 3D DIVISION—MAJ. GEN. LEWIS WALLACE—/ ARMY OF THE TENNESSEE. / INDIANA.

. . . APRIL 6TH, 1862, THIS BATTERY LEFT STONY LONESOME / AT 12 M., BY SHUNPIKE ROAD; COUNTER-MARCHING AT A / POINT NEAR CLEAR CREEK, IT REACHED THE / BATTLEFIELD VIA / SAVANNA ROAD. AT 7:30 P.M. FROM THIS POSITION APRIL 7TH, 5:30 A.M. IT OPENED BATTLE WITH FIRST SHOT OF THE / DAY. IN JONES FIELD, NEAR OGLESBY HEADQUARTERS, AFTER / 1100 ROUNDS FIRED BY THE BATTERY, AMMUNITION BEING / EXHAUSTED IT RETIRED BY GEN. LEWIS WALLACE'S ORDERS / CASUALTIES: 1 MAN KILLED; 5 MEN WOUNDED; TOTAL 6.

Organized at Indianapolis, mustered in December 20, 1861. Shiloh. Corinth. Central Mississippi Campaign. Meridian. Red River. Nashville. Mustered out June 25, 1865. Lost 61 officers or enlisted men killed, mortally wounded, or by disease.

1.4.2 Subject: Battery I, 1st Regt., Illinois Vol. Artillery, Stele
Location: N 35 09 11 95 / W 88 20 16 92
Dedicated: May 17–18, 1904
Media: Bronze, granite
Monument is a decorated stele surmounting a base.

Inscription

ILLINOIS / BATTERY "I," / 1ST REGIMENT LT. ARTILLERY / UNASSIGNED / ARMY OF THE TENNESSEE

BOUTON'S BATTERY "I," / COMMANDED BY / CAPT. EDWARD BOUTON. / THIS BATTERY OF JAMES RIFLES, 6 POUNDERS / REACHED THE LANDING APRIL 5, 1862. ABOUT 3:00 / P.M., ON THE 6TH, IT WAS ORDERED FORWARD AND / WENT INTO ACTION ON THIS LINE, DOING / GOOD SERVICE UNTIL 5.00 P.M. 2 MEN WERE WOUNDED.

Organized at Camp Douglas, mustered in February 10, 1862. Shiloh. Corinth. Central Mississippi Campaign. Vicksburg. Chattanooga. Franklin. Nashville. Mustered out July 26, 1865. Lost 14 enlisted men mortally wounded or by disease.

East of TN 22, West of Woolf Field

1.5.1 Subject: 23rd Indiana VI, Obelisk
Location: N 35 08 26 24 / W 88 21 25 90
Dedicated: April 6–7, 1903
Medium: Limestone
Monument is a decorated obelisk surmounting a base.

Inscription

23RD / REGIMENT / INFANTRY / COMMANDED BY / COL. WILLIAM L. SANDERSON / 2ND BRIGADE—COL. J. M. THAYER— / 3RD DIVISION—MAJ. GEN. LEWIS WALLACE— / ARMY OF THE TENNESSEE / INDIANA.

Organized at New Albany, mustered in July 29, 1861. Shiloh. Corinth. Central Mississippi Campaign. Vicksburg. Meridian. Atlanta. March to the Sea. Carolinas Campaign. Grand Review. Mustered out July 23, 1865. Lost 217 officers or enlisted men killed, mortally wounded, or by disease.

1.5.2 Subject: 78th Ohio VI, Stele
Location: N 35 08 30 56 / W 88 21 32 18
Dedicated: June 6, 1902
Medium: Granite
Monument is a decorated obelisk with adjoining shafts surmounting a base.

Inscription

[Relief of laurel wreath] [Flanking stacked muskets with canteens and cartridge boxes]

OHIO / 78TH INFANTRY, / COMMANDED BY / COL. MORTIMER D. / LEGGETT / WITTLESEY'S / (3D) BRIGADE / L. WALLACE'S / (3D) DIVISION / ARMY OF THE / TENNESSEE

THIS REGIMENT WAS ENGAGED / NORTH OF JONES FIELD AT 8 A.M., / APRIL 7, 1862; WAS TRANSFERRED / TO THE RIGHT AND WAS ENGAGED / HERE FROM 2 P.M. TO 3 P.M. / PRESENT FOR DUTY, 635 / OFFICERS AND MEN. / *[LOST]* 1 MAN KILLED; / 9 WOUNDED; TOTAL, 10.

Organized at Zanesville, mustered in January 11, 1862. Fort Donelson. Shiloh. Corinth. Central Mississippi Campaign. Vicksburg. Meridian. Atlanta. March to the Sea. Carolinas Campaign. Grand Review. Mustered out July 11, 1865. Lost 355 officers or enlisted men killed, mortally wounded, or by disease.

Wicker Field and Environs, Hamburg-Savannah Road

1.6.1 Subject: 20th Ohio VI, Stele
Location: N 35 08 29 67 / W 88 21 34 10
Dedicated: June 6, 1902
Medium: Granite
Monument is a decorated stele with cornice surmounting a base.

Inscription

[Sculpture of two drums set between two knapsacks]

OHIO / 20TH INFANTRY / COMMANDED BY / LT. COL. MANNING F. FORCE / WHITTLESEY'S (3D) BRIGADE / L. WALLACE'S (3D) DIVISION / ARMY OF THE TENNESSEE

[Relief of laurel wreath and crossed muskets]

. . . ENGAGED NORTHWEST OF JONES FIELD AT / 8 A.M. APRIL 7, 1862. . . . SUPPORTED THE LEFT OF THE DIVISION / UNITL ABOUT NOON WHEN IT RETURNED TO THE EXTREME RIGHT / OF THE ARMY AND WAS ENGAGED HERE FROM 2 TO 3 P.M. . . . PRESENT FOR DUTY, OFFICERS AND MEN, 491. / *[LOST]* 1 MAN KILLED, 1 OFFICER AND 18 MEN / WOUNDED: TOTAL 20.

Organized at Columbus, September 21, 1861. Fort Donelson. Shiloh. Central Mississippi Campaign. Vicksburg. Meridian. Atlanta. Carolinas Campaign. Grand Review. Lost 360 officers or enlisted men killed, mortally wounded, or by disease.

1.6.2 Subject: 24th Indiana VI, Obelisk
Location: N 35 08 26 61 / W 88 21 15 46
Dedicated: April 6–7, 1903
Medium: Limestone
Monument is a decorated obelisk surmounting a base.

Inscription

24TH / REGIMENT / INFANTRY / COMMANDED BY / COL. ALVIN P. HOVEY, / 1ST BRIGADE—COL. M. L. SMITH— / 3D DIVISION—MAJ. GEN. LEWIS WALLACE— / ARMY OF THE TENNESSEE. / INDIANA

. . . FROM CRUMP'S LANDING, APRIL 6, 1862, THIS REG- / IMENT MARCHED TO STONY LONESOME, THENCE 12M . TO A / POINT NEAR CLEAR CREEK; COUNTERMARCHED THERE IT / REACHED BATTLEFIELD, VIA SAVANNAH ROAD, 7.30 P.M. APRIL / 7TH, ENGAGED THE ENEMY AT 5.30 A.M., DROVE HIM BACK TO / THIS / POSITION, WHERE IT WAS FURIOUSLY ASSAULTED FOR TWO / HOURS. ENEMY GAVE WAY, PURSUED HIM TILL NIGHTFALL, HALT- / ING ON SOUTH SIDE OF SHILOH BRANCH. CASUALTIES—KILLED / 3 OFFICERS AND 3 MEN; WOUNDED, 1 OFFICER AND 44 MEN; / TOTAL, 51.

Organized at Vincennes, mustered in July 31, 1861. Fremont's Missouri Campaign. Shiloh. Vicksburg. Western Louisiana. Spanish Fort. Fort Blakely. Mustered out November 15, 1865. Lost 295 officers or enlisted men killed, mortally wounded, or by disease.

1.6.3 Subject: 11th Indiana VI, Obelisk
Location: N 35 08 28 02 / W 88 21 13 12
Dedicated: April 6–7, 1903
Medium: Limestone
Monument is a decorated obelisk surmounting a base.

Inscription

11TH / REGIMENT / INFANTRY / (ZOUAVES), / COMMANDED BY / COL. GEORGE F. MCGINNIS, / 1ST BRIGADE—COL. M. L. SMITH— / 3D DIVISION—MAJ. GEN. LEWIS WALLACE— / ARMY OF THE TENNESSEE. / INDIANA

. . . FROM CRUMP'S LANDING, APRIL 6TH, 1862, THIS REGIMENT MARCHED TO STONY LONESOME; THENCE, 12 M., TO A POINT NEAR CLEAR CREEK; COUNTER- MARCHING THERE, IT REACHED BATTLEFIELD, VIA SAVANNAH ROAD, 7.30 P.M. APRIL 7TH, ENGAGED / ENEMY 5.30 A.M., DROVE HIM BACK TO THIS POSITION, WHERE / IT WAS FURIOUSLY ASSAILED FOR TWO HOURS. ENEMY GAVE / WAY. PURSUED HIM TILL NIGHTFALL, HALTING ON SOUTH SIDE / OF SHILOH BRANCH. CASUALTIES—KILLED, 11 MEN; WOUNDED, / 1 OFFICER, 50 MEN; TOTAL, 62

The 11th Infantry, "Wallace's Zouaves," organized at Indianapolis, August 31, 1861. Fort Donelson. Shiloh. Corinth. Vicksburg. Western Louisiana Campaign. Shenandoah Valley: Winchester; Fisher's Hill; Woodstock; Cedar

Creek. Mustered out July 26, 1865. Lost 288 officers or enlisted men killed, mortally wounded, or by disease.

1.6.4 Subject: 76th Ohio VI, Stele
Location: N 35 08 27 75 / W 88 21 09 48
Dedicated: June 6, 1902
Medium: Granite
Monument is a decorated shaft surmounting a two-tiered base.

Inscription

76TH / INFANTRY, / COMMANDED BY / COL. CHARLES R. WOODS / WHITTLESEY'S (3D) BRIGADE / L. WALLACE'S (3D) DIVISION / ARMY OF THE TENNESSEE

[Relief of crossed muskets with canteen, cartridge belt] [Two flanking sculptures of blanket rolls and knapsacks]

THIS REGIMENT WAS ENGAGED NORTH OF JONES FIELD AT / 8 A.M., APRIL 7, 1862. IT THEN SUPPORTED STUART'S BRIGADE / UNTIL ABOUT 2 P.M., WHEN IT WAS ENGAGED HERE IN FRONT / LINE. / [LOST] 4 MEN WOUNDED; 1 MISSING; TOTAL, 5.

Organized at Camp Sherman, Newark, February 3, 1862. Fort Donelson. Shiloh. Corinth. Vicksburg. Chattanooga. Atlanta. Carolinas Campaign. Grand Review. Mustered out July 15, 1865. Lost 216 officers or enlisted men killed, mortally wounded, or by disease.

1.6.5 Subject: 58th Ohio VI, Stele
Location: N 35 08 25 67 / W 88 21 18 76
Dedicated: June 6, 1902
Medium: Granite
Monument is an inscribed stele with relief of flanking columns.

Inscription

OHIO / 58TH INFANTRY, / COMMANDED BY / COL. VALENTINE BAUSENWEIN, / THAYER'S (2D) BRIGADE, / L. WALLACE'S (3D) DIVISION, / ARMY OF THE / TENNESSEE.

THIS REGIMENT WAS ENGAGED AT / NORTH END OF JONES FIELD AT 8 A.M., / APRIL 7, 1862. IT ADVANCED TO THIS / PLACE, WHERE IT WAS ENGAGED / FROM 10 A.M. TO 2 P.M. / IT HAD PRESENT FOR DUTY, OFFICERS / AND MEN, 630. / [LOST] 9 MEN KILLED; / 2 OFFICERS AND 40 MEN WOUNDED; / TOTAL, 51.

Organized at Camp Sherman, Newark, February 3, 1862. Fort Donelson. Shiloh. Vicksburg. Chattanooga. Atlanta. Carolinas Campaign. Grand Review. Mustered out July 15, 1865. Lost 305 officers or enlisted men killed, mortally wounded, or by disease.

1.7.1 Subject: 6th Battery, Indiana Vol. Artillery, Shaft
Location: N 35 08 14 21 / W 88 21 18 76
Dedicated: April 6–7, 1903
Medium: Limestone
Monument is a decorated obelisk surmounting a base.

Inscription

6TH / BATTERY, / MORTON'S / COMMANDED BY / CAPTAIN FREDERICK BEHR / 1ST BRIGADE COL. J. A. MCDOWELL / 5TH DIVISION GEN. SHERMAN / ARMY OF THE TENNESSEE

. . . ORDERED INTO ACTION AT THIS PLACE, / BY GEN. W. T. SHERMAN AT 10.30 A.M., APRIL 6TH 1862. / CAPTAIN BEHR WAS SHOT FROM HIS HORSE AND FELL DEAD. / CASUALTIES 1 OFFICER KILLED, 5 MEN WOUNDED: TOTAL 6.

Organized at Evansville, mustered in at Indianapolis, September 7, 1861. Shiloh. Corinth. Central Mississippi Campaign. Vicksburg. Meridian. Tishomingo Creek. Tupelo. Oxford. Mustered out July 22, 1861. Lost 17 officers or enlisted men killed or by disease.

1.7.2 Subject: Battery E, 2nd Regt., Illinois Vol. Artillery, Stele
Location: N 35 08 13 31 / W 88 21 09 00
Dedicated: May 17–18, 1904
Media: Bronze, granite
Monument is a decorated stele surmounting a base.

Inscription

ILLINOIS / BATTERY E / 2D REGIMENT LT. ARTILLERY / 1ST DIVISION MCCLERNAND / ARMY OF THE TENNESSEE

SCHWARTZ'S BATTERY, "E" / COMMANDED BY / LIEUT. G. L. NISPEL. / WENT INTO ACTION HERE ABOUT 9:00 A.M., APRIL 6, / 1862, MAINTAINING THEIR POSITION UNTIL 11:00 A.M., / WHEN IT WAS FORCED TO RETIRE, LEAVING 2 GUNS. / [LOST] 1 MAN / KILLED AND 4 WOUNDED; TOTAL 5.

Organized at St. Louis, mustered in August 20, 1861. Forts Henry and Donelson. Shiloh. Corinth. Britton's Lane. Central Mississippi Campaign. Vicksburg. Louisiana Campaign. Mustered out September 29, 1864. Lost 17 officers or enlisted men killed, mortally wounded, or by disease.

1.7.3 Subject: 43rd Illinois VI, Stele
Location: N 35 08 13 22 / W 88 21 07 54
Dedicated: May 17–18, 1904
Media: Bronze, granite
Monument is a decorated stele surmounting a base.

Inscription

ILLINOIS / 43D INFANTRY

3D BRIGADE—RAITH / 1 ST DIVISION—MCCLERNAND / ARMY OF THE TENNESSEE

. . . COMMANDED BY / LIEUT. COL. A. ENGELMAN. / THIS REGIMENT FORMED ON ITS
COLOR LINE ON THE / MORNING OF APRIL 6, 1862, AND MOVED FORWARD TO A /
POSITION SUPPORTING WATERHOUSE'S BATTERY, WHICH / WAS HELD UNTIL 10:00
A.M., WHEN IT FELL BACK TO / THIS POINT AND FORMED A LINE WITH THE REST
OF / THE BRIGADE. [LOST] 5 OFFICERS / AND 45 KILLED; 7 OFFICERS AND 111 MEN
WOUNDED; / 29 MEN MISSING; TOTAL 197.

Organized at Camp Butler, mustered in October 12, 1861. Shiloh. Central
Mississippi Campaign. Operations against Forrest, Salem Cemetery. Vicksburg.
Steele's Expedition. Mustered out December 14, 1865. Lost 246 officers or en-
listed men killed, mortally wounded, or by disease.

1.7.4 Subject: 49th Illinois VI, Stele
Location: N 35 08 13 08 / W 88 21 05 44
Dedicated: May 17–18, 1904
Media: Bronze, granite
Monument is a decorated stele surmounting a base.

Inscription

ILLINOIS / 49TH INFANTRY

3D BRIGADE—RAITH / 1 ST DIVISION—MCCLERNAND / ARMY OF THE TENNESSEE

. . . COMMANDED BY / LIEUT. COL. PHINEAS PEASE, / WOUNDED. / THIS REGIMENT
FELL IN FOR BATTLE ON ITS COLOR / LINE ABOUT 8.30 A.M., APRIL 6, 1862, AND
HELD IT BUT / A SHORT TIME WHEN IT MOVED BACK FIGHTING / TO THIS PLACE.
[LOST] 2 OFFICERS / AND 17 MEN KILLED; 4 OFFICERS AND 79 MEN WOUNDED; / 8
MEN MISSING. TOTAL, 110.

Organized at Camp Butler, mustered in December 31, 1861. Fort Donelson.
Shiloh. Corinth. Meridian. Red River Campaign. Smith's expedition: Tupelo,
Oxford. Mustered out September 9, 1865. Lost 254 officers or enlisted men
killed, mortally wounded, or by disease.

11th Illinois VI, Stele

1.7.5 Subject: 11th Illinois VI, Stele
Location: N 35 08 13 11 / W 88 21 03 88
Dedicated: May 17–18, 1904
Media: Bronze, granite
Monument is a decorated stele surmounting a base.

Inscription

ILLINOIS / 11TH INFANTRY
2D BRIGADE—MARSH / 1ST DIVISION—MCCLERNAND / ARMY OF THE TENNESSE

. . . COMMANDED BY / 1. LIEUT.-COL. T. E. G. RANSOM, / WOUNDED. / 2. MAJOR
GARRETT NEVINS, / WOUNDED. / 3. CAPT. L. D. WADDELL. / WENT INTO BATTLE
ON THIS LINE WITH 9 COMPANIES / (ONE COMPANY ON PICKET) ABOUT 9.00
A.M., APRIL 6, 1862, / RECEIVING A FIRE THAT KILLED OR WOUNDED, IN A FEW /
MINUTES, THE LIEUT. COLONEL, MAJOR, FOUR LINE OFFICERS / AND MANY MEN.
THIS POSITION WAS HELD ABOUT TWO HOURS / WHEN THEY FELL BACK 500 YARDS.
[LOST] 1 OFFICER AND 16 MEN KILLED; 4 OFFICERS AND 65 / MEN WOUNDED; 17
MEN MISSING; TOTAL, 103.

Organized at Cairo, July 30, 1861. Forts Henry and Donelson. Shiloh. Central
Mississippi Campaign. Vicksburg. Mobile. Mustered out July 14, 1865. Lost 471
officers or enlisted men killed, mortally wounded, or by disease.

1.7.6 Subject: State of Illinois, Shaft and Statue, Female

Location: N 35 08 14 18 / W 88 21 02 28

Dedicated: May 17–18, 1904

Media: Bronze, granite

Monument is a woman, seated, holding a scepter, surmounting a shaft and base.

Inscription

[Bronze tablet displaying battlefield relief]

ILLINOIS / ERECTS THIS MONUMENT TO COMMEMORATE HER SONS, / WHO HERE GAVE THEIR SERVICES, TO PERPETUATE / THE HONOR AND GLORY OF THE UNITED STATES.

ILLINOIS HAD IN THIS BATTLE 27 REGIMENTS / OF INFANTRY, 10 BATTERIES OF ARTILLERY AND / 6 DETACHMENTS OF CAVALRY. HER LOSS IN KILLED / AND WOUNDED WAS 3,957.—IN MISSING 410.

1776 / 1861–1865

[RELIEF OF STATE SEAL OF ILLINOIS FLANKED BY TWO TORCHES IN RELIEF]

"THE WORLD WILL LITTLE NOTE, NOR LONG / REMEMBER WHAT WE SAY HERE, BUT IT / CAN NEVER FORGET WHAT THEY DID HERE."

Among the Northern state monuments at Shiloh, Wisconsin's sculpture of a stricken, dying Union officer may be the most dramatic, the Iowa column the most attractive, the Minnesota artillerist the most understated, and the Michigan common soldier the most orthodox. The Illinois monument in Woolf Field, however, may be the most regal. The sculptor is Richard W. Bock of Chicago. Working in a Beaux-Arts style, Bock depicted a presiding sculpture of a woman "representing the mother of Illinois" holding a scepter. The figure was modeled on the sculptor's wife, Martha Bock. The state monument is described as follows:

> The crowning figure, of standard bronze and weighing nearly 7,000 pounds, is twelve feet high and is designed to represent Illinois, whose record of her sons' achievements on this field can be found on the pages of the book where her finger parts the leaves. The sword is sheathed, but the scabbard is held with a firm grasp, as if in readiness for release of the blade again and renewal of the battle should occasion at any time require. Watchfully, guardingly, her gaze is bent toward the south, from whence her enemies came, and the look upon her face is one of admonition. The splendid countenance has a definite expression to its dignity. Over her shoulders is thrown a military cape, cast back to leave the arms free.

Shiloh is not mentioned by name in the inscription, but the cause for which it was fought is certainly declared, the commemoration of Illinois soldiers

State of Illinois, Shaft and Statue, Female

who "gave their services" is given tribute, and a summary of Illinois's contribution is displayed. The quotation beginning "The World Will Little Note" is excerpted from the Gettysburg Address and also appears on the Iowa state monument. The monument is distinctive for its triumphalist declaration on behalf of Illinois's "sons" who here gave their services, to perpetuate the honor and glory of the United States—not victory, not reconciliation. It is the only Union monument to make direct reference to 1776, inscribed on the back, to harken back, one may imagine, to the "new birth of freedom" declared with the independence of the thirteen colonies as a new nation.

The sculpture of the female figure is twelve feet high, in bronze, surmounting a base twenty-three feet high and twelve feet square. The monument was erected at a cost of $18,810.26. The granite work was done by the Culver Construction Company, the bronze work by the American Bronze Foundry Company of Chicago.

1.7.7 Subject: 20th Illinois VI, Stele
Location: N 35 08 14 22 / W 88 21 01 36
Dedicated: May 17–18, 1904
Media: Bronze, granite
Monument is a decorated stele surmounting a base.

Inscription

ILLINOIS / 20TH INFANTRY

2D BRIGADE—MARSH / 1ST DIVISION—MCCLERNAND / ARMY OF THE TENNESSEE

COMMANDED BY / 1. LIEUT. COL. E. RICHARDS, WOUNDED. / 2. MAJOR F. A. BARTLESON, WOUNDED. / 3. CAPT. O. FRISBIE. / WENT INTO POSITION HERE ABOUT 9.00 A.M., APRIL 6, 1862, / AND HELD IT UNTIL 11 A.M., WHEN IT WITHDREW, GOING / TO THE REAR OF ITS OWN CAMP WHERE IT FORMED A NEW / LINE. *[LOST]* 1 OFFICER / AND 21 MEN KILLED; 5 OFFICERS AND 102 MEN WOUNDED; / 7 MEN MISSING; TOTAL, 136.

Organized at Joliet, mustered in June 13, 1861. Forts Henry and Donelson. Shiloh. Corinth. Britton's Lane. Central Mississippi Campaign. Vicksburg. Meridian. Atlanta. March to the Sea. Carolinas Campaign. Grand Review. Mustered out July 16, 1865. Lost 331 officers or enlisted men killed, mortally wounded, or by disease.

1.7.8 Subject: 39th Indiana VI, Obelisk
Location: N 35 08 10 17 / W 88 20 58 48
Dedicated: April 6–7, 1903
Medium: Limestone
Monument is a decorated obelisk surmounting a base.

Inscription

39TH / REGIMENT / INFANTRY, / COMMANDED BY / COL. THOMAS J. HARRISON, / 6TH BRIGADE—COL. W. H. GIBSON—/ 2D DIVISION—GEN. MCCOOK— / ARMY OF THE OHIO. / INDIANA.

. . . THIS REGIMENT ARRIVED ON THE BATTLEFIELD AT 10.30 / A.M., MONDAY, APRIL 7, 1862. AT 12 M. REGIMENT MOVED / IN LINE OF BATTLE UNDER A GALLING FIRE, DRIVING / THE ENEMY A QUARTER / OF A MILE. IT THEN FELL BACK 150 YARDS TO THIS POSITION, / WHERE IT WAS ENGAGED UNTIL 2 P.M. REGIMENT AGAIN ADVANCED CAPTURING / 15 PRISONERS. CASUALTIES—KILLED, 1 OFFICER AND 1 / MAN; WOUNDED, / 1 OFFICER AND 33 MEN; TOTAL, 36.

Organized at Indianapolis, August 29, 1861. Shiloh. Corinth. Stones River. Tullahoma. Chickamauga. Atlanta. McCook's raid. March to the Sea. Carolinas Campaign. Mustered out July 20, 1865. Lost 398 officers or enlisted men killed, mortally wounded, or by disease.

1.7.9 Subject: 49th Ohio VI, Stele

Location: N 35 08 07 63 / W 88 20 55 74

Dedicated: June 6, 1902

Medium: Granite

Monument is a decorated obelisk with adjoining shafts surmounting a base.

Inscription

OHIO

[Relief of crossed muskets, laurel wreath, cartridge box]

49TH INFANTRY / COMMANDED BY / LT. COL. A. M. BLACKMAN / GIBSON'S (6TH) BRIGADE / MCCOOK'S (2D) DIVISION / ARMY OF THE OHIO

THIS REGIMENT ARRIVED ON / THIS FIELD AT 11 A.M., APRIL 7, / 1862. IT BECAME / ENGAGED HERE / ABOUT NOON, AND FOUGHT ITS WAY / FORWARD ABOUT 80 YARDS / WHERE THE BATTLE ENDED / AT 3 P.M. / *[LOST]* 6 MEN KILLED; / 34 WOUNDED; TOTAL, 40.

Organized at Tiffin, September 1861. Shiloh. Corinth. Stones River. Tullahoma. Chickamauga Campaign. Atlanta. Franklin. Nashville. Mustered out November 30, 1865. Lost 363 officers or enlisted men killed, mortally wounded, or by disease.

1.7.10 Subject: 14th Battery, Ohio Vol. Artillery, Stele

Location: N 35 08 12 83 / W 88 20 59 50

Dedicated: June 6, 1902

Medium: Granite

Monument is two granite blocks, decorated, surmounting a base.

Inscription

[Raised letters on unfolded scroll]

OHIO / 14TH BATTERY / LIGHT ARTILLERY / COMMANDED BY / CAPT. JEROME B. BURROWS / (WOUNDED) / MCCLERNAND'S / (1ST) DIVISION / ARMY OF THE TENNESSEE

THIS BATTERY OF 6 GUNS / WENT INTO ACTION HERE / AT 9 A.M., APRIL 6, 1862. / *[LOST]* 4 MEN KILLED; / 1 OFFICER AND 25 MEN WOUNDED; / AND 70 HORSES KILLED. / AT 11 A.M. IT WAS OBLIGED / TO RETIRE LEAVING ITS GUNS / ON THE FIELD.

Organized at Cleveland, mustered in September 10, 1861. Shiloh. Corinth. Atlanta. Nashville Campaign. Mustered out August 11, 1865. Lost 49 officers or enlisted men killed, mortally wounded, or by disease.

1.7.11 Subject: 15th Ohio VI, Stele
Location: N 35 08 13 84 / W 88 21 00 18
Dedicated: June 6, 1902
Medium: Granite
Monument is a decorated shaft with an inverted V-shaped peak, surmounting a base.

Inscription

[Surmounting sculpture of drum with two knapsacks]

15 / OHIO / 15TH / INFANTRY / COMMANDED BY / MAJOR / WILLIAM WALLACE / GIBSON'S / (6TH) BRIGADE / MCOOK'S / (2D) DIVISION / ARMY OF THE / OHIO

[Relief of laurel wreath]

[Relief of two stacked muskets with cartridge box sling]

THIS REGIMENT ARRIVED / UPON THE FIELD AT 11 A.M., / APRIL 7, 1862, AND BECAME ENGAGED HERE ABOUT NOON. / IT ADVANCED FIGHTING TO SHERMAN'S HEADQUARTERS / AT 3 P.M. / [LOST] 7 MEN / KILLED; 1 OFFICER AND 65 / MEN WOUNDED; 2 MEN MISSING; / TOTAL, 75.

[Relief of two stacked muskets with cartridge box sling]

ORGANIZED AT MANSFIELD, SEPTEMBER 1861. SHILOH. CORINTH. STONES RIVER. TULLAHOMA. CHICKAMAUGA. CHATTANOOGA. ATLANTA. FRANKLIN. NASHVILLE. MUSTERED OUT NOVEMBER 21, 1865. LOST 315 OFFICERS OR ENLISTED MEN KILLED, MORTALLY WOUNDED, OR BY DISEASE.

1.7.12 Subject: 46th Illinois VI, Stele
Location: N 35 08 14 98 / W 88 21 00 68
Dedicated: May 17–18, 1904
Media: Bronze, granite
Monument is a decorated stele surmounting a base.

Inscription

ILLINOIS / 46TH INFANTRY / 2D BRIGADE—VEATCH / 4TH DIVISION—HURLBUT / ARMY OF THE TENNESSEE

. . . COMMANDED BY / COL. JOHN A. DAVIS, WOUNDED. / LIEUT.-COL. J. J. JONES. / FORMED HERE FOR BATTLE AT 9:30 A.M., APRIL 6, 1862 / AND MAINTAINED ITS POSITION UNTIL 11:00 A.M., THEN / WITHDREW NORTHWARD, TO JONES FIELD AND FORMED / A NEW LINE. ITS LOSS IN THE BATTLE WAS 25 MEN / KILLED; 10 OFFICERS AND 124 MEN WOUNDED; 1 MAN / MISSING; TOTAL 160.

Organized at Camp Butler, December 28, 1861. Fort Donelson. Shiloh. Corinth. Central Mississippi Campaign. Vicksburg. Red River. Mobile. Mustered out January 20, 1866. Lost 335 officers or enlisted men killed, mortally wounded, or by disease.

15th Ohio VI, Stele

1.7.13 Subject: 32nd Indiana VI, Obelisk
Location: N 35 08 15 59 / W 88 21 00 96
Dedicated: April 6–7, 1903
Medium: Limestone
Monument is a decorated obelisk surmounting a base.

Inscription

32ND / REGIMENT / INFANTRY, / COMMANDED BY / COL. AUGUST WILLICH, / 6TH BRIGADE—COL. W. H. GIBSON—/ 2ND DIVISION—GEN. MCCOOK— / ARMY OF THE OHIO. / INDIANA.

. . . THIS REGIMENT ARRIVED ON THE BATTLEFIELD AT 10 A.M., / APRIL 7TH, 1862; WAS ORDERED TO THE FRONT BY MAJOR / GENERAL GRANT. IT FORMED ON THIS LINE ABOUT 12 M., WHEN / THE REGIMENT REPULSED AN ASSAULT BY THE ENEMY. DURING / THE DAY THIS REGIMENT MADE SEVERAL CHARGES UPON THE / ENEMY, DRIVING HIM BACK. CASUALTIES—KILLED, 2 OFFICERS / AND 8 MEN; WOUNDED, 4 OFFICERS AND 82 MEN; TOTAL, 96.

The 32nd Indiana, the "1st German Regiment," organized at Indianapolis, mustered in August 24, 1861. Shiloh. Corinth. Stones River. Tullahoma. Chickamauga. Chattanooga. Atlanta. Mustered out December 4, 1865. Lost 268 officers or enlisted men killed, mortally wounded, or by disease.

1.7.14 Subject: Battery D, 2nd Regt., Illinois Vol. Artillery, Stele
Location: N 35 08 16 24 / W 88 21 99 14
Dedicated: May 17–18, 1904
Media: Bronze, granite
Monument is a decorated stele surmounting a base.

Inscription

ILLINOIS / BATTERY "D" / 2D REGIMENT LT. ARTILLERY / 1ST DIVISION—
MCCLERNAND / ARMY OF THE TENNESSEE

DRESSER'S BATTERY, "D" / COMMANDED BY / CAPT. J. P. TIMONY. / THIS BATTERY OF
JAMES RIFLES, 6 POUNDERS, WENT / INTO ACTION HERE ABOUT 9.00 A.M., APRIL 7,
1862 / AND HELD THIS POSITION FOR TWO HOURS, AND THEN / RETIRED TO CAMP
OF 20TH ILLINOIS. [LOST] 4 MEN KILLED AND 9 / WOUNDED; TOTAL, 13.

Organized at Cairo, mustered in December 17, 1861. Forts Henry and Donelson.
Shiloh. Corinth. Central Mississippi Campaign. Meridian. Mustered out
November 21, 1864. Lost 19 enlisted men killed, mortally wounded, or by
disease.

1.7.15 Subject: 11th Iowa VI, Stele
Location: N 35 08 16 68 / W 88 20 58 96
Dedicated: November 23, 1906
Media: Bronze, granite
Monument is a decorated stele surmounting a base.

Inscription

IOWA / TO HER / 11TH INFANTRY, / HARE'S (1ST) BRIGADE, / MCCLERNAND'S (1ST)
DIVISION, / ARMY OF THE TENNESSEEE.

11TH REGIMENT INFANTRY VOLUNTEERS, / COMMANDED BY LIEUT. COL. WM. HALL,
(WOUNDED) / THIS REGIMENT, DETACHED FROM ITS BRIGADE, WAS PLACED IN
POSITION HERE BY ORDER / OF GENERAL MCCLERNAND ABOUT 9.30 A.M., APRIL 6,
1862. / IT WAS AT ONCE STRONGLY ATTACKED BY THE ENEMY, SUFFERING HERE ITS
MOST SEVERE LOSS. IT HELD THIS POSITION UNTIL 11 A.M. WHEN IT RETIRED TO
ITS SECOND POSITION 100 YARDS IN FRONT OF ITS CAMP IN JONES FIELD. IT HAD
PRESENT FOR DUTY 763. ITS LOSS WAS, 1 OFFICER AND 32 MEN KILLED; 5 OFFICERS
AND 155 MEN WOUNDED; 1 MAN MISSING; TOTAL, 195.

Organized at Davenport, October 18, 1861. Shiloh. Corinth. Central Mississippi
Campaign. Vicksburg. Meridian. Atlanta. March to the Sea. Carolinas
Campaign. Grand Review. Mustered out July 15, 1865. Lost 259 officers or en-
listed men killed, mortally wounded, or by disease.

Battery D, 1st Illinois Artillery, 2nd Division, Stele

11th Iowa VI, Stele

1.7.16 Subject: 14th Illinois VI, Stele
Location: N 35 08 15 92 / W 88 20 55 66
Dedicated: May 17–18, 1904
Media: Bronze, granite
Monument is a decorated stele surmounting a base.

Inscription

ILLINOIS / 14TH INFANTRY, / 2D BRIGADE—VEATCH, / 4TH DIVISION—HURLBUT / ARMY OF THE TENNESSEE

. . . COMMANDED BY / COL. CYRUS HALL. / WENT INTO BATTLE ON THIS LINE ABOUT 9.30 A.M., / APRIL 6, 1862, AND WITH SLIGHT CHANGES OF POSITION / HELD IT UNTIL 11 A.M., WHEN THE REGIMENT FELL / BACK TO THE ROAD AND FORMED A NEW LINE. IT LOST / IN THE BATTLE 9 OFFICERS AND 117 MEN WOUNDED; / 35 MEN KILLED; 4 MISSING; TOTAL, 165.

Organized at Jacksonville, mustered in May 25, 1861. Fremont's Missouri Campaign. Fort Donelson. Shiloh. Corinth. Central Mississippi Campaign. Vicksburg. Meridian. Atlanta. March to the Sea. Carolinas Campaign. Grand Review. Mustered out September 18, 1865. Lost 223 officers or enlisted men killed, mortally wounded, or by disease.

1.7.17 Subject: 34th Illinois VI, Stele
Location: N 35 08 19 78 / W 88 21 00 22
Dedicated: May 17–18, 1904
Media: Bronze, granite
Monument is a decorated stele surmounting a base.

Inscription

ILLINOIS / 34TH INFANTRY, / 5TH BRIGADE—KIRK, / 2D DIVISION—MCCOOK, / ARMY OF THE OHIO.

. . . COMMANDED BY / 1. MAJOR CHAS. N. LEVANWAY, / KILLED. / 2. CAPT. H. W. BRISTOL. / THIS REGIMENT REACHED PITTSBURG LANDING AT 5:00 / A.M., APRIL 7, 1862, FORMED LINE ON THE CORINTH ROAD / NEAR HURLBUT'S HEADQUARTERS, ADVANCED TO THE EDGE / OF THIS FIELD WHERE IT RELIEVED ROUSSEAU ABOUT 11.50 / A.M. THEN IT AGAIN ADVANCED TO THIS POINT AND / CHARGED THROUGH AND BEYOND THE POND. ITS LOSS / IN THE BATTLE WAS 1 OFFICER AND 14 MEN KILLED; / 7 OFFICERS AND 105 MEN WOUNDED; TOTAL, 127.

Organized as the "Red River Rifles" at Camp Butler, mustered in September 7, 1861. Shiloh. Corinth. Perryville. Stones River. Tullahoma. Chattanooga. Atlanta. March to the Sea. Carolinas Campaign. Grand Review. Mustered out July 12, 1865. Lost 261 officers or enlisted men killed, mortally wounded, or by disease.

1.7.18 Subject: 30th Indiana VI, Obelisk
Location: N 35 08 22 05 / W 88 21 03 10
Dedicated: April 6–7, 1903
Medium: Limestone
Monument is a decorated obelisk surmounting a base.

Inscription

30TH / REGIMENT / INFANTRY, / COMMANDED BY / COL. SION S. BASS, / 5TH
BRIGADE—COL. E. N. KIRK—/ 2D DIVISION—GEN. MCCOOK—/ ARMY OF THE OHIO.
/ INDIANA

. . . THIS REGIMENT ARRIVED ON THE BATTLEFIELD MONDAY, / APRIL 7, 1862,
AT 6 A.M.; WENT TO THE FRONT AND RIGHT CENTER / OF ARMY. AT 10 A.M. WAS
IN LINE IN RESERVE ON THE RIGHT OF / GEN ROUSSEAU'S BRIGADE; ADVANCED
AND FORMED ON THIS / LINE ABOUT 12 M. IT WAS FURIOUSLY ASSAULTED BY THE
ENEMY FOR / TWO HOURS, WHEN THE ENEMY GAVE WAY IN RETREAT. HERE / COL.
BASS FELL MORTALLY WOUNDED. CASUALTIES—KILLED, 12 / MEN; WOUNDED, 6
OFFICERS AND 109 MEN; MISSING, 2 MEN; TOTAL 129.

Organized at Fort Wayne, mustered in September 24, 1861. Shiloh. Corinth.
Perryville. Stones River. Tullahoma. Chickamauga. Atlanta. Franklin;
Nashville. Mustered out November 25, 1865. Lost 442 officers or enlisted men
killed, mortally wounded, or by disease.

1.7.19 Subject: 29th Indiana VI, Obelisk
Location: N 35 08 24 51 / W 88 21 06 22
Dedicated: April 6–7, 1903
Medium: Limestone
Monument is a decorated obelisk surmounting a base.

Inscription

29TH / REGIMENT / INFANTRY, / COMMANDED BY / LIEUT. COL. DAVID M. DUNN, /
5TH BRIGADE—COL. E. N. KIRK— / 2D DIVISION—GEN. MCCOOK— / ARMY OF THE
OHIO. / INDIANA.

. . . THIS REGIMENT ARRIVED ON BATTLEFIELD AT / 6.30 A.M., APRIL 7, 1862. IT
WENT TO THE / FRONT AND / CENTER OF THE ARMY, WHERE IT WAS HELD IN
RESERVE. / IT FORMED ON THIS LINE ABOUT 12 M., AND WAS HEAVILY / ASSAILED
/ BY THE ENEMY FOR TWO HOURS, WHEN THE ENE- / MY RETIRED. / CASUALTIES—
KILLED, 4 MEN; WOUNDED, 4 OFFI- / CERS AND 72 MEN; TOTAL, 80.

Organized at La Porte, mustered in August 27, 1861. Shiloh. Corinth. Stones
River. Tullahoma. Chickamauga. Mustered out December 2, 1865. Lost 304
officers or enlisted men killed, mortally wounded, or by disease.

1.7.20 Subject: Trenches Interring Confederate Dead, Stele, #3
Location: N 35 08 24 14 / W 88 21 06 26
Dedicated: May 17, 1917
Medium: Granite
Monument is a stele surmounting a base.

Inscription

TO THE CONFEDERATE DEAD / IN THE TRENCHES / ERECTED BY THE U.D.C. / A.D. 1917

This is believed to be the largest known mass grave of Confederate dead on the Shiloh battlefield, with an estimated 721 bodies.

1.7.21 Subject: State of Tennessee, three Common Soldiers Statues, Confederate
Location: Woolf Field near the Water Oaks Pond   N 35 08 17 34 / W 88 21 04 58
Dedicated: June 3, 2005
Media: Bronze, black granite, steel
Monument displays three soldiers, infantrymen: one bearing a musket and gazing to the southwest; a second soldier, older, bearing a Confederate national flag and shouldering a third soldier, younger, wounded; the whole surmounting a granite base.

Inscriptions

[Front]

TENNESSEE

ERECTED BY THE SOVEREIGN STATE OF TENNESSEE. / WITH ASSISTANCE FROM THE TENNESSEE / UNITED DAUGHTERS OF THE CONFEDERACY, AND / SONS OF CONFEDERATE VETERANS, / THIS MONUMENT IS DEDICATED, / WITH EVERLASTING GRATITUDE AND RESPECT, TO THE TENNESSEANS WHO FOUGHT HERE.

TENNESSEE ORGANIZATIONS ENGAGED AT / THE BATTLE OF SHILOH, APRIL 6TH AND 7TH, 1862 / ARTILLERY: BANKHEAD'S BATTERY, MCCLUNG'S (CASWELL ARTILLERY) BATTERY, MILLER'S (PILLOW FLYING ARTILLERY) BATTERY, POLK'S BATTERY, RUTLEDGE'S BATTERY. / CAVALRY: 3RD (FORREST'S) REGIMENT.

INFANTRY: 1ST (MANEY'S BATTALION) REGIMENT, 2ND (BATE'S) REGIMENT, 2ND (WALKER'S) REGIMENT, 4TH REGIMENT, 5TH (VENABLE'S) REGIMENT, 5TH *[35TH]* (HILL'S) REGIMENT, 6TH REGIMENT, 9TH REGIMENT, 12TH REGIMENT, 13TH REGIMENT, 15TH REGIMENT, 19TH REGIMENT, 20TH REGIMENT, 22ND REGIMENT, 23RD REGIMENT, 24TH REGIMENT, 27TH REGIMENT, 28TH REGIMENT, 33RD REGIMENT, 38TH REGIMENT, 44TH REGIMENT, 45TH REGIMENT, 47TH REGIMENT, 51ST REGIMENT, 52ND REGIMENT, 55TH REGIMENT, 154TH SENIOR REGIMENT, CREW'S BATTALION.

"THE TENNESSEANS HAD MORE TO FIGHT FOR. THE FIGHT WAS FOR THEIR HOMES AND FIRESIDES." / BRIGADIER GENERAL PATRICK R. CLEBURNE, / AS RECOUNTED BY A SOLDIER IN THE 23RD TENNESSEE INFANTRY.

State of Tennessee, Three Common Soldiers, Statues, Confederate

This monument, titled "Passing of Honor" and sculpted by G. L. Sanders, depicts a fallen flag-bearer, a comrade who is picking up the flag and comforting the fallen soldier, and a third standing by, alert to the action on the battlefield. It redresses the long-standing absence of a monument to Tennessee Confederates who fought at Shiloh.

The Tennessee UDC initiated the project. Present-day Park Service regulations stipulate that states must sponsor new monuments, so the UDC applied to the State of Tennessee for support. The state agreed and provided $125,000 in matching funds for the $280,000 project, the larger sum including contributions from the UDC, the Sons of Confederate Veterans, private individuals, and the federal government.

The figures stand nine feet high. The flag, in the First National pattern, is sculpted in bronze, but its eleven stars are of stainless steel. It is a Confederate Tennessee monument: Tennessee soldiers who fought for the Union are not represented. The "Tennessee Organizations Engaged at the Battle of Shiloh" are from the Confederate order of battle.

1.7.22 Subject: 15th Illinois VI, Stele
Location: N 35 08 15 35 / W 88 21 04 38
Dedicated: May 17–18, 1904
Media: Bronze, granite
Monument is a decorated stele surmounting a base.

Inscription

ILLINOIS / 15TH INFANTRY / 2D BRIGADE—VEATCH / 4TH DIVISION—HURLBUT / ARMY OF THE TENNESSEE

. . . COMMANDED BY / LIEUT.-COL. E. F. W. ELLIS, KILLED. / MAJOR WM. R. GODDARD, KILLED. / CAPT. LOUIS D. KELLY. / THIS REGIMENT WAS ATTACKED ON THIS LINE ABOUT 9.30 / A.M., APRIL 6, 1862, AND OFERED MOST STUBBORN RESIST- / ANCE FOR MORE THAN ONE HOUR, THE ENEMY ATTACKING / BOTH FRONT AND FLANK. IN THIS ACTION BOTH FIELD / OFFICERS AND SEVERAL LINE OFFICERS WERE LOST. THE REGI- / MENT RETIRED IN GOOD ORDER AND FORMED A NEW LINE. / ITS LOSS IN THE BATTLE WAS 5 OFFICERS AND 44 MEN KILLED; / 8 OFFICERS AND 109 MEN WOUNDED; TOTAL, 166.

Organized at Freeport, mustered in May 24, 1861. Fremont's Missouri Campaign. Fort Donelson. Shiloh. Corinth. Central Mississippi Campaign. Vicksburg. Meridian. Atlanta. March to the Sea. Carolinas Campaign. Grand Review. Mustered out September 16. 1865. Lost 227 officers or enlisted men killed, mortally wounded, or by disease.

Shiloh Church, Shiloh Spring, Rhea Spring, and Environs

1.8.1 Subject: Battery B, Illinois Vol. Artillery
Location: N 35 08 02 19 / W 88 21 19 36
Dedicated: May 17–18, 1904
Media: Bronze, granite
Monument is a decorated stele surmounting a base.

Inscription

ILLINOIS / BATTERY "B," / 5TH DIVISION—SHERMAN, / ARMY OF THE TENNESSEE

TAYLOR'S BATTERY, "B". / COMMANDED BY / CAPT. SAM'L E. BARRETT. / OPENED FIRE FROM THIS POSITION APRIL 6, 1862, AND / HELD IT FROM ABOUT 7.30 UNTIL 10.00 A.M., WHEN / THE BATTERY RETIRED AND LATER MOVED TO ASSIST / MCCLERNAND. IT LOSS IN THE BATTLE WAS 1 MAN / KILLED AND 5 WOUNDED; TOTAL, 6.

Organized at Chicago, mustered in May 2, 1861. Belmont. Forts Henry and Donelson. Shiloh. Corinth. Central Mississippi Campaign. Vicksburg. Chattanooga. Atlanta Campaign until mustered out July 23, 1864. Lost 9 enlisted men killed or mortally wounded; 1 officer and 17 enlisted men by disease. Total 27.

1.8.2 Subject: 70th Ohio VI, Stele
Location: N 35 07 59 18 / W 88 21 23 20
Dedicated: June 6, 1902
Medium: Granite

Inscription

OHIO / 70TH INFANTRY, / COMMANDED BY / COL. JOSEPH R. COCKERILL / BUCKLAND'S (4TH) BRIGADE / SHERMAN'S (5TH) DIVISION / ARMY OF THE TENNESSEE
[Relief of crossed muskets surmounted by knapsack with "70" inscribed]

THIS REGIMENT WAS ENGAGED HERE FROM 7 A.M. / TO 10 A.M., APRIL 6, 1862. / IT HAD PRESENT FOR DUTY, OFFICERS AND MEN, 647. / [LOST] 2 OFFICERS AND 13 MEN KILLED; 3 / OFFICERS AND 70 MEN WOUNDED; 45 MEN MISSING; TOTAL, 77.

Organized at West Union, October 14, 1861. Mustered out August 14, 1865. Shiloh. Central Mississippi Campaign. Vicksburg. Chattanooga. Atlanta. March to the Sea. Carolinas Campaign Grand Review. Lost 265 officers or enlisted men killed, mortally wounded, or by disease.

1.8.3 Subject: 2nd Tennessee Infantry CSA, Common Soldier Statue, Confederate
Location: N 35 07 58 77 / W 88 21 23 20
Dedicated: October 1903
Medium: Granite
Monument is a common soldier surmounting a base.

Inscription

[Front]

CSA / [CSA SECOND NATIONAL FLAG] / TO THE MEMORY AND IN HONOR OF OUR / COMRADES OF THE SECOND TENNESSEE / INFANTRY REGIMENT, C.S.A., WHO FELL / NEAR THIS SPOT EARLY ON THE MORNING OF / THE BATTLE OF SHILOH APRIL 6, 1862. / GO, STRANGER, AND TELL TENNESSEE / THAT HERE WE DIED FOR HER. / SECOND TENNESSEE / REGIMENT [BATE]. / ARMY OF THE MISSISSIPPI.

[Blank]

[36 names, Companies A, C, D, F, G, H, I, K]

"TENNESSEE CAN NEVER MOURN FOR / A NOBLER BAND THAN FELL THIS DAY / IN HER SECOND REGIMENT." / (FROM GENERAL CLEBURNE'S REPORT / OF THE BATTLE OF SHILOH). / "DIGNUM ET JUSTUM EST / PRO PATRIA MORI."

Tennessee was the first former Confederate state to be represented by a monument, this one. It is still one of only two Confederate regimental monuments on this field. At Shiloh, the regiment was led by Col. William B. Bate, who was wounded in action here. After the war, Bate became governor of Tennessee and

2nd Tennessee Infantry CSA, Common Soldier Statue, Confederate

a US senator, as well as chairing the committee that led to this monument. The regiment mustered 385 men on the first day of the battle, according to historian Stacy W. Reeves, and reported casualties of 235 killed, wounded, or missing—65 percent of the total on the field.

Three thousand people attended the unveiling. Former Confederate Brig. Gen. Basil W. Duke accepted the monument on behalf of the United States.

The exhortation "Go, Stranger, and Tell Tennessee" is attributed to Maj. Gen. Pat Cleburne, but it is similar not only to the Thermopylae epitaph to the Spartans, but also to the Great Commission of Matthew 28:19 ("Go ye therefore, and teach all nations"). Simonides of Ceos (556–468 BC) is credited with the epitaph on the monument marking the battle of Thermopylae (480 BC). Translated, it reads, "Go and tell the Spartans, stranger passing by, that here, obedient to their laws, dead we lie."

The sculpture stands seven feet high and is eighteen inches wide. The shaft and base stand twenty-one feet high. The monument is composed of light Barre granite on gray Mount Airy granite. The Morriss Bros. Company served as fabricator. The sculptor is unknown.

1.8.4 Subject: 48th Ohio VI, Stele
Location: N 38 08 00 28 / W 88 21 27 46
Dedicated: June 6, 1902
Medium: Granite
Monument is a granite stele with common soldier in high relief, the whole surmounting a base.

Inscription

OHIO

[Relief of soldier in kneeling position aiming a musket]

48TH INFANTRY, / COMMANDED BY / COL. PETER J. SULLIVAN (WOUNDED) LT. COL. JOB. R. PARKER, / BUCKLAND'S (4TH) BRIGADE / SHERMAN'S (5TH) DIVISION / ARMY OF THE TENNESSEE.

THIS REGIMENT / WAS ENGAGED HERE FROM 7 A.M. / TO 10 A.M., APRIL 6, 1862. / *[LOST]* 1 OFFICER AND 11 MEN KILLED; / 3 OFFICERS AND 70 MEN WOUNDED; 2 OFFICERS / AND 16 MEN MISSING; TOTAL, 103.

Organized at Camp Dennison by December 1861, mustered in February 17, 1862. Shiloh. Corinth. Central Mississippi Campaign. Vicksburg. Western Louisiana. Red River Campaign 1864: regiment captured, Sabine Cross Roads, April 8; prisoners of war until exchanged, October 1864. Fort Blakely. Mobile. Mustered out May 9, 1866. Lost 180 officers or enlisted men killed, mortally wounded, or by disease.

1.8.5 Subject: 72nd Ohio VI, Stele
Location: N 35 07 58 00 / W 88 21 27 46
Dedicated: June 6, 1902
Medium: Granite

Inscription

[Surmounting sculpture of drum with two knapsacks]

72 / OHIO / 72D INFANTRY, / COMMANDED BY / LT. COL. HERMAN CANFIELD (KILLED), / COL. RALPH P. BUCKLAND, / BUCKLAND'S (4TH) BRIGADE—SHERMAN'S (5TH) DIVISION / ARMY OF THE TENNESSEE

[Relief of crossed muskets, canteen, and cartridge belt]

THIS REGIMENT WAS ENGAGED HERE FROM 7 A.M. / TO 10 A.M., APRIL 6, 1862. / IT HAD PRESENT FOR DUTY, OFFICERS AND MEN, 647. / *[LOST]* 2 OFFICERS AND 13 MEN KILLED; 3 / OFFICERS AND 70 MEN WOUNDED; 45 MEN MISSING; TOTAL, 133.

Organized at Fremont, February 1862. Shiloh. Corinth. Central Mississippi Campaign. Vicksburg. Brice's Cross Roads. Nashville. Mobile. Mustered out September 11, 1865. Lost 298 officers or enlisted men killed, mortally wounded, or by disease.

1.8.6 Subject: 17th Illinois VI, Stele
Location: N 35 07 59 79 / W 88 21 16 42
Dedicated: May 17–18, 1904
Media: Bronze, granite
Monument is a decorated stele surmounting a base.

Inscription

ILLINOIS / 17TH INFANTRY, / 3D BRIGADE—RAITH, / 1 ST DIVISION—MCCLERNAND, / ARMY OF THE TENNESSEE.

. . . COMMANDED BY / 1. LIEUT. COL. ENOS P. WOOD. / 2. MAJOR FRANCIS M. SMITH. / THIS REGIMENT FORMED THE RIGHT OF THE THIRD / BRIGADE, 1ST DIVISION, AND WENT INTO BATTLE ON / THIS LINE ABOUT 8.30 A.M., APRIL 6, 1862, HOLDING / IT UNTIL 10 A.M., WHEN IT FELL BACK ABOUT 60 YARDS. / [LOST] 5 OFFICERS AND / 113 MEN WOUNDED; 15 MEN KILLED; 5 MISSING; TOTAL, 138.

Organized at Peoria, mustered in May 24, 1861. Forts Henry and Donelson. Shiloh. Corinth. Central Mississippi Campaign. Vicksburg. Meridian. Mustered out June 4, 1864. Lost 146 officers or enlisted men killed, mortally wounded, or by disease.

1.8.7 Subject: 29th Illinois VI, Stele
Location: N 35 07 58 14 / W 88 21 14 64
Dedicated: May 17–18, 1904
Media: Bronze, granite
Monument is a decorated stele surmounting a base.

Inscription

ILLINOIS / 29TH INFANTRY / 3D BRIGADE—RAITH / 1 ST DIVISION—MCCLERNAND / ARMY OF THE TENNESSEE

. . . COMMANDED BY / LIEUT. COL. CHAS. M. FERRELL. / WENT INTO BATTLE ON THIS LINE AT 8.30 A.M., APRIL 6, 1862, / AND HELD IT UNTIL 10.00 A.M., THEN RETREATED TO A / POSITION NORTH OF CORINTH ROAD FACING PURDY ROAD. IT / [LOST] 3 OFFICERS AND 9 MEN KILLED; 2 / OFFICERS AND 71 MEN WOUNDED; 4 MEN MISSING; TOTAL, 89.

Organized at Camp Butler, mustered in August 19, 1861. Forts Henry and Donelson. Shiloh. Corinth. Central Mississippi Campaign. Most of regiment surrendered at Holly Springs, December 20, 1862. Paroled July 1863. Vicksburg. Mobile. Mustered out November 28, 1865. Lost 300 officers or enlisted men killed, mortally wounded, or by disease.

1.8.8 Subject: 77th Ohio VI, Stele
Location: N 35 07 56 99 / W 88 21 16 88
Dedicated: June 6, 1902
Medium: Granite

Inscription

77 / OHIO / 77TH INFANTRY / COMMANDED BY / LT. COL. WILLS / DE HASS / MAJ. BENJAMIN D. / FEARING / HILDEBRAND'S / (3D) BRIGADE / SHERMAN'S / (5TH) DIVISION / ARMY OF THE / TENNESSEE.

[Relief of two stacked muskets and cartridge strap]

THIS REGIMENT WAS ENGAGED / HERE FROM 7 A.M. TO 9.30 A.M., / APRIL 6, 1862. ON THE 8TH IT / JOINED IN PURSUIT OF THE ENEMY / AND WAS ENGAGED IN FIGHT / NEAR MICKEY'S. / ITS LOSS ON 6TH, 7TH, AND 8TH / WAS 1 OFFICER AND 50 MEN / KILLED; 7 OFFICERS AND / 48 MEN MISSING; TOTAL, 218.

[Relief of two stacked muskets and cartridge strap]

Organized at Marietta, January 5, 1862. Shiloh. Corinth. Guarded military prisons at Alton. Steele's Expedition: most of regiment captured at Mark's Mills, April 25, 1864; exchanged February 1865. Mobile. Mustered out March 8, 1866. Lost 280 officers or enlisted men killed, mortally wounded, or by disease.

1.8.9 Subject: 57th Ohio VI, Stele
Location: N 35 07 53 26 / W 88 21 13 24
Dedicated: June 6, 1902
Medium: Granite
Monument is a decorated stele with flanking relief of columns, the whole surmounting a base.

Inscription

[Two flanking reliefs of stacked muskets, canteen, and cartridge box]

OHIO / 57TH INFANTRY / COMMANDED BY / LT. COL. AMERICUS V. RICE / HILDEBRAND'S (3D) BRIGADE / SHERMAN'S (5TH) DIVISION / ARMY OF THE / TENNESSEE.

THIS REGIMENT WAS ENGAGED / HERE FROM 7 A.M. TO 9.30 A.M., / APRIL 6, 1862. / IT HAD PRESENT FOR DUTY, / OFFICERS AND MEN, 542. / [LOST] 2 OFFICERS / AND 8 MEN KILLED; 4 OFFICERS / AND 68 MEN WOUNDED; 12 / MEN MISSING; TOTAL, 94.

Organized at Camp Vance, Findlay, September 16, 1861. Shiloh. Corinth. Central Mississippi Campaign. Vicksburg. Chattanooga. Atlanta. March to the Sea. Carolinas Campaign. Grand Review. Mustered out August 14, 1865. Lost 319 officers or enlisted men killed, mortally wounded, or by disease.

1.8.10 Subject: Battery E, 1st Regt. Vol. Illinois Artillery, Stele
Location: N 35 07 54 68 / W 88 21 10 62
Dedicated: May 17–18, 1904
Media: Bronze, granite
Monument is a decorated stele surmounting a base.

Inscription

ILLINOIS / BATTERY "E" / 1ST REGIMENT LT. ARTILLERY / 5TH DIVISION—SHERMAN / ARMY OF THE TENNESSEE

WATERHOUSE'S BATTERY, "E". / COMMANDED BY / 1. CAPT. A.C. WATERHOUSE, WOUNDED. / 2. LIEUT. A.E. ABBOTT, WOUNDED. / 3. LIEUT. JOHN A. FITCH / TWO GUNS OF THIS BATTERY WERE ADVANCED ABOUT / 300 YARDS BUT SOON FELL BACK TO THIS POSITION / WHERE THE WHOLE BATTERY WENT INTO ACTION. / THIS GROUND WAS HELD FROM 7.00 A.M. TO 9.30 A.M., APRIL 6, / 1862, WHEN THE BATTERY LOST 2 GUNS AND MOVED BACK / ABOUT 100 YARDS. [LOST] 1 MAN KILLED; 3 / OFFICERS AND 14 MEN WOUNDED; TOTAL, 18.

Organized at Chicago, mustered in December 19, 1861. Shiloh. Corinth. Central Mississippi Campaign. Vicksburg. Sturgis' Expedition: Tishomingo Creek, Tupelo, Oxford. Mustered out July 15, 1865. Lost 30 enlisted men killed, mortally wounded, or by disease.

1.8.11 Subject: Trenches Interring Confederate Dead, Stele, #4
Location: N 35 08 00 56 / W 88 21 04 38
Dedicated: May 17, 1917
Medium: Granite
Monument is a stele surmounting a base.

Inscription

TO THE CONFEDERATE DEAD / IN THE TRENCHES / ERECTED BY TENN. DIVISION / U.D.C. 1935

1.8.12 Subject: 53rd Ohio VI, Stele
Location: N 35 07 44 06 / W 88 21 11 44
Dedicated: June 6, 1902
Medium: Granite

Inscription

OHIO

[Relief of crossed muskets, cartridge box, canteen, blanket roll, and knapsack, framed by two Ionic columns]

53D INFANTRY, / COMMANDED BY / COL. J. J. APPLER, / LT. COL. ROBT. A. FULTON, / HILDEBRAND'S (3D) BRIGADE, / SHERMAN'S (5TH) DIVISION, / ARMY OF THE TENNESSEE.

THIS REGIMENT FORMED HERE AT 8 A.M., APRIL 6, 1862, / BUT SOON FELL BACK ACROSS THE RAVINE IN THE REAR. / [LOST] 9 MEN KILLED; 1 OFFICER AND 32 MEN / WOUNDED; 2 MEN MISSING; TOTAL, 44.

Organized at Jackson, February 11, 1862. Shiloh. Corinth. Central Mississippi Campaign. Vicksburg. Chattanooga. Atlanta. March to the Sea. Carolinas Campaign Grand Review. Mustered out August 11, 1865. Lost 276 officers or enlisted men killed, mortally wounded, or by disease.

1.8.13 Subject: Trenches Interring Confederate Dead, Stele, #5
Location: N 35 07 42 66 / W 88 21 12 54
Dedicated: May 17, 1917
Medium: Granite
Monument is a stele surmounting a base.

Inscription

TO THE CONFEDERATE DEAD / IN THE TRENCHES / ERECTED BY TENN. DIVISION / U.D.C. 1935

State of Mississippi, three Common Soldier Statues, Confederate

---

1.8.14 Subject: State of Mississippi, three Common Soldier Statues, Confederate

Location: N 35 07 48 75 / W 88 21 14 16

Installed or dedicated: October 2015

Media: Bronze, granite

Monument displays three soldiers, infantrymen, in bronze, advancing under fire, the whole surmounting a granite base.

Inscriptions

MISSISSIPPI

"THE NIGHT CAME ON, AND THE CONFEDERATES LAY DOWN IN / LINE OF BATTLE TO REST AND SLUMBER, REALIZING THE DANGER / OF THE COMING MORN AND THE CERTAINTY THAT FOR MANY / THE NEXT SUNRISE WOULD BE THEIR LAST ON EARTH."
THOMAS D. DUNCAN, PVT
TISHMONINGO RANGERS

IN MEMORY OF ALL MISSISSIPPIANS WHO BATTLED / UPON THIS HALLOWED GROUND THE SIXTH AND SEVENTH OF APRIL / EIGHTEEN HUNDRED SIXTY TWO / ERECTED BY THE CITIZENS OF THE GREAT STATE OF MISSISSIPPI / MISSISSIPPI UNITS, ARMY OF THE MISSISSIPPI

[Base:]
J KIM SESSUMS / ISAIAH 53:6 2015

INFANTRY
3RD INFANTRY BATTALION, WOOD'S BRIGADE / 5TH INFANTRY REGIMENT, CHALMER'S BRIGADE / 6TH INFANTRY REGIMENT, / CHALMER'S BRIGADE / 7TH INFANTRY REGIMENT, CHALMER'S BRIGADE / 9TH INFANTRY REGIMENT, CHALMER'S BRIGADE / 10TH INFANTRY REGIMENT, CHALMER'S BRIGADE / 15TH INFANTRY REGIMENT, CHALMER'S BRIGADE / 22ND INFANTRY REGIMENT, CHALMER'S BRIGADE

/ BLYTHE'S INFANTRY REGIMENT, JOHNSON'S BRIGADE / 2ND CONFEDERATE
INFANTRY REGIMENT, COS. A, H, & I, BOWEN'S BRIGADE / 3RD CONFEDERATE
INFANTRY REGIMENT, COS. E & G, SHAVER'S BRIGADE

ARTILLERY
BAINS' (VAIDEN) BATTERY, GIBSON'S BRIGADE / BYRNE'S BATTERY, TRABUE'S
BRIGADE / HARPER'S (JEFFERSON LIGHT ARTILLERY) BATTERY, WOOD'S BRIGADE
/ SMITH'S BATTERY, STEPHENS' BRIGADE / STANFORD'S BATTERY, STEWART'S
BRIGADE / SWETT'S (WARREN LIGHT ARTILLERY) BATTERY, SHAVER'S BRIGADE

CAVALRY
ADAMS' CAVALRY REGIMENT, UNATTACHED / BREWER'S (MISS. & ALA.) CAVALRY
BATTALION, CHEATHAM'S DIVISION

LINDSAY'S 1ST CAVALRY REGIMENT, CHEATHAM'S DIVISION

" . . . NEVER BEFORE DID I GAZE SO EARNESTLY / MENTALLY INTO THAT DARK
UNKNOWN WORLD / & SEEK TO THE POSITION I MUST OCCUPY THERE. / AT THIS
MOMENT I TRUST I MADE A SINCERE, / HONEST SURRENDER OF MYSELF TO GOD,
THE / MAKER OF MY & THE PRESERVER OF MY LIFE. / . . . I ASKED FOR LIFE IF
THAT MIGHT BE A USEFUL / ONE. LET ME REMEMBER THIS IN FUTURE YEARS." /
AUGUSTUS H. MECKLIN, PVT. / CO. I, 15TH MISS. INF. REGIMENT

Mississippi native Kim Sessums completed the sculpture composition of a trio
of eight-foot soldiers honoring the participation of Mississippians at Shiloh.
The central figure, a color-bearer, is recoiling from a bullet wound as his col-
or-guard comrades reach to support him and keep the flag from falling.

The memorial was unveiled and dedicated in the fall of 2015 at Rhea Springs,
near a mass grave of Confederate soldiers. The cost of the monument was
$425,000, including $250,000 from the Mississippi State Legislature and approximately $175,000 by the Col. W. P. Rogers SCV Camp 321 in Corinth along
with the Mississippi Division of the SCV.

Sessums, a practicing physician, maintains parallel careers in art and medicine. His proposal, "Why a Mississippi Monument at Shiloh?" includes the
following observations:

> Monuments, by their very nature, are often history made visible whether
> they commemorate specific individuals or people groups, or whether they
> commemorate significant events in history. The best of such monuments
> lead us as visitors on a path to better comprehend the past and somehow
> apply that knowledge and wisdom to our present. . . . Should monuments
> not be designed so as to draw the viewer in for a closer look and consid-
> eration? Should they be instructive to a point but not quenching intellec-
> tual, spiritual, and emotional curiosity? Should they not exist so that we
> all might, as T. S. Eliot once wrote, "Kneel where prayer has been valid"?
> Surely any War Memorial is a sacred challenge.

· Isaiah 53:6, inscribed on the base, is both an accusation and condemnation. It takes terse and pointed measure of the prophet Isaiah's

generation, and it has applications to the generations that follow: "All we like sheep have gone astray; we have turned every one to his own way; and the LORD hath laid on him the iniquity of us all." By some Judeo-Christian interpretations, the prophet saw redemption for his people's failings only by way of a transcendent instrument—a messiah.

· Sessums's attention to detail includes a ring worn on the little finger of the right-hand figure's left hand. During the Victorian era, single men and women planning to remain single would express this preference by wearing such a ring.

Spain's Field

1.9.1 Subject: 61st Illinois VI, Stele
Location: N 35 07 24 70 / W 88 20 20 44
Dedicated: May 17–18, 1904
Media: Bronze, granite
Monument is a decorated stele surmounting a base.

Inscription

ILLINOIS / 61ST INFANTRY / 2D BRIGADE—MILLER / 6TH DIVISION—PRENTISS / ARMY OF THE TENNESSEE

. . . COMMANDED BY / COL. JACOB FRY. / FORMED IN LINE OF BATTLE ABOUT 8.00 A.M., APRIL 6, / 1862, ADVANCED THROUGH THE OPEN FIELD IN FRONT / AND ENGAGED THE ENEMY A SHORT TIME, THEN FELL / BACK TO THIS LINE AND HELD IT MORE THAN ONE / HOUR, WHEN THE REGIMENT RETIRED TO SOUTH SIDE / OF CORINTH ROAD. [LOST] 12 / MEN KILLED; 3 OFFICERS AND 42 MEN WOUNDED; / 18 MEN MISSING; TOTAL 75.

Organized at Carrollton, mustered in February 5, 1862. Shiloh. Corinth. Central Mississippi Campaign. Salem. Vicksburg. Steele's Expedition. Action against Forrest, Murfreesboro. Mustered out and discharged September 27, 1865. Lost 224 officers or enlisted men killed, mortally wounded, or by disease. At Shiloh, Col. Jacob Fry said to the regiment as the Confederates approached, "Gentlemen, remember your state and do your duty today like brave men."

Hamburg-Purdy Road, Review Field

1.10.1 Subject: 15th Indiana VI, Obelisk
Location: N 35 07 59 25 / W 88 20 40 96
Dedicated: April 6–7, 1903
Medium: Limestone
Monument is a decorated obelisk surmounting a base.

Inscription

15TH / INFANTRY, / COMMANDED BY / LIEUT. COL. GUSTAVUS A. WOOD, / 21ST BRIGADE—COL. GEORGE D. WAGNER— / 6TH DIVISION—GEN. WOOD— / ARMY OF THE OHIO. / INDIANA

... ARRIVED ON THE BATTLEFIELD FROM SAVANNAH, / ABOUT 12 M., APRIL 7, 1862. WAS ORDERED TO THE FRONT / BY MAJOR GENERAL GRANT. IT FORMED ON THIS POSITION IN / LINE OF BATTLE AT 2 P.M., AND ASSISTED IN DRIVING / THE ENEMY FROM THE FIELD. THE REGIMENT WAS UNDER FIRE / OF BOTH INFANTRY AND ARTILLERY, BUT SUSTAINED / NO LOSS.

Organized at Lafayette, mustered in June 14, 1861. West Virginia: Cheat Mountain. Shiloh. Corinth. Perryville. Stones River. Tullahoma. Chickamauga. Chattanooga. Mustered out June 16, 1864. Lost 183 officers or enlisted men killed, mortally wounded, or by disease.

1.10.2 Subject: 40th Indiana VI, Obelisk
Location: N 35 08 00 31 / W 88 20 43 02
Dedicated: April 6–7, 1903
Medium: Limestone
Monument is a decorated obelisk surmounting a base.

Inscription

40TH / REGIMENT / INFANTRY, / COMMANDED BY / COL. JOHN. W. BLAKE, / 21ST BRIGADE—COL. GEORGE D. WAGNER— / 6TH DIVISION—GEN. WOOD— / ARMY OF THE OHIO. / INDIANA.

... ARRIVED ON THE BATTLEFIELD FROM / SAVANNAH, ABOUT 12M., APRIL 7, 1862; WAS ORDERED, / WITH ITS BRIGADE, TO THE FRONT BY MAJOR GENERAL / GRANT. IT FORMED ON THIS LINE AT 2 P.M., AND ASSISTED IN / DRIVING THE ENEMY FROM THE FIELD. IT WAS UNDER FIRE / OF INFANTRY AND ARTILLERY, BUT SUSTAINED NO LOSS.

Organized at Lafayette and Indianapolis, mustered in December 30, 1861. Shiloh. Corinth. Perryville. Stones River. Tullahoma. Chattanooga. Atlanta. Franklin. Nashville. Mustered out December 21, 1865. Lost 359 officers or enlisted men killed, mortally wounded, or by disease.

1.10.3 Subject: 57th Indiana VI, Obelisk
Location: N 35 08 02 85 / W 88 20 48 9
Dedicated: April 6–7, 1903
Medium: Limestone
Monument is a decorated obelisk surmounting a base.

Inscription

57TH / REGIMENT / INFANTRY, / COMMANDED BY / COL. CYRUS C. HINES, / 21ST BRIGADE—COL. GEORGE D. WAGNER— / 6TH DIVISION—GEN. WOOD— / ARMY OF THE OHIO. / INDIANA.

... ARRIVED ON THE BATTLEFIELD ABOUT 12 M., / MONDAY, APRIL 7, 1862. IT FORMED ON THIS LINE AT / 2 P.M. AND ASSISTED IN DRIVING THE ENEMY FROM THE FIELD; WAS / ENGAGED WITH ENEMY'S INFANTRY AND ARTILLERY. IT HAD / FOUR MEN WOUNDED.

40th Indiana VI, Obelisk

Organized at Richmond, mustered in November 18, 1861. Shiloh. Perryville. Stones River. Tullahoma. Chickamauga. Chattanooga. Atlanta. Franklin. Nashville. Mustered out December 14, 1865. Lost 275 officers or enlisted men killed, mortally wounded, or by disease.

1.10.4 Subject: 77th Pennsylvania VI, Common Soldier Statue
Location: N 35 08 05 62 / W 88 20 52 50
Installed: 1902; dedicated: November 13, 1903
Media: Bronze, granite
Monument is a common soldier surmounting a base.

Inscription

PENNSYLVANIA /[Coat of arms]
77TH REGIMENT INFANTRY, / 5TH BRIGADE (KIRK'S), / 2D DIVISION (MCCOOK'S), / ARMY OF THE OHIO.
ORGANIZED AUGUST 1, 1861. DISCHARGED JANUARY 18, 1866.
ERECTED 1902.

. . . ARRIVED AT PITTSBURG LANDING AT 7 A.M., APRIL 7, / 1862. IT WAS THE ONLY PENNSYLVANIA REGIMENT ON THE FIELD. / ABOUT 2 P.M. THE REGIMENT CHARGED UPON, AND CAPTURED TWO / GUNS OF A CONFEDERATE BATTERY. / "BEING NOW SATISFIED THAT THE ENEMY HAD CHANGED HIS POINT / OF ATTACK FROM THE RIGHT TO MY LEFT, I ORDERED THE 77TH / PENNA. / TO TAKE A POSITION ON MY EXTREME LEFT AND REPEL THE ASSAULT / THERE BEING MADE. IT IMMEDIATELY

ENGAGED THE ENEMY. AT THIS / MOMENT THE CONTEST ALONG THE WHOLE LINE BECAME TERRIBLE. / THIS REGIMENT PARTIALLY ISOLATED FROM THE DIVISION, MOVED / STEADILY OVER AN OPEN FIELD UNDER A HEAVY FIRE; WHILE HERE / THE ENEMY'S CAVALRY CHARGED IT TWICE, BUT WERE EACH TIME / REPULSED WITH HEAVY LOSS. COLONEL STUMBAUGH HAD THE / SATISFACTION OF RECEIVING THE SWORD OF COLONEL BATTLE OF THE / 20TH TENN. WHO SURRENDERED AS A PRISONER." / GENERAL MCCOOK'S REPORT.

[Relief of 77th PVI soldiers in line, unarmed on left, armed on right. Caption: "Col. Stumbaugh receives the sword of Col. Battle of the 20th Tenn. who surrendered as a prisoner."]

[Relief of battle scene: 77th PVI advancing]

The 77th Pennsylvania was the only eastern regiment on the field at Shiloh. Commanded by Col. Frederick M. Stumbaugh at Shiloh, the 77th had present for duty, officers, men, 504. Its loss at Shiloh was 3 men killed; 7 men wounded; total 10. A delegation from Pennsylvania, led by Governor Samuel W. Pennypacker, arrived by river steamer for the dedication of the monument on Review Field, where it was accepted on behalf of the Secretary of War by Commission Chairman Cornelius Cadle.

The base is made of Vermont granite. The bronze work was done by Julius C. Loester; the granite is by W. Liance Cottrell.

The 77th organized at Pittsburgh. Shiloh. Corinth. Stones River. Tullahoma. Chickamauga. Chattanooga. Atlanta. Franklin. Nashville. Lost 319 officers or enlisted men killed, mortally wounded, or by disease.

Corinth Road

1.11.1 Subject: 48th Illinois VI, Stele
Location: N 35 08 14 98 / W 88 20 51 40
Dedicated: May 17–18, 1904
Media: Bronze, granite
Monument is a decorated stele surmounting a base.

Inscription

ILLINOIS / 48TH INFANTRY, / 2D BRIGADE—MARSH, / 1ST DIVISION— MCCLERNAND, / ARMY OF THE TENNESSEE.

WENT INTO LINE OF BATTLE HERE ABOUT 9.00 A.M., / APRIL 6, 1862, AND HELD IT UNTIL 10.50 A.M., WHEN IT WAS DRIVEN BACK 300 YARDS. THE REGIMENT LOST . . . 1 OFFICER AND 17 MEN KILLED; 6 OFFICERS AND 108 MEN / WOUNDED; 2 MEN MISSING; TOTAL, 133.

The 48th Illinois organized at Camp Butler, September 1861. Fort Donelson. Shiloh. Corinth. Operations against Forrest, West Tennessee. Chattanooga. Atlanta Campaign. March to the Sea. Carolinas Campaign. Grand Review. Mustered out August 15, 1865. Lost 380 officers, enlisted men killed, mortally wounded, or by disease.

1.11.2 Subject: 45th Illinois VI, Stele
Location: N 35 08 14 98 / W 88 20 51 40
Dedicated: May 17–18, 1904
Media: Bronze, granite
Monument is a decorated stele surmounting a base.

Inscription

ILLINOIS / 45TH INFANTRY, / 2D BRIGADE—MARSH, / 1ST DIVISION—
MCCLERNAND, / ARMY OF THE TENNESSEE.

. . . COMMANDED BY / COL. JOHN E. SMITH. / WENT INTO BATTLE ON THIS LINE
ABOUT 9.00 A.M., APRIL 6, / 1862, AND MAINTAINED THIS POSITION UNTIL 11.00
A.M., WHEN / IT JOINED THE DIVISION ON A NEW LINE. THE REGIMENT LOST 1
/ OFFICER AND 22 MEN KILLED; 17 OFFICERS AND 170 MEN / WOUNDED; 3 MEN
MISSING; TOTAL, 213.

The 45th Illinois, the "Washburn Lead Mine Regiment," organized at Galena,
mustered in at Camp Douglas, December 25, 1861. Fort Donelson. Shiloh.
Corinth. Central Mississippi Campaign. Vicksburg. Meridian. Atlanta. March
to the Sea. Carolinas Campaign. Grand Review. Mustered out July 12, 1865.
Lost 223 officers or enlisted men killed, mortally wounded, or by disease.

1.11.3 Subject: 25th Indiana VI, Obelisk
Location: N 35 09 03 75 / W 88 19 24 36
Dedicated: April 6–7, 1903
Medium: Limestone
Monument is a decorated obelisk surmounting a base.

Inscription

25TH / REGIMENT / INFANTRY, / COMMANDED BY / LIEUT. COL. WILLIAM H.
MORGAN, / 2D BRIGADE—COL. J. C. VEATCH—/ 4TH DIVISION—GEN. HURLBUT— /
ARMY OF THE TENNESSEE. / INDIANA.

. . . THIS REGIMENT TOOK THIS POSITION AT 9 A.M., APRIL 6, / 1862, AND HELD IT
AGAINST A FIERCE ASSAULT OF THE ENEMY / FOR TWO HOURS. BEING FLANKED,
FELL BACK 100 YARDS; / AGAIN IT FELL BACK 100 YARDS. HERE REGIMENT WAS /
FURIOUSLY ASSAILED BY INFANTRY AND ARTILLERY WHICH / CAUSED IT TO FALL
BACK SLOWLY TO THE RIGHT OF THE SIEGE / GUNS, WHERE IT RESTED SUNDAY
NIGHT. ON MONDAY, APRIL 7, / REGIMENT CONTINUED IN BATTLE DURING THE DAY.
/ CASUALTIES—KILLED, 2 OFFICERS AND 19 MEN; WOUNDED, 4 / OFFICERS AND 111
MEN; MISSING, 3 MEN; TOTAL, 139.

Organized at Evansville, mustered in August 19, 1861. Fremont's Missouri
Campaign. Fort Donelson. Shiloh. Central Mississippi Campaign. Meridian.
Atlanta. March to the Sea. Carolinas Campaign. Grand Review. Mustered out
July 17, 1865. Lost 7 officers, 81 enlisted men killed or mortally wounded; 3
officers, 270 enlisted men by disease. Total 361.

1.12.1 Subject: Battery D, 1st Illinois Vol. Artillery, Stele
Location: N 35 08 15 21 / W 88 20 48 52
Dedicated: May 17–18, 1904
Media: Bronze, granite
Monument is a decorated stele surmounting a base.

Inscription

ILLINOIS / BATTERY "D" / 1ST REGIMENT LT. ARTILLERY / 1ST DIVISION—MCCLERNAND / ARMY OF THE TENNESSEE

MCALLISTER'S BATTERY, "D" / COMMANDED BY / CAPT. E. MCALLISTER, WOUNDED. / THIS BATTERY OF FOUR 24 POUNDERS WENT INTO / ACTION HERE ABOUT 9.00 A.M., APRIL 6, 1862, HOLDING / HIS POSITION UNTIL ABOUT 11.00 A.M., WHEN IT / RETIRED ALONG THE CORINTH ROAD, LEAVING ONE GUN. / [LOST] ONE OFFICER AND THREE MEN WOUNDED.

Organized at Cairo, mustered in July 30, 1861. Forts Henry and Donelson. Shiloh. Corinth. Central Mississippi Campaign. Vicksburg. Meridian. Atlanta. Ordered to Nashville, duty there until December: battle of Nashville. Mustered out July 28, 1865. Lost 1 officer, 7 enlisted men killed or mortally wounded; 28 enlisted men by disease. Total 36.

1.12.2 Subject: 13th Iowa VI, Stele
Location: N 35 08 14 76 / W 88 20 44 66
Dedicated: November 23, 1906
Media: Bronze, granite
Monument is a decorated stele surmounting a base.

Inscription

IOWA / TO HER / 13 TH INFANTRY, / HARE'S (1ST) BRIGADE, / MCCLERNAND'S (1ST) DIVISION, / ARMY OF THE TENNESSEE.

. . . COMMANDED BY COL. MARCELLUS M. CROCKER. THIS REGIMENT HELD THIS POSITION FROM 9 A.M. TO 11 A.M. APRIL 6, 1862. RETIRED UNDER ORDERS ABOUT TWO HUNDRED YARDS, AND MAINTAINED ITS POSITION UNTIL ABOUT 2.30 P.M. MOVED TO A POINT NEAR THE CAMP OF THE 15TH ILLINOIS INFANTRY WHERE IT REPELLED A CHARGE OF WHARTON'S CAVALRY. / UNDER ORDERS, MOVED TO A POINT NEAR, AND WEST OF, CAMP OF THE 3RD IOWA INFANTRY, WHERE IT FOUGHT ITS SEVEREST ENGAGEMENT, AND REMAINED UNTIL ABOUT 4.30 P.M., WHEN BOTH FLANKS BEING TURNED, IT FELL BACK, BY ORDER, TO THE CORINTH ROAD AND JOINED A PORTION OF COLONEL TUTTLE'S COMMAND; ADVANCED TOWARD THE ENEMY; THEN RETIRED TO THE LAST LINE OF THE DAY, ITS RIGHT IN FRONT OF THE CAMP OF THE 14TH IOWA. WAS IN RESERVE LINE ON THE 7TH WITH SLIGHT LOSS. / PRESENT FOR DUTY, INCLUDING OFFICERS, MUSICIANS, TEAMSTERS, ETC., 760. ITS LOSS WAS, 1 OFFICER AND 23 MEN KILLED; 1 OFFICER AND 15 MEN MORTALLY WOUNDED; 8 OFFICERS AND 118 MEN WOUNDED; 5 MEN MISSING; TOTAL, 171.

Organized at Davenport, November 2, 1861. Shiloh. Central Mississippi Campaign. Vicksburg. Meridian. Atlanta. March to the Sea. Carolinas Campaign. Grand Review. Mustered out July 21, 1865. Lost 5 officers, 114 enlisted men killed or mortally wounded; 4 officers, 205 enlisted men by disease. Total 328.

1.12.3 Subject: 8th Illinois VI, Stele
Location: N 35 08 13 67 / W 88 20 32 72
Dedicated: May 17–18, 1904
Media: Bronze, granite
Monument is a decorated stele surmounting a base.

Inscription

ILLINOIS / 8TH INFANTRY / 1ST BRIGADE—HARE / 1ST DIVISION—MCCLERNAND / ARMY OF THE TENNESSEE

. . . COMMANDED BY / 1. CAPT. J. M. ASHMORE, WOUNDED. / 2. CAPT. W. H. HARVEY, KILLED. / 3 CAPT. R. H. STURGESS. / THIS LINE WAS HELD FROM 9.30 A.M. UNTIL 11.00 A.M., / APRIL 6, 1862, WHEN THE REGIMENT WAS FORCED BACK / TO A POSITION BEHIND DUNCAN FIELD. IT LOST IN / THE BATTLE, 1 OFFICER AND 29 MEN KILLED; 1 OFFICER / AND 90 MEN WOUNDED; 3 MEN MISSING; TOTAL, 124.

Organized at Cairo, July 25, 1861. Fort Donelson. Shiloh. Central Mississippi Campaign. Vicksburg. Meridian. Mobile. Mustered out May 13, 1866. Lost 321 officers or enlisted men killed, mortally wounded, or by disease.

1.12.4 Subject: 18th Illinois VI, Stele
Location: N 35 08 14 48 / W 88 20 38 84
Dedicated: May 17–18, 1904
Media: Bronze, granite
Monument is a decorated stele surmounting a base.

Inscription

ILLINOIS / 18TH INFANTRY / 1ST BRIGADE—HARE / 1ST DIVISION—MCCLERNAND / ARMY OF THE TENNESSEE

. . . COMMANDED BY / 1. MAJOR S. EATON, WOUNDED. / 2. CAPT. D. H. BRUSH, WOUNDED. / 3. CAPT. WM. J. DILLON, KILLED. / 4. CAPT. J. J. ANDERSON. / THIS REGIMENT RETURNED THE FIRE OF THE ENEMY / WHILE MARCHING BY THE FLANK TO TAKE THIS POSITION / IN LINE OF BATTLE. IT HELD THIS LINE FROM ABOUT 9.30 / TO 11.00 A.M., APRIL 6, 1862, WHEN IT RETIRED, / SKIRMISHING, ABOUT ONE-FOURTH OF A MILE. ITS LOSS / IN THE BATTLE WAS 1 OFFICER AND 16 MEN KILLED; 7 / OFFICERS AND 61 MEN WOUNDED; 2 MEN MISSING; TOTAL, 87.

Organized at Aurora, mustered in May 28, 1861. Fort Henry. Fort Donelson. Shiloh. Corinth. Central Mississippi Campaign. Operations against Forrest, West Tennessee. Vicksburg. Steele's Expedition, Little Rock. Mustered out December 31, 1865. Lost 394 officers or enlisted men killed, mortally wounded, or by disease.

18th Illinois VI, Stele

6th Indiana VI, Obelisk

1.12.5 Subject: 6th Indiana VI, Obelisk
Location: N 35 08 18 60 / W 88 20 33 74
Dedicated: April 6–7, 1903
Medium: Limestone
Monument is a decorated obelisk surmounting a base.

Inscription

6TH / REGIMENT / INFANTRY, / COMMANDED BY / COL. THOMAS T. CRITTENDEN, / 4TH BRIGADE—GEN. ROUSSEAU—/ 2D DIVISION—GEN. MCCOOK—/ ARMY OF THE OHIO / INDIANA.

. . . ARRIVED ON THE BATTLEFIELD AT 6 A.M. / APRIL 7, 1862. AT 8 A.M. ADVANCED UNDER THE FIRE OF / A BATTERY OF ARTILLERY. OCCUPIED THIS POSITION FROM 10 / A.M. TO 11.30 A.M. ENEMY GAVE WAY; REGIMENT FOLLOWED / UNTIL LATE IN THE DAY. CASUALTIES—KILLED 4; WOUNDED 36; / MISSING 2; TOTAL, 42.

Organized at Madison, mustered in September 20, 1861. Shiloh. Corinth. Stones River. Tullahoma. Chickamauga. Chattanooga. Atlanta. Mustered out September 22, 1864. Lost 267 officers or enlisted men killed, mortally wounded, or by disease.

1.12.6 Subject: 1st Ohio VI, Stele
Location: N 35 08 22 05 / W 88 20 24 06
Dedicated: June 6, 1902
Medium: Granite
Monument is a decorated stele surmounting a base.

Inscription

OHIO / 1ST INFANTRY / COMMANDED BY / COL. B. F. SMITH / ROUSEAU'S (4TH) BRIGADE / MCCOOK'S (2D) DIVISION / ARMY OF THE OHIO

[Relief of crossed muskets, cartridge belt, canteen]

THIS REGIMENT WAS ENGAGED HERE / ABOUT 10 A.M., APRIL 7, 1862. / *[LOST]* 2 MEN KILLED; 2 OFFICERS / AND 45 MEN WOUNDED; 1 MAN MISSING; / TOTAL, 50.

Organized at Dayton, October 30, 1861. Shiloh. Corinth. Perryville. Stones River. Tullahoma. Chickamauga. Chattanooga. Atlanta. Mustered out October 14, 1864. Lost 5 officers, 116 enlisted men killed or mortally wounded; 130 enlisted men by disease. Total 251.

1st Ohio VI, Stele

1.12.7 Subject: US Infantry, Shaft
Location: N 35 08 23 56 / W 88 20 23 02
Dedicated: December 9, 1910
Medium: Granite
Monument is an obelisk surmounting a base.

Inscription

U.S.

[Relief of laurel wreath] [Relief of two muskets, bayonets affixed, with surmounting shield]

15TH U.S. INFANTRY. / 1ST BATTALION, / CAPT. PETER SWAIN. / 16TH U.S. INFANTRY. / 1ST BATTALION, / CAPT. EDWIN F. TOWNSEND. / 19TH U.S. INFANTRY, / 1ST BATTALION / MAJ. STEPHEN D. CARPENTER. . . . / 4TH BRIGADE (ROUSSEAU), / 2ND DIVISION (MCCOOK), / ARMY OF THE OHIO.

THESE BATTALIONS OF U.S. INFANTRY, / ACTING AS A REGIMENT, UNDER THE / COMMAND OF MAJ. JOHN H. KING, / WERE ENGAGED HERE FROM ABOUT / 9:30 TO 11:30 A.M., APRIL 7, 1862. / CASUALTIES 15 KILLED, 141 WOUNDED, TOTAL 156.

These units organized by direction of President Lincoln, May 4, 1861, confirmed by act of Congress July 29, 1861. The 15th Infantry organized at Wheeling. Lost 280 officers or enlisted men killed, mortally wounded, or by disease. The 19th Infantry organized at Indianapolis. Lost 184 officers or enlisted men killed, mortally wounded, or by disease. Regiments' combined service: Shiloh. Corinth. Perryville. Stones River. Tullahoma. Chickamauga. Chattanooga. Atlanta.

1.12.8 Subject: 7th Illinois VI, Stele
Location: N 35 08 21 25 / W 88 20 21 25
Dedicated: May 17–18, 1904
Media: Bronze, granite
Monument is a decorated stele surmounting a base.

Inscription

ILLINOIS / 7TH INFANTRY / 3D BRIGADE—SWEENY / 2D DIVISION—W. H. L. WALLACE / ARMY OF THE TENNESSEE

. . . COMMANDED BY / MAJOR RICHARD ROWETT. / WENT INTO POSITION HERE ABOUT 9.00 A.M., APRIL 6, / 1862; ADVANCED TO RIGHT AND FRONT, AND AFTER / A SHARP ENCOUNTER FELL BACK TO THIS POSITION / WHERE ITS GREATEST LOSS OCCURRED. ABOUT 4:00 / P.M. IT MOVED TO ASSIST MCCLERNAND. *[LOST]* 2 OFFICERS KILLED; 2 / WOUNDED; 15 MEN KILLED; 79 WOUNDED; 1 MISSING; TOTAL, 99.

Regiment organized at Cairo, July 25, 1861. Forts Henry and Donelson. Shiloh. Corinth. Dodge's operations against Forrest. Dodge's expedition, northern Alabama. March to the Sea. Carolinas Campaign. Grand Review. Mustered out July 9, 1865. Lost 266 officers or enlisted men killed, mortally wounded, or by disease.

1.12.9 Subject: 58th Illinois VI, Stele
Location: N 35 08 19 23 / W 88 20 26 02
Dedicated: May 17–18, 1904
Media: Bronze, granite
Monument is a decorated stele surmounting a base.

Inscription

ILLINOIS / 58TH INFANTRY / 3D BRIGADE—SWEENY / 2D DIVISION—W. H. L. WALLACE / ARMY OF THE TENNESSEE

. . . COMMANDED BY / COL. WM. F. LYNCH. / THIS REGIMENT HELD THIS LINE WITH SLIGHT CHANGES / OF POSITION FROM ABOUT 9:00 A.M., APRIL 6, 1862, UNTIL / ITS CAPTURE ABOUT 5:30 P.M. THE REGIMENT LOST IN / BATTLE 20 MEN KILLED; 8 OFFICERS AND 39 MEN / WOUNDED; 223 MEN MISSING; TOTAL, 290.

Organized at Camp Douglas, February 11, 1862. Fort Donelson. Shiloh: mostly captured. Regiment consolidated with other units. Corinth. Meridian. Red River. Nashville. Mobile. Mustered out April 15, 1866. Lost 298 officers or enlisted men killed, mortally wounded, or by disease.

1.12.10 Subject: 2nd Iowa VI, Stele
Location: N 35 08 17 34 / W 88 20 24 62
Dedicated: November 23, 1906
Media: Bronze, granite
Monument is a decorated stele surmounting a base.

Inscription

IOWA / TO HER / 2D INFANTRY, / TUTTLE'S (1ST) BRIGADE, / W. H. L. WALLACE'S (1ST) DIVISION, / ARMY OF THE TENNESSEE.

. . . COMMANDED BY LIEUT. COL. JAMES BAKER. THIS REGIMENT HELD THIS POSITION FROM ABOUT 9 A.M. UNTIL 4.30 P.M., APRIL 6, 1862, SUCCESSFULLY RESISTING REPEATED ASSAULTS FROM THE ENEMY'S INFANTRY AND THE HEAVY FIRE OF HIS ARTILLERY. THEN, BEING NEARLY SURROUNDED, IT WAS ORDERED TO FALL BACK, WHICH IT DID IN GOOD ORDER, THROUGH A HEAVY CROSS FIRE FROM BOTH FLANKS, TO A POINT ABOUT ONE MILE FROM THIS PLACE, WHERE IT FORMED IN LINE AND HELD ITS POSITION UNTIL DARKNESS CLOSED THE FIGHTING FOR THAT DAY. / ON APRIL 7TH THE REGIMENT MOVED OUT EARLY IN RESERVE AND WAS AT DIFFERENT TIMES UNDER FIRE. ABOUT 2 P.M. IT WAS ORDERED BY GENERAL NELSON TO CHARGE ACROSS A FIELD ON THE ENEMY IN THE WOODS BEYOND, WHICH WAS DONE IN MOST GALLANT MANNER, THE ENEMY RETIRING. THIS ENDED THE TWO DAYS FIGHTING FOR THIS REGIMENT. NUMBER ENGAGED, 490. ITS LOSS WAS, KILLED AND WOUNDED, 68; MISSING, 4; TOTAL, 72.

Organized at Keokuk, mustered in May 27, 1861. Fort Donelson. Shiloh. Corinth. Dodge's Expedition. Atlanta. March to the Sea. Carolinas Campaign. Grand Review. Mustered out July 20, 1865. Lost 283 officers or enlisted men killed, mortally wounded, or by disease.

1.12.11 Subject: UDC Memorial Tableau: One Officer, Three Common Soldiers, Three Female Figures in Mourning
Location: N 35 08 25 10 / W 88 20 05 52
Dedicated: May 17, 1917
Media: Bronze, granite, marble
Monument is a tableau sculpture of four soldiers, three female figures in mourning.

Inscriptions

[Front]

[TABLEAU OF FIGURES, MALE AND FEMALE, AND HIGH RELIEFS IN THREE GROUPS OF FIGURES. IN THE CENTRAL GROUP, A FEMALE FIGURE REPRESENTING VICTORY IS FLANKED BY TWO SHROUDED MALE FIGURES SYMBOLIZING DEATH AND NIGHT. A BUST OF GEN. ALBERT S. JOHNSTON IS DISPLAYED AT THE CENTER. AT EITHER SIDE OF THE CENTRAL GROUP ARE CARVED RELIEFS OF HEADS OF SOLDIERS. STATUES OF TWO SOLDIERS, REPRESENTING ARTILLERY AND INFANTRY ON THE RIGHT; TWO SOLDIERS REPRESENTING THE CAVALRY AND OFFICERS ARE ON THE LEFT.]

UDC Tableau: One Officer, Three Common Soldiers, Three Female Figures in Mourning

This is the preeminent Confederate monument on the Shiloh battlefield and one of the most significant in the South. It stands at a high-water mark of the battle for Southern arms, near the point where the Confederates secured the surrender of over twenty-three hundred Union soldiers, at what later came to be known as the Hornet's Nest. It is also—indirectly—tribute to the UDC for erecting a monument at a site that was otherwise neglected by Southern state legislatures and is a counterpoint to the plethora of Union monuments on the field.

Fundraising for the project began in 1905. The ambitious projected goal of $50,000 was reached "little by little," the UDC reported, with no assistance from other private organizations and with no state appropriation.

Frederick Hibbard's first major success as a sculptor came when he was selected by the UDC to erect the monument. Hibbard eventually designed and produced the eagle surmounting the portico of the Illinois State Memorial and Temple at Vicksburg, the equestrian statue of General Ulysses S. Grant at Vicksburg, and county seat Civil War monuments at Raymond, Mississippi, and Forsyth, Georgia. Hibbard later commented on the Shiloh commission, observing that the "subject was a difficult one, for the Battle of Shiloh did not result in a Confederate victory. I went weeks studying Civil War history and biography, deciding at last to use symbolic figures typifying the reasons for the defeat."

The director of the UDC's Shiloh Monument Committee declared that visitors came "on boats, on horseback, in carriages and in automobiles from distant points in Alabama, Mississippi, Kentucky and Tennessee." Sculptor Frederick Hibbard was in attendance. Mrs. Cordelia Powell Odenheimer bestowed the monument to the War Department, represented by Park Superintendent DeLong Rice. The governor of Tennessee, Tom Rye, was present and gave the opening address. A letter from President Woodrow Wilson was read. The principal address was given by the Rt. Rev. Thomas F. Gailor.

The monument is an unusual design: the base is eighteen feet, six inches high by fifty feet wide. Many Tennessee monuments are taller; this is the longest. The figures are in bronze; the panels and base are of Georgia marble and Mount Airy granite. The highly symbolic tableau is in front. The inscription is on the reverse, facing east, away from the roadway. However, viewers from the reverse side looking at the monument face the field of battle of the first day; viewers of the monument from the roadside front see a visual, symbolic interpretation and narration of what occurred behind them.

The Park Service offers the following description of the symbolism of the monument:

> The monument's central figures depict "Defeated Victory." In front, the South surrenders the laurel wreath of victory to Death on her right, and Night on her left. Death took away the Confederate commander-in-chief; while Night, having brought re-enforcements for the Federals, stands waiting to complete the defeat. Below them, in low relief, appears the figure of General Albert Sidney Johnston, the southern commander, Johnston, the highest-ranking American officer ever killed in action. The panel of heads on the right represents the spirit of the first day. How hopefully and fearlessly the 11 young Confederates rushed into battle! The panel of heads on the left represents the second day of the battle and the sorrow of the men, now reduced to 10, over the victory so nearly won and so unexpectedly lost.

· Frederick Hibbard also sculpted the Confederate monument in Forsyth, Georgia; the eagle surmounting the Illinois monument in Vicksburg; the bronze plaque on the Confederate monument in Raymond, Mississippi; and the equestrian statue of Maj. Gen. Ulysses S. Grant in the Vicksburg National Military Park.

Intersection of Cavalry and Corinth-Pittsburg Roads

1.13.1 Subject: State of Michigan, Common Soldier Statue, Union
Location: N 35 08 36 33 / W 88 19 58 20
Dedicated: May 30, 1919
Media: Bronze, granite
Monument is statue of common soldier surmounting a shaft and base.

Inscription

MICHIGAN

[State seal of Michigan]

E PLURIBUS UNUM

TUEBAR / SI QUAERIS PENINSULAM AMOENAM / CIRCUMSPICE

THIS MONUMENT / IS ERECTED AND DEDICATED BY / THE PEOPLE OF MICHIGAN / TO THE MEMORY OF / HER SOLDIERS / WHO FOUGHT AND FELL IN / THE BATTLE OF SHILOH

THE 12TH MICHIGAN INFANTRY MET THE FIRST CONFEDERATE LINE IN THE EARLY MORNING OF APRIL 6, 1862, AND HELPED TO RESIST ITS SUDDEN ADVANCE. 27 KILLED, 54 WOUNDED, 109 MISSING—TOTAL, 190 MEN.

THE 15TH MICHIGAN INFANTRY, UNASSIGNED, ALTHOUGH NOT SUPPLIED WITH AMMUNITION, MOVED TO THE FRONT AS THE BATTLE OPENED, ENDEAVORING TO MEET THE CONFEDERATES WITH BAYONETS, BUT WAS FORCED TO RETURN TO THE LANDING FOR AMMUNITION, AFTER WHICH IT "FOUGHT WITH CONSPICUOUS GALLANTRY" UNTIL THE CLOSE OF THE BATTLE. / LOSING 23 KILLED, 74 WOUNDED, 5 MISSING—TOTAL, 102 MEN.

ROSS' BATTERY B, MICHIGAN LIGHT ARTILLERY WAS CONSPICUOUS IN THE DESPERATE STRUGGLES OF THE FIRST DAY IN THE "PEACH ORCHARD" AND NEAR THE "BLOODY POND," FIGHTING UNTIL ORDERED TO RETIRE. WHILE PREPARING TO EXECUTE THIS ORDER, IT WAS CHARGED AND CAPTURED BY CONFEDERATE CAVALRY WITHIN A FEW FEET OF THIS MONUMENT, LOSING FOUR OF ITS SIX GUNS. / LOSSES: 5 WOUNDED, 56 MISSING—TOTAL, 102 MEN.

MORE ENDURING THAN THIS GRANITE WILL BE THE GRATITUDE OF MICHIGAN, TO HER SOLDIERS OF SHILOH.

The state of Michigan dedicated the last state monument erected at Shiloh in the twentieth century on Memorial Day 1919. Erected on behalf of the three Michigan units on the field, it was also the last Northern state monument. It is an imposing monument on a county courthouse model, facing south, at the corner of Cavalry and Corinth-Pittsburg Roads, a staunch-looking tribute to the stalwartness of the Union soldier.

The monument stands seventeen feet, nine inches high. The Detroit Granite Company executed the monument in light Barre granite. The Michigan delegation was led by Michigan governor Albert E. Sleeper. He presented the

State of Michigan, Common Soldier Statue, Union

monument to Park Director DeLong Rice, who accepted on behalf of the War Department.

The 12th Michigan organized at Niles, Dowagiac, and Buchanan, mustered in March 5, 1862. Shiloh. Corinth. Vicksburg. Steele's Expedition. Mustered out February 15, 1866. Lost 1 officer, 52 enlisted men killed or mortally wounded; 3 officers, 372 enlisted men by disease. Total 428.

The 15th Michigan organized at Detroit, Monroe, and Grand Rapids, mustered in March 20, 1862. Shiloh. Corinth. Vicksburg. Chattanooga. Atlanta. March to the Sea. Carolinas Campaign. Grand Review. Mustered out August 18, 1865. Lost 3 officers, 60 enlisted men killed or mortally wounded; 4 officers, 268 enlisted men by disease. Total 335.

Battery B, 1st Light Artillery organized at Grand Rapids and Detroit, December 14, 1861. Battery captured at Shiloh except Lang's Section. Reorganized at Detroit, December 1862. Atlanta. March to the Sea. Carolinas Campaign. Grand Review. Mustered out June 14, 1865.

Eastern Corinth Road, Sunken Road, and Vicinity

1.14.1 Subject: State of Arkansas, Common Soldier Statue, Confederate
Location: N 35 08 06 93 / W 88 20 17 02
Installed: 1910; dedicated: September 6, 1911
Medium: Granite

Monument is a statue of common soldier facing northeast, surmounting a shaft and base.

Inscriptions

[Front]
[Relief of CS national flag] [Relief of state seal of Arkansas]

CONFEDERATE TROOPS FROM / ARKANSAS PRESENT AT THE BATTLE OF / SHILOH. / REMARKS / THE FOLLOWING FIELD OFFICERS / OF ARKANSAS TROOPS WERE KILLED OR / DIED OF WOUNDS RECEIVED ON THE / BATTLEFIELD OF SHILOH *[List of five officers]*

[Relief of musket, canteen, and bayonet]

TO THE BRAVE CONFEDERATE DEAD / OF ARKANSAS WHO FELL UPON / THIS BATTLEFIELD, / THIS MONUMENT IS ERECTED BY / THE ARKANSAS DIV. UNITED / DAUGHTERS OF THE CONFEDERACY / IN THE YEAR 1910.

[Relief of crossed swords]

INFANTRY / 1ST ARKANSAS (FAGAN) / GIBSON'S BRIGADE, BRAGG'S CORPS / 15TH ARKANSAS (PATTON) / CLEBURNE'S BRIGADE, HARDEE'S CORPS / 2ND ARKANSAS (COWAN) / 6TH ARKANSAS (HAWTHORN) / 7TH ARKANSAS (DEAN) / SHAIER'S BRIGADE, HARDEE'S CORPS / 8TH ARKANSAS (PATTERSON) / 9TH (14TH) ARKANSAS BATTALION (KELLY) / WOOD'S BRIGADE, HARDEE'S CORPS, / 9TH ARKANSAS (DUNLOP) / BOWEN'S BRIGADE, BRECKINRIDGE'S CORPS / 13TH ARKANSAS (TAPPAN) / STEWART'S BRIGADE, POLK'S CORPS

[Relief of two cannon barrels]

ARTILLERY / CALVERT'S BATTERY (SHOUP'S BATTALION) / HUBBARD'S BATTERY, CLEBURNE'S BRIG. / TRIGG'S BATTERY / HARDEE'S CORPS. / ROBERTS' BATTERY (UNASSIGNED)

This memorial "to the brave Confederate dead of Arkansas who fell on this battlefield" was dedicated by the state's UDC chapters on September 6, 1911. The dedication address was given by Brig. Gen. Robert G. "Fighting Bob" Shaver, commander of a brigade at Shiloh, which included the 2nd, 6th, and 7th Arkansas Infantry.

The monument stands near the Hornet's Nest figure and faces northeast, toward the Union last line of defense and the Tennessee River. There is a present-tense dynamic to the monument: the soldier's hand shields his eyes as he looks toward the river, as if the distance were daunting and the opposition of uncertain strength, or as if the smoke of battle obscures his way forward. The battle flag, as sculpted, is still waving.

State of Arkansas, Common Soldier Statue, Confederate

The monument is composed of light Barre granite on gray Mount Airy granite. The Morriss Bros. Company of Memphis served as fabricator. The sculpture stands seven feet high and is eighteen inches wide. The shaft and base stand twenty-one feet high. The sculptor is unknown.

1.14.2 Subject: 14th Iowa VI, Stele
Location: N 35 08 07 52 / W 88 20 15 96
Dedicated: November 23, 1906
Media: Bronze, granite
Monument is a decorated stele surmounting a base.

Inscription

IOWA / TO HER / 14TH INFANTRY, / TUTTLE'S (1ST) BRIGADE, / W. H. L. WALLACE'S (2D) DIVISION, / ARMY OF THE TENNESSEE.

THIS REGIMENT, (SEVEN COMPANIES), HELD THIS POSITION AGAINST REPEATED ATTACKS FROM 9 A.M. UNTIL 4 P.M., APRIL 6, 1862. / IN ATTEMPTING TO FOLLOW THE REST OF THE BRIGADE, WHICH WAS BEING WITHDRAWN, / IT BECAME HOTLY ENGAGED ABOUT 200 YARDS EAST OF THIS POSITION. REPULSING THIS ATTACK / IT CONTINUED TO RETIRE TOWARDS THE HAMBURG ROAD, FIGHTING HEAVILY. REACHING THE / CAMP OF THE 32D ILLINOIS INFANTRY IT FOUND ITSELF ENTIRELY SURROUNDED BY THE JUNCTION OF THE CONFEDERATE RIGHT AND LEFT WINGS. IT WAS CAPTURED ABOUT 6.00 P.M. / PRESENT ON DUTY, INCLUDING MUSICIANS, TEAMSTERS, ETC., 442. ITS LOSS WAS, KILLED, 8 MEN; WOUNDED, 2 OFFICERS AND 37 MEN; CAPTURED, 15 OFFICERS AND 211 MEN; TOTAL, 273. OF THE WOUNDED, 5 DIED OF THEIR WOUNDS; OF THE CAPTURED, 15 DIED IN PRISON.

Organized at Davenport, mustered in November 6, 1861. Forts Henry and Donelson. Shiloh. Regiment mostly captured. Paroled October 12, 1862; exchanged November 19, 1862. Remaining elements: Corinth. Meridian. Red

River Campaign: Pleasant Hill. Smith's expedition: Tupelo, Oxford. Regiment mustered out November 16, 1864; two companies mustered out August 8, 1865. Lost 203 officers or enlisted men killed, mortally wounded, or by disease.

1.14.3 Subject: 8th Iowa VI, Stele
Location: N 35 08 05 14 / W 88 20 15 14
Dedicated: November 23, 1906
Media: Bronze, granite
Monument is a decorated stele surmounting a base.

Inscription

IOWA / IN MEMORY OF HER / 8TH INFANTRY, / SWEENY'S (3D) BRIGADE, / W. H. L. WALLACE'S (2D) DIVISION, / ARMY OF THE TENNESSEE.

. . . COMMANDED BY COL. JAMES L. GEDDES. / THE REGIMENT HELD THIS POSITION FROM ABOUT 11 A.M., APRIL 6, 1862, UNTIL ABOUT 4 P.M., / WHEN IT CHANGED FRONT TO THE LEFT / AND HELD THIS SECOND POSITION UNTIL ABOUT 5 P.M. / WHEN NEARLY SURROUNDED IT ATTEMPTED TO RETREAT, BUT FINDING ALL AVENUES OF / ESCAPE CUT OFF, SURRENDERED ABOUT 6 P.M. / THE REGIMENT ENTERED THE ENGAGEMENT WITH AN AGGREGATE OF ABOUT 600 MEN. ITS LOSS WAS, KILLED, 40; WOUNDED, 95 (18 MORTALLY). MISSING, 340; TOTAL, 493.

The 8th Iowa organized at Davenport, September 1861. Fremont's Missouri Campaign. Shiloh: most of regiment captured. Paroled October 18, 1862; exchanged November 10, 1862. Corinth. Vicksburg. Red River. Forrest's attack, Memphis. Mobile. Mustered out April 20, 1866. Lost 276 officers or enlisted men killed, mortally wounded, or by disease.

1.14.4 Subject: 5th Battery, 1st Regt., Ohio Vol. Artillery, Stele
Location: N 35 08 04 74 / W 88 20 14 40
Dedicated: June 6, 1902
Medium: Granite
Monument is a decorated stele surmounting a base.

Inscription

[Inscription on a scroll relief, framed by two cannon barrels in vertical position, high relief]

OHIO / 5TH BATTERY LIGHT ARTILLERY / COMMANDED BY / CAPT. ANDREW HICKENLOOPER / PRENTISS'S (5TH) DIVISION / ARMY OF THE TENNESSEE

[High relief of two crossed ramrods with wheel, two cannonballs]

THIS BATTERY WENT INTO ACTION AT 7:30 A.M. APRIL 6, 1862, / IN SPAIN FIELD. AT 9 A.M. IT RETIRED TO THIS PLACE WITH 4 GUNS AND WAS / HOTLY ENGAGED UNTIL 4 P.M., WHEN IT RETIRED WITH 3 GUNS TO MCARTHUR'S HEADQUARTERS, WHERE IT WAS ENGAGED IN LAST ENCOUNTER OF THE DAY. / [LOST] 1 MAN KILLED; 1 OFFICER AND 18 MEN WOUNDED; TOTAL 20. / IT HAD 2 GUNS CAPTURED AND 1 DISABLED.

The 5th Independent Battery organized at St. Louis, mustered in September 22, 1861. Shiloh. Corinth. Central Mississippi Campaign. Vicksburg. Steele's expedition. Mustered out July 31, 1865. Lost 5 enlisted men killed or mortally wounded; 36 enlisted men by disease. Total 41.

- The barrel on this monument was vandalized and has been missing since at least 1984.

1.14.5 Subject: 31st Indiana VI, Obelisk
Location: N 35 07 59 69 / W 88 20 10 84
Dedicated: April 6–7, 1903
Medium: Limestone
Monument is a decorated obelisk surmounting a base.

Inscription
31ST / REGIMENT / INFANTRY / COMMANDED BY / COL. CHARLES CRUFT, / 3D BRIGADE—GEN. LAUMAN—/ 4TH DIVISION—GEN. HURLBUT—/ ARMY OF THE TENNESSEE. / INDIANA.

[. . .] TOOK THIS POSITION SUNDAY, APRIL 6, 1862, AT / 8.30 A.M., AND HELD IT AGAINST REPEATED CHARGES / OF THE ENEMY UNTIL 2.30 P.M. DURING THIS TIME THE WOODS / IN FRONT CAUGHT FIRE, AND MANY DEAD AND WOUNDED / WERE BURNED THE REGIMENT WAS THEN TRANSFERRED TO / THE LEFT AND WAS ENGAGED EAST OF THE HAMBURG ROAD / UNTIL 4 P.M. WHEN IT SLOWLY RETIRED TO THE SUPPORT OF / THE SIEGE GUNS. ON MONDAY, APRIL 7, 1862, IT WAS ENGAGED / DURING THE DAY ON THE RIGHT CENTER OF THE ARMY, / CASUALTIES: KILLED, 2 OFFICERS AND 19 MEN; TOTAL, 138.

Organized at Terre Haute, mustered in September 15, 1861. Fort Donelson. Shiloh. Corinth. Perryville. Stones River. Tullahoma. Chickamauga. Chattanooga. Atlanta. Franklin. Nashville. Mustered out December 8, 1865. Lost 378 officers or enlisted men killed, mortally wounded, or by disease.

1.14.6 Subject: 44th Indiana VI, Obelisk
Location: N 35 07 55 68 / W 88 20 09 60
Dedicated: April 6–7, 1903
Medium: Limestone
Monument is a decorated obelisk surmounting a base.

Inscription
44 TH / REGIMENT / INFANTRY, / COMMANDED BY / COL. HUGH B. REED, / 3D BRIGADE—GEN. LAUMAN— / 4TH DIVISION—GEN. HURLBUT—/ ARMY OF THE TENNESSEE / INDIANA

. . . FORMED IN THIS LINE SUNDAY, APRIL 6TH / 1862, AT 8.30 A.M. IT REPULSED SEVERAL CHARGES MADE BY / THE ENEMY, WHICH, UNDER ORDERS OF GEN. BRAGG, WAS / ATTEMPTING TO FORCE THIS PART OF THE LINE BACK. DURING / THESE ENGAGEMENTS THE WOODS CAUGHT FIRE. AT 2.30 / P.M. REGIMENT FELL BACK TO A LINE WITH 1ST BRIGADE, THEN TO / REAR AND LEFT OF BLOODY POND, WHERE IT CHARGED ON / ENEMY'S INFANTRY AND ARTILLERY. HERE SEVEN FLAG- / BEARERS

3rd Iowa VI, Stele

WERE SHOT DOWN. AT 4.30 P.M. SLOWLY FELL BACK / AND SUPPORTED SIEGE GUNS. MONDAY, APRIL 7TH, REGIMENT / FOUGHT THE ENEMY TILL 3 P.M. NUMBER [OF] MEN IN ACTION, / 478. CASUALTIES—KILLED, 1 OFFICER AND 33 MEN; WOUNDED, / 6 OFFICERS AND 171 MEN; MISSING, 1 MAN; TOTAL, 212.

Organized at Fort Wayne, mustered in November 22, 1861. Fort Donelson. Shiloh. Corinth. Stones River. Tullahoma. Chickamauga. Chattanooga. Mustered out September 14, 1865. Lost 309 officers or enlisted men killed, mortally wounded, or by disease.

1.14.7 Subject: 3rd Iowa VI, Stele
Location: N 35 07 53 58 / W 88 20 05 52
Dedicated: November 23, 1906
Media: Bronze, granite
Monument is a decorated stele surmounting a base.

Inscription

IOWA / TO HER / 3D INFANTRY, / WILLIAMS' (1ST) BRIGADE, / HURLBUT'S (4TH) DIVISION, / ARMY OF THE TENNESSEE.

. . . COMMANDED BY MAJOR WILLIAM M. STONE, (CAPTURED) / LIEUT. GEORGE W. CROSLEY

. . . WENT INTO ACTION SUNDAY, APRIL 6, 1862, ON THE SOUTH SIDE OF THIS FIELD AT ABOUT 9 A.M. IT SOON FELL BACK TO THIS PLACE WHICH IT HELD AGAINST REPEATED / ATTACKS UNTIL 2 P.M. WHEN IT FELL BACK 200 YARDS AND ONE HOUR LATER WITHDREW TO THE WICKER FIELD. HERE IT WAS ENGAGED UNTIL 4 P.M. WHEN IT RETIRED, FIGHTING, TO ITS CAMP, WHERE IT WAS NEARLY SURROUNDED BUT BROKE THROUGH THE RANKS OF THE ENEMY AND JOINED THE COMMAND OF COL. M. M. CROCKER IN FRONT OF THE 2D IOWA CAMP, WHERE IT BIVOUACKED SUNDAY NIGHT. ON MONDAY IT WAS ENGAGED UNDER LIEUT. CROSLEY, HE BEING SENIOR OFFICER FOR DUTY. PRESENT FOR DUTY, INCLUDING OFFICERS, MUSICIANS, TEAMSTERS, ETC., 560. ITS LOSS WAS, 23 MEN KILLED; 6 OFFICERS AND 128 MEN WOUNDED; 3 OFFICERS AND 27 MEN MISSING: TOTAL, 187.

Organized at Keokuk, mustered in June 8, 1861. Guard duty, operations against partisans in Missouri. Shiloh. Corinth. Central Mississippi Campaign. Vicksburg. Meridian. Red River. Veterans consolidated with 2nd Iowa, November 4, 1864. Lost 249 officers or enlisted men killed, mortally wounded, or by disease.

1.14.8 Subject: 32nd Illinois VI, Stele
Location: N 35 07 53 06 / W 88 20 00 18
Dedicated: May 17–18, 1904
Media: Bronze, granite
Monument is a decorated stele surmounting a base.

Inscription

ILLINOIS / 32D INFANTRY / 1ST BRIGADE—WILLIAMS / 4TH DIVISION—HURLBUT / ARMY OF THE TENNESSEE

. . . COMMANDED BY / COL. JOHN LOGAN, WOUNDED. ADVANCED IN LINE OF BATTLE APRIL 6, 1862, THROUGH THIS / FIELD TO THE TIMBER, THEN FELL BACK TO THIS POSITION / AND ENGAGED THE ENEMY FROM ABOUT 9.30 TO 11.30 A.M., / WHEN IT MOVED TO THE LEFT AND REAR OF THE 41ST / ILLINOIS. THE REGIMENT LOST IN THE BATTLE 3 OFFICERS / AND 36 MEN KILLED; 6 OFFICERS AND 108 MEN WOUNDED; / 5 MEN MISSING; TOTAL, 158.

Organized at Camp Butler, mustered in December 31, 1861. Shiloh. Corinth. Central Mississippi Campaign. Meridian. Atlanta. March to the Sea. Carolinas Campaign. Grand Review. Mustered out September 16, 1865. Lost 268 officers or enlisted men killed, mortally wounded, or by disease.

1.14.9 Subject: 28th Illinois VI, Stele
Location: N 35 07 52 87 / W 88 19 55 86
Dedicated: May 17–18, 1904
Media: Bronze, granite
Monument is a decorated stele surmounting a base.

Inscription

ILLINOIS / 28TH INFANTRY / 1ST BRIGADE—WILLIAMS / 4TH DIVISION—HURLBUT / ARMY OF THE TENNESSEE

. . . COMMANDED BY / COL. A. K. JOHNSON. / HELD THIS LINE AND ONE ABOUT 200 YARDS SOUTH / AGAINST HEAVY AND CONSTANT FIRE FROM 9.30 A.M. TO 2.00 P.M., / APRIL 6, 1862, THEN RETREATED TO THE WOODS ON THE NORTH / SIDE OF THIS FIELD. THE REGIMENT LOST IN THE BATTLE / 2 OFFICERS AND 27 MEN KILLED; 8 OFFICERS AND 203 MEN / WOUNDED; 1 OFFICER AND 4 MEN MISSING; TOTAL, 245.

Organized at Camp Butler, mustered in August 15, 1861. Shiloh. Corinth. Central Mississippi Campaign. Vicksburg. Mobile. Mustered out March 15, 1866. Lost 290 officers or enlisted men killed, mortally wounded, or by disease.

1.14.10 Subject: State of Minnesota, Common Soldier, Relief, Union
Location: N 35 08 09 78 / W 88 20 16 10
Installed or dedicated: April 10, 1908
Media: Bronze, granite
Monument is two tiered shafts, the fore shaft surmounted by a common soldier, an artillerist, flanked by two field artillery pieces.

Inscription

MINNESOTA

FIRST MINNESOTA BATTERY LIGHT ARTILLERY, / CAPT. EMIL MUNCH, / BRIG. GEN. B. M. PRESTISS' DIVISION, / ARMY OF THE TENNESSEE. / ENGAGED FROM EARLY IN THE MORNING, WHEN CAPT. MUNCH / WAS WOUNDED; DISABLED, IN THE FIRST DAY'S BATTLE / OF SHILOH, APRIL 6, 1862. THE RIGHT AND LEFT SECTIONS UNDER / COMMAND OF 1ST LIEUT. WILLIAM PFAENDER PARTICIPATED IN / THE STRUGGLE OF THE "HORNET'S NEST" WHERE THIS MON- / UMENT STANDS. THE TWO GUNS OF THE CENTER SECTION / WERE DISABLED EARLY IN THE DAY, BUT ONE OF THEM TOOK / PART IN THE EVENING IN REPELLING THE LAST CHARGE OF / THE CONFEDERATES. CAPT. E. MUNCH AND 1ST LIEUT. F. E. PEEBLES / WOUNDED; THREE MEN KILLED AND SIX MEN WOUNDED.

The First Minnesota Light Artillery was that state's only unit at Shiloh. The monument was dedicated on April 10, 1908, and accepted by Commissioner Cadle. Addresses were given by Minnesota's Governor Johnson and Confederate Brig. Gen. Basil Duke.

John K. Daniels was the sculptor of the monument. Daniels also designed monuments at the Memphis and Nashville national cemeteries. Using Minnesota granite and United States standard bronze, Daniels created a figure who looks more workmanlike than warlike. He bears a sponge for the cannon, of course, but his appearance is less bellicose than would be the case if he held a rifle. The figure gives the appearance of the ideal of the citizen-soldier as a kind of reluctant warrior.

The battery organized at Fort Snelling, November 21, 1861. Shiloh. Corinth. Central Mississippi Campaign. Vicksburg. Atlanta. March to the Sea. Carolinas Campaign. Grand Review. Mustered out July 1, 1865. Lost 38 officers or enlisted men killed, mortally wounded, or by disease.

1.14.11 Subject: 12th Iowa VI, Stele
Location: Eastern Corinth Road at the Sunken Road   N 35 08 10 58 / W 88 20 17 98
Dedicated: November 23, 1906
Media: Bronze, granite
Monument is a decorated stele surmounting a base.

IOWA / TO HER / 12TH INFANTRY, / TUTTLE'S (1ST) BRIGADE, / W. H. L. WALLACE'S (2D) DIVISION, / ARMY OF THE TENNESSEE.

. . . COMMANDED BY COL. J. J. WOODS (WOUNDED; CAPTURED) / CAPT. S. R. EDGINGTON (CAPTURED) . . . HELD THIS POSITION AGAINST REPEATED ATTACKS FROM 9 A.M. TO 5 P.M. APRIL 6, 1862. IT THEN ABOUT-FACED TO MEET AN ATTACK COMING FROM THE REAR, AND FOUGHT ITS WAY BACK TO THE CAMP OF THE 41ST ILLINOIS, WHERE IT WAS SURROUNDED AND CAPTURED AT 5.30 P.M. TOTAL NUMBER REPORTED PRESENT FOR DUTY[:] 489. ITS LOSS IN THE BATTLE WAS 2 OFFICERS AND 15 MEN KILLED; 1 OFFICER AND 42 MEN WOUNDED; LEFT ON THE FIELD; 33 MEN WOUNDED; CAPTURED; 20 OFFICERS AND 366 MEN MISSING; TOTAL 479. OF THE WOUNDED, 16 DIED OF THEIR WOUNDS; OF THE MISSING, 4 WERE NEVER AFTERWARDS HEARD FROM; THEY WERE DOUBTLESS KILLED; OF THE MISSING, 71 DIED IN PRISON.

Organized at Dubuque, mustered in November 25, 1861. Forts Henry and Donelson. Shiloh. Most of regiment captured. Paroled October 26; exchanged November 10. Vicksburg. Smith's expedition: Tupelo, Oxford. Operations against Price in Arkansas, Missouri. Nashville. Mobile. Mustered out January 20, 1866. Lost 348 officers or enlisted men killed, mortally wounded, or by disease.

- After the battle, the regiment's senior officer, Col. Joseph Woods, reported, "Again and again did he attack us, trying vainly to drive us from our position. He failed to move us one inch from our position. On the contrary, we repulsed every attack of the enemy and drove him back in confusion."

1.14.12 Subject: 7th Iowa Volunteer Infantry, Stele
Location: N 35 08 12 21 / W 88 20 19 94
Dedicated: November 23, 1906
Media: Bronze, granite
Monument is a decorated stele surmounting a base.

Inscription

IOWA / TO HER / 7TH INFANTRY, / TUTTLE'S (1ST) BRIGADE, / W. H. L. WALLACE'S (1ST) DIVISION, / ARMY OF THE TENNESSEE.

. . . COMMANDED BY LT. COL. J. C. PARROTT. ON THE MORNING OF APRIL 6, 1862, THE REGIMENT, AS PART OF THE BRIGADE, FORMED IN LINE OF BATTLE ON THE LEFT OF THE 2D IOWA VOLUNTEER INFANTRY, ON A SUNKEN ROAD, THE CENTER OF THE REGIMENT BEING WHERE THIS MONUMENT STANDS. IT HELD ITS POSITION, REPELLING A NUMBER OF ATTACKS, UNTIL LATE IN THE AFTERNOON, WHEN THE BRIGADE WAS ORDERED TO FALL BACK. IN THE RETREAT THE REGIMENT WAS SUBJECTED TO A SEVERE FIRE FROM BOTH SIDES. IT REFORMED IN A NEW LINE OF BATTLE ALONG A ROAD LEADING TO THE LANDING, AND HELD THAT POSITION DURING THE NIGHT. ON THE MORNING OF APRIL 7TH THE REGIMENT WAS

ASSIGNED TO THE RESERVE AND, UNDER ORDERS FROM GENERAL CRITTENDEN, CHARGED AND CAPTURED ONE OF THE ENEMY'S BATTERIES. PRESENT FOR DUTY[:] 383. ITS LOSS WAS, 1 OFFICER AND 9 MEN KILLED; 17 MEN WOUNDED; 7 MEN MISSING; TOTAL 34.

Organized at Burlington, August 4, 1861. Belmont. Fort Donelson. Shiloh. Corinth. Expedition against Forrest, West Tennessee. Atlanta. March to the Sea. Carolinas Campaign. Grand Review. Mustered out July 12, 1865. Lost 305 officers or enlisted men killed, mortally wounded, or by disease.

1.14.13 Subject: State of Wisconsin, Statues of Common Soldier, Union, and Female
Location: N 35 08 09 58 / W 88 20 12 42
Dedicated: April 7, 1906
Media: Bronze, granite
Monument is a sculpture of a woman bearing a flag and holding a fallen soldier, the whole surmounting a base.

Inscriptions
[Front]
[State seal of Wisconsin]

DEDICATED BY THE STATE OF WISCONSIN / TO HER VALIANT SONS / WHO ON / APRIL 6TH AND 7TH 1862 / FOUGHT ON THIS BATTLEFIELD / FOR THE PRESERVATION AND PERPETUITY / OF THE UNION. / A.D. / MDCCCCV

[Relief of infantry, with officer leading, moving forward, and engaging opposing infantry and artillery]

THE 14TH WISCONSIN VOLUNTEER INFANTRY PARTICIPATED IN THE BATTLE OF SHILOH APRIL 7TH 1862. IT LOST 16 KILLED, 74 WOUNDED, 3 MISSING: TOTAL, 93.

[Relief of infantry firing on and engaging opposing infantry; an officer—Saxe—has just been shot]

THE 16TH WISCONSIN VOLUNTEER INFANTRY PARTICIPATED IN THE BATTLE OF SHILOH APRIL 6TH AND 7TH 1862. IT LOST 40 KILLED, 188 WOUNDED, 26 MISSING: TOTAL, 254.

[Relief of infantry, with officer on horseback, moving forward]

THE 18TH WISCONSIN VOLUNTEER INFANTRY PARTICIPATED IN THE BATTLE OF SHILOH APRIL 6TH AND 7TH 1862. IT LOST 23 KILLED, 83 WOUNDED, 174 MISSING: TOTAL, 280.

This is another notable and visually dynamic Beaux-Arts state monument on the Shiloh battlefield. It is less prominent in location than the Iowa or Illinois monuments, but a vivid, romantic, distinctive scene is depicted all the same. A sculptured figure of a female—called Columbia or Victory—holding a US flag, leans down to a figure representing Capt. Edward A. Saxe of the 16th Wisconsin, the first Federal officer killed at Shiloh. The soldier has been shot and is still conscious—eyes open, clutching his chest. But he is dying in her

State of Wisconsin, Statues of Common Soldier, Union and Female

arms—that is, he is held, as Wisconsin veteran F. H. Magdeburg put it, "by Victory holding aloft the flag he carried, where, in his last moments he can gaze upon it and glory in the comforting thought of victory won." Preservation of the union, not states' rights, is the stated cause for the war, but fraternity to Southern veterans was a feature of the dedication ceremonies. In his remarks at the event, Confederate General Basil W. Duke observed, "This National Park was established in order that it might be made a memorial of the valor and devotion shown by those who fell on either side, and no testimonial which human wisdom might devise could more perfectly attest the restoration of fraternal feeling and the existence of that unity of national sentiment without which mere political union would be of slight avail."

The base is made of Westerly Rhode Island granite; the statue of United States standard bronze. Charles A. Fink of Milwaukee designed the pedestal, including the reliefs. F. H. Magdeburg worked with W. R. Hodges to conceive the design. Robert Porter Bringhurst was the sculptor.

· Six Wisconsin color-bearers, all killed in action at Shiloh, are interred in the national cemetery. Near them is the grave of Capt. Edward Saxe.

The soldiers of the Wisconsin regiments—like many at Shiloh—were recent recruits, mustered in only earlier in the year. Wisconsin troops suffered 627 casualties at Shiloh.

The 14th Wisconsin organized at Fond du Lac, mustered in January 30, 1862. Shiloh. Corinth. Iuka. Corinth. Central Mississippi Campaign. Vicksburg. Red River Campaign. Smith's expedition Tupelo, Oxford. Operations against Price in Arkansas and Missouri. Nashville. Mustered out October 9, 1865. Lost 319 officers or enlisted men killed, mortally wounded, or by disease. The 16th Wisconsin organized at Madison, mustered in January 31, 1862. Mustered out July 12, 1865. Lost 399 officers or enlisted men killed, mortally wounded, or

13th Ohio VI, Stele

by disease. The 18th Wisconsin organized at Milwaukee, mustered in March 15, 1862. Mustered out July 18, 1865. Lost 225 officers or enlisted men killed, mortally wounded, or by disease.

Regiments' combined service: Shiloh. Corinth. Central Mississippi Campaign. Vicksburg. Atlanta. March to the Sea. Carolinas Campaign. Grand Review.

Sunken Road, East

1.15.1 Subject: 13th Ohio VI, Stele
Location: N 35 08 08 66 / W 88 20 05 96
Dedicated: June 6, 1902
Medium: Granite
Monument is a decorated stele surmounting a two-tiered base.

Inscription

OHIO / 13TH INFANTRY / LT. COL. JOS. G. HAWKINS / W. S. SMITH'S (14) BRIGADE / CRITTENDEN'S (5TH) DIVISION / ARMY OF THE OHIO

[High relief: crossed rifles, cartridge box, wreath]

THIS REGIMENT BIVOUACKED SUNDAY NIGHT IN / FRONT OF THE SIEGE GUNS. IT ADVANCED MONDAY, / MORNING, APRIL 7, 1862, AND BECAME ENGAGED / HERE AT ABOUT 10:30 A.M. / ITS LOSS WAS 11 MEN KILLED; 4 OFFICERS AND / 44 MEN WOUNDED: 7 MEN MISSING; TOTAL 66.

[High relief: crossed rifles, cartridge box, wreath]

Organized at Camp Dennison, June 22, 1861. West Virginia. Shiloh. Corinth. Perryville. Stones River. Tullahoma. Chickamauga. Chattanooga. Atlanta. Franklin. Nashville. Mustered out December 5, 1865. Lost 221 officers or enlisted men killed, mortally wounded, or by disease.

1.15.2 Subject: Battery G, 1st Ohio Vol. Light Artillery
Location: N 35 08 15 10 / W 88 20 13 44
Dedicated: June 6, 1902
Medium: Granite
Monument is a decorated stele surmounting a base.

Inscription

OHIO

[High relief of flanking cannon barrels, rammers, wagon wheel, cannonballs; text is on high relief of scroll]

BATTERY G / 1ST LIGHT ARTILLERY / COMMANDED BY / CAPT. JOSEPH BARTLETT / CRITTENDEN'S (5TH) DIVISION / ARMY OF THE OHIO

THIS BATTERY OF 6 GUNS WENT INTO / ACTION HERE AT 10 A.M., APRIL 7, 1862, / AND WAS ENGAGED TWO HOURS, WHEN / IT RETURNED FOR AMMUNITION. / TWO MEN WOUNDED.

Organized at Camp Dennison, mustered in December 17, 1861. Shiloh. Corinth. Repulse of Forrest, Edgefield. Stones River. Tullahoma. Chickamauga. Chattanooga. Franklin. Nashville. Mustered out August 31, 1865. Lost 6 enlisted men killed or mortally wounded; 1 officer, 26 enlisted men by disease. Total 33.

1.15.3 Subject: 59th Ohio VI, Stele
Location: N 35 08 15 35 / W 88 20 12 94
Dedicated: June 6, 1902
Medium: Granite
Monument is a decorated stele surmounting a base.

Inscription

OHIO

[Relief of laurel wreath, muskets, canteen, cartridge box and strap]

59TH INFANTRY / COMMANDED BY / COL. J. P. FYFFE / BOYLE'S (11TH) BRIGADE / CRITTENDEN'S (5TH) DIVISION / ARMY OF THE OHIO

THIS REGIMENT FORMED HERE IN SUPPORT OF BARLETT'S BATTERY / AT 10 A.M., APRIL 7, 1862, AND HELD THE POSITION UNTIL ABOUT / 12 M., WHEN IT ADVANCED TO LEFT AND FRONT, AND WAS ENGAGED / NEAR HAMBURG ROAD, WHERE ITS GREATEST LOSS OCCURRED. / *[LOST]* 6 MEN KILLED; 51 WOUNDED; TOTAL, 57.

Organized at Ripley, September 12, 1861. Shiloh. Corinth. Stones River. Tullahoma. Chickamauga. Chattanooga. Atlanta. Mustered out October 31, 1864. Lost 157 officers or enlisted men killed, mortally wounded, or by disease.

59th Ohio VI, Stele

1.15.4 Subject: 19th Ohio VI, Stele
Location: N 35 08 17 78 / W 88 20 13 94
Dedicated: June 6, 1902
Medium: Granite
Monument is two decorated granite slabs surmounting a base.

Inscription

OHIO

[Sculpture of two blanket rolls and knapsack] [Relief of crossed muskets and laurel wreath]

19TH INFANTRY / COMMANDED BY / COL. SAMUEL BEATTY / BOYLE'S (11TH) BRIGADE / CRITTENDEN'S (5TH) DIVISION / ARMY OF THE OHIO

THIS REGIMENT ARRIVED ON THE FIELD ABOUT MIDNIGHT. MONDAY / MORNING, APRIL 7, 1862, IT ADVANCED TO THIS POSITION WHERE IT /

WAS ENGAGED FROM ABOUT 10 A.M. TO 12 M. IT THEN MOVED TO THE / LEFT SUPPORTING NELSON'S DIVISION. / *[LOST]* 1 OFFICER (MAJOR T. D. EDWARDS) AND 3 MEN / KILLED; 1 OFFICER AND 43 MEN WOUNDED; 7 MEN MISSING; TOTAL, 55.

Organized at Alliance, September 25, 1861. Shiloh. Corinth. Perryville. Stones River. Tullahoma. Chickamauga. Chattanooga. Atlanta. Franklin. Nashville. Mustered out October 24, 1865. Lost 279 officers or enlisted men killed, mortally wounded, or by disease.

Pvt. J. D. Putnam, 14th Wisconsin VI, Sculpture

1.15.5 Subject: J. D. Putnam, 14th Wisconsin VI, Sculpture
Location: N 35 08 02 57 / W 88 20 20 58
Dedicated: April 7, 1906
Medium: Granite
Monument is an inscribed tree stump.

Inscription

J. D. PUTNAM / CO. F. 14 / W. V.

J. D. PUTNAM, CO. F., / 14TH WISCONSIN VOL. INF., / WAS KILLED HERE APRIL 7, / 1862, WHILE REGIMENT / WAS ADVANCING IN LINE / OF BATTLE AGAINST A / CONFEDERATE BATTERY. / HIS COMRADES BURIED / HIM WHERE HE FELL AND / CUT HIS NAME IN AN OAK / TREE WHICH STOOD HERE. / IN 1901, THOMAS STEELE / RECOGNIZED THE BURIAL / PLACE, THE NAME HE / HELPED CUT IN 1862 / STILL BEING LEGIBLE ON / THIS STUMP. THIS ENABLED / THE WISCONSIN COM- / MISSION TO FIX LINE OF / REGIMENT'S ADVANCE, AND ITS / LAST TABLET, AND / PLACE FOR STATE / MONUMENT.

Pvt. J. D. Putnam was killed in action at Shiloh and is interred in the National Cemetery. His friends originally buried him here and inscribed a burial inscription on the foot of a tree. It was still legible in 1901 and was replaced by this replica in 1906. This modest but distinctive sculpture is one of two monuments to individuals and the only monument on either side to an individual common soldier. The Wheeler monument (1.20.2) is the only tribute to an officer.

1.16.1 Subject: Crescent Louisiana Regiment, Stele
Location: N 35 07 47 51 / W 35 20 17 92
Dedicated: May 31, 1915
Medium: Granite
Monument is a stele with crescent surmounting a base.

Inscription

[Relief of crescent wraps around inscription]

CRESCENT REGIMENT / LOUISIANA INFANTRY / COL. MARSHALL J. SMITH / POND'S
BRIGADE / RUGGLES' DIVISION / BRAGG'S CORPS. / ARMY OF THE MISSSISSIPPI / PRO
/ PATRIA / MORI

[Relief of two muskets pointed up, crossed, with wreath, set against a formée cross with raised text]

6 & 7 / APRIL / 1862

ON LEFT OF CONFEDERATE LINE / SUNDAY MORNING, TO GUARD / BRIDGE OVER
OWL CREEK. AT 2 P.M. / ORDERED TO CENTER NEAR DUNCAN / HOUSE TO ENGAGE
RIGHT OF THE ENEMY / UNDER GEN. PRENTISS IN HORNETS' NEST / WHERE AT
ABOUT 5.30 P.M. HE SURREN- / DERED. ON MONDAY JOINED THE 19TH LOUI- /
SIANA HERE IN SUPPORT OF WASHINGTON / ARTILLERY. LATER, WITH COL.
WHEELER'S / COMMAND FORMED REAR GUARD OF RETREAT / CASUALTIES, BOTH
DAYS, 127. / ERECTED BY A PRIVATE OF CO. B.

Dr. Yves R. Lemonnier, who served in the Crescent Regiment at Shiloh, personally sponsored this monument, which was dedicated on Memorial Day 1915.

Crescent Louisiana Regiment, Stele

Lemonnier is referenced in the inscription only as a "Private of Co. B." He received little support for the project; he received no support at the state level. Lemonnier was unable to attend the dedication ceremonies due to ill health, and it is not even certain if anyone from Louisiana attended the service.

The Albert Weiblen Marble & Granite Company of New Orleans designed and erected the monument at Lemonnier's direction. The stele stands six feet, four inches high and four feet wide.

1.16.2 Subject: State of Texas, Shaft
Location: N 35 07 42 46 / W 88 19 51 37
Installed or dedicated: November 9, 1964
Medium: Bronze, pink granite
Monument is a stele surmounting a base.

Inscription

TEXAS / *[Star set in a wreath]* /REMEMBERS THE VALOR AND DEVOTION OF / HER SONS WHO SERVED AT SHILOH / APRIL 6–7, 1862 / HERE THE RANGERS UPHELD THE FAME OF / THE NAME THEY BORE, THE 2ND TEXAS / FOUGHT WITH GALLANTRY AND THE 9TH / TEXAS RESPONDED TO ANY DEMAND UPON / ITS COURAGE AND ENDURANCE. / GENERAL ALBERT SIDNEY JOHNSTON OF / TEXAS GAVE HIS LIFE IN THIS BATTLE.

TEXAS TROOPS AT SHILOH WERE: / 9TH TEXAS INFANTRY, / COLONEL WRIGHT A. STANLEY. / (BRIG. GEN. PATTON ANDERSON'S BRIGADE, / RUGGLES' DIVISION, BRAGG'S CORPS) / 2ND TEXAS INFANTRY, COL. JOHN C. MOORE, / LIEUTENANT COLONEL WILLIAM P. ROGERS, / MAJOR HAL G. RUNNELS / (BRIG. GEN. JOHN K. JACKSON'S BRIGADE, WITHERS' DIVISION, BRAGG'S CORPS) / 8TH TEXAS CAVALRY (RANGERS), / COLONEL JOHN A. WHARTON. / (UNATTACHED)

A MEMORIAL TO TEXANS / WHO SERVED THE CONFEDERACY / ERECTED BY THE STATE OF TEXAS 1964

Eleven markers of this design were erected by the State of Texas at battlefields across the South and in Pennsylvania between 1963 and 1965.

The 2nd Texas organized in Galveston in September 1861. Shiloh. Corinth. Vicksburg: Regiment surrendered and furloughed as paroled prisoners of war. Exchanged November 1863, reassembled and stationed in Galveston. Disbanded rather than surrender at the cessation of hostilities in May 1865. The 9th Texas organized in Northeast Texas on November 4, 1861. Mustered into Confederate service on December 1, 1861. Losses at Shiloh: 14 killed, 42 wounded, 11 missing. Perryville, Stones River. Chickamauga. Franklin. Nashville. Spanish Fort and Blakely. Paroled at Meridian, Mississippi, May 11, 1865.

Larkin Bell's Field and Vicinity

1.17.1 Subject: 55th Illinois VI, Stele
Location: N 35 07 42 18 / W 88 19 23 64
Dedicated: May 17–18, 1904
Media: Bronze, granite
Monument is a decorated stele surmounting a base.

Inscription

ILLINOIS / 55TH INFANTRY, / 2D BRIGADE—STUART / 5TH DIVISION—SHERMAN / ARMY OF THE TENNESSEE

. . . COMMANDED BY / LIEUT.—COL. MALMBORG. / THIS POSITION WAS ASSUMED AND DEFENDED FROM / 11.30 A.M., UNTIL ABOUT 2.00 P.M., APRIL 6, 1862, WHEN THE / REGIMENT WAS WITHDRAWN ACROSS THE RAVINE, THEN / BACK TO THE LAST LINE AT THE LANDING. THE REGIMENT / LOST IN THE BATTLE 51 MEN KILLED; 7 OFFICERS AND / 190 MEN WOUNDED; 27 MEN MISSING; TOTAL, 275.

Organized at Camp Douglas, mustered in October 31, 1861. Shiloh. Corinth. Vicksburg. Chattanooga. Atlanta. March to the Sea. Carolinas Campaign. Grand Review. Mustered out August 14, 1865. Lost 286 officers or enlisted men killed, mortally wounded, or by disease.

1.17.2 Subject: 54th Ohio VI, Zouaves, Stele with Common Soldier Relief
Location: N 35 07 40 92 / W 88 19 16 94
Dedicated: June 6, 1902
Medium: Granite
Monument is a granite slab with relief figure of Zouave, the whole surmounting a base.

Inscription

OHIO

[Relief of soldier in Zouave uniform bearing a musket with bayonet fixed]

54TH INFANTRY (ZOUAVES) / COMMANDED BY / COL. THOS. KILBY SMITH—LT. COL. JAS. A FARDEN / STUART'S (2D) BRIGADE / SHERMAN'S (5TH) DIVISION / ARMY OF THE TENNESSEE

THIS REGIMENT, WITH SIX OF ITS COMPANIES AT THIS PLACE / AND FOUR COMPANIES / 300 YARDS TO THE LEFT, DEFENDED THE POSITION, ON EXTREME LEFT OF / UNION ARMY, FROM 11.30 A.M. TO 2 P.M., APRIL 6, 1862. / [LOST] 2 OFFICERS AND 23 MEN KILLED; 5 OFFICERS AND / 128 MEN WOUNDED; 32 MEN MISSING; TOTAL, 190. KILLED / [List By Name of Men Killed In Action]

Organized at Camp Dennison, October 1861. Shiloh. Corinth. Central Mississippi Campaign. Vicksburg. Chattanooga. Atlanta. March to the Sea. Carolinas Campaign. Grand Review. Mustered out August 15, 1865. Lost 233 officers or enlisted men killed, mortally wounded, or by disease.

54th Ohio VI, Zouaves, Stele with Common Soldier Relief

1.17.3 Subject: 71st Ohio VI, Stele
Location: N 35 07 42 80 / W 88 19 33 70
Dedicated: June 6, 1902
Medium: Granite
Monument is a stele with flanking relief of columns, the whole surmounting a base.

Inscription
[Two flanking reliefs of stacked muskets, canteen, and cartridge box]

OHIO / 71ST INFANTRY / COMMANDED BY / COL. RODNEY MASON / STUART'S (2D) BRIGADE / SHERMAN'S (5TH) DIVISION / ARMY OF THE TENNESSEE.

THIS REGIMENT FORMED LINE OF BATTLE HERE AT 11 A.M., / APRIL 6, 1862, BUT WAS SOON DRIVEN BACK TO THE RAVINE / IN THE REAR. LT. COL. BARTON S. KYLE WAS KILLED WHILE / ATTEMPTING TO RALLY THE REGIMENT. / *[LOST]* 1 OFFICER AND 13 MEN KILLED; 44 MEN WOUNDED; 1 OFFICER AND 50 MEN MISSING; TOTAL, 109.

Organized at Camp Todd, Troy, mustered in February 1, 1862. Shiloh. Atlanta. Franklin. Nashville. Mustered out November 30, 1865. Lost 206 officers or enlisted men killed, mortally wounded, or by disease.

Sarah Bell's Old Cotton Field and Vicinity

1.18.1 Subject: Lt. Gen. Albert Sydney Johnston, Mortuary Monument
Location: N 35 07 48 32 / W 88 19 46 72
Dedicated: n.a.
Media: Concrete, cast iron
Monument is an inverted cannon barrel surmounting a base.

Inscription

C.S. / ALBERT SIDNEY JOHNSTON / COMMANDING / THE / CONFEDERATE ARMY / WAS MORTALLY WOUNDED HERE / AT 2:30 P.M., APRIL 6, 1862 / DIED IN RAVINE, 50 YARDS / SOUTH-EAST, AT / 2:45 P.M.

This is one of five mortuary monuments on the field. It marks the site of the death of the highest-ranking officer in US history. Johnston was shot in the leg while personally leading an attack near this site. Initially, he thought the wound minor, but by the time the severity of the wound was recognized, little could be done; Johnston bled to death in minutes.

The base is eighteen feet, seven inches by eighteen feet, seven inches; the barrel is seven feet, eleven inches high.

1.18.2 Subject: 41st Illinois VI, Stele
Location: N 35 07 52 76 / W 88 19 51 68
Dedicated: May 17–18, 1904
Media: Bronze, granite
Monument is a decorated stele surmounting a base.

Inscription

ILLINOIS / 41ST INFANTRY / 1ST BRIGADE—WILLIAMS / 4TH DIVISION—HURLBUT / ARMY OF THE TENNESSEE

. . . COMMANDED BY / COL. ISAAC PUGH. / 1. LIEUT.-COL. A TUPPER, KILLED. / MAJOR WARNER. / 2. CAPT. JOHN N. HALE. / THIS POSITION WAS FIRST ATTACKED ABOUT 9.00 A. / M., APRIL 6, 1862, ON A LINE 100 YARDS IN FRONT, BUT / SOON FELL BACK TO THIS POSITION WHICH IT HELD / UNTIL 2.00 P.M., WHEN IT WITHDREW TO REPAIR GUNS / AND GET AMMUNITION. [LOST] 2 OFFICERS AND 19 MEN KILLED; 2 OFFICERS AND 71 MEN / WOUNDED; 3 MEN MISSING; TOTAL, 97.

Organized at Decatur, mustered in August 5, 1861. Forts Henry and Donelson. Shiloh. Corinth. Central Mississippi Campaign. Vicksburg. Meridian. Smith's expedition to Tupelo, Oxford. March to the Sea. Consolidated with 53rd Illinois, December 1864. Lost 275 officers or enlisted men killed, mortally wounded, or by disease.

41st Illinois VI, Stele

1.18.3 Subject: Battery A, 1st Regt., Illinois Vol. Artillery
Location: N 35 07 52 65 / W 88 19 48 86
Dedicated: May 17–18, 1904
Media: Bronze, granite
Monument is a decorated stele surmounting a base.

Inscription

ILLINOIS / BATTERY "A" / 1ST REGIMENT LT. ARTILLERY / 2ND DIVISION—W. H. L. WALLACE / ARMY OF THE TENNESSEE

WILLARD'S BATTERY, "A" / COMMANDED BY / LIEUT. P. P. WOOD. / WENT INTO ACTION ABOUT 9.00 A.M., APRIL 6, 1862, / AND VIGOROUSLY ENGAGED THE ENEMY IN THIS AND / OTHER POSITIONS [IN] THE IMMEDIATE VICINITY UNTIL / 4:00 P.M. [LOST] 4 MEN / KILLED; 1 OFFICER, AND 25 MEN WOUNDED; TOTAL, 30.

Mustered into state service for three months, April 17, 1861, as Battery A, 1st Illinois Light Artillery, July 1861. Forts Henry and Donelson. Shiloh. Corinth. Central Mississippi Campaign. Vicksburg. Chattanooga. Atlanta. Mustered out July 3, 1865. Lost 37 enlisted men killed, mortally wounded, or by disease.

1.18.4 Subject: 9th Illinois VI, Stele
Location: N 35 07 50 70 / W 88 19 44 94
Dedicated: May 17–18, 1904
Media: Bronze, granite
Monument is a decorated stele surmounting a base.

Inscription

ILLINOIS / 9TH INFANTRY / 2D BRIGADE—MCARTHUR / 2D DIVISION—W. H. L. WALLACE / ARMY OF THE TENNESSEE

. . . COMMANDED BY / COL. AUGUST MERSY. / WENT INTO ACTION ABOUT 10.30 A.M., APRIL 6, 1862, / IN THE RAVINE IN FRONT, HOLDING THAT LINE / UNTIL 2.00 P.M. AFTER GREAT LOSS THEY FELL / BACK ABOUT 55 YARDS WHEN THE REGIMENT / RE-FORMED AND WENT TO THEIR CAMP. THEIR / [LOST] 1 OFFICER AND 60 MEN / KILLED; 19 OFFICERS AND 281 WOUNDED; / 1 OFFICER AND 4 MEN MISSING; / TOTAL 366.

Organized at Cairo, August 31, 1861. Fort Donelson. Shiloh. Corinth. Central Mississippi Campaign. Atlanta. March to the Sea. Carolinas Campaign. Grand Review. Mustered out July 9, 1865. Lost 417 officers or enlisted men killed, mortally wounded, or by disease.

- This regiment sustained the highest casualties of any Federal unit at Shiloh. Another monument to the 9th Illinois stands in the national cemetery.

1.18.5 Subject: 12th Illinois VI, Stele
Location: N 35 07 51 29 / W 88 19 41 78
Dedicated: May 17–18, 1904
Media: Bronze, granite
Monument is a decorated stele surmounting a base.

Inscription

ILLINOIS / 12TH INFANTRY / 2D BRIGADE—MCARTHUR / 2D DIVISION—W. H. L. WALLACE / ARMY OF THE TENNESSEE

. . . COMMANDED BY / 1. LIEUT.-COL. A. L. CHETLAIN. / 2. CAPT. J. R. HUGUNIN. / HELD THIS LINE AND ONE IN THE RAVINE ABOUT 75 / YARDS TO THE FRONT FROM 10.30 A.M. UNTIL 2.00 P.M., / APRIL 6, 1862, WHEN THE REGIMENT WAS FORCED TO / TAKE A NEW POSITION ABOUT 400 YARDS TO THE REAR. / [LOST] 2 OFFICERS AND 20 MEN / KILLED; 5 OFFICERS AND 71 MEN WOUNDED; 1 OFFICER / AND 3 MEN MISSING; TOTAL, 102.

The 12th Illinois, the "1st Scotch Regiment," organized at Cairo, August 1, 1861. Forts Henry and Donelson. Shiloh. Corinth. Central Mississippi Campaign. Atlanta. March to the Sea. Carolinas Campaign. Grand Review. Mustered out July 18, 1865. Lost 5 officers, 143 enlisted men killed or mortally wounded; 3 officers, 109 enlisted men by disease. Total 260.

1.18.6 Subject: 50th Illinois VI, Stele
Location: N 35 07 54 81 / W 88 19 39 74
Dedicated: May 17–18, 1904
Media: Bronze, granite
Monument is a decorated stele surmounting a base.

Inscription

ILLINOIS / 50TH INFANTRY / 3D BRIGADE—SWEENY / 2D DIVISION—W. H. L. WALLACE / ARMY OF THE TENNESSEE

. . . COMMANDED BY / 1. COL. M. M. BANE, WOUNDED. / 2. CAPT. T. W. GAINES. / WENT INTO POSITION ON THIS LINE ABOUT 10.30 A.M., / APRIL 6, 1862, AND HELD ITS GROUND UNTIL 2:00 / P.M., WHEN THE REGIMENT RETIRED TOWARD THE LANDING. / [LOST] 12 MEN KILLED; 2 OFFICERS / AND 66 MEN WOUNDED; 4 MEN MISSING; TOTAL, 84.

The 50th Infantry, the "Blind Half-Hundred," organized at Quincy, mustered in September 12, 1861. Forts Henry and Donelson. Shiloh. Corinth. Central Mississippi Campaign. Expedition against Forrest, West Tennessee. Atlanta. Carolinas Campaign. Grand Review. Mustered out July 13, 1865. Lost 191 officers or enlisted men killed, mortally wounded, or by disease.

Wicker Field and Vicinity

1.19.1 Subject: 4th US Artillery, Shaft
Location: N 35 08 02 64 / W 88 19 54 26
Dedicated: December 9, 1910
Medium: Granite
Monument is an obelisk surmounting a base.

Inscription

4TH U.S. ARTILLERY. / BATTERIES "H" AND "M" / CAPTAIN JOHN MENDENHALL. / 5TH DIV. (CRITTENDEN) / 5TH U.S. ARTILLERY, / BATTERY "H" / CAPTAIN WM. R. TERRILL. / 2ND DIV. (MCCOOK) / ARMY OF THE OHIO.

THESE BATTERIES WERE ENGAGED / NEAR HERE FROM ABOUT 9 A.M. / TO 1.30 P. M., APRIL 7, 1862 / CASUALTIES / 3 KILLED, 19 WOUNDED. TOTAL 22.

Battery "H," Battery "M," 4th Artillery: Shiloh. Corinth. Perryville. Stones River. Tullahoma. Chickamauga. Chattanooga. Franklin. Nashville.

- Capt. John Mendenhall was chief of artillery to Maj. Gen. Thomas L. Crittenden during the battle of Stones River where, on the last day of the battle, he oversaw the artillery at McFadden's Ford that stopped a Confederate assault on the Union left flank.

1.19.2 Subject: 9th Indiana VI, Obelisk
Location: N 35 08 05 77 / W 88 19 57 42
Dedicated: April 6–7, 1903
Medium: Limestone
Monument is a decorated obelisk surmounting a base.

Inscription

9TH / REGIMENT / INFANTRY, / COMMANDED BY / COL. GIDEON C. MOODY, / 19TH BRIGADE—COL. HAZEN—/ 4TH DIVISION—GEN. NELSON—/ ARMY OF THE OHIO. / INDIANA.

. . . THIS REGIMENT ARRIVED ON THE BATTLEFIELD AT 9 P.M., 6, / APRIL, 1862, MOVED UPON THE ENEMY AT DAYLIGHT OF THE / 7TH, WAS HOTLY ENGAGED AT THIS PLACE 10 A.M. REPULSED A / HEAVY ATTACK FROM THE FRONT (SOUTH), AND CHARGED / WITH BRIGADE TO THE RIGHT (WEST), AND DROVE BACK THE / ENEMY. AT 12:30 P.M. WAS SENT BY GEN. NELSON ACROSS / THE ROAD TO THE LEFT TO THE AID OF COL. AMMEN. CASUAL- / TIES: KILLED, 1 OFFICER AND 16 MEN: WOUNDED, / 7 OFFICERS AND 146 MEN: TOTAL, 170.

Organized at La Porte, September 5, 1861. West Virginia. Shiloh. Corinth. Perryville. Stones River. Tullahoma. Chickamauga. Chattanooga. Atlanta. Franklin. Nashville. Mustered out September 28, 1865. Lost 11 officers, 120 enlisted men killed or mortally wounded; 2 officers, 220 enlisted men by disease. Total 353.

1.19.3 Subject: 41st Ohio VI, Stele
Location: N 35 08 07 38 / W 88 19 59 84
Dedicated: June 6, 1902
Medium: Granite
Monument is a shaft and stele surmounting a base.

Inscription

OHIO

[Sculpture of drum] [Two reliefs of laurel wreath, muskets, canteen, cartridge box and strap]

41ST INFANTRY, / COMMANDED BY / LT. COL. GEORGE S. / MYGATT / HAZEN'S / (19TH) BRIGADE / NELSON'S / (4TH) DIVISION / ARMY OF THE / OHIO

THIS REGIMENT ADVANCED / TO THIS POINT MONDAY / MORNING, APRIL 7, 1862, WHERE / IT BECAME ENGAGED AT 10 A.M. / IT HAD PRESENT 18 OFFICERS AND 355 MEN. / [LOST] 1 OFFICER / AND 20 MEN KILLED; 6 OFFICERS / AND 105 MEN WOUNDED; 1 MAN / MISSING; TOTAL, 133.

Organized at Camp Wood, Cleveland, October 29, 1861. Shiloh. Corinth. Perryville. Stones River. Tullahoma. Chickamauga. Chattanooga. Atlanta. Franklin. Nashville. Mustered out November 27, 1865. Lost 330 officers or enlisted men killed, mortally wounded, or by disease.

1.19.4 Subject: Battery F, 2nd Regiment Illinois Artillery, Stele
Location: N 35 08 10 29 / W 88 19 59 44
Dedicated: May 17–18, 1904
Media: Bronze, granite
Monument is a decorated stele surmounting a base.

Inscription

ILLINOIS / BATTERY "F" / 2D REGIMENT LT. ARTILLERY / UNASSIGNED / ARMY OF THE TENNESSEE

. . . COMMANDED BY / CAPT. J. W. POWELL, WOUNDED. / REACHED THIS POSITION ABOUT 10:00 A.M., APRIL 6, / 1862, AND UNTIL 4 P.M. WAS IN ACTION ON THIS / LINE. [LOST] 1 OFFICER / AND 5 MEN WOUNDED; 3 MEN MISSING; TOTAL, 9.

Organized at Cape Girardeau, mustered in December 11, 1861. Shiloh. Corinth. Central Mississippi Campaign, Vicksburg. Meridian. Atlanta. Mustered out July 27, 1865. Lost 298 enlisted men killed, mortally wounded, or by disease.

- Capt. John Wesley Powell (1834–1902) was wounded in the arm at Shiloh; ultimately the limb was amputated. He recovered, however, and rose to the rank of major by war's end. After the war he was a scientist and explorer, best known for his explorations of the Green and Colorado Rivers in 1869 and 1872.

1.19.5 Subject: 57th Illinois VI, Stele
Location: N 35 08 05 18 / W 88 19 46 46
Dedicated: May 17–18, 1904
Media: Bronze, granite
Monument is a decorated stele surmounting a base.

Inscription

ILLINOIS / 57TH INFANTRY / 3D BRIGADE—SWEENY / 2D DIVISION—W. H. L. WALLACE / ARMY OF THE TENNESSEE

. . . COMMANDED BY / 1. COL. S. D. BALDWIN. / 2. CAPT. G. A. BUSSE. THIS REGIMENT WAS HELD IN RESERVE BEHIND RICHARD- / SON'S BATTERY UNTIL ABOUT 2 P.M., APRIL 6, 1862, WHEN / IT WAS MOVED TO THIS POINT IN THE LINE, AND HELD ITS / POSITION UNTIL ABOUT 4 P.M., WHEN IT FELL BACK TO THE / LANDING. THE REGIMENT [LOST] / 3 OFFICERS AND 24 MEN KILLED; 7 OFFICERS AND 103 / MEN WOUNDED; 3 MEN MISSING; TOTAL, 140.

Organized at Camp Douglas, mustered in December 26, 1861. Fort Donelson. Shiloh. Corinth. Central Mississippi Campaign. Atlanta. March to the Sea. Carolinas Campaign. Grand Review. Mustered out July 7, 1865. Lost 180 officers or enlisted men killed, mortally wounded, or by disease.

1.19.6 Subject: 36th Indiana VI, Obelisk
Location: N 35 08 02 33 / W 88 19 44 60
Dedicated: April 6–7, 1903
Medium: Limestone
Monument is a decorated obelisk surmounting a base.

Inscription

36TH / REGIMENT / INFANTRY / COMMANDED BY / COL. WILIAM GROSS 10TH BRIGADE—COL. JACOB AMMEN—/ 4TH DIVISION—GEN. NELSON— ARMY OF THE OHIO. / INDIANA.

. . . THIS REGIMENT ARRIVED ON THE BATTLEFIELD AT 5.30 / P.M., APRIL 6, 1862; WAS ORDERED BY MAJ. GEN. / GRANT 150 YARDS TO THE LEFT TO SUPPORT CAPT. STONE'S / BATTERY, WHERE IT WAS ENGAGED UNTIL DARK. AT 5.30 / A.M., APRIL 7TH, IT MOVED FORWARD IN LINE OF BATTLE, / ARRIVING AT THIS POSITION ABOUT 10 A.M. REGIMENT / CHARGED THE ENEMY AND ASSISTED IN DRIVING HIM / FROM THE FIELD. CASUALTIES—KILLED, 1 OFFICER AND 8 / MEN; WOUNDED, 1 OFFICER AND 35 MEN; TOTAL, 45.

Organized at Richmond, mustered in September 16, 1861. Shiloh. Corinth. Stones River. Tullahoma. Chickamauga. Chattanooga. Atlanta. Franklin. Nashville. Transferred to 30th Indiana, July 12, 1865. Lost 245 officers or enlisted men killed, mortally wounded, or by disease.

1.19.7 Subject: 24th Ohio VI, Stele
Location: N 35 08 01 44 / W 88 19 46 74
Dedicated: June 6, 1902
Medium: Granite
Monument is two decorated granite slabs surmounting a base.

Inscription

[Drum, with flanking blanket rolls and knapsacks leaning against it, along with canteens and cartridge boxes]
OHIO *[Crossed muskets and laurel wreaths]*
. . . 24TH INFANTRY, / COMMANDED BY / COL. F. C. JONES, / AMMEN'S (10TH) BRIGADE, / NELSON'S (4TH) DIVISION, / ARMY OF THE OHIO.

THIS REGIMENT ADVANCED TO THIS POINT / MONDAY, APRIL 7, 1862, WHERE IT WENT INTO / ACTION ABOUT 10 A.M. / [LOST] 5 MEN KILLED; 5 OFFICERS / AND 60 MEN WOUNDED; 6 MEN MISSING; / TOTAL, 76.

Organized at Camp Chase and Jackson, June 17, 1861. West Virginia Campaign. Nashville. Shiloh. Corinth. Perryville. Stones River. Tullahoma. Chickamauga. Chattanooga. Mustered out June 24, 1864. Lost 176 officers or enlisted men killed, mortally wounded, or by disease.

1.19.8 Subject: 6th Ohio VI, Stele
Location: N 35 08 01 44 / W 88 19 49 32
Dedicated: June 6, 1902
Medium: Granite
Monument is two decorated granite slabs surmounting a base.

Inscription

OHIO / 6TH INFANTRY / COMMANDED BY / LT. COL. N. L. ANDERSON, / AMMEN'S (10TH) BRIGADE, / NELSON'S (4TH) DIVISION, / ARMY OF THE OHIO.

. . . ADVANCED TO THIS POINT MONDAY, APRIL 7, / 1862, WHERE IT WAS ENGAGED AT 10 A.M., / SUPPORTING TERRILL'S U.S. BATTERY. / [LOST] 2 MEN KILLED; 5 WOUNDED; 2 MISSING; / TOTAL, 9.

Organized at Camp Dennison, June 18, 1861. West Virginia. Fort Donelson. Nashville: the first unit to enter city. Shiloh. Corinth. Perryville. Stones River. Tullahoma. Chickamauga. Chattanooga. Mustered out June 23, 1864. Lost 144 officers or enlisted men killed, mortally wounded, or by disease.

State of Missouri, Stele

1.19.9 Subject: State of Missouri, Stele
Location: N 35 08 11 87 / W 88 19 51 60
Installed or dedicated: April 1, 1971
Media: Limestone, red and black marble, concrete
Monument is a granite stele sculpted in the shape of the state of Missouri.

Inscription

UNION ARMY OF THE TENNESSEE. / 2ND. DIVISION 2ND. BRIGADE / 13TH MO.,
COL. CRAFTS WRIGHT / 14TH MO., BIRGE SHARP SHOOTERS / COL. B. COMPTON
/ 1ST MO. LIGHT ARTILLERY / BATTY. D., CAPT. HENRY RICHARDSON / BATTY. H,
CAPT. FREDERICK WELKER / BATTY. K., CAPT. GEORGE STONE / 3RD. DIVISION /
1ST BRIGADE, COL. MORGAN SMITH, 8TH MO. / 8TH MO., LT. COL. JAMES PECKHAM
/ 1ST MO. LIGHT ARTILLERY, / BATTY. I., LT. CHARLES THURBER / 4TH DIVISION,
1ST MO. LIGHT ARTILLERY, / MANN'S BATTY. C., LT. EDWARD BROTZMANN / 6TH
DIVISION, 1ST BRIGADE, / COL. E. PEABODY, LT. COL. H. WOODYARD / 21ST MO., COL.
DAVID MOORE / 25TH MO., LT. COL. ROBERT VANHO / 2ND BRIGADE, COL. MADISON
MILLER, 18TH MO. / 18TH MO., LT. COL. ISSAC PRATT. / UNATTACHED INFANTRY
23RD MO. / COL. JACOB TINDALL, LT. COL. QUIN MORTON. / CONFEDERATE ARMY
OF THE MISSISSIPPI. / RESERVE CORPS, 2ND BRIGADE, / 1ST MO. COL. LUCIUS RICH /
MISSOURI.

[Inscribed images: light artillery piece, hornet's nest, rifled musket]

IN MEMORY OF HER SONS / WHO FOUGHT AND DIED / TO PRESERVE THOSE
FREEDOMS / IN WHICH THEY BELIEVED / BATTLE OF SHILOH / APRIL 6TH AND 7TH,
1862.

Like the State of Kentucky's Shiloh monument, the Missouri monument was
erected in the 1970s, at a time when political divisions within the United States
were especially sharp. This inscription is careful to declare its bipartisanship: it

was erected "In Memory Of Her Sons Who Fought And Died To Preserve Those Freedoms *In Which They Believed*" (italics added).

The project was initiated by Boy Scouts from Missouri who noted the absence of a monument from their state during a field trip to Shiloh. Efforts to interest the state legislature to support the project were unavailing, but the Scouts' private fund-raising efforts resulted in this tribute.

- The gray stands for Confederate soldiers, the blue for Union soldiers, the red for the blood that was shed—gray Mount Airy granite, blue Norwegian granite, and red Missouri granite. The monument is seven feet, one inch high; the base is seven feet by four feet, six inches.

Cloud Field and Vicinity

1.20.1 Subject: State of Alabama, Shaft
Location: N 35 08 23 68 / W 88 19 55 44
Installed or dedicated: Unveiled May 7, 1907
Medium: Granite
Monument is a tiered shaft surmounted by a sculpture of stacked cannonballs.

Inscription

[Front]
C.S.A. / ALABAMA
[Relief of crossed sword, musket with bayonet, battle flag unfurled on staff]

C.S.A. / ALABAMA INFANTRY. / 4TH BATTALION, MAJ. JAMES M. CLIFTON. / 16TH REGIMENT LIEUT. COL. JOHN W. HARRIS. / 17TH REGT., LIEUT. COL. ROBERT C. FARISS. / 18TH REGT., COL. ELI S. SHORTER. / 19TH REGT., COL. JOSEPH WHEELER. / 21ST REGT. (LIEUT. COL. STEWART W. CAYCE. / (MAJ. FREDERICK STEWART. / 22ND REGT. (COL. ZACH C. DEAS. (WOUNDED) / (LIEUT. COL. JOHN C. MARRAST. / 25TH REGT. (COL. JOHN D. LOOMIS. (WOUNDED) / (MAJ. GEORGE D. JOHNSTON. / 26TH REGT. (COL. JOHN G. COLTART. (WOUNDED) [SIC] / 31ST REGT. LIEUT. COL. MONTGOMERY GILBREATH.

C.S.A. / ALABAMA / TO THE LASTING MEMORY OF THE HEROES / FROM ALABAMA / WHO FOUGHT AT SHILOH, / APRIL 6–7, 1862. ERECTED BY THE ALABAMA / DIVISION, / UNITED DAUGHTERS OF THE CONFEDERACY / 1907.

C.S.A. / ALABAMA GENERAL OFFICERS / AT SHILOH. / BRIG. GEN. JONES M. WITHERS, 2ND DIV. 2ND ARMY CORPS. / BRIG. GEN. STERLING A. M. WOOD, 3RD BRIG. 3RD ARMY CORPS. / ALABAMA CAVALRY. / GEN. BRAGG'S ESCORT, COMPANY, CAPT. ROBERT W. SMITH. / FIRST BATTALION, CAPT. THOMAS F. JENKINS. / MISS. AND ALA. BATTALION, LIEUT. COL. RICHARD H. BREWER. / FIRST REGIMENT, COL. JAMES H. CLANTON. / ALABAMA ARTILLERY. / GAGE'S BATTERY, CAPT. CHARLES P. GAGE. / KETCHUM'S BATTERY, CAPT. WM. H. KETCHUM. / ROBERTSON'S BATTERY, CAPT. FELIX ROBERTSON.

The Alabama Monument, erected with donations from the state's chapters of the UDC, was only the second tribute erected to the Confederate soldiers who

State of Alabama, Shaft

Col. Joseph Wheeler, Shaft

fought at Shiloh. The monument displays a roster of units from Alabama—
nine regiments and one battalion of infantry—a list of general officers present,
and a tribute to the "Heroes Who Fought at Shiloh." Cornelius Cadle accepted
the memorial on behalf of the federal government on May 7, 1907, a rainy
day in Tennessee, when a delegation from Alabama presented this relatively
modest monument.

1.20.2 Subject: Col. Joseph Wheeler, Shaft
Location: N 35 08 23 08 / W 88 19 55 32
Dedicated: October 9, 1930
Medium: n.a.
Monument is a stele surmounting a base.

Inscription

IN LOYAL MEMORY OF / GENERAL JOSEPH WHEELER / 1836–1906 / COLONEL IN COMMAND OF THE / 19TH REGIMENT, ALABAMA INFANTRY / APRIL 6–7, 1862 / ERECTED BY / THE GENERAL JOSEPH WHEELER / MEMORIAL ASSOCIATION / OCT. 9, 1930

WHEELER

The General Joseph Wheeler Association received permission to erect this monument to Wheeler, who fought on the Shiloh battlefield and went on to become the senior cavalry officer of the Army of Tennessee. It was erected decades after the peak of the battlefield monument movement. Some of the stringent standards for monument erection were relaxed for this commemoration: there are no monuments to any individual officers on the field. However, the inscription is modest: there is no praise for Wheeler, nor is there any reference to the virtue of the cause(s) for which Wheeler fought as colonel of the 19th Alabama at Shiloh or in the US Army after the Civil War. Instead, Wheeler, who later entered federal service in the Spanish American War and the Philippine War, has a simple remembrance and inferred tribute.

Brown's Ferry Road

1.21.1 Subject: State of Kentucky, Stelae and Obelisks
Location: N 35 08 28 43 / W 88 19 33 76
Installed or dedicated: 1974
Media: Aluminum, granite
Monument is two granite posts flanking or supporting panels with maps and narratives.

Inscription

[Front]
KENTUCKY REGIMENTS / AT / BATTLE OF SHILOH / FIRST DAY APRIL 6, 1862. / *[Map]*

[TEXT EXCERPT:] *AS A BORDER SLAVE STATE THAT REMAINED IN THE UNION, KENTUCKY WAS SHARPLY DIVIDED IN ITS LOYALTY DURING THE CIVIL WAR. THE STATE PROVIDED MANY TROOPS TO BOTH SIDES AT SHILOH: APPROXIMATELY 6,500 TO THE FEDERAL FORCES; APPROXIMATELY 2,000 TO THE CONFEDERATE FORCES. CONFEDERATE COMMANDING GENERAL ALBERT SIDNEY JOHNSTON, WHO WAS KILLED IN ACTION ON APRIL 6 AT SHILOH, THOUGH A TEXAN BY ADOPTION, WAS A KENTUCKIAN BY BIRTH. . . . CASUALTIES AMONG KENTUCKY TROOPS AT SHILOH:*

UNION, 115 KILLED, 636 WOUNDED, 29 MISSING; CONFEDERATE, 137 KILLED, 627 WOUNDED, 45 MISSING.

KENTUCKY HISTORICAL SOCIETY 1974

KENTUCKY REGIMENTS / AT / BATTLE OF SHILOH / SECOND DAY APRIL 7, 1862. *[Map]*

Kentucky did not secede from the Union, but many of its citizens fought for the Confederacy, and this monument of the 1970s—when many Americans were divided over domestic and international issues—gives tribute to Kentucky regiments on both sides of the Union / Confederate divide. There are no tributes; the inscription is limited to narratives of the activities of Kentucky Confederate and Union soldiers—one narrative, repeated on the reverse side, as well as two maps of the Shiloh battlefield on the successive days of the engagement.

Twelve Kentucky infantry regiments fought on the Union side at Shiloh. Five infantry regiments fought on the Confederate side, along with an artillery battery and cavalry elements led by Colonel John Hunt Morgan.

· The monument comprises field stone, concrete metal alloy; the dimensions are five feet, eight inches high; the base is nine feet wide. The presentation and materials have been problematic. The Kentucky granite has been replaced with Georgia granite, and the maps are weathered and difficult to read.

State of Kentucky, stelae and obelisks on Brown's Ferry Road. The inscriptions on the reverse and the front are identical: the maps are different: the shows depicts the battlefield on April 6; the reverse depicts the battlefield on April 7.

8th Battery Ohio Vol. Artillery

1.21.2 Subject: 8th Battery, Ohio Vol. Artillery, Stele
Location: N 35 08 49 27 / W 88 19 10 96
Dedicated: June 6, 1902
Medium: Granite
Monument is a decorated obelisk with battlements surmounting a base.

Inscription
[Relief of flanking cannon barrels]
OHIO / 8TH BATTERY / LIGHT ARTILLERY / COMMANDED BY / CAPT. LOUIS
MARKGRAF / UNASSIGNED / ARMY OF THE TENNESSEE
[Relief of crossed rammers and laurel wreaths]

THIS BATTERY OF 6 GUNS WAS IN / ACTION HERE FROM 5:30 P.M. TO
6:30 P.M., APRIL 6, 1862. / 3 MEN WOUNDED.

Organized at Camp Dennison, mustered in March 11, 1862. Shiloh. Corinth.
Central Mississippi Campaign. Vicksburg. Mustered out August 7, 1865.

Mass Grave, Confederate Soldiers, UDC Stele

Cavalry Road

1.22.1 Subject: Trenches Interring Confederate Dead, #1, Stele
Location: N 35 08 43 84 / W 88 20 04 74
Dedicated: May 17, 1917
Medium: Granite
Monument is a stele surmounting a base.

Inscription
TO THE CONFEDERATE DEAD / IN THE TRENCHES
ERECTED BY TENN. DIVISION / U.D.C. 1935

1.22.2 Subject: 52nd Illinois VI, Stele
Location: N 35 08 45 01 / W 88 20 14 12
Dedicated: May 17–18, 1904
Media: Bronze, granite
Monument is a decorated stele surmounting a base.

Inscription
ILLINOIS / 52D INFANTRY / 3D BRIGADE—SWEENY / 2D DIVISION—W. H. L.
WALLACE / ARMY OF THE TENNESSEE

. . . COMMANDED BY / MAJOR H. STARK. / CAPT. E. A. BOWEN. / THIS REGIMENT WAS
HELD IN RESERVE UNTIL 4:00 / P.M., APRIL 6, 1862, WHEN IT FORMED FOR BATTLE
ON / THIS LINE AND RESISTED THE ATTACK OF THE ENEMY / UNTIL WITHDRAWN
FOR THE NIGHT. [LOST] 1 OFFICER AND 22 MEN KILLED; 3 OFFICERS / AND 120 MEN
WOUNDED; 9 MEN MISSING; TOTAL 155.

Organized at Geneva, mustered in November 19, 1861. Fort Donelson. Shiloh.
Corinth. Dodge's expedition against Forrest. Atlanta. March to the Sea.
Carolinas Campaign. Grand Review. Mustered out July 5, 1865. Lost 180 offi-
cers or enlisted men killed, mortally wounded, or by disease.

1.22.3 Subject: 16th Iowa VI, Stele
Location: N 35 08 44 14 / W 88 20 43 02
Dedicated: November 23, 1906
Media: Bronze, granite
Monument is a decorated stele surmounting a base.

Inscription

IOWA / TO HER / 16TH INFANTRY, / MILLER'S (2D) BRIGADE, / PRENTISS' (6TH) DIVISION, / ARMY OF THE TENNESSEE.

. . . COMMANDED BY COLONEL ALEXANDER CHAMBERS, (WOUNDED) / LIEUT. COLONEL ADD H. SANDERS / THIS REGIMENT EARLY IN THE MORNING OF APRIL 6, 1862, FORMED ON THE BLUFF AT PITTSBURG LANDING AND FOR THE FIRST TIME RECEIVED AMMUNITION. . . . BY ORDERS OF GENERAL GRANT IT MARCHED WITH THE 15TH IOWA TO THE SUPPORT OF MCCLERNAND'S (1ST) DIVISION. . . . THE REGIMENT FORMED LINE OF BATTLE HERE ABOUT 10:30 IN THE FORENOON, AND ADVANCING TO THE EDGE OF TIMBER HELD THAT POSITION FOR AN HOUR OR MORE, AND THEN RETIRED UNDER ORDERS. LATER IN THE DAY . . . IT SUPPORTED SCHWARTZ'S BATTERY. . . . / PRESENT FOR DUTY 785. [LOST] 2 OFFICERS AND 15 MEN KILLED; 11 OFFICERS AND 90 MEN WOUNDED; 13 MEN CAPTURED OR MISSING; TOTAL 131.

Organized at Davenport, March 1862. Shiloh. Corinth. Central Mississippi Campaign. Vicksburg. Meridian. Atlanta. March to the Sea. Carolinas Campaign. Grand Review. Mustered out July 19, 1865. Lost 323 officers or enlisted men killed, mortally wounded, or by disease.

1.22.4 Subject: 15th Iowa VI, Stele
Location: N 35 08 41 95 / W 88 20 43 02
Dedicated: November 23, 1906
Media: Bronze, granite
Monument is a decorated stele surmounting a base.

Inscription

IOWA / TO HER / 15TH INFANTRY, / HARE'S (1ST) BRIGADE, / PRENTISS (6TH) DIVISION, / ARMY OF THE TENNESSEE.

. . . THIS REGIMENT ARRIVED AT PITTSBURG LANDING ON THE MORNING OF APRIL 6, 1862. IT DISEMBARKED, FORMED ON THE BLUFF, AND THERE RECEIVED ITS FIRST AMMUNITION. . . . UNDER THE ORDERS OF GENERAL GRANT, AND CONDUCTED BY ONE OF HIS STAFF OFFICERS, IT MARCHED TO JOIN MCCLERNAND'S HEADQUARTERS AND WHILE CROSSING IT WAS FIRED UPON BY ARTILLERY AND MUSKETRY. IT FORMED LINE OF BATTLE AND ADVANCED UNDER FIRE INTO THE WOODS, ITS COLONEL COMMANDING OFFICIALLY REPORTED THAT THE REGIMENT HELD ITS POSITION FROM 10 O'CLOCK IN THE FORENOON UNTIL 12 O'CLOCK NOON, AND THEN UNDER ORDERS RETURNED TO A NEW LINE. PORTIONS OF THE REGIMENT FOUGHT WITH OTHER DIVISIONS LATER IN THE DAY AND ON MONDAY. / PRESENT

FOR DUTY 760. [LOST] 2 OFFICERS AND 19 MEN KILLED; 7 OFFICERS AND 149 WOUNDED; 2 OFFICERS AND 6 MEN CAPTURED OR MISSING; TOTAL 185.

Organized at Keokuk, February 22, 1862. Shiloh. Corinth. Central Mississippi Campaign. Vicksburg. Meridian. Atlanta. March to the Sea. Carolinas Campaign. Grand Review. Mustered out July 24, 1865. Lost 387 officers or enlisted men killed, mortally wounded, or by disease.

Sherman Road and Vicinity

1.23.1 Subject: 46th Ohio VI, Stele
Location: N 35 08 35 97 / W 88 21 01 78
Dedicated: June 6, 1902
Medium: Granite
Monument is a decorated granite shaft surmounting a base.

Inscription
[Sculpture of two drums set between two knapsacks]
OHIO / 46TH INFANTRY, / COMMANDED BY / COL. THOMAS / WORTHINGTON, / MCDOWELL'S / (1ST) BRIGADE / SHERMAN'S / (5TH) DIVISION, / ARMY OF THE / TENNESSEE.
[Relief of laurel wreath]

[Relief of stacked muskets with canteen, and cartridge box]

THIS REGIMENT FELL BACK / FROM ITS CAMP AND DEFENDED / THIS POSITION, WHERE IT DID / ITS MOST SEVERE FIGHTING, / FROM ABOUT NOON UNTIL 2 / P.M., APRIL 6, 1862. / IT HAD PRESENT FOR DUTY, / OFFICERS AND MEN, 701. / [LOST] 2 OFFICERS / AND 35 MEN KILLED; / 4 OFFICERS AND 181 MEN WOUNDED; / 24 MEN MISSING; TOTAL, 246.
[Relief of stacked muskets with canteen, and cartridge box]

Organized at Worthington, January 28, 1862. Shiloh. Corinth. Central Mississippi Campaign. Vicksburg. Chattanooga. Atlanta. March to the Sea. Carolinas Campaign. Grand Review. Mustered out July 22, 1865. Lost 290 officers or enlisted men killed, mortally wounded, or by disease.

1.23.2 Subject: 6th Iowa VI, Stele
Location: N 35 08 32 47 / W 88 21 02 24
Dedicated: November 23, 1906
Media: Bronze, granite
Monument is a decorated stele surmounting a base.

Inscription

IOWA / TO HER / 6TH INFANTRY, / MCDOWELL'S (1ST) BRIGADE, / SHERMAN'S (5TH) DIVISION, / ARMY OF THE TENNESSEE.

. . . THIS REGIMENT HELD A POSITION NEAR ITS CAMP ON THE PURDY ROAD, THE EXTREME RIGHT OF THE ARMY, UNTIL 10 O'CLOCK A.M., APRIL 6, 1862. THEN IT MOVED TO THE LEFT AND REAR, AND WAS ENGAGED IN THIS VICINITY AGAINST A STRONG FORCE OF THE ENEMY'S INFANTRY AND ARTILLERY, FOR FOUR HOURS;— ITS LAST POSITION BEING IN JONES FIELD, FROM WHICH IT WAS ORDERED TO RETIRE ABOUT 2.30 P.M. IT THEN FELL BACK TO THE SUPPORT OF WEBSTER'S LINE OF ARTILLERY, WHERE IT WAS ENGAGED WHEN THE BATTLE CLOSED AT SUNDOWN. / IN DETACHMENTS, / COMMANDED BY COMPANY OFFICERS, THE REGIMENT PARTICIPATED IN THE MOVEMENTS OF THE ARMY THROUGHOUT THE 7TH. / PRESENT FOR DUTY, OFFICERS 27; MEN 605; TOTAL, 632. / ITS LOSS WAS, KILLED 52; WOUNDED 100; CAPTURED 37; TOTAL, 189.

Organized at Burlington, mustered in July 17, 1861. Fremont's Missouri Campaign. Shiloh. Corinth. Central Mississippi Campaign. Vicksburg. Chattanooga. Atlanta. March to the Sea. Carolinas Campaign. Grand Review. Mustered out July 21, 1865. Lost 280 officers or enlisted men killed, mortally wounded, or by disease.

1.23.3 Subject: Trenches Interring Confederate Dead, #2, Stele
Location: N 35 08 31 59 / W 88 21 02 32
Dedicated: May 17, 1917
Medium: Granite
Monument is a stele surmounting a base.

Inscription

TO THE CONFEDERATE DEAD / IN THE TRENCHES
ERECTED BY TENN. DIVISION / U.D.C. 1935

1.23.4 Subject: 22nd Ohio VI (ex-13th Missouri Vol.), Stele
Location: N 35 08 29 39 / W 88 21 02 00
Dedicated: June 6, 1902
Medium: Granite
Monument is a granite stele with common soldier in high relief, the whole surmounting a base.

Inscription

OHIO
[Relief of Union soldier bearing musket with bayonet]
13TH MISSOURI INFANTRY, / (AFTERWARD DESIGNATED 22D OHIO) / COMMANDED BY COL. CRAFTS J. WRIGHT / MCARTHUR'S (2D) BRIGADE, / W. H. L. WALLACE'S (2D) DIVISION, / ARMY OF THE TENNESSEE.

. . . ORDERED TO / REPORT TO GEN. SHERMAN. [THIS REGIMENT] BECAME ENGAGED HERE ABOUT 11 A.M., / APRIL 6, 1862. IT WAS DRIVEN BACK TO JONES FIELD, RALLIED / AND RETURNED TO THIS PLACE, WHERE IT WAS ENGAGED / UNTIL 2 P.M. / IT HAD PRESENT FOR DUTY, OFFICERS AND MEN, 538. [LOST] 10 MEN KILLED; 3 OFFICERS AND 67 MEN WOUNDED; 1 MAN MISSING; TOTAL, 81.

Organized at Benton Barracks, Missouri as the 13th Missouri VI, mustered in November 5, 1861. Fort Donelson. Shiloh. Corinth. Vicksburg. Steele's expedition. Mustered out August 28, 1865. Lost 207 officers or enlisted men killed, mortally wounded, or by disease.

1.23.5 Subject: 40th Illinois VI, Stele
Location: N 35 08 28 08 / W 88 21 01 64
Dedicated: May 17–18, 1904
Media: Bronze, granite
Monument is a decorated stele surmounting a base.

Inscription

ILLINOIS / 40TH INFANTRY / 1ST BRIGADE—MCDOWELL / 5TH DIVISION—SHERMAN / ARMY OF THE TENNESSEE

. . . COMMANDED BY / 1. COL. S. G. HICKS, WOUNDED. / 2. LIEUT. COL. J. M. BOOTHE. / OCCUPIED THIS, THEIR THIRD POSITION, ABOUT 12.00 M., APRIL 6, / 1862, AND HELD IT UNTIL 1.30 P.M., SUSTAINING THEIR HEAVIEST / LOSS. THE REGIMENT THEN FELL BACK TO THE LANDING. [LOST] / 1 OFFICER AND 46 MEN KILLED; 11 / OFFICERS AND 149 MEN WOUNDED; 9 MEN MISSING; TOTAL, 216.

Organized at Springfield, mustered in August 10, 1861. Corinth. Vicksburg. Chattanooga. Atlanta. March to the Sea. Carolinas Campaign. Grand Review. Mustered out July 24, 1865. Lost 246 officers or enlisted men killed, mortally wounded, or by disease.

1.23.6 Subject: 81st Ohio VI, Stele
Location: N 35 08 28 01 / W 88 20 57 44
Dedicated: June 6, 1902
Medium: Granite

Monument is a granite stele with common soldier in high relief, the whole surmounting a base.

Inscription

OHIO / 81ST INFANTRY / COMMANDED BY / COL. THOMAS MORTON MCARTHUR'S (2D) BRIGADE / W. H. L. WALLACE'S (2D) DIVISION / ARMY OF THE TENNESSEE
[Relief of Union soldier advancing south, bearing a musket]

THIS REGIMENT GUARDED SNAKE CREEK BRIDGE DURING / FORENOON APRIL 6, 1862; ASSISTED IN REPELLING ENEMY'S / ADVANCE AT ARMY'S EXTREME RIGHT AFTER NOON; BY PER- / SONAL ORDER OF GEN. GRANT, RECEIVED AT 3 P.M., DEVELOPED / ENEMY'S POSITION AT CROSSING OF HAMBURG & SAVANNAH / AND MAIN CORINTH ROADS; FORMED LEFT OF MCCLERNAND'S / COMMAND APRIL 7TH; DROVE ENEMY FROM A BATTERY / SHORTLY BEFORE END OF BATTLE, WHERE ITS GREATEST LOSS / OCCURRED. / [LOST] 2 OFFICERS AND 2 MEN KILLED; 17 MEN / WOUNDED; 2 MEN MISSING; TOTAL, 23.

Organized in Ohio, September 1861. Shiloh. Corinth. Atlanta. March to the Sea. Carolinas Campaign. Grand Review. Mustered out July 13, 1865. Lost 222 officers or enlisted men killed, mortally wounded, or by disease.

81st Ohio VI, Stele

Chattanooga

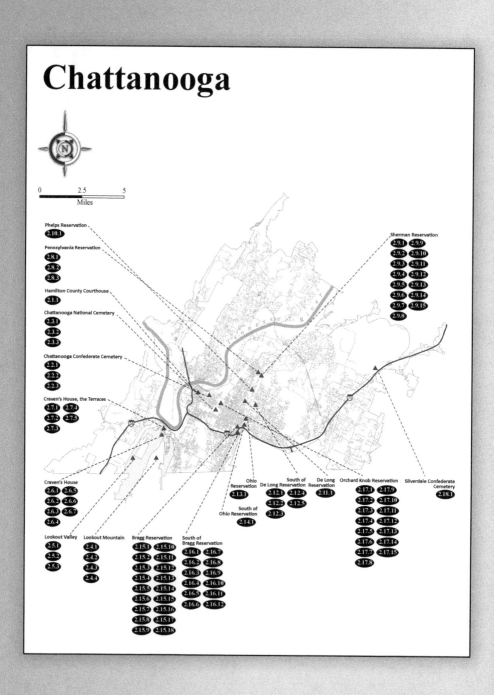

0   2.5   5
Miles

Phelps Reservation
2.10.1

Pennsylvania Reservation
2.8.1
2.8.2
2.8.3

Hamilton County Courthouse
2.1.1

Chattanooga National Cemetery
2.3.1
2.3.2
2.3.3

Chattanooga Confederate Cemetery
2.2.1
2.2.2
2.2.3

Craven's House, the Terraces
2.7.1 2.7.4
2.7.2 2.7.5
2.7.3

Sherman Reservation
2.9.1 2.9.9
2.9.2 2.9.10
2.9.3 2.9.11
2.9.4 2.9.12
2.9.5 2.9.13
2.9.6 2.9.14
2.9.7 2.9.15
2.9.8

Craven's House
2.6.1 2.6.5
2.6.2 2.6.6
2.6.3 2.6.7
2.6.4

Lookout Valley
2.5.1
2.5.2
2.5.3

Lookout Mountain
2.4.1
2.4.2
2.4.3
2.4.4

Bragg Reservation
2.15.1 2.15.10
2.15.2 2.15.11
2.15.3 2.15.12
2.15.4 2.15.13
2.15.5 2.15.14
2.15.6 2.15.15
2.15.7 2.15.16
2.15.8 2.15.17
2.15.9 2.15.18

South of
Bragg Reservation
2.16.1 2.16.7
2.16.2 2.16.8
2.16.3 2.16.9
2.16.4 2.16.10
2.16.5 2.16.11
2.16.6 2.16.12

Ohio
Reservation
2.13.1

South of
Ohio Reservation
2.14.1

South of
De Long Reservation
2.12.1 2.12.4
2.12.2 2.12.5
2.12.3

De Long
Reservation
2.11.1

Orchard Knob Reservation
2.17.1 2.17.9
2.17.2 2.17.10
2.17.3 2.17.11
2.17.4 2.17.12
2.17.5 2.17.13
2.17.6 2.17.14
2.17.7 2.17.15
2.17.8

Silverdale Confederate
Cemetery
2.18.1

CHATTANOOGA

INCLUDING CHICKAMAUGA
AND CHATTANOOGA
NATIONAL MILITARY PARK

"NOV. 25, 1863 5 P.M."

C HATTANOOGA monumentation merits a separate chapter. The Chattanooga Campaign, November 23–25, 1863, was a decisive event in the war. Fought between Union forces under Maj. Gen. Ulysses S. Grant against Confederate troops commanded by General Braxton Bragg, the battle ended the Confederate Army of Tennessee's siege of Chattanooga that had begun some two months earlier.

Geographically speaking, this is a very Southern city, but relatively few Southern monuments stand here: the cemetery markers at Chattanooga and Silverdale and the Stewart monument at the courthouse are prominent exceptions to the host of Union monuments. The Chattanooga division of the Chickamauga and Chattanooga National Military Park was established by act of Congress on August 19, 1890, and was superintended by the War Department until 1933, when it was transferred to the National Park Service. Presented in this chapter are thirty-eight monuments from Illinois, six from Ohio, three from Iowa, five from New York, eight from Pennsylvania, thirteen from Missouri (one Confederate), three from Wisconsin, two from Kansas, and one each from New Jersey, Connecticut, Maryland (to Federal and Confederate soldiers), and Massachusetts.

The Area: The Events

The Confederate Army of Tennessee, victorious at the Battle of Chickamauga on September 18–20, 1863, laid siege to the Union Army of the Cumberland, which was ensconced but trapped and ill-supplied at Chattanooga, under the command of Maj. Gen. William S. Rosecrans. Grant was appointed to command of the Military Division of the Mississippi on October 18. He reinforced the army at Chattanooga and replaced Rosecrans with Maj. Gen. George H. Thomas. A new supply line was established by force, Maj. Gen. William T. Sherman arrived with four divisions in mid-November, and the Federals took the offensive: Union troops seized Orchard Knob and Lookout Mountain on November 23–24. On the following day, the Union troops were repulsed on the grounds of what is now the Sherman Reservation. However, the Federals then assaulted and, at length, seized the Southern positions on Missionary Ridge. As dusk fell at 5:00 p.m. on November 25, the Confederates were defeated. They withdrew and were pursued to Ringgold, Georgia, November 26–27. Their army was still intact, but their reversal was another blow to Southern hopes for independence. Chattanooga, gateway to the South, served as the Federal supply and logistics base for the Atlanta Campaign, which in turn led to the March to the Sea, the Carolinas Campaign, and the fall of the Confederacy.

Illinois Monuments

The most common markers (as is also the case at Shiloh) are thirty-eight battery or regimental monuments from Illinois, dedicated in 1899. On May 22, 1895, the Illinois state legislature voted to allocate $65,400 for "marking by appropriate monuments and markers of granite, the positions of the several commands of Illinois volunteers." The unit monuments were erected by the J. S. Culver Company of Springfield, at an average cost of $877.87 per stele. The state's contract with the company stipulated that unit monuments be seven feet, six inches wide by four feet, four inches high by three feet, eight inches deep. The design principles also stipulated that the

> monuments of the Illinois troops should be exact duplicates, (excepting the lettering to indicate each command), so that those visiting those historic battlefields might distinguish the Illinois Monuments as far as the eye could see them. . . . The monuments, all alike, are of dark Quincy Granite, two pieces, base and die . . . the top and three sides quarry face, the other side highly polished, bearing four lines of three inch sunk letters . . . and on the bevel face of each die the word ILLINOIS cut in raised polished letters 6 inches high, 2 inches base and 3 inch raise[d]. . . . The markers consist of one piece of dark Quincy granite . . . exact duplicates of the monuments except in size.

Three Distinct Features

There are at least three distinct features to the monumentation at Chattanooga. First, monuments exist where none should be expected: on steep, wooded slopes at the end of seldom-walked trails of the Sherman Reservation (2.9.12: 116th Illinois; 2.9.13: 127th Illinois; 2.9.14: 63rd Illinois), emplaced on hillside terraces above the Cravens House on Lookout Mountain (2.7.1, 2.7.2: 28th and 147th Pennsylvania; 2.7.3: 96th Illinois), or along cliffsides of trails farther up Lookout Mountain (2.4.3, 2.4.4: 29th and 111th Pennsylvania). These locations are not in plain sight; they require physical exertion and prior knowledge to find. In fact, previous to this book there were no public maps or guides to their locations. At all events, they are of equal import with their more prominent counterparts.

Second, several cryptic, seemingly innocuous phrases have momentous import and are repeated on numerous monuments along Missionary Ridge. The satisfaction of the ridge being won by Union forces is discernible but subtle. The climactic moment of the battle of Chattanooga when the crest was gained—"NOV. 25, 1863 5 P. M."—is inscribed on no fewer than seventeen Illinois and Wisconsin monuments along the ridge. Third, there is an understated note of victory, even triumph, discernible in Missouri's regimental markers on the Bragg Reservation—3rd, 12th, 17th, 29th, 31st, and 32nd Missouri (2.15.13, 2.15.14, 2.15.15, 2.15.16, 2.15.17, and 2.15.18, respectively). The inscriptions on these marble stelae are weathered and difficult to read. They stand only three feet high, but they take note, for example, that by day's end their fighting earned the "32ND MO. INFTY. / U.S.A." the right to rest here, "Near This Point / Night of Nov. 25, 1863." The victory was not complete, and the war was not over: the Confederates withdrew—hard pressed, but not crushed—to fight another day. However, the achievement of Union troops in storming Missionary Ridge is repeatedly commemorated on this site: here Union soldiers bivouacked on grounds that only a few hours earlier had been occupied by Confederate lines near the site of Bragg's army headquarters.

- Particular caution should be exercised when touring Missionary Ridge. Most of the tour is on Crest Road, a winding, two-lane road in a residential neighborhood with limited provisions for visitation. In this area the national military park consists of a narrow strip of ground sixty feet wide, reduced in many places by grading for the roadway to twenty feet.

- Missing from this study is the 27th Pennsylvania Light Artillery stele, erected in 1896, on the north bank of the Tennessee River, on private property.

Hamilton County Courthouse

2.1.1 Subject: Lt. Gen. Alexander P. Stewart, Portrait Bust
Location: 300 Courthouse, 37402   N 35 02 56 23 / W 85 18 24 86
Installed or dedicated: 1917
Media: Bronze, marble
Monument is a waist-length portrait bust of Stewart, in military uniform with a cape over his shoulders.

Inscription

A.P. STEWART / LT. GENERAL / C.S.A. / 1861–1865

Lt. Gen. Alexander P. Stewart (1821–1908), born in Rogersville, Tennessee, was a West Point graduate and Regular Army officer who opposed secession but sided with the Confederacy when the war came. He fought in numerous battles, including Chickamauga, where he was wounded, and Ezra Church—where he was wounded again. He commanded the Third Corps during the 1864 Nashville Campaign and the Carolinas Campaign in 1865. After the war, he served as commissioner of the Chickamauga and Chattanooga National Military Park.

Lt. Gen. Alexander P.
Stewart, Portrait Bust

Upon his death, county leaders elected to erect a monument inside the Hamilton County Courthouse. The monument was dedicated in 1913. However, the seven-ton sculpture with a marble base surmounted by a bronze bust was deemed too heavy for the courthouse structure to support, so it was placed outside, in front of the building. The sculptor of his monument was Belle Kinney of Nashville; it was cast by Tiffany & Co. Stewart's biographer, Sam Davis Elliott, notes that it "is noticed by few—an ornament ignored by most people who walk by it." Elliott laments that "only children and tourists from out-of-state seem to really look" at the statue. However, Stewart—"Old Straight," as he was affectionately called by his men—was respected by his peers for his integrity and "quiet competence." Today the figure of Stewart faces southeast, in line of sight of Missionary Ridge, where units under his command strove, unsuccessfully, to stem the onrushing tide of elements of Thomas's Army of the Cumberland as they came over the slopes during the battle of Chattanooga.

Chattanooga Confederate Cemetery

2.2.1 Subject: The Obelisk
Location: East Fifth Street   N 35 02 56 98 / W 85 17 45 62
Installed or dedicated: May 10, 1877
Medium: Granite
Monument is an obelisk surmounting a base.

Inscription
OUR / CONFEDERATE / DEAD.

The stark, impressive obelisk is the centerpiece of the Confederate cemetery on grounds adjacent to the campus of the University of Tennessee at Chattanooga. The Confederate Memorial Association, formed May 14, 1874, raised $2,500 for the memorial, which was designed by G. C. Conner and dedicated May 10, 1877. Attendees included Union and Confederate veterans as well as residents of Chattanooga and the surrounding communities.

The dead of Chattanooga Confederate hospitals were originally buried in a plot beside the Tennessee River, but floodwaters washed over the site, and wooden headboards for about 141 graves were lost. A veterans group purchased the current site for $750 in 1867, and the dead were reinterred there. In the 1890s, Confederate dead found during work for the national military park were also reinterred here along with at least two Union soldiers who died while prisoners of war at Chattanooga. Individual graves have not been identified. The stelae are representative of the dead. Today, twenty-four plaques are emplaced in two rows: one from North Carolina with 15 names; one from South Carolina with 14 names; four from Tennessee with 151 names; six from Alabama with 288 names; one from Texas with 11 names; one from Arkansas with 30 names; one from Florida with 18 names; two from Georgia with 46 names; one from Kentucky with 15 names; one from Louisiana with 27 names; three from Mississippi with 106 names. These are the only state commemorations of Confederate soldiers in Chattanooga. A typical plaque reads as follows:

TO THE MEMORY OF OUR CONFEDERATE DEAD / FROM THE STATE OF ALABAMA, WHOSE NAMES / AND COMMANDS ARE HERE RECORDED

2.2.2 Subject: The Cross, Cemetery Grounds
Location: N 35 02 54 39 / W 85 17 46 5
Installed or dedicated: 1997
Medium: Granite
Monument is an inscribed cross surmounting a base.

"PEACE BE TO THE ASHES OF / OUR CONFEDERATE DEAD AND / HONOR BE TO THEIR MEMORY." / 1997 / N. B. FORREST #3 / SONS OF CONFEDERATE VETERANS / PATRICK R. CLEBURNE #158, / MILITARY ORDER OF THE STARS & BARS

Two tombstones inscribed "Hospital Matron CSA" and "Negro Man CSA" respectively, stand on both sides of the monument.

- Another tribute, a cast-iron plaque, offers a background narrative of the cemetery grounds and reads in part:

TO THE MEMORY OF OUR CONFEDERATE DEAD / IN THESE SACRED GROUNDS THE SONS OF ELEVEN / SOUTHERN STATES ARE BURIED.
THE MOST OF THEM DIED IN HOSPITALS AT CHATTANOOGA, FROM / WOUNDS RECEIVED IN THE BATTLE OF MURFREESBORO AND FROM SICKNESS AND / WOUNDS INCURRED IN THE CAMPAIGNS FROM JANUARY 1ST TO SEPTEMBER 7TH, / 1863, WHEN CHATTANOOGA WAS EVACUATED BY THE CONFEDERATE TROOPS.

2.2.3 Subject: The Arch
Location: N 35 02 53 24 / W 85 17 47 52
Installed or dedicated: 1901
Media: Limestone, wrought iron
Monument is an arch as a gateway and central element of the cemetery wall.

Inscription

ERECTED IN 1901 / BY THE / DAUGHTERS OF THE CONFEDERACY / CHAPTER 81 / CHATTANOOGA TENNESSEE / TO COMMEMORATE THE VALOR / AND HEROISM THAT OUR / CONFEDERATE SOLDIERS / DISPLAYED IN THEIR BATTLE FOR OUR / BELOVED SOUTHLAND / IN THE WAR FROM 1861 TO 1865. / IN FRATERNAL RECOGNITION OF / N. B. FORREST CAMP U.C.V. / IT IS NOT IN THE POWER OF MORTALS / TO COMMAND SUCCESS. / THE CONFEDERATE SOLDIER DID MORE. / HE DESERVED IT.

The Arch

- The Masonic stone at the base reads:

MAY 22 / A.D.A.L. / 19015901

This distinctive limestone structure and wrought-iron battle-flag gate with thirteen stars was designed by Lawrence Thompson Dickinson and erected in 1901. It stands directly across the street from the campus of the University of Tennessee at Chattanooga.

Chattanooga National Cemetery

2.3.1 Subject: Memorial Arch, Entryway
Location: 1200 Bailey Avenue, 37404   N 35 02 02 59 / W 85 17 32 58
Installed or dedicated: 1880
Media: Iron, limestone
Monument is an arch with Doric columns, surmounting keystone and iron gates.

Inscription

NATIONAL MILITARY CEMETERY / CHATTANOOGA A.D. 1863.

HERE REST IN PEACE 12,956 CITIZENS / WHO DIED FOR THEIR COUNTRY / IN THE YEARS 1861 TO 1865.

This is one of five archways, each standing thirty-five feet high, designed to serve as the formal entrance to national cemeteries in the South. The others are at Marietta National Cemetery, Marietta, Georgia, 1883; Nashville National Cemetery, circa 1870; Arlington National Cemetery, 1879; and Vicksburg National Cemetery, circa 1880.

Major General George H. Thomas is said to have selected this site for a cemetery during the assault of his troops on Missionary Ridge on November 25, 1863. Missionary Ridge is visible to the east; Lookout Mountain is visible to the west. On December 25, 1863, General Order No. 296 officially designated the site as a cemetery. By 1870, there were more than 12,800 interments: 8,685 known and 4,189 unknown. The dead include casualties of the battles of Chickamauga, Missionary Ridge, and Lookout Mountain. In addition there are reinterments from Athens, Charleston, and other sites surrounding Chattanooga, as well as locations along the line of the Atlanta Campaign of 1864.

- This is the largest cemetery in the state, with more than 37,000 interments on 121 acres. It was closed to new interments in 2015.

Memorial Arch

2.3.2 Subject: Union Fourth Army Corps, Obelisk
Location: Between Sections C and F   N 35 02 09 91 / W 85 17 22 54
Installed or dedicated: 1868
Medium: Marble
Monument is an obelisk surmounting a base.

Inscription
FOURTH / ARMY / CORPS. / IN MEMORY OF / OUR FALLEN COMRADES

[Order of battle]

The IV Corps, Maj. Gen. Gordon Granger commanding, was organized at Chattanooga on October 9, 1863, after the battle of Chickamauga, by consolidating the XX and XXI Corps and elements of the Reserve Corps. The IV Corps saw extensive action under various commanders from its establishment to the end of the war. It served with great distinction in the famous unordered attack on Missionary Ridge, which this cemetery faces, but its hardest test may have occurred on the Franklin battlefield on November 30, 1864, when the Corps withstood the full-scale frontal assault by the Army of Tennessee. Most of the regiments were mustered out in December 1865.

- The IV Corps of the Army of the Potomac—no relation—was organized in March 1862 and was discontinued in August 1863.

Tribute to Andrews Raiders

2.3.3 Subject: Tribute to Andrews' Raiders, Union
Location: Section H   N 35 02 03 18 / W 85 17 11 70
Installed or dedicated: n.a.
Media: Bronze, marble
Monument is a train engine, in bronze, surmounting a marble base.

Inscriptions
[Front]
OHIO'S TRIBUTE / TO THE / ANDREWS' RAIDERS. / 1862. / ERECTED 1890.

ESCAPED [8 names] / R. D. BARR / SC / BUREAU BROS. BRONZE FOUNDERS

EXECUTED [7 names]

EXCHANGED [6 names]

The only sculpture of a train on a Civil War monument appears here, on the Andrews monument. The site marks the graves of eight soldiers who were executed as Union spies, along with James J. Andrews, a civilian, who planned and led the operation. Under his direction, a train locomotive, the "General," was seized on April 12, 1862, by twenty-two men dressed in civilian clothes. The scheme was only partially successful, but it disrupted Confederate logistics and created great notoriety. Andrews, the leader of the plot, was captured and eventually hanged in Atlanta. Four of the men were awarded the Medal of Honor.

- The train is approximately two feet by six feet by one foot; the base is approximately eight by nine by five feet.
- The state legislature of Ohio passed a resolution to have the executed raiders' remains moved to Chattanooga cemetery in 1866. The Chattanooga Post 45 of the Grand Army of the Republic (GAR) held a ceremony for Andrews's reburial on October 16, 1887, and in March

1889 the Ohio state legislature appropriated $5,000 for the monument. Some four thousand people attended the ceremonies; thousands of miniature flags decorated the gravesites, according to historian James G. Bogle, who also noted that the replica train surmounting the base is modeled on trains of the 1880s, not that of the 1860s when, as he notes, the balloon stack prevailed and wood was the fuel.

Lookout Mountain, Point Park

2.4.1 Subject: State of New York, Peace Monument, Column and Common Soldier Statues, Union and Confederate
Location: N 35 00 40 10 / W 85 20 38 98
Dedicated: November 15, 1910
Media: Bronze, granite, marble
Monument is two sculpted figures, a Union and a Confederate soldier, shaking hands under the flag of the United States, the whole surmounting a shaft and colonnade with stelae and base.

Inscriptions

[Front]
UNION TROOPS IN BATTLE OF LOOKOUT MOUNTAIN
MAJ. GEN. JOSEPH HOOKER COMMANDING. / 2ND DIVISION, 12TH CORPS (SLOCUM)—BRIG. GEN. JOHN W. GEARY [ORDER OF BATTLE] / 1ST DIVISION 15TH CORPS (BLAIR)—BRIG. GEN. PETER J. OSTERHAUS [ORDER OF BATTLE] / 1ST DIVISION 4TH CORPS (GRANGER)—BRIG. GEN. CHARLES CRUFT [ORDER OF BATTLE] / 1ST DIVISION 14TH CORPS (PALMER)—BRIG. GEN. RICHARD W. JOHNSON [ORDER OF BATTLE] / ARTILLERY [ORDER OF BATTLE]

[Narrative plaque]

CONFEDERATE TROOPS IN BATTLE OF LOOKOUT MOUNTAIN
MAJ. GEN. CARTER L. STEVENSON, COMMANDING. / STEVENSON'S DIVISION (HARDEE'S CORPS)—BRIG. GEN. JOHN C. BROWN [ORDER OF BATTLE] / CHEATHAM'S DIVISION (HARDEE'S CORPS)—BRIG. GEN. JOHN K. JACKSON [ORDER OF BATTLE] / STEWART'S DIVISION (BRECKINRIDGE'S CORPS)—MAJ. GEN. ALEXANDER P. STEWART [ORDER OF BATTLE] / ARTILLERY [ORDER OF BATTLE]

[Narrative plaque]

"IN GRATEFUL COMMEMORATION OF SOLDIERS FROM THE STATE OF NEW YORK IN THE ARMY OF THE POTOMAC OF THE ELEVENTH AND TWELFTH CORPS WHO TOOK PART IN THE OPERATIONS ABOUT CHATTANOOGA, OCT.–NOV. 1863" [ORDER OF BATTLE: NEW YORK UNITS]

"REUNITED—ONE COUNTRY AGAIN AND ONE COUNTRY FOREVER."
PRESIDENT MCKINLEY ATLANTA, DEC. 15, 1898.

The New York Peace Memorial is the largest monument in the Chickamauga and Chattanooga National Military Park and the tallest in Tennessee. Its place in Point Park on Lookout Mountain stands at the highest elevation of any Civil War monument.

State of New York, Peace Monument, Column and Common Soldier Statues, Union and Confederate

Lookout Point was purchased as part of what became the Chickamauga and Chattanooga National Military Park on August 3, 1898. Monuments were prohibited on the crest at first, but an exception was made for the state of New York's "Peace Memorial," and later for the 96th Illinois regimental stele.

The monument stands approximately ninety-five feet high; the sculptures of common soldiers are approximately nine feet tall; marble stairs lead up to the colonnade and a base that is fifty feet in diameter. Sixteen columns support the shaft, and bronze stelae on the pedestal display the names of units from New York. The bronze group crowning the marble shaft is called "Reconciliation" and is the work of sculptor Hinton Perry. A. J. Zabriskie prepared plans and specifications; the G. H. Cutting Granite Company served as the contractor. The sculpture is in bronze, the column in pink granite, the base in Tennessee marble. The cost of the monument was $80,000.

Copious detail and an extended narrative are features of this monument and, in general, of state monuments from the North on the Chattanooga battlefield. They are more than commemorations: this is a New York commemoration of victory in war while offering the ideal of reconciliation in its aftermath.

· The inscription ascribed to President William McKinley, a Union veteran who served in the 23rd Ohio VI during the war, is taken from a speech given at a "peace jubilee" in Atlanta, Georgia, on December 15, 1898: "Reunited—One Country Again And Forever." The larger context reads as follows: "Reunited—One country again and one country forever! Proclaim it from the press and the pulpit; teach it in the schools; write it across the skies! The world sees and feels it; it cheers every heart North and South, and brightens the life of every American home! Let nothing ever stain it again! At peace with all the world and with each other, what can stand in the pathway of our progress and prosperity?"

2.4.2 Subject: 96th Illinois VI, Tablet
Location: North of the Peace Monument   N 35 00 37 86 / W 85 20 37 60
Dedicated: 1899
Medium: Granite
Monument is a granite stele.

Inscription

ILLINOIS / 96TH INFANTRY, / 2ND BRIGADE / 1ST DIVISION, / 4TH CORPS / NOV. 25, 1863

This is the only unit monument surmounting Lookout Mountain; the regiment was among the first units to reach the crest of the mountain on November 25, 1863. The 96th Illinois is also commemorated with a granite stele at the Cravens Reservation (2.7.2).

Palisades below the Point on Lookout Mountain

2.4.3 Subject: 29th Pennsylvania VI, Tablet
Location: N 35 00 46 21 / W 85 20 37 80
Installed: 1910
Medium: Bronze
Monument is a bronze plaque on a natural rock wall.

Inscriptions

[First Panel]
[Bronze panel relief of soldiers scaling heights]
[Relief of state seal of Pennsylvania]
111TH REGIMENT PENNSYLVANIA VETERAN VOLUNTEER INFANTRY, LIEUTENANT COLONEL THOMAS M. WALKER, COMMANDING.
COBHAM'S 2ND BRIGADE, GEARY'S SECOND DIVISION. SLOCUM'S 12TH CORPS.

[Second Panel]
. . . ON THE 24TH OF NOV., 1863, THE REGIMENT WAS ORDERED TO ASSAULT THE RUGGED SIDES OF LOOKOUT MOUNTAIN. UNDER COVER OF THE FOG IT MARCHED TO LIGHT'S MILLS AND UP THE MOUNTAIN SIDE UNTIL THE RIGHT OF THE LINE RESTED UNDER THE PALISADES, WHEN, FACING TO THE FRONT THE LINE EXTENDING UP AND DOWN THE MOUNTAIN, IT ADVANCED, AND FORCING BACK THE ENEMY, GAINED A POINT EXTENDING FROM THE PALISADES TOWARD AND NEAR THE CRAVEN [SIC] HOUSE. FACING TO THE RIGHT IT GAINED A POSITION UNDER THE PALISADES, WHERE THE ENEMY ON THE TOP OF THE MOUNTAIN

111th Pennsylvania VI, Tablets

ROLLED ROCKS, AND DROPPED LIGHTED SHELLS ON THE MEN AS THEY STOOD
WITH THEIR BACKS AGAINST THE PALISADES, WHILE THEY WERE UNDER THE
FIRE OF THE SHARPSHOOTERS, AND THE ENEMY ON THE WORKS FURTHER DOWN
THE MOUNTAIN. EARLY IN THE MORNING OF THE 25TH IT WAS DISCOVERED THAT
THE ENEMY HAD EVACUATED HIS WORKS AND SOME OF THE ADVENTUROUS ONES
CLIMBED UP RUDE LADDERS AND GAINED THE SUMMIT. LEAVING LOOKOUT THE
REGIMENT CROSSED THE VALLEY TOWARD MISSIONARY RIDGE. / LOSS ONE KILLED;
EIGHT WOUNDED.

This large bronze tablet, technically an *aedicula*, or framed shrine, is four feet
by four feet in diameter and is emplaced on a sheer natural rock wall along the
trail below the crest of Lookout Mountain.

The 111th organized at Erie, January 1862. Cedar Mountain. Maryland
Campaign. Chancellorsville. Gettysburg. Chattanooga. Atlanta. March to the
Sea. Carolinas Campaign. Grand Review. Mustered out July 19, 1865. Lost 304
officers or enlisted men killed, mortally wounded, or by disease.

2.4.4 Subject: 29th Pennsylvania VI, Tablet
Location: N 35 00 46 21 / W 85 20 37 80
Installed: 1910
Medium: Bronze
Monument is two bronze plaques on a natural rock wall.

Inscription

[First panel]
[RELIEF OF STATE SEAL OF PENNSYLVANIA]
TWENTY NINTH REGIMENT / PENNSYLVANIA VOLUNTEER INFANTRY / COLONEL
WILLIAM RICKARDS, JR., COMMANDING / COBHAM'S BRIGADE, GEARY'S DIVISION
/ SLOCUM'S TWELFTH CORPS / HOOKER'S DETACHMENT / FROM THE ARMY OF THE
POTOMAC / BATTLE ABOVE THE CLOUDS
[Bronze relief of officer and infantry]

[Second Panel]
TWENTY NINTH REGIMENT PENNSYLVANIA VOLUNTEER INFANTRY
THIS REGIMENT WAS THE PICKET OF GEARY'S WHITE STAR DIVISION, ON THE NIGHT
OF OCTOBER 28TH, 1863, AT WAUHATCHIE, AND RECEIVED THE FIRST ATTACK OF
HOOD'S FORCE UPON THAT DIVISION ABOUT MIDNIGHT.
. . . EARLY ON THE MORNING OF NOVEMBER 24TH, 1863, THE REGIMENT LED THE
ADVANCE OF HOOKER'S ASSAULT ON LOOKOUT MOUNTAIN, CROSSING LOOKOUT
CREEK AT LIGHT'S MILL, ABOUT THREE MILES SOUTH OF THIS POINT AT THE BASE
OF THE MOUNTAIN. ASCENDED UP THE MOUNTAIN TO THE PALISADES, THEN
FACING NORTH ADVANCED TOWARDS THE LEFT FLANK OF THE CONFEDERATE
LINE NEARLY TWO MILES DISTANT. ASSISTED IN FORCING THE ENEMY FROM HIS
WORKS, FINALLY REACHING THIS POINT, THE HIGHEST THEN ACCESSIBLE. THE
REGIMENT CONTINUED THE ATTACK ON THE NARROW LEDGE TO THE LEFT OF THIS
TABLET, REACHING A POINT 500 YARDS SOUTH, HOLDING IT UNTIL RELIEVED AT
9.30 P.M. TO REPLENISH AMMUNITION. . . . THE BATTLE OF MISSIONARY RIDGE
OPENED ON THE EXTREME LEFT. THE REGIMENT DESCENDED THE MOUNTAIN,
CROSSED THE VALLEY DIRECTLY EAST OF THIS POINT AND JOINED IN THE ASSAULT
ON MISSIONARY RIDGE, BREAKING THE ENEMY'S LINE AND REACHING THE CREST
ABOUT 6 P.M. ON NOVEMBER 27, 1863.

This is another dramatic aedicula, or framed shrine, like its 111th PVI counterpart nearby, along the trail below the crest of Lookout Mountain. The plaque's
dimensions are four feet by six feet. Reliefs of pilasters frame the inscription
and battle scene, which is described in the narrative. Iron rods drilled into the
stone have secured its place since its installation in 1910.

The 29th organized at Philadelphia, July 1, 1861. Shenandoah Valley. Cedar
Mountain. Antietam. Chancellorsville. Gettysburg. Chattanooga. Atlanta.
March to the Sea. Carolinas Campaign. Grand Review. Mustered out July 11,
1865. Lost 187 officers or enlisted men killed, mortally wounded, or by disease.

· Tablets for these two regiments also stand on Missionary Ridge, near
   the monument to Ireland's New York VI (2.16.8).

Lookout Valley

2.5.1 Subject: New York Troops in Howard's Eleventh Corps, Shaft
Location: Monument is off I-24, Exit 75   N 35 00 51 09 / W 85 20 30 88
Installed or dedicated: 1899
Media: Bronze, granite
Monument is a granite shaft surmounting a base.

Inscription

[Front (Excerpts)]
TO THE NEW YORK TROOPS IN HOWARD'S ELEVENTH CORPS OF HOOKER'S
COMMAND, 11TH AND 12TH CORPS, ARMY OF THE POTOMAC, AT WAUHATCHIE,
OCTOBER 28–29, 1863. / STEINWEHR'S DIVISION. / 134TH N.Y. INFANTRY, / 154TH
N.Y. INFANTRY, BUSCHBECK'S BRIGADE / 136TH N.Y. INFANTRY, ORLAND SMITH'S
BRIGADE / SCHURZ'S DIVISION. / 45TH N.Y. INFANTRY, / 143RD N.Y. INFANTRY,
TYNDALE'S BRIGADE / 58TH N.Y. INFANTRY / 119TH N.Y. INFANTRY / 141ST N.Y.
INFANTRY, KRZYZANOWSKI'S BRIGADE / 68TH N.Y. INFANTRY, HECKER'S BRIGADE /
CO. A 8TH N.Y. INFANTRY, HEADQUARTERS GUARD

SCHURZ'S DIVISION. / SOON AFTER FIRING WAS HEARD IN THE DIRECTION OF
WAUHATCHIE, GEN. SCHURZ WAS ORDERED TO PUSH HIS LEADING BRIGADE TO THE
RELIEF OF GEN. GEARY.
TYNDALE'S BRIGADE WAS IN THE ADVANCE. ITS LEFT, WHILE PASSING
SMITH'S HILL, WAS FIRED UPON BY THE ENEMY CONCEALED IN THE WOODS;
THE BRIGADE PROCEEDED TO THE HILL ON THE RIGHT OF THIS MONUMENT
(KNOWN AS TYNDALE'S HILL) FROM WHICH THE ENEMY WAS SPEEDILY DRIVEN.
KRZYZANOWSKI'S BRIGADE WAS THEN PLACED IN THE GAP BETWEEN SMITH'S AND
TYNDALE'S HILLS AND GEN. SCHURZ, INSTRUCTED BY GEN. HOOKER IN PERSON,
SENT HECKER'S BRIGADE TO EFFECT A JUNCTION WITH GEARY'S DIVISION, WHICH
WAS ACCOMPLISHED ABOUT 5 A.M. THE OPERATIONS OF HOWARD'S CORPS AND
THOSE OF GEARY'S DIVISION, 12TH CORPS, DISLODGED THE ENEMY FROM EVERY
POSITION THIS SIDE OF LOOKOUT CREEK, AND, IN CONJUNCTION WITH THE
TROOPS AT BROWN'S FERRY UNDER GEN. W. F. SMITH, REOPENED THE UNION LINES
OF COMMUNICATION TO CHATTANOOGA.

ON THE AFTERNOON OF OCTOBER 28, 1863, / TWO DIVISIONS OF THE 11TH CORPS
. . . MOVED DOWN / THIS VALLEY TOWARD BROWN'S FERRY, WHERE JUNCTION
/ WAS EFFECTED WITH HAZEN'S AND TURCHIN'S / BRIGADES . . . UNDER / GEN.
W. F. SMITH. . . . A DETACHMENT . . . FROM THE 141ST NEW YORK . . . ADVANCING
/ BEYOND THESE FOOTHILLS ABOUT 500 YARDS / EAST FROM WHERE THIS
MONUMENT STANDS, / DISCOVERED AND SKIRMISHED WITH THE ENEMY, /
SHORTLY BEFORE MIDNIGHT, MOVING TO ATTACK / THE UNION FORCES IN THE
VALLEY.

STEINWEHR'S DIVISION
BETWEEN MIDNIGHT AND 1 A.M. HEAVY FIGHTING WAS HEARD IN THE DIRECTION
OF GEARY'S DIVISION, AND SHORTLY AFTERWARD STEINWEHR'S DIVISION WAS
MOVED TOWARD ELLIS' HOUSE AND THE LEADING BRIGADE ORDERED TO CAPTURE
THE HILL TO THE LEFT OF THIS MONUMENT (KNOWN AS SMITH'S HILL) ALREADY
OCCUPIED BY LAW'S ALABAMA BRIGADE, LONGSTREET'S CORPS. ORLAND SMITH'S
BRIGADE CHARGED UP THE HILL UNDER HEAVY FIRE WITHOUT RETURNING IT

New York Troops in Howard's Eleventh Corps, Shaft, Lookout Valley

UNTIL THE CREST WAS GAINED, WHEN THE ENEMY RETREATED DOWN THE SLOPE AND FELL BACK ACROSS LOOKOUT CREEK. ABOUT FIFTY PRISONERS AND SOME ARMS WERE CAPTURED. THE ATTACKING FORCE NUMBERED NOT QUITE 700 MUSKETS. BUSCHBECK'S BRIGADE HELD IN RESERVE, WAS ADVANCED INTO THE GAPS TO THE RIGHT AND LEFT OF THE HILL TO PREVENT A FLANKING MOVEMENT OF THE ENEMY.

This monument commemorates the actions of the New York regiments of Steinwehr's division in this area, including their role in the reopening of Federal supply lines into Chattanooga during the siege, as well as a rare night action during the campaign. The names of nine regiments and one company of New York infantry are wrapped around the shaft. The effect is to display a startling kind of panache, especially for travelers on I-24, who are normally subjected to so many other, more contemporary notices or advertisements as they drive.

The monument was moved about three hundred feet to make way for the construction of I-24. Today it stands beside the interstate on Park Service ground and remains accessible via a dirt road extending from I-24, Exit 75. Beyond it stands Tyndale's Hill, named for Brig. Gen. Hector Tyndale, which is also the site of the scene depicted in the James Walker painting "Battle Above the Clouds." Designed by A. J. Zabriskie, New York, and erected at a cost of $2,700, it stands seven feet, two inches by seven feet, two inches by twenty-two feet, nine inches.

- A granite shaft, privately erected, off US 41 near Garden Road (N 35 01 14 05 / W 85 21 16 12), displays a summary of the action near the railroad and Lookout Creek:

DURING THE LAST HALF OF THE 60 DAY / SIEGE OF CHATTANOOGA IN 1863, UNION TROOPS / ON THE WEST SIDE OF LOOKOUT CREEK FOUGHT / ALMOST DAILY WITH CONFEDERATES ON THIS / SIDE. EACH SIDE WANTED CONTROL OF THE / CREEK'S BRIDGES. / HOOKER'S CORPS REPORTS

2.5.2 Subject: Greene's Third Brigade, New York VI, Stele
Location: Wauhatchie Pike, south of US 41, near 320 Wauhatchie   N 35 00 34 81 / W 85 22 27 94
Installed or dedicated: 1898
Media: Bronze, granite, limestone
Monument is a stele with plaque surmounting a base.

Inscription

[Front]
[Relief of state seal of New York]
78TH NEW YORK INFANTRY / 137TH NEW YORK INFANTRY / 149TH NEW YORK INFANTRY / GREENE'S—THIRD BRIGADE / GEARY'S—SECOND DIVISION / SLOCUM'S—TWELFTH CORPS / HOOKER'S COMMAND / 11TH AND 12TH CORPS / ARMY OF THE POTOMAC / OCT. 28–29 1863

TWO SECTIONS OF KNAP'S PENNA. BATTERY AND SIX REGIMENTS OF GEARY'S DIVISION ENCAMPED HERE ON EVENING OF OCTOBER 28, 1863, AND HERE ATTACKED AT MIDNIGHT BY BRATTON'S SOUTH CAROLINA BRIGADE, LONGSTREET'S CORPS. THE BATTERY HELD SUMMIT OF KNOLL A FEW YARDS SOUTH-WEST OF THIS POINT. THE INFANTRY BATTLE LINE ENVELOPED POSITION OCCUPIED BY BATTERY IN FORM OF A HORSESHOE, CENTRE FACING NORTH. THE 137TH N.Y. INFANTRY HELD THE LEFT OF THE LINE ALONG A FENCE FACING NORTHERLY AND WESTERLY. THE 149TH N.Y. INFANTRY WERE ON THE RIGHT OF THE LINE ALONG RAILROAD EMBANKMENT, FACING EASTERLY WITH ITS LEFT NEAR THIS MONUMENT; THE 78TH N.Y. INFANTRY IN RESERVE, OCCUPIED THREATENED POSITIONS ALTERNATELY ON EXTREME LEFT AND RIGHT DURING ENGAGEMENT WHICH LASTED THREE HOURS, THE CONFEDERATES RETIRING. / BRIG.-GEN. GEO. S. GREENE WAS WOUNDED; COL. DAVID S. IRELAND ASSUMED COMMAND OF THIRD BRIGADE DURING THE BATTLE.

CASUALTIES
[Order of battle: casualties]
TOTAL KILLED AND WOUNDED, 106
THE NEW YORK REGIMENTS ENGAGED HERE / NUMBERED 44 OFFICERS AND 745 MEN.

This monument also commemorates action by New York infantry on the night of October 28–29, 1863, against South Carolina troops led by Col. John Bratton. It was designed by A. J. Zabriskie of New York and erected at a cost of $900.

As is typical of the six New York monuments at Chattanooga, a narrative of events is displayed, as well as a systematic delineation of units and commanders. "Greene" is Brig. Gen. George S. Greene, second cousin to the Revolutionary

Greene's Third Brigade, New York VI, Stele

Wiedrich's Battery, New York Vol. Artillery, Smith's Hill, Stele

War's General Nathanael Greene, for whom Greeneville, Tennessee, is named. A statue of Brig. Gen. George S. Greene stands at Culp's Hill at Gettysburg, as do monuments to each of the New York regiments here and statues of Brig. Gen. John W. Geary; and Maj. Gen. Henry W. Slocum.

2.5.3 Subject: Wiedrich's Battery, New York Vol. Artillery, Smith's Hill, Stele
Location: Near the summit of Smith's Hill in Lookout Valley
N 35 01 41 45 / W 85 21 20 54
Installed or dedicated: 1898
Media: Bronze, granite
Monument is a stele surmounting a base.

Inscription
NEW YORK

[Bronze plaque: removed, text missing]

This monument stands at a hilltop, in woods, at an off-road site that is virtually inaccessible by vehicle and has no public access. It can be reached on foot by a trail along a power line uphill from an unpaved one-lane service road east of the Ireland's New York Brigade monument (2.5.1). The monument stands six feet, four inches by four feet, four inches by eleven feet and was erected at a cost of $1,500.

- The bronze plaque is missing. Park Service officials report that there are no plans to replace it because of the remoteness of the location. It read as follows:

WIEDRICH'S BATTERY / 1ST NEW YORK LIGHT ARTILLERY / OSBORN'S ARTILLERY / STEINWHER'S 2ND DIVISION / HOWARD'S 11TH CORPS / HOOKER'S COMMAND / 11TH AND 12TH CORPS / ARMY OF THE POTOMAC / NOVEMBER 24, 1863 / NEW YORK

The battery also has a monument on Cemetery Hill at Gettysburg. Wiedrich's Battery I, 1st New York Light Artillery organized at Buffalo, October 1861. Cross Keys. Manassas. Fredericksburg. Chancellorsville. Gettysburg. Chattanooga. Atlanta. March to the Sea. Carolinas Campaign. Grand Review. Mustered out June 23, 1865. Lost 29 officers or enlisted men killed, mortally wounded, or by disease.

Cravens House

2.6.1 Subject: State of New York, Twelfth Corps Column and Common Soldier
Location: N 35 00 51 09 / W 85 20 30 88
Dedicated: 1899
Media: Bronze, granite
Monument is a figure of a Union soldier standing, holding a furled flag, surmounting a shaft and base.

Inscription
[Front (Excerpts)]
[Relief of state seal of New York]

State of New York, Twelfth Corps Column and Common Soldier Statue, Union

TO IRELAND'S (FORMERLY GREENE'S) BRIGADE, / GENTRY'S DIVISION, SLOCUM'S
CORPS, HOOKER'S COMMAND, / 11TH AND 12TH CORPS, ARMY OF THE POTOMAC,
IN THE / BATTLE OF LOOKOUT MOUNTAIN, NOVEMBER 24, 1863 / 60TH NEW YORK
INFANTRY. . . . 78TH NEW YORK INFANTRY. . . . / 102ND NEW YORK INFANTRY / . . . .
137TH NEW YORK INFANTRY. . . . / 149TH NEW YORK INFANTRY / ERECTED BY THE
STATE [STAR BADGE OF THE XII CORPS] OF NEW YORK

EFFECTIVE FORCE OF BRIGADE / 47 OFFICERS 728 ENLISTED MEN
[Order of battle]
TOTAL LOSS, 121. . . .
THIS BRIGADE, EXCEPTING THE 78TH NEW YORK, / LEFT ON PICKET, CROSSED
LOOKOUT CREEK ABOUT 9 A.M., / NOVEMBER 24, 1863, AT LIGHT'S DAWN,
FORMING THE CENTRE / OF THE FIRST LINE OF BATTLE, CONSISTING OF GEARY'S /
DIVISION. AFTER ABOUT TWO MILES, PART OF / WALTHALL'S MISSISSIPPI BRIGADE
WAS CONFRONTED BEHIND / BREASTWORKS, ABOUT 80 RODS IN REAR OF THIS
POSITION. / A SHARP ENGAGEMENT FOLLOWED. BATTLE-FLAGS, A NUMBER
OF PRISONERS AND TWO ABANDONED GUNS WERE CAPTURED. / THE BRIGADE
ADVANCED UNDER FIRE AROUND THE NORTHERN / POINT OF THE MOUNTAIN AND
ACROSS THE PLATEAU TO A / POSITION ABOUT 100 YARDS BEYOND CRAVEN'S [SIC]
HOUSE, WHERE LINE OF BATTLE WAS HALTED ABOUT NOON AND RE-ALIGNED . . .
THE LEFT WAS ATTACKED ABOUT 1 P.M., BY MOORE'S / ALABAMA BRIGADE, WHICH
WAS REPELLED BY THE / 149TH NEW YORK.

This is the preeminent monument on the grounds of the Cravens House. The
monument, in granite with bronze plaques and a bronze seal of the State of
New York, stands forty-five feet high. Its plaques offer a clear narrative of the

actions of the five New York regiments in this vicinity during the battle. The Iowa or Ohio state monument may be more impressive as works of art, but the New York monument is the one that is visible from as far away as Chattanooga. The monument, under state sponsorship was erected at a cost of $10,000, in Vermont granite by the Bureau Brothers of Philadelphia. The bronze statue is by a man known only by his last name, Burbere.

The 60th New York, the "St. Lawrence Regiment," organized at Ogdensburg, mustered in October 30, 1861; mustered out July 17, 1865. Lost 168 officers or enlisted men killed, mortally wounded, or by disease. The 78th New York, "Cameron Highlanders," organized at New York City, April 1862. Consolidated with 102nd New York, July 12, 1864. The 137th New York organized at Binghamton, mustered in September 25, 1862; mustered out June 9, 1865. Lost 294 officers or enlisted men killed, mortally wounded, or by disease. The 149th New York, "the 4th Onondagas," organized at Syracuse, mustered in September 18, 1862; mustered out June 12, 1865. Lost 211 officers or enlisted men killed, mortally wounded, or by disease. Regiments variously engaged at Harpers Ferry, Cedar Mountain, Second Manassas. Antietam. Chancellorsville. Gettysburg. Chattanooga. Atlanta. March to the Sea. Carolinas Campaign. Grand Review.

2.6.2 Subject: 75th Illinois VI, Stele
Location: Terrace near the New York monument   N 35 00 52 02 / W 85 20 30 24
Dedicated: 1899
Media: Bronze, granite
Monument is a stele surmounting a base.

Inscription

ILLINOIS / 75TH INFANTRY. / 3RD BRIGADE—GROSS, / 1ST DIVISION—CRUFT, / 4TH ARMY CORPS—GRANGER

COMMANDED BY / COL. JOHN E. BENNETT / REACHED GENERAL HOOKER'S COMMAND FROM / CHATTANOOGA SOON AFTER DARK NOVEMBER / 24TH. MOVED TO MISSIONARY RIDGE VIA / ROSSVILLE ON THE MORNING OF / NOVEMBER 25TH, 1863. / LOSS 21

Organized at Dixon, mustered in September 2, 1862. Perryville. Stones River. Tullahoma. Chickamauga. Chattanooga. Atlanta. Franklin. Nashville. Mustered out June 12, 1865. Lost 205 officers or enlisted men killed, mortally wounded, or by disease.

2.6.3 Subject: 84th Illinois VI, Stele

Location: Slope near the New York monument   N 35 00 52 39 / W 85 20 30 46

Dedicated: 1899

Media: Bronze, granite

Monument is a stele surmounting a base.

Inscription

ILLINOIS / 84TH INFANTRY. / 3RD BRIGADE—GROSS, / 1ST DIVISION—CRUFT, / 4TH ARMY CORPS—GRANGER

COMMANDED BY / COL. LOUIS H. WATERS / WITH GEARY'S DIVISION NEAR CRAVENS HOUSE / FROM 3 UNTIL 6.30 P.M. NOVEMBER 24TH. / MOVED TO MISSIONARY RIDGE VIA ROSSVILE / ON THE MORNING OF NOVEMBER 25TH, 1863 / LOSS 4.

Organized at Quincy, mustered in September 1, 1862. Perryville. Stones River. Tullahoma. Chattanooga. Atlanta. Franklin. Nashville. Mustered out June 16, 1865. Lost 269 officers or enlisted men killed, mortally wounded, or by disease.

2.6.4 Subject: 92nd Illinois VI, Stele

Location: N 35 00 51 64 / W 85 20 30 88

Dedicated: 1899

Media: Bronze, granite

Monument is a stele surmounting a base.

Inscription

ILLINOIS / 92D INFANTRY / CO. F DETACHED AT GEN. / CRUFT'S HEADQUARTERS / NOV. 24, 1863

Co. F was the only unit from the 92nd Illinois on the battlefield. Organized at Rockford, mustered in September 4, 1862. Served as mounted infantry after July 1863. Atlanta. March to the Sea. Mustered out June 22, 1865.

2.6.5 Subject: 104th Illinois VI, Stele
Location: Slope above the Cravens House Reservation   N 35 00 48 92 / W 85 20 31 30
Dedicated: 1899
Media: Bronze, granite
Monument is a stele surmounting a base.

Inscription

ILLINOIS / 104 TH INFANTRY. / 1ST BRIGADE—CARLIN. / 1ST DIVISION—JOHNSON. / 14TH ARMY CORPS—PALMER.

COMMANDED BY / LT. COL-DOUGLAS HAPEMAN / REACHED GENERAL HOOKER'S COMMAND FROM / CHATTANOOGA SOON AFTER DARK NOVEMBER / 24TH. MOVED TO MISSIONARY RIDGE VIA / ROSSVILLE ON THE MORNING OF / NOVEMBER 25TH, 1863. / LOSS 21

Organized at Ottawa, mustered in August 27, 1862. Action at Hartsville, December 7, 1862: regiment captured, paroled, sent to Camp Douglas, Chicago, as paroled prisoners of war until April 1863, when declared exchanged. Chickamauga. Chattanooga. Atlanta. March to the Sea. Carolinas Campaign. Grand Review. Mustered out July 11, 1865. Lost 194 officers or enlisted men killed, mortally wounded, or by disease.

· Another monument to the 104th stands on Missionary Ridge (2.16.7).

2.6.6 Subject: State of Ohio, Column
Location: Cravens House   N 35 00 47 90 / W 85 20 28 60
Installed or dedicated: October 17, 1917
Media: Bronze, granite
Monument is a sculpture of an eagle, in bronze, surmounting a granite column set atop a two-tiered granite base.

Inscription
[Front (Excerpts)]
[State seal of Ohio] / [Woman, relief]
OHIO

ERECTED BY THE STATE OF OHIO IN MEMORY OF THE OHIO TROOPS THAT WERE ENGAGED IN THE BATTLE OF LOOKOUT MOUNTAIN, TENNESSEE NOV. 24, 1863. / 1ST BRIGADE 2ND DIVISION 12TH ARMY CORPS / 5TH OHIO COL. / 7TH OHIO COL. / 66TH OHIO / 1ST BRIGADE 1ST DIVISION 14TH ARMY CORPS / 2ND OHIO COL. / 33RD OHIO / 94TH OHIO / OHIO

[Common soldier, relief]

ERECTED BY THE STATE OF OHIO IN MEMORY OF THE OHIO TROOPS THAT WERE ENGAGED IN THE BATTLE OF LOOKOUT MOUNTAIN, TENNESSEE NOV. 24, 1863. / 2ND BRIGADE 1ST DIVISION 4TH ARMY CORPS / 40TH OHIO / 51ST OHIO / 99TH

Sponsored by veterans of three brigades to commemorate their participation
in the battle of Lookout Mountain, there was enormous difficulty in assembling the impressive monument at this mountainside site. The date for dedicating it was pushed back several times; it was also delayed by US involvement
in World War I.

The monument is a shaft set on a two-tiered base and surmounted by an
eagle in bronze. The bronze tablet displays a relief of a female figure, symbolic
of peace; the rear tablet displays a relief of a common soldier. The approximate
height of the whole of the monument is seventy-five feet. Erected at a cost of
$20,000, the Bunnel Company of Cleveland, Ohio, served as founder.

State of Ohio, Column

2.6.7 Subject: State of Iowa, Column and Common Soldier Statue, Union

Location: N 35 00 51 57 / W 85 20 26 34

Installed: 1903; dedicated: November 19, 1906

Medium: Granite

Monument is a Union soldier surmounting a shaft and base.

Inscription

[Front (Excerpts)]

IOWA / IOWA REMEMBERS HER PATRIOT SONS / WHO WENT FORTH AT THE CALL OF DUTY / TO HONOR THEIR COUNTRY / IN THE DREADFUL CARNAGE OF WAR / 4TH INFANTRY 9TH INFANTRY

IOWA / IN THE BATTLE ABOVE THE CLOUDS / WILLIAMSON'S BRIGADE / OSTERHAUS' DIVISION / 15TH ARMY CORPS / LOOKOUT MOUNTAIN NOVEMBER 24TH 1863 / MISSIONARY RIDGE NOVEMBER 25TH 1863 / RINGOLD [SIC], GA. NOVEMBER 27TH, 1863 / 1ST BATTERY / FORTY ROUNDS

IOWA / WILLIAMSON'S BRIGADE ASSISTED / IN THE CAPTURE OF THIS POSITION / AND WAS ENGAGED / ON THE UNION RIGHT AND FRONT / THROUGHOUT THE AFTERNOON AND EVENING. / THE 31ST IOWA ON THE RIGHT / REACHING THE FOOT OF THE PALISADES / 25TH INFANTRY

IOWA / MAY THE HEROISM / WHICH DEDICATED THIS LOFTY FIELD / TO IMMORTAL RENOWN / BE AS IMPERISHABLE / AS THE UNION IS ETERNAL / 30TH INFANTRY 31ST INFANTRY

"Iowa Remembers" is a theme of the state of Iowa's monument on Lookout Mountain, which stands just below the Cravens House, at the farthest point reached by Iowa infantry during the battle of November 25, 1863.

Erected at a cost of $8,000, the monument's overall height is seventy-two feet. The figure of the common soldier is life-size; the base has a width of twenty by twenty feet. The Van Amringe Granite Company served as fabricator. A second Iowa monument stands on the Sherman Reservation (2.9.7), and a third stands at Rossville Gap, on the Georgia side of the battlefield (2.16.11).

The 4th Iowa organized at Council Bluffs, mustered in August 8, 1861. Lost 402 officers or enlisted men killed, mortally wounded, or by disease.

The 9th Iowa organized at Dubuque, mustered in September 24, 1861. Lost 386 officers or enlisted men killed, mortally wounded, or by disease.

The 1st Battery Light Artillery organized at Burlington, August 17, 1861. Lost 61 officers or enlisted men killed, mortally wounded, or by disease.

The 25th Iowa organized at Mount Pleasant, mustered in September 27, 1862. Lost 274 officers or enlisted men killed, mortally wounded, or by disease.

The 30th Iowa organized at Keokuk, mustered in September 20, 1862. Lost 317 officers or enlisted men killed, mortally wounded, or by disease.

The 31st Iowa organized at Davenport, mustered in October 13, 1862. Lost 303 officers or enlisted men killed, mortally wounded, or by disease.

Cravens House, the Terraces; Left to right: Monuments to the 28th and 147th Pennsylvania VI, 96th and 59th Illinois VI

These units mustered out June–July 1865. Service included Pea Ridge, Vicksburg, Chattanooga, Atlanta, March to the Sea, Carolinas Campaign, and Grand Review.

The Terraces above the Cravens House

2.7.1 Subject: 28th Pennsylvania VI, Stele
Location: N 35 00 46 55 / W 85 20 32 02
Installed or dedicated: 1897
Media: Bronze, granite
Monument is a granite stele surmounted by a granite star.

Inscription

[Front]
28TH, PENNSYLVANIA INFANTRY / 1ST, BRIGADE / 2ND, DIVISION / 12TH, CORPS
[Fatigue cap, sculpture]

[Bronze relief of state seal of Pennsylvania]

MUSTERED IN AT PHILADELPHIA, PA., JUNE 28TH, 1861. / RE-ENLISTED AS VETERAN VOLUNTEERS AT WAHATCHIE, TENNESSEE, DECEMBER 23, 1863 / MUSTERED OUT AT PHILADELPHIA, PA, JULY 18TH, 1865. PARTICIPATED IN THE CHATTANOOGA CAMPAIGN OF NOVEMBER 1863. ASSAULT AND CAPTURE OF LOOKOUT MOUNTAIN NOVEMBER 24TH, 1863. ROSSVILLE GAP NOVEMBER 25TH, 1863. / ENGAGED AT PEA VINE CREEK NOVEMBER 26TH, 1863. ASSAULT AND CAPTURE OF (TAYLOR'S RIDGE) RINGGOLD NOVEMBER 27TH, 1863. / IN THE CAMPAIGN: KILLED AND DIED OF WOUNDS 13, WOUNDED 21, TOTAL 34.

[Bronze relief of XII Corps' star badge]

The contractor and designer was J. E. Harrison & Co., Adrian, Michigan; the monument was erected at a cost of $4,040, and stands eight feet, six inches by nine feet, six inches.

The "Goldstream Regiment": Antietam. Chancellorsville. Gettysburg. Chattanooga. Atlanta. March to the Sea. Carolinas Campaign. Grand Review. Mustered out July 18, 1865. Lost 284 officers or enlisted men killed, mortally wounded, or by disease.

2.7.2 Subject: 96th Illinois VI, Stele
Location: N 35 00 46 72 / W 85 20 33 28
Dedicated: 1899
Media: Bronze, granite
Monument is a stele surmounting a base.

Inscription

ILLINOIS / 96TH INFANTRY. / 2ND BRIGADE—WHITAKER. / 1ST DIVISION—CRUFT. / 4TH ARMY CORPS—GRANGER

COMMANDED BY / COL. THOMAS E. CHAMPION / WITH ITS BRIGADE TEMPORARILY ATTACHED TO / GEARY'S DIVISION. AMONG THE FIRST TROOPS / TO OCCUPY THE CREST OF LOOKOUT MOUNTAIN / WHERE THEY REMAINED DURING / NOVEMBER 25TH, 1863 / LOSS 15

Organized at Rockford, mustered in September 6, 1862. Tullahoma. Chickamauga. Chattanooga. Atlanta. Franklin. Nashville. Mustered out June 10, 1865. Lost 241 officers or enlisted men killed, mortally wounded, or by disease.

2.7.3 Subject: 147th Pennsylvania VI, Stele
Location: N 35 00 46 06 / W 85 20 32 74
Installed or dedicated: n.a.
Media: Bronze, granite
Monument is a granite stele surmounting a base.

Inscriptions

[Front]

THE COMMONWEALTH OF PENNSYLVANIA / TO HER / 147TH INFANTRY REGIMENT / COLONEL ARIO PARDEE, COMMANDING / 1ST BRIGADE / 2D DIVISION / 12TH CORPS.

[Relief of state seal of Pennsylvania]

THIS REGIMENT WAS TRANSFERRED FROM THE ARMY OF THE / POTOMAC TO THE ARMIES OPERATING NEAR CHATTANOOGA, / TENNESSEE, ARRIVING AT WAHATCHIE OCTOBER 29TH, 1863. / IT PARTICIPATED WITH GENERAL GEARY'S WHITE STAR / DIVISION IN THE CAPTURE OF LOOKOUT MOUNTAIN, / NOVEMBER 24, 1863. ON THE 25TH, CROSSED THE / CHATTANOOGA VALLEY TO THE FOOT OF MISSIONARY RIDGE, / NORTH OF ROSSVILLE GAP, GAINING THE CREST ABOUT / THREE-FOURTHS OF A MILE NORTH OF THAT POINT, AND / ASSISTING IN THE CAPTURE OF MANY PRISONERS DURING / AND AFTER THE CHARGE OF THE ARMY OF THE CUMBERLAND / WHICH DROVE THE ENEMY FROM THE RIDGE, THEN FOLLOWED / THE RETREATING CONFEDERATE ARMY ON THE 26TH, AND 27TH, / ENGAGING IN ITS FINAL DEFEAT AT RINGGOLD, GEORGIA.

Erected by the Smith Granite Company at a cost of $1,500, the monument stands seven feet, six inches by four feet, three inches by ten feet, six inches.

Organized October 10, 1862, from elements of the 28th Pennsylvania. Fredericksburg. Chancellorsville. Gettysburg. Chattanooga. Atlanta. March to the Sea. Carolinas Campaign. Grand Review. Mustered out July 15, 1865. Lost 142 officers or enlisted men killed, mortally wounded, or by disease.

2.7.4 Subject: 59th Illinois VI, Stele
Location: N 35 00 47 15 / W 85 20 33 62
Dedicated: 1899
Media: Bronze, granite
Monument is a stele surmounting a base.

Inscription

ILLINOIS / 59TH INFANTRY. / 3RD BRIGADE—GROSE, / 1ST DIVISION—CRUFT, / 4TH ARMY CORPS—GRANGER

COMMANDED BY / MAJOR CLAYTON HALE. / WITH GEARY'S DIVISION NEAR CRAVENS' HOUSE / FROM 3 UNTIL 6.30 P.M. NOVEMBER 24 TH. / MOVED TO MISSIONARY RIDGE VIA ROSSVILLE / ON THE MORNING OF NOVEMBER 25 TH, 1863. / LOSS 18.

Organized at St. Louis as 9th Missouri VI, September 18, 1861; designation changed to 59th Illinois, February 1862. Pea Ridge. Corinth. Perryville. Stones River. Tullahoma. Chattanooga. Atlanta. Franklin. Nashville. Mustered out December 1865. Lost 230 officers or enlisted men killed, mortally wounded, or by disease.

2.7.5 Subject: 13th Illinois VI, Stele
Location: N 35 00 47 42 / W 85 20 33 00
Dedicated: 1899
Media: Bronze, granite
Monument is a stele surmounting a base.

Inscription

ILLINOIS / 13TH INFANTRY / 1ST BRIGADE—WOODS / 1ST DIVISION–OSTERHAUS / 15TH CORPS—BLAIR

COMMANDED BY / LT. COL. FREDERIC W. PARTRIDGE / WITH GEARY'S DIVISION NEAR CRAVENS' HOUSE / FROM 3 UNTIL 6.39 P.M. NOVEMBER 24TH. / MOVED TO MISSIONARY RIDGE VIA ROSSVILLE / ON THE MORNING OF NOVEMBER 25TH 1863. / LOSS 63.

The 13th Illinois, "Fremont's Grey Hounds," organized at Dixon. Mustered in April 1861; mustered into Federal service by Capt. John Pope, May 24, 1861, the first three-year regiment from Illinois. Fremont's Missouri Campaign. Vicksburg. Chattanooga. Mustered out June 18, 1864, expiration of term. Lost 192 officers or enlisted men killed, mortally wounded, or by disease.

Missionary Ridge

Pennsylvania Reservation

Glass Street and North Crest Road: Regiments here were not in action at this site, but elsewhere. The monuments were placed here for access.

2.8.1 Subject: 73rd Pennsylvania VI, Shaft
Location: N 35 04 01 31 / W 85 14 35 96
Installed or dedicated: 1903
Media: Bronze, granite
Monument is a granite shaft surmounted by a sculpture of the half-moon badge of the XI Corps.

Inscription

[Inscribed star badge of the XII Corps] [State seal of Pennsylvania]

The 73d Regiment originally known as the 45th Pennsylvania was recruited in Philadelphia; organized August 8th, 1861, entered the service September 19th, 1861; and was attached to the army of the Potomac. After participating in the battle of Gettysburg, Pennsylvania, was ordered to Chattanooga, Tennessee, September, 1863. On November 25th, 1863, assisted in the storming of these hills, then moved to this position. Losses in killed, wounded; captured, 181. / January 1864, re-enlisted as a veteran regiment and joined the 2d Brigade, 2d Division, 20th Army Corps. / From Raleigh, N.C. it marched to Alexandria, Va. where on the 14th of July, 1865, it was mustered out of service.

73RD REGT. PENN. VET. VOL. / 1ST BRIGADE—2ND DIVISION / 11TH ARMY CORPS

[Inscribed half-moon badge of the XI Corps]

[Inscribed star badge of the XII Corps]

Service notes: Cross Keys. Cedar Mountain. Bull Run. Fredericksburg. Chancellorsville. Gettysburg. Chattanooga. Mostly captured on November 25 at Tunnel Hill. Remaining elements: Atlanta. March to the Sea. Carolinas Campaign. Grand Review. Lost 216 officers or enlisted men killed, mortally wounded, or by disease.

The monument stands four feet, six inches by four feet, six inches by thirteen feet, five inches. It was erected by the Joss Brothers of Quincy, Massachusetts, at a cost of $1,500.

- Park Service notes record that this regiment, veterans of Second Manassas, Antietam, and Gettysburg, "charged Confederate rifle pits in the hills at the north end of Missionary Ridge. . . . Nearly the entire regiment was killed, wounded, or captured. Only twenty-five men avoided capture."

73rd Pennsylvania VI, Shaft. A staid monument, like others here, but near the site of where the regiment was cut off from the rest of its brigade Another example of monumentation understating—practically by definition of the genre—the import of the deeds done on the battlefield.

2.8.2 Subject: 26th Illinois VI, Stele
Location: Pennsylvania Reservation, Glass Street and North Crest Road
Dedicated: 1899
Media: Bronze, granite
Monument is a stele surmounting a base.

Inscription

ILLINOIS / 26TH INFANTRY. / 1ST BRIGADE—LOOMIS, / 4TH DIVISION—EWING, / 15TH ARMY CORPS—BLAIR.

COMMANDED BY / LIEUT. COL. R. A. GILLMORE. / PASSED TO THE RIGHT OF THIS POINT / ABOUT 1 P.M. NOVEMBER 25, 1863, AND / BECAME ENGAGED ON OR NEAR THE / RAILROAD SOUTHWEST OF THIS [SIC] / LOSS 93.

Organized at Camp Butler, mustered in August 31, 1861. Island No. 10. Corinth. Vicksburg. Chattanooga. Atlanta. March to the Sea. Carolinas Campaign. Grand Review. Mustered out July 28, 1865. Lost 286 officers or enlisted men killed, mortally wounded, or by disease.

2.8.3 Subject: 90th Illinois VI, Stele
Location: Pennsylvania Reservation, Glass Street and North Crest Road
Dedicated: 1899
Media: Bronze, granite
Monument is a stele surmounting a base.

Inscription

ILLINOIS / 90TH INFANTRY. / 1ST BRIGADE—LOOMIS, / 4TH DIVISION—EWING, / 15TH ARMY CORPS—BLAIR.

COMMANDED BY / COL. TIMOTHY O'MEARA KILLED / LIEUT. COL. OWEN STUART. / PASSED TO THE RIGHT OF THIS POINT / ABOUT 1 P.M. NOVEMBER 25, 1863, AND / BECAME ENGAGED ABOUT 220 YARDS / SOUTHWEST, BETWEEN THIS AND / THE RAILROAD. LOSS 117.

Organized at Chicago, mustered in September 7, 1862. Vicksburg. Chattanooga. Atlanta. March to the Sea. Carolinas Campaign. Mustered out June 10, 1865. Lost 148 officers or enlisted men killed, mortally wounded, or by disease.

Sherman Reservation

At this writing the Sherman Reservation is closed to automobile traffic. For visitors, parking is available near the entry point; visitors must dismount and move on foot approximately a quarter mile to the site, either by a trail to the hilltop or the service road.

2.9.1 Subject: 10th Missouri VI, Union, Shaft
Location: Adjacent service road, slope   N35 04 08 06 / W 85 14 28 60
Installed or dedicated: circa 1896
Medium: Marble
Monument is a stele surmounting a base.

Inscription

10TH MO. INFANTRY / U.S.A. / IN ACTION NEAR TUNNEL / NOV. 25, 1863 / CO. E 24TH MO. / INFANTRY

Organized at St. Louis, August 1861. Corinth. Grant's Central Mississippi Campaign. Vicksburg. Chattanooga. Regiment mustered out October 31, 1864, expiration of term. Lost 331 officers or enlisted men killed, mortally wounded, or by disease.

2.9.2 Subject: 26th Missouri VI, Union, Shaft
Location: Adjacent service road, slope, Crest Road Extension   N35 04 10 42 /
W 85 14 25 58
Installed or dedicated: circa 1896
Medium: Marble
Monument is a stele surmounting a base.

Inscription
26TH MO. INFANTRY / U.S.A. / ON THIS LINE / NOV. 25, 1863

Organized in Missouri at-large, December 1861. Island No. 10. Corinth. Grant's
Central Mississippi Campaign. Vicksburg. Chattanooga. March to the Sea.
Carolinas Campaign. Grand Review. Regiment mustered out August 13, 1865.
Lost 303 officers or enlisted men killed, mortally wounded, or by disease.

2.9.3 Subject: 93rd Illinois VI, Stele
Location: On west hillside service road, slope   N35 04 10 10 / W 85 14 26 74
Dedicated: 1899
Media: Bronze, granite
Monument is a stele surmounting a base.

Inscription
ILLINOIS / 93RD INFANTRY. / 3RD BRIGADE—MATHIES, / 4TH DIVISION—JOHN E.
SMITH, / 17TH ARMY CORPS—MCPHERSON.

[Bronze plaque: removed, missing]

· The missing plaque read as follows:

COMMANDED BY / COL. HOLDEN PUTMAN (KILLED) / LIEUT. COL. NICHOLS C.
BUSHWELL / REACHED THIS POSITION ABOUT 1.30 P.M. / NOVEMBER 25, 1863,
WITHDRAWING ABOUT 4 P.M. / LOSS 93.

The location of this monument—a steep slope, in dense brush above the service road—is a particularly difficult place to reach. However, it marks the spot
where Col. Holden Putman was killed in action and is suggestive of the ferocity of the action at this site as well as an intimation of the purpose of these
commemorations.

Regiment organized at Chicago, mustered in October 13, 1862. Central
Mississippi Campaign. Vicksburg. Chattanooga. March to the Sea. Carolinas
Campaign. Grand Review. Mustered out June 23, 1865. Lost 294 officers or
enlisted men killed, mortally wounded, or by disease.

93rd Illinois VI, Stele

2.9.4 Subject: Battery D, 1st Missouri Vol. Artillery, Union, Shaft
Location: On west hillside service road, slope   N35 04 10 76 / W 85 14 26 96
Installed or dedicated: n.a.
Medium: n.a.
Monument is a stele surmounting a base.

Inscription

BATTERY D. 1ST MO. / LIGHT ARTILLERY / U.S.A. / WAS IN ACTION 1200 YDS. / NORTHWEST OF THIS POINT

Organized at St. Louis, from 1st Missouri VI, September 1, 1861. Fort Henry. Fort Donelson. Shiloh. Corinth. Chattanooga. Service until April 1865. Losses not reported.

2.9.5 Subject: 56th Illinois VI, Stele
Location: On west hillside, service road, slope   N35 04 12 80 / W 85 14 23 26
Dedicated: 1899
Media: Bronze, granite
Monument is a stele surmounting a base.

Inscription

ILLINOIS / 56TH INFANTRY. / 2ND BRIGADE—RAUM, / 4TH DIVISION—JOHN E. SMITH, / 17TH ARMY CORPS—MCPHERSON.

[Bronze plaque: removed, missing]

· The missing plaque read as follows:

COMMANDED BY / MAJ. PICKNEY J. WELSH / WAS IN THE SECOND LINE OF THE BRIGADE / IN THE ASSAULT OF NOV. 25TH, 1863, / AND ASSISTED IN REPULSING THE FINAL / ATTACK OF THE ENEMY / LOSS 19.

Organized at Shawneetown, mustered in February 27, 1862. Corinth. Vicksburg. Chattanooga. Atlanta. March to the Sea. Carolinas Campaign. Grand Review. Mustered out August 12, 1865. Lost 389 officers or enlisted men killed, mortally wounded, or by disease.

Sherman Reservation, the Crest and Plateau

2.9.6 Subject: 40th Illinois VI, Stele
Location: Left of Iowa facing north   N 35 04 14 13 / W 85 14 23 20
Dedicated: 1899
Media: Bronze, granite
Monument is a stele surmounting a base.

Inscription

ILLINOIS / 40TH INFANTRY. / 2ND BRIGADE—CORSE, / 4TH DIVISION—EWING, / 15TH ARMY CORPS—BLAIR.

[Bronze plaque: removed, missing]

Organized at Springfield, mustered in August 10, 1861. Shiloh. Corinth. Vicksburg. Atlanta. March to the Sea. Carolinas Campaign. Grand Review. Mustered out July 24, 1865. Lost 246 officers or enlisted men killed, mortally wounded, or by disease.

- The inscription of the missing plaque is not archived or was not accessible.

2.9.7 Subject: State of Iowa, Column and Common Soldier Statue, Union
Location: N 35 04 13 99 / W 85 14 22 38
Installed: 1903; dedicated: November 19, 1906
Medium: Granite
Monument is a granite figure of a Union soldier holding a flag, surmounting a shaft and base.

Inscription
[Front (Excerpts)]
IOWA DEDICATES THIS MONUMENT / IN HONOR OF HER SONS / WHO ON THIS AND OTHER FIELDS / PROVED THEMSELVES WORTHY SONS / OF PATRIOTIC SIRES / IOWA / YOU HAVE MADE IT A HIGH PRIVILEGE / TO BE / A CITIZEN OF IOWA.

THIS MONUMENT MARKS THE POSITION / CARRIED BY THE 6TH IOWA / IN THE ASSAULT OF CORSE'S BRIGADE / THE MORNING OF NOV. 25, 1863. / REPEATED CHARGES WERE MADE LATER / ON THE ENEMY'S LINE NORTH OF THE TUNNEL. / THE 5TH 10TH AND 17TH IOWA / WERE HOTLY ENGAGED AND LOST HEAVILY / ON THE IMMEDIATE RIGHT.

IOWA LOSSES ON SHERMAN HEIGHTS / NOVEMBER 25, 1863 / KILLED-WOUNDED-
MISSING-TOTAL [291]
5TH INFANTRY / 3RD BRIGADE, 2ND DIVISION, 17TH ARMY CORPS / 6TH INFANTRY /
2ND BRIGADE, 4TH DIVISION, 15TH ARMY CORPS / 10TH INFANTRY / 3RD BRIGADE,
2ND DIVISION, 17TH ARMY CORPS / 17TH INFANTRY / 3RD BRIGADE, 2ND DIVISION,
17TH ARMY CORPS

This is the most prominent monument on the Sherman Reservation and is an eloquent symbol of the ferocity of the action at this somewhat neglected site. Federal assaults were not successful in this area. The ground was won only in conjunction with successful assaults by Union troops farther south along Missionary Ridge.

The life-size figure of a Union soldier holding a flag in both hands surmounts a column approximately fifty feet high; the base is approximately six feet by sixteen feet square. The Van Amringe Granite Company of Boston served as fabricator. The monument was erected at a cost of $8,000.

The 5th Iowa organized at Burlington, July 15, 1861. Fremont's Missouri Campaign. Island No. 10. Corinth. Iuka. Corinth. Central Mississippi Campaign. Fort Pemberton. Vicksburg. Chattanooga. Consolidated with 5th Iowa Cavalry, August 1864. Lost 250 officers or enlisted men killed, mortally wounded, or by disease.

The 6th Iowa organized at Burlington, mustered in July 17, 1861. Fremont's Missouri Campaign. Shiloh. Corinth. Central Mississippi Campaign. Regiment mounted. Vicksburg. Chattanooga. Atlanta. March to the Sea. Carolinas Campaign. Grand Review. Mustered out July 21, 1865. Lost 280 officers or enlisted men killed, mortally wounded, or by disease.

The 10th Iowa organized at Iowa City and Montezuma, September 1861. Island No. 10. Corinth. Iuka. Central Mississippi Campaign. Vicksburg. Chattanooga. March to the Sea. Carolinas Campaign. Grand Review. Mustered out August 15, 1865. Lost 235 officers or enlisted men killed, mortally wounded, or by disease.

The 17th Iowa organized at Keokuk, mustered in April 16, 1862. Corinth. Iuka. Grant's Central Mississippi Campaign. Vicksburg. Chattanooga. Attack on Tilton, Georgia, October 1864: most of regiment captured. Remnant: Carolinas Campaign. Grand Review. Mustered out July 25, 1865. Lost 194 officers or enlisted men killed, mortally wounded, or by disease.

- Historian William C. Lowe notes that the parks commission would not permit the Iowa monuments commission to inscribe a tribute to the women of Iowa. The inscription would have read, "In memory of the brave women of Iowa who met their country's call by offering on the altar of freedom their prayers, their hearts, and their honor." It was replaced with the badge of the 15th Army Corps.

State of Iowa, Column and Common Soldier Statue, Union

2.9.8 Subject: 103rd Illinois VI, Stele
Location: Right of Iowa monument, facing north   N 35 04 14 06 / W 85 14 22 02
Dedicated: 1899
Media: Bronze, granite
Monument is a stele surmounting a base.

Inscription
ILLINOIS / 103RD INFANTRY. / 2ND BRIGADE—CORSE, / 4TH DIVISION—EWING, / 15TH ARMY CORPS—BLAIR.

[Bronze plaque: removed, missing]

Organized at Peoria, mustered in October 2, 1862. Grant's Central Mississippi Campaign. Vicksburg. Chattanooga. March to the Sea. Carolinas Campaign. Grand Review. Mustered out June 1865. Lost 8 officers, 87 enlisted men killed or mortally wounded; 1 officer, 153 enlisted men by disease. Total 249.

· The missing plaque read as follows:
COMMANDED BY / COL. WILARD A. DICKERSON / REACHED THIS POSITION ABOUT 11:30 A.M. / NOVEMBER 25, 1863, ADVANCED WITHIN 50 STEPS / OF CONFEDERATE BATTERIES IN ITS FRONT / AND RETIRED UNDER CREST OF HILL ABOUT 4 P.M. / LOSS 89

2.9.9 Subject: 6th Missouri VI, Union, Shaft
Location: Plateau   N 35 04 16 85 / W 85 14 21 80
Installed or dedicated: circa 1896
Medium: Marble
Monument is a stele surmounting a base.

Inscription
6TH MISSOURI INFANTRY / U.S.A. / IN ACTION 1000 YARDS N. E. / OF THIS POSITION / NOV. 25, 1863

Organized at St. Louis, July 9, 1861. Fremont's Missouri Campaign. Corinth. Central Mississippi Campaign. Vicksburg. Chattanooga. Atlanta. March to the Sea. Carolinas Campaign. Grand Review. Mustered out August 17, 1865. Lost 269 officers or enlisted men killed, mortally wounded, or by disease.

2.9.10 Subject: 8th Missouri VI, Union, Shaft
Location: Plateau   N 35 04 10 42 / W 85 14 25 58
Installed or dedicated: circa 1896
Medium: Marble
Monument is a stele surmounting a base.

Inscription

8TH MO. INFANTRY / U.S.A. / IN ACTION 1000 YARDS / EAST OF THIS POSITION / NOV. 25, 1863

Organized at St. Louis, August 14, 1861. Fort Donelson. Shiloh. Corinth. Grant's Central Mississippi Campaign. Vicksburg. Chattanooga. Atlanta. Carolinas Campaign. Grand Review. Mustered out August 14, 1865. Lost 206 officers or enlisted men killed, mortally wounded, or by disease.

2.9.11 Subject: 55th Illinois VI, Stele
Location: Plateau   N 35 04 16 98 / W 85 14 21 46
Dedicated: 1899
Media: Bronze, granite
Monument is a stele surmounting a base.

Inscription

ILLINOIS / 55TH INFANTRY. / 1ST BRIGADE—GILES A. SMITH, / 2ND DIVISION—MORGAN L. SMITH, / 15TH ARMY CORPS—BLAIR.

[Bronze plaque: removed, missing]

· The missing plaque read as follows:

COMMANDED BY / COL. OSCAR MALMBERG / REACHED THIS POSITION ABOUT / SUNSET NOVEMBER 25, 1863

Organized at Springfield, mustered in August 10, 1861. Shiloh. Corinth. Vicksburg. Chattanooga. Atlanta. March to the Sea; Carolinas Campaign. Grand Review. Mustered out July 24, 1865. Lost 246 officers or enlisted men killed, mortally wounded, or by disease.

North Slope of Sherman Reservation

2.9.12 Subject: 116th Illinois VI, Stele
Location: N 35 04 09 77 / W 85 14 26 18
Dedicated: 1899
Media: Bronze, granite
Monument is a stele surmounting a base.

Inscription

ILLINOIS / 116TH INFANTRY / 1ST BRIGADE—GILES A. SMITH. / 2ND DIVISION—MORGAN L. SMITH. / 15TH ARMY CORPS—BLAIR.

[Bronze plaque: removed, missing]

· The missing plaque read as follows:

COMMANDED BY COL. JAMES F. BOYD / REACHED THIS POSITION ABOUT / SUNSET, NOVEMBER 15, 1863

Organized at Decatur, mustered in September 30, 1862. Central Mississippi Campaign. Vicksburg. Chattanooga. Atlanta. March to the Sea. Carolinas Campaign. Grand Review. Mustered out June 7, 1865. Lost 295 officers or enlisted men killed, mortally wounded, or by disease.

2.9.13 Subject: 127th Illinois VI, Stele
Location: N 35 04 19 28 / W 85 14 19 26
Dedicated: 1899
Media: Bronze, granite
Monument is a stele surmounting a base.

Inscription

ILLINOIS / 127TH INFANTRY / 1ST BRIGADE—GILES A. SMITH. / 2ND DIVISION—MORGAN L. SMITH. / 15TH ARMY CORPS—BLAIR.

[Bronze plaque: removed, missing]

· The missing plaque read as follows:

COMMANDED BY / LIEUT. COL. FRANK S. CURTISS. / CROSSED THE TENNESSEE RIVER ON / THE AFTERNOON OF NOVEMBER 25, / 1863 AND WAS HELD IN RESERVE

Organized at Camp Douglas, mustered in September 6, 1862. Grant's Mississippi Central Campaign. Vicksburg. Chattanooga. Atlanta. March to the Sea. Carolinas Campaign. Grand Review. Mustered out June 4, 1865. Lost 218 officers or enlisted men killed, mortally wounded, or by disease.

2.9.14 Subject: 63rd Illinois VI, Stele
Location: N 35 04 19 46 / W 85 14 18 38
Dedicated: 1899
Media: Bronze, granite
Monument is a stele surmounting a base.

Inscription

ILLINOIS / 63RD INFANTRY. / 1ST BRIGADE—ALEXANDER, / 2ND DIVISION—JOHN E. SMITH, / 17TH ARMY CORPS—MCPHERSON.

[Bronze plaque: removed, missing]

· The missing plaque read as follows:

COMMANDED BY / COL. JOSEPH B. MCCOWN / REACHED THIS POSITION ABOUT / SUNSET, NOVEMBER 25, 1863.

Organized at Camp Dubois, mustered in April 10, 1862. Central Mississippi Campaign. Vicksburg. Chattanooga. March to the Sea. Carolinas Campaign. Grand Review. Mustered out July 13, 1865. Lost 144 officers or enlisted men killed, mortally wounded, or by disease.

2.9.15 Subject: Barrett's Battery, Missouri, CSA, Shaft
Location: Crest Road, south gate of Sherman Reservation   N 35 03 57 17 /
W 85 14 26 18
Installed or dedicated: circa 1896
Medium: Marble
Monument is a stele surmounting a base.

Inscription
BARRETT'S BATTERY / C.S.A. / COMMANDED BY / ISAAC LIGHTNER / MORTALLY
WOUNDED / ON CREST OF HILL / NOV. 25, 1863

There are many iron NPS stelae on the Chattanooga battlefield, but this is
the only single monument to an individual Confederate unit in Chattanooga.

"Barrett" is Captain Overton Barrett. Barrett's Battery—the 10th Missouri
Light Artillery—mustered into military service on April 1, 1862. Service:
Pea Ridge, Corinth, Perryville, Stones River, Tullahoma, Chickamauga,
Chattanooga, Atlanta. Last engaged at the battle of Columbus, Georgia, April
16, 1865.

Historian James E. McGhee notes that at Chattanooga the battery fought
on the right flank with Brig. Gen. Preston Smith's brigade and then on the
left with Maj. Gen. Patrick Cleburne's Division. It also engaged Union troops
on the right center and formed part of the rear guard during the retreat from
Missionary Ridge.

Phelps Reservation

2.10.1 Subject: Col. Edward H. Phelps, Shaft
Location: Opposite 280 North Crest Road   N 35 02 59 65 / W 85 15 08 24
Installed or dedicated: 1908
Media: Bronze, granite
Monument is an inverted cannon barrel surmounting a base.

Inscription
COL. E. H. PHELPS / MORTALLY WOUNDED NEAR / THIS SPOT / ABOUT 5:30 P.M. /
NOV. 25TH / 1863

The monument, which features a cannonball surmounting an upright cannon
tube, stands near the site where Col. Edward H. Phelps was killed in action.
Phelps commanded the 3rd Brigade, XIV Corps at the time (4th Kentucky, 10th
Kentucky, 74th Indiana, 38th Ohio VI). Park historian James Ogden states that
the original monument here was a shell pyramid design similar to those that
mark the headquarters locations at Chickamauga. It was removed and replaced
with the present monument in 1908, when North Crest Road was widened.

Col. Edward H. Phelps, Shaft

De Long Reservation

2.11.1 Subject: 2nd Minnesota VI, Obelisk
Location: 1.9 miles south of the Sherman Reservation   N 35 02 34 22 /
W 85 15 15 58
Installed or dedicated: 1896
Media: Bronze, granite
Monument is a four-sided granite shaft.

Inscription

[Front (Excerpts)]
ERECTED / BY / THE STATE OF MINNESOTA / 1893. . . . / THE SECOND MINNESOTA
/ REGIMENT OF VETERAN VOLUNTEER / INFANTRY DEPLOYED AS SKIRMISHERS /
(COVERING VAN DERVEER'S BRIGADE) ATTACKED / AND CAPTURED THE LINE OF
BREASTWORKS / AT THE FOOT OF THIS RIDGE ABOUT 4 O'CLOCK P.M. NOV. 25, 1863,
AND SOON / AFTERWARDS PARTICIPATED WITH THE BRIGADE IN THE SUCCESSFUL
ASSAULT OF / THE MAIN RIDGE AND IN THE SUBSEQUENT FIGHTING THEREON
WITH THE ENEMY COMING / FROM THE NORTH END OF THE RIDGE. THE REGIMENT
CAPTURED 14 PRISONERS / AND 2 CANNON AND LOST 8 MEN KILLED AND 31
WOUNDED: OF THE SEVEN MEN IN THE COLOR / GUARD, ALL BUT ONE WERE KILLED
OR WOUNDED.

BARD'S DIVISION / MAJ. GEN. A. BAIRD COMD'G / VAN DERVEER'S BRIGADE / 2D
BRIG. 3D DIV. 14TH A.C. / 2D MINNESOTA VOLUNTEERS / 9TH OHIO VOLUNTEERS
/ 35TH OHIO VOLUNTEERS / 87TH ILLINOIS VOLUNTEERS / 75TH ILLINOIS
VOLUNTEERS / 101ST ILLINOIS VOLUNTEERS / 105TH OHIO VOLUNTEERS

4 KILLED IN ASSAULT OF MISSION RIDGE / NOVEMBER 25, 1863 / [LIST OF TEN MEN]
/ COMPANIES F & G ABSENT ON DETACHED / SERVICE—185 MEN ENGAGED

2nd Minnesota VI, Obelisk

This imposing shaft—standing alone in a parklike setting—was erected at a cost of $6,000 and stands eight feet by eight feet by three feet, six inches.

It was here that the 2nd Minnesota overran Waters's Alabama Battery, which was supported by Deas's Brigade of Hindman's Division. Hand-to-hand fighting broke out. Five of the battery's six artillery pieces were captured.

The 2nd Minnesota organized at Fort Snelling, mustered in August 1861. Mill Springs. Corinth. Perryville. Tullahoma. Chickamauga. Chattanooga. Atlanta. March to the Sea. Carolinas Campaign. Grand Review. Mustered out July 11, 1865. Lost 281 officers or enlisted men killed, mortally wounded, or by disease.

2.12.1 Subject: 35th Illinois VI, Stele
Location: 122 North Crest Road   N 35 02 14 61 / W 85 15 15 90
Dedicated: 1899
Medium: Granite
Monument is a stele surmounting a base.

Inscription

ILLINOIS / 35TH INFANTRY, / 1ST BRIGADE, / 3D DIVISION, / 4TH CORPS. / NOV. 25, 1863, 5 P. M.

Organized at Decatur, July 3, 1861. Pea Ridge. Stones River. Tullahoma. Chickamauga. Chattanooga. Atlanta. Mustered out September 27, 1864. Lost 267 officers or enlisted men killed, mortally wounded, or by disease.

2.12.2 Subject: 25th Illinois VI, Stele
Location: 122 North Crest Road   N 35 02 13 65 / W 85 15 15 98
Dedicated: 1899
Medium: Granite
Monument is a stele surmounting a base.

Inscription

ILLINOIS / 25TH INFANTRY / 1ST BRIGADE / 3D DIVISION / 4TH CORPS / NOV. 25, 1863, 5 P. M.

Organized at St. Louis, mustered in August 4, 1861. Fremont's Missouri Campaign. Pea Ridge. Stones River. Tullahoma. Chickamauga. Chattanooga. Atlanta. Mustered out September 5, 1864. Lost 232 officers or enlisted men killed, mortally wounded, or by disease.

The crest of Missionary Ridge, 25th Illinois VI, Stele

2.12.3 Subject: 8th Kansas VI, Common Soldier Statue, Union
Location: 120 North Crest Road   N 35 02 13 65 / W 85 15 15 98
Installed or dedicated: 1896
Media: Bronze, granite
Monument is a Union soldier surmounting a base.

Inscription
THE 8TH KANSAS VOL. INFTY., / COL. JOHN A. MARTIN COMMANDING / WILLICH'S
BRIG., WOOD'S DIV., GRANGER'S CORPS / NOVEMBER 25TH, 1863 / ADVANCED FROM
ORCHARD KNOB AT 3:00 P.M., AND WITH THE / BRIGADE CARRIED THE WORKS
AT THE FOOT OF THE RIDGE, / AND CONTINUED THE ASSAULT UP ITS FACE. THE
REGIMENT / BROKE THROUGH THE OPPOSING LINE ON THE CREST AT / THIS POINT
AND A PORTION OF IT PURSUED THE ENEMY / 200 YARDS BEYOND, AND THERE
ENGAGED IN A LIVELY BUT / SHORT FIGHT, WHILE THE REST ASSISTED IN DRIVING
/ THE ENEMY FROM THE LEFT. THE REGIMENT BIVOAUCKED / ON THE RIDGE NEAR
THIS POINT.
TOTAL NUMBER ENGAGED 219, 1 COMMISSIONED OFFICER / WOUNDED, 3 ENLISTED
MEN KILLED. / 23 ENLISTED MEN WOUNDED.

This common soldier statue gives tribute to the 8th Kansas Infantry, the only Kansas unit at Chattanooga. Regiment organized August 1861. Perryville. Tullahoma. Chickamauga. Chattanooga. Atlanta. Franklin. Nashville. Mustered out January 9, 1866. Lost 244 officers or enlisted men killed, mortally wounded, or by disease.

The contractor was William Van Amringe for the Smith Granite Company. The medium is believed to be blue Westerly granite. Total cost for the three monuments to the 8th Kansas monuments—here, on Missionary Ridge, at Orchard Hill, and at Chickamauga—was $3,600. Other 8th Kansas monuments stand on the Chickamauga battlefield, as well as Orchard Knob (2.17.15).

2.12.4 Subject: 89th Illinois VI, Stele
Location: N 35 02 10 35 / W 85 15 16 86
Dedicated: 1899
Medium: Granite
Monument is a stele surmounting a base.

Inscription
ILLINOIS / 89TH INFANTRY / 1ST BRIGADE / 3D DIVISION / 4TH CORPS / NOV. 25,
1863, 5 P. M.

The 89th Infantry, the "Railroad Regiment," organized at Chicago, mustered in August 27, 1862. Perryville. Stones River. Tullahoma. Chickamauga. Chattanooga. Atlanta. Franklin. Nashville. Mustered out June 10, 1865. Lost 306 officers or enlisted men killed, mortally wounded, or by disease.

8th Kansas VI, Common Soldier Statue, Union

2.12.5 Subject: 15th Wisconsin VI, Stele

Location: 100 North Crest Road, corner of Shallowford Road   N 38 02 07 95 / W 85 15 17 86

Dedicated: July 24, 1889

Medium: Granite

Monument is a stele surmounting a base.

Inscription

WISCONSIN / 15TH INFANTRY / 1ST BRIGADE / 3RD DIVISION / NOV. 25TH 1863 / 5 P. M.

The crest of Missionary Ridge, 89th Illinois VI

Recruits for the 15th Wisconsin, the "Scandinavian Regiment," came from Eau Claire, Chippewa, and Stockholm. Organized at Madison, mustered in February 14, 1862. Island No. 10. Perryville. Stones River. Tullahoma. Chickamauga. Chattanooga. Atlanta. Mustered out February 1865. Lost 336 officers or enlisted men killed, mortally wounded, or by disease.

Ohio Reservation

2.13.1 Subject: State of Ohio, Column, One Officer, Three Common Soldiers: Statues, Union
Location: N 35 01 41 05 / W 85 15 29 52
Installed: 1903; dedicated: October 21, 1903
Media: Bronze, granite
Monument is a granite obelisk surrounded by four life-size granite figures mounted on individual platforms.

Inscription
[Front]
[State seal of Ohio]
OHIO
[Infantryman]

OHIO
[Cavalryman]

OHIO
[Drummer]

OHIO
[Artilleryman]

Ohio Reservation: State of Ohio, Column, One Officer, Three Common Soldiers: Statues, Union

The sculpture cost $27,000 and was erected at the direction of the Ohio Missionary Ridge & Lookout Mountain Monument Commission. The over-all height of the monument is forty-five feet; the four figures stand six feet by thirty inches by thirty-six inches. The Van Amringe Granite Company of Boston and Leland & Hall Company of New York served as designers and fab-ricators. Edward L. A. Pausch served as sculptor.

On the south side of the Ohio Reservation facing west are plaques for the 3rd, 98th, 108th, 113th, and 121st Ohio VI. On the north side facing west are plaques for the 1st, 3rd, 4th, and 10th Ohio Cavalry; 1st Sharpshooters; the 18th, 10th, 21st, 4th Ohio Cavalry; and the 52nd Ohio VI. A tribute to Ohio soldiers at Chattanooga near the Ohio monument reads

> The battle of Chattanooga occupied three days; the first, Nov. 23d, Orchard Knob; the second, Lookout Mountain; the third, Missionary Ridge. Gen. Rosecrans who commanded the Army of the Cumberland until relieved be-fore the battle by Gen. Thomas, and Gen. Sherman, commanding the Army of the Tennessee, were from Ohio. Gen. Grant, commanding the combined forces, was born in Ohio and appointed thence to West Point. Three of the 15 Divisions, ten of 38 Brigades were commanded by Ohio officers. Of 227 Infantry organizations, 65 were from Ohio; of 54 Batteries 13; of the 8 Cavalry regiments 4. . . . Of the total [Union casualties], 5,475, killed and wounded, 31.1 percent were Ohio Soldiers. Of 115 officers killed or mortally wounded, 45 were from Ohio.

South of Ohio Reservation

2.14.1 Subject: 100th Illinois VI, Stele
Location: 107 South Crest Road. near East Main Street   N 35 01 23 47 /
W 85 15 38 32
Dedicated: 1899
Medium: Granite
Monument is a stele surmounting a base.

Inscription

ILLINOIS / 100TH INFANTRY / 2D BRIGADE / 2D DIVISION / 4TH CORPS / NOV. 25,
1863, 5 P. M.

Organized at Joliet, mustered in August 30, 1862. Stones River. Tullahoma
Campaign. Chickamauga. Chattanooga. Atlanta. Franklin. Nashville. Mustered
out June 1865. Lost 214 officers or enlisted men killed, mortally wounded, or
by disease.

Bragg Reservation

2.15.1 Subject: State of Illinois, Column, Female and Common Soldiers, Statues
Location: N 35 01 10 49 / W 85 15 46 96
Installed or dedicated: circa 1898–99
Media: Bronze, granite, marble, white bronze (zinc)
Monument is a granite shaft set on a Georgia marble base with bronze
figures.

Inscription

[Front]
[Eagle with flags] [Bronze medallion: state seal of Illinois]
ILLINOIS

THE COMMANDS INSCRIBED ON THIS MONUMENT WERE ENGAGED IN THE ASSAULT
/ ON MISSIONARY RIDGE, NOVEMBER 25, 1863.
WILLICH'S BRIGADE: / 25TH INFANTRY / COL. RICHARD N. NODINE, / LOSS 67; /
35TH INFANTRY, / LIEUT. COL. WILLIAM P. CHANDLER, / LOSS 54; / 89TH INFANTRY,
/ LIEUT. COL. WILLIAM D. WILLIAMS, / LOSS 34. / WAGNER'S BRIGADE / 100TH
INFANTRY, / MAJ. CHAS. M. HAMMOND / LOSS 32. / GROSE'S BRIGADE: 59TH
INFANTRY, / MAJ. CLAYTON HALE, / LOSS 18; / 75TH INFANTRY, / COL. JOHN E.
BENNETT, / LOSS 2; / 84TH INFANTRY, / COL. LOUIS H. WATERS, / LOSS 4.

SHERMAN'S BRIGADE: / 44TH INFANTRY, / COL. WALLACE W. BARRETT, / LOSS 21;
/ 88TH INFANTRY, / LIEUT. COL. GEO. W. CHANDLER, / LOSS 51; / 36TH INFANTRY,
/ COL. SILAS MILLER, / LOSS 29; / 73RD INFANTRY, / COL. JAMES F. JAQUESS, /
LOSS 27; / 74TH INFANTRY, / COL. WALLACE W. BARRETT, / LOSS 49; / HARKER'S
BRIGADE: / 27TH INFANTRY / COL. JONATHAN R. MILES / LOSS 78; / 22ND INFANTRY
/ LIEUT. COL. FRANCIS SWANWICK / LOSS 18; / 42ND INFANTRY / COL. NATHAN H.
WALWORTH / (COMDNG. DEMI BRIGADE) / CAPT. EDGAR D. SWAIN / LOSS 51; / 51ST

Bragg Reservation: State of Illinois, Column, Female, One Officer, Three Common Soldiers, Statues

INFANTRY / MAJ. CHARLES W. DAVIS, WOUNDED / CAPT. ALBERT M. TILTON / LOSS 5; / 79TH INFANTRY / COL. ALLEN BUCKNER / LOSS 7;

CARLIN'S BRIGADE: / 104TH INFANTRY, / LIEUT. COL. DOUGLASS HAPEMAN / LOSS 21; / WOOD'S BRIGADE / (OSTERHAUS DIV.) / 13TH INFANTRY, / LIEUT. COL. FREDERICK W. PARTRIDGE, / CAPT. GEO. P. BROWN, / LOSS 63; MOORE'S BRIGADE: / 19TH INFANTRY, / LIEUT. COL. ALEXANDER W. RAFFEN / LOSS 26

The state of Illinois's central monument on Missionary Ridge stands near the grounds of the headquarters of the Army of Tennessee, General Braxton Bragg commanding, and is emblematic of the sweeping victory that was obtained by Union troops at the battle of Chattanooga. The language is commemorative; the appearance is triumphant. It may well draw upon Trajan's Column in

Rome, erected circa AD 113, which commemorates Emperor Trajan's military campaigns. This column is less bellicose, surmounted as it is by a bronze female figure of Peace holding an olive wreath.

Numerous regimental monuments surround the hilltop's central edifice, giving this column all the more stature and prominence.

The figures are in bronze, the shaft is of white Barre granite, the base is gray Georgia marble. The height of the monument is eighty feet, with the bronze figure of Peace at the top and four bronze figures at the base: an infantryman, an artilleryman, a cavalryman, and an engineer officer. Each figure is nine feet in height. The base stands twenty-one feet by twenty-one feet by six feet, three inches. The American Bronze Company was the founder, the J. S. Culver Company served as fabricator, Robert A. Bullard was the designer, and Sigvald Asbjornsen was the sculptor. Estimated cost: $50,000.

- The actual site of Bragg's headquarters was three hundred yards to the northeast, at the Moore House, near where I-24 now passes through Missionary Ridge. The house no longer stands, and nothing marks the site.

2.15.2 Subject: 97th Ohio VI, Stele
Location: N 35 01 11 45 / W 85 15 46 70
Installed or dedicated: 1915
Medium: Granite
Monument is a granite stele with common soldier relief surmounting a base.

Inscription

97TH OHIO VOL. INF'Y
[Two common soldiers in high relief]
THIS REGIMENT OF WAGNER'S BRIGADE, WOOD'S DIVISION, WAS THE FIRST INFANTRY / REG'T TO CROSS THE TENNESSEE RIVER AND OCCUPY CHATTANOOGA SEPT. 9TH, 1863. / NOV. 25TH 1863 IN SHERIDAN'S DIV. CHARGED MISSIONARY RIDGE GAINING THE CREST / AS SHOWN BY BRONZE TABLET NORTH END OF VIADUCT AND PURSUING THE ENEMY TO CHICKAMAUGA CREEK, LOSS 149 KILLED AND WOUNDED OUT OF 434.

The 97th Ohio's monument, with its high relief sculpture of a Union soldier in motion toward the view, also overlooks the downtown at a particularly picturesque point on the ridge, as well as I-24 below. The monument stands six feet, two inches by four feet by ten feet. It is a stele with high relief carving surmounting a two-tiered base.

The 97th OVI organized at Zanesville, September 1, 1862. Perryville. Stones River. Tullahoma. Chattanooga. Atlanta. Franklin. Nashville. Mustered out June 10, 1865. Lost 254 officers or enlisted men killed, mortally wounded, or by disease.

22nd Illinois VI, Stele, with city of Chattanooga in background

West Side, Bragg Reservation

2.15.3 Subject: 22nd Illinois VI, Stele
Location: N 35 01 12 21 / W 85 15 46 28
Dedicated: 1899
Medium: Granite
Monument is a stele surmounting a base.

Inscription

ILLINOIS / 22D INFANTRY / 3D BRIGADE / 2D DIVISION / 4TH CORPS / NOV. 25, 1863
5 P. M.

Organized at Belleville, mustered in June 25, 1861. Belmont. Island No. 10. Corinth. Stones River. Tullahoma. Chickamauga. Chattanooga. Atlanta. Mustered out July 7, 1864, expiration of term. Lost 250 officers or enlisted men killed, mortally wounded, or by disease.

2.15.4 Subject: 51st Illinois VI, Stele
Location: N 35 01 11 80 / W 85 15 47 10
Dedicated: 1899
Medium: Granite
Monument is a stele surmounting a base.

Inscription

ILLINOIS / 51ST INFANTRY / 3D BRIGADE / 2D DIVISION / 4TH CORPS / NOV. 25, 1863
5 P. M.

Organized at Camp Douglas, mustered in December 24, 1861. Island No. 10. Corinth. Stones River. Tullahoma. Chickamauga. Chattanooga. Atlanta. Franklin. Nashville. Mustered out October 15, 1865. Lost 250 officers or enlisted men killed, mortally wounded, or by disease.

2.15.5 Subject: 79th Illinois VI, Stele
Location: N 35 01 10 34 / W 85 15 47 92
Dedicated: 1899
Medium: Granite
Monument is a stele surmounting a base.

Inscription

ILLINOIS / 79TH INFANTRY / 3D BRIGADE / 2D DIVISION / 4TH CORPS / NOV. 25, 1863
5 P. M.

Organized at Mattoon, mustered in August 28, 1862. Perryville. Stones River. Tullahoma. Chickamauga. Chattanooga. Atlanta. Franklin. Nashville. Mustered out June 12, 1865. Lost 297 officers or enlisted men killed, mortally wounded, or by disease.

2.15.6 Subject: 27th Illinois VI, Stele
Location: N 35 01 09 76 / W 85 15 48 32
Dedicated: 1899
Medium: Granite
Monument is a stele surmounting a base.

Inscription

ILLINOIS / 27TH INFANTRY / 3D BRIGADE / 2D DIVISION / 4TH CORPS / NOV. 25, 1863
5 P. M.

Organized at Camp Butler, August 10, 1861. Belmont. Island No. 10. Corinth. Stones River. Tullahoma. Chickamauga. Chattanooga. Atlanta. Mustered out September 20, 1864. Lost 188 officers or enlisted men killed, mortally wounded, or by disease.

2.15.7 Subject: 42nd Illinois VI, Stele
Location: N 35 01 09 69 / W 85 15 48 49
Dedicated: 1899
Medium: Granite
Monument is a stele surmounting a base.

Inscription

ILLINOIS / 42D INFANTRY / 3D BRIGADE / 2D DIVISION / 4TH CORPS / NOV. 25, 1863
5 P. M.

Organized at Chicago, July 22, 1861. Fremont's Missouri Campaign. Island No. 10. Stones River. Tullahoma. Chickamauga. Chattanooga. Atlanta. Franklin. Nashville. Mustered out January 10, 1866. Lost 387 officers or enlisted men killed, mortally wounded, or by disease.

2.15.8 Subject: 36th Illinois VI, Stele
Location: N 35 01 09 46 / W 85 15 48 58
Dedicated: 1899
Medium: Granite
Monument is a stele surmounting a base.

Inscription

ILLINOIS / 36TH INFANTRY / 3D BRIGADE / 2D DIVISION / 4TH CORPS / NOV. 25, 1863
5 P. M.

The Fox River Regiment organized at Aurora, mustered in September 23, 1861.
Pea Ridge. Perryville. Stones River. Tullahoma. Chickamauga. Chattanooga.
Atlanta. Franklin. Nashville. Mustered out October 27, 1865. Lost 332 officers
or enlisted men killed, mortally wounded, or by disease.

2.15.9 Subject: 73rd Illinois VI, Stele
Location: N 35 01 08 80 / W 85 15 48 80
Dedicated: 1899
Medium: Granite
Monument is a stele surmounting a base.

Inscription

ILLINOIS / 73RD INFANTRY / 3D BRIGADE / 2D DIVISION / 4TH CORPS / NOV. 25, 1863
5 P. M.

The 73rd Infantry, the "Persimmon" or "Preachers" Regiment, organized at
Camp Butler, mustered in August 21, 1862. Perryville. Stones River. Tullahoma.
Chickamauga. Chattanooga. Atlanta. Franklin. Nashville. Mustered out June
12, 1865. Lost 281 officers or enlisted men killed, mortally wounded, or by
disease.

2.15.10 Subject: 44th Illinois VI, Stele
Location: N 35 01 08 29 / W 85 15 49 02
Dedicated: 1899
Medium: Granite
Monument is a stele surmounting a base.

Inscription

ILLINOIS / 44TH INFANTRY / 3D BRIGADE / 2D DIVISION / 4TH CORPS / NOV. 25,
1863 5 P. M.

Organized at Chicago, mustered in September 13, 1861. Fremont's Missouri
Campaign. Pea Ridge. Perryville. Stones River. Tullahoma. Chickamauga.
Chattanooga. Franklin. Nashville. Mustered out September 25, 1865. Lost 292
officers or enlisted men killed, mortally wounded, or by disease.

Missouri Vol. Infantry and Artillery, Union, Stele, looking east toward Georgia

Crest, Bragg Reservation

2.15.11 Subject: Missouri Vol. Infantry and Artillery, Union, Stele
Location: N 35 01 08 71 / W 85 15 45 54
Installed or dedicated: circa 1896
Medium: Granite
Monument is a stele surmounting a base.

Inscription

MISSOURI / TO HER 2ND AND 15TH INFTY. / U.S.A. / WHO REACHED THIS POSITION IN THE ASSAULT / NOV. 25, 1863.

MISSOURI / TO HER 6TH 8TH 10TH AND 26TH INFTY. BATTERY F / ENGAGED ON THE NORTH END OF MISSIONARY RIDGE

This state monument stands at the crest of the ridge of the Bragg Reservation. It is understated by comparison to the Illinois state monument, but other Missouri regimental stelae stand just beyond it, marking the point of bivouac for each unit after the assault on Missionary Ridge.

The monument's dimensions are seven feet by four feet by eight feet, six inches. It was erected by the Union Marble and Granite Co., Atlanta, at a cost of $1,366.

2.15.12 Subject: 13th Illinois VI, Stele
Location: 107 South Crest Road   N 35 01 06 92 / W 85 15 47 62
Dedicated: 1899
Medium: Granite
Monument is a stele surmounting a base.

Inscription
ILLINOIS / 13TH INFANTRY, / 1ST BRIGADE, / 1ST DIVISION, / 15TH CORPS. / NOV. 25, 1863, BIVOUAC.

Like other regiments, the 13th Illinois, "Fremont's Grey Hounds," was also engaged at Lookout Mountain, near the Cravens House, where another monument stands (2.7.5). They fought here the following day and bivouacked, then pushed on toward Ringgold Gap after the two-day campaign.

East Side, Bragg Reservation

2.15.13 Subject: 32nd Missouri VI, Shaft
Location: N 35 01 06 39 / W 85 15 47 82
Installed or dedicated: circa 1896
Medium: Marble
Monument is a stele surmounting a base.

Inscription
32ND MO. INFTY. / U.S.A. / NEAR THIS POINT / NIGHT OF NOV. 25, 1863

Organized at Benton Barracks, December 8, 1862. Vicksburg. Chattanooga. Atlanta. March to the Sea. Carolinas Campaign. Grand Review. Mustered out July 18, 1865. Lost 434 officers or enlisted men killed, mortally wounded, or by disease.

2.15.14 Subject: 31st Missouri VI, Shaft
Location: N 35 01 06 29 / W 85 15 47 92
Installed or dedicated: circa 1896
Medium: Marble
Monument is a stele surmounting a base.

Inscription
31ST MO. INFTY. / U.S.A. / NEAR THIS POINT / NIGHT OF NOV. 25, 1863

Organized at St. Louis, Carondelet, and Ironton, October 7, 1862. Vicksburg. Chattanooga. Atlanta. March to the Sea. Carolinas Campaign. Review. Mustered out July 18, 1865. Lost 283 officers or enlisted men killed, mortally wounded, or by disease.

2.15.15 Subject: 29th Missouri VI, Shaft
Location: N 35 01 06 66 / W 85 15 47 16
Installed or dedicated: circa 1896
Medium: Marble
Monument is a stele surmounting a base.

Inscription

29TH. MO. INFTY. / U.S.A. / NEAR THIS POINT / NIGHT OF NOV. 25, 1863

Organized at St. Louis, October 1862. Vicksburg. Chattanooga. Atlanta. March to the Sea. Carolinas Campaign. Grand Review. Mustered out June 12, 1865. Lost 369 officers or enlisted men killed, mortally wounded, or by disease.

2.15.16 Subject: 17th Missouri VI, Shaft
Location: N 35 01 06 02 / W 85 15 47 94
Installed or dedicated: circa 1896
Medium: Marble
Monument is a stele surmounting a base.

Inscription

17TH MO. INFTY. / U.S.A. / NEAR THIS POINT / NIGHT OF NOV. 25, 1863

Organized at St. Louis, August 1861. Fremont's Missouri Campaign. Pea Ridge. Vicksburg. Chattanooga. Atlanta. March to the Sea. Consolidated with 15th Missouri VI, December 1864. Lost 219 officers or enlisted men killed, mortally wounded, or by disease.

2.15.17 Subject: 12th Missouri VI, Shaft
Location: N 35 01 06 39 / W 85 15 47 82
Installed or dedicated: circa 1896
Medium: Marble
Monument is a stele surmounting a base.

Inscription

12TH MO. INFTY. / U.S.A. / NEAR THIS POINT / NIGHT OF NOV. 25, 1863

Organized at St. Louis, August, 1861. Fremont's Missouri Campaign. Pea Ridge. Vicksburg. Chattanooga. Atlanta. Mustered out November 14, 1864. Lost 208 officers or enlisted men killed, mortally wounded, or by disease.

2.15.18 Subject: 3rd Missouri VI, Shaft
Location: N 35 01 08 77 / W 85 15 46 34
Installed or dedicated: circa 1896
Medium: Marble
Monument is a stele surmounting a base.

Inscription
3RD MO. INFTY. / U.S.A. / NEAR THIS POINT / NIGHT OF NOV. 25, 1863

Organized at St. Louis, September 3, 1861, to January 18, 1862. Pea Ridge. Vicksburg. Chattanooga. Atlanta. Lost 240 officers or enlisted men killed, mortally wounded, or by disease.

South of Bragg Reservation

2.16.1 Subject: 24th Wisconsin VI, Stele
Location: 188 South Crest Road   N 35 01 07 22 / W 85 15 50 82
Dedicated: July 24, 1889
Medium: Granite
Monument is a stele surmounting a base.

Inscription
WISCONSIN / 24TH INFANTRY / 1ST BRIGADE / 2D DIVISION / 4TH CORPS / NOV. 24TH, 1863, / 5 P. M.

Organized at Milwaukee, mustered in August 15, 1862. Perryville. Stones River. Tullahoma. Chickamauga. Chattanooga. Atlanta. Franklin. Nashville. Mustered out June 10, 1865. Lost 201 officers or enlisted men killed, mortally wounded, or by disease.

- · As adjutant of the 24th Wisconsin at Chattanooga, Arthur MacArthur, father of Douglas MacArthur, was awarded the Medal of Honor for inspiring his unit, seizing "the colors of his regiment at a critical moment," according to his citation, "and plant[ing] them on the captured works on the crest of Missionary Ridge."

2.16.2 Subject: 88th Illinois VI, Stele
Location: 195 South Crest Road   N 35 01 07 29 / W 85 15 52 32
Dedicated: 1899
Medium: Granite
Monument is a stele surmounting a base.

Inscription
ILLINOIS / 88TH INFANTRY, / 1ST BRIGADE, / 2ND DIVISION, / 4TH CORPS, / NOV. 25, 1863, 5 P. M.

The crest of Missionary Ridge, 24th Wisconsin VI

The 88th Illinois, the "2nd Board of Trade Regiment," organized at Camp Douglas, mustered in September 4, 1862. Perryville. Stones River. Tullahoma. Chickamauga. Chattanooga. Atlanta. Franklin. Nashville. Lost 191 officers or enlisted men killed, mortally wounded, or by disease.

2.16.3 Subject: 74th Illinois VI, Stele
Location: 195 South Crest Road   N 35 01 06 15 / W 85 15 53 98
Dedicated: 1899
Medium: Granite
Monument is a stele surmounting a base.

Inscription
ILLINOIS / 74TH INFANTRY, / 1ST BRIGADE, / 2ND DIVISION, / 4TH CORPS, / NOV. 25, 1863, 5 P. M.

Organized at Rockford, mustered in September 4, 1862. Perryville. Stones River. Tullahoma. Chickamauga. Chattanooga. Atlanta. Franklin. Nashville. Mustered out June 10, 1865. Lost 202 officers or enlisted men killed, mortally wounded, or by disease.

2.16.4 Subject: 19th Illinois VI, Stele and Relief
Location: 212 South Crest Road   N 35 01 02 73 / W 85 15 55 86
Installed or dedicated: 1899
Media: Bronze, granite
Monument is a stele surmounting a base.

Inscription
THIS REGIMENT FORMED THE EXTREME LEFT OF JOHNSON'S DIVISION, 14TH A. C.
AND GAINED THE CREST OF THE RIDGE AT THIS POINT. THEIR COLORS BEING THE
FIRST OVER THE CONFEDERATE WORKS SOUTH OF BRAGG'S HEADQUARTERS.
THIS MONUMENT ERECTED BY THE SURVIVING MEMBERS OF THE REGIMENT AND
FRIENDS IN MEMORY OF THE BRAVE COMRADES WHO FELL DURING THE WAR.
[4 names] COMMITTEE.

THE FIRST UNION FLAG WAS PLACED ON THE CONFEDERATE WORKS BY CAPT. D. F.
BREMNER FOLLOWED BY PRIVATE JOHN BROSNAHAN OF CO. E., BEARING THE STATE
COLORS AFTER THE FOLLOWING COLOR BEARERS HAD BEEN KILLED OR WOUNDED
IN THE ORDER NAMED:
[4 names]
19TH ILLINOIS INFTY. / JOHNSON'S DIVISION, 14TH A.C.
[25 names]
THEIR COLORS BEING THE FIRST OVER THE CONFEDERATE WORKS SOUTH OF
BRAGG'S HEADQUARTERS.

This is the only privately funded regimental monument on Missionary Ridge.
David Bremner, a veteran of the regiment and postwar banker, sponsored the
monument and commissioned sculptor Julia M. Brachen to execute the bas-relief of the Missionary Ridge assault.

Many units claimed to be the first to surmount the crest of Missionary
Ridge. The 19th, a Zouave regiment, is said to have "carried a vicious charge into
the enemy works on the Federal right," according to historian Victor Hicken.
Capt. Bremner "snatched a falling flag from a wounded bearer and carried it
to the top despite the blood which streamed from a wound on his own face."

2.16.5 Subject: 19th Illinois VI, Stele
Location: 212 South Crest Road   N 35 01 02 73 / W 85 15 55 86
Dedicated: 1899
Medium: Granite
Monument is a stele surmounting a base.

Inscription
ILLINOIS / 19TH INFANTRY, / 2ND BRIGADE, / 1ST DIVISION, / 14TH CORPS, / NOV.
25, 1863, 5 P. M.

Regiment organized at Chicago, mustered in June 17, 1861. Stones River.
Tullahoma. Chickamauga. Chattanooga. Mustered out July 9, 1864. Lost 169
officers or enlisted men killed, mortally wounded, or by disease.

2.16.6 Subject: 11th Michigan VI, Stele
Location: 240 South Crest Road   N 35 00 58 26 / W 85 15 59 52
Installed or dedicated: n.a.
Medium: Granite
Monument is a stele surmounting a base.

Inscription
ELEVENTH MICHIGAN / INFANTRY / NOV. 25, 1863 / MAJOR B. G. BENNETT /
COMMANDING WAS KILLED ON THE / SLOPE BENEATH THIS POSITION

The 11th Michigan organized at White Pigeon, mustered in September 24, 1861.
Stones River. Tullahoma. Chickamauga. Chattanooga. Atlanta. Mustered out
September 30, 1864. Lost 308 officers or enlisted men killed, mortally wound-
ed, or by disease.

2.16.7 Subject: 104th Illinois VI, Stele
Location: South Crest Road   N 35 00 48 79 / W 85 16 04 92
Dedicated: 1899
Medium: Granite
Monument is a stele surmounting a base.

Inscription
ILLINOIS / 104TH INFANTRY, / 1ST BRIGADE, / 1ST DIVISION, / 14TH CORPS, / NOV.
25, 1863, 5 P. M.

The 104th was also engaged at Lookout Mountain, near the Cravens House,
where another monument stands (2.6.5).

2.16.8 Subject: Ireland's Brigade New York VI, Shaft
Location: 444 South Crest Road   N 35 00 11 63 / W 85 16 17 02
Installed or dedicated: 1897
Media: Bronze, granite, limestone
Monument is a stele surmounting a plinth and base.

Inscription
[State seal of New York]
80TH NEW YORK INFANTRY / 102ND NEW YORK INFANTRY / 137TH / W YORK
INFANTRY / 149TH NEW YORK INFANTRY / IRELAND'S-THIRD BRIGADE / GEARY'S-
SECOND DIVISION / SLOCUM'S-TWELFTH CORPS / HOOKER'S COMMAND / 11TH AND
12TH CORPS / ARMY OF THE POTOMAC / NOVEMBER 25, 1863
[Bronze relief of XII Corps' star badge]
NEW YORK

THE NEW YORK INFANTRY REGIMENTS / OF IRELAND'S BRIGADE . . . ON
AFTERNOON OF / NOVEMBER 25, 1863, ADVANCED AND / CONNECTED WITH THE
RIGHT OF PALMER'S / 14TH CORPS. THEY ASSISTED IN BREAKING / THE LINES

OF BRECKINRIDGE'S CONFEDERATE / CORPS, THE DIVISION CAPTURING MANY PRISONERS. / THE SKIRMISHERS OF THE BRIGADE / REACHED THIS POINT AND BEYOND. / THE MAIN BODY OF THE BRIGADE / BIVOUACKED AT THE FOOT OF THE HILL, / IN THE CONFEDERATE CAMPS.

This is the New Yorkers' commemoration of reaching the crest of Missionary Ridge. It is a more modest counterpoint to their majestic column and common soldier monument on the Cravens Reservation (2.6.1). Like other monuments along the ridge, it stands on a precipice between the road and the steep slope of the ridge. The inscription takes an understated note of the successful, even triumphant breaking of Confederate lines on Missionary Ridge and the units' bivouac that night in the Confederate camps.

· Adjacent to the New York monument are bronze shafts to the 111th PVI and 29th PVI, respectively, at corner of East View and South Crest Drive. Each unit has an aedicula, or framed shrine, on the trail below Lookout Point (2.4.3, 2.4.4).

29TH REGIMENT / PENNSYLVANIA INFANTRY / REACHED THIS POINT AT 6 P.M. / BATTLE OF MISSIONARY RIDGE / NOVEMBER 25, 1863

111TH REGIMENT PENNSYLVANIA / VETERAN VOLUNTEER INFANTRY / NO LOSS OCCURRED IN THE ENGAGMENT

2.16.9 Subject: Co. F, 2nd Missouri Vol. Light Artillery
Location: 604 South Crest Road, west side   N 34 59 33 21 / W 85 16 33 99
Installed or dedicated: circa 1896
Medium: Marble
Monument is a stele surmounting a base.

Inscription
CO. F 2ND MO. / LIGHT ARTILLERY / U.S.A.

Organized at St. Louis, January 1862. Chattanooga. Atlanta. Mustered out August 25, 1865.

2.16.10 Subject: Missouri Vol. Infantry and Artillery, Union, Stele
Location: Corner of South Crest and West Crest   N 35 00 11 63 / W 85 16 17 02
Installed or dedicated: 1895
Medium: Granite
Monument is a stele surmounting a base.

Inscription
MISSOURI
TO HER 3RD, 12TH, 17TH, 27TH, 29TH, 31ST AND 32ND INFTY. / AND BATTERY F. 2ND MO. U.S.A. / WHO OCCUPIED A POSITION NEAR THIS POINT NOV. 25, 1863.

This stele, flanked by two field artillery pieces, stands at the southern end of Missionary Ridge, just north of the Rossville Gap and the Tennessee-Georgia state line. Erected at a cost of $1,386 by the Union Marble and Granite Company, it commemorates units that also have individual markers on the Bragg Reservation.

2.16.12 Subject: State of Iowa, Column and Common Soldiers Statue, Union
Location: East side of Rossville Boulevard / US 27, Rossville Gap, Georgia
N 34 59 01 40 / W 85 16 46 30
Installed: 1903; dedicated: November 19, 1906
Medium: Granite
Monument is a granite figure of a Union soldier holding a flag, surmounting a shaft and base.

Inscription

[Front]
[Relief of state seal of Iowa]
IOWA ERECTS THIS MONUMENT IN MEMORY / OF ALL HER SOLDIERS WHO TOOK PART / IN THE BATTLES OF LOOKOUT MOUNTAIN, / MISSIONARY RIDGE AND RINGGOLD / 9TH INFANTRY / COL. / DAVID CARSKADDON / 10TH INFANTRY / LIEUT. COL. / P. P. HENDERSON
IOWA
[Statue: Common soldier, cavalryman]

IOWA LOSSES [TOTAL: 446 OFFICERS AND MEN KILLED, WOUNDED, OR MISSING] 4TH INFANTRY, 5TH INFANTRY, 8TH INFANTRY, 9TH INFANTRY, 10TH INFANTRY 17TH INFANTRY, 25TH INFANTRY, 26TH INFANTRY, 30TH INFANTRY, 31ST INFANTRY, 1ST BATTERY / 17TH INFANTRY / COL. CLARK R. WEVER / 25TH INFANTRY / COL. GEORGE A. STONE / 26TH INFANTRY / COL. MILO SMITH / 30TH INFANTRY / LIEUT. COL. / AURELIUS ROBERTS
IOWA
[Statue: Common soldier, infantryman]

IN THE FINAL CONTEST FOR MISSIONARY / RIDGE FOUR IOWA REGIMENTS WERE ENGAGED / ON THE CONFEDERATE RIGHT FLANK. SIX / OTHERS WITH BATTERY ON THE CONFEDERATE / LEFT AND REAR. THE MOVEMENT FROM / ROSSVILLE BROUGHT THE LATTER PAST THIS / POSITION. ENDING LATER IN THE ASSAULT / UPON THE RIDGE AND TWO DAYS AFTERWARDS / THE BATTLE OF RINGOLD [SIC] GA. THE STATE OF IOWA IS PROUD OF YOUR / ACHIEVEMENTS AND RENDERS YOU HER / HOMAGE AND GRATITUDE AND WITH EXULTANT / HEART CLAIMS YOU AS HER SONS.
[40 rounds]
31ST INFANTRY / LIEUT. COL. / JEREMIAH W. JENKINS / 1ST BATTERY / LIEUT. / JAMES M. WILLIAMS
[Statue: Common soldier, artillerist]
IOWA

MAY THIS SHAFT REGISTER ALIKE / THE SACRIFICE OF OUR FALLEN BROTHERS / AND OUR PURPOSE / TO PERPETUATE THEIR MEMORY / BY CITIZENSHIP WORTHY

State of Iowa, Column and Common Soldiers Statue, Union

/ OF THE HERITAGE THEY LEFT US. / A RE-UNITED AND GLORIOUS UNION / IOWA / 4TH INFANTRY / LIEUT. COL. / GEORGE BURTON / 5TH INFANTRY / COL. JABEZ BANBURY

[Statue: Common soldier, infantryman]

The service of Iowa soldiers at Chattanooga is commemorated with three state-sponsored monuments, one each at Sherman Heights and on Lookout Mountain, and this one, the largest of the three. Standing seventy-two feet high on the south edge of Missionary Ridge, at Rossville Gap, it is 120 yards south of the Tennessee-Georgia state line.

It is another triumphant Union monument celebrating the common soldier, in this case the ten regiments of infantry and one battery from Iowa. The monument displays five statues of common soldiers of various ages and service branches, as well as a tribute to the Iowa soldier's sacrifice in leaving "us a Re-united and Glorious Union." Note the direct address to the veterans in the inscription, as if the ceremony is ongoing—perpetual—and the participants are still present: "The State Of Iowa Is Proud Of Your Achievements And Renders You Her Homage And Gratitude."

Participating in the dedication services of the Iowa monuments was a delegation from Iowa that successively dedicated monuments to Iowa troops at Andersonville, Georgia, the former prison camp; Vicksburg, Mississippi; and the Shiloh battlefield in Tennessee. Funding for the monuments was appropriated by the state legislature. Historian William C. Lowe notes that the monuments' construction at Chattanooga was overseen by an eleven-member Lookout Mountain and Missionary Ridge commission, which was given a budget of $35,000 for three monuments, $10,000 more than the marking commission had recommended. The commission selected the designs of the Van Amringe Granite Company of Boston. Lowe notes that the commissioners originally planned to divide the funding appropriation for Chattanooga equally among three monuments, but ultimately decided that the majority of the funds should be invested in one "immortal" work of art at "the most sightly place."

- The designs and inscriptions were subject to the approval of the park commission and the War Department. Among the changes mandated by the park commission, as William C. Lowe notes, was the deletion of the phrase "in a holy cause" and Lincoln's "malice towards none" passage from the Second Inaugural. The commission also ruled that "although a quotation from Iowa's wartime governor Kirkwood (supplied by Benjamin F. Shambaugh) was appropriate, Kirkwood's name would have to be left off the monument as he was not involved in the battle."

- By way of US 27, Rossville Gap still provides quick passage through the barrier of Missionary Ridge into Georgia and the Chickamauga battlefield, although other avenues—a tunnel for US 41, a new gap for I-24—have been added in recent decades. In September 1863, Rossville Gap had major strategic value in deciding the course of the war in the west. The gap was a major objective of Lt. Gen. Braxton Bragg's Confederate Army of Tennessee during the Chickamauga Campaign. The Confederate forces' effort to block the Federal Army's way to Chattanooga was unsuccessful. Although Bragg's forces won a victory at Chickamauga, decisive results could not be achieved. Maj. Gen. William Rosecrans'

Federal Army of the Cumberland retreated through the pass after the defeat to fight another day. The last act of the wartime drama involving Rossville Gap occurred when Federal troops drove Confederate forces back through the pass, as marked by the adjacent commemoration of the 27th Missouri VI (marble stele nearby on the Georgia side) and this monument. Park Service notes record that after the victorious assault on Missionary Ridge, Iowa troops celebrated their feat of arms with a grand review through the Rossville Gap. Iowa troops did not fight in the gap during the battle, but the recollection of this march was a factor in erecting the monument at this site.

Orchard Knob Reservation

The Orchard Knob Reservation stands in a residential neighborhood approximately one mile west of Missionary Ridge. Federal troops commanded by Maj. Gen. George H. Thomas seized the hill on November 23, 1863. It then served as Grant's headquarters during the assault on Missionary Ridge on November 24. Monuments on this hill commemorate units who fought here as well as those who were present during the Chattanooga Campaign but were not engaged in combat.

2.17.1 Subject: 46th Pennsylvania VI, Stele and Common Soldier Statue, Union
Location: Northwest corner   N 35 02 25 84 / W 85 16 25 56
Dedicated: 1897
Media: Bronze, granite
Monument is a figure of a Union soldier, in bronze, standing at parade rest, surmounting a granite base.

Inscription

46TH PENNSYLVANIA INFANTRY / 1ST BRIGADE [KNIPES] / 1ST DIVISION [WILLIAMS] / 12TH CORPS SLOCUM / JOE HOOKER'S COMMAND / M. J. POWER FOUNDER, N.Y.

THIS REGIMENT RENDERED IMPORTANT SERVICE AS REAR GUARD IN THE MOVEMENT AND ACTION OF THE 11TH & 12TH CORPS IN OPENING AND MAINTAINING COMMUNICATIONS WITH THE ARMY OF THE CUMBERLAND AT CHATTANOOGA.

The 46th Pennsylvania organized at Harrisburg, October 31, 1861. Shenandoah Valley. Cedar Mountain. Antietam. Fredericksburg "Mud March." Chancellorsville. Gettysburg. Atlanta. March to the Sea. Carolinas Campaign. Grand Review. Mustered out July 16, 1865. Lost 317 officers or enlisted men killed, mortally wounded, or by disease.

The monument, placed by veterans of the battle of Chattanooga, stands six feet, eight inches high on a base that is twenty-four inches by twenty-four

46th Pennsylvania VI,
Stele and Common Soldier
Statue, Union

inches. Erected at a cost of $4,000 by the M. J. Power. Co., of New York. Monuments to the 46th PVI also stand at Gettysburg and the Cedar Mountain battlefields.

2.17.2 Subject: 75th Pennsylvania VI, Stele
Location: Orchard Hill, south side   N 35 02 25 64 / W 85 16 26 02
Installed or dedicated: 1897
Media: Bronze, granite
Monument is a stele surmounting a base.

Inscription

[State seal of Pennsylvania]
THE COMMONWEALTH OF PENNSYLVANIA / TO HER SEVENTY-FIFTH REGIMENT, /
INFANTRY VOLUNTEERS. / MAJOR AUGUST LEDIC COMMANDING
WAHATCHIE / LOOKOUT MOUNTAIN / MISSIONARY RIDGE
ORGANIZED AT PHILADELPHIA / IN AUGUST 1861 BY / COL. HENRY BOHLEN /
DISCHARGED AT MURFREESBORO, TENNESSEE / SEPTEMBER 1, 1865
75TH PENNSYLVANIA INFANTRY / 3RD BRIGADE, 3RD DIVISION, 11TH CORPS

The monument was erected at a cost of $4,040; its dimensions are seven feet by four feet, eight inches by four feet.

The 75th Infantry (formerly 40th Pennsylvania). Cross Keys. Pope's campaign, northern Virginia. Fredericksburg "Mud March." Chancellorsville. Gettysburg. Chattanooga. Nashville. Franklin. Mustered out September 1, 1865. Lost 161 officers or enlisted men killed, mortally wounded, or by disease.

2.17.3 Subject: State of New York, Eleventh Corps Column and Common Soldier Statue, Union
Location: Orchard Knob, hilltop   N 35 02 23 65 / W 85 16 26 02
Installed or dedicated: 1899
Medium: Granite
Monument is a figure of a Union soldier surmounting a Corinthian column and base.

Inscription

[Front]
TO THE NEW YORK TROOPS IN HOWARD'S ELEVENTH CORPS OF HOOKER'S
COMMAND, 11TH AND 12TH CORPS, ARMY OF THE POTOMAC, AT CHATTANOOGA
AND MISSIONARY RIDGE, / NOV. 23, 24, 25, 1863. / STEINWEHR'S—2ND DIVISION
/ BUSCHBECK'S—1ST BRIGADE / 134TH N.Y. INFANTRY—LT. COL. A. H. JACKSON, /
154TH N.Y. INFANTRY—COL. P. H. JONES / ORLAND SMITH'S—2ND BRIGADE / 136TH
N.Y. INFANTRY—COL. JAS. WOOD JR. / SCHURZ'S—3RD DIVISION / TYNDALE'S—1ST
BRIGADE / 45TH N.Y. INFANTRY—MAJ. CHAS. KOCH / 143RD N.Y. INFANTRY—COL.
HORACE BOUGHTON / KRZYZANOWSKI'S—2ND BRIGADE / 58TH N.Y. INFANTRY—
CAPT. M. ESEMBAUX / 119TH N.Y. INFANTRY—COL. J. T. LOCKMAN / 141ST N.Y.
INFANTRY—COL. W. K. LOGIE / HECKER'S—3RD BRIGADE / 68TH N.Y. INFANTRY—
LT. COL. A. VON STEINHAUSEN / OSBURN'S—ARTILLERY / 15TH N.Y. BATTERY—
CAPT. WM. WHEELER / HEADQUARTERS GUARD / CO. A, 8TH N.Y. INFANTRY—CAPT.
A. BRUHN

State of New York,
Eleventh Corps Column
and Common Soldier
Statue, Union

THE INFANTRY AND THREE BATTERIES OF THE ELEVENTH CORPS. MAJOR GENERAL
O. O. HOWARD, COMMANDING, LEFT LOOKOUT VALLEY ONE P.M., NOVEMBER 22,
1863, CROSSING THE RIVER AT BROWN'S FERRY. . . . ABOUT NOON NOVEMBER 23RD,
THE CORPS FORMED NORTH OF FORT WOOD IN CLOSE COLUMN, WITH STEINWEHR'S
DIVISION ON THE RIGHT AND SCHURZ'S DIVISION ON THE LEFT, IN SUPPORT
OF WOOD'S DIVISION, FOURTH CORPS, AND ASSISTED IN CAPTURING ORCHARD
KNOB. . . . .

SHERMAN'S ARMY HAVING CROSSED THE TENNESSEE RIVER NEAR CHICKAMAUGA
CREEK DURING NIGHT OF THE 23RD., GENERAL HOWARD WAS DIRECTED TO
OPEN COMMUNICATION WITH IT. . . . THE ENEMY WAS DRIVEN FROM HIS

WORKS IMMEDIATELY IN FRONT OF THE CORPS. . . . ON THE MORNING OF NOV. 25TH, HECKER'S BRIGADE DROVE THE ENEMY OUT OF HIS RIFLE PITS IN FRONT OF SCHURZ'S DIVISION AND KRZYZANOWSKI'S BRIGADE REJOINED THAT COMMAND. THE CORPS THEN MARCHED BEYOND THE NORTHERN TERMINATION OF MISSIONARY RIDGE TO SHERMAN'S SUPPORT. . . . THREE REGIMENTS OF BUSCHBECK'S BRIGADE, . . . SUPPORTED LOOMIS'S BRIGADE OF THAT DIVISION IN / THE ATTACK ON TUNNEL HILL. THE 73RD PENNA., TEMPORARILY COMMANDED BY LT. COL. J. B. TAFT OF THE 143RD NEW YORK, DROVE THE ENEMY FROM THE "GLASS BUILDINGS" AND FOLLOWED HIM NEARLY TO THE SUMMIT OF THE HILL. IN THIS ACTION LT. COL. TAFT WAS KILLED.

The monument was placed by veterans to commemorate the actions of the XI Corps at Chattanooga, actions that served as a point of pride for the corps, which had earned notoriety, even enmity for its performance in the battles of Chancellorsville and Gettysburg.

The monument was erected at a cost of about $10,000. The monument's column stands thirty-five feet high; the dimensions of the base are twelve by fourteen by fourteen feet. The sculptor of the common soldier figure is unknown, the firm of C. E. & R. E. Taylor served as fabricator, and Caspar Buberl of New York served as designer.

2.17.4 Subject: State of Maryland, Column and Common Soldier Statue, Union
Location: Orchard Knob, hilltop   N 35 02 22 96 / W 85 16 26 22
Installed or dedicated: 1903
Media: Bronze, granite
Monument is a common soldier surmounting a column and base.

Inscription

[Front]
THE STATE OF MARYLAND: IN HONORED RECOGNITION OF THE HISTORIC VALOR OF HER SONS WHO IN BLUE AND GRAY NOBLY SUSTAINED THE MARTIAL GLORY OF THEIR WAR FOR THE UNION 1861–1865 THE PROUD HERITAGE BEQUESTED TO WORTHY SONS OF ILLUSTRIOUS SIRES ARISE PHOENIX-LIKE FROM THE FIERCE FRATERNAL STRIFE. REDEEMED AND REGENERATED AND NOW AND FOREVER VICTOR AND VANQUISHED ARE INDISSOLUBLY UNITED, KNOWING BUT ONE GOD, ONE COUNTRY, ONE DESTINY.

TO THIS REGIMENT, WITH THE DIVISION TO / WHICH IT BELONGED, WAS ASSIGNED THE ARDUOUS / AND IMPORTANT DUTIES OF HOLDING THE / NASHVILLE AND CHATTANOOGA RAILROAD FROM / WARTRACE BRIDGE, TENN., TO BRIDGEPORT, ALA. . . . THEREBY CONTRIBUTING MATERIALLY TO THE / ACHIEVEMENTS THAT CULMINATED IN THE / DEFEAT OF GEN. BRAGG'S ARMY . . . ON / MISSIONARY RIDGE NOVEMBER 25TH, 1863.

THIRD / MARYLAND REGIMENT / VETERAN VOLUNTEER INFANTRY / COL. JOSEPH M. SUDSBURG. / FIRST BRIGADE / FIRST DIVISION / TWELFTH CORPS / U.S.A.

BY ACT OF / THE GENERAL ASSEMBLY / OF MARYLAND / SESSION OF 1902
[8 names]

State of Maryland, Column and Common Soldier Statue

THIS BATTERY, WITH ITS DIVISION, / WAS ASSIGNED TO THE RIGHT OF BRAGG'S LINE / ON MISSIONARY RIDGE. ARRIVING SHORTLY / AFTER 2 O'CLOCK P.M. OF NOVEMBER 25TH. / IT WAS ASSIGNED TO AND WENT INTO POSITION / ON THE CREST OF THE RIDGE IMMEDIATELY / SOUTH OF THE TUNNEL WHERE STEVENSON'S / DIVISION SUPPORTED GEN. CLEBURNE / . . . AGAINST THE / ASSAULT OF GEN. SHERMAN. / AFTER GEN. BRAGG'S LINE HAD BEEN BROKEN / ON THE LEFT AND CENTRE, THIS BATTERY, / TOGETHER WITH ITS DIVISION, WITHDREW / UNDER FIRE IN GOOD ORDER, TOWARD / CHICKAMAUGA STATION.

THIRD BATTERY / MARYLAND ARTILLERY, / C.S.A. / CAPTAIN JOHN B. ROWAN / 1ST LIEUT. WILLIAM L. RITTER / ARTILLERY BATTALION / STEVENSON'S DIVISION / HARDEE'S CORPS.

This monument to Maryland units at the battle of Chattanooga commemorates Federal and Confederate soldiers. It is the only bipartisan monument on the Chattanooga battlefield, with narrative descriptions and tributes to the two Maryland units—one Confederate, one Federal—on the battlefield.

The monument is a common soldier, a color-bearer, holding a Federal flag in both hands, surmounting a column and base. Apart from the iron stelae of the Park Service, this is one of only two unit monuments for Confederate soldiers in Chattanooga, the other being for Barrett's Missouri Artillery (2.9.15). Ironically, they were erected by states that did not secede from the Union.

The monument is forty-five feet high; the base is approximately five by sixteen by twelve feet. The Smith Granite Company served as contractor; the Van Amringe Granite Company served as fabricator and used Westerly granite as its medium. Erected at a cost of $7,000.

The 3rd Maryland Battery (CS) mustered into Confederate service on January 14, 1862. Surrendered at Vicksburg, July 4, 1863. Reorganized at Decatur, Georgia, October 1863. Missionary Ridge. Atlanta. Hood's Middle Tennessee Campaign. Battery surrendered May 4, 1865.

The 3rd Maryland Infantry (US) organized at Baltimore and Williamsport, February 17, 1862. Shenandoah Valley. Cedar Mountain. Antietam. Fredericksburg "Mud March." Chancellorsville. Gettysburg. Chattanooga. Wilderness. Spotsylvania. North Anna. Cold Harbor. Petersburg. Appomattox. Grand Review, May 23. Mustered out July 31, 1865. Lost 225 officers or enlisted men killed, mortally wounded, or by disease.

2.17.5 Subject: State of Illinois, Column and Common Soldier Statue, Union
Location: Orchard Knob, hilltop   N 35 02 22 66 / W 85 16 25 96
Dedicated: 1899
Media: Bronze, granite
Monument is a figure of a Union soldier surmounting a Corinthian column and canopy base.

Inscription

[Front (Excerpts)]
THE COMMANDS INSCRIBED HERE WERE / ENGAGED IN CAMPAIGN, BUT NOT IN / THE ASSAULT ON MISSIONARY RIDGE, / NOVEMBER 25TH, 1863.
MORGAN'S BRIGADE: / 10TH INFANTRY, / 16TH INFANTRY, / 60TH INFANTRY, / STARKWEATHER'S BRIGADE: / 24TH INFANTRY, / J. BEATTY'S BRIGADE: / 34TH INFANTRY / 78TH INFANTRY, / HECKER'S BRIGADE: / 80TH INFANTRY, / 82ND INFANTRY, / DANIEL MCCOOK'S BRIGADE: / 85TH INFANTRY, / 86TH INFANTRY, / 110TH INFANTRY, / 125TH INFANTRY,

WHITAKER'S BRIGADE: / 96TH INFANTRY, / 115TH INFANTRY, / TYNDALE'S BRIGADE: / 101ST INFANTRY, / WILDER'S BRIGADE: / 92ND INFANTRY, (MOUNTED) / CO. "E" DETACHED, / ESCORT TO GEN. CRUFT; / 123RD INFANTRY, (MOUNTED) / LONG'S BRIGADE: / 98TH INFANTRY (MOUNTED) / ENYART'S BRIGADE: / 21ST INFANTRY, / 38TH INFANTRY, / CO. "K" 15TH CAVALRY / ESCORT TO GEN. HOOKER. / 1ST ILLS. LIGHT BATTERY (BRIDGES' BATTERY.) / 2ND ILLS. LIGHT BATTERY I / 1ST ILLS. LIGHT BATTERY A, B, C, F, H, I, M / COGSWELL'S, CHICAGO BOARD OF TRADE

State of Illinois,
Column and Common
Soldier Statue, Union

Erected at a cost of $10,000 by the J. S. Culver and Company, Springfield, this state monument was dedicated to "commands [who] were engaged in the campaign, but not in the assault on Missionary Ridge, November 25th, 1863." The Illinois commission stated,

> Many regiments and batteries engaged in the campaign at Chattanooga were not fortunate enough to be in the assaulting line that swept the enemy off from the summit of Missionary Ridge, and the National

Commission made Orchid [*sic*] Knob in the valley in front of Missionary Ridge a part of the Military Park, and gave to each State, room for a monument there for such commands, and the Illinois Commissioners have there erected a Canopy Monument of highly polished Quincy granite 11 feet square at base, 50 feet high, surmounted by a bronze figure of a private soldier. There are many handsome monuments on Orchard Knob, but it is believed by many that the Illinois monument is the handsomest one there.

2.17.6 Subject: State of New Jersey, Column and Common Soldier Statue, Union
Location: Orchard Knob, hilltop   N 35 02 21 31 / W 85 14 26 49
Dedicated: November 23, 1896
Medium: Granite
Monument is a figure of a Union soldier, in granite, bearing a furled flag, surmounting a granite base.

Inscription
[Front]
NEW JERSEY

33D. / N.J. INFANTRY / 1ST. BRIGADE / 2D. DIVISION / 11TH. CORPS

ERECTED / BY / THE STATE OF / NEW JERSEY / 1896

13TH. / N.J. INFANTRY / 3D. BRIGADE / 1ST. DIVISION / 12TH. CORPS

The first state battlefield monument in Chattanooga was this column, erected by the State of New Jersey, standing thirty-eight feet high, dedicated November 23, 1896. Two regiments of New Jersey infantry participated in the battle of Chattanooga. Of the New Jersey common soldier, one dedication address noted at the ceremonies that the duty they were called to "was simple but sacred." For these "citizens in uniform" were simply "performing upon the field of action the obligations they owed their country, just as at other times and in other capacities they might perform at the ballot box, in the forum, in Legislative halls, or in a court of justice."

On the other hand, what they did was also a sacred duty: "We do well to come long distances to dedicate in this spirit; for it is in this spirit that New Jersey rears this monument and makes her contribution to this National Park, this sacred spot, this Westminster Abbey of the New World. O, fortunate Tennessee, in that within your borders lie such hallowed grounds."

Its overall height is approximately thirty-eight feet, and the statue itself stands approximately ten feet high. The project was completed for about $5,000. The statue is in Maine granite; the base is Quincy granite. The Badger Brothers served as fabricators.

State of New Jersey,
Column and Common
Soldier Statue, Union

The 13th VI organized at Camp Frelinghuysen, Newark, mustered in August 25, 1862. Antietam. Chancellorsville. Gettysburg. Chattanooga. Atlanta. March to the Sea. Carolinas Campaign. Grand Review. Mustered out June 8, 1865. Lost 118 officers or enlisted men killed, mortally wounded, or by disease.

The 33rd VI, the "2nd Zouaves," organized at Newark, mustered in September 3, 1863. Antietam. Fredericksburg. Chancellorsville. Gettysburg. Chattanooga. Atlanta. March to the Sea. Carolinas Campaign. Grand Review. Mustered out July 17, 1865. Lost 163 officers or enlisted men killed, mortally wounded, or by disease.

· Three granite-and-bronze stelae mark the 13th New Jersey's movements and positions on the field at Antietam. A granite monument commemorates the regiment's service on Culp's Hill at Gettysburg.

2.17.7 Subject: 109th Pennsylvania VI, Stele
Location: Orchard Knob, slope   N 35 02 20 12 / W 85 16 26 02
Dedicated: 1896
Media: Bronze, granite
Monument is a pyramid surmounting a four-sided shaft.

Inscription

[Front]
109TH / PENNSYLVANIA / INFANTRY. / 2D BRIGADE. / 2D DIVISION 12TH CORPS.
[State seal of Pennsylvania] [Relief of star badge of the XII Corps]

THE REGIMENT, UNDER COMMAND OF CAPTAIN FREDERICK L. GIMBER, WAS ENGAGED AT WAUHATCHIE, SEVEN / MILES FROM HERE, FROM 11.15 / P.M. OCTOBER 28TH TO / 3 A.M. OF THE 29TH, AND AT LOOKOUT MOUNTAIN / NOVEMBER 24TH, 1863.

THE STATE OF PENNSYLVANIA HAS ERECTED THIS MONUMENT / IN GRATEFUL REMEMBRANCE OF THE OFFICERS AND MEN OF / THE 109TH PENNSYLVANIA VETERAN VOLUNTEER INFANTRY, / WHO, IN THE TIME OF THEIR COUNTRY'S PERIL, OFFERED THEIR / LIVES UPON THIS FIELD AND MANY OTHER BATTLEFIELDS / TO SAVE FOR THE BENEFIT OF POSTERITY, A GOVERNMENT / FOUNDED UPON THE / CONSENT OF THE / GOVERNED AND DEDICATED / TO THE PRINCIPLES OF / PERSONAL LIBERTY AND / HUMAN FREEDOM. / CURTIN LIGHT GUARDS. RECRUITED IN PHILADELPHIA, / PENNSYLVANIA. MUSTERED IN THE U.S. SERVICE, DECEMBER / 1861. RE-ENLISTED JANUARY 1864 . . . MUSTERED OUT OF SERVICE / JULY 19TH 1865.

Erected at a cost of $4,040, the monument stands seven feet high with dimensions of four feet, eight inches by four feet.

The 109th PVI organized at Philadelphia, May 1862. Cedar Mountain. Chancellorsville. Gettysburg. Chattanooga. Atlanta. March to the Sea. Carolinas Campaign. Consolidated with 111th PVI, March 31, 1865. Lost 135 officers and enlisted men killed and mortally wounded and by disease.

2.17.8 Subject: 27th Pennsylvania VI, Stele
Location: Orchard Knob, slope   N 35 02 21 82 / W 85 16 27 72
Installed or dedicated: n.a.
Media: Bronze, granite
Monument is a decorated shaft surmounting a base.

Inscription

[Relief of minié balls]
[Relief of half-moon badge of the XI Corps] [State seal of Pennsylvania]
27TH REGIMENT / PENNSYLVANIA / VOL. INFANTRY / 1ST BRIGADE, 2ND DIVISION, / 11TH ARMY CORPS. / THIS REGIMENT TOOK AN ACTIVE PART AT / WAHATCHIE AND MISSIONARY RIDGE.

[Relief of minié balls] [Sculpture of knapsack, blanket roll, and cartridge box]

[Relief of minié balls]

NUMBERS OF OFFICERS AND MEN IN / ACTION AT MISSIONARY RIDGE 240. / ONE OFFICER AND 45 MEN KILLED, / 6 OFFICERS AND 80 MEN WOUNDED

[Relief of minié balls] [Sculpture of knapsack, blanket roll, and cartridge box]

The monument was erected by Badger Bros., West Quincy, Illinois, at a cost of $4,040. Its dimensions are seven feet by four feet, ten inches by ten feet, two inches.

The 27th Infantry, the "Washington Brigade," organized at Philadelphia, January 1861. Manassas. Cross Keys. Second Manassas. Chancellorsville. Gettysburg. Chattanooga. Atlanta, until mustered out June 11, 1864. Lost 134 officers or enlisted men killed, mortally wounded, or by disease.

2.17.9 Subject: 10th Michigan VI, Stele
Location: Orchard Knob N 35 02 21 45 / W 85 16 27 94
Installed or dedicated: 1896
Media: Bronze, granite
Monument is a granite shaft with relief of a Union common soldier, surmounting two granite blocks.

Inscription

[Relief of knapsack, with pick, axe, sword, bayonet, shovel, and laurel wreath] [Bronze relief of Union soldier]
TENTH MICHIGAN INFANTRY / MORGAN'S BRIGADE, DAVIS' DIVISION, / PALMER'S CORPS.

[Bronze relief of state seal of Michigan]
MICHIGAN / TO HER TENTH REGIMENT OF INFANTRY / COMMANDED / BY LIEUT. COLONEL CHRISTOPHER J. DICKERSON, / MORGAN'S BRIGADE, DAVIS' DIVISION, PALMER'S CORPS.
THE REGIMENT CROSSED THE TENNESSEE RIVER WITH ITS BRIGADE NOVEMBER 24TH, 1863, AFTER A FORCED MARCH OF 58 MILES AND BIVOUACKED IN LINE OF BATTLE AT THE BASE OF MISSIONARY RIDGE UNTIL 2 O'CLOCK A.M. OF THE 26TH; THEN WITH ITS BRIGADE ADVANCED UPON CHICKAMAUGA STATION, AND TO THE RELIEF OF KNOXVILLE RETURNING TO CHATTANOOGA AFTER 29 DAYS ACTIVE OPERATIONS.

The monument was erected at a cost of $3,075 by the M. J. Powers MFG. Co., New York with dimensions of four feet, six inches by four feet by six inches by four feet.

The 10th Michigan organized at Flint, mustered in February 6, 1862. Corinth. Chattanooga. Atlanta. March to the Sea. Carolinas Campaign. Grand Review. Mustered out August 1, 1865. Lost 327 officers or enlisted men killed, mortally wounded, or by disease.

2.17.10 Subject: Battery E, Pennsylvania Vol. Artillery, Stele
Location: Orchard Knob, east side   N 35 02 21 13 / W 85 16 28 16
Installed or dedicated: 1897
Medium: Vermont granite
Monument is a sculpture of a cannon draped with an American flag surmounting a base.

Inscription
BATTERY E, PA, VOL. / KNAP'S / GEARY'S DIV. HOOKER'S COM.

1861 / TO / 1865

WAUHATCHIE—MISSIONARY RIDGE / LOOKOUT MOUNTAIN—RINGGOLD

ERECTED / 1895

The Battery E monument is a Vermont granite sculpture of a light artillery piece draped with an American flag surmounting a base shaped like the walls of a fort. The design is by Sylvester W. McCluskey, a member of Knap's Battery. Built at a cost of approximately $4,000 by the American Granite Company, the whole of the sculpture stands approximately six feet high by eight feet wide and surmounts a base approximately six by eight by two feet.

Battery E was recruited at Pittsburgh and organized in 1861. Cedar Mountain. Antietam. Chancellorsville. Gettysburg. Chattanooga. Atlanta. March to the Sea. Carolinas Campaign. Mustered out June 14, 1865.

2.17.11 Subject: 5th and 20th Connecticut VI, Stele
Location: Orchard Knob slope, east side   N 35 02 20 42 / W 85 16 28 54
Installed or dedicated: October 15, 1904
Medium: Granite
Monument is an inscribed stele.

Inscription
[State seal of Connecticut]
ERECTED BY THE STATE OF CONNECTICUT / TO HER / FIFTH AND TWENTIETH
INFANTRY REGIMENTS / CHATTANOOGA CAMPAIGN / 1863–1864
[Relief of laurel wreath and crossed muskets with bayonets]

The monument was erected at a cost of $5,000 and stands eight feet by seven feet by two feet, six inches.

The 5th Connecticut organized at Hartford, July 26, 1861. Cedar Mountain. Bull Run. Chancellorsville. Gettysburg. Chattanooga. Atlanta. March to the Sea. Carolinas Campaign. Grand Review. Mustered out July 19, 1865. Lost 193 officers or enlisted men killed, mortally wounded, or by disease.

The 20th Connecticut organized at New Haven, September 8, 1862. Gettysburg. Chattanooga. Atlanta. March to the Sea. Carolinas Campaign.

Grand Review. Mustered out June 13, 1865. Lost 168 officers or enlisted men killed, mortally wounded, or by disease.

2.17.12 Subject: 2nd and 33rd Massachusetts VI, Stele
Location: Orchard Knob, Hawthorne and Ivy St.   N 35 02 20 14 / W 85 16 28 22
Installed or dedicated: September 20, 1895
Media: Bronze, granite
Monument is a stele with plaque.

Inscription
MASSACHUSETTS / TO HER / SECOND AND / THIRTYTHIRD [*SIC*] / INFANTRY / IN THE CAMPAIGNS OF / CHATTANOOGA

The monument was erected at a cost of $2,500, and stands eight feet wide by six feet high, by two feet, six inches deep. The designer was John A. Fox, a Boston architect and veteran of the 2nd Massachusetts who also served at Chattanooga.

The 2nd Massachusetts organized at Camp Andrew, mustered in May 25, 1861. Cedar Mountain. Antietam. Fredericksburg "Mud March." Chancellorsville. Gettysburg. Duty in New York City. March to the Sea. Carolinas Campaign. Grand Review. Mustered out July 1865. Lost 288 officers or enlisted men killed, mortally wounded, or by disease.

The 33rd Massachusetts organized at Springfield, August 6, 1862. Fredericksburg "Mud March." Chancellorsville. Gettysburg. Chattanooga. Atlanta. March to the Sea. Carolinas Campaign. Grand Review. Mustered out July 2, 1865. Lost 188 officers or enlisted men killed, mortally wounded, or by disease.

2.17.13 Subject: 1st Michigan Engineers, Stele
Location: Orchard Knob slope, east side   N 35 02 20 14 / W 85 16 28 22
Installed or dedicated: 1899
Media: Bronze, granite
Monument is granite stele.

Inscription
[Bronze relief of engineers engaged in pontoon bridge building]
[Two emblems of crossed oars, anchor, and emblem of the engineers]
FIRST MICHIGAN ENGINEERS / ARMY OF THE CUMBERLAND / WILLIAM P. INNES COLONEL COMMANDING

[State seal of Michigan]
A DETACHMENT OF THIS REGIMENT, CAPTAIN PERRIN V. FOX COMMANDING, PREPARED THE MATERIALS AND CONSTRUCTED THE PONTOON BRIDGES AT THIS CITY AND BROWN'S FERRY, / AND THE SOUTH CHICKAMAUGA RIVER NEAR THE NORTH END OF MISSIONARY RIDGE / OTHER DETACHMENTS OF THE

REGIMENT WERE ENGAGED DURING THE CAMPAIGNS ALONG THE RAILROAD FROM CHATTANOOGA TO MURFREESBORO BUILDING BRIDGES AND OTHER ENGINEER DUTIES.

The monument was erected at a cost of $3,075 by the M. J. Powers MFG. Co., New York. It stands eight feet, nine inches by four feet, three inches by five feet. It commemorates the work of the 1st Michigan Engineers, organized at Marshall, mustered in October 29, 1861. Engaged in construction and maintenance of bridges, roads, trains, track, fortifications. Perryville, Stones River, Chattanooga. March to the Sea. Carolina Campaign. Grand Review. Mustered out September 22, 1865. Lost 364 officers or enlisted men killed, mortally wounded, or by disease.

2.17.14 Subject: State of Wisconsin, Column and Stelae
Location: Orchard Knob, east side   N 35 02 20 12 / W 85 16 24 90
Dedicated: July 24, 1889
Media: Bronze, granite
Monument is a column surmounting a base.

Inscription

[Front]
[State seal of Wisconsin]
WISCONSIN / ERECTS THIS / MONUMENT TO / ITS BRAVE AND / STEADFAST / SONS WHO / PARTICIPATED / IN THE / ENGAGEMENTS / AT AND ABOUT / CHATTANOOGA / 1863

1ST WIS INF / 3RD BRIGADE / 1ST DIVISION / 14TH CORPS / 10TH WIS INF / 1ST BRIGADE / 1ST DIVISION / 14TH CORPS / 21ST WIS INF / 3RD BRIGADE / 1ST DIVISION / 14TH CORPS

15TH WIS INF / 1ST BRIGADE / 3RD DIVISION / 4TH CORPS / 24TH WIS INF / 1ST BRIGADE / 2ND DIVISION / 4TH CORPS /

18TH WIS INF / 1ST BRIGADE / 2ND BRIGADE / 17TH CORPS / 26TH WIS INF / 2ND BRIGADE / 3RD DIVISION / 11TH CORPS

5TH WIS INF / 3RD BRIGADE / 2ND DIVISION / 14TH CORPS

6TH WIS BAT / 3RD BRIGADE / 2ND DIVISION / 17TH CORPS / 12TH WIS BAT / 3RD BRIGADE / 2ND DIVISION / 17TH CORPS

1ST WISCONSIN / HEAVY ART / COMPANY C / 2ND BRIGADE / 2ND DIVISION / ART RESERVE / 1ST WISCONSIN / CAVALRY / 2ND BRIGADE / 1ST DIVISION / CAVALRY CORPS

3RD WIS BAT / 1ST BRIGADE / 2ND DIVISION / ART DIVISION / 8TH WIS BAT / 1ST BRIGADE / 2ND DIVISION / ART RESERVE / 10TH WIS BAT / 1ST BRIGADE / 2ND DIVISION / ART RESERVE

The monument is an elegant three-tiered square marble base surmounted by an octagonal granite shaft. Surmounting the shaft is a polished marble column

State of Wisconsin,
Column and Stelae

with a Corinthian capital; a sphere surmounts the capital. Erected at a cost of $4,072. Approximate total height is thirty-two feet; the base is thirteen by thirteen feet. The sculptor is unknown. The designer was Buemming and Dick of Milwaukee. The American Granite Company served as fabricator.

All of these units were present at Chattanooga; not all of them saw combat. However, among the first units to reach the crest of Missionary Ridge was the 24th Wisconsin, led by Capt. Arthur MacArthur—father of the future Gen. Douglas MacArthur.

Other Wisconsin monuments, granite stelae to the 15th VI (2.12.5) and 24th VI (2.16.1), stand on Missionary Ridge.

2.17.15 Subject: 8th Kansas VI, Stele
Location: Orchard Knob, west side   N 35 02 23 95 / W 85 16 21 50
Installed or dedicated: 1896
Media: Bronze, granite
Monument is a stele surmounting a base.

Inscription

THE 8TH KANSAS VOL. INFTY., / COL. JOHN A MARTIN, COMMANDING / 1ST
BRIGADE GEN. AUGUST WILLICH / 3RD DIV. GEN. T. J. WOOD, / NOVEMBER 23, 1863
/ MOVED ON THIS POINT AT 2.00 O'CLOCK P.M. FROM / THE RAILROAD TRACK IN
FRONT OF FORT WOOD AS SKIRMISHERS FOR THE BRIGADE AND SUP- / PORTED
BY THE BRIGADE CAPTURED THIS KNOB / AND LINE OF WORKS WITHOUT MUCH
RESIST- / ANCE AND BEFORE THE MAIN LINE ARRIVED. / THE REGIMENT REMAINED
IN THIS POSITION / UNTIL 3 O'CLOCK IN THE AFTERNOON OF THE / 25TH WHEN IT
MOVED WITH THE BRIGADE TO / ASSAULT THE ENEMY'S WORKS AT THE FOOT / OF
MISSIONARY RIDGE.

Erected by the Smith Granite Company, Westerly, Rhode Island, this monument describes the advance of the 8th Kansas in this area. The stone is believed
to be blue Westerly granite. The contractor was William Van Amringe of Boston
for the Smith Granite Company. Another Kansas monument, the common
soldier statue to the 8th Kansas VI (2.12.3), stands on Missionary Ridge.

2.18.1 Subject: Memorial Arch, Entryway, Silverdale Confederate Cemetery
Location: 7710 Lee Highway, 37421   N 35 02 23 39 / W 85 07 50 62
Installed or dedicated: 1901
Medium: Bronze, limestone
Monument is an archway and bronze tablet.

Inscription

ERECTED IN 1901 / BY THE / DAUGHTERS OF THE CONFEDERACY / CHAPTER 81 /
CHATTANOOGA TENNESSEE / TO COMMEMORATE THE VALOR / AND HEROISM THAT
OUR / CONFEDERATE SOLDIERS / DISPLAYED IN THEIR BATTLE FOR OUR / BELOVED
SOUTHLAND / IN THE WAR FROM 1861 TO 1865 / IN FRATERNAL RECOGNITION OF /
N. B. FORREST CAMP U.C.V. / IT IS NOT IN THE POWER OF MORTALS / TO COMMAND
SUCCESS, / THE CONFEDERATE SOLDIER DID MORE, / HE DESERVED IT.

Interred here are the bodies of approximately 155 Confederate soldiers who died while the Confederate Army of Mississippi was based in this area in the summer of 1862. In addition, body parts from Stout's hospitals were buried here. The grounds are adjacent to and briefly visible (to the discerning but still-prudent eye) to travelers on I-75 southbound.

The site was abandoned after the war, and the original wooden markers deteriorated or were vandalized. However, the N. B. Forrest Confederate Veterans Camp eventually purchased the site, and in 1901, a limestone and wrought-iron gate adorned with a Confederate battle flag was installed. A fieldstone wall and arch replaced wire fencing in the 1920s; a concrete archway and cast-iron commemorative plaques were installed in the 1930s. Today the Chattanooga Area Relic and Historical Association maintains the grounds.

East Tennessee

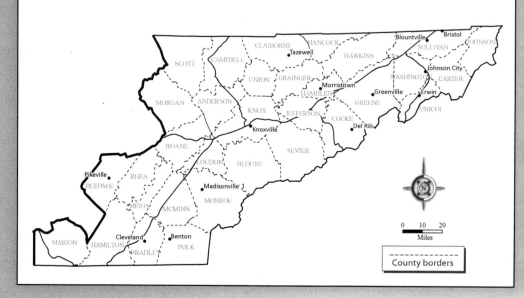

EAST
TENNESSEE

THE "LOYAL AND TRUE"

A T LEAST TWENTY-FIVE monuments stand in East Tennessee, including seven courthouse locations (Blountville, Erwin, Greeneville, Tazewell, Morristown, Madisonville, and Cleveland) several battlefield monuments in the Fort Sanders neighborhood of Knoxville, as well as Confederate and national cemeteries at Knoxville, and Confederate cemeteries at Bristol, Cleveland, Morristown, and Tazewell. The encampment of troops commanded by Lt. Gen. James Longstreet during the winter of 1862–63 is marked at Russellville.

East Tennessee describes the eastern third of the three Grand Divisions of Tennessee. Its succession of mountains, valleys, and ridges are geographically associated with Appalachia. Chattanooga and Knoxville were key population centers at the time of the war and remain so today. The area was crucial as a transportation and communication corridor between Tennessee, Georgia, and Virginia. The East Tennessee and Virginia Railway connected Virginia—and the Confederate capital at Richmond—with Tennessee and points farther south and west.

The region also had political and strategic value. East Tennesseans were much divided in their sentiments and convictions regarding slavery and secession, more so than Middle or West Tennessee, and arguably more so than any other section in the South. The legacy of those divisions persists: to this day the courthouse grounds of Greeneville display monuments to Union soldiers—"the Loyal and True"—as well as a tribute to Confederate general John H. Morgan, the "Thunderbolt of the Confederacy."

East Tennesseans voted against a referendum calling for secession on February 9, 1861. They rejected the Ordinance of Secession on June 8, 1861, although it won approval on a statewide vote. A petition to the state legislature was drawn up, demanding that East Tennessee be allowed to secede and form a separate Union-aligned state. The legislature rejected the petition, and Tennessee governor Isham Harris ordered state military units to occupy East Tennessee. East Tennessee political leaders took umbrage and strong countermeasures. Although Tennessee seceded from the Union, Senator Andrew Johnson and Congressman Horace Maynard retained their seats in Congress and pressed President Abraham Lincoln to "liberate" East Tennessee. Lincoln acceded.

East Tennessee proved to be a point of vulnerability for the Confederacy. The loss of control of the railroad crippled Confederate communications between the capital in Richmond and the western Confederacy. The defeat of Confederate forces at Chattanooga on November 25, 1863, effectively ended Southern efforts to retain control of East Tennessee, although the climax of the campaign arguably occurred four days later. At Fort Sanders in Knoxville on November 29, 1863, troops under the command of Lt. Gen. James Longstreet were turned back in a scant forty minutes in a valiant but vain and bloody assault. Other episodes that are commemorated include that of the "Five Union Men" at Afton who were hanged by Confederate authorities for their attempt to blow up a series of East Tennessee railroad bridges; Confederate partisans who were taken by surprise and ambushed by Union soldiers high up in what is now Cherokee Forest in Polk County; and Union soldiers who died in the sinking of the SS *Sultana* and are commemorated at Mount Olive Cemetery in Knoxville.

Sullivan County

3.1.1 Subject: Bristol, East Hill Cemetery, Confederate, Pyramid
Location: East State Street at Georgia Avenue, 37620   N 36 35 41 62 / W 82 10 26 68
Dedicated: May 29, 2010
Media: Brick and mortar, bronze, and concrete
Monument is a four-sided brick-and-mortar pyramid with bronze tablets, surmounting a concrete base.

Inscription

[Front]
[Seal of SCV] [72 names]
THIS MONUMENT DEDICATED / TO THE CONFEDERATE VETERANS / BURIED IN THIS CEMETERY / VETERANS BURIED IN UNKNOWN GRAVE[S] IN THE FIELD OF HONOR

[Seal of SCV] [80 names]
VETERANS BURIED IN UNKNOWN GRAVE[S] IN THE FIELD OF HONOR

ERECTED BY THE MEMBERS OF JAMES KEELING CAMP #52 / SONS OF CONFEDERATE VETERANS / BRISTOL, TENNESSEE *[68 names]*
VETERANS BURIED IN UNKNOWN GRAVE[S] IN THE FIELD OF HONOR

This hilltop cemetery straddles Bristol, Tennessee, and Bristol, Virginia. The first burials at East Hill Cemetery took place in 1857. The Confederate Medical Corps established facilities here in 1862, and the first burials of Civil War soldiers took place that same year. A phalanx of 105 headstones marking unknown and unmarked graves stands here and may include unknown Union soldiers. Standing on the west crest of the cemetery, facing downtown

Bristol, East Hill Cemetery, Pyramid, Confederate

Bristol, the monument honors the Confederate soldiers interred here from Virginia, North Carolina, Kentucky, Tennessee, South Carolina, Georgia, and Mississippi. Among those listed on the plaques are doctors, surgeons, a cadet of the Virginia Military Institute, members of the home guard, "Mrs. Legrand Sexton, Nurse, CSA.," and the Rev. Milton Clendenon, Company G, 22nd Virginia Infantry.

James Keelan (also spelled Keeling) is buried here. Keelan was called the "South's Horatius" as sole defender of the Strawberry Plains railroad bridge against "Unionist" bridge-burners in 1861.

3.1.2 Subject: Blountville, Courthouse Stele, Confederate
Location: 3411 TR 126, 37617   N 36 31 08 19 / W 17 38 12 23 40
Dedicated: June 6, 1928
Media: Bronze, granite
Monument is a bronze plaque set in a granite shaft.

Inscription
[Laurel wreath with unfurled Confederate battle flag]
DEDICATED TO / THE MEMORY OF THE / CONFEDERATE SOLDIERS / OF / SULLIVAN COUNTY, / TENNESSEE / WAR OF 1861–1865 / BATTLE OF BLOUNTVILLE / SEPTEMBER 22, / 1863 / ERECTED BY / NINETEENTH TENNESSEE CHAPTER / U.D.C. / JUNE 6, 1928

This UDC monument stands directly in front of the courthouse and is also on the site of the battle of Blountville, which took place on September 22, 1863. The inscription has two elements: a tribute to Confederate veterans of the

Blountville, Courthouse Stele, Confederate

"War of 1861–1865" and a commemoration of the battle. Here Union forces under Col. John W. Foster (2nd Brigade, 4th Division, 23rd Corps, including Tennessee troops fighting on the Union side) contended with approximately twelve hundred Confederate soldiers commanded by Col. James E. Carter (including the 1st Tennessee Cavalry and accompanying artillery) in the course of a four-hour conflagration. Union troops shelled the town and then undertook a flanking movement that compelled the Confederates to withdraw. Estimated casualties were 192 men—27 Union and 165 Confederate soldiers.

- The 19th Tennessee Infantry, from which the local UDC chapter took its name, was formed from companies enlisted from counties in East Tennessee. The regiment was present or engaged in every major battle of the Army of Tennessee. It was encamped with the Army of Tennessee at Greensboro, North Carolina, when the army surrendered on April 26, 1865.

Washington County

3.2.1 Subject: Johnson City, UDC Stele
Location: University Parkway and Lamont Street, 37601   N 36 18 45 14 / W 82 21 57 26
Installed or dedicated: October 8, 1931
Medium: Limestone
Monument is an inscribed boulder.

Johnson City, UDC Stele

Inscription

1861 / HERE WAS TRAINING / CAMP OF CONFEDERATE / REGIMENTS FROM THE / SOUTH ON THEIR WAY BY / RAIL TO VIRGINIA TO JOIN / GENERAL LEE.

IN FRONT OF THIS MARKER WAS THE PARADE GROUND / ERECTED BY U.C. CHAPTER OF THE / UNITED DAUGHTERS OF THE CONFEDERACY

This marker stands on a bluff of a residential neighborhood near the site of a Confederate training campsite at what is now University Parkway and Lamont Street. The railway still runs nearby; the neighborhood is residential and adjacent to East Tennessee State University. What troops these "Confederate Regiments" were is not specified and may derive from distant or secondhand memory. The reference to "Confederate Regiments from the South" is general; "General Lee" is the only name mentioned, although Robert E. Lee did not take command of what was to be the Army of Northern Virginia until June 1, 1862.

The Johnson City chapter of the United Daughters of the Confederacy dedicated the monument on October 8, 1931, on the occasion of the annual reunion of the Tennessee Division of the United Confederate Veterans that met in Johnson City. A description of the ceremonies was published in the Knoxville *Journal*, October 9, 1931: "A granite marker, erected by the Johnson City chapter, U.D.C., at the corner Lamont and Tennessee streets was dedicated formally, with veterans in attendance at five o'clock. The dedication address was made by Judge Samuel C. Williams, who reviewed the incident of 1861 when troops under General John H. Savage camped and trained on the spot, prior to joining in the campaign of Virginia."

"General John H. Savage," it should be noted, was a colonel in the Provisional Army of Tennessee and did not serve in Virginia.

Obelisk, Union, Mountain Home National Cemetery

3.2.2 Subject: Obelisk, Union, Mountain Home National Cemetery
Location: 53 Memorial Avenue, Mountain Home, 37684 N 36 18 46 17 /
W 82 22 33 80
Installed or dedicated: n.a.
Medium: Granite

Inscription

WALTER PRESTON BROWNLOW / MARCH 27, 1851, / JULY 8, 1910 / BROWNLOW

CLAYETTA ASHLAND BROWNLOW / NOV. 10, 1851 / OCT. 25, 1913

The obelisk at Mountain Home in Johnson City is the only monument, as such, on the grounds of this national cemetery, which was founded as a resting place for the bodies of Union soldiers. It is a lofty, dignified monument. There is no reference to the war in the inscription, however, and no sentiment or tribute to the figures interred here.

Walter Preston Brownlow did not serve in the military, but he was buried in the cemetery via a special dispensation to honor his work in founding what became known as the Mountain Home Branch of the National Home for Disabled Volunteer Soldiers. Brownlow was born in Abingdon, Virginia. In 1862, at the age of thirteen, he attempted to join the Union Army but was rejected due to his age. In 1901, Congress approved a bill introduced by Brownlow, by then a US congressman, to establish a national home in the Johnson City area. The home opened October 15, 1903. It recorded its first interment, Francis Conaty, on September 18, 1903, nearly one month before the first resident of the home arrived. The former congressman Brownlow and his wife Clayetta occupy the only graves inside Monument Circle.

The Mountain Home Branch was one of nine facilities funded by Congress to care for Union veterans of the Civil War. In 1973, it was transferred to the Veterans Administration, and the cemetery was designated a national cemetery. It covers nearly ninety-two acres and contains the remains of more than ten thousand veterans. Today the facilities of the former National Home are part of the James H. Quillen Veterans Affairs Medical Center, which is affiliated with the James H. Quillen College of Medicine at East Tennessee State University.

· Historian Suzanne Julin notes the "Soldiers Home" developed in the United States was modeled on a European tradition of maintaining government institutions caring for and supporting disabled veterans.

Greene County

Greeneville

3.3.1 Subject: Courthouse Stele to Brig. Gen. John H. Morgan
Location: 101 South Main Street, 37743
Installed: Late 1920s; dedicated: May 10, 1931
Medium: Tennessee marble
Monument is an inscribed marble stele.

Inscription

GENERAL / JOHN H. MORGAN / 1825–1864 / "THE THUNDERBOLT OF THE / CONFEDERACY" / FIRST LIEUTENANT, MARSHAL'S REGIMENT / OF CAVALRY IN THE MEXICAN WAR / CAPTAIN THE "LEXINGTON RIFLES" 1857 / CAPTAIN COMPANY A OF THE KENTUCKY / CAVALRY 1861 / COLONEL 2ND KENTUCKY CAVALRY 1862 / BRIGADIER GENERAL APPOINTED FROM / TENNESSEE DECEMBER 11 1862 / HIS COMMAND, NEVER EXCEEDING 4000 / MEN, WAS COMPOSED LARGELY OF KEN- / TUCKIANS AND TENNESSEANS. IT WAS / RENOWNED FOR BOLDNESS AND CELERITY / ON RAID, CARRYING TERROR INTO THE RE- / GION NORTH OF THE OHIO. / THE "GREAT RAIDER" WAS SURPRISED AT / NIGHT AND KILLED BY A DETACHMENT OF / THE COMMAND OF GEN. A. C. GILLEM ON / THE PREMISES OF THE WILLIAMS HOME / NEAR THIS SPOT SEPTEMBER 4 1864 / HIS HEROISM IS THE HERITAGE OF / THE SOUTH
[Erected by a group of private citizens in 1932]

This imposing courthouse homage to Brig. Gen. John H. Morgan, "Thunderbolt of the Confederacy," stands eight feet high by four feet by eighteen inches, weighs three tons, and is of rose-speckled Tennessee marble. Sam Highbarger was the sculptor.

Alabama-born John H. Morgan was courageous, personable, and a natural leader. The monument's praise is justified, but Morgan left a mixed legacy. The judgment of historian Wilmer L. Jones is that "for Southerners, he was a chivalrous knight, the gallant cavalier of romantic literature. To Northern citizens, he was a rogue. To his own army, he was a maverick. The real John

Courthouse Stele to Brig. Gen. John H. Morgan

Hunt Morgan was a little of each." He was shot and killed here, at Greeneville, on September 4, 1864, by night, by troops under the command of the other name mentioned on the monument, Maj. Gen. Alvin C. Gillem, a native of Middle Tennessee and a West Point graduate who sided with the Union when the war began. Morgan was defenseless at the time and offered surrender, but he was shot down by a Union soldier. No blame, however, is directly ascribed to Gillem, only to "a detachment of the command."

- The monument is said to have been erected in the middle of the night. This story remains unconfirmed, however, because of a lack of records of the event.

- An equestrian statue of Morgan stands in Lexington, Kentucky. Another monument to Morgan's command stands at Alexandria (see chap. 4).

Courthouse Common
Soldier Statue, Union

3.3.2 Subject: Courthouse Common Soldier Statue, Union
Location: Courthouse lawn, 101 South Main Street, 37743   N 36 09 46 16 /
W 82 49 51 64
Installed or dedicated: circa 1916
Media: Bronze, granite
Monument is a statue of a Union soldier standing at parade rest, surmounting a base.

Inscription
[Front]
TO THE MEMORY OF / THE UNION SOLDIERS / WHO ENLISTED IN / THE UNION ARMY / FROM GREENE COUNTY / WAR 1861–1865

IN THE HOUR OF / THEIR COUNTRY'S PERIL / THEY WERE LOYAL / AND TRUE.

ERECTED BY THE / UNION SOLDIERS' / MONUMENT ASSOCIATION: / *[3 names].*

[Seal of G.A.R.]
BURNSIDE POST NO. 8: G.A.R. / GREENEVILLE, TENNESSEE

Erected by the local Union veterans' organization, the Grand Army of the Republic, this is the only statue of a Union soldier at a courthouse site in Tennessee. Along the line of the Great Appalachian Valley from north to south, Pennsylvania to Alabama, this is the only Union monument at a courthouse site for nearly five hundred miles. The soldier faces north, looking alert, bearing a rifle, and carrying a knapsack, ready to move. Until the US Colored Troops (USCT) common soldier was dedicated at Madison in 2003 (4.22.10), this was the only sculpture of a Tennessee Union soldier in the state.

- The W. H. Mullins Company of Salem, Ohio, which served as the founder, produced numerous Union and Confederate monuments.
- The Grand Army of the Republic ("GAR") was founded in 1866. Membership was limited to honorably discharged veterans of military service who served between April 12, 1861, and April 9, 1865. The GAR exercised enormous political power: five GAR members were elected president of the United States.
- A state marker notes that Greeneville was the site of a convention that opposed secession and advocated the establishment of East Tennessee as a new Unionist state.

3.3.3 Subject: Statue, Andrew Johnson
Location: corner of College and Depot Streets, Greeneville, 37743
N 36 09 45 32 / W 82 49 46 42
Installed or dedicated: n.a.
Media: Bronze, granite
Monument is a statue surmounting a base.

Inscription
ANDREW JOHNSON / 1808–1875 / 17TH PRESIDENT / OF THE / UNITED STATES OF AMERICA / 1865–1869

This statue of Andrew Johnson, wartime governor of Tennessee, was sculpted by Jim Gray. The figure of Johnson stands on the corner of College and Depot Streets in downtown Greeneville, overlooking the Andrew Johnson National Historic Site.

A bronze tablet adjacent to the statue notes that Margaret Johnson Patterson Bartlett, great-granddaughter of Andrew Johnson, is the donor of this memorial as a tribute to "her illustrious ancestor." This "ageless image," the inscription declares, is dedicated to "an unsurpassed legend in American history to all mankind for generations upon generations yet unborn."

- Another cast of this statue stands on the state capitol grounds in Nashville.

Statue, Andrew Johnson

3.3.4 Subject: Andrew Johnson, National Cemetery, Shaft
Location: Andrew Johnson National Cemetery, 121 Monument Ave, 37743
N 36 09 19 78 / W 82 50 14 92
Installed or dedicated: 1878
Media: Granite, marble
Monument is an eagle surmounting a US flag–draped shaft and base.

Andrew Johnson, Shaft, National Cemetery

Inscription

[Relief of scroll, inscribed]
CONSTITUTION / OF THE / UNITED STATES
[Urn] [Relief of open book with hand]
ANDREW JOHNSON / SEVENTEENTH PRESIDENT / OF THE UNITED STATES / BORN
DEC. 29, 1808 / DIED JULY 31, 1875 / HIS FAITH IN THE PEOPLE NEVER WAVERED.

Andrew Johnson's remains were interred here at the crest of a hill on August 3, 1875. The site, known now as Monument Hill because of this family monument, was purchased by Johnson in 1852. It affords views of the surrounding area and was used during the war for observation and signaling.

This tombstone marking the grave of Andrew and Eliza Johnson makes no mention of the war, slavery, secession, Andrew Johnson's impeachment, or the role that this controversial figure played as a wartime governor of Tennessee. It is focused instead only—simply—on praising Johnson for his faith in the people.

- The hilltop cemetery was owned by the family until 1906, when it came under the jurisdiction of the War Department. The Park Service took charge of the cemetery in 1942. The site is still used for interments.

- Another statue of Johnson stands on the state capitol grounds in Nashville.

3.3.5 Subject: Afton, Lick Creek Hexagonal Shaft, "Five Union Men"
Location: 1270 Pottertown Road, east of Bridge Burners Boulevard, Mosheim, 37809   N 36 12 01 97 / W 83 00 49 52
Dedicated: January 1, 1980
Medium: Granite
Monument is a hexagonal shaft set on a base.

Inscription

[Front]

"IN THE HOUR / OF THEIR / COUNTRY'S / PERIL, THEY / WERE LOYAL / AND TRUE" ON THE NIGHT OF NOVEMBER / 8TH, 1861, THESE FIVE UNION / MEN ALONG WITH OTHERS, WHO / MOSTLY REMAIN UNKNOWN, / CARRIED OUT THE ORDERS OF / PRESIDENT ABRAHAM LINCOLN, / TRANSMITTED TO GENERAL / GEORGE H. THOMAS AND GIVEN / TO THEIR LEADER CAPTAIN DAVID / FRY, TO BURN THE EAST / TENNESSEE AND VIRGINIA / RAILROAD BRIDGE OVER / NEARBY LICK CREEK. ALL / FIVE MEN WERE SUMMARILY / EXECUTED BY CONFEDERATE / AUTHORITIES. THE FIVE EXE- / CUTIONS LEFT NEARLY TWENTY / FATHERLESS CHILDREN.

JACOB HARMON / PVT CO F 2 TENN VOL INF USA JUNE 2, 181 / DECEMBER 17, 1861 / HANGED AT KNOXVILLE, / TENNESSEE

HENRY HARMON / PVT CO F 2 TENN VOL INF USA / SEPTEMBER 3, 1839 / DECEMBER 17, 1861 / HANGED AT KNOXVILLE, / TENNESSEE

CHRISTOPHER A. HAUN / PVT CO F 2 TENN VOL INF USA / SEPTEMBER 5, 1821 / DECEMBER 11, 1861 / HANGED AT KNOXVILLE, / TENNESSEE

HENRY FRY / PVT CO F 2 TENN VOL INF USA / DECEMBER 7, 1823 / NOVEMBER 30, 1861 / HANGED AT GREENEVILLE, / TENNESSEE

JACOB M. HINSHAW / PVT CO F 2 TENN VOL INF USA / DECEMBER 8, 1840 / NOVEMBER 30, 1861 / HANGED AT GREENEVILLE, / TENNESSEE

Union sentiments are clearly described here: these "Five Union Men"—Jacob Hinshaw, Jacob and Henry Harmon (two brothers), Christopher Haun, and Henry Fry—are described as Union soldiers acting under the orders of President Lincoln. Their actions formed one element of a conspiracy to burn nine railroad bridges in Tennessee and northeast Alabama, with the goal of severing rail and telegraph connection between Virginia and the western

Afton, Lick Creek Hexagonal Shaft, "Five Union Men"

Confederacy as well as facilitating the invasion of the area by Federal troops stationed in Kentucky. The plot failed. A planned movement of Union troops into the area was canceled. The response by Confederate authorities was swift and decisive: the Harmon brothers and Christopher Haun were hanged at Knoxville; Henry Fry and Jacob Hinshaw were hanged in Greeneville. Their legacy remains mixed. The case raised concern about how to adjudicate between legitimate military acts of war and civilian acts of terror. The stand on this hexagonal shaft is clear: these men were Union soldiers acting under Federal authority. The full text of the wraparound inscription reads, "In the hour of their country's peril, they were loyal and true."

Unicoi County

3.4.1 Subject: Erwin, Courthouse Monument, Common Soldier, Confederate
Location: Unaka Way Street and Ohio Avenue, 37650   N 36 08 19 22 /
W 82 24 47 74
Installed or dedicated: June 3, 1930
Medium: Granite
Monument is a granite obelisk.

Inscription
[Front]
[Relief of Confederate battle flag]
1861–1865 / CONFEDERACY
TO THOSE WHO DIED FOR A SA- / CRED CAUSE, AND / TO THOSE WHO / LIVED TO
WIN A / NOBLER VICTORY / IN TIME OF PEACE.

[Relief of US flag]
1917–1918 / WORLD WAR

ERECTED BY / ROSALIE BROWN / CHAPTER, / UNITED DAUGHTERS OF / THE
CONFEDERACY, / JUNE 3, 1930.

TO THE WOMEN OF / THE CONFEDERACY / WHOSE FIDELITY, WHOSE / PURITY,
WHOSE GENTLE GENIUS IN / LOVE AND IN COUNSEL, / KEPT THE HOME SECURE, /
THE FAMILY A SCHOOL OF / VIRTUE, THE STATE A COURT / OF HONOR; WHO MADE
OF / WAR A SEASON OF HERO- / ISM AND OF PEACETIME / OF HEALING—THE GUAR-
/ DIANS OF OUR TRANQUIL- / ITY AND OF OUR STRENGTH.

[Relief of cross and hatchet]
"IN A RIGHTEOUS / CAUSE THEY WON / IMMORTAL GLORY, / AND NOBLY SERV- / ED"
THEIR NATION / IN SERVING MAN- / KIND." / WILSON.

This obelisk, eleven feet high, stands in a small park at the corner of Ohio
Avenue and Unaka Way Street in Erwin. Historian Mark A. Stevens reports
that the founding figure behind this monument was Mrs. R. W. Brown, president of the Rosalie Brown Chapter, United Daughters of the Confederacy,
whose aspiration for several years was to erect a monument in tribute to soldiers of the Confederacy as well as veterans of World War I. Along with the
monument commemorating the battle of Nashville, this is one of only two
Tennessee tributes to soldiers of both wars.

The quotation beginning "In a righteous cause" is taken from a Thanksgiving
address given by President Woodrow Wilson on November 17, 1918, six days
after the armistice ending World War I. The larger context reads, "Our gallant
armies have participated in a triumph which is not marred or stained by any
purpose of selfish aggression. In a righteous cause they have won immortal
glory and have nobly served their nation in serving mankind. God has indeed
been gracious.

Erwin, Courthouse Monument, Common Soldier, Confederate

"We have cause for such rejoicing as revives and strengthens in us all the best traditions of our national history. A new day shines about us, in which our hearts take new courage and look forward with new hope to new and greater duties."

Historian Kelli Nelson reports that approximately three hundred people attended the dedication ceremonies. During the event, Dr. J. L. Rosser of Bristol gave a speech entitled "The Inspiration of the Confederate Soldier." Rosser spoke of "the influence of Jefferson Davis, and the beloved leader of the Southland, Robert E. Lee[,] not forgetting the great part the heroic women of the South played during the four years of unceasing warfare." D. H. Rosier of the Unaka Post American Legion spoke for local World War I veterans who held "deep honor and reverence . . . for those who wore the gray of the Confederacy." During the ceremony, Mrs. Brown pinned the Southern Cross of Honor on Elbert L. Bailey, the county's only living Confederate veteran. A "saxophonic 'Dixie' rang through the air as the feeble old man [the last veteran], proudly erect, with eyes shining like the stars, stepped forward to have this badge of honor pinned on his coat."

3.5.1 Subject: Del Rio, Dixie Highway Stele to Robert E. Lee
Location: US 70, US 25, TR 9, at Tennessee / North Carolina state line
N 35 55 04 76 / W 82 54 45 10
Installed or dedicated: 1928
Media: Bronze, fieldstone
Monument is a bronze plaque mounted on a fieldstone stele.

Inscription

[Relief of Robert E. Lee on horseback, facing due east]
ERECTED AND DEDICATED BY THE / UNITED DAUGHTERS OF THE CONFEDERACY /
AND FRIENDS / IN LOVING MEMORY OF / ROBERT E. LEE / AND TO MARK THE ROUTE
OF THE / DIXIE HIGHWAY / THE SHAFT MEMORIAL AND HIGHWAY STRAIGHT /
ATTEST HIS WORTH—HE COMETH TO HIS OWN / LITTLEFIELD / ERECTED 1928

This marker stands on the crest of the ridge between Cocke County, Tennessee, and Madison County, North Carolina, elevation 1,512 feet, about twenty feet inside Tennessee. The network of roads called the Dixie Highway was an early twentieth century network linking north and south before the advent of systematized numbered routes. The name Dixie Highway was chosen to mark "Fifty Years of Peace" between the North and South; this UDC marker is duly inscribed "In loving memory of Robert E. Lee." Continued road development as well as the system of numbered roads rendered the system redundant. Only vestiges like this sign remain to mark this stretch of highway, which follows US 25W from Jellico to Knoxville and US 27 from Rockwood to Chattanooga.

Del Rio, Dixie Highway Stele to Robert E. Lee

Tazewell, Irish Cemetery, Confederate, Shaft

Claiborne County

3.6.1 Subject: Tazewell, Irish Cemetery, Confederate, Shaft
Location: Irish Cemetery Rd, off TR 33, south of intersection with US
25E   N 36 27 01 14 / W 83 24 28 56
Installed or dedicated: n.a.
Media: Fieldstone blocks, mortared
Monument is a tapered four-sided column, in stone, surmounted by a
cannonball.

Inscription
"SACRED TO THE MEMORY OF / UNKNOWN CONFEDERATE DEAD / WHO LAID DOWN
THEIR LIVES / AMONG STRANGERS FOR THE 'LOST CAUSE.'"

Scant history or documentation is available on the monument located in the
Tazewell Irish memorial cemetery. A county historian observes that Claiborne
County, like other East Tennessee counties, favored the Union and furnished
many soldiers to the Federal Army. No major military actions took place in
the county, but quartermaster units foraged in the area and company-size
engagements occurred in or near Tazewell; in addition, engagements between
regimental-sized forces took place for control of the Cumberland Cap.

· A granite footstone reads as follows:

REBUILT AND REDEDICATED / BY THE / SONS OF CONFEDERATE VETERANS / JUNE
3, 2000

Hamblen County

Morristown, Bethesda Cemetery

3.7.1 Subject: Unknown Confederate Dead, Stele
Location: Bethesda Cemetery, 4990 Bethesda Road, Morristown, 37814
N 36 14 52 19 / W 83 13 38 40
Installed or dedicated: 1989
Medium: Granite
Monument is a granite stele surmounting a base.

Inscription

WE REMEMBER / THE UNKNOWN C.S.A. SOLDIERS / WHO ARE HERE IN THESE [*SIC*] / HALLOWED GROUND / GIVEN IN MEMORY / BY / DISABLED AMERICAN VETERANS / AND AUXILARY CHAPTER 59 / 1989

Bethesda Presbyterian Church, completed 1835, was the scene of several actions during the war and served as a hospital after the battle of Bean's Station on December 14, 1863. Troops under Confederate Gen. James Longstreet wintered here in 1863–64. In October 1864, Federal troops pursued Confederate forces near here ("Vaughn's Stampede"); in November 1864, Confederates chased Union troops westward toward Knoxville ("Gillem's Stampede"). During one of these engagements, a cannonball struck the east wall of the church and caused structural damage.

The congregation is cited as a reminder of the effect of the Civil War on the Tennessee home front. The church closed during the war and resumed services from 1866 to 1871, but, it is said, the congregation divided on the issue of secession and never reconciled, and the church closed permanently in 1875.

Records of the war dead interred here are incomplete, but they include at least eighty unknown dead, most of whom are believed to be Confederate soldiers. They are given tributes by the three monuments in the cemetery, which collectively serve to indicate the uncertainty of the interments, including the possibility that Union soldiers are interred together with their Confederate counterparts.

3.7.2 Subject: Unknown Confederate Dead, Stele
Location: Bethesda Cemetery, 4990 Bethesda Road, Morristown, 37814
Installed or dedicated: 1921
Medium: Granite
Monument is a granite stele surmounting a base.

Inscription

IN HONOR OF THE 17 SOLDIERS / WHO DIED IN 1863 IN DEFENCE [*SIC*] / OF THE SOUTHLAND. THE NAMES / OF ONLY TWO ARE KNOWN, / 1ST GEORGIA CAVALRY.
[2 names]

Unknown Confederate Dead, Stele, Bethesda Church

THESE MARKERS WERE PLACED / BY THE SAM DAVIS CHAPTER / UNITED
DAUGHTERS OF THE / CONFEDERACY IN 1921.

3.7.3 Subject: Unknown Dead, Stele
Location: Bethesda Cemetery, 4990 Bethesda Road, Morristown, 37814
Installed or dedicated: n.a.
Medium: Granite
Monument is a granite stele surmounting a base.

Inscription
UNKNOWN DEAD / THIS PLOT IS SACRED TO / THE MEMORY OF SIXTY-FIVE /
UNKNOWN DEAD, MOST OF / WHOM ARE BELIEVED TO BE / CONFEDERATE SOLDIERS

3.7.4 Subject: Russellville, Campsite of the Army of Tennessee, Stele
Location: US 11E near Depot Street   N 34 15 23 17 / W 83 11 47 52
Dedicated: June 3, 1928
Media: Bronze, granite
Monument is a granite shaft with bronze plaque.

Inscription
CAMP SITE / OF THE / ARMY OF TENNESSEE / C.S.A. / 1863–64 / COMMANDED BY /
LIEUT. GEN. JAMES A. LONGSTREET / MAJ. GEN. LAFAYETTE MCLAWS, / BRIG. GEN. /
J. B. KERSHAW / ERECTED BY / SAM DAVIS CHAPTER / U.D.C.

After the battle of Bean's Station on December 14, 1863, twenty-five thousand
Confederate troops under the command of Lt. Gen. James Longstreet encamped in the area until February 1864. Longstreet used Russellville as his winter
quarters. His troops camped along the railroad and from the Holston to the
Nolichucky Rivers. Although the troops are associated in this inscription with
the Army of Tennessee, they were detached at this point, returned to Virginia
in 1864, and served thereafter with the Army of Northern Virginia.

Russellville, Campsite of the Army of Tennessee, Stele

Common Soldier Statue,
Confederate Cemetery, Knoxville

Knoxville

BETHEL CONFEDERATE CEMETERY

3.8.1 Subject: Common Soldier Statue, Confederate
Location: 1917 Bethel Avenue, 37915   N 35 58 28 51 / W 83 54 03 86
Cornerstone laid: May 21, 1891; dedicated: May 19, 1892
Medium: Marble
Monument is a common soldier, Confederate, surmounting a shaft and base.

Inscription

THIS SHAFT,
PLACED HERE WITH REVEREND [SIC] HANDS / MAY 19, 1892 / BY THE LADIES
MEMORIAL ASSOCIATION, / OF KNOXVILLE, TENNESSEE / COMMEMORATES /
THE HEROIC COURAGE AND THE UNSHAKEN CONSTANCY / OF MORE THAN 1600
SOLDIERS OF THE SOUTH, / WHO IN THE GREAT WAR BETWEEN THE STATES / 1861
TO 1865 / WERE INSPIRED / BY THE HOLINESS OF A PATRIOTIC AND IMPERSONAL
LOVE, / AND IN THE MOUNTAIN PASSES OF TENNESSEE, / WHETHER ON STRICKEN
FIELD OR IN A HOSPITAL WARD, / GAVE UNGRUDGINGLY THEIR LIVES / TO THEIR
COUNTRY.
"AND THEIR DEEDS, PROUD DEEDS, SHALL REMAIN WITH US, / AND THEIR NAMES,
DEAR NAMES, WITHOUT STAIN FOR US, / AND THE GLORIES THEY WON SHALL NOT
WANE FOR US, / IN LEGEND AND LAY, / OUR HEROES IN GRAY, / THOUGH DEAD,
SHALL LIVE OVER AGAIN FOR US."

"FORGOTTEN! NO! WE CANNOT ALL FORGET, / OR WHEN WE DO, FAREWELL TO
HONOR'S FACE / TO HOPE'S SWEET TENDANCE, VALOR'S UNPAID DEBT, / AND EV'RY
NOBLEST GRACE, / WHICH NURSED IN LOVE, MIGHT STILL BENIGNLY BLOOM /
ABOVE A NATION'S TOMB."
OUR CONFEDERATE DEAD

This imposing but weathered Tennessee marble edifice stands over the burial
site of more than sixteen hundred Confederate soldiers, including approximately one hundred killed in the assault on Fort Sanders. The graves of an
estimated fifty Union prisoners of war and Civil War veterans are also interred
here.

The statue, facing north, stands eight feet, six inches high and surmounts a
shaft forty-eight feet high. Knoxville artist Lloyd Branson served as the sculptor; Geo. W. Callahan & Bros. served as fabricators. The monument cost $4,500.
Located on Bethel Avenue in East Knoxville, Bethel Confederate Cemetery
is adjacent to Calvary Catholic Cemetery to the west and Knox County's
Pauper (Belleview) Cemetery to the east. The monument was erected by the
Ladies' Memorial Association and was unveiled on May 19, 1892. It is the largest Confederate monument in East Tennessee and is comparable only to the
Mount Olivet memorial in Nashville as the largest Confederate monument in
the state.

The Winstead family superintended the grounds from 1886 to 1989. The family's white frame house was erected circa 1886 and stands atop several unmarked graves. The last family descendent and caretaker, Miss Mamie Winstead, died in 1989 and willed the cemetery to the Hazen Historical Museum Foundation. The foundation, which also operates the Mabry-Hazen House, oversees care of the grounds to the present day.

· Poetic, even lyrical and effusive affections are displayed in the inscription. The excerpt beginning "And Their Deeds, Proud Deeds" is excerpted from Father Abram Joseph Ryan's poems "Our Dead" and "C.S.A." Ryan (1839–86) was a Roman Catholic priest and poet with a reputation as the "Poet Priest of the Lost Cause" and "Poet-Priest of the South." A Confederate soldier, Ryan also lost a brother in the war. He served at Saints Peter and Paul's parish in Knoxville from 1872 to 1878.

· The panel facing west is weathered, but the passage beginning "Forgotten No! We cannot all forget" seems to be an excerpt of the poem "Forgotten" by the Southern American writer Paul Hamilton Hayne (1830–86), poet, critic, and editor. His service in the Confederate Army was cut short by illness, but he too was a poet of the Lost Cause.

· At this writing, the cemetery is locked and closed weekdays and Sundays but is open Saturdays and by appointment.

3.8.2 Subject: Roster of Confederate Soldiers, Four Stelae
Installed or dedicated: 1961
Media: Bronze, granite
Monuments are four stelae displaying bronze plaques.

Inscription

[Left (excerpts)]
CONFEDERATE DEAD KILLED IN THE BATTLE OF KNOXVILLE
ALABAMA *[320 names]* ARKANSAS *[35 names]* FLORIDA *[9 names]*
FLORIDA *[153 names]* GEORGIA *[215 names]*
[Plaque at center:]
THESE TABLETS COMMEMORATE / THE CONFEDERATE DEAD KILLED / IN THE
BATTLE OF KNOXVILLE / 1861–1865 / ALSO INTERRED ARE FIFTY / CONFEDERATE
SOLDIERS AND / FIFTY FEDERAL PRISONERS OF WAR / WHOSE NAMES ARE
UNKNOWN / ERECTED 1961 THROUGH THE EFFORTS / OF / *[3 names]*

CONFEDERATE DEAD KILLED IN THE BATTLE OF KNOXVILLE
GEORGIA *[263 names]* KENTUCKY *[16 names]* LOUISIANA *[17 names]* MISSISSIPPI
[65 names]

CONFEDERATE DEAD KILLED IN THE BATTLE OF KNOXVILLE
MISSISSIPPI *[7 names]* / NORTH CAROLINA *[77 names]* / TENNESSEE *[137 names]* / TEXAS
[26 names] / VIRGINIA *[12 names]* / STATES UNKNOWN *[96 names]*

The 1892 monument was appended in 1961, during the centennial of the war, with these four marble stelae inscribed with the names of approximately sixteen hundred soldiers whose bodies are interred here.

FORT SANDERS

3.8.3 Subject: Fort Sanders, UDC Battlefield Stele
Location: Laurel Avenue, near 505 South 17th Street SW   N 35 57 31 08 / W 83 56 01 40
Installed or dedicated: November 29, 1914
Medium: Marble
Monument is a shaft surmounted by a sculpture of a draped Confederate battle flag.

Inscription
[Seal of UDC]
TO THE MEMORY OF THE CONFEDERATE SOLDIERS / WHO FELL IN THE ASSAULT ON FORT SANDERS / NOVEMBER 29, 1863.
NOR WRECK NOR CHANGE, NOR WINTER'S BLIGHT, / NOR TIME'S REMORSELESS DOOM, / SHALL DIM ONE RAY OF GLORY'S LIGHT / THAT GILDS YOUR GLORIOUS TOMB.
ERECTED BY KNOXVILLE CHAPTER NO. 89, / UNITED DAUGHTERS OF THE CONFEDERACY,
NOV. 29, 1914.

The hilltop UDC monument of Tennessee marble was erected in memory of an assault by Confederate soldiers against Fort Sanders on November 29, 1863. Confederate Lt. Gen. James Longstreet judged that a dawn assault could surprise and seize Fort Sanders, a key element of the Knoxville defenses held by forces under the command of Maj. Gen. Ambrose E. Burnside. The attack was

UDC Battlefield Stele, Fort Sanders, Knoxville

valiant but ill-planned and unsuccessful. Union wire entanglements frustrated the advance. The fort's outer ditch—twelve feet wide and four to ten feet deep with vertical sides—was an additional challenge as was the fort's nearly vertical exterior slope. Rifle and artillery fire was vigorous. A few Confederates got into the fort only to be wounded, killed, or captured. For all that took place, it was over in less than forty minutes. The Confederates suffered 813 casualties: 129 killed, 458 wounded, 226 missing.

- · The tribute beginning "Nor Wreck Nor Change, Nor Winter's Blight" is taken from Theodore O'Hara's poem, "The Bivouac of the Dead." O'Hara was an attorney, reporter, editor, and writer; he also served as a soldier in the Mexican War as well as in the Confederate Army.

3.8.4 Subject: 79th New York VI, Battlefield Shaft
Location: Corner of 16th Street and Clinch Avenue   N 35 57 32 62 / W 83 56 01 40
Dedicated: September 23, 1918
Medium: Marble
Monument is a four-sided shaft.

Inscription
[Front]
[Relief of Union and Confederate soldiers shaking hands, an unfurled US flag waving behind them]
THE HANDS THAT ONCE WERE RAISED IN STRIFE / NOW CLASP A BROTHER'S HAND, / AND LONG AS FLOWS THE TIDE OF LIFE— / IN PEACE, IN TOIL, WHEN WAR IS RIFE— / WE SHALL AS BROTHERS STAND, / ONE HEART, ONE SOUL FOR OUR FREE LAND

79TH N.Y. INFANTRY / (HIGHLANDERS) / FIRST BRIGADE (MORRISON'S) / FIRST DIVISION (FERRERO'S) / NINTH CORPS (POTTER'S) / BURNSIDE'S COMMAND ARMY OF THE OHIO / COMMANDED BY CAPTAIN WILLIAM S. / MONTGOMERY, THE 79TH N.Y. VOL. INF. / TOOK A PROMINENT PART IN THE OPER- / ATIONS OF THE SIEGE OF KNOXVILLE, / AND WAS STRENUOUSLY ENGAGED IN / THE DEFENSE OF FORT SANDERS, HOLD- / ING THE NORTHWEST BASTION, / NOVEMBER 29, 1863 / NEW YORK

[Ninth Corps emblem: light artillery gun barrel crossed with ship's anchor]

[Relief of Scottish emblem of thistles and shields]
E LACESSET IMPUNE

[Emblem of State of New York]
EXCELSIOR

This impressive hilltop monument of Tennessee marble to the 79th New York—the "Cameron Highlanders"—stands in a residential neighborhood near the grounds of Fort Sanders and was sponsored by the 79th New York Veterans Organization. Organized in 1858, the 79th modeled itself after the

79th New York VI, Battlefield Shaft

British Army's original 79th Cameron Highlanders and adopted the British unit's name and number. The unit comprised primarily immigrant Scots and Irishmen who claimed Celtic ethnicity. The 79th has three monuments in Knoxville but none at any other battlefields, although the regiment fought in over thirty battles during the war.

Funding of $5,000 was appropriated for the project by the New York State legislature. James F. R. Vosper served as designer. Veterans in attendance at the ceremonies for the monument were said to have "evinced pardonable pride and unbounded glee gazing on their marble memorial as it was being brilliantly dedicated." One account noted that the "exercises alternated between addresses by veterans—Confederate and Federal—and those contributed by civilians, representing a later generation. For both natives and visitors, let alone the Highlanders themselves, this was an interstate function that makes for lasting and fond recollection."

The 79th mustered in May 29, 1861. First Manassas. Second Manassas. Chantilly. South Mountain. Antietam. Fredericksburg "Mud March." Vicksburg. Knoxville. Petersburg. Surrender of Lee. Grand Review. Mustered out July 14, 1865. Lost 198 officers and enlisted men killed, mortally wounded, or by disease.

- The inscription beginning "The Hands" was composed by poet Joseph I. C. Clarke. "Nemo Me Lacesset Impune" is translated as "No one attacks me with impunity" and is the motto of Scotland and of the Order of the Thistle. "Excelsior," translated as "Ever Upward," is the motto of New York State.

- No apparent trace of Fort Sanders remains apart from the name for a mostly residential neighborhood adjacent to the Knoxville campus of the University of Tennessee—"the Fort," locals call it. However, three columns (two at Clinch Avenue, corner of 11th Street, and one at 11th Street and World Fair Park Drive) give visitors and residents some notice of the venerability and significance of the ground, which the UDC and 79th New York monuments elaborate. The columns are inscribed "FORT SANDERS / ERECTED 2003."

KNOXVILLE NATIONAL CEMETERY

3.8.5 Subject: Common Soldier Statue, Union
Location: 939 Tyson Street, 37917   N 35 58 32 30 / W 83 55 34 90
Dedicated: October 15, 1906
Media: Bronze, marble
Monument is a granite tower surmounted by the figure of a soldier, in bronze, facing west.

Inscription
[Front]
E PLURIBUS UNUM
IN MEMORIAM / UNION SOLDIERS / OF / TENNESSEE / OCTOBER 15, 1896.

"REST ON EMBALMED AND SAINTED DEAD, / DEAR AS THE BLOOD YE GAVE; / NO IMPIOUS FOOTSTEP HERE SHALL TREAD / THE HERBAGE OF YOUR GRAVE; / NOR SHALL YOUR GLORY BE FORGOT / WHILE FAME HER RECORD KEEPS, / OR HONOR POINTS THE HALLOWED SPOT / WHERE VALOR PROUDLY SLEEPS."
TENNESSEE FURNISHED FOR THE UNION ARMY 31092 MEN. / CASUALTIES 6776.
US / 1861–1865

Common Soldier Statue, Union

TO THE TENNESSEE MEN / WHO LAID DOWN THEIR LIVES A VOLUNTARY /
SACRIFICE ON / FREEDOMS [*SIC*] ALTAR: / WHO ENDURED WITH FORTITUDE
TEMPORARY BANISH- / MENT FROM THEIR MOUNTAIN HOMES; WHO FOLLOWED /
THE FLAG THEY LOVED / IN SCORES OF BATTLE-FIELDS AND WHO FELL / VALIANTLY
CONTENDING FOR NATIONAL UNITY, / THIS MONUMENT / IS LOVINGLY ERECTED BY
THEIR SURVIVING / COMRADES AND FRIENDS.
US / 1896–1901

This is one of the largest monuments in Tennessee; it is the largest Civil War
monument east of Chattanooga. It was practically destroyed by lightning on
August 22, 1904, but was re-erected by the federal government at a cost of
$4,300. The earlier monument was surmounted by the figure of an eagle; the
present version has a sculpted figure of a common soldier. East Tennessee
Unionist sentiments are clear: "Tennessee Men . . . fell valiantly contending
for the National Unity."

- The monument, sometimes referred to as the Wilder Monument, was
  sponsored by the Grand Army of the Republic, Department of Tennessee, and was initially erected by dint of contributions of $11,000,
  from more than seven thousand donors. The monument's sixty-foot
  tall crenulated tower is taller by design than the Confederate cemetery monument in Knoxville and surmounts a memorial chamber. The
  interior chamber is accessed through iron gates on two sides of the
  tower and features a stained-glass window. Inscribed in the chamber
  are names of "Tennessee Union Troops Cavalry."

79th New York VI, Shaft

- · The inscription beginning "Rest on Embalmed" is taken from the poem "The Bivouac of the Dead" (1847) by Theodore O'Hara.
- · Knoxville National Cemetery is notable for its layout, by Capt. E. B. Chamberlain, in which burials and headstones are arranged in concentric circles around a central flagpole. The site predates Arlington Cemetery; Maj. Gen. Ambrose Burnside established the grounds as a cemetery shortly after the siege of Knoxville. Remains were interred or reinterred from Knoxville and the surrounding area, as well as from Kentucky, Virginia, and North Carolina. Today it contains the graves of more than eight thousand soldiers of the Civil War, the Spanish-American War, World War I, World War II, Korea, and Vietnam. The cemetery closed to new interments in 1990.

3.8.6 Subject: 79th New York VI, Shaft
Location: Section A   N 35 58 31 64 / W 83 55 36 88
Installed or dedicated: circa 1864
Media: Marble, Tennessee limestone
Monument is a common headstone-shaped memorial, several inches higher than the adjacent tombstones, facing southeast.

Inscription

BY / ALL THE THOUSANDS THAT HAVE / DIED FOR THEE, / O LOVED REPUBLIC, BE THOU JUST AND FREE!

SACRED / TO THE MEMORY OF / DECEASED SOLDIERS / OF THE / 79TH N.Y. VOLS. / "HIGHLANDERS."
THEIR COUNTRY'S SOLDIERS, (LIVING, / THIS THEIR SIMPLE STORY,) / BUT DEAD, HER BEST DEFENSE AND HER UNDYING GLORY.

Mount Olive Cemetery, *Sultana* Memorial Stele

At least thirteen graves of soldiers of the 79th Infantry surround the monument, including two men who are described as having "died in defense of Fort Sanders, Nov. 29, 1863." Stonecutters in the regiment prepared the stele; the quotations are attributed to the regimental chaplain, Rev. Crammond Kennedy.

3.8.7 Subject: Mount Olive Cemetery, SS *Sultana* Memorial Stele
Location: 2500 Maryville Pike, 37920, near Mount Olive Baptist Church
N 35 54 32 42 / W 83 56 11 16
Installed or dedicated: July 4, 1916
Medium: Tennessee marble
Monument is a marble stele set on a base.

Inscription

[Front]
IN MEMORY OF THE MEN WHO WERE ON THE SULTANA THAT WAS DESTROYED /
APRIL 27 1865 BY EXPLOSION ON THE MISSISSIPPI RIVER NEAR MEMPHIS TENN /
FROM IND 352 KY 125 MICH 243 OHIO 460 TENN 365 VA 50 MO 2
[Relief of steamship with Sultana inscribed and US flag with thirteen stars on the stern]
[4 names] TRUST / THIS STONE WAS DONATED BY GRAY EAGLE MARBLE CO
CARVED BY JOSEPH HENRY TROUTT
1916 / MEMORIAL TO THE SULTANA INCIDENT
1ST, 2ND, 3RD TENN CAV *[83 names]*

3RD, 4TH, 7TH, 8TH, 11TH, 12TH TENN CAV, 2ND TENN MTD INF, 3RD TENN VI
[89 names]

3RD TENN CAV *[175 names]*

3RD TENN CAV *[74 names]*

The steamboat SS *Sultana* was en route north, near Memphis on the Mississippi River, two hours before dawn on April 27, 1865, when it exploded, killing some eighteen hundred men, most of them former prisoners of war newly freed from camps at Andersonville, Georgia, and Cahaba. Journalist Jack Neely notes that one quarter of the passengers on the SS *Sultana*, and about a quarter of the dead, were members of the 3rd Tennessee Volunteer Cavalry. (Most of the regiment had been captured in the course of operations against Forrest, September 16–25, at Athens and Sulphur Branch Trestle, Georgia.) There are no plaques: all the names are inscribed by hand. These are common soldiers—citizen soldiers. There are no ranks inscribed, just names and units of Tennessee men.

OLD GRAY CEMETERY

3.8.8 Subject: Common Soldier Statue, Confederate, Tombstone
Location: 543 North Broadway, 37917 N 35 58 28 28 / W 83 55 35 40
Installed or dedicated: n.a.
Medium: Marble
Monument is a statue of a Confederate soldier standing at parade rest, surmounting a base.

Inscription
HORNE

The Horne monument is distinctive for the near life-size representation of a Confederate soldier, adjacent to the graves of Confederate veterans William and John Horne. William Asbury Horne (1845–91) was an assistant quartermaster with the 42nd Georgia Infantry, and John Fletcher Horne (1843–1906) was a sergeant with what is called the "Kansas Bottom Tennessee Artillery," although no official record for the unit is known at this writing. Reflecting a tendency to depict veterans as they were at the time of the sculpting rather than during the war, the marble figure is older and heavier than was typical of wartime Confederate soldiers.

- An estimated fifty-seven hundred Confederate and Union veterans, including military and wartime civilian personnel, are interred here. The first burial at Old Gray Cemetery dates from 1851; marble is a common medium of the stonework. The thirteen-acre site adjacent to the national cemetery was named in honor of English poet Thomas Gray (1716–1771), author of "Elegy Written in a Country Churchyard."

3.8.9 Subject: UDC Stele, Dr. Harvey Baker
Location: Baker-Peters House, 9000 Kingston Pike, US 11 / TR 1
N 35 54 45 16 / W 84 04 55 34
Installed or dedicated: 1926
Medium: Granite
Monument is a shaft surmounting a base.

Common Soldier Statue, Confederate, Tombstone

Inscription

[CS battle flag]

IN MEMORY OF / ABNER BAKER / A / CONFEDERATE SOLDIER / DIED SEP. 4, 1865 / AGED 22 YEARS / A MARTYR FOR MANLINESS / AND / PERSONAL RIGHTS / "COWARDS DIE MANY TIMES / THE BRAVE BUT ONCE"

ERECTED 1926 / BY / THE ABNER BAKER CHAPTER / UNITED DAUGHTERS OF THE CONFEDERACY

Standing at this busy suburban intersection is the venerable Baker-Peters House, a two-story Greek Revival structure constructed circa 1849 by Dr. Harvey Baker. The house served as a hospital during the war. Harvey Baker, a civilian, was killed on this site on June 19, 1863, by Federal soldiers. His son Abner Baker served as a private in Co. I, 2nd Tennessee Cavalry. Baker may have been seeking to avenge his father's death when he killed a Union veteran at the courthouse in Knoxville. He was arrested and hanged. His remains are interred at First Presbyterian Church Cemetery in Knoxville.

· The Abner Baker Chapter No. 1404 of the UDC remains active at this writing.

IN MEMORY OF
ABNER BAKER
A
CONFEDERATE SOLDIER
DIED SEPT. 4, 1865
AGED 22 YEARS
A MARTYR FOR MANLINESS
AND
PERSONAL RIGHTS
"COWARDS DIE MANY TIMES
THE BRAVE BUT ONCE"
ERECTED 1926
BY
THE ABNER BAKER CHAPTER
UNITED DAUGHTERS OF THE CONFEDERACY

UDC Stele, Dr. Harvey Baker

Madisonville, Courthouse Stele, Confederate

Monroe County

3.9.1 Subject: Madisonville, Courthouse Stele, Confederate
Location: 310 Tellico Street South, 37354   N 35 31 11 93 / W 84 21 46 50
Installed or dedicated: January 1, 2004
Medium: Granite
Monument is a granite stele.

Inscription

[Front]
IN MEMORY OF THOSE WHO SERVED / CIVIL WAR 1861–1865 / MONROE COUNTY /
CONFEDERATE
4TH (BRANNER'S) TENNESSEE CAVALRY BATTALION . . . / 3RD (VAUGN'S) TENNESSEE
INFANTRY REGIMENT / COMPANIES "B," "F," "H" AND 2ND "K". / 39TH (W.M.
BRADFORD'S) TENNESSEE INFANTRY / REGIMENT COMPANY "K". / 59TH TENNESSEE
INFANTRY REGIMENT / COMPANIES "B," "E" AND "G". / 62ND TENNESSEE INFANTRY
REGIMENT / COMPANIES "C," "D," "H" AND "K" / MONROE COUNTY / FEDERAL /
9TH TENNESSEE CAVALRY REGIMENT / COMPANY "L" / 12TH TENNESSEE CAVALRY
REGIMENT / COMPANY "K" / 3RD TENNESSEE MOUNTED INFANTRY REGIMENT /
COMPANIES "C," "D," "G" AND "H".
ERECTED NOV. 2004 / BY MONROE COUNTY TENNESSEE

Sponsored by the county, and reflecting divisions of loyalty within East
Tennessee, this granite stele credits the service of Monroe County soldiers
on both sides of the war. No major battles were fought in Monroe County, but
Union and Confederate troops occupied the town at various times, and Federal
troops burned down the courthouse at this site in 1864.

Polk County

3.10.1 Subject: Benton, Confederate, Stele
Location: Confederate campsite, Cherokee National Forest   N 35 08 51 22 /
W 84 37 00 66
Installed or dedicated: n.a.
Medium: Fieldstone
Monument is an inscribed fieldstone.

Inscription

T. B. HANEY, / A CONFEDERATE / SOLDIER WAS KILL / ED HERE FEB. 15, 1865 /
SOLDIERS / CAMPSITE, FEB. 15, 1865 / CAPTEN [SIC] P. L. BIBLE / LIEUTENANT A.
D. DONALDSON / TOM HANEY KILLED / W. M. CROCKETS LEG SHOT / CRAWLED TO
GRASSEY CREEK. / JASPER MCCONNELL. / GEORGE RENFRO CAPTURED. / CO. B, 62,
TENN. C.S.A.

Standing near the crest of a ridge of Chilhowee Mountain, elevation 2,084
feet, this inscribed stone tells the story of an engagement in which Union
soldiers alleged to be bushwhackers attacked Confederates also alleged to be

Benton, Stele, Confederate

bushwhackers. The Confederates were attacked while they were encamped. At least one Confederate soldier was killed, another was wounded, but four others escaped. The official records indicate that this was a local conflict: the participants—both Union and Confederate—were from Bradley and Polk Counties. The Federals may have been from Co. D, 5th Tennessee Mounted Infantry. The Confederates were believed to be part of the 1864 "Polk County Murders," also known as the "Madden Branch Massacre," when marauding forces under command of Capt. John Gatewood raided local communities and killed as many as twenty-seven citizens.

Bradley County

Cleveland

3.11.1 Subject: Courthouse Common Soldier Statue, Confederate
Location: Robert E. Lee, Ocoee and Broad Street, 37311   N 35 09 50 61 / W 84 52 23 38
Installed: 1910; dedicated: May 31, 1911 or June 3, 1911
Media: Granite, marble
Monument is a common soldier surmounting a shaft and base.

Inscription
[Front]
CSA / 1861 / 1865
TO OUR KNOWN / AND UNKNOWN / CONFEDERATE DEAD

MAN WAS NOT BORN TO HIMSELF ALONE, BUT TO HIS COUNTRY

ERECTED BY THE / JEFFERSON DAVIS CHAPTER / UNITED DAUGHTERS / OF THE CONFEDERACY

Cleveland, Courthouse
Common Soldier Statue,
Confederate

The Jefferson Davis Chapter No. 900 of the UDC, founded on April 15, 1905, remains active at this writing and sponsored this monument, located several blocks from the courthouse. It is the only courthouse common soldier in East Tennessee. The UDC's motto, "Man was not born to himself alone, but unto his country," is inscribed on the monument. The first initiative in the project was taken on April 15, 1905, when "Mrs. J. H. Hardwick invited a number of women to her home to consider organizing a Cleveland Chapter of the UDC." Looking back in 1930, a history of the chapter further observed that "we got up a county fair[,] published a cook book, gave entertainments with local talent, and in various ways raised the money, and it was a happy day for our Chapter when we unveiled the five-thousand dollar monument on June 3, 1911." The John D. Traynor Camp, UCV, lent assistance to the project, and a delegation from the Oviatt Post, GAR, attended the dedication ceremonies. Four years later, the GAR Oviatt Post erected their own monument at Fort Hill Cemetery.

The monument is of Italian marble on an Elberton gray granite base, weighing about fifteen thousand pounds and standing twenty-eight feet high, surmounting a base that is twelve feet square. The McNeel Marble Works served as the fabricator. The sculpture was made in Italy, but the sculptor is unknown.

Fort Hill Cemetery

3.11.2 Subject: Grand Army of the Republic, Shaft, Union
Location: Ninth Street SE, 37311, corner of Park and Worth Streets
N 35 09 21 95 / W 84 52 49 52
Installed or dedicated: May 30, 1914
Media: Concrete, fieldstone
Monument is a tablet set between two shafts.

Inscription

THIS MONUMENT TO / PERPETUATE THE MEMORY / OF THE BOYS IN BLUE / IN THE WAR OF 1861–65 / WHO HAVE LIVED IN / BRADLEY COUNTY WAS / DEDICATED BY OVIATT / POST NO 20 G.A.R. / MAY 30 1914

The Grand Army of the Republic (GAR) erected Tennessee monuments here and at Knoxville but at few other cemeteries in the South and none elsewhere in Tennessee or Virginia. No causes are espoused. The restoration of the Union is not celebrated. By this modest monument, the "Boys in Blue" are simply remembered.

· Fort Hill Cemetery was established in 1836. The high ground was occupied by Federal troops because of its commanding views of the town, the valley, railroad, and adjacent road network.

3.11.3 Subject: Unknown Confederate Soldiers, Memorial Headstone
Location: Veterans Drive and Glaze Street   N 35 09 21 03 / W 84 52 54 72
Installed or dedicated: circa 1990
Medium: Marble
Monument is a marble tombstone.

Inscription

[SCV seal]
270 / UNKNOWN / CONFEDERATE / SOLDIERS / C.S.A.

A large number of unknown Confederate dead are interred here with only this modest, undated monument to mark their place. No major battles were fought in Bradley County during the war, but numerous raids, skirmishes, foraging expeditions, occupations, and encampments occurred, beginning at least in September 1863, when Union troops first arrived in the area, and continuing for the rest of the war.

Grand Army of the Republic, Shaft, Union

Unknown Confederate Soldiers, Memorial Headstone

33rd Alabama Infantry, Shaft

3.11.4 Subject: 33rd Alabama Infantry, Shaft
Installed or dedicated: November 4, 1989
Medium: Granite

Monument is a granite shaft.

Inscription

CSA
[Crossed flags: CS battle flag and regimental flag, 33rd Alabama]
IN MEMORY / THE 33RD ALA. VOLUNTEERS / WHO DIED NOV. 4, 1862 / IN A TRAIN /
WRECK SOUTH OF CLEVELAND, / ENROUTE TO CHATTANOOGA
[17 names]
DEDICATED NOV. 4, 1989

Another monument sponsored by the Jefferson Davis Chapter No. 900 of the
UDC, this one is to soldiers of the 33rd Alabama Infantry who were killed
in a train derailment near Cleveland and whose bodies were buried here. At
the time of the accident "there was no time for burials," according to Larry
Holcomb, who played an influential role in establishing the monument. The
regiment was compelled to move on. "These men were apparently laid in their
graves and returned to earth . . . known only to God."

A contemporary account was published by journalist Allen M. Banner in
the *Cleveland Daily Banner* at the dedication of the monument. It notes that
the "train wrecked and the cars piled on top of each other. We took axes to
chop the wood and get the dead out. Then we took the 67 men (injured) and
brought them to a hospital in Cleveland, and the 17 dead we buried in a long
ditch we dug and marked their grave . . . and they moved on to join the battle
in Murfreesboro."

Confederate Cemetery, Isabella T. Hardwick, Stele

The 33rd Alabama was organized at Pensacola, Florida, on April 23, 1862. The regiment served in the campaigns of Stones River, Chattanooga, Atlanta, and Middle Tennessee. Surviving elements of the regiment were with the army when it surrendered in North Carolina in April 1865.

3.11.5 Subject: Confederate Cemetery, Isabella T. Hardwick, Stele
Installed or dedicated: 2009
Medium: Granite
Monument is a granite shaft.

Inscription
CSA / ISABELLA TUCKER / HARDWICK / CONFEDERATE CEMETERY / EST. 1862

Extant records are incomplete on this site. The Hardwick family of Cleveland is believed to have donated the land for this cemetery. Emma L. Hampton's history of the UDC notes that a predecessor group, the Ladies Confederate Memorial Association, was established on March 15, 1898, "for the purpose of caring for and beautifying the graves of the Confederate dead who are buried in our cemetery." The records also indicate that Cooksey A. Harris, first president of the local UDC chapter, chaired the first meeting, at which the chapter apparently nominated Isabella Minerva Tucker (1835–1915) to be "Chapter Mother." She was "a real daughter of the Confederacy, who was always ready, not only with her wise counsel, but with her means, to help in every undertaking."

Pikeville City Cemetery, Unknown Confederate Dead, Two Stelae

Bledsoe County

3.12.1 Subject: Pikeville City Cemetery, Unknown Confederate Dead, Shaft
Location: Adjacent TR 127 bypass, Pikeville   N 35 36 06 87 / W 85 11 44 36
Installed or dedicated: n.a.
Medium: Limestone
Monument is a stele facing east.

Inscription
16 UNKNOWN / CONFEDERATE / DEAD

Virtually nothing is known about the dead soldiers interred on a rise of the
Pikeville City Cemetery in the Sequatchie Valley of East Tennessee. A local
history indicates that these may be cavalrymen of Forrest's command who
passed through the area. An adjacent marble stele reads

Inscription
SIXTEEN UNKNOWN / CONFEDERATE / SOLDIERS / C.S.A.

Middle Tennessee

Fort Donelson National Battlefield · Clarksville · Springfield · Lafayette · CLAY · PICKETT

STEWART · MONTGOMERY · ROBERTSON · SUMNER · MACON

Gallatin · Hartsville · JACKSON · OVERTON · FENTRESS

HOUSTON · CHEATHAM · TROUSDALE · Carthage · SMITH

Charlotte · DAVIDSON · Nashville · Lebanon · WILSON · PUTNAM

DICKSON · DEKALB · Smithville · WHITE

HUMPHREYS · Franklin · Stones River National Battlefield · Murfreesboro · Woodbury

HICKMAN · WILLIAMSON · RUTHERFORD · CANNON · McMinnville · Spencer

PERRY · MAURY · Spring Hill · Chapel Hill · Beech Grove · WARREN · VAN BUREN

Columbia · Mount Pleasant · Wartrace · COFFEE · Altamont

LEWIS · Farmington · Shelbyville · Manchester

Lewisburg · BEDFORD · Tullahoma · GRUNDY · SEQUATCHIE

Waynesboro · MARSHALL · University of the South (Sewanee)

GILES · Lynchburg · Winchester

WAYNE · LAWRENCE · Pulaski · Mulberry · MOORE · FRANKLIN

Fayetteville · LINCOLN

Minor Hill

County borders

MIDDLE
TENNESSEE
"VALOROUS GRAY, GLORIOUS BLUE"

CHAPTER 4 describes monuments at seventeen courthouse sites;
the battlefields at Murfreesboro, Franklin, Nashville, and Fort
Donelson; the state capital at Nashville; the Confederate cemeteries
at Clarksville, Fort Donelson, Franklin, Murfreesboro, and Nashville; and the
national cemeteries at Fort Donelson, Nashville, and Stones River.

Dramatic advances and retreats were characteristic of the war in Middle
Tennessee; its landscape is characterized by rolling hills and fertile stream
valleys. There were also skilled maneuvers, hard-earned victories, tactical and
strategic blunders, bloodletting, political infighting, and military triumphs on
both sides. Among the key campaigns, actions, or engagements that took place
were Fort Henry (February 6, 1862); Fort Donelson (February 13–15, 1862);
the fall of Nashville on February 25, 1862; the battles of Hartsville (December
7, 1862) and Stones River (December 31, 1862, and January 1–2, 1863); the
Tullahoma Campaign of June 23–June 30, 1863; and the Nashville Campaign,
November–December 1864, including the battles of Franklin (November 30)
and Nashville (December 15–16). Cavalry forays were led by Confederate generals Nathan B. Forrest, Joseph Wheeler, and John H. Morgan. Raids by Union
cavalry were led by Brig. Gen. Samuel P. Carter and Col. William P. Sanders.
None of these raids changed the overall course of events in the war, but they af-
fected logistics; absorbed time, resources, and flesh and blood; caused what we
would call collateral damage among civilians; and almost certainly lengthened
the conflict. The movement of Union and Confederate armies, cavalry, raiders,
or marauders across the landscape afflicted many communities. Partisan bushwhacking, guerilla warfare and harassment, and criminal depredations and
vandalism against the population and its property were common.

Political sentiments were divided: although Middle Tennessee voters favored secession in 1861, the monuments at Crossville, Cumberland County,
and at Spencer, Van Buren County, evince diverse loyalties. Unity is the theme
of the battle of Nashville monument on the Granny White Pike and Battlefield
Drive. In a gesture of reconciliation, it gives tribute to Union and Confederate
soldiers: "Oh, Valorous Gray, in the Grave of Your Fate, Oh, Glorious Blue."

Crossville, Cumberland County

Cumberland County

4.1.1 Subject: Crossville, Courthouse Stelae, Confederate and Union
Location: Opposite the courthouse, 20 South Main Street, 38555
N 35 56 53 75 / W 85 01 36 08
Installed or dedicated: May 28, 2001
Medium: Bronze, sandstone
Monument comprises three sandstone block stelae with bronze panels.

Inscription

CONFEDERATE STATES ARMY / 1861–1865 / C.S.A.
[99 names in 5 columns]

[SCV seal]
ERECTED BY THE / SGT. WILLIAM A. HAMBY CAMP 1750 / SONS OF CONFEDERATE
VETERANS / AND THE SCV LADIES AUXILIARY / IN HONOR OF THOSE FROM /
CUMBERLAND COUNTY / WHO SERVED IN THE CIVIL WAR / STONE DONATED BY THE
ROSE FAMILY / OF TENNESSEE BUILDING STONE / IN MEMORY OF / SGT. MCKENZIE
ROSE CO. B 5TH INF. U.S.A. / DESIGNED BY DON R. HEPBURN / STONEWORK BY BREN
DAUGHTERY / DEDICATED MAY 28, 2001

UNITED STATES ARMY / 1861–1865 / U.S.A.
[89 names in 4 columns]

Crossville stands along the Cumberland Plateau at the intersection of the east-west stage road between Knoxville and Nashville, and the north-south Kentucky Stock road between Middle Tennessee and Kentucky. Today US 70, TN 127, and I-40 pass through or near the town. During the war, the crossroads attracted the attention of Union and Confederate troops as well as marauding irregulars. Divided loyalties in the area led to vicious local conflicts and much suffering on the part of the local population.

Erected by the Sons of Confederate Veterans (SCV), this monument reflects the divisions, with ninety-nine names in four Confederate columns and eighty-nine names in five Union columns.

Van Buren County

4.2.1 Subject: Spencer, Courthouse Stele, Confederate
Location: Courthouse grounds, 38585   N 35 44 51 10 / W 85 28 01 92
Dedicated: June 1, 1988
Medium: Granite
Monument is a granite stele surmounting a concrete base.

Inscription

IN MEMORY OF THOSE WHO WERE KILLED / OR MISSING IN ACTION FROM VAN BUREN / COUNTY DURING THE CIVIL WAR
[81 names in 2 columns]
ERECTED BY THE VAN BUREN COUNTY / HISTORICAL SOCIETY—1988

[Crossed sword and musket]
C.S.A.

Spencer stands on the western edge of the Cumberland Plateau, and this soldiers' memorial is on the lawn of the 1906 courthouse. The monument stands adjacent to World War I and World War II memorials, as well as a flagpole flying the US flag. The 1988 stele gives tribute to those killed or missing in action. Ranks are inscribed for the men, but no distinctions are offered between Union or Confederate loyalties. There are bipartisan overtones to the inscription—no tributes or causes are espoused—but the reverse side of the stone is plainly inscribed "CSA."

Warren County

McMinnville

4.3.1 Subject: Courthouse Obelisk, 16th Tennessee Infantry, CSA
Location: N 35 40 54 10 / W 85 46 24 02
Installed or dedicated: 1904
Medium: Marble
Monument is an obelisk.

McMinnville: Warren County Courthouse Obelisk, 16th Tennessee Infantry, CSA

Inscription

IN MEMORY OF / THOSE MEMBERS OF THE / 16TH TENN. REGT. C.S.A. / KILLED IN BATTLE, / WHOSE NAMES ARE INSCRIBED HEREON. / ERECTED BY / THEIR COLONEL / JOHN H. SAVAGE, / 1904.
[217 names]

The 16th Tennessee Infantry organized June 1861, served throughout the war, and was paroled May 1, 1865, at Greensboro, North Carolina. John H. Savage served as colonel of the 16th Tennessee. Savage petitioned the state legislature to fund this, the only courthouse regimental monument in Tennessee. The project was approved; Savage, however, died on March 26, 1904, just six weeks before the monument's unveiling on May 10, 1904.

Warren County voted against secession, but after the election of Abraham Lincoln as president, the community sent an estimated two thousand soldiers to fight for the Confederacy. The 16th, 35th, and 84th Infantry were raised in Warren County, in addition to the 22nd Infantry Battalion and two companies of the 11th Cavalry.

4.3.2 Subject: Jesse Walling Tablet, Confederate
Location: Between 108 and 110 East Main Street, 37110   N 35 40 52 60 / W 85 46 20 56
Dedicated: circa 1925
Medium: granite
Monument is a granite plaque set between two buildings.

Jesse Walling Tablet, Confederate

Inscription

JESSE / WALLING

I ENLISTED / IN THE LORD'S / CAUSE WHEN / YOUNG. LATER / I ENLISTED / IN THE / CONFEDERATE / CAUSE AND / WAS WOUNDED / AT / MURFREESBORO / AND LATER / DISCHARGED / BY PRESIDENT / DAVIS. / THE LORD / HAS BEEN / GOOD TO ME / 85 YEARS. / THIS STONE IS NOT / TO BE MOVED FOR / LOVE OR MONEY.

This unusual monument—a granite wall slab, about twenty-five inches wide and twelve feet high—is set in a gap between two Main Street office buildings. It stands as a testimony to the two professed causes in Jesse Walling's life. Walling (1841–1930) served with Company E, 16th Tennessee. After the war, he was a businessman and mayor of McMinnville.

Smith County

4.4.1 Subject: Carthage, Courthouse Stele, Confederate
Location: Main and Second Streets, off US 70   N 36 15 04 75 / W 85 57 08 00
Installed or dedicated: circa 1940
Medium: Granite
Monument is a granite stele.

Inscription
CONFEDERACY / 1861–1865 / CAPT. HENRY W. HART / CHAPTER U.D.C.

The records of the Capt. Henry W. Hart Chapter of the United Daughters of the Confederacy (UDC) extend only from 1941 to 1953, but the women left this granite legacy on the courthouse lawn. An estimated twelve hundred men from Smith County served in the Confederate Army. An undetermined number joined the Federal Army. "A Veterans of all wars" obelisk on the courthouse grounds, dedicated in 1976, has a "Civil War" roster with 138 names inscribed.

- During the war, Carthage served as a base for military and partisan operations. The Confederate Army of Mississippi passed through Carthage en route to Kentucky during the Kentucky Campaign of 1862. Union Brig. Gen. George Crook established a military base here in March 1863 to contest Confederate partisan activity in East and Middle Tennessee.

DeKalb County

4.5.1 Subject: Smithville, Courthouse Shaft, Confederate
Location: South Public Square, Smithville, 37166   N 35 57 38 25 / W 85 48 47 16
Installed or dedicated: 1996
Medium: Granite, limestone
Monument is an inscribed obelisk.

Inscription
[Front]
ATLANTA / CHICKAMAUGA / MURFREESBORO
THIS MONUMENT IS DEDICATED / TO THE MEMORY OF ALL / DEKALB COUNTIANS WHO / SERVED THE CONFEDERACY. / THEY SACRIFICED MUCH FOR / THE CAUSE OF AN INDEPENDENT SOUTH. / THEIR COURAGE AND / PATRIOTISM TO THE STATE OF / TENNESSEE IS AN EXAMPLE / TO ALL GENERATIONS.
[SCV seal]
ERECTED BY / SONS OF CONFEDERATE VETERANS / SAVAGE-GOODEN CAMP #1513 / 1996

ANTIETAM / SEVEN PINES / SPOTSYLVANIA
CONFEDERATE INFANTRY UNITS / RAISED IN DEKALB COUNTY
[Roster]

Smithville Courthouse Shaft

MILL SPRINGS / PERRYVILLE / GETTYSBURG
SHILOH / FRANKLIN / NASHVILLE
CONFEDERATE CAVALRY UNITS / RAISED IN DEKALB COUNTY
[Roster]

MILL SPRINGS / PERRYVILLE / GETTYSBURG
CONFEDERATE CAVALRY UNITS / RAISED IN DEKALB COUNTY
[Roster]

Erected in 1996, this monument might be described as a retro design that har-
kens back to fiftieth-year commemorations of the war, when many Southern
monuments were rich and expansive in visual detail, and sentimental but still
defiant in their inscriptions. Like many SCV monuments, this one substitutes
regimental detail for grandeur of design or scale.

The monument shows a profound loyalty to the Confederacy: over one hundred years after Appomattox, the defense of "an Independent South" is still
invoked as a just cause. DeKalb County was bitterly divided regarding secession; the rancor began before the war, and continued during and after, but
these rosters testify to the county's commitment to the CSA.

· With one exception, all of the units displayed served in what is today
  referred to as the western theater of war. The 7th Tennessee Infantry
  was sent east and served with the Army of Northern Virginia.

Alexandria Town Square Obelisk

4.5.2 Subject: Alexandria, Brig. Gen. John H. Morgan Obelisk
Location: City square, Main Street, between High and Church Streets, 37010
N 36 04 39 71 / W 86 02 01 12
Installed or dedicated: 1999
Medium: Bronze, granite
Monument is an obelisk set on a three-tiered base.

Inscription
[Front]
GEN. / JOHN H. / MORGAN

[Inscribed figure of cavalryman riding a horse, moving at a gallop]
GEN. MORGAN'S / GREAT / INDIANA AND OHIO / RAID BEGAN HERE / JUNE 11, 1863, / AND ENDED LESS / THAN 100 MILES / FROM LAKE ERIE / JULY 26, 1863 /

[SCV seal]
ERECTED BY / SAVAGE—GOODNER / CAMP 1513 / 1999

[SCV seal]
GEN. MORGAN LEFT / HERE DEC. 21, 1862, / WITH 2,500 / HORSEMEN ON HIS / KENTUCKY / CHRISTMAS / RAID. THE RAID / CONCLUDED IN / SMITHVILLE / JAN. 5, 1863, / AFTER THE RAIDERS / CAPTURED 1887 / ENEMY SOLDIERS / AND DE-STROYED / $2,000,000 IN / FEDERAL PROPERTY.

John H. Morgan's rise through the ranks of the Confederate Army was meteoric. As a captain he led a cavalry squadron in central Kentucky; at Shiloh he was promoted to colonel. He commanded a regiment during the Corinth siege, then took two regiments on a raid through Kentucky from July 4 to August 1, 1862. For the "Christmas Raid," an effort to disrupt Union supply lines, December 21, 1862–January 5, 1863, he was promoted to brigadier general and also received the thanks of the Confederate Congress.

The Ohio Raid mentioned in the inscription was epic, dramatic, and disastrous. Morgan exceeded his authority by initiating the raid, then violated explicit orders not to cross the Ohio River. Along with most of his command, he was captured near New Lisbon, Ohio, on July 26, 1863, notwithstanding the fact, as the monument states, that the raid "ended less than 100 miles from Lake Erie." He was imprisoned in the Ohio State Penitentiary but escaped on November 26, 1863.

The 4.5-ton obelisk stands in the middle of a shopping square in Alexandria. Another monument to Morgan (3.3.1) stands at the Greeneville Courthouse. Two others commemorate the battle of Hartsville, fought under Morgan's command (4.20.1 and 4.20.2).

Grundy County

4.6.1 Subject: Altamont, Cemetery Stele, Confederate, Stele
Location: Town cemetery off Fitchtown Road, Veterans Park, 37301
N 35 25 48 10 / W 85 43 21 70
Dedicated: September 24, 2004
Medium: Bronze, granite
Monument is a stele surmounting a base.

Inscription
STARS AND BARS 1861–1863 [Flag icon]
STAINLESS BANNER [Flag icon]
GREAT SEAL OF THE CONFEDERACY [Bronze seal]
3RD NATIONAL 1865–PRESENT 1863–1865 [Flag icon]
2ND NAVAL JACK 1863–1865 [Flag icon]
CS BATTLE FLAG 1861–1865 [Flag icon]
"SURRENDER MEANS THAT THE HISTORY OF / THIS HEROIC STRUGGLE WILL BE WRITTEN BY / THE ENEMY, THAT OUR YOUTH WILL BE TRAINED / BY NORTHERN SCHOOL TEACHERS, LEARN FROM / NORTHERN SCHOOL BOOKS, THEIR VERSION OF THE / WAR, AND TAUGHT TO REGARD OUR GALLANT DEAD AS / TRAITORS AND OUR MAIMED VETERANS AS FIT / SUBJECTS OF DERISION."
GENERAL PATRICK CLEBURNE, CSA / KILLED NOV 30, 1864

TO / THE MEMORY OF / ALL MEN, WOMEN AND CHILDREN / FROM GRUNDY COUNTY / THAT CONTRIBUTED TO THE / DEFENSE OF THEIR HOMELAND / DURING THE WAR FOR / SOUTHERN INDEPENDENCE
[SCV seal]

Standing in Altamont, the county seat of Grundy County, this monument displays a staunch and ominous warning attributed to Irish-born Confederate soldier Maj. Gen. Patrick R. Cleburne, circa 1861. It also gives a broad tribute to the men, women, and children from Grundy County who contributed to the war effort "for Southern Independence."

Including children in the commemoration is unique, but it is consistent with the nature of the American Civil War as an all-consuming conflict—"total war," as later historians would call it.

Franklin County

Winchester, Confederate Memorial Cemetery

4.7.1 Subject: Stele and Roster, SCV
Location: South Vine and 6 Avenue SW   N 35 10 49 50 / W 86 06 43 88
Dedicated: April 5, 2003
Medium: Granite
Monument is a granite stele surmounting a base.

Inscription
[CSA battle flag]
THE / FRANKLIN COUNTY / CONFEDERATE / MEMORIAL CEMETERY
IN MEMORY OF THE BRAVE MEN / FROM THE FRANKLIN COUNTY / AREA WHO DEFENDED THEIR / HOMELAND AGAINST / NORTHERN AGGRESSION / 1861–1865

THE FOLLOWING CSA UNITS WERE / COMPOSED OF MEN FROM / FRANKLIN COUNTY AND THE / SURROUNDING AREA. SOME MEN / FROM FRANKLIN COUNTY SERVED / IN OTHER CSA UNITS. / CO. K, 4TH TN CAVALRY / CO. B, C, D, AND E, 1ST CONF. INF. REGT. (TURNEY'S) / CO. E, 23D TN. INF. BN. / CO. K 32D TN. INF. REGT. / CO. G & I, 41TH TN INF. REGT. / CO. D, 44TH TN INF. REGT.

The UDC monument to Confederate soldiers from Winchester Cemetery is nearby and was erected in 1950, only five years after the end of World War II. The UDC cross is evocative of the marble headstones erected for the dead of World War II in national cemeteries, but this SCV example, erected fifty-five years later, offers a strong advocacy for the Franklin County Confederate soldiers' defense of "their homeland against Northern Aggression."

· A granite stele erected November 12, 2007, at the base of the monument displays the following text and roster:

IN MEMORY OF THE CONFEDERATE SOLDIERS OF FRANKLIN COUNTY WHO ANSWERED THE CALL TO DEFEND THE HOMELAND BUT WHO NEVER RETURNED. THEY DIED IN BATTLE—FROM WOUNDS—FROM DISEASE—IN POW CAMPS
[SCV Seal]
[Roster of 332 soldiers in five columns, by name, unit, and cause of death]
ERECTED BY GEN. A. P. STEWART CAMP 1411 SONS OF CONFEDERATE VETERANS ON NOVEMBER 12, 2007

Stele and Roster, SCV, Winchester, Confederate Memorial Cemetery, Franklin County

The cemetery also maintains gravesites with headstones of soldiers from Tennessee, Alabama, Georgia, Arkansas, Mississippi, Louisiana, Florida, and Kentucky.

4.7.2 Subject: Lt. Gen. Alexander P. Stewart, Stele
Installed or dedicated: 2007
Medium: Granite
Monument is a stele surmounting a base.

Inscription
"OLD STRAIGHT"
[Inscribed CSA battle flag]
LIEUTENANT GENERAL / ALEXANDER P. STEWART
OCTOBER 2, 1821 / AUGUST 30, 1908
GENERAL STEWART WAS A RELUCTANT MILITARIST, EDUCATOR, / AND DEFENDER
OF THE SOUTH. / HE GRADUATED WEST POINT ACADEMY [SIC] IN 1842

Confederate Lt. Gen. Alexander P. Stewart had extensive service in Middle Tennessee with the Army of Tennessee during the war. He participated in the Tullahoma Campaign of 1863 as division commander, then passed through Middle Tennessee again as commander of the Third Corps during Hood's Campaign of 1864. "Old Straight" was respected by officers and rank-and-file soldiers alike as a solid, dependable leader.

· A bust of Stewart is outside the courthouse at Chattanooga (see chap.
   2); a stele to him stands at Hoover's Gap.

4.7.3 Subject: Granite Cross, UDC
Location: N 35 10 49 68 / W 86 06 43 82
Installed or dedicated: 1950
Medium: Granite
Monument is a cross and funereal urn surmounting a base.

Inscription
TO THE CONFEDERATE / SOLDIERS / 1861–1865 / ERECTED BY / PETER TURNEY
CHAPTER / U.D.C. 1950

This is one of only a few crosses on a Confederate monument in Tennessee—
another is on the courthouse podium at Lafayette. Crosses were destined to be
common features of tombstones in the twentieth century, especially military
tombstones during World War II, but Calvinist theological decorum may have
influenced design in such a way as to make them uncommon in Tennessee.

4.7.4 Subject: Unknown, Unmarked Graves, Confederate, Stele
Installed or dedicated: June 4, 2000
Medium: Granite
Monument is a granite stele.

Inscription
ERECTED BY PETER TURNEY CHAPTER UDC / IN MEMORY OF THE CONFEDERATE
SOLDIERS BURIED IN THIS CEMETERY / WHOSE TOMBSTONES NO LONGER EXIST /
JUNE 4, 2000
[6 names]

The Peter Turney Chapter of the UDC was founded in 1927 and remains active
at this writing. This granite stele, adjacent to the UDC's 1950 granite cross,
offers a testimony to the fidelity and care of commemorative groups who continue to take note of the missing and unrecovered names of those interred here
and elsewhere in the South.

University of the South, Sewanee

4.7.5 Subject: Lt. Gen. Edmund Kirby Smith, Relief
Location: 735 University Avenue, Sewanee, 37383   N 35 12 16 02 / W 85 54 56 78
Unveiled: May 5, 1939; dedicated: May 16, 1940
Media: Bronze, sandstone
Monument is a plaque with a relief portrait.

Inscription
[Front, relief:]
GENERAL EDMUND KIRBY-SMITH, C.S.A. 1824–1893
[Plaque at base:]
KIRBY-SMITH

Lt. Gen. Edmund Kirby Smith, Relief, University of the South, Sewanee

EDMUND KIRBY-SMITH / 1824–1893 / WEST POINT—1845 / TWICE BREVETTED
MEXICAN WAR—1848 / BRIGADIER GENERAL C.S.A.—1861 / GENERAL C.S.A.—1864
/ PROFESSOR, SEWANEE, 1875–1893 / THIS MEMORIAL ERECTED BY / UNITED
DAUGHTERS OF THE CONFEDERACY / TENNESSEE DIVISION

Edmund Kirby Smith was a professor at Sewanee, a position given equal status
with his military service to the United States and his rank as the last full general of the Confederate Army. This monument is a rectangular wall with a bronze
relief portrait of the general in uniform emplaced on the face of an obelisk
made of Tennessee sandstone blocks; the whole surmounts a circular sandstone base with a semicircular seating area in back. The sculptor is unknown.

Kirby Smith served the Confederacy from its inception to the end of the
conflict. He was wounded in action at First Manassas and served in the eastern
and western theaters of the war. He is perhaps best known as commander of
the Trans-Mississippi Department of the Confederacy—Arkansas, western
Louisiana, and Texas. The area became known as "Kirby Smithdom" because
of its isolation from the rest of the Confederacy after the fall of Vicksburg.

- Smith's remains are interred at the university cemetery. Also buried
  there is Brig. Gen. Francis A. Shoup, chief of artillery under Maj. Gen
  William Hardee, Episcopal rector, and professor of math at Sewanee.
  Shoup's body is interred under two crosses: the Christian cross and the
  crossed cannons of the artillery.

- "Kirby Smith" is the usual spelling. The hyphenation of Kirby Smith,
  here and on his tombstone, appears to be irregular.

- Clergy and lay delegates from southern Episcopal dioceses founded
  Sewanee, the University of the South, in 1857. Bishop Leonidas Polk,

destined to serve as a Confederate lieutenant general, was a founding figure and laid the cornerstone for the university's central building in October 1860. A monument to the cornerstone is nearby, off University Avenue. The opening was delayed by the war, however, and Federal troops who occupied the area in 1863 are said to have vandalized the cornerstone, breaking it up for souvenirs. The building was never completed, but the university opened in 1868.

Lincoln County
Fayetteville

4.8.1 Subject: Courthouse Common Soldier Statue, Confederate
Location: Courthouse, Confederate Park, College Street and Elk Avenue, 37334
N 35 09 06 16 / W 86 34 10 54
Installed or dedicated: 1904
Medium: Marble
Monument is figure of a Confederate common soldier, surmounting a base.

Inscription

[Front]
THIS CARVEN STONE IS HERE TO TELL / TO ALL THE WORLD THE LOVE WE BEAR / TO THOSE WHO FOUGHT AND BLED AND FELL / WHOSE BATTLE CRY WAS DO AND DARE / WHO FEARED NO FOE, BUT FACED THE FRAY / OUR GALLANT MEN WHO WORE THE GRAY / A TRIBUTE FROM THE ZOLLICOFFER-FULTON CHAPTER, U.D.C.

PRESERVE THE TRUTH IN HISTORY / 1861–1865 / IN LOVING MEMORY OF / THE THREE THOUSAND / CONFEDERATE SOLDIERS / OF LINCOLN COUNTY / WHOSE PATRIOTISM AND / HEROISM ARE HELD IN / PERPETUAL REMEMBRANCE.
CREST TO CREST THEY BORE OUR BANNER / SIDE BY SIDE THEY FELL ASLEEP / HAND TO HAND WE REAR THIS TOKEN / HEART TO HEART WE KNEEL AND WEEP.
CONFEDERATE SOLDIERS

IN PERPETUAL REMEMBRANCE

Confederate Park, established in 1905, forms a kind of outdoor museum of local Civil War history. This monument is its centerpiece. Erected by the Zollicoffer-Fulton Chapter of the UDC, which is no longer extant, it displays a Confederate soldier facing north. The statue was made in Carrara, Italy. Lewis Peach, a local Confederate veteran, erected the monument. An accompanying plaque states that the pedestal is of white Georgia marble and the base is "Bedford stone."

Of the dedication ceremonies, the Fayetteville *Observer* published this report on September 13, 1906:

There were fully three thousand people present at the unveiling of the Monument and the exercises were of a character that was gratifying in the extreme to those [who] were participants in the bloody drama of forty years ago. . . . As the clock in the tower struck eleven the cord was pulled

Fayetteville: Lincoln County Courthouse Common Soldier Statue, Confederate. At left: UDC Stele: Tribute to CSA Partisans

and the drapery floated down, revealing the statue in all its beauty. The thirteen states which furnished troops for the Southern cause were represented by thirteen little girls dressed in white. In their beauty and purity they fittingly represented the justice of the Southern Cause and the purity of Southern motives. They came forward, removed their crowns of roses, and laid them at the base of the monument.

· The inscription beginning "Crest to Crest" is excerpted from the poem "Pro Memoria," by Ina M. Porter, published in 1867 in *War Poetry of the South*. It also appears on the Mount Pleasant monument.

4.8.2 Subject: UDC Stele: Tribute to CSA Partisans
Location: Courthouse grounds
Dedicated: June 15, 1914
Medium: Limestone

Inscription
JOHN MASSEY / WILLIAM PICKETT / FRANK BURROUGHS
MARTYRED / JUNE 15, 1864
ORIGINAL MARKER ERECTED / JUNE 15, 1914 BY U.D.C.

This frail fieldstone marker commemorates another example of righteous grievances lodged against occupying Union troops during the war. The marker formerly stood at the site of the hanging of three Confederate partisans.

The wartime compatriot of these "martyrs," as the monument describes them, is Sam Davis. The figures here are placed in context with the example set by Davis of Southerners conducting themselves with a spirit of sacrifice in the face of almost implacable opposition.

· An adjacent plaque explains the story behind the "martyrdom":

ON JUNE 15, 1864, THOMAS MASSEY, WILLIAM PICKETT, AND FRANK / BURROUGHS WERE ARRESTED AND WERE TO BE EXECUTED WITHOUT TRIAL BY / UNION GENERAL E. A. PAYNE FOR THE ALLEGED CHARGE OF BUSHWHACKING. / HEARING OF THE ORDER, JOHN MASSEY, THE OLDER BROTHER OF THOMAS / MASSEY OF THE FIRST TENNESSEE REGIMENT WENT TO PAYNE TO TELL HIM / THAT THOMAS, HIS YOUNGER BROTHER, HAD NEVER BEEN IN THE / ARMY, AND WAS A HUSBAND AND FATHER. HE OFFERED HIS BLOOD INSTEAD OF / HIS BROTHER'S. PAYNE RELEASED THOMAS AND ARRESTED JOHN. AT 3:00 P.M., THE THREE MEN WERE EXECUTED TWO BLOCKS NORTH OF HERE WHERE / THIS ORIGINAL STONE WAS FIRST PLACED.

4.8.3 Subject: Courthouse UDC Statue, Female
Location: Southwest side of the courthouse square   N 35 09 04 92 / W 86 34 13 56
Installed or dedicated: 1904
Medium: Cast iron
Monument is a standing female figure surmounting a shaft with two flanking fountains and base.

Inscription
TO THE WOMEN OF THE CONFEDERACY, / WHO KEPT INTACT THE HOMES OF THE / SOUTH, WHILE THE MEN OF THE SOUTH / WERE FIGHTING HER BATTLES, AND / WHO GAVE TO THEIR SOLDIERS, THEIR / CHILDREN, AND THEIR LAND THE / WATER OF LIFE, HOPE AND COURAGE, / THIS FOUNTAIN IS ERECTED BY THEIR / GRATEFUL DESCENDANTS, THE / DAUGHTERS OF THE CONFEDERACY.

Erected by the Zollicoffer-Fulton Chapter of the UDC, this extravagant tribute to the wartime generation of women is notable for blending neoclassical features with contemporary industrial materials as well as a gesture to temperance by dint of the fountain. The monument is a cast-iron figure of a female surmounting a painted cast-iron base. A plaque at the base indicates that it was made by the J. L. Mott Iron Works of the Mott-Haven section of the Bronx, New York. It may be modeled on a cast-iron fountain, twenty-five feet tall, that the company displayed at the Philadelphia Centennial Exposition in 1876.

· Smithsonian records note that the statue stands approximately four feet; the base is approximately four by two by two feet. The tiered rectangular base has a drinking fountain on either side.

Mulberry

4.8.4 Subject: Town Square Common Soldier Statue, Confederate
Location: South of TN 50, Mulberry Town Square, 37359   N 35 12 37 82 N / W 86 27 37 10
Installed or dedicated: September 27, 1909
Medium: Granite, marble
Monument is a common soldier surmounting a base.

Inscription

61–65
IN GRATEFUL / REMEMBRANCE / OF THE 300 / CONFEDERATE / UNCONQUERED / SOLDIERS / WHO WENT OUT / FROM MULBERRY
ERECTED SEPT. 27, 1909 / BY MULBERRY CHAPTER NO. 996 / U.D.C.

1861–1865 / WE KEPT THE SOUTHLAND'S FAITH: FELL AT THE POST OF DUTY

The marble figure of a common soldier, sculptor unknown, stands approximately four feet tall on a granite base that elevates the figure by four feet, six inches. The common soldier faces north; a period photograph shows a solemn crowd standing alongside the monument on the day of its dedication.

The Smithsonian archive describes the Confederate soldier as "slightly smaller than life-sized, very youthful looking." To a visitor, it may seem to be on the scale of the town itself: at present Mulberry is the smallest community in Tennessee with a statue of a Confederate soldier.

The figure appears to be youthful in movement, ardent and oversized by his hip-length coat, baggy trousers, brimmed hat, and CSA belt buckle. He also appears to be ready for what may come. To judge by the tree stump that reaches to just below hip level—a typical symbol of monumentation—he is destined to be cut down by the course of life he will face. However, the community's proclamation is strident and unambiguous: "We Kept the Southland's Faith . . . 300 Confederate Unconquered Soldiers Who Went Out From Mulberry."

Wayne County

4.9.1 Subject: Waynesboro, Courthouse Shaft, Confederate
Location: 100 Court Circle, 38485   N 35 19 10 89 / W 87 45 45 34
Installed or dedicated: 2004
Medium: Granite
Monument is a granite stele surmounting a base.

Inscription
[SCV seal]
THE MONUMENT ERECTED IN HONOR OF THE / GALLANT CONFEDERATE SOLDIERS
OF WAYNE COUNTY / WHO FOUGHT, DIED AND SUFFERED IN THE WAR FOR /
SOUTHERN INDEPENDENCE. 1861–1865
CONFEDERATE UNITS FORMED IN WAYNE COUNTY
[Order of battle]
SACRED IS THE MEMORY OF THE CITIZENS / OF WAYNE COUNTY FOR THE
SACRIFICES / THEY MADE IN DEFENDING THEIR HOMELAND / ERECTED 2004 AD BY
THE / COL. JACOB B. BIFFLE CAMP, 1603 / SONS OF CONFEDERATE VETERANS

Not until 2004 were those who "Who Fought, Died and Suffered" in the "War For Southern Independence" commemorated with a monument in Wayne County. The granite stele erected by the local Sons of Confederate Veterans stands today in front of the 1975 courthouse. The memories are nevertheless "sacred," and the sacrifices of these citizen soldiers for the defense of "Their Homeland" are lavishly venerated.

Moore County

4.10.1 Subject: Lynchburg, Courthouse Stele, Confederate
Location: 196 Main Street, 37352   N 35 16 57 92 / W 86 22 24 50
Installed or dedicated: 1927
Medium: Marble
Monument is an inscribed marble stele.

Inscription
1861–1865
IN LOVING MEMORY / CONFEDERATE SOLDIERS / OF MOORE COUNTY / ERECTED 1927.

1861–1865
IN PERPETUAL REMEMBRANCE. / PRESERVE THE TRUTH / IN HISTORY / ERECTED 1927.

The Lynchburg Courthouse stele's inscription is at once brief and sentimental—"In Loving Memory." There is no attribution and no UDC chapter with extant records on this site, but this modestly sized monument of the commemorative era is perhaps most notable for its staunch exhortation to the viewer to "preserve the truth in history."

Records indicate that sentiment for secession was almost unanimous in Moore County. Confederate units with Moore County soldiers included

Manchester, Courthouse Stele, UDC, Coffee County

Companies D and E, 1st Tennessee Infantry; Company C, 4th Infantry; Company H, 8th Infantry; and Companies A and G, 41st Infantry.

Coffee County

4.11.1 Subject: Manchester, Courthouse Stele, UDC
Location: 300 Hillsboro Boulevard, 37355   N 35 29 00 33 / W 86 05 18 68
Installed or dedicated: 1991
Medium: Granite
Monument is shaft surmounting a base.

Inscription

TO HONOR THE MEMORY / OF THE MEN AND WOMEN / WHO SERVED AND SACRIFICED / DURING THE WAR / BETWEEN THE STATES / 1861–1865 / LEST WE FORGET / ERECTED AND DEDICATED / BY THE / CAPT. CALVIN C. BREWER / CHAPTER 2505 / UNITED DAUGHTERS / OF / THE CONFEDERACY / 1991

1861–1865 / WITH AFFECTION, REVERENCE, / AND AN UNDYING REMEMBRANCE. / UDC

This stele, erected in 1991 by the UDC, remains at the site of the former county courthouse erected in 1871. New courthouse facilities have replaced this site, but at this writing, the county's war memorials are expected to remain here.

The monument offers tributes to the "Men and Women Who Served and Sacrificed," doing so with no apparent distinction between the causes the men and women served. However, it defines the conflict not as a civil war that was fought for the union, but a "War Between the States." Is it nonpartisan? Not quite. It is a monument of the United Daughters of the Confederacy after all, using the Southern designation for the war.

Tullahoma, Maplewood Cemetery

Tullahoma

MAPLEWOOD CEMETERY

4.11.2 Subject: Presiding Stele
Location: Maplewood Avenue, 37388   N 35 20 57 59 / W 86 12 32 34
Installed or dedicated: 1964
Medium: Granite

Monument is a granite stele set on a three-tiered base.

CONFEDERATE MEMORIAL
ON THIS GROUND ARE BURIED 407 / UNKNOWN CONFEDERATES. MANY OF / THESE
DIED IN ONE OF THE HOSPITALS / ESTABLISHED HERE WHEN TULLAHOMA / WAS
HEADQUARTERS FOR THE ARMY OF / TENNESSEE DURING THE FIRST SIX / MONTHS
OF 1863 FOLLOWING THE / BATTLE OF MURFREESBORO AND / PRECEDING THE
WITHDRAWAL OF THE / ARMY TO CHATTANOOGA.
ERECTED BY / TULLAHOMA CIVIL WAR CENTENNIAL / COMMISSION / 1964

The graves of over four hundred Confederate soldiers are interred in Maplewood Cemetery. This is the presiding monument on a field that is now a veritable mass grave, part of the legacy of time spent here by the Army of Tennessee, January–June 1863, after the Stones River Campaign and prior to the Tullahoma Campaign.

The army's headquarters and logistical base was near here, and hospitals were established in the town. The roster of the dead is listed as unknown in this centennial-era monument, but late twentieth-century research of extant documents brought to light the names of many of the unknown, enabling the establishment of a roster of the dead at the base of this monument. The names of 380 of them are now inscribed on bronze tablets.

Affectionate tributes from state UDC chapters are displayed from Arkansas, Georgia, Louisiana, Alabama, Florida, Tennessee, Texas, North Carolina, and Mississippi. Recently installed audio recordings accessible by dint of a solar-powered audio digital repeater have enhanced the visual effect of the presiding monument and stelae.

4.11.3 Subject: State of Arkansas, Stele

Inscription

IN LOVING MEMORY OF THE BRAVE ARKANSANS / WHO VALIANTLY LEFT THEIR NATIVE STATE / TO FIGHT AND DIE ON TENNESSEE SOD.
ARKANSAS DIVISION, UDC / WILLIAM F. SIEMONS CH. 977 / MONTICELLO, DREW COUNTY / DEDICATED JULY 7, 2012

4.11.4 Subject: State of Georgia, Stele

Inscription

GEORGIA DIVISION, UNITED DAUGHTERS OF THE CONFEDERACY / PROUDLY HONORS THE MEMORY OF THE SOLDIERS BURIED HERE. / MAY THE FAITHFUL AND LOYAL SERVICE OF THE GALLANT, / FALLEN HEROES ALWAYS BE REMEMBERED.
JUNE 26, 2010

4.11.5 Subject: State of Louisiana, Stele

Inscription

IN REMEMBRANCE OF LOUISIANA'S CONFEDERATE SONS: / THEY SERVED WITH COURAGE / AND DIED WITH HONOR. / LET US NOT FORGET . . .
JUNE 3, 2009 / CALCASIEU CHAPTER NO. 1519, LA DIV, UDC

- "Let us not forget" is an apparent paraphrase of the traditional tribute taken from the Kipling poem "Lest We Forget," published in 1901.

4.11.6 Subject: State of Alabama, Stele

Inscription

DEDICATED TO THE MEMORY AND TO HONOR OUR ALABAMA / SOLDIERS BURIED IN THE TULLAHOMA, TN CONFEDERATE CEMETERY
ALABAMA DIVISION / UNITED DAUGHTERS OF THE CONFEDERACY / THIS MAY 17, 2008

4.11.7 Subject: State of Florida, Stele

Inscription

SACRED TO THE MEMORY OF OUR FLORIDA / SOLDIERS BURIED HERE IN TENNESSEE SOIL
UNITED DAUGHTERS OF THE CONFEDERACY / FLORIDA DIVISION / APRIL 5, 2008

4.11.8 Subject: Roster of the Dead, Confederate, Stele

Inscription

THE CONFEDERATE SOLDIERS BURIED HERE WERE IDENTIFIED / THROUGH
RESEARCH OF MILITARY SERVICE RECORDS
*[Relief of roster of the known dead: from Alabama, 65; Arkansas, 6; Florida, 47; Georgia,
13; Kentucky, 6; Louisiana, 20; Mississippi, 47; North Carolina, 37; South Carolina, 4;
Tennessee, 94; and Texas, 11]*

4.11.9 Subject: State of Tennessee, Stele

Inscription

IN MEMORY OF THE TENNESSEE CONFEDERATES WHO DIED HERE / IN HOS-
PITALS AND OF THE P.O.W.'S AND CIVILIANS WHO WERE / MURDERED BY THE
PROVOST MARSHAL FORCES / OF THE UNITED STATES / DEDICATED 26 JULY 2008 /
TULLAHOMA CONFEDERATE ASSOCIATION

- The Tullahoma Confederate Association offers a sharp rebuke of
  Provost Marshal of the United States and, by implication, the injustice
  perpetrated by the federal government.

4.11.10 Subject: State of Texas, Stele

Inscription

TREAD LIGHTLY, THIS IS HALLOWED GROUND! / BRAVE TEXANS HERE, A REST HATH
FOUND, / WAR'S RICHEST SPOILS LIE BENEATH THIS SOD; / THEIR SOULS FOREVER
AT REST WITH GOD.
"WE REMEMBER"
THE TEXAS DIVISION / UNITED DAUGHTERS OF THE CONFEDERACY
JUNE 27, 2009

- The tribute beginning "Tread Lightly" may be taken from William Hubbard's "At the Grave of William Hubbard," although that poem may
  draw from a poem published in 1839 by William T. Coggeshall.

4.11.11 Subject: State of North Carolina, Stele

Inscription

[Relief of state of North Carolina]
DEDICATED TO THE MEMORY, GLORY AND HONOR OF OUR / NORTH CAROLINA
CONFEDERATE SOLDIERS / BURIED IN THE TULLAHOMA CONFEDERATE CEMETERY
/ UNITED DAUGHTERS OF THE CONFEDERACY / NORTH CAROLINA DIVISION /
NOVEMBER 11, 2009

4.11.12 Subject: State of Mississippi, Stele

Inscription

[Relief of state of Mississippi]

DEDICATED TO THE MEMORY OF OUR MISSISSIPPI SOLDIERS / WHO SUFFERED ALL, SACRIFICED ALL, ENDURED ALL, AND DIED HERE. / MISSISSIPPI DIVISION / UNITED DAUGHTERS OF THE CONFEDERACY / MAY 22, 2010

- The phrase beginning "Who suffered all" is attributed to Rev. Randolph Harrison McKim, a Confederate veteran (2nd Virginia Cavalry). The passage is taken from a speech McKim gave to a United Confederate Veterans reunion at Nashville, Tennessee, on June 14, 1904. An excerpt also appears on the Confederate monument at Arlington Cemetery and at Thornrose Cemetery in Staunton, Virginia.

4.11.13 Subject: Headquarters, Army of Tennessee, Stele
Location: US 41A, near Carroll Street   N 35 21 24 75 / W 86 12 26 86
Installed or dedicated: n.a.
Medium: Granite
Monument is a stele surmounting a base.

Inscription

[Polk's battle flag]

HEADQUARTERS / ARMY OF TENNESSEE / JAN–JULY 1863 / LT. GEN. BRAXTON BRAGG / COMMANDER

[Hardee's Corps, blue with white circle]

LT. GEN. W. J. HARDEE / LT. GEN. LEONIDUS POLK / CORPS COMMANDERS
[Confederate battle flag]

After the battle of Stones River, Gen. Bragg placed his army headquarters here, from January to June 1863, and the Army of Tennessee established a fortified line along the Duck River from Shelbyville to Wartrace and points east. The monument stands on the grounds of a former public school / civic center on present-day US 41A near Carroll Street and near the wartime Nashville and Chattanooga Railroad.

BEECH GROVE CONFEDERATE CEMETERY

4.11.14 Subject: Maj. Gen. Alexander P. Stewart, Stele
Location: 116 Confederate Cemetery Road, I-24, Exit 97, confluence of TR 64 / US 41   N 35 37 33 06 / W 86 14 30 12
Dedicated: April 24, 2010
Medium: Granite
Monument is a granite stele surmounting a base.

Beech Grove Confederate Cemetery, General Nathan B. Forrest, Farewell Address, Stele

Inscription

[Front]
GENERAL A. P. STEWART / STEWART'S DIVISION
[Flag of Second Corps, Army of Tennessee]
2ND ARMY CORPS / (HARDEE) / ARMY OF TENNESSEE / CSA / DEDICATED 24TH DAY
OF APRIL 2010 / BY BENJAMIN F. CHEATHAM CAMP 72 / SONS OF CONFEDERATE
VETERANS / MANCHESTER TENNESSEE

BATTLE OF HOOVER'S GAP / JUNE 24–26, 1863
[Order of battle]
NO FAINT OF HEARTS EXISTED IN THE BRAVE SOLDIERS OF / STEWART'S DIVISION
AS THEY [MADE] THREE / FRONTAL ASSAULTS AGAINST THE ENTRENCHED
INVADING UNION FORCES OF JOHN WILDER'S MOUNTED INFANTRY AND ELI /
LILLY'S / 18TH INDIANA ARTILLERY. CONFEDERATES FOR THE FIRST TIME / EVER
IN THE WAR FACED THE NEW 7-SHOT SPENCERS IN THE / HANDS OF WILDER'S
TWO THOUSAND MOUNTED INFANTRY AND / ELI LILLY'S SIX 3-INCH RIFLES AND
FOUR MOUNTAIN HOWITZERS. / THE RIFLE FIRE AND 350 DOUBLE-SHOT CANISTER
ROUNDS / BARELY PREVENTED CONFEDERATE FORCES FROM OVERRUNNING /
UNION POSITIONS. DARKNESS ENDED THE FIGHTING. / DEO VINDICE

Beech Grove was the site of an attack by Union Col. John T. Wilder's brigade of mounted infantry in the opening movements of the Tullahoma Campaign. Union soldiers armed with seven-shot Spencer rifles fought for and secured Hoover's Gap, then withstood counterattacks by Confederate troops commanded by Brig. Gen. William B. Bate and Bushrod R. Johnson of Stewart's Division, Hardee's Corps. The advance and subsequent stand allowed decisive elements of the Union Army of the Cumberland to move south through the gap, down the Manchester Pike and thus to outflank the Army of Tennessee.

Construction of I-24, which traverses Hoover's Gap, destroyed much of the original landscape in the middle of the twentieth century. Today the highway runs adjacent to these grounds. The Beech Grove Cemetery remains, however, and the seventy-four unknown Confederate dead who were reinterred in this antebellum graveyard in 1866 are undisturbed.

- The inscription notes that "Darkness ended the fighting" here, as if fate or nature intervened to prevent the Southerners from concluding the action. It's something of an ominous note, but the seal of the Confederacy, "Deo Vindice"—"With God as Our Judge," the motto of the Confederate States—ends the narrative.

4.11.15 Subject: Unknown Confederate Soldiers, Stele
Installed or dedicated: 2010
Medium: Bronze, granite
Monument is a bronze plaque on a granite stele.

Inscription

IN HONOR OF THE CONFEDERATE 1ST / 3RD KENTUCKY / CALVARY [SIC] (CONSOLIDATED) WHO FIRST ENCOUNTERED THE / ONSLAUGHT OF WILDER'S BRIGADE, THOMAS'S CORPS OF THE / UNION ARMY, NORTH OF HOOVER'S GAP JUNE 24, 1863 / DEDICATED JUNE 3, 2010 / B. F. CHEATHAM SCV CAMP 72

Praise and recognition are tendered here to the unknown Confederate dead of the 1st / 3rd Kentucky in meeting Wilder's Brigade, armed with the notorious Spencer rifles, as it moved through Hoover's Gap.

4.11.16 Subject: General Nathan B. Forrest, Farewell Address, Stele
Installed or dedicated: 1954
Medium: Granite
Monument is a stele with adjoining exedra, surmounting a base.

Inscription
[Confederate battle flag]
FORREST'S FAREWELL ORDER / TO HIS CAVALRY CORPS / EXTRACT / GAINESVILLE, ALA., MAY 9, 1865[:] / CIVIL WAR, SUCH AS YOU HAVE PASSED / THROUGH, NATURALLY ENGENDERS / FEELINGS OF ANIMOSITY, HATRED, AND / REVENGE. IT IS OUR DUTY TO DIVEST / OURSELVES OF ALL SUCH FEELINGS, AND, / SO FAR AS IT IS IN OUR POWER TO DO / SO, TO CULTIVATE FRIENDLY FEELINGS / TOWARD THOSE WITH WHOM WE HAVE SO / LONG CONTESTED AND HERETOFORE SO / WIDELY BUT HONESTLY DIFFERED. / NEIGHBORHOOD FEUDS, PERSONAL / ANIMOSITIES AND PRIVATE DIFFERENCES / SHOULD BE BLOTTED OUT, AND WHEN / YOU RETURN HOME A MANLY, / STRAIGHTFORWARD COURSE OF CONDUCT / WILL SECURE YOU THE RESPECT EVEN OF / YOUR ENEMIES. / I HAVE NEVER ON THE FIELD OF BATTLE / SENT YOU WHERE I WAS UNWILLING TO / GO MYSELF, NOR WOULD I NOW ADVISE /

YOU TO A COURSE WHICH I MYSELF·FELT / UNWILLING TO PURSUE. YOU HAVE BEEN / GOOD SOLDIERS; YOU CAN BE GOOD / CITIZENS.
N. B. FORREST, LIEUTENANT GENERAL.

ERECTED TO THE MEMORY / OF THE UNKNOWN / CONFEDERATE SOLDIERS / BURIED HERE, WHO FELL IN / THE BEECH GROVE AND / HOOVER'S GAP ENGAGEMENTS / OF JUNE 24–26, 1863 AND TO / THE OTHER CONFEDERATES / WHO FELL IN THIS BATTLE / AND NOW REST IN HONORED / GRAVES ELSEWHERE. / 1954

This farewell address from Forrest to his troops was given at Gainesville, Alabama, May 9, 1865. Apart from Sam Davis, another native Tennessean, Forrest is the most widely quoted soldier on Tennessee Confederate monuments. This speech is also excerpted at Chapel Hill, Forrest's birthplace. Another speech, his last public address, is inscribed at Covington (5.9.3).

4.11.17 Subject: 20th Tennessee Infantry, CSA, Stele
Dedicated: November 1, 2008
Medium: Bronze, granite
Monument is a bronze plaque on a granite stele.

Inscription
20TH TENNESSEE VOLUNTEER INFANTRY / A REGIMENT OF MANY HEROES INCLUDING / TOD CARTER / DEWITT S. JOBE / WILLIAM SHY / THOMAS B. SMITH / THEIR BRAVERY WILL NEVER DIE
DEDICATED NOVEMBER 1, 2008 / TENNESSEE DIVISION SONS OF CONFEDERATE VETERANS

Tributes to individual Tennessee units are uncommon. The 20th Infantry was organized in May–June 1861 at Camp Trousdale and served across the breadth of the war, including the battles of Shiloh, Baton Rouge, Stones River, Franklin, and Nashville. The regiment surrendered with the Army of Tennessee on April 26, 1865.

Capt. Tod Carter was mortally wounded at the battle of Franklin. While serving with Coleman's Scouts, Pvt. Dewitt S. Jobe was captured, tortured, and executed by Union soldiers on August 29, 1864. Col. William Shy was killed in action at the battle of Nashville; Brig. Gen. Thomas B. Smith was taken prisoner at the battle of Nashville, was abused by his captors, and suffered permanent injuries.

4.11.18 Subject: 18th Indiana Vol. Artillery, Union, Tablet
Location: N 35 37 34 56 / W 86 14 29 02
Installed or dedicated: June 28, 2008
Medium: Bronze
Monument is a bronze plaque.

Inscription

[Relief of light artillery piece being transported, by horse, with soldiers attending, in mud and rain]

18TH INDIANA BATTERY

HOOVER'S GAP, TN. JUNE 24, 1863. THE 18TH INDIANA BATTERY, / COMMANDED BY CAPT. ELI LILLY, DISLODGED ONE CONFEDERATE / ARTILLERY PIECE AND FORCED THE CONFEDERATE BATTERIES TO CHANGE / POSITION. THE BATTERY, ALONG WITH WILDER'S BRIGADE, DID / CONSIDERABLE DAMAGE TO THE ADVANCING CONFEDERATE INFANTRY / WITH DOUBLE ROUNDS OF CANISTER. THIS BATTLE OPENED MIDDLE / TENNESSEE TO THE UNION FORCES, RESULTING IN THE ADVANCE OF / THE UNION ARMY TO CHATTANOOGA AND GEORGIA. / THE BATTERY WAS FORMED IN INDIANAPOLIS, IN. IN 1862 BY / CAPT. ELI LILLY. THE 18TH INDIANA BATTERY WAS THE LARGEST / BATTERY IN THE ARMY OF THE CUMBERLAND COMPRISED OF SIX / 3 INCH ORDNANCE RIFLES AND 4 MOUNTAIN HOWITZERS. THE / BATTERY SERVED IN KENTUCKY, TENNESSEE, GEORGIA AND ALABAMA. / THIS PLAQUE IS DEDICATED TO THE MEMORY OF THE MEN OF THE / 18TH INDIANA BATTERY AND TO ALL AMERICAN SOLDIERS WHO FOUGHT / ON THIS SITE. PRESENTED BY / THE MIDWEST CIVIL WAR ARTILLERY ASSOCIATION

Commemorating the action at Hoover's Gap during the Tullahoma Campaign are these monuments and the Confederate cemetery. The hill on which the present-day cemetery stands was seized and held by the 72nd Indiana Infantry and this artillery battery, the 18th Indiana. In a conciliatory gesture, the inscription concludes with a tribute to "all American soldiers who fought on this site."

The 18th Independent Battery Vol. Light Artillery was organized at Indianapolis and was mustered in August 20, 1862. It was mustered out June 23, 1865. Capt. Eli Lilly, who established and commanded the battery, was also destined to found Eli Lilly & Company, the modern-day international pharmaceutical company.

Bedford County

4.12.1 Subject: Shelbyville, Courthouse Column, Confederate
Location: Courthouse lawn, 1 Public Square, 37160 N 35 28 58 08 / W 86 27 39 40
Unveiled: July 23, 1937 Media: Bronze, limestone
Monument is a bronze plaque emplaced on three limestone blocks surmounting a base.

Inscription

IN MEMORY OF THE / "SHELBYVILLE REBELS," CO. F / 41ST TENN. REGT., C.S.A. AND / ALL SOLDIERS FROM BEDFORD / COUNTY WHO FOUGHT FOR THE / CONFEDERACY IN THE WAR / BETWEEN THE STATES, 1861–1865

ERECTED AND AFFECTIONATELY DEDICATED / BY THE AGNES L. WHITESIDE CHAPTER, U.D.C.

"LORD GOD OF HOSTS, BE WITH US YET, / LEST WE FORGET, LEST WE FORGET."

Shelbyville Courthouse Column

Bedford County voted against secession by a large majority on June 8, 1861; when the war came, the county furnished almost as many soldiers to Federal service as to the Confederacy. Its pro-Union stance earned it the nickname "Little Boston."

The "Shelbyville Rebels," organized in September 1861, were the first Confederate company raised in the county. Other companies joined the 2nd and 17th Tennessee Infantry. A company of artillery was organized in Shelbyville in 1862, and elements of the company known as "Forrest's Escort" were recruited from Bedford County. Bedford County volunteers for the Union Army served with the 4th, 5th, and 10th Tennessee Mounted Infantry.

Like many Middle Tennessee towns, Shelbyville was occupied at various times by Confederate and Federal forces. The city's location along the Duck River and along the Nashville and Chattanooga Railroad gave it tactical and strategic value.

- The three limestone blocks of this monument formed part of a column of the former county courthouse. The courthouse was burned down in December 1934 by a mob of incensed white citizens after town officials rescued an African American prisoner from a lynch mob. The present-day courthouse, a neoclassical structure, was built the following year.

- "Lest We Forget" is from the Rudyard Kipling poem of the same title, published in 1901.

Willow Mount Cemetery, Shelbyville, Confederate Common Soldier Statue, Bedford County

4.12.2 Subject: Willow Mount Cemetery, Common Soldier Statue, Confederate
Location: 321 Dover Street, 37160   N 35 29 28 80 / W 86 28 16 98
Dedicated: October 17, 1899
Medium: Granite, marble
Monument is figure of a Confederate common soldier, surmounting a base.

Inscription

[Front]
CSA
[Thirteen stars]
"THIS MARBLE SOLDIER'S VOICELESS STONE / IN DEATHLESS SONG SHALL TELL / WHEN MANY A VANISHED YEAR HATH FLOWN, / THE STORY HOW YE FELL." / IN MEMORY OF / OUR CONFEDERATE DEAD

GATHER THE SACRED DUST / OF THE WARRIORS TRIED AND TRUE, / WHO BORE THE FLAG OF OUR NATION'S TRUST / AND FELL IN A CAUSE, THOUGH LOST, STILL JUST.

1861–1865
"BUT THE BUGLE CALL, AND THE BATTLE BALL / AGAIN SHALL ROUSE THEM NEVER; / THEY FOUGHT AND FELL, THEY SERVED US WELL, / THEIR FURLOUGH LASTS FOREVER."

THEY ROSE TO DEFEND THEIR HOMES AND / FIRESIDES; THEY ENDURED EVERY HARDSHIP / WITHOUT COMPLAINT, THEIR SOULS REST / WITH GOD; THEIR FAME IS IMMORTAL.

This monument overlooks the graves of Confederate soldiers from the rise on which it stands. It is festooned with tributes to the common soldier in consonance with the latter days of the cemetery monument movement between 1867 and 1890.

Mourning became praise and laudation in many of the monuments erected in the late nineteenth century. Later monuments would more often be placed at courthouse sites, but this is still a Southern military cemetery, with graves of soldiers from every Confederate state apart from Virginia.

- The bodies of some six hundred unknown Confederate soldiers are interred on the north side of Confederate Lane. The monument stands approximately thirty-six feet high, and the base is approximately four by twelve by twelve feet. The statue of the Confederate soldier is of white marble, the stele is marble, the base is granite. The sculpture stands approximately eight feet high, and its sculptor is unknown.

- The inscription beginning "In deathless song shall tell" is taken from "The Bivouac of the Dead" (1847), by Theodore O'Hara. The inscription beginning "Gather the sacred dust" is taken from the poem "The Conquered Banner" (1865), by Father Abram Joseph Ryan. The inscription beginning "But the bugle call, and the battle ball" is taken from the poem "Dirge for a Soldier," by Samuel P. Merrill.

- Adjacent to the statue is a stele—a bronze tablet surmounting a granite base, erected in 2004—listing soldiers whose names have been recovered:

IN MEMORY OF THE CONFEDERATE SOLDIERS / THAT REST HERE IN SHELBYVILLE, TN / THE EPITAPH OF THE SOLDIER WHO FALLS WITH HIS COUNTRY IS / WRITTEN IN THE HEARTS OF THOSE WHO / LOVED THE RIGHT AND HONOR THE BRAVE. / THE SONS OF CONFEDERATE VETERANS CAMP #1620
[Alabama, 92; Arkansas, 24; Florida, 2; Georgia, 13; Kentucky, 13; Louisiana, 1; Mississippi, 108; North Carolina, 21; South Carolina, 11; Tennessee, 94; Texas, 21; unknown, 21]

- A granite stele with bronze tablets stands over the grave of S. A. Cunningham, a Confederate soldier and founder and editor of *Confederate Veteran*, also buried here (N 35 29 28 50 / W 86 28 20 88). The epitaph reads in part, "He Felt the Heart Throb of the South."

4.12.3 Subject: Wartrace, Maj. Gen. Patrick R. Cleburne, Stele
Location: West TR 269 and US 64, 37183   N 35 31 42 42 / W 86 20 04 24
Installed or dedicated: December 10, 2011
Medium: Granite
Monument is an inscribed stele.

Inscription
MAJOR GENERAL PATRICK R. CLEBURNE / "STONEWALL OF THE WEST" / CLEBURNE'S DIVISION
[Flag of 2nd Corps]
2ND ARMY CORPS / (HARDEE) / ARMY OF TENNESSEE / DEDICATED DECEMBER 10, 2011 / MAJ[.] / GEN[.] BENJAMIN F. CHEATHAM / CAMP 72 SONS OF CONFEDERATE VETERANS / MANCHESTER, TENNESSEE

This monument stands in Wartrace's Memorial Park, at the corner of Spring and Bridgeview and, according to a wayside plaque, is "Dedicated to those Brave and Gallant Soldiers in Butternut and Gray!" The park is across the road from the Chockley Tavern, Cleburne's headquarters during the Tullahoma Campaign, and adjacent to the tracks of the wartime Nashville and Chattanooga Railroad, now run by CSX Transportation. Cleburne's staff officers camped here from January 9, 1863, after the Stones River Campaign, until the morning of June 27, 1863, when Union troops forced their flank and compelled a withdrawal. The memorial includes a solar-powered audio digital repeater that can be prompted to play recordings of "Dixie" and narratives of the life of "Pat Cleburne."

· Cleburne's reputation as the "Stonewall of the West" originated with Jefferson Davis. He is commemorated with another monument on Winstead Hill on the Franklin battlefield (4.14.21) and is quoted on the courthouse monument at Altamont (4.6.1).

Cannon County

4.12.1 Subject: Woodbury, Hutchenson, Battlefield Stele, Confederate
Location: US 70S, TR 53, 1 Massy Drive and Old Murfreesboro Road, 37190
N 35 49 32 19 / W 86 05 10 28
Installed or dedicated: July 1926
Medium: Granite
Monument is a granite stele surmounting a base.

Inscription
[Relief of battle flag draped across the top]
THIS BOULDER MARKS THE SPOT / WHERE THE GALLANT TENNESSEAN / LIEUT. COL. JOHN B. HUTCHENSON / OF COMPANY E 2ND KY. REGT. MORGAN'S / CAVALRY WAS KILLED IN BATTLE / JAN. 25, 1863 / ERECTED BY CANNON COUNTY CHAP- / TER, UNITED DAUGHTERS OF THE / CONFEDERACY / JULY 1926

TO HONOR THE MEMORY, THE / PATRIOTISM, THE DEEDS OF VALOR / AND SACRIFICES OF CANNON COUNTY'S / CONFEDERATE SOLDIERS OF THE PERIOD / OF 1861–65. / ERECTED BY CANNON COUNTY CHAP- / TER, UNITED DAUGHTERS OF THE / CONFEDERACY / JULY 1926 / "NOR SHALL YOUR MEMORY BE FORGOT / WHILE FAME HER RECORDS KEEP"

Woodbury, county seat of Cannon County, displays this monument one half mile west of the courthouse. The inscribed boulder is said to mark the spot where Lt. Col. John B. Hutchenson of Morgan's cavalry was killed in action January 1863. The 2nd Kentucky Cavalry had extensive wartime service, but there is no record of a battle here on January 25, 1863. There were, however, numerous skirmishes in the area in the wake of the Stones River Campaign, and this monument may be a reference to these actions.

- The inscription beginning "Nor Shall Your Memory" is taken from O'Hara's "Bivouac of the Dead."
- The Cannon County UDC Chapter No. 1812, no longer extant, dated from at least 1923.

Chapel Hill

4.13.2 Subject: Stele, Tribute to CSA Veterans, Lt. Gen. N. B. Forrest
Location: Chapel Hill Town Hall, 2202 Unionville Road, 37034   N 35 37 54 76 / W 86 41 30 00
Installed or dedicated: n.a.
Medium: Brick, bronze, copper
Monument is a copper disc with a relief of Forrest mounted on a galloping horse, the whole affixed to a brick wall.

Inscription
NATHAN BEDFORD FORREST / LT. GEN. CSA
JULY 13, 1821 CHAPEL HILL TN / OCTOBER 29, 1877 MEMPHIS, TN
[Bronze plaque:]
IN HONOR OF ALL CONFEDERATE SOLDIERS / PRESENTED BY / SONS OF CONFEDERATE VETERANS

This tribute to Nathan B. Forrest stands in front of the Chapel Hill Town Hall. Discomfort with Forrest's legacy led to this monument's being moved from its original site on the campus of Middle Tennessee State University to this location in Forrest's hometown.

- A duplicate of this monument stands at the entryway to Nathan B. Forrest State Park.

4.13.3 Subject: Lt. Gen. Nathan B. Forrest, Obelisk
Location: 127 North Horton Parkway, 37034   N 35 37 39 38 / W 86 41 35 46
Installed or dedicated: July 13, 1928
Medium: Granite
Monument is an obelisk.

Inscription
FORREST

The site of Nathan Bedford Forrest's boyhood home is here, marked with a granite obelisk displaying the shortest inscription on any Tennessee Civil War monument. On the day of the monument's dedication in 1928, a tribute to Forrest was given by "local district Congressional Judge E[d]win L. Davis." Davis praised Forrest as a soldier and as "a man of unimpeachable integrity, high moral courage, and constructive citizenship."

Chapel Hill: Lt. Gen. Nathan B. Forrest, Obelisk

4.13.4 Subject: Lt. Gen. Nathan B. Forrest, Stele
Location: 127 North Horton Parkway, 37034
Installed or dedicated: July 13, 1927
Medium: Bronze, marble
Monument is a stele with plaque.

Inscription

ON THIS SPOT / STOOD THE PIONEER CABIN HOME / OF / WILLIAM AND MARIAN BELL FORREST / HERE WAS BORN / ON THE 13, DAY OF JULY 1821, / THEIR SON / NATHAN BEDFORD FORREST / LIEUTENANT-GENERAL, CONFEDERATE STATES OF AMERICA / AND CAVALRY LEADER OF WORLD-WIDE FAME / WHOSE MILITARY TACTICS HAVE BECOME / THE STANDARD / OF INTERNATIONAL ARMIES. / TO HIS CAUSE FEARLESS IN HIS DUTY, / IMPREGNABLE IN HIS HONOR, / SIMPLE IN HIS GREATNESS, / INCARNATION OF COURAGE IN BATTLE. / DIED / MEMPHIS, TENNESSEE, OCT. 25, 1877. / HIS GREATNESS / PROCLAIMED IN THE TEARS OF HIS FRIENDS / AND THE PRAISE OF HIS FOES.

This tablet was erected by the State of Tennessee as an appropriation secured by Mrs. J. A. Hargrove, president of the UDC Chapter at Chapel Hill. It conveys much praise to this native son. The praise may seem provocative today, but it is not unjust in declaring Forrest to be an innovative tactician of international reputation.

The property and house were privately owned until the State of Tennessee acquired the site in the 1970s. Plans called for its restoration and incorporation into Henry Horton State Park, but those plans came to naught, and the house lay vacant until it was transferred to the care of the SCV in 1997.

Marshall County

4.14.1 Subject: Lewisburg, Courthouse Common Soldier Statue, Confederate
Location: Courthouse grounds, Lewisburg, 37091   N 35 26 59 01 / W 86 47 17 82
Installed and dedicated: 1904
Media: Bronze, granite, Tennessee limestone, white bronze
Monument is a Confederate soldier surmounting a tiered granite base.

Inscription
[Front]
TO THE PATRIOTISM, VALOR AND SELF- / SACRIFICE OF OUR SOLDIERS. IN DEFENSE / OF THE SOVEREIGN RIGHTS OF THE STATES / UNDER THE FLAG FURLED AT APPOMATTOX. / VICTIS / LEST WE FORGET

TO THE WOMEN OF THE SOUTH, WHOSE / PATRIOTISM, DEVOTION, SACRIFICE AND / COURAGE—UNSURPASSED IN HISTORY—/ FURNISHED THE INSPIRATION TO THOSE / DARING DEEDS OF THE CONFEDERATE SOLDIER.
[90 names]
1861–1865

LIST OF THOSE KILLED OR DIED IN / THE CONFEDERATE ARMY / FROM MARSHALL COUNTY
[108 names]

ERECTED AND DEDICATED / A.D. 1904.
[96 names]

The sovereign rights of the states in a glorious, collective national defeat is the theme of the inscription on this courthouse monument. Latin exhortations, French history, and the British Empire have a prominent place. "Gloria Victis" is translated from the Latin as "Glory to the defeated." The use of the phrase may draw from an 1874 sculpture by Marius Jean Antonin Mercié, a tribute to French soldiers who fought in the Franco-Prussian War. Equal praise is conveyed to the "Women of the South" as to "Our Soldiers." "Lest We Forget" is taken from the Rudyard Kipling poem of the same title, published in 1901 on the occasion of the Golden Jubilee of Queen Victoria. It is intended here as an exhortation to remember the dead, but the poem was originally composed as a warning by Kipling about the hazards of pride that can befall an empire.

· The monument faces southeast. The sculpture stands approximately six feet tall. The sculptor is unknown. It surmounts a base approximately sixteen feet by seven feet by seven feet.

Lewisburg: Marshall County Courthouse Common Soldier Statue, Confederate

4.14.2 Subject: Battle of Farmington, Obelisk
Location: East of US 31A, TR 40 off TR 64, 37091   N 35 29 53 77 / W 86 41 54 36
Installed or dedicated: July 4, 1874
Medium: Concrete, marble
Monument is an obelisk surmounting a base.

Inscription

IN MEMORY OF / THE GALLANT DEAD / OF MAJ. GEN. / WHEELER'S CAVALRY CORPS, WHO FELL / IN AN ENGAGEMENT / WITH THE FEDERAL / FORCES ON THIS FIELD

ERECTED / JULY 1874

NO USELESS COFFINS / ENCLOSE THEIR BREAST, / NOR IN SHEET NOR SHROUD / WE WO[U]ND THEM, / BUT THEY LIE LIKE WARRIORS / TAKING THEIR REST / WITH THEIR MARTIAL / CLOAK AROUND THEM. / THEY SLEEP THEIR LAST SLEEP / THEY HAVE FOUGHT / THEIR LAST BATTLE / NO SOUND CAN AWAKE / THEM TO GLORY AGAIN.

THEY FELL / OCT. 7, 1863 / SEALING WITH / THEIR BLOOD / THEIR DEVOTION / TO THE / LOST CAUSE

Farmington is said to be the oldest village in Tennessee south of the Duck River. The voters opposed secession. Not surprisingly, perhaps, there was, according to *Confederate Veteran*, "very little sympathy manifested for the

Confederates Buried here" after the battle of Farmington, in particular, the bodies of "nine gallant martyrs whose identity could not be ascertained. . . . Messrs. Bennet Chapman, Cols. J. R. Neil, J. H. Lewis and others, [however,] erect[ed] a monument to their memory."

The battle of Farmington was a Confederate defeat at the hands of veteran Union cavalry under the command of brigadier generals George Crook and Robert B. Mitchell. The Southern troopers, part of Maj. Gen. Joseph Wheeler's command, were in transit to Confederate lines after their otherwise successful October 1863 raid.

- An undated plaque emplaced in a fieldstone wall surrounding the monument has the following inscription:

NAMES OF CONFEDERATE SOLDIERS / KILLED ON THIS FIELD IN BATTLE / BETWEEN CONFEDERATE AND FEDERAL / CAVALRY ON OCT. 7TH, 1863.
[12 names]

- The excerpt beginning "No useless Coffins" is from the 1843 poem "The Grave of Bonaparte," by American poet Lyman Heath (1804–70).

Giles County
Pulaski

4.15.1 Subject: Courthouse Common Soldier Statue, Sam Davis, Confederate
Location: 1 Public Square, 222 East Madison Street, Pulaski, 38478
N 35 11 57 24 / W 87 01 52 82
Installed or dedicated: October 11, 1906
Medium: Granite, marble
Monument is a statue of Sam Davis surmounting a shaft and base.

Inscription
[Front]
BORN OCT. 6, 1842, NEAR SMYRNA, / RUTHERFORD COUNTY TENNESSEE / THOUGH A CONFEDERATE STATES / SOLDIER IN THE LINE OF DUTY, / HE WAS EXECUTED AS A SPY / BY THE FEDERALS AT / PULASKI, NOV. 27, 1863 / "LET COME WHAT MUST, / I KEEP MY TRUST." / SAM DAVIS

"IF I HAD A THOUSAND LIVES, / I WOULD LOSE THEM ALL HERE / BEFORE I WOULD BETRAY MY / FRIEND OR THE CONFIDENCE / OF MY INFORMER."

ERECTED BY THE GILES CO. / CHAPTER U.D.C. OCT. 11, 1906.

"GREATER LOVE HATH NO / MAN THAN THIS; THAT A / MAN LAY DOWN HIS LIFE / FOR HIS FRIENDS."

Sam Davis is the most extensively quoted common soldier on any Civil War monument in Tennessee or Virginia. In fact, he is the only common soldier whose spoken words are inscribed on any monument in either state. His execution was judged to be unjust and illegal, and Tennesseans considered Davis

Pulaski: Giles County Courthouse Statue of Sam Davis

a hero. He seems to be something more, something of a representational figure who was caught up in a conflict in which he emerged the more noble, and which defines him. The figure of Davis bears no weapon, he has a pensive countenance, and he stands erect with arms crossed. The statement "Greater Love" is taken from the New Testament, John 15:13.

The sculpted figure of Italian marble stands approximately six feet tall and surmounts a tiered base of Georgia granite. The sculptor is unknown.

The neoclassical courthouse with its Corinthian columns was erected in 1909, three years after this monument's dedication.

Variations occur in the wording of his vow, "If I had," but the substance is the same, and the attestation to his saying it is sound.

His statement, alleged and witnessed and apparently spontaneous, is evocative of the American Revolutionary hero Nathan Hale's last words. Hale, hanged by the British for spying, declared that, "I only regret that I have but one life to lose for my country." A bronze statue of Hale, dedicated in 1893, stands at City Hall Park, New York City.

4.15.2 Subject: Sam Davis Museum, Tablet
Location: 134 Sam Davis Avenue, corner of Highland Avenue   N 35 11 48 52 / W 87 01 40 80
Installed or dedicated: 1950
Medium: Bronze, limestone
Monument is two bronze plaques adjoining the door to the museum.

Inscription
BORN / OCTOBER 6, 1842, / NEAR SMYRNA, / RUTHERFORD COUNTY, / TENNESSEE / THOUGH A / CONFEDERATE SOLDIER / IN THE LINE OF DUTY / HE WAS EXECUTED AS A / SPY BY THE FEDERALS / AT PULASKI NOVEMBER / 27, 1863 / HAD I A THOUSAND / LIVES TO LIVE, / HAD I A THOUSAND / LIVES TO GIVE, / I'D GIVE—NAY, / I'D GLADLY DIE, / BEFORE I'D LIVE / ONE LIFE A LIE

Two bronze tablets are displayed on the adjoining doors to the Sam Davis Memorial Museum, which was erected by the Tennessee Historical Commission in 1950. The museum stands at the hilltop site where Davis was hanged and is said to have opened eighty-seven years to the minute after his execution. Among the memorabilia on display are the leg shackles Davis wore to the gallows and the block on which he stood for his execution.

4.15.3 Subject: Maplewood Cemetery, UDC Tablet
Location: 500 Ballentine Street, 38478   N 35 11 30 08 / W 87 01 39 38
Installed or dedicated: 1913
Medium: Marble

Inscription
OUR HONORED CONFEDERATE DEAD / GILES CO. CHAPTER U.D.C. 1913

This simple flat tablet marks the graves of Confederate soldiers in what was originally the "white pauper section" at the southeast corner of Maplewood Cemetery. Sources indicate that at least eighty-five Confederate soldiers are buried in Maplewood—soldiers' graves here, as marked, and those buried in family plots elsewhere on the grounds. In the latter category are Brig. Gen.

UDC Tablet, Maplewood Cemetery, Pulaski. The USCT section is near the trees to the right in the photograph

John Adams and Maj. Gen. John C. Brown. Adams was killed in action at the battle of Franklin. Brown was wounded in the same battle but survived and went on to serve as Tennessee's postwar governor. Adams's grave is marked with a cross; a statue stands over the grave of Maj. Gen. John C. Brown (N 35 11 36 74 / W 87 01 43 32).

In addition, the graves of approximately forty United States Colored Troops are adjacent to the Confederate area, just south of the original boundaries of the grounds, in what would become the African American portion of the cemetery. Like the white soldiers, some of these African American soldiers were buried in the area especially designated for them, while others were buried with their families in the 1878 section. A Pulaski Heritage Trail wayside marker stands over the US Colored Troops (USCT) soldiers' site (N 35 11 30 08 / W 87 01 39 38).

4.15.4 Subject: Tarpley's Shop, Battlefield Cemetery Stele
Location: US 31, TR 7, south of Pulaski   N 35 08 38 12 / W 86 59 48 68
Installed or dedicated: 1911
Medium: Granite
Monument is a stele surmounting a base.

Inscription
DIED IN THE PERFORMANCE OF A FAITHFUL SERVICE / ON THE MORNING OF
SEPTEMBER 27, 1864 / THE SEVENTH KENTUCKY MOUNTED INFANTRY, / FORRESTS'
CAVALRY, CONFEDERATE STATES ARMY ENGAGED THE ENEMY ON THIS FIELD, /
AND THE FOLLOWING IS A LIST OF ITS DEAD, / WHOSE REMAINS REPOSE NEAR THIS
STONE. [8 names] AND AN UNKNOWN MISSISSIPPIAN.
ERECTED BY A COMRADE 1911

Minor Hill, Sam Davis, Stele

The monument on this roadside gravesite south of Pulaski was erected by Col. V. Y. Cook of Arkansas, a veteran of the engagement. Here an advance guard of Maj. Gen. Nathan B. Forrest's cavalry—Brig. Gen. Abraham Buford commanding—met Federal troops during Forrest's raid into northern Alabama and Middle Tennessee, September 16–October 10, 1864. The Southerners were unable to advance and withdrew to the line of the Nashville and Chattanooga Railroad. The cemetery inters Confederate dead who were collected and buried in this area.

4.15.5 Subject: Minor Hill, Sam Davis, Stele
Location: Off TR 11, intersection of Sam Davis Circle and Monument Drive
N 35 02 20 19 / W 87 10 24 66
Installed or dedicated: July 22, 1925
Medium: Marble
Monument is an inscribed stele surmounting a base.

Inscription
PLACE WHERE / SAM DAVIS WAS / CAPTURED NOV. 19, 1863 / MINOR HILL, TENNESSEE / EXECUTED AT PULASKI / TENN. NOV. 27, 1863 / WHEN OFFERED HIS FREEDOM / FOR INFORMATION, HIS / ANSWER WAS, "NO, I CANNOT, / I WOULD RATHER DIE A / THOUSAND DEATHS THAN / BETRAY A FRIEND OR BE / FALSE TO A DUTY." / NO GREATER LOVE HATH MAN / THAN THIS: LIFE FOR ONE'S / FRIEND TO GIVE, THAT SOUL / DIVINE, SPEAKS TO HIS FOE, / "I DIE THAT YOU MAY LIVE." *[Relief of rifle]*

This marker, fourteen miles south of Pulaski and just four miles north of the Alabama state line, marks the site where Sam Davis was captured by troopers of the notorious 7th Kansas Cavalry. He was imprisoned, tried, and hanged within eight days, but his legacy remains prominent on the Tennessee Civil War landscape.

Columbia, Maury County: Rose Hill Cemetery, Common Soldier Statue, Confederate

This monument is relatively modest in size, but a short four-lane divided roadway leads up to the site from the two-lane roadway of TR 11, and the 1926 dedication of the monument was attended by some twenty-five hundred people, including the governor of Tennessee, Austin Peay. In his remarks, Peay is said to have counseled young people in the audience to live their lives as Davis did, to "be loyal to their country and true to their friends."

Maury County

4.16.1 Subject: Columbia, Rose Hill Cemetery, Common Soldier Statue, Confederate
Location: Cemetery Avenue, 3rd Avenue, between C and B Streets, 38401
N 35 36 10 79 / W 87 01 47 62
Dedicated: May 7, 1882
Medium: Marble, Tennessee limestone
Monument is a Confederate soldier surmounting a shaft and base.

Inscription
OUR FALLEN HEROES. / 1861–1865.

CSA / DEDICATED MAY 7, 1882 / MULDOON MNT CO. / FOR / CONFEDERATE
MEMORIAL ASSN.

Columbia, the home of the national headquarters for the Sons of Confederate Veterans, has this 1882 monument to the "Fallen Heroes 1861–1865" on sloping ground overlooking scores of graves of Confederate soldiers. The statue of a Confederate soldier in full uniform stands at funeral parade rest, facing south.

The monument offers terse inscription but a particularly effective silent narrative. Manifest signs of the struggle that the war brought are displayed

Mount Pleasant, Town Square Common Soldier Statue, Confederate

in the reliefs. Of particular note are the signs of a past struggle: a broken staff of the Confederate battle flag draped over a cannon with broken wheel; weapons fallen or lying on the ground; swords; a bugle, drum, and hat. Other than the statue of the presiding soldier, there are no figures on the reliefs, as if the statue presides over the departed in solemn, solitary vigil.

· Extensive maneuvers and skirmishing occurred in this area during Hood's 1864 Tennessee Campaign, although no major battle occurred. On November 25, Hood advanced on the Federal earthworks erected here but did not attack.

· At this writing, the SCV plans to erect a full-sized statue of a Confederate soldier at its National Confederate Museum at Historic Elm Springs.

4.16.2 Subject: Mount Pleasant, Town Square, Common Soldier Statue, Confederate
Located: Town square, Main Street, 38474   N 35 32 03 60 / W 87 12 26 06
Dedicated: September 27, 1907
Medium: Granite
Monument is a Confederate soldier surmounting a shaft and base.

Inscription
[Front]
[Relief of staff, broken, and battle flag of the Confederacy]
[Seal of the Confederacy]

CSA / ERECTED IN MEMORY OF OUR / CONFEDERATE SOLDIERS / BY THE / BIGBY GRAY CHAPTER U.D.C.

THE LOVE, GRATITUDE, AND MEMORY / OF THE PEOPLE OF THE SOUTH / SHALL GILD THEIR FAME IN ONE / ETERNAL SUNSHINE.

1861–1865 / CONFEDERACY / IN OUR PERPETUAL REMEMBRANCE.

[Relief of crossed muskets]
CREST TO CREST THEY BORE OUR / BANNER; / SIDE BY SIDE THEY FELL ASLEEP / HAND TO HAND WE REAR THIS TOKEN / HEART TO HEART WE KNEEL AND / WEEP.

[Relief of capstan and anchor]
HISTORY HAS ENSHRINED THEM / IMMORTAL.

Faith, hope, affection, and mourning characterize the tone of this town square monument erected in 1907. It is an opulent, confident monument for a town that to this day displays the monument on its official seal.

- The inscription beginning "Crest to Crest" is drawn from the poem "Pro Memoria," by Ina M. Porter, published in 1867 in *War Poetry of the South*. The relief of a capstan and anchor may be a symbol of hope, pursuant to the New Testament book of Hebrews 6:19. Southern Granite and Marble served as fabricator. "Darricoat" was the sculptor. The monument dimensions are approximately twenty by five by five feet.

Spring Hill

4.16.4 Subject: UDC Stele, Confederate Dead, Battle of Franklin, Spring Hill Cemetery
Location: McLemore Avenue at end of Walnut Street   N 35 45 00 16 / W 86 55 35 04
Installed or dedicated: August 2014
Medium: Granite
Monument is an inscribed stele.

Inscription

IN MEMORY OF UNKNOWN / CONFEDERATE SOLDIERS / BURIED HERE / THE BATTLE OF FRANKLIN / NOV. 30, 1864 / SPARKMAN CHAPTER / UDC 1971

Unknown Confederate soldiers killed or mortally wounded in the battle of Franklin are believed to be buried in a mass grave at this site. Some observers discern a slight mounding of the earth in front and to the right of the stele. The UDC monument was erected during a period of low ebb in the commemoration of the war—after the centennial, during the Vietnam War. It was the first monument in this cemetery. More recent research indicates that a number of Confederate soldiers now buried here had been exhumed and transferred from several battlefields, mainly from Spring Hill and Thompson's Station. The Sam Freeman camp of the SCV in Savannah, Tennessee, used a local newspaper

UDC Stele, Confederate Dead, Battle of Franklin, Spring Hill Cemetery

article written in 1866 that listed the names, dates, and ranks of thirty-nine Confederate soldiers who were buried in 1864 at Spring Hill cemetery. Based on this research, the headstones or cenotaphs were added by dint of efforts by the Nathaniel Cheairs Camp of the SCV.

- Near here on the night of November 28, 1864, troops commanded by Lt. Gen. John Bell Hood, the Army of Tennessee, marched toward Spring Hill in an effort to interdict the supply lines of Maj. Gen. John M. Schofield's Union army. Cavalry skirmishing and several piecemeal attacks occurred. During the evening, however, most of Schofield's command passed unvexed through Spring Hill to Franklin—within shouting distance of Hood's troops, it appears, who were encamped nearby. Veterans and historians alike have described the near encounter as Hood's best opportunity to isolate and defeat the Union forces commanded by Schofield. The two armies would later meet in battle at Franklin on November 30, but the Spring Hill episode has long been described as "one of the most controversial non-fighting events of the entire war."

4.16.3 Subject: Capt. Samuel L. Freeman, Shaft
Location: N 35 45 00 16 / W 86 55 35 04
Installed or dedicated: May 2013
Medium: Bronze, granite

Inscription
IN THIS HALLOWED GROUND / ARE THE MORTAL REMAINS OF / SAMUEL L. FREEMAN, GEN. N. B. FORREST'S FIRST ARTILLERY / CAPTAIN. FREEMAN'S FAVORITE

CANNONS WERE 12 PDR. FIELD / HOWITZERS. WHILE ADVANCING / ON FRANKLIN, TN. APRIL 10, 1863, / ON THE LEWISBURG PIKE, THE / BATTERY WAS CAPTURED BY THE / 4TH U.S. CAVALRY. 29 CAPTURED / CANNONEERS, THE DOCTOR AND / FREEMAN WERE ORDERED TO RUN / OR BE SHOT. TO PREVENT BEING / SAVED BY FORREST'S MEN. HAVING / HURT HIS KNEE WHILE TRYING TO GET / THE GUNS IN ACTION, / FREEMAN WAS UNABLE TO RUN. / SURRENDERED AND UNARMED, CAPTAIN FREEMAN WAS SHOT IN THE MOUTH AND MURDERED BY HIS CAPTORS. HE / WAS BURIED IN SPRINGHILL, TN. / APRIL 11, 1863. / THE BATTERY ALWAYS HELD / TO THE NAME OF FREEMAN

DEO VINDICE.

PLACED APRIL 11, 2013 BY / FREEMAN'S BATTERY / FORREST'S ARTILLERY / CAMP 1939 / SONS OF CONFEDERATE VETERANS

In recent decades, monumentalized eulogies and tributes to Samuel L. Freeman and the battery of artillery bearing his name—"Freeman's Battery, Forrest's Artillery"—have been erected at Franklin and Parkers Crossroads in Tennessee, and at Brice's Corner in Mississippi. Regarded as a promising young teacher and law student, the Nashville native was killed in 1863 by Union soldiers after his artillery unit was captured on Lewisburg Pike. The manner of his death— vividly described in the inscription above—and his potential as a young man have parallels with his fellow Tennessee Confederate soldier Sam Davis. Like Davis, Freeman is remembered as a patriot whose death was simply tragic. He is not characterized as a firebrand, zealot, or advocate for the cause, just a capable young man whose life might have taken a more placid and productive course had war not come to Tennessee in 1861. Standing over Freeman's lifeless body, Nathan Bedford Forrest was heard to say, "Brave man, none braver."

· Members of the SCV camp report that Freeman was thought to be buried in this plot but had no confirmation. However, historian Andrew Sherriff at Spring Hill's Rippavilla Plantation found an 1866 newspaper article, also cited above, listing Freeman as one of thirty-nine men interred here.

Williamson County, Including the Franklin Battlefield
Franklin

4.17.1 Subject: Courthouse Common Soldier Statue, Confederate
Location: Main Street and 3rd Avenue, 37964   N 35 55 30 67 / W 86 52 08 30
Dedicated: November 30, 1899
Medium: Granite, marble
Monument is a Confederate soldier surmounting a shaft and base.

Inscription
[Front]
[Unfurled national flag]

ERECTED TO / CONFEDERATE SOLDIERS / BY FRANKLIN CHAPTER / NO 14 /
DAUGHTERS OF / THE CONFEDERACY / NOV. 30, A.D. 1899
OUR CONFEDERATE SOLDIERS

[Crossed rifles]
WOULD NOT IT BE / A BLAME FOR US / IF THEIR MEMORY PART / FROM OUR LAND
AND HEARTS / AND A WRONG TO THEM / AND A SHAME FOR US, / THE GLORIES
THEY WON / SHALL NOT WANE FROM US, / IN LEGEND AND LAY, / OUR HEROES IN
GRAY / SHALL EVER LIVE / OVER AGAIN FOR US.

IN HONOR AND MEMORY / OF OUR HEROES / BOTH PRIVATE AND CHIEF / OF THE
/ SOUTHERN CONFEDERACY. / NO COUNTRY EVER HAD / TRUER SONS. / NO CAUSE
/ NOBLER CHAMPIONS, / NO PEOPLE / BOLDER DEFENDERS / THAN THE BRAVE
SOLDIERS / TO WHOSE MEMORY / THIS STONE IS ERECTED

WE WHO SAW / AND KNEW THEM WELL, / ARE WITNESSES / TO COMING AGES OF
THEIR VALOR / AND FIDELITY. / TRIED AND TRUE. / GLORY CROWNED. / 1861–1865.

The prototypical Confederate monument, it stands on ground that the Army of
Tennessee sought but could not reach during the battle of Franklin on November
30, 1864, and it is surmounted by the sculpted figure of a Confederate common
soldier, holding the barrel of a rifle, facing south, toward the battlefield.

Franklin was the site of a climactic late-war act of desperation by
Confederate arms in November 1864. The battle changed nothing in terms of
the outcome of the war, but at a cost of some eighty-five hundred casualties
it became, by some Southern accounts, the war's "most hallowed and bloody
ground." This monument offers what may be one of the most moving testa-
ments to Confederate arms in the South. Confederate soldiers suffered more
casualties in this charge here than in Pickett's Charge during the Battle of
Gettysburg.

The sculpture, of Italian marble by an unknown sculptor, faces south toward
the battlefield. The figure is approximately six feet, six inches tall. The whole
of the monument stands approximately thirty-seven feet, eight inches high.
Four cannon barrels, set in concrete bases, surround it.

- During the dedication ceremonies, the "Address of Welcome by
  Dr. Hanner" included a tribute to the UDC: "All the enthusiasm of your
  nature and kindle afresh that patriotism that never fails. Ennoble the
  history of our common country in the future as you have done in the
  past, and coming ages will proclaim that you were as noble as citizens
  as you were brave as soldiers."
- Confederate Brig. Gen. George W. Gordon's dedication address was
  "eloquent, chaste, and evoked high enthusiasm." He said, in part: "Let
  no man, unchallenged, asperse the memory of our sacred dead, our
  fallen comrades, with the charge of treason and rebellion. They fell in

defense of the liberty and independence of their country consequently were heroes and patriots. But let their history in granite, so fittingly summarized in the mottoes on this monument, vindicate their memory, pronounce their eulogy, and perpetuate their example. Peace to their spirits! Honor to their ashes!"

· The excerpt beginning "Would it not be" is from the poem "C.S.A.," by Father Abram Ryan. The inscription beginning "We Who Saw And Knew Them" may be a reference to John 19:35: "He who saw it has borne witness—his testimony is true, and he knows that he is telling the truth—that you also may believe."

4.17.2 Subject: Federal Lines, Main Entrenchment, Stele, Union
Location: Carter House, 1140 Columbia Avenue, 37064   N 35 54 58 07 / W 86 52 24 10
Installed or dedicated: 1922
Medium: Bronze, limestone
Monument is a plaque surmounting a stele.

Inscription

MAIN ENTRENCHMENT FEDERAL BATTLE LINE / BATTLE OF FRANKLIN, NOVEMBER 30, 1864, FEDERAL / COMMANDER, GEN. JOHN M. SCHOFIELD, CONFEDERATE / COMMANDER, GEN. JOHN B. HOOD, BLOODIEST BATTLE / OF THE WAR BETWEEN THE STATES FOR NUMBERS / INVOLVED. IN THIS BATTLE FELL SIX CONFEDERATE / GENERALS; CLEBURNE, STRAHL, GIST, ADAMS, / GRANBERRY AND CARTER TENNESSEE HISTORICAL COMMISSION 1922 / RESTORED BY S. S. ORWIG 1938.

This marker near the Carter House is at the practical center of the site of the fighting that took place during the battle of Franklin. Elements of the IV Corps were driven to this ground from their main line of entrenchments, which stood about 260 feet south of this marker. The Confederates had the initiative. However, reinforcements—in this area it was Col. Emerson Opdycke's Brigade (1st Brigade, 2nd Division)—rushed forward and countercharged, repelling the Southern onslaught and sealing the breakthrough they had forged. Historian Victor Hicken observes that there was "no finer example of the initiative of the Union soldier in the entire war," than along this ridge and near this site.

4.17.3–4.17.16 McGavock Confederate Cemetery
Location: 1345 Carnton Lane, 37064   N 35 54 17 21 / W 86 51 42 12
Markers installed: 1890

McGavock Confederate Cemetery is the largest private Confederate cemetery in the South and is devoted almost entirely to the Confederate dead from the battle of Franklin. The site was on the field of battle and is near the Carnton

McGavock Confederate Cemetery, Overview

House, where the bodies of three dead Confederate generals were brought and laid out on the veranda after the battle: Maj. Gen. Patrick Cleburne, Brig. Gen. Hiram B. Granbury, and Brig. Gen. Otho F. Strahl.

A committee formed to collect and reinter the Confederate dead in April 1866, although some 150 had already been buried on these grounds immediately after the battle. John McGavock, a member of the committee and owner of Carnton Plantation, donated two acres for the cemetery. With the assistance of his wife, Caroline Winder "Carrie" McGavock, he supervised the reinterment of 1,496 dead. George Cuppett and a crew of laborers did the actual work of locating the dead, exhuming the remains, and moving them. The cost was $3,000, about $2 per grave. The dead are arranged by state, buried in platoon formation: 15 graves in each row. Thus the 230 graves from Tennessee have equal place and status with those from North Carolina (2), Florida (4) or Kentucky (6). Mississippi, with 424 graves, is the largest state gravesite.

The name of each soldier was officially registered in what came to be known as the "Book of the Dead," which Caroline W. McGavock maintained during her lifetime.

Excerpt from the 1911 book *Historic Monuments*:

John McGavock and his noble wife [Caroline Winder "Carrie" McGavock], old residents of Franklin, conceived the laudable idea of dead heroes. With that object in view, Colonel McGavock donated the necessary ground near his residence, one mile south of the public square of Franklin and joining his family burying-ground. . . . establish[ed] a cemetery for the bodies of [1,418] soldiers. Each grave was marked with a painted headboard, bearing the name and command of the dead when known. A list of the names of every known body was compiled, together with the name of the regiment and company to which the soldier belonged.

According to historian Eric Jacobson's research of the grounds and the Book of the Dead, 780 graves are positively identified, 558 graves are unknown, and 143 "have some sort of identification, genuine or otherwise." The John L. McEwen Bivouac of the United Confederate Veterans assisted in maintaining the graves. Limestone headstones replaced the wooden headboards over each grave in about 1890. An iron fence was "secured through the efforts of Miss M[ary] A. H. Gay, of Decatur, Ga." Mary Ann Harris Gay, whose half-brother, Tommy Stokes, was killed at Franklin, was active in fund-raising and aid to social and religious causes during and after the war.

The state monuments were erected in 1890. Funding was solicited from the Southern states, but responses came from only three: South Carolina, Mississippi, and Louisiana. The base of each monument is twenty-three by twenty-three inches square; the shaft and base are five feet high, and the shaft is twelve by twelve inches square. Regardless of plot size—Mississippi the largest; North Carolina the smallest—each state monument is the same size. The cost and cause are also identical: the relentless synthetic parallelism of "Killed At Franklin" on each state monument is notable; so too is the repetition of CSA as the representative cause for which they died.

Today the McGavock Confederate Cemetery Corporation serves as the official organization that maintains the cemetery. Trustees are elected by the board from the Franklin Chapter No. 14 UDC.

4.17.3 Subject: State of North Carolina, Shaft

Inscription

CSA / 2 / KILLED AT FRANKLIN / N. CAROLINA

One of only two monuments in Tennessee to North Carolina; the other is at Tullahoma.

4.17.4 Subject: State of Kentucky, Shaft

Inscription

CSA / 6 / KILLED AT FRANKLIN / KENTUCKY

4.17.5 Subject: State of Florida, Shaft

Inscription

CSA / 4 / KILLED AT FRANKLIN / FLORIDA

McGavock Confederate Cemetery, Unknown Soldiers

4.17.6 Subject: Unknown, Shaft
Installed or dedicated: 1890
Medium: Marble
Monument is a four-sided shaft surmounted by sculpted cannonballs.

Inscription
[Four cannon barrels, upturned]
1861–1865 / KILLED AT FRANKLIN / 225 / UNKNOWN

The large number of "Unknown" at Franklin is accounted for, to some extent, by the fact that many of the headboards were burned or otherwise destroyed after Federal troops returned to Franklin after the battle of Nashville.

4.17.7 Subject: State of Louisiana, Shaft

Inscription
CSA / 18 / KILLED AT FRANKLIN / LOUISIANA

4.17.8 Subject: State of South Carolina, Shaft

Inscription
CSA / 51 / KILLED AT FRANKLIN / S. CAROLINA

4.17.9 Subject: Fifteen Unknown, Shaft

Inscription
THIS SECTION / CONTAINS 15 / UNKNOWN

4.17.10 Subject: State of Georgia, Shaft

Inscription

CSA / 69 / KILLED AT FRANKLIN / GEORGIA

4.17.11 Subject: State of Mississippi, Shaft

Inscription

CSA / 424 / KILLED AT FRANKLIN / MISSISSIPPI

4.17.12 Subject: State of Alabama, Shaft

Inscription

CSA / 129 / KILLED AT FRANKLIN / ALABAMA

4.17.13 Subject: State of Arkansas, Shaft

Inscription

CSA / 104 / KILLED AT FRANKLIN / ARKANSAS

4.17.14 Subject: State of Missouri, Shaft

Inscription

CSA / 130 / KILLED AT FRANKLIN / MISSOURI

McGavock Confederate Cemetery, Missouri Soldiers

Winstead Hill: Left to right: Stelae: Freeman, Tennessee, Mississippi, Alabama, Arkansas, Cockrell, Cleburne

4.17.15 Subject: State of Tennessee, Shaft

Inscription

CSA / 230 / KILLED AT FRANKLIN / TENNESSEE

4.17.16 Subject: State of Texas, Shaft

Inscription

CSA / 89 / KILLED AT FRANKLIN / TEXAS

Winstead Hill
4023 Columbia Pike, 37064

The infantry of the Army of Tennessee formed on this hill prior to the battle of Franklin. Winstead Hill Park looks out on the open ground over which the Army of Tennessee infantry advanced in a charge as dramatic as that of "Pickett's Charge" at Gettysburg. It was from here that Lt. Gen. John B. Hood observed the battle. This is not a national battlefield site: it requires more imagination to envision what happened than the arguably equally dramatic grounds preserved at Gettysburg. Today the Franklin site is given over to light industry, retail establishments, and residential neighborhoods. The contours of the terrain remain largely intact, however: Winstead Hill stands, the slope up to the Carter House is evident; even the forward ground of the Union skirmish line as a rise in the terrain is clearly discernible.

The surface features of the landscape visible from this eminence are ever changing, of course. The site where Confederate general Patrick Cleburne was killed in action, for example, was a fast-food restaurant parking lot but is today a park with a memorial. The city's 110-acre Eastern Flank Battlefield Park—once a golf course and athletic facility—opened in 2014 and is today marked with numerous wayside tablets along expansive walkways. In the past two decades, Winstead Hill Park has been lavished with monuments, many erected by the Sons of Confederate Veterans. Many are undated, but most were erected circa 2000.

A bronze plaque notes that the plot of nine acres forming Winstead Hill Park was donated to the Franklin Chapter No. 14 of the UDC by Walter A. Roberts on May 7, 1948. The UDC in turn donated the hill as a "Confederate Memorial Park" to the Sam Davis Camp No. 1293, May 5, 1982.

4.17.17 Subject: Army of Tennessee, Stele
Location: N 35 53 19 31 / W 86 52 40 36
Installed or dedicated: n.a.
Medium: Bronze, fieldstone

Inscription

TENNESSEE: A GRAVE OR A FREE HOME
NO WORDS CAN DESCRIBE THE COURAGE, ENDURANCE, AND GALLANTRY OF THE
/ ARMY OF TENNESSEE. THEY MARCHED, FOUGHT, BLED, AND DIED FOR A CAUSE /
THEY KNEW WAS RIGHT. ON THAT INDIAN SUMMER AFTERNOON OF NOVEMBER /
20, 1864, THE COURAGEOUS ARMY OF TENNESSEE DEPLOYED INTO LINE OF BATTLE
AND MARCHED OVER THESE OPEN FIELDS INTO IMMORTALITY. THE / MEMORY OF
THESE HEROIC SOULS IS AS ENDURING AS TIME. THEIR LEGACY IS / ASSURED; IT IS
ONLY THAT OF EVERLASTING GLORY.
"A LIFE GIVEN FOR ONE'S COUNTRY IS NEVER LOST"- / SAM WATKINS, 1ST
TENNESSEE INFANTRY, C.S.A.

This tribute is excerpted from Sam Watkins' *Company Aytch: Or, a Side Show of the Big Show*, a vivid account of his service with the 1st Tennessee Infantry during the war.

Brigadier's Walk

This is a preeminent example of SCV monumentation in the South: granite monuments to the six generals killed at Franklin stand here, practically adjacent to one another. Tributes to field-level courage and leadership in the face of death are prominent themes of the SCV inscriptions. The materials—granite, inscribed—are less grand than the statue-oriented monuments of the court-house era, for example, but the sense of location and descriptive prose and narratives is provocative in the same way.

The six monuments are granite stelae, installed or dedicated circa 2000, each surmounting a base, in various shades of granite, each approximately thirty-six inches wide by fifty-five inches tall. Narratives, praises, last words, and tributes are common notes of commemoration on these monuments.

Winstead Hill: Brigadier's Walk: Left to right: Brig. Gen. Hiram B. Grandbury, Brig. Gen. John C. Carter, Stele, Brig. Gen. John Adams, Stele, Brig. Gen. Otho Strahl, Stele, Brig. Gen. States Rights Gist, Stele

Winstead Hill: Brig. Gen. States Rights Gist, SCV Stele

4.17.18 Subject: Brig. Gen. Hiram B. Grandbury, Stele
Location: N 35 53 19 49 / W 86 52 42 06
Monument is a granite stele surmounting a base.

Inscription

[Wreath with Star of Texas]
BRIGADIER GENERAL HIRAM B. GRANBURY / CONFEDERATE STATES OF AMERICA
/ COMMANDER, TEXAS BRIGADE, / ARMY OF TENNESSEE / BORN MARCH 1, 1831 /
DIED ON THIS FIELD, NOVEMBER 30, 1864 / A MOMENT BEFORE HE FELL, HE URGED
HIS TEXANS ON: "FORWARD, MEN, FORWARD! NEVER LET IT BE SAID / THAT TEXANS
LAG IN A FIGHT!" THEY NEVER DID, AND NEITHER DID HE. / GOD REST HIS SOUL.
[Texas Star]
THIS MONUMENT ERECTED THROUGH THE DEDICATION OF:
[List of donors]

Granbury was killed at the head of his Texas brigade in the first assault, near
Columbia Pike. The thirty-three-year-old Granbury was on foot, urging his
men on when he was shot. Historian Wiley Sword reports that a bullet struck
him just under the right eye, passing through and carrying off the top of his
head. According to reports, General Granbury threw both hands to his face
and sank to his knees in death. He was buried in a pauper's grave in Ashwood
Cemetery in Columbia. In 1893, his body was moved to Granbury, Texas—
named for him—and was reinterred.

4.17.19 Subject: Brig. Gen. States Rights Gist, Stele

Inscription

[CS national flag]
STATES RIGHTS GIST
THE TRAGEDY OF FRANKLIN QUITE POSSIBLY MAY HAVE BEEN / AVERTED HAD THIS
SCHOLARLY SOUTH CAROLINA BLUE BLOOD / BEEN GIVEN THE PROMOTION TO
DIVISION COMMAND THAT / HIS SERVICE RECORD WARRANTED. . . . [HIS] BRIGADE,
MADE UP OF [T]HE 46TH, 65TH & 2ND BATTALION / GEORGIA SHARPSHOOTERS,
AND THE 16TH AND [C]RACK 24TH / SOUTH CAROLINA SLAMMED INTO THE 72ND
ILLINOIS & 111TH / OHIO CAUSING THE 72ND TO "BREAK AND RUN". HAVING HIS /
HORSE SHOT FROM UNDER HIM, GIST SPRINTED FOR THE LOCUST / ABATIS IN HIS
FRONT. ADVANCING TO WITHIN A FEW YARDS OF / THE ABATIS, GIST WENT DOWN
WITH A BULLET IN THE CHEST. HE / DIED THE NEXT MORNING AT [T]HE HARRISON
HOUSE. HE WAS / BURIED, FIRST IN A PRIVATE CEMETERY IN FRANKLIN, THEN AND
/ FINALLY, AT THE TRINITY EPISCOPAL CHURCH IN COLUMBIA, / SOUTH CAROLINA.

Brig. Gen. States Rights Gist (1831–64) was highly regarded in his time. The
speculation on this stele that the battle of Franklin "quite possibly may have
been averted" is not explained, but there is much praise, historically, for Gist
as a leader, an intellect, and a man of courage. Gist had no military training

before the war, but his leadership and courage were well noted, and he was often given command responsibilities beyond his nominal rank. He served at First Manassas, coastal defense commands, at Vicksburg, Chickamauga, Chattanooga, and the Atlanta Campaign.

- This is the only mention of Abraham Lincoln on a Confederate monument in Tennessee. And, other than the Jefferson Davis monument in Memphis, there is no other mention of the Confederacy's only president in Tennessee monumentation.

4.14.20 Subject: Brig. Gen. Otto F. Strahl, Stele

Inscription

[Confederate battle flag]
OTTO F. STRAHL
COMMISSIONED BRIGADIER TO RANK FROM JULY 28, 1863, / THIS OHIO BORN "STATES RIGHTER" COMMANDED ONE OF / THE "HARDEST HITTING BRIGADES" IN THE ARMY OF / TENNESSEE. . . . / DURING THE ILL FATED MIDDLE TENNESSEE CAMPAIGN OF / LATE 1864, THE BRIGADE CONSISTED OF THE 24TH, 5TH, / 19TH, 4TH, 31ST, 33RD, 38TH & 41ST TENNESSEE / REGIMENTS. . . . ALTHOUGH REDUCED IN / NUMBERS BY THE TIME THE BRIGADE SLAMMED INTO THE / FINAL LINE OF FEDERAL WORKS THEY MANAGED TO HOLD / ONTO THE OUTER PORTION OF THE WORKS DESPITE VICIOUS / ENFILADING FIRE FROM THE AREA OF THE GIN HOUSE. / STRAHL WAS SEVERELY WOUNDED IN THE NECK WHILE / PASSING A LOADED ENFIELD TO S. A. CUNNINGHAM. / WHILE BEING CARRIED TO THE REAR, STRAHL WAS STRUCK / BY TWO MORE BULLETS, THE SECOND BRINGING DEATH. / FIRST BURIED AT ST. JOHNS WITH CLEBURNE, STRAHL WAS / LATER REINTERRED AT HIS BELOVED DYERSBURG, TENNESSEE.

"Boys, this will be short but desperate," Brig. Gen. Otho F. Strahl predicted before the advance of his brigade from Winstead Hill. He led his troops into the Federal works and was wounded during the fight there. He was carried to the rear but was hit twice en route and finally killed.

Strahl, a German American, was born in McConnelsville, Ohio, but moved to Dyersburg and was practicing law there at the outbreak of the war. He sided with the South, enlisted and rose from captain to colonel while serving with the 4th Tennessee Infantry at Shiloh, Bentonville, and Stones River, and then to general during the Atlanta Campaign.

His body was first interred in the potter's field section of Rose Hill Cemetery, reinterred at Ashwood Cemetery of St. John's Episcopal Church near Columbia, and was finally settled in Dyersburg in 1901.

- S. A. Cunningham, mentioned in the inscription, served as founder and editor of *Confederate Veteran*, described his place near Strahl at his death.

4.14.21 Subject: Brig. Gen. John C. Carter, Stele

Inscription

JOHN C. CARTER
COMMISSIONED BRIGADIER TO RANK FROM JULY 7, 1864 / CARTER HAD WORKED
HIS WAY UP FROM THE RANK OF / CAPTAIN BY DISTINGUISHING HIMSELF WITH
THE ARMY / OF TENNESSEE AT SHILOH, PERRYVILLE, MURFREESBORO / &
CHICKAMAUGA. . . . / ATTACKING TO THE LEFT OF GIST'S BRIGADE AT FRANKLIN, /
CARTER'S REGIMENTS; THE 1ST, 4TH PROVISIONAL, 6TH, / 8TH, 9TH, 16TH, 27TH,
28TH, AND 50TH TENNESSEE / WERE "TORN BY CANISTER AND MUSKETRY BEFORE
THEY / REACHED THE LOCUST ABATES". CARTER RODE RECKLESSLY / IN FRONT OF
HIS BRIGADE ESPOUSING THE "LEAD BY / EXAMPLE" CREDO THAT HAD COME TO
BE THE NORM IN / THE ARMY OF TENNESSEE. LESS THAN 150 YARDS FROM / THE
WORKS CARTER TUMBLED FROM HIS HORSE, SHOT / THROUGH THE BODY. SHORTLY
THEREAFTER "HIS BOYS" OF / THE 1ST TENNESSEE PENETRATED THE FEDERAL
WORKS. / HE DIED ON DECEMBER 10, 1864 AT THE HARRISON / HOUSE AND WAS
LAID TO REST AT ROSE HILL CEMETERY / IN COLUMBIA, TENNESSEE.

Brig. Gen. John C. Carter (1837–64) was born in Waynesboro, Georgia, but
was practicing law in Memphis in 1861 and entered the war as a captain in
the 38th Tennessee Infantry. He commanded the 28th at Shiloh, Perryville,
and Stones River, and during the Atlanta Campaign. Mortally wounded at
Franklin, Carter was taken from the battlefield to the Harrison House, where
he died several days later.

4.14.22 Subject: Brig. Gen. John Adams, Stele

Inscription

JOHN ADAMS
TENNESSEE BORN JOHN ADAMS WAS A WEST POINT / GRADUATE. HE WAS COMMIS-
SIONED BRIGADIER TO / RANK FROM DECEMBER 29, 1862, AFTER ASSUMING / COM-
MAND OF MARYLAND BORN LLOYD TILGHMAN'S / BRIGADE. JOINING THE ARMY
OF TENNESSEE AT / RESACA IN MAY OF 1864, THE BRIGADE SERVED / GALLANTLY
THROUGHOUT THE ATLANTA CAMPAIGN. AT / FRANKLIN THE BRIGADE CONSISTED
OF ALL MISSISSIPPI / REGIMENTS; 6TH, 14TH, 15TH, 20TH, 23RD, & 43RD. / HAVING
BEEN FORCED TO ANGLE TOWARD THE CENTER / DUE TO THE OSAGE HEDGES,
THE BRIGADE MADE ONE / OF THE MOST SPECTACULAR ASSAULTS OF THE DAY! /
DESPITE TAKE A SEVERE WOUND IN THE ARM, / ADAMS REMAINED MOUNTED AND
DROVE STRAIGHT / FOR THE COLORS OF THE 65TH ILLINOIS. LESS THAN / 50 FEET
FROM THE PARAPET ADAMS SPURRED HIS / BELOVED "OLD CHARLEY" TO JUMP
THE DITCH AND / PARAPET. THE LEAPING HORSE CRASHED DEAD ON / TOP OF THE
WORKS AS ADAMS WAS RIDDLED WITH / BULLETS. HE FELL AND WAS PINNED BE-
NEATH HIS / HORSE, AS THE UNION COLONEL OF THE 65TH LOOKED / ON, AND DIED
SHORTLY THEREAFTER. ADAMS IS / BURIED IN PULASKI, TENNESSEE.

Adams (1825–64), who, when dying on the field below still had the presence of
mind to thank his men for their service, was also quoted as saying that "it is
the fate of a soldier to die for his country." He left a widow with six children

Winstead Hill: State of Mississippi, SCV Stele

at his death. His body was taken directly from the battlefield to his home in Pulaski, Tennessee. A bronze state marker to Adams stands over his grave at Maplewood Cemetery, Pulaski.

4.17.23 Subject: State of Mississippi, Stele
Location: N 35 53 19 12 / W 86 52 80 84
Installed or dedicated: November 30, 1994
Medium: Granite, fieldstone

Inscription

[Inscribed CS battle flag]
TWAS NOVEMBER THIRTIETH, EIGHTEEN SIXTY-FOUR. / MISSISSIPPI'S SONS AND FATHERS INTO BATTLE AGAIN / WERE POURED. THE YOUNG AND THE OLD, THE BRAVE AND / THE BOLD, THEIR MISSION ALL TOO PLAIN–TO CHARGE / ACROSS WHAT WOULD BECOME FRANKLIN'S BLOODY PLAIN. / AT FOUR O'CLOCK, EIGHTEEN BRIGADES THAT FORMED / THE RANKS OF GRAY MOVED AGAINST THE YANKEE FOE. / FLAGS FLYING IN GRAND ARRAY, THE SIGHT SWELLS / THE HEART WITH PRIDE FOR THE VICTORY THEY MIGHT / GAIN, THEN BREAKS IT WITH SORROW FOR THOSE LOST / ON FRANKLIN'S BLOODY PLAIN.
MISSISSIPPI
NOVEMBER 30, 1994 / SPONSORED BY SONS OF CONFEDERATE VETERANS

[Order of battle]

Another tribute to Confederate soldiers, in this instance from Mississippi, with an order of battle of Mississippi units on the field, a poetic narrative, and a Confederate battle flag framing a message of admiration for men who could see the mortal risks before them and courageously confront them.

4.17.24 Subject: State of Tennessee, Confederate Stele
Location: N 35 53 18 57 / W 86 52 41 10

Inscription

TENNESSEE
ON A NOVEMBER AFTERNOON IN 1864, BRAVE CONFEDERATE SONS OF / TENNESSEE MOVED FORWARD INTO BATTLE AGAINST FEDERAL LINES ENTRENCHED TWO MILES NORTH. WINSTEAD HILL SERVED AS THE PLACE OF ASSEMBLY AND WAS AN OBSERVATION POINT DURING THE BATTLE. / CONFEDERATE REGIMENTS FORMED IN TENNESSEE AND PRESENT FOR THE CAMPAIGN
[Order of battle]
COURAGE AND SACRIFICE BECAME THE ORDER OF THE DAY AS NEARLY 7,000 CONFEDERATE SOLDIERS FAILED TO LEAVE THE FIELD OF BATTLE. THIS BATTLE AT FRANKLIN WAS THE MOST BRUTAL OF THE DECISIVE TENNESSEE CAMPAIGN[S] OF THE WINTER OF 1864. THE ARMY OF TENNESSEE WOULD FIGHT ON UNTIL WAR'S END IN 1865.
ERECTED BY SAM DAVIS CAMP #1293 AND THE TENNESSEE DIVISION, SONS OF CONFEDERATE VETERANS

The admiration and affection of the Tennessee Division of the SCV for their Confederate ancestors is perhaps epitomized in this monument, which details the roster of Tennessee Confederate units who were on the field for the battle of Franklin. It might be compared to the Pennsylvania monument at Gettysburg in the broad sweep of its ambition: it is like a state monument to Tennessee Confederate soldiers. The focus is on Tennessee soldiers fighting on Tennessee soil, with a description of six brigades of infantry, three units of cavalry, and three units of artillery. Notable, too, is how dynamic the inscription is: there is emphasis on "Courage and Sacrifice" as well as an assertion that the battle of Franklin was the most brutal of the 1864 Tennessee Campaign and that Tennessee soldiers were unyielding, playing a crucial role here and on other fields, and "Fight[ing] On Until War's End in 1865."

4.17.25 Subject: Freeman's Battery, Forrest's Artillery, Stele
Location: N 35 53 19 88 / W 86 52 40 44
Installed or dedicated: November 30, 2003
Medium: Granite

Inscription

[Relief of six cannonballs]
FREEMAN'S BATTERY
[SCV Seal]
FORREST'S ARTILLERY / DEDICATED TO / FREEMAN'S BATTERY / AND / SAMUEL L. FREEMAN. / GEN. NATHAN BEDFORD / FORREST'S FIRST ARTILLERY / CAPTAIN. THE

BATTERY WAS / CAPTURED ON THE LEWISBURG PIKE / NEAR FRANKLIN, TN / APRIL 10, 1863

[Inscribed light artillery piece with five men attending]
WHILE ADVANCING TOWARD FRANKLIN, TN ON THE / LEWISBURG PIKE, APRIL 10, 1863, GENERAL N. B. / FORREST'S COMMAND WAS ATTACKED BY THE 4TH U.S. / REGULARS. . . . OF CAPT. FREEMAN [KILLED IN ACTION HERE], FORREST SAID, "BRAVE MAN, / NONE BRAVER." YEARS AFTER THE WAR, ONE OF THE / BATTERY'S CANNONEERS STATED, "WE ALWAYS HELD / TO THE NAME OF FREEMAN"
ERECTED BY FREEMAN'S BATTERY FORREST'S / ARTILLERY CAMP 1939, SONS OF CONFEDERATE VETERANS / NOVEMBER 30, 2003

This is the only monument on Winstead Hill that is not related to the battle of Franklin in 1864. The 1863 engagement was the result of a reconnaissance by Confederate Maj. Gen. Earl Van Dorn, leading the 1st Cavalry Corps, Army of Tennessee. Van Dorn's force encountered Federal skirmishers under the overall command of Union Maj. Gen. Gordon Granger. The 4th US Cavalry attacked and captured Freeman's Tennessee Battery on the Lewisburg Road just outside Franklin. Freeman was killed in the incident. Brig. Gen. Nathan Bedford Forrest's troopers counterattacked and recovered the battery. The results of the operation were indecisive. The Union cavalry withdrew. Van Dorn cut short his movements and withdrew to Spring Hill.

- Monuments to Freeman's Battery, which fought with Forrest, also stand on the Salem battlefield and at Brice's Corner in Mississippi.

4.17.26 Subject: Cockrell's Missouri Brigade, Confederate, Stele
Location: Upper walk   N 35 53 19 84 / W 86 52 41 92
Installed or dedicated: n.a.
Medium: Granite

Inscription
[Inscribed crossed flags: CS battle flag and the Missouri battle flag]
COCKRELL'S MISSOURI / BRIGADE / CSA
ON THIS FIELD OF HONOR / MISSOURI MEN OF / COCKRELL'S BRIGADE / FOUGHT AND DIED FOR / SOUTHERN INDEPENDENCE / NOVEMBER 30, 1864 / FRANKLIN, TENNESSEE
PRESENTED BY MISSOURIANS OF THE SONS OF / CONFEDERATE VETERANS AND HIS FRIENDS / IN MEMORY OF / GAYLORD PATRICK O' CONNOR, 1916–1994

The Missouri Brigade, commanded for most of the war by Brig. Gen. Francis M. Cockrell, fought in numerous actions in the west, including Shiloh, Iuka, Port Gibson, Champion Hill, Vicksburg, the Atlanta Campaign, Franklin, and Nashville.

Cockrell was highly regarded, as was his brigade. He was wounded in the battle of Franklin but survived to return to active duty, and would go on to serve in the US Senate from 1875 to 1905.

- The Missouri Brigade was "the best on either side, including the Stonewall Brigade and the Iron Brigade of the North," according to historian Ed Bearss.

4.14.27 Subject: Maj. Gen. Patrick R. Cleburne, Stele
Location: Brigadier's Walk   N 35 53 19 26 / W 86 52 42 34
Installed or dedicated: n.a.
Medium: Granite
Monument is a granite stele surmounting a base.

Inscription

CSA
MAJOR GENERAL / PATRICK R. / CLEBURNE / CSA
WELL GOVAN IF WE ARE TO DIE / LET US DIE LIKE MEN / NOV 30, 1864
PRESENTED AS A TRIBUTE TO / GENERAL CLEBURNE AND HIS / GALLANT DIVISION
BY DR. AND / MRS[.] DAVID R. WATTS

Cleburne's remains were interred at St. John's Church, Mount Pleasant, Tennessee. In 1870, his body was reinterred in Helena, Arkansas. Historian Shelby Foote describes his last moments: "When his second horse was killed by a shot from a cannon he went ahead on foot through the smoke and din, waving his cap. The hope of his veterans, who idolized him, was that he had been wounded for the third time in the war, or even captured; but this hope collapsed next morning, when his body was found beside the Columbia Pike just short of the enemy works. A single bullet had gone through his heart."

"Govan" is Brig. Gen. Daniel C. Govan (1829–1911). The recollection is postwar and was published in the Southern Historical Society Papers in 1880, when Govan recalled his last meeting with his division commander. Cleburne was "greatly depressed" as he briefed his brigade commanders about the pending assault, and Govan recalled saying, "Well, General, few of us will ever return to Arkansas to tell the story of this battle." Cleburne replied, "Well, Govan, if we are to die, let us die like men." Govan survived the battle, was later wounded at the battle of Nashville, recovered and returned to active service before the war ended, and survived the war.

4.17.28 Subject: State of Arkansas, Stele
Location: N 35 53 19 26 / W 86 52 41 94
Dedicated: October 25, 2014
Medium: Granite

Inscription

ARKANSAS
THE BATTLE OF FRANKLIN WAS THE MOST TRAGIC CHAPTER OF THE ARMY OF
TENNESSEE. THESE WERE BATTLE-HARDENED VETERANS. THEY KNEW THE

ENEMY THEY FACED AND THE STRENGTH OF THEIR DEFENSES. HONOR, VALOR, PATRIOTISM, DEVOTION TO DUTY, AND THE SPIRIT OF SELF SACRIFICE / WERE NEVER MORE EVIDENT THAN HERE AT FRANKLIN. / THEIR NAMES ARE WRITTEN IN STONE AND BLOOD

ARKANSAS INFANTRY UNITS AT FRANKLIN / GEN. DANIEL C. GOVAN'S BRIGADE / 1ST ARKANSAS INF. 2ND ARKANSAS INF. 5TH ARKANSAS INF. / 6TH ARKANSAS INF. 7TH ARKANSAS INF. 8TH ARKANSAS INF. / 13TH ARKANSAS INF. 15TH ARKANSAS INF. 19TH ARKANSAS INF. / 24TH ARKANSAS INF. / GEN. DANIEL H. REYNOLD'S BRIGADE / 4TH ARKANSAS INF. 9TH ARKANSAS INF. 25TH ARKANSAS INF.

"NOT MANY OF US WILL GET BACK TO ARKANSAS" / GEN. DANIEL C. GOVAN

"IF WE ARE TO DIE LET US DIE LIKE MEN." GEN. PATRICK R. CLEBURNE / NOVEMBER 30TH, 1864

ERECTED IN LOVING MEMORY TO THE / MEN OF ARKANSAS BY THE / ARKANSAS DIVISION, SONS OF CONFEDERATE VETERANS / AND THE ARKANSAS DIVISION UNITED DAUGHTERS OF THE CONFEDERACY

"WHERE THIS DIVISION DEFENDED, NO ODDS BROKE ITS LINE, / WHERE IT AT-TACKED, NO NUMBERS RESISTED ITS ONSLAUGHT, / SAVE ONLY ONCE: AND THERE IS THE GRAVE OF CLEBURNE" / —GEN. WILLIAM J. HARDEE

Members of the Jo Shelby Camp of the SCV and the Boston Mountain UDC sponsored this monument and attended the dedication ceremonies for it during the sesquicentennial of the battle of Franklin. The cause is not mentioned, the leadership of men like Cleburne or Govan is praised or cited, but the senior leadership—that is, Hood—is not indicted. Like other SCV monuments on Winstead Hill, detailed rosters of participants are displayed along with tributes to the Confederate soldier's devotion and courage in the course of the valiant but failed assault on the fields to the north.

· Historian Wiley Sword concludes that "never on a Civil War battle-field, and in few moments in American history, were the elements of contradiction so evident. Franklin witnessed a full embodiment of the Confederacy's power and glory, and abject disparagement of intelligent reason."

4.17.29 Subject: State of Alabama, Stele
Location: N 35 53 18 88 / W 86 52 41 78
Installed or dedicated: circa 2014
Medium: Granite

Inscription
IN MEMORY OF THE MEN OF ALABAMA / WHO BRAVELY FOUGHT AND DIED AT THE / BATTLES OF FRANKLIN & NASHVILLE
[Crossed battle flag and flag of Alabama]
ALABAMA INFANTRY REGIMENTS / 1ST, 10TH, 16TH, 17TH, 18TH, 19TH, 20TH, 22ND, 23RD, 24TH, / 25TH, 26TH, 27TH, 28TH, 29TH, 30TH, 31ST, 32ND, 33RD, 34TH, / 35TH, 36TH, 38TH, 39TH, 45TH, 46TH, 49TH, 50TH, 55TH, 57TH, 58TH / ALABAMA ARTILLERY BATTERIES / DENT'S ALABAMA BATTERY / GARRITY'S ALABAMA

BATTERY / EUFAULA ALABAMA BATTERY / LUMSEN'S ALABAMA BATTERY / SELDEN'S
ALABAMA BATTERY / KOLB'S ALABAMA BATTERY / PHELAN'S ALABAMA BATTERY /
GOLDWAITE'S ALABAMA BATTERY / 7TH ALABAMA CAVALRY
MOURN NOT THAT THESE GREAT MEN DIED, / BUT BE THANKFUL THEY LIVED.
ERECTED BY / ALABAMA DIVISION / SONS OF / CONFEDERATE / VETERANS /
MECHANIZED CAVALRY, 1ST BATTALION, COMPANY D
[Alabama state flag]
WE DARE DEFEND / OUR RIGHTS

This SCV monument makes no claim to being state sponsored, but its display of the Alabama state flag and state motto along with the detailed rosters of Alabama units gives it that appearance. States' rights are an apparent theme. "We Dare Defend Our Rights"—translated from the Latin, *Audemus jura nostra defendere*—is the state motto and is depicted on the official coat of arms. The state flag, crimson St. Andrew's cross on a white field, is patterned after the Confederate battle flag and was officially adopted in 1895.

The monument is unique—perhaps surprisingly—in giving equal tribute to the units' service in the battle of Nashville.

· Pvt. Calvin J. C. Munroe of Company G, 25th Alabama, remembered the battle of Franklin in this fashion:

> The line was formed in a few minutes. Bates' Division, French's Division, and Cleburne's Division led the way. Our Division was to support Bates. We drove them from one line of works and had charged them in the second line . . . we was ordered to charge and we rushed upon them and drove them from their position. We crossed over into the ditch, we was obliged to lie down in the ditch to protect ourselves, but the ditch was not deep enough to shelter us. We lay there and fought them about 2 hours when they took advantage of the darkness and withdrew their force in the direction of Nashville.

Rest Haven Cemetery

4.17.30 Subject: Rest Haven Cemetery, Unknown Soldier, Column
Location: N. Margin Street between 4th and 5th Avenues   N 35 55 40 97 / W 86 52 25 30
Dedicated: October 2009
Medium: Granite, marble
Monument is granite headstone and a marble column.

Although prodigious efforts were made to inter the dead on the Franklin battlefield, records and recovery remain incomplete, and not all bodies were recovered. The remains of "Franklin's Unknown Soldier" were found during the course of a construction project on Columbus Avenue. His identity is unknown, but forensic examination established that he was a Civil War soldier. Whether he was a Confederate or a Union soldier is also unknown. He was given a

Unknown Soldier, Column, Rest Haven Cemetery

funeral at St. Paul's Episcopal Church, which was erected 1831–34 and used as a hospital after the battle of Franklin, and a burial with military honors.

The uninscribed monument is constructed of segments of the original columns of the Tennessee State Capitol, which were discarded during a restoration of the building. The soldier's tombstone is inscribed:

Inscription

UNKNOWN SOLDIER / FRANKLIN BATTLEFIELD / CIVIL WAR / 1864

· Also buried at Rest Haven are Theodrick "Tod" Carter, 20th Tennessee Infantry, mortally wounded at Franklin, and whose home, the Carter House, is on the battlefield; and George Cuppet, who superintended the burial of Confederate soldiers at McGavock Cemetery.

Rutherford County, Including Murfreesboro and Stones River National Battlefield

Murfreesboro

4.18.1 Subject: Courthouse Common Soldier Statue, Confederate
Location: County courthouse, 26 North Public Square, 37130   N 35 50 46 67 / W 86 23 29 76
Installed or dedicated: November 7, 1901
Medium: Bronze, granite, limestone, marble
Monument is a figure of a private soldier, Confederate, in bronze, surmounting a granite base.

Inscription

[Front]
IN COMMEMORATION OF THE VALOR OF / CONFEDERATE SOLDIERS / WHO FELL IN THE GREAT BATTLE OF MURFREESBORO, / DEC. 31, 1862, AND JANUARY 2, 1863, / AND IN MINOR ENGAGEMENTS IN THIS VICINITY, / THIS MONUMENT IS ERECTED.

Murfreesboro: Rutherford County Courthouse Common Soldier Statue, Confederate

Erected in 1859 from a design by architect James H. Yeaman, this is one of only six prewar courthouses still standing in Tennessee. It retains much of its wartime appearance and was the site of extensive activity during the war. The courthouse square was repeatedly occupied, seized, and reoccupied by both sides during the war. The courthouse itself served as a hospital and headquarters and was a battlefield site as well.

· The statue of the soldier—sculptor unknown—bears an aggressive stance: in midstride, heading north, bearing a musket. The figure stands approximately five by three by two feet on a base approximately twelve by five by five feet. Granite slabs at the base of the monument were placed by the Murfreesboro Camp, SCV No. 33, and are inscribed with rosters of units raised in Rutherford County.

· "Minor Engagements in the Area" includes Forrest's raid on the city on July 13, 1862, which is commemorated with a courthouse plaque (4.18.2). A second sortie, during Hood's Middle Tennessee Campaign, on December 4, 1864, was less successful and was stoutly resisted by troops commanded by Maj. Gen. Lovell H. Rousseau and Brig. Gen. Robert Milroy. The phrase "Honor Decks The Turf That Wraps Their Clay" is taken from George Gordon Byron's "Childe Harold's Pilgrimage," Canto One.

4.18.2 Subject: Courthouse Plaque to General Nathan B. Forrest
Location: On east side of the courthouse

Inscription

ERECTED TO THE MEMORY / OF / GEN. NATHAN BEDFORD FORREST / BY / THE
DAUGHTERS OF THE CONFEDERACY / FOR HEROIC SERVICES / RENDERED THE
CITIZENS / OF MURFREESBORO ON JULY 13, 1862
JULY 13, 1912

Arguably the most dramatic of Forrest's cavalry raids occurred here, on July
13, 1862, when troops under his command surprised a Federal garrison commanded by Brig. Gen. Thomas T. Crittenden, including elements of the 9th
Michigan VI who were stationed at this site and sustained heavy casualties.
It was to no avail: all Federal troops at Murfreesboro surrendered to Forrest
by late afternoon.

4.18.3 Subject: James Garfield, Tablet
Location: East Main Street Church of Christ   N 35 50 44 24 / W 86 23 20 98
Installed or dedicated: n.a.
Medium: Bronze
Monument is an inscribed tablet.

Inscription

JAMES GARFIELD / TWENTIETH PRESIDENT / OF THE UNITED STATES / AND A
MINISTER / IN THE CHURCH OF CHRIST / PREACHED HERE IN 1863
PLAQUE PLACED BY THIS CHURCH AND A.P.T.A.

The inscription on this tablet may seem inaccurate. Union Brig. Gen. James
Garfield attended services at East Main Street Church of Christ while he was
stationed here with the Army of the Cumberland in 1863. Garfield "preached"
in a broader sense of the word; he was an elder but was not ordained to the min-
istry. However, he is said to have offered homiletical remarks at communion
services. Secondly, he did not preach "here": he spoke at an earlier church edifice erected in 1859, not at the present edifice, erected in the twentieth century.

He was certainly present for services, however, and the tablet is not inaccurate. "We had an eyewitness," according to Rev. Dr. George W. Dehoff, minister
of East Main in the 1940s, who noted that Mrs. Ben Johnson related her memories of Garfield in 1945. "As a child," Dehoff remembered, "she was sitting on
the Lord's Day with other children in the pew behind that occupied by Gen.
Garfield. She reminisced that when he arose to preach or preside at the Lord's
Table, he would remove his saber and his side arms, leaving them in the pew."

Garfield's wartime effort to cross the lines of faith and worship with
his Southern counterparts despite the war is well noted here. His efforts

at conciliation continued after the war as well. After he became president, Garfield sent an embossed pewter communion set to the congregation: an eighteen-inch-high pewter wine container and two wine goblets. Some church members "objected to the 'Yankee Gift' however. It was given to a black congregation in the outskirts of Murfreesboro, who used it for several years. In the 1950's, it was acquired by A. N. Miller who subsequently gave it to the East Main Street Church of Christ."

- His religious convictions notwithstanding, Garfield's faith was shaken by the war. In a letter to William Dean Howells after the war, he wrote that at the sight of "dead men whom other men had killed, something went out of him, the habit of his lifetime, that never came back again: the sense of the sacredness of life and impossibility of destroying it."

Evergreen Cemetery, Confederate Circle

4.18.4 Subject: Unknown Confederate Dead, Shaft
Location: 519 Greenland Drive, 37130   N 35 51 04 75 / W 86 22 52 32
Installed or dedicated: May 12, 1915
Medium: Marble
Monument is a plinth, base, dado, and shaft surmounted by ball.

Inscription
[Unfurled battle flag]
OUR / UNKNOWN / DEAD / 1861–1865

ERECTED BY THE MURFREESBORO / CHAPTER UNITED DAUGHTERS OF / THE CONFEDERACY.

This site inters the remains of two thousand soldiers, including nonbattle casualties before the battle of Stones River, and those killed or mortally wounded during the battle. Many of these soldiers' remains were first buried on the battlefield, but the Ladies' Memorial Association of Murfreesboro arranged for them to be moved to a Confederate cemetery established two miles south of Murfreesboro in 1867. The site was neglected and subject to flooding by the Stones River. The present cemetery plot was granted to the Association Confederate Soldiers, Tennessee Division, Joseph Palmer Bivouac No. 10 in February 1890. The LMA arranged for the reinterment of the graves at this site in 1891. This marble shaft was unveiled during the UDC Tennessee Division Convention of May 1915.

4.18.5 Subject: Stele, Roster, Confederate
Monument is granite shaft surmounting base.

Inscription
[72 names]

Two granite stelae were placed here during a renovation by the SCV, Murfreesboro Camp No. 33, in November 1982. Renovations, including a flag pole and granite posts, were completed by the SCV Camp No. 33 in 2006, dedicated on the 144th anniversary of the battle of Murfreesboro. Granite posts, clockwise from the north are inscribed as follows: "Tennessee, CSA"; 'Texas, CSA"; "Virginia, CSA"; "Alabama, CSA"; "Arkansas, CSA"; "Florida, CSA"; "Georgia, CSA"; "Kentucky, CSA"; "Louisiana, CSA"; "Mississippi, CSA"; "Missouri, CSA"; "North Carolina, CSA"; "South Carolina, CSA."

Stones River National Cemetery
3501 Old Nashville Highway, 37129

This sixteen-acre site stands between the railroad and the Nashville Pike. Maj. Gen. George H. Thomas formally established this cemetery in 1864. Between 1865 and 1867, Chaplain William Earnshaw, the first superintendent, and the 111th USCT were charged with the task of locating and reburying Union soldiers from the battlefield and the surrounding area, including Franklin, Shelbyville, Tullahoma, and Cowan. Today more than 6,100 Union soldiers are buried here, of whom 2,562 are unknown. In addition, approximately 1,000 postwar veterans and some family members are also interred. The railroad site was chosen as a point of access during the reinterments, for visitors to the battlefield and as a legacy to remind train passengers as they passed by.

4.18.6 Subject: 43rd Wisconsin and 180th Ohio VI, Stele
Location: N 35 52 55 21 / W 86 25 55 26
Installed or dedicated: 1865
Medium: Limestone
Monument is a limestone stele.

Inscription
ERECTED BY THE / 43RD REG'T WIS. / VOL. INF. IN MEMORY / OF DECEASED SOLDIERS / IN THAT REG'T AND / OF THE 180TH, OHIO. / TENNESSEE / UNION SOLDIERS. / RAILROAD / EMPLOYEES, & C. / 1865.

These regiments were not present at the battle of Stones River, and this monument was not originally erected on this site. This limestone shaft stood at Dechard, Tennessee, until it was moved, along with the associated graves, to Stones River with the establishment of the national cemetery. These units were detailed to railroad guard duty in the area in 1863–64.

Stones River National Cemetery: Regular Army Brigade Shaft, with Surmounting Eagle

4.18.7 Subject: Regular Army Brigade, Shaft, Eagle
Location: N 35 52 53 19 / W 86 25 57 50
Installed or dedicated: 1882
Medium: Bronze, granite
Monument is a granite base surmounted by a cylinder and sculpted eagle.

Inscription

IN MEMORY / OF THE OFFICERS AND ENLISTED MEN OF THE / 15TH, 16TH, 18TH, & 19TH U.S. INFANTRY AND / BATTERY H, 5TH U.S. ARTILLERY, WHO / WERE KILLED OR DIED OF WOUNDS, / RECEIVED AT / THE BATTLE OF STONE RIVER, / TENNESSEE, / DECEMBER 31ST 1862 TO JANUARY 3RD 1863.

ERECTED / BY / THEIR COMRADES / OF THE / REGULAR BRIGADE / ARMY OF / THE CUMBERLAND.

This monument in Section C of the national cemetery displays an eagle, inscribed "Bronze Bros. Phila.," surmounting a granite cylinder that is "carved in the motion of taking flight." The location is significant as the Round Forest, also known as "Hell's Half-Acre."

- A fund-raising scandal led to prison time for embezzlement for Col. Oliver L. Shepherd, who commanded the US Regular Brigade at Stones River, but who, after the war, was tried, convicted, and served time for misuse of funds raised for this monument.

- Regular Army monuments at Civil War battlefields are uncommon. Shiloh has three, for example; Gettysburg has one, Chattanooga none.

Stones River National Battlefield: The Hazen Monument

Stones River National Battlefield

4.18.8 Subject: The Hazen Monument
Location: Off US 41, south of the National Cemetery   N 35 52 35 62 /
W 86 25 38 44
Erected: Spring 1863; completed: Fall 1863
Medium: Limestone
Monument is an inscribed shaft.

Inscription
[Front]
HAZEN'S BRIGADE, / TO / THE MEMORY OF ITS SOLDIERS / WHO FELL AT / STONE RIVER DEC. 31, 1862. / "THEIR FACES TOWARD HEAVEN, / THEIR FEET TO THE FOE."

THE BLOOD OF ONE THIRD OF ITS SOLDIERS TWICE SPILLED IN TENNESSEE CRIMSONS THE BATTLE FLAG OF THE BRIGADE AND INSPIRES TO GREATER DEEDS. KILLED AT STONES RIVER DEC. 31ST 1862 *[7 names]*

ERECTED IN 1863 UPON THE GROUND WHERE THEY FELL BY THEIR COMRADES FORTY FIRST INFANTRY OHIO VOLUNTEERS, LT. COL. A. WILEY / SIXTH INFANTRY KENTUCKY VOLUNTEERS, COL. W. E. WHITAKER / NINTH INFANTRY INDIANA VOLUNTEERS, COL. W. H. BLAKE / ONE HUNDRED AND TENTH INFANTRY ILLINOIS VOLUNTEERS, COL. T. S. CASEY / NINETEENTH BRIGADE BUELL'S ARMY OF THE OHIO. / COL. WILLIAM B. HAZEN 41ST INF'TRY O. VOLS. COMMANDING

THE VETERANS OF SHILOH / HAVE LEFT A DEATHLESS HERITAGE OF / FAME UPON THE FIELD OF / STONES RIVER
KILLED AT SHILOH APRIL 7TH 1862 *[6 names]*

This Egyptian-style "pyramidal shaft" is the oldest extant Civil War battlefield monument and one of the most prominent and well known. The Hazen Monument was erected using local limestone during the spring of 1864, at the time of the construction of Fortress Rosecrans. The Hazen Brigade Monument is located one-third of a mile south of the cemetery along Old Nashville Highway. The monument, erected in 1863, is thought to be one of the oldest existing Civil War memorials. The faces of the 10-foot cube, constructed of limestone blocks, carry inscriptions listing and honoring the men who fought under the command of Union Colonel W. B. Hazen. The Hazen Brigade is notable as being the only Union unit in the Battle of Stones River to hold its ground and not retreat. The graves of 55 members of the brigade surround the monument. Soldiers of the 9th Indiana VI built it; they also interred the graves of at least fifty-five soldiers of Hazen's Brigade within the limestone enclosure. Soldiers of the 115th Ohio VI carved the inscription, which includes a listing of the officers killed at the battle of Stones River.

Col. William B. Hazen's brigade (9th Indiana, 41st Ohio, 6th Kentucky, and 110th Illinois VI) held a position here, at the Round Forest, between the Nashville Pike—present-day Old Nashville Highway—and the wartime Nashville and Chattanooga Railroad. Union troops withstood four Confederate attacks in this area—"Hell's Half-Acre," it was called. Hazen and Col. Isaac C. B. Suman of the 9th Indiana conceived the idea of the monument while the army was stationed here in the aftermath of the battle. Hazen originally envisioned a bronze sculpture of a common soldier surmounting the shaft; this has not been fulfilled. As completed, it was described as a "quadrangular pyramidal shaft, 10 feet square at the base and 11 feet in height, surmounted by a neat coping."

- What may have been the war's first monument was erected by Confederate soldiers, to acting Brig. Gen. Francis Bartow, on September 4, 1861, on the First Manassas battlefield. That monument was vandalized by Union soldiers after the Confederates withdrew from the area in March 1862. The 32nd Indiana VI monument, erected in January 1862, after the battle of Rowlett's Station in Munfordville, Kentucky, is extant but no longer stands on the original site.

4.18.9 Subject: Obelisk, Union Artillery
Location: Off Van Cleave Lane and US 41 / 70   N 35 53 16 98 / W 86 25 33 34
Installed or dedicated: July 1906
Medium: Bronze, concrete
Monument is an obelisk with an inscribed bronze plaque.

Inscription

ON JANUARY 2ND, 1863, AT 3:00 P. M., / THERE WERE STATIONED ON THIS HILL / FIFTY-EIGHT CANNON, COMMANDING THE FIELD / ACROSS THE RIVER, AND AS THE CONFEDERATES / ADVANCED OVER THIS FIELD, THE SHOT AND SHELL / FROM THESE GUNS RESULTED IN A LOSS OF / EIGHTEEN-HUNDRED, KILLED AND WOUNDED, / IN LESS THAN AN HOUR.
SHOPS OF N.C. & STL. RY JULY 1906.

The Artillery Monument, Obelisk, Union Artillery

The "Artillery Monument" was erected within the sightline of the railroad to commemorate the closing action of the three-day battle of Stones River. Union infantry retreated across this field on January 2, 1863, pursued by Confederate troops under the command of Maj. Gen. John C. Breckinridge. The Southern advance across the West Fork Stones River by dint of McFadden's Ford was stopped—climactically—by a stout line of field artillery assembled and directed by Capt. John Mendenhall. More than eighteen hundred Southern casualties were sustained in the assault. Historian Kent Masterson Brown notes that in forty-two minutes of fighting, the Confederate Kentucky Brigade—the "Orphans"—lost 431 of the 1,197 men who took the field, over one-quarter of the command.

John W. Thomas, president of the Nashville, Chattanooga and St. Louis Railroad, a major and a former master of transportation for the Confederate Army of Tennessee, is credited with initiating the project for the monument. Park historians observe that Thomas may have intended to honor the Confederate soldiers who made the assault rather than the Union artillery, which stopped them.

The obelisk, designed by Hunter McDonald, of Portland cement concrete, stands thirty-four feet high on a square base thirteen by thirteen feet. It was erected at a cost of $859.

4.18.10 Subject: State of Michigan, Stele
Location: Park Road, near the Slaughter Pen   N 35 52 10 32 / W 86 25 55 52
Installed: July 1, 1966
Medium: Bronze
Monument is a bronze stele.

Inscription

THE / STATE OF MICHIGAN / HAS ERECTED / THIS MARKER / TO HER BRAVE AND / COURAGEOUS SONS / WHO FOUGHT AT / STONES RIVER TO / PRESERVE THE UNION ERECTED 1966 BY MICHIGAN CIVIL WAR CENTENNIAL OBSERVANCE COMMISSION. (MARKER NUMBER 279.)

THIS MARKER IS DEDICATED TO ALL THE MICHIGAN / SOLDIERS ENGAGED IN THIS GREAT BATTLE, TO THE / 71 MEN WHO LOST THEIR LIVES AND TO THE 6 REG- / IMENTS WHICH FOUGHT BRAVELY FOR THEIR COUNTRY:
/ 21ST MICHIGAN INFANTRY, COMMANDED BY / LT. COL. WILLIAM B. MCCREERY (FLINT), 18 KILLED, / 89 WOUNDED, 36 MISSING / 11TH MICHIGAN INFANTRY, COM- MANDED BY / COL. WILLIAM L. STOUGHTON (STURGIS), 30 KILLED, / 84 WOUND- ED, 25 MISSING / 13TH MICHIGAN INFANTRY, COMMANDED BY COL. / MICHAEL SHOEMAKER (JACKSON), 17 KILLED, / 72 WOUNDED / 4TH MICHIGAN CAVALRY, COMMANDED BY / COL. ROBERT H. G. MINTY (DETROIT), 1 KILLED, 7 WOUNDED, / 12 MISSING / 1ST MICHIGAN ENGINEERS AND MECHANICS, / COMMANDED BY COL. WILLIAM P. INNES (GRAND RAPIDS), / 2 KILLED, 9 WOUNDED, 5 MISSING / 1ST MICHIGAN ARTILLERY BATTERY, / COMPANY A, COMMANDED BY COL. CYRUS O. / LOOMIS (COLDWATER), 1 KILLED, 10 WOUNDED, 2 MISSING

MICHIGAN MEN FOUGHT AT STONES RIVER / FOR THE PRESERVATION AND PERPE- TUITY / OF THE UNION
[*Erected 1966 by Michigan Civil War Centennial Observance Commission. (Marker Number 279.)*]
MICHIGAN HISTORICAL REGISTERED MARKER NO. 279

This centennial tribute to Michigan soldiers is the only state monument on the Stones River battlefield. It stands near but is not on the present-day driving tour of the battlefield.

The initiative to erect this marker was undertaken in 1965. At the time that the monument was proposed, Stones River was said to be the "only major battlefield of the Civil War which lacks a Michigan Monument." The sum of $5,000 was allocated by the Michigan state legislature to redress that shortfall. After all, it was noted, "historic monuments are the grappling irons that bind one generation to another," according to Charles S. Marshall of the National Park Service, in remarks given at the dedication service.

Cited on the stele are Michigan units deemed to have played particular "active" or "dramatic" roles in the battle; these units also had the heaviest ca- sualties. Other units from Michigan on the field were the 5th and 6th Batteries, the 1st Engineers, and the 10th and 25th Infantries.

U.S. Army Assistant Quartermaster Captain John Means selected the site and designed the cemetery layout. The cemetery is roughly rectangular in shape, bordered on the east by the lines of the Nashville and Chattanooga Railroad (now CSX) and to the west by the Nashville Pike (now the Old Nashville Highway). A stone wall dating from the late 1860s lines the perimeter. Tree-lined paths radiate both diagonally and perpendicularly from the central flagpole; additional paths create sections of squares, rectangles, trapezoids, and triangles.

Two monuments stand in the cemetery. The U.S. Regulars Monument, erected in 1882, is a sandstone cylindrical shaft crowned with a bronze eagle. The monument honors the men of the Union's Western Regular Brigade killed during the Battle of Stones River. A second memorial is dedicated to the soldiers of the 43rd Wisconsin and the 108th Ohio who protected the Nashville and Chattanooga Railroad line during the Union occupation of Murfreesboro.

4.18.11 Subject: Sam Davis, Cemetery Obelisk
Location: Sam Davis Memorial Association, 1399 Sam Davis Road
N 35 59 25 16 / W 86 30 03 48
Installed or dedicated: 1896
Medium: Marble
Monument is an obelisk surmounting a base.

Inscription
IN / MEMORY OF / SAMUEL DAVIS
A MEMBER OF THE 1ST / TENN. REGT. OF VOLUNTEERS
BORN OCT. 6, 1842, / DIED NOV. 27, 1863, / AGED / 21 YRS, 1 MONTH & 21 DAYS
"HE LAID DOWN HIS LIFE / FOR HIS COUNTRY." / A TRUER SOLDIER, A PURER /
PATRIOT, A BRAVER MAN NEVER / LIVED, WHO SUFFERED DEATH / ON THE GIBBET
RATHER THAN / BETRAY HIS FRIENDS AND COUNTRY

After Sam Davis was hanged as a spy, his body was returned to Smyrna and interred here, in the family cemetery outside the 1810 neoclassical farmhouse where he was raised, one of Tennessee's most significant Confederate memorial properties. The obelisk was erected by Davis's father, Charles Davis. A memorial service was held in May 1896. The *Confederate Veteran* describes the proceedings as follows:

> The gathering of more than one thousand people at a country home on a quiet Sunday afternoon to do homage to the character of a plain young man, who was a private soldier in the Confederate army, nearly one-third of a century after his death, is an extraordinary event. The presence of Veteran associations and ministers eminent in various Christian churches gave it the dignity that was fitting the sacred occasion.

The address of Dr. Barbee on that day has been read in thousands of homes, and becomes the history of Samuel Davis, and of an important chapter in the history of the great war.

The names of Davis's mother, Jane Simmons Davis, grandmother, and his father, Charles Louis Davis, are also inscribed on the stone. The grounds were purchased by the State of Tennessee in 1927 and opened for tours as a state museum in 1930.

Wilson County

Lebanon

4.19.1 Subject: Lebanon Courthouse Statue, Robert H. Hatton, Confederate
Location: US 70A and US 231   N 36 12 28 81 / W 86 17 28 18
Dedicated: May 20, 1912
Medium: Limestone
Monument is a figure of Robert Hatton surmounting a shaft and base.

Inscription

[Front]
GEN'L HATTON
ERECTED IN HONOR OF THE / CONFEDERATE VETERANS / OF / WILSON COUNTY / AND ALL OTHER / TRUE SOUTHERN SOLDIERS / 1861–1865

AS LONG AS HONOR OR COURAGE IS CHERISHED / THE DEEDS OF THESE HEROES WILL LIVE / "WHETHER ON THE SCAFFOLD HIGH / OR IN THE BATTLES VAN / THE FITTEST PLACE FOR MAN TO DIE / IS WHERE HE DIES FOR MAN"

TO OUR / MOTHERS AND DAUGHTERS / OF THE CONFEDERACY FROM / 1861 TO THE PRESENT

ERECTED BY THE / S. G. SHEPARD CAMP / NO. 941. UCV / WITH CONTRIBUTIONS FROM TRUE FRIENDS / OF THE SOUTHERN SOLDIER COMMITTEE [4 names]

This UCV Confederate Monument stands in the city square of Lebanon. The surmounting figure is of Robert Hatton, who was born in Ohio but raised in Tennessee and was a graduate of Cumberland University. A lawyer and member of Congress, he opposed secession but sided with secessionism when Lincoln was elected president and called for volunteers to form an army. Hatton formed the Lebanon Blues, which became a part of the 7th Tennessee.

He was promoted to brigadier general in the Army of Northern Virginia, but the appointment was not confirmed by the Confederate Congress before he was killed in action.

· The figure of Hatton faces west, leaning back, not quite standing straight. The sculpture stands approximately six feet; the base is approximately six feet by eight feet, five inches by eight feet, five inches. The sculptor is unknown.

Lebanon: Wilson County Courthouse Statue, Robert H. Hatton, Confederate

- The inscription beginning "Whether On The Scaffold High" is taken from "God Save Ireland," an Irish rebel song written by T. D. Sullivan, published in 1867, and an unofficial Irish national anthem popular in the late nineteenth and early twentieth century.

- A bronze plaque set on a granite base reads as follows:

THE 20TH OF MAY 2012 BEING 100 YEARS FROM ITS / UNVEILING, DEDICATION
AND CONVEYANCE TO / THE UNITED DAUGHTERS OF THE CONFEDERACY, / THIS
MONUMENT AND PARK IS REDEDICATED BY / THE UNITED DAUGHTERS OF THE
CONFEDERACY / AND THE SONS OF CONFEDERATE VETERANS IN / MEMORY OF
CONFEDERATE VETERANS OF / WILSON COUNTY AND ALL OTHER TRUE / SOUTHERN
SOLDIERS OF 1861–1865.
GENERAL ROBERT H. HATTON SCV CAMP 723 / GENERAL ROBERT H. HATTON UDC
CHAPTER 329 / MAY 12, 2012

4.19.2 Subject: Cedar Grove Cemetery, Common Soldier Statue, Confederate
Location: South Maple west of South Cumberland Street (US 231 / TN 10)
N 36 11 36 35 / W 86 17 52 54
Installed or dedicated: July 27, 1899
Medium: Limestone, marble base
Monument is a figure of a private soldier surmounting a shaft and base.

Inscription

SACRED / TO MEMORY OF / CONFEDERATE SOLDIERS / WHO SLEEP IN THIS /
CEMETERY / AND, TO THEIR / SURVIVING COMRADES / WHO SHALL REST HERE.
/ IMMORTAL HEROES! / YOUR UNPARALLELED / COURAGE, YOUR BLOOD, /
YOUR PATRIOTISM, / HAVE BEQUEATHED TO ALL / GENERATIONS AN EXAMPLE
/ OF SUBLIME HEROISM AND / TO YOUR COUNTRY AN / ETERNITY OF FAME. /
CONFEDERATE DEAD / THE CONFEDERACY / WITHOUT AN ARMY, NAVY, / OR
GOVERNMENT 600,000 VOLUNTEERS / SUSTAINED THE ASSAULT / OF 2,778,304 MEN,
/ SUPPORTED BY THE / STRONGEST GOVERNMENT IN / THE WORLD FOR FOUR YEARS.
/ ITS DESTRUCTION RENDERED / NECESSARY A PUBLIC DEBT / OF $2,708,393,885.00,
/ THE SACRIFICE OF 349,944 / LIVES AND 1,366,443 / PENSIONERS.
[2 names]

[26 names]

[51 names]

[55 names]

The graves of more than one hundred fifty Confederate soldiers are said to be located here; one hundred thirty names are inscribed on the monument. There are no separate grounds for Confederate soldiers, and recent civilian interments have occurred close by the monument, so it is evident that the monument commemorates burials throughout the cemetery, including the graves of nine men of the 2nd Kentucky Cavalry (CS) killed during the battle of Lebanon, May 5, 1862.

The defiance is evident. The inscription takes the form of a direct address, followed by a declaration. Praise for the Confederate soldier is contrasted with the great profligacy of blood and money expended by the Federal government—which goes unnamed—in prosecuting the war against the South.

The names on the shaft are those of soldiers whose remains are buried in the cemetery. Blank spaces on the south and west sides were left for those buried after the monument was emplaced, but they remain uninscribed. The presiding sculpture of a common soldier stands approximately six feet by two feet by two feet; the base of the monument is approximately twenty by five by five feet. The sculptor is unknown. The pedestal is twelve feet high.

· Also here is the grave of Brig. Gen. Robert Hatton (N 36 11 38 91 / W 86 17 58 80). A plaque adjacent to his tombstone reads as follows:

ERECTED BY / SURVIVORS OF 7TH TENN REG.
IN YOUTH HE EMBRACED CHRISTIANITY AS / THE TRUE SCIENCE OF MANHOOD

Trousdale County

Hartsville

4.20.1 Subject: Courthouse Shaft, Confederate
Location: 240 Broadway, Hartsville, 37074   N 36 23 26 29 / W 86 09 59 36
Installed or dedicated: 1930
Medium: Bronze, granite
Monument is an inscribed obelisk.

Inscription

[Front]
THE BATTLE OF HARTSVILLE
HERE DEC. 7TH 1862 / 1500 CONFEDERATES UNDER / GEN. JOHN H. MORGAN /
SWIMMING THE ICY CUMBERLAND / SURPRISED AND CAPTURED / A LARGE FEDERAL
GARRISON / MAJ. JOHN D. ALLEN CHAPTER U.D.C. / MARKS THE SPOT / TO HONOR
THE HEROIC VICTORY / 1861–1865

1846–1848 / 1898–1899

1812 / 1775–1783

1917–1918

Erected by the County Court of Trousdale County in 1930, this monument
commemorates the battle of Hartsville, a Confederate victory fought in the
early days of the Stones River Campaign. Other wars are not named but are
commemorated by dint of inscribed dates.

In this vicinity, about thirteen hundred Union soldiers of the 39th Brigade
of the XIV Corps (106th Ohio, 108th Ohio, 104th Illinois infantry, and 2nd
Indiana Cavalry) guarded the Cumberland River crossing at Hartsville in
December 1862. Under cover of darkness, two cavalry brigades, mainly
Kentuckians, under the command of Brig. Gen. John H. Morgan crossed the
river on the morning of December 7, 1862, and took the Federals by surprise.
Fighting commenced at 6:45 AM and continued until about 8:30 AM, when the
outnumbered Confederates had surrounded the Federals and compelled their
surrender. Estimated casualties: 2,004 total (Union 855, including prisoners,
nearly the whole of the Federal force, including the commander, Col. Absalom
B. Moore; Confederates 149, including 30 names inscribed on the cemetery
monument south of the town).

- The battlefield retains much of its integrity and can be toured. The
  action at Hartsville was a prelude to cavalry raids commanded by Brig.
  Gen. Nathan B. Forrest in West Tennessee, December 1862–January
  1863, and Brig. Gen. John H. Morgan into Kentucky, December 1862–
  January 1863.

4.20.2 Subject: Battlefield Cemetery Stele
Location: Hartsville Cemetery, off TN 141, south of Hartsville
N 36 33 57 96 / W 86 09 55 96
Installed or dedicated: December 7, 1997
Medium: Granite
Monument is a triptych.

Inscription
[Crossed CS national and battle flags]
BATTLE OF HARTSVILLE / DECEMBER 7, 1862, / THE BOLDEST AND MOST
SUCCESSFULLY EXECUTED / CAVALRY RAIDS OF THE WAR BETWEEN THE STATES. /
WE SALUTE THE / CONFEDERATE VETERANS / WITH AFFECTION, REVERENCE, AND /
UNDYING DEVOTION TO THE / CAUSE FOR WHICH THEY STOOD
DEDICATED / DECEMBER 7, 1997 / BATTLE OF HARTSVILLE PRESERVATION
COMMITTEE / AND / SONS OF CONFEDERATE VETERANS
[Extended narrative of the battle]
IN MEMORY OF THOSE WHO FELL IN THE BATTLE OF HARTSVILLE
[Roster of casualties]

THE BURIAL PLACE IS SACRED GROUND, AND THE MEMORY / OF THEIR GENEROUS
AND CHIVALROUS SPIRITS IS ON / PERPETUAL RECORD IN THE HEARTS OF OUR
PEOPLE / NEAR OUR QUIET VILLAGE AND CLOSE TO THE HOMES OF / THOSE WHO
LOVED THEM, THEY SLEEP WELL, AND TENNESSEANS DO REVERENCE TO THE
LOWLY GRAVES / OF KENTUCY'S [*SIC*] SONS. / "THE NEIGHING STEED, THE FLASHING
BLADE, / THE TRUMPET'S STIRRING BLAST, / THE CHARGE, THE DREADFUL
CANNONADE, / THE DIN AND SHOUT ARE PAST; / NO WAR'S WILD NOTE, NOR
GLORY'S PEAL, / SHALL THRILL WITH FIERCE DELIGHT / THOSE BREAST [*SIC*] THAT
NEVER MORE SHALL FEEL / THE RAPTURE OF THE FIGHT. / REST ON, EMBALMED
AND SAINTED DEAD! / DEAR AS THE BLOOD YOU GAVE, / NO IMPIOUS FOOTSTEPS
HERE SHALL TREAD / THE HERBAGE OF YOUR GRAVE; / NOR SHALL YOUR GLORY
BE FORGOT / WHILE FAME HER RECORD KEEPS. [*SIC*] / OR HONOR POINTS THE
HALLOWED SPOT / WHERE VALOR PROUDLY SLEEPS."

This monument standing at the east end of this local cemetery commemorates
casualties taken in the battle of Hartsville, justly praising the initiative and
effectiveness of their action taken against Union forces and taking particular
note of the otherwise unmarked "lowly graves" of Kentucky soldiers. An estimated fifty Confederate veterans are also interred here.

· The excerpt beginning "The Neighing Steed, The Flashing Blade" is
  taken from Theodore O'Hara's "The Bivouac of the Dead" (1847).

4.21.1 Subject: Lafayette, Courthouse Stele, Podium, Confederate
Location: 104 County Courthouse, 37083   N 36 31 14 40 / W 86 01 33 94
Installed or dedicated: 2001
Medium: Granite
Monument is a podium.

Inscription
THIS MONUMENT DEDICATED IN MEMORY OF THE MEN WHO SERVED / IN THE CONFEDERATE STATES ARMY FROM MACON COUNTY TENNESSEE / DURING THE WAR BETWEEN THE STATES 1861–1865 / THESE UNITS WERE COMPRISED OF LOCAL MEN SERVING IN / THE ARMY OF TENNESSEE
[Roster of casualties]
YOU WILL NOT BRAND THEM TRAITORS, / YOU WHO BATTLED SIDE BY SIDE. / FOR TENNESSEE YOU FOUGHT AND LIVED, / FOR TENNESSEE THEY DIED.
MAJOR GENERAL BENJAMIN FRANKLIN CHEATHAM / CORP. [SIC] / COMMANDER, ARMY OF TENNESSEE
[SCV seal]
ERECTED BY / CAMP JIM DAVIS 1425 / IN THE YEAR OF OUR LORD / 2001
[Inscribed cross]

Macon County loyalties were divided during the war: about five hundred men served on the opposing sides in the conflict. The Highland Rim Ridge as well as family loyalties generally served as the lines of division. This SCV Camp monument in the form of a podium is, however, absolute in its claim that the cause of the Confederacy was just, citing Maj. Gen. Benjamin F. Cheatham in declaring that "You Will Not Brand Them Traitors."

· The inscribed cross is—perhaps surprisingly—an unusual feature of Civil War monumentation, notwithstanding its place on the Confederate battle flag.

Davidson County

Nashville

STATE CAPITOL

4.22.1 Subject: Sam Davis Statue, Confederate
Location: State capitol grounds   N 36 09 54 39 / W 86 47 03 40
Unveiled: April 30, 1909
Media: Bronze, granite
Monument is a statue of Davis surmounting a base.

Inscription
[Front]
SAM DAVIS
SAM DAVIS OF TENNESSEE / BORN OCTOBER 6, 1842, NEAR MURFREESBORO, TENN. / EDUCATED AT THE WESTERN MILITARY INSTITUTE AT NASHVILLE. / EARLY IN THE

CIVIL WAR HE JOINED THE CONFEDERATE ARMY / COMPANY I, FIRST TENNESSEE REGIMENT. / IN 1863 HE WAS ASSIGNED TO SHAW'S SCOUTS, CHEATHAM'S DIVISION. / IN NOVEMBER 1863, WHEN ON DUTY / UNIFORMED IN CONFEDERATE BUTTERNUT AND GRAY, / DAVIS WAS CAPTURED IN HIS NATIVE STATE, THEN WITHIN FEDERAL LINES. / IMPORTANT PAPERS, DESCRIPTIVE OF THE FEDERAL FORTIFICATIONS AND FORCES, / WERE FOUND UPON HIS PERSON. / THESE PAPERS HAD BEEN GIVEN DAVIS BY CAPTAIN SHAW / WHO HAD ALSO BEEN CAPTURED AND WAS CONFINED IN THE SAME PRISON.

DAVIS WAS TRIED BY COURT MARTIAL, / COMDEMNED TO DEATH AND EXECUTED AT PULASKI, NOVEMBER 27. / THE FEDERAL COMMANDER OFFERED DAVIS HIS LIFE, IF HE WOULD TELL / WHO GAVE HIM THE PAPERS. TO THIS OFFER, UNDER THE VERY SHADOW OF / THE GALLOWS, DAVIS MADE HIS IMMORTAL REPLY: / "I WOULD DIE A THOUSAND DEATHS / BEFORE I WOULD BETRAY A FRIEND." / "GREATER LOVE HATH NO MAN THAN THIS— / THAT A MAN LAY DOWN HIS LIFE FOR HIS FRIENDS."

1842 SAM DAVIS 1863
"THE BOYS WILL HAVE TO FIGHT / THE BATTLES WITHOUT ME."
HE GAVE ALL HE HAD— / LIFE; / HE GAINED ALL HE LACKED— / IMMORTALITY.
THIS MONUMENT IS ERECTED / BY CONTRIBUTIONS FROM CITIZENS / OF EVERY STATE IN THE AMERICAN UNION, / ON THE SITE AUTHORIZED / BY THE 51ST GENERAL ASSEMBLY / OF THE STATE OF TENNESSEE. / 1909

SAM DAVIS.
WHEN THE LORD CALLS UP EARTH'S HEROES / TO STAND BEFORE HIS FACE, / O, MANY A NAME, UNKNOWN TO FAME / SHALL RING FROM THAT HIGH PLACE; / THEN OUT OF A GRAVE IN THE SOUTHLAND / AT THE JUST GOD'S CALL AND BECK, / SHALL ONE MAN RISE WITH FEARLESS EYES / WITH A ROPE ABOUT HIS NECK; / O SOUTHLAND! BRING YOUR LAURELS, / AND ADD YOUR WREATH, O NORTH! / LET GLORY CLAIM THE HERO'S NAME / AND TELL THE WORLD HIS WORTH
G. J. ZOLNAY SCULPTOR. 1908
ROMAN BRONZE WORKS N—Y—/ ELLA WHEELER WILCOX.

This may be the most prominent Confederate monument in Tennessee. It stands on the south side of the capitol, facing southwest. References to Davis's Tennessee background are many; that he was "Captured in his Native State" by Federal forces and unjustly executed is clear. He is more than a symbol of injustice, however. Something of the time and perspective on Davis can be found in the entry on Sam Davis in the 1911 book *Historic Southern Monuments*, in which the UDC author concludes that the "martyrdom of Sam Davis is not equaled in the annals of war." Extracts from the address of Governor Patterson at the unveiling of the monument further this theme:

> [Davis] seemed to have filled every conception of the flower and chivalry of young manhood, and his very presence was suggestive of romance and valorous deeds. His habits were pure, his affections strong, his disposition singularly quiet and reticent. . . . On Calvary the Son of God died with cruel nails driven through his quivering flesh, the crown of thorns pressing down upon his agonized brow, and since then the cross has been the

Statue of Sam Davis, State Capitol

Christian's sign in every land; [If Jesus taught] men how to live could [God] not also give this son of Tennessee to teach men how to die?

The statement "Greater Love" is taken from the New Testament book of John 15:13. "He Gave All He Had" is an apparent paraphrase of Matthew 16:26.

4.22.2 Subject: Andrew Johnson, Statue
Location: State capitol facing south   N 36 09 56 26 / W 86 47 59 86
Installed or dedicated: 1995
Medium: Bronze, granite
Monument is a statue surmounting a base.

Inscription

ANDREW JOHNSON / 1808–1875 / 17TH PRESIDENT / OF THE / UNITED STATES OF
AMERICA / 1865–1869 / STATE CAPITOL

Andrew Johnson is commemorated as the 17th president of the United States
on the monument sculpted by artist Jim Gray and dedicated in 1995. There is,
however, no mention of Johnson's service in Nashville as wartime governor of
Tennessee. When the city fell under Union occupation in 1862, Johnson was
appointed military governor and used the heavily fortified capitol building—
Fort Andrew Johnson—as the seat of government.

4.22.3 Subject: "Tribute to the Women of Tennessee," Two Females,
Common Soldier, Statues
Location: Vietnam Veterans Memorial Park, Seventh Ave and Union
N 36 09 49 32 / W 86 47 00 74
Dedicated: October 10, 1926
Medium: Bronze, copper, granite
Monument is three seated figures surmounting a base.

Inscription

ERECTED BY THE STATE OF TENNESSEE / TO COMMEMORATE THE HEROIC
DEVOTION AND / SELF-SACRIFICE OF THE WOMEN OF TENNESSEE / DURING THE
WAR BETWEEN THE STATES
DEDICATED OCTOBER 10, 1926 / BELLE KINNEY, SCULPTOR / THIS PLAQUE PLACED
BY THE TENNESSEE HISTORICAL COMMISSION

Belle Kinney is the sculptor of this work, titled "Tribute to the Women of
Tennessee during the War Between the States." The sculpture is bronze, painted copper over patina; the base is granite. It stands adjacent to the military
branch of the Tennessee State Museum.

Smithsonian records note that the monument is approximately eight by
seven by six feet and is set on a base that is approximately eleven by seven by
six feet. Three seated figures are depicted. On the right a male figure, a soldier, leans back, apparently seriously wounded. The male figure is attired in
unidentifiable, nonpartisan garb. The man grasps a partially rolled up flag that
is unidentifiable as a Union or Confederate banner. In the center is a presiding
female figure wearing classical drapery and a laurel wreath on her head. She

"Tribute to the Women of Tennessee" Statues

Centennial Park, Sam Davis, Common Soldier

holds a wreath over the head of the other female figure. The woman on the left holds a palm branch over the soldier.

- Also on the capitol grounds is a UDC plaque erected in 1969 commemorating the 75th anniversary of the founding of the UDC in Nashville. Tennessee-born Belle Kinney Scholz (1890–1959) is also sculptor of the Lt. Gen. Alexander P. Stewart sculpture in Chattanooga (2.1.1).

4.22.4 Subject: Centennial Park, Common Soldier Statue, Sam Davis, Confederate
Location: Centennial Park, West End and 25th Avenue North, 37201
N 36 08 52 29 / W 86 48 45 46
Dedicated: June 19, 1909
Medium: Bronze, granite, limestone
Monument is a common soldier surmounting a base.

Inscription

TO THE HEROISM / OF THE / PRIVATE CONFEDERATE SOLDIER

ERECTED / BY / FRANK CHEATHAM BIVOUAC NUMBER 1 / ASSOCIATION OF CONFEDERATE SOLDIERS / CAMP NUMBER 35 / UNITED CONFEDERATE VETERANS, / NASHVILLE, TENNESSEE
[541 names in 8 columns]

DUTY DONE HONOR WON / 1861–1865 / FAITHFUL TO THE END

When it was dedicated, this monument to the Frank Cheatham Bivouac No. 1 of the Tennessee Confederate soldiers, and Camp No. 35, UCV, was called the "private soldiers' monument." Today it stands near a full-scale replica of the Parthenon, erected in 1897, on the occasion of the Tennessee Centennial Exposition.

The tablet displays the names of 540 officers and men, all members of the two organizations; of that number, 328 were still living at the time of the dedication. It is the largest roster of veterans in Tennessee. A summary statement of their deeds faces south: "Duty Done Honor Won."

The monument is surmounted by a seated portrait of Sam Davis, also facing south, wearing a military uniform and holding the barrel of a rifle in his right hand.

- The ceremony was said to be brief. Rev. R. Lin Cave, chaplain general of the United Confederate Veterans, gave the invocation, and Judge S. F. Wilson, of the Tennessee Court of Appeals, was the orator. Maj. B. M. Hord, chairman of the committee, was master of ceremonies.
- The monument was commissioned June 19, 1903, but was not dedicated until 1909. Fundraising was prolonged, uneven, and incomplete until

the UDC took a leadership role and completed the task. George Julian Zolnay served as sculptor. The Foster & Herbert Cut Stone Company served as contractor. The monument's sculpture stands approximately six feet; the base is approximately eight feet by six feet by eight feet inches.

4.22.5 Subject: The Hermitage, Confederate Cemetery, Stele
Location: 4580 Rachel's Lane, off Lebanon Pike, 37076
Dedicated: June 3, 1941
Medium: Granite
Monument is a granite boulder surmounting a three-tiered granite base.

Inscription

THIS CRUDE, UNHEWN PIECE OF EVERLASTING GRANITE IS HERE TO MARK THE RESTING PLACE OF THE MANLY MEN. MEN LIKE IT, FIRM, SOLID, TRUE MEN WHO, IN SUPPORT / OF PRINCIPLE, UNCOMPLAININGLY ENDURED HUNGER; / COLD AND PRIVATION WHICH HISTORY CANNOT RECORD. / THE STURDY MEN GROUPED ABOUT THIS RUGGED STONE DIED IN / THE TENNESSEE HOME FOR CONFEDERATE SOLDIERS. / THIS STONE WILL STAND THE TEST OF TIME / THE SOULS OF THE TRIED MEN GROUPED AROUND IT WILL ENDURE THROUGHOUT ETERNITY.

The Confederate Soldiers' Home and Cemetery opened in 1892 and closed in 1933. The Frank Cheatham Bivouac of the Association of Confederate Soldiers proposed the project to the Tennessee General Assembly to establish this home in January 1889. It was approved. Funding came from the state, several Confederate veterans organizations, and the United Daughters of the Confederacy.

The cemetery, adjacent to the Hermitage Presbyterian Church, contains the remains of deceased veterans. The monument was dedicated June 3, 1941, Jefferson Davis's birthday, to commemorate the site of the graves of the 487 veterans—"Firm, Solid, True Men"—who spent their last days at the home.

· A granite stele surmounting a base reads as follows:

"MAY THESE / SOLDIERS / BURIED HERE / NEVER BE FORGOTTEN / FOR THEIR SACRIFICES MADE." / IN COMMEMORATION OF THE / 100TH ANNIVERSARY / HONORING OUR VALIANT / CONFEDERATE ANCESTORS / DEDICATED / JUNE 3, 2011 COL. RANDALL MCGAVOCK #1713. SCV CAPT. JOHN / S. DONELSON #2608 UDC TRAVELLER'S RIDER #963

4.22.6 Subject: "The Peace Monument": Battlefield Tribute, Bipartisan, Statue
Location: Granny White Pike and Battlefield Drive   N 36 06 51 53 / W 86 47 33 50
Installed: 1926–1927; dedicated and unveiled: November 11, 1927

"The Peace Monument": Battlefield Tribute, Bipartisan, Statue

Media: Bronze, granite, marble

Monument is sculptures of two horses, a youth, and presiding angel surmounting an obelisk, the whole surmounting a base.

Inscription

[Front]

UNITY / BATTLE / OF / NASHVILLE / 1864

"OH, VALOROUS GRAY, IN THE GRAVE OF YOUR FATE, / OH, GLORIOUS BLUE, IN THE LONG DEAD YEARS, / YOU WERE SOWN IN SORROW AND HARROWED IN HATE, / BUT YOUR HARVEST TODAY IS A NATION'S TEARS, / FOR THE MESSAGE YOU LEFT

THROUGH THE LAND HAS SPED, / FROM THE LIPS OF GOD TO THE HEART OF MAN: / LET THE PAST BE PAST, LET THE DEAD BE DEAD—/ NOW AND FOREVER, AMERICAN!"

ERECTED A.D. 1926 / BY / THE LADIES BATTLEFIELD MEMORIAL ASSOCIATION / AIDED BY CONTRIBUTIONS FROM PATRIOTIC CITIZENS / THE STATE OF TENNESSEE / AND / THE COUNTY OF DAVIDSON

THE SPIRIT OF YOUTH HOLDS IN CHECK THE CONTENDING / FORCES THAT STRUGGLED HERE IN THE FIERCE BATTLE OF / NASHVILLE, DECEMBER 16TH, 1864, SEALING FOREVER THE / BONDS OF UNION BY THE BLOOD OF OUR HEROIC DEAD OF THE / WORLD WAR 1917–1918.

A MONUMENT LIKE THIS, STANDING ON SUCH MEMORIES, / HAVING NO REFERENCE TO UTILITIES BECOMES A SENTIMENT, / A POET, A PROPHET, AN ORATOR TO EVERY PASSERBY.

The Peace Monument is the most prominent of the relatively few commemorations of the engagement fought on December 15–16, 1864. With a design by sculptor Giuseppe Moretti, it is unusual for its abstract, modernist style. A square marble base is emplaced at the foot of a granite obelisk surmounted by an "Angel of Peace" in white Georgia granite. Surmounting the marble base is a bronze sculpture of a nude male youth holding the reins of two rearing horses. The horses are said to represent the North and the South, and the youth represents unity and holds them in them together.

The monument is also a tribute to Americans who fought in World War I. The inscription is unique in its bipartisan claims, that is, that the battle "Seal[ed] Forever the Bonds of Union by the Blood of Our Heroic Dead of the World War 1917–1918."

The project was sponsored by the Ladies Battlefield Association under the supervision of Mrs. James E. Caldwell, who purchased the original grounds for the site after the war.

The youth and horses are bronze, the base is marble, the obelisk is granite. The sculpture of the youth and horses is approximately fourteen by seven by five feet. The base is approximately ten by fifteen by thirteen feet; the obelisk stands approximately forty feet high. There is something messianic about Moretti's "spirit of youth": the pose, the lack of weaponry, the presumed innocence of the figure, and the fact that Moretti also sculpted the *Head of Christ* in 1907.

- This unusual monument has had an eventful history. A tornado brought down the structure in 1974. Highway construction in the 1980s isolated the site from public access. However, the monument was restored and moved to its present location in 1998–1999. A forty-foot granite obelisk replaced the original thirty-foot obelisk of Carrara marble, and a new "Angel of Peace" was carved in white Georgia granite by Nashville sculptor Coley Coleman. The monument was rededicated June 26, 1999.

· The excerpt beginning "Oh, Valorous Gray" is taken from the poem "Reunited," by John Trotwood Moore. It was first read at a monument dedication to Forrest's artillery on the Chickamauga battlefield in 1898. The excerpt beginning "A Monument Like This" is attributed to Ralph Waldo Emerson.

4.22.8 Subject: Battle of Nashville, Line of Redoubts, Stele
Location: Calvary United Methodist Church, Hillsboro Pike and Graybar Lane
N 36 06 40 56 / W 86 48 41 18
Installed: 1940
Medium: Sandstone
Monument is an inscribed stele.

Inscription

[UDC seal]

BATTLE OF NASHVILLE / ON HILLS S.W. AND N.E. OF HERE STOOD THE REDOUBTS /
OF THE LINE OF GEN. JOHN B. HOOD, DEC. 15, 1864
ERECTED BY GEN. WM. B. BATE CHAP. U.D.C. / 1940

Gen. John B. Hood led Confederate soldiers of the Army of Tennessee north from the Franklin battlefield to this line of hills south of Nashville in December 1864. Near here a series of redoubts was erected by Confederate troops in anticipation of attacks by Union forces defending Nashville. Maj. Gen. George H. Thomas's Army of the Cumberland obliged. This stone marks the site where troops commanded by Maj. Gen. Edward C. Walthall (Walthall's Division) stood behind the stonewall on December 15, illustrated above, during the battle, facing east, parallel to the Hillsborough Pike. A valiant defense could not prevent Union forces from driving them from this position.

Battle of Nashville, Line of Redoubts

4.22.9 Subject: Mt. Olivet Cemetery, Common Soldier Statue, Confederate
Location: 1011 Lebanon Road, 37210   N 36 08 54 65 / W 86 44 04 82
Dedicated: May 16, 1889; unveiled: May 16, 1892
Medium: Granite, marble
Monument is a Confederate soldier, facing north, surmounting a shaft and base.

Inscription
[Front]
CSA
THIS SHAFT HONORS THE VALOR, DEVOTION, AND SACRIFICE UNTO DEATH / OF CONFEDERATE SOLDIERS OF TENNESSEE. / THE WINDS OF HEAVEN KISSING ITS SIDES, HYMN AN EVERLASTING REQUIEM / IN MEMORY OF THE UNRETURNING BRAVE. / CONFEDERATE MEMORIAL

CSA
ERECTED, THROUGH THE EFFORTS OF WOMEN OF THE STATE, / IN ADMIRATION OF THE CHIVALRY OF MEN / WHO FOUGHT IN DEFENSE OF HOME AND FIRESIDE, / AND IN THEIR FALL / SEALED A TITLE TO UNFADING AFFECTION.

CSA
IN THE MAGNANIMOUS JUDGEMENT OF MANKIND, / WHO GIVES UP LIFE UNDER A SENSE OF DUTY / TO A PUBLIC CAUSE DEEMED JUST, / IS A HERO.

CSA
THE MUSTER-ROLL OF OUR DAUNTLESS DEAD IS LOST, / AND THEIR DUST DISPERSED ON MANY FIELDS. / THIS COLUMN SENTINELS EACH SOLDIER GRAVE / AS A SHRINE.

Mt. Olivet Cemetery, Common Soldier Statue, Confederate

"Erected through efforts of the women of the south," this circular burial ground at the highest point in Mt. Olivet Cemetery was a project of the Ladies' Memorial Society of Nashville, who purchased the site in 1869. Confederate Circle was eventually laid out with thirteen rows of graves encircling a central square. The first six rows inter soldiers from outside Tennessee; the seventh row contains the graves of the unknown; the remaining rows contain the graves of Tennessee Confederate soldiers.

The presiding forty-five-foot high monument, a marble statue surmounting a Barre granite shaft and base, was dedicated on May 16, 1889. An estimated ten thousand people attended the ceremonies, including Confederate Col. John Overton and Brig. Gen. William H. Jackson.

- Fifteen hundred Confederate veterans are buried here, including seven Confederate generals: Maj. Gen. William B. Bate; Brig. Gen. William N. R. Beall; Maj. Gen. Benjamin F. Cheatham; Brig. Gen. William H. Jackson; Brig. Gen. George E. Maney; Brig. Gen. James E. Rains; Brig. Gen. Thomas B. Smith. Other Nashville Confederates such as Colonels Adolphus Heiman and Randall McGavock are interred nearby.

- Carlo Nicoli served as the statue's carver. The monument stands approximately nine feet; the base is approximately thirty-six by sixteen by sixteen feet. A Confederate battle flag with a broken shaft is carved in relief around the shaft.

- Some of the dead from the battle of Nashville are interred in Old City Cemetery. Also interred there are Brig. Gen. Samuel R. Anderson; Lt. Gen. Richard S. Ewell; Maj. Gen. Bushrod R. Johnson; and Brig. Gen. Felix K. Zollicoffer.

4.22.10 Subject: Fort Negley Stele
Location: 1100 Fort Negley Boulevard, 37203   N 36 08 36 59 / W 86 46 31 08
Installed or dedicated: 1936
Medium: Limestone
Monument is a stele.

Inscription

FORT NEGLEY
BUILT / BY FEDERAL FORCES / 1862
RESTORED BY W. P. A. / 1936

Nashville was abandoned by Confederate authorities and was surrendered to Union troops on February 25, 1862. Some twenty miles of trenches or breastworks were erected to defend it. The centerpiece of the defenses was here, behind this modest stone: Fort Negley was constructed between August and

Fort Negley, Stele

December 1862 on a site formerly known as St. Cloud Hill, a recreation area before the war.

The fort covers some four acres, is six hundred feet long and three hundred feet wide, and is the largest inland stone fort in the Americas. Construction involved Union troops and some twenty-seven hundred conscript laborers. Most of the latter were contrabands (former slaves) and free blacks. It served as a fort and military base until September 1867. The site was allowed to deteriorate until the City of Nashville purchased the grounds in 1928. The Works Progress Administration restored it during the 1930s, and a fieldstone gate and this stele were erected at that time. The site was not maintained, and it was allowed to decay again, but was restored in the 1990s. Today it is landscaped and interpreted and stands near the confluence of I-65 and I-40. Fort Negley Visitors Center and Park is adjacent to the Cumberland Science Museum as well as Greer Stadium.

- Most of the fighting during the battle of Nashville took place in the hills south of the city, although initial shots may have been fired from this site.
- Other Nashville fortifications: A blockhouse stood on Casino Hill, southwest of Fort Negley, now the site of a city reservoir. Fort Morton stood near the Franklin Pike. Fort Houston was at 16th Avenue South and Division Street.

- Nashville City Cemetery nearby, at 1001 Fourth Avenue South, interred more than fifteen thousand Union and Confederate soldiers by war's end. Most of the bodies of the Union and Confederate soldiers were eventually reinterred at Nashville National Cemetery and Mt. Olivet Cemetery, respectively.

MADISON, NASHVILLE NATIONAL CEMETERY

4.22.11 Subject: Memorial Arch, Entryway
Location: 1420 Gallatin Road, South Madison, 37115   N 36 14 30 16 / W 86 43 25 82
Installed or dedicated: 1870
Medium: Granite
Monument is a granite arch.

Inscription

NASHVILLE MILITARY CEMETERY
NASHVILLE A.D. 1867.

HERE REST IN PEACE 16,516 CITIZENS / WHO DIED FOR THEIR COUNTRY, / IN THE YEARS 1861 TO 1865.

This postwar cemetery inters the remains of soldiers removed from temporary burial grounds around Nashville's general hospitals, the battlefields at Franklin and Gallatin, and those from Bowling Green and Cave City, Kentucky. The site was formally established as a US military cemetery on January 28, 1867. There are 4,141 unknowns.

The neoclassical arch is approximately thirty-five feet high, with Doric columns, a pair of ornamental iron gates, and the inscriptions cited above. Note the status of the men as citizens not soldiers, and that they "died for their country."

Railroad tracks divide the cemetery. As with other Tennessee national cemeteries—for example, Stones River—the railroad site was chosen as a point of access as well as a point of recognition for the dead to passersby.

4.22.12 Subject: Common Soldier Statue, US Colored Troops
Location: Section J   N 36 14 28 74 / W 86 43 42 36
Installed or dedicated: January 1, 2003
Medium: Bronze, granite
Monument is a sculpture of a Union soldier, in bronze, surmounting a granite base.

Inscription

IN MEMORY / OF THE 20,133 WHO SERVED AS / UNITED STATES COLORED TROOPS / IN THE UNION ARMY
DEDICATED 2003

Common Soldier Statue, US Colored Troops (USCT), Nashville National Cemetery

SCULPTOR: ROY W. BUTLER / MODEL: WILLIAM C. RADCLIFFE
PRESENTED BY: THE AFRICAN AMERICAN CULTURAL ALLIANCE / UNITED
ASSOCIATION FOR BLACK VETERANS / CREATIVE ARTISTS OF TENNESSEE

More than fifteen hundred African American soldiers are buried in the Nashville cemetery; of these, some four hundred are unknown. This nine-foot cast-bronze statue, the work of Middle Tennessee artist Roy Butler, is one of a very few monuments to African American soldiers in the country; it is the only statue of an African American soldier in a national cemetery. It is, at this writing, the only statue of a Union Civil War soldier erected in Tennessee in the twenty-first century, and it is one of only two statues erected to Tennessee Union soldiers in Tennessee (the other is at Greeneville).

Erected at a cost of $80,000, the statue's construction was coordinated and sponsored by the African American Cultural Alliance of Nashville. William C. Radcliffe, a Nashville firefighter and 13th USCT reenactor, served as the model for the sculpture. Norm Hill, chairman of the Tennessee Historical Commission averred that the project "was a grassroots effort which included church contributions, individual citizens, businesses and other Civil War groups including the Sons of Confederate Veterans (SCV)."

- Nashville National Cemetery was established shortly after the war. There are 12,769 listings for Civil War–era soldiers. Most of the reinternments came from Middle Tennessee and Kentucky battlefields, including the battles of Nashville and Franklin, and at least 251 sites, according to cemetery documents.

State of Minnesota, Statue

4.22.13 Subject: State of Minnesota, Statue, Female
Location: Section MM   N 36 14 23 84 / W 86 43 36 80
Installed or dedicated: 1920
Medium: Bronze, granite
Monument is a sculpted figure of a woman surmounting a base.

Inscription

ERECTED A.D. 1920 BY THE / STATE OF MINNESOTA / IN MEMORY OF HER SOLDIERS / HERE BURIED WHO LOST THEIR LIVES / IN THE SERVICE OF THE UNITED STATES / IN THE WAR FOR THE / PRESERVATION OF THE UNION / A D 1861–1865

JOHN K. DANIELS SR. / FLORENTINE BROTH. FOUNDRY

John K. Daniels designed this sculpted figure of a woman bearing a laurel wreath in bronze, who is depicted as if she is approaching or wishing to approach and offer the wreath. The name of the conflict is precise and reflective of higher principles articulated in the Gettysburg Address: Minnesota soldiers fought in a "War for the Preservation of the Union."

· Daniels also sculpted the Minnesota figure at Memphis National Cemetery (5.16.5).

Sumner County

4.23.1 Subject: Gallatin, Courthouse Common Soldier Statue, Confederate
Location: 183 W Main Street, Trousdale House, South Locust Avenue, 37066
N 36 23 14 41 / W 86 26 56 92
Installed or dedicated: September 19, 1903
Medium: bronze, granite
Monument is a Confederate Soldier, in bronze, surmounting a granite base.

Inscription

[Front]
[Relief of Confederate battle flag]
"THERE IS NO NOBLER / SPOT OF GROUND, / THAN WHERE EXALTED / VALOR LIES."
[Inscribed on relief of a granite scroll]
CONFEDERATE / SOLDIERS

CSA

ERECTED / BY THE / DAUGHTERS.

[Wreath surrounding]
1861 / 1865

This handsome monument, which appears on this book's cover, stands twenty feet, six inches high and faces almost due north. It is the northernmost statue of a Confederate soldier in the state and is believed to be positioned to face the wartime encampment of occupying Federal troops in Gallatin.

The sculpture, in bronze with a green patina on a Vermont granite base, was erected at a cost of $2,000. The Daniel S. Donelson Bivouac No. 6, UCV initiated the project, but their fund-raising efforts fell short and the UDC—the Clark Chapter No. 13—succeeded them and served as the Monument Committee. (The Clark Chapter continues as an active organization at this writing.) Senator Edward W. Carmack delivered the oration at the festive dedication ceremonies on September 19, 1903.

The statue is seven feet in height. The sculptor is unknown. Smithsonian records note that the soldier appears to have an 1830s model Harpers Ferry Musket.

The excerpt on the front panel was written by Henry Timrod (1828–67), Confederate soldier and poet, known unofficially as the "Laureate of the Confederacy." The passage is taken from his "Ode Sung at Magnolia Cemetery," written in 1867 and composed on the occasion of the decoration of the graves of the Confederate dead in Magnolia Cemetery, Charleston, South Carolina.

- Trousdale Place, erected circa 1813, was the home of an early governor of Tennessee, William Trousdale (1790–1872). Trousdale's two sons served as Confederate soldiers. The house was deeded to the Clark Chapter No. 13, UDC, in 1889 and is listed on the National Register of Historic Places. A bronze plaque on the wall of the Trousdale house reads as follows:

  IN MEMORY / JULIUS AUGUSTUS TROUSDALE
  THIS HOME WAS GIVEN / BY HIS WIFE / ANNIE BERRY TROUSDALE / AS A
  LASTING TRIBUTE / TO HIS EXALTED PATRIOTISM / AS CITIZEN, STATESMAN,
  AND SOLDIER / OF THE SOUTHERN CONFEDERACY / TO HONOR HIM AND IN
  GRATEFUL / RECOGNITION OF THE GIFT / THIS TABLET IS DEDICATED BY /
  CLARK CHAPTER NO. 13 / UNITED DAUGHTERS OF / THE CONFEDERACY

Robertson County

4.24.1 Subject: Springfield, Elmwood Cemetery Stele, Confederate
Location: 1029 Richard Street, corner of Central Avenue   N 36 30 16 18 /
W 86 53 30 67
Unveiled: January 1958
Medium: Granite
Monument is an inscribed stele.

Inscription
CONFEDERATE / VETERANS / SPRINGFIELD CHAPTER / #1741 / UNITED DAUGHTERS
/ OF THE / CONFEDERACY / JAN. 1958

This low, modest monument faces east, off Richard Street in Springfield. The
cemetery dates from at least 1890, was deeded to the city in June 1987, and
comprises approximately thirty acres. There is no separate Confederate cemetery section, but there are numerous graves of Confederate soldiers on the
grounds. The local UDC chapter, which is still active at this writing, offered an
inscribed tribute to "Confederate Veterans." It still holds them in memory as
survivors, veterans—note the present tense—although all known Confederate
veterans had passed away by 1958.

- Most Robertson County men who enlisted in the armed forces served
  with the Confederacy. Springfield was occupied by Union forces early
  in 1862, served as a base for the training of US Colored Troops, and
  remained garrisoned by Federal troops for the duration of the war.

Montgomery County
Clarksville

4.25.1 Subject: Greenwood Cemetery, Common Soldier Statue, Confederate
Location: 984 Greenwood Avenue, 37040   N 36 80 26 68 / W 87 20 55 35 46
Unveiled: October 25, 1893
Media: Bronze, granite
Monument is a common soldier surmounting a shaft and base with two
soldiers.

Inscription
IN HONOR OF / THE HEROES WHO FELL / WHILE FIGHTING FOR US / IN THE ARMY
OF THE / CONFEDERATE / STATES / CONFEDERATE MEMORIAL

THOUGH ADVERSE FORTUNE / DENIED FINAL VICTORY / TO THEIR UNDAUNTED
/ COURAGE, HISTORY PRES- / ERVES THEIR FAME, MADE / GLORIOUS FOREVER. /
1861–1865

This opulent fifty-foot monument—in Barre granite and bronze—was erected by Forbes Bivouac, UCV, and a "committee of other Montgomery County

Clarksville: Greenwood Cemetery, Three Common Soldier Statues, Confederate

citizens." The surmounting bronze sculpture of a Confederate common soldier, an infantryman, faces west, toward Fort Defiance and Fort Donelson. In
addition, statues of two other common soldiers sculpted in granite—a cavalryman and an artillerist—face north and south. The three figures—six feet,
six inches in height—were modeled on photographs of members of Forbes
Bivouac, United Confederate Veterans. The infantryman was modeled on W. R.
Bringhurst; the cavalryman, Clay Stacker; the artillerist, Charles H. Bailey.

4.24.2 Subject: Riverview Cemetery, Shaft and Urn, Confederate
Location: 635 North Spring Street, 37040, near US 41A, North Riverside Drive
N 36 30 26 68 / W 87 290 35 46
Dedicated: November 10, 1889
Medium: Marble
Monument is a shaft with surmounting urn.

Inscription

IN MEMORY OF / 127 UNKNOWN / CONFEDERATE SOLDIERS / WHO SLEEP HERE.
[CS battle flag inscribed]

ERECTED BY FORBES BIVOUAC, / NOVEMBER 1899

These two bronze plaques, listing 307 names of the dead from Clarksville Confederate Hospital, were dedicated at Riverview Cemetery on May 26, 2001. The dedication service was held by the Clarksville, Montgomery County chapter of the SCV, the Frank P. Gracey Camp 225.

Inscription

THEY GAVE ALL IN THE DEFENSE OF THE CONFEDERATE STATES OF AMERICA AND IN THEIR FINAL HOURS ON EARTH THEY RECEIVED TENDER LOVING CARE FROM MISS BLANCHE LEWIS AT THE CLARKSVILLE FEMALE ACADEMY
TEXAS 7TH *[Three columns, 55 names]* TENNESSEE *[Three columns, 111 names]*
ALABAMA *[6 names]* ARKANSAS *[1 name]* KENTUCKY *[17 names]*
MISSISSIPPI *[76 names]* VIRGINIA *[17 names]* UNKNOWN *[24 names]*

More than 305 Confederate soldiers were buried in a garden behind the Clarksville Female Academy, which served as the Confederate hospital in Clarksville. Many were casualties of the battle at Fort Donelson. At least 105 of the deaths occurred before February 11, 1862, when the battle began and were likely the result of disease. The graves were marked with wooden headboards but burial locations were lost when these deteriorated. After a landslide in 1897 exposed some of the burial locations, 127 unidentified remains were found, disinterred, and reinterred here.

The remaining graves of an estimated 180 soldiers were left undisturbed until 2000, when construction of a bridge by the City of Clarksville resulted in the burial site being covered with additional soil and structural debris. In response to protests, the city agreed to name the bridge the "Confederate Soldier Memorial Bridge."

· Two African American sisters, who contracted disease and died while caring for the ill and wounded, are also interred there.

4.25.3 Subject: Cemetery Stele, Confederate Memorial Bridge
Location: 537 Cumberland Drive   N 36 31 26 90 / W 87 21 08 32
Dedicated: December 15, 2002
Medium: Bronze, granite
Monument is a bronze plaque and stele.

Inscription
DURING THE WAR FOR SOUTHERN INDEPENDENCE, 1861 TO 1865, THIS SA-
CRED GROUND WAS USED AS A BURIAL SITE FOR CONFEDERATE SOLDIERS. THE
CLARKSVILLE FEMALE ACADEMY WAS USED AS A CONFEDERATE HOSPITAL LOCATED
200 YARDS DUE NORTH. . . . IN THIS CORNER OF THE ACADEMY GARDEN, A TOTAL
OF 307 WERE LAID TO REST. IN 1897, A LANDSLIDE EXPOSED SOME OF THE SOL-
DIERS' REMAINS. UNDER THE SUPERVISION OF COMMANDER CLAY STACKER AND
THE CONFEDERATE VETERANS OF FORBES BIVOUAC, THE BODIES OF 127 SOLDIERS
WERE FOUND, REINTERRED, AND HONORED WITH A MONUMENT AT RIVERVIEW
CEMETERY. MANY YEARS LATER THE REMAINING GRAVES WERE COVERED WHEN
THE FIRST BRIDGE WAS BUILT HERE. IN 2001 . . . THIS BRIDGE WAS NAMED IN HON-
OR OF THE 180 CONFEDERATE SOLDIERS INTERRED HERE.
ERECTED BY FRANK P. GRACEY CAMP 225, / SONS OF CONFEDERATE VETERANS /
2002
[UDC seal] [SCV seal]

The monument honors an estimated one hundred eighty Confederate soldiers,
names unknown, and two nurses whose graves are beneath the western approach to the Confederate Soldiers Memorial Bridge on Cumberland Drive.
The monument is located near their burial site, about two hundred yards south
of the campus of the Clarksville Female Academy, which served as a wartime
hospital.

Stewart County, Including Fort Donelson National Military Park
Fort Donelson National Military Park

4.26.1 Subject: UDC Common Soldier Statue and Obelisk
Location: 120 Fort Donelson Shores Road, Dover, 37058   N 36 29 05 38 /
W 87 51 46 30120
Erected: 1932–33; dedicated: June 3, 1933
Media: Bronze, marble
Monument is a statue of a Confederate soldier in front of an obelisk.

Inscription
CSA
[Battle flag unfurled with broken staff]
THIS SHAFT IS DEDICATED / AS AN ALTAR OF REMEMBRANCE / TO THE
CONFEDERATE SOLDIERS / WHO FOUGHT AT FORT DONELSON / FEBRUARY, 1862 /
BY THE DAUGHTERS OF THE CONFEDERACY / OF TENNESSEE / "THERE IS NO HOLIER
SPOT OF GROUND / THAN WHERE DEFEATED VALOR LIES."

CSA

"HERE / WAS THE PLACE OF BATTLE. YOU WHO / HAVE NEVER KNOWN THE SCOUR AND / PIERCE OF BATTLE MAY ONLY / REMEMBER MOMENTS BY NAMES, / PLACES BY MONUMENTS, BUT I WHO / WAS BORN BY THE BATTLE-FIELDS / CANNOT ESCAPE A SORROW THAT / DWELLS, A VALOR THAT LINGERS, / A HOPE THAT SPOKE ON LIPS NOW STILL."

CSA

FEBRUARY 13TH, 1862 / FEBRUARY 14TH, 1862 / FEBRUARY 15TH, 1862 / SOMEWHERE OUR UNKNOWN / DEAD WILL LIE FOREVER, / WITH ARMS UNSTACKED FOREVER, WITH / COLORS THAT CANNOT BE FURLED.

CSA

HONOR THEIR VALOR, EMULATE / THE DEVOTION WITH WHICH THEY GAVE / THEMSELVES TO THE SERVICE OF / THEIR COUNTRY, NEVER LET IT BE / SAID THAT THEIR SONS IN THESE / SOUTHERN STATES HAVE FORGOTTEN / THEIR NOBLE EXAMPLE.

CAST BY AM-ART / BRONZE FDY / CHICAGO

After capturing Fort Henry on February 6, 1862, Brig. Gen. Ulysses S. Grant advanced Union forces cross-country to attack Fort Donelson. The fort's twelve-thousand-man garrison surrendered unconditionally ten days later, after the failure of their attack aimed at breaking through Union lines. The loss of Fort Donelson was a major victory for the North. It was catastrophic for the South. With its surrender, Kentucky was destined to remain in the Union, the Tennessee and Cumberland Rivers were destined to be used for riverine invasion and supply, and the fall of Nashville was assured.

It's unconfirmed whether this site is a mound interring Confederate dead, but this monument gives tribute to those who remain here: the Confederate dead who are interred at various sites—most of them unknown—on the grounds of what is today a Federal national park.

UDC Common Soldier Statue and Obelisk, Fort Donelson National Military Park

This was the last original design of a statue of a Confederate soldier to be erected in Tennessee in the twentieth century. Among statues of Confederate soldiers, it is second only to the 2012 concrete statue at Confederate Plaza, Dyer County, as the most recent.

The monument stands approximately thirty-one feet high on a base twelve by twelve feet; the statue is in bronze and bears a resemblance to a common soldier of World War I; the obelisk and base are in Georgia silver gray; the obelisk is surmounted by what appears to be a funereal urn. The Muldoon Monument Company served as the fabricator; the American Bronze Company was the founder.

- The excerpt beginning "There Is No Holier Spot Of Ground" is taken from Henry Timrod's "Ode Sung at Magnolia Cemetery," written in 1867.

- The excerpt beginning "Here Was The Place Of Battle" is from the poem "The Sod of Battlefields" by Donald Davidson.

4.26.2 Subject: State of Texas Monument, Shaft
Location: Natcor Drive, at Stop 9, Forge Road, on the Fort Donelson driving tour   N 36 28 50 39 / W 87 50 23 72
Installed or dedicated: 1964
Medium: Bronze, granite
Monument is a granite shaft set on a pedestal.

Inscription

TEXAS
[Star set in a wreath]
REMEMBERS THE VALOR AND DEVOTION OF / HER SONS WHO SERVED AT FORT DONELSON / AND OTHER ENGAGEMENTS OF THIS THEATER / OF THE CIVIL WAR. / DURING THE BATTLE AT FORT DONELSON / FEBRUARY 12–16, 1862 COL. JOHN GREGG'S / 7TH TEXAS INFANTRY OF DAVIDSON'S / BRIGADE, JOHNSON'S DIVISION, WERE THE / RIGHT OF A GALLANT LINE WHICH DROVE / THE ENEMY FROM A HILL UNDER TERRIFIC / FIRE. IN SUPPORT OF CONFEDERATE GENERAL / WHEELER'S ATTACK ON THE FEDERAL GARRISON / AT FORT DONELSON, FEBRUARY 3, 1863, THE / 8TH TEXAS CAVALRY—TERRY'S TEXAS RANGERS—/ OF WHARTON'S BRIGADE SET UP A ROAD BLOCK / EIGHT MILES WEST OF DOVER AND SUCCESSFULLY / STOPPED THE UNION LAND REINFORCEMENTS / FROM REACHING THE BATTLE AREA. ALTHOUGH / COL. B. F. TERRY WAS KILLED AT THE BATTLE OF / WOODSONVILLE MORE THAN A YEAR BEFORE / THIS ACTION, THE RANGERS CONTINUED TO BE / KNOWN AS TERRY'S TEXAS RANGERS TO THE / WAR'S END. IN GENERAL HARDEE'S SPECIAL / ORDERS IT WAS SAID OF TERRY: "HIS / REGIMENT DEPLORES THE LOSS OF A BRAVE / AND BELOVED COMMANDER; THE ARMY OF ONE OF / ITS ABLEST OFFICERS."
A MEMORIAL TO TEXANS / WHO SERVED THE CONFEDERACY / ERECTED BY THE STATE OF TEXAS 1964

State of Texas Monument, Shaft

This is one of two Confederate centennial-era granite shafts erected by the State of Texas in Tennessee. The other stands on the Shiloh battlefield (1.16.2). It is the only unit monument and the only state monument on this battlefield.

The 7th Texas Infantry organized at Waco during the summer of 1861, formed part of the garrison at Fort Donelson, and was taken prisoner when the garrison was surrendered. Regiment exchanged, reconstituted, and engaged at the battles of Raymond and Jackson. Other service included Chickamauga, Chattanooga, Atlanta, Hood's 1864 campaign, and in North Carolina in 1865. The regiment surrendered on April 26, 1865.

The 8th Texas Cavalry, also known as Terry's Texas Rangers, was organized at Houston in December 1861. It served at Shiloh, Murfreesboro, and Chickamauga as well as the Knoxville, Atlanta, and Carolinas campaigns. The regiment was surrendered on April 26, 1865, with only about thirty men.

Dickson County

4.27.1 Subject: Charlotte, Courthouse Shaft, Confederate
Location: 100 West Main Street, Charlotte Courthouse Square, 37036
N 36 10 41 84 / W 86 20 21 90
Dedicated: March 1, 2001
Medium: Granite
Monument is a stele.

Inscription

CSA
DEO VINDICE
TO ALL WHO SERVED / IN MEMORY OF THE / CONFEDERATE SOLDIER / OF DICKSON
COUNTY, TN / 11TH TENNESSEE INFANTRY, CO. C, E, H, K / 49TH TENNESSEE
INFANTRY, CO. B, D / 50TH TENNESSEE INFANTRY, CO. A / 10TH TENNESSEE
CAVALRY / 24TH TENNESSEE SHARPSHOOTERS / BAXTER'S CO. TN. LIGHT ARTILLERY
/ BAXTER'S BATT. TN. LIGHT ARTILLERY / ROSS' CAVALRY BRIGADE, CO. A / 1861—
1865 / ERECTED IN MARCH 2001

[SCV seal]
"OFFERED IN THEIR MEMORY" / BY W.Y. MCCAULEY CAMP 260 / SONS OF
CONFEDERATE VETERANS

Confederate sentiments were strong in Dickson County; the legacy is manifested by dint of the two UDC monuments on the courthouse square and the roster of Confederate units formed in the county. No major actions occurred in Dickson County, but partisan Confederates operated in the area, and Brig. Gen. Nathan Bedford Forrest's command moved through during the retreat from Fort Donelson in February 1862. They came again a year later, when troops commanded by Forrest and Brig. Gen. Joseph Wheeler came through after their unsuccessful campaign against Fort Donelson and Dover in February 1863. In 1864, Federal troops established Camp Gillem in Tennessee City to protect the locomotive yard and railroad.

- An adjacent UDC obelisk erected in 2011 gives tribute to "To Our Gallant Soldiers, Veterans and their Families." It makes oblique reference to the Civil War by dint of "All Conflicts Domestic and Foreign."

West Tennessee

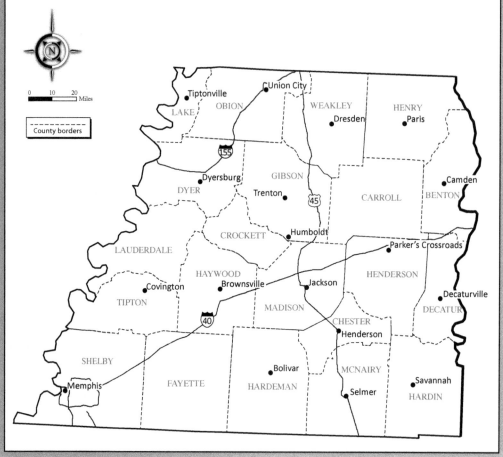

WEST
TENNESSEE

"HISTORY IS AN IMPARTIAL WITNESS"

TWELVE CIVIL WAR courthouse monuments—eleven Confederate, one bipartisan—stand in West Tennessee. The area has many distinctions. By some accounts, the earliest postwar monuments in the country were erected in West Tennessee, at Bolivar and Union City. Memphis, the largest city, displayed the only equestrian Civil War monument in Tennessee, to Lt. Gen. Nathan B. Forrest, until its removal in 2017. Tributes to the Confederate dead are at Elmwood Cemetery, and to the Union dead at Memphis National Cemetery. The largest tribute to the Confederacy west of Richmond's Monument Avenue or Stone Mountain, Georgia, is at a hilltop location north of Dyersburg, where an enormous Confederate battle flag and shrine dominate the landscape.

The largest engagement in West Tennessee was at Shiloh (see chap. 1), but other West Tennessee battlefield monuments are at Island No. 10 (April 8, 1862), Memphis (June 6, 1862), Britton Lane (September 1, 1862), Davis Bridge (October 5, 1862), Salem Cemetery (December 19, 1862), Trenton (December 20, 1862), Parker's Crossroads (December 31, 1862), and Pilot Knob (November 4, 1864).

The twenty-one counties of West Tennessee were less divided in their sentiments and convictions regarding slavery and secession than their Middle or East Tennessee brethren. The voters supported the ordinance of secession on June 8, 1861. The Mississippi and Tennessee Rivers were vital strategic arteries, but railways also served as avenues of logistics, strategy, and conflict. Various actions were fought at Humboldt, Jackson, Trenton, Union City, Dyersburg, and Memphis. These towns or cities retain monuments that reflect the sentiments of the wartime generation's secession convictions.

Is history "an Impartial Witness," as the Jackson courthouse monument inscription declares (5.12.1)? Perhaps. Perhaps God will vindicate—"Deo Vindice"—as the motto of the Confederacy affirms. Whatever course Providence takes, these monuments seem to be static, but they are not: they have import. A resolution of the Memphis city council on February 6, 2013, changed the name of Confederate Park to Memphis Park; Jefferson Davis Park to Mississippi River Park; and Nathan Bedford Forrest Park to Health Sciences Park. The Davis and Forrest monuments were removed in 2017.

· Conspicuous for its absence of monuments is Fort Pillow, a state park. Fort Pillow continues to cast a shadow on the history of the Confederate military in the wake of the shooting of unarmed black troops during the battle fought there on April 12, 1864. The engagement is cited on several monuments in West Tennessee, but no monument is on the battlefield as of this writing.

Benton County

5.1.1 Subject: Pilot Knob, General Nathan B. Forrest, Obelisk
Location: 1825 Pilot Knob Road, Eva, 38333   N 36 05 18 67 / W 87 58 26 56
Dedicated: October 21, 1931
Medium: Granite
Monument is a granite obelisk.

Inscription
[Front]
COMMEMORATING THE CAPTURE / OF FEDERAL GUNBOATS / BY FORREST'S CAVALRY IN THE / JOHNSONVILLE EXPEDITION / NOVEMBER 4, 1864.

ERECTED BY / MONUMENT AND MEMORIAL / COMMISSION AND DIVISION / OF HISTORY / STATE OF TENNESSEE 1930

FAITH IS THE DUTY OF THE HOUR / N. B. FORREST, MAJOR-GENERAL / TO / LIEUTENANT-GENERAL / RICHARD TAYLOR / NOVEMBER 12, 1864

Nathan Bedford Forrest State Park was established in 1929 on land acquired in part from Benton County. The high ground where this obelisk stands overlooks what is presently the western shore of the Kentucky Lake impoundment of the Tennessee River. It was from here, in the vicinity of the park and the town of Eva, that forces under the command of Forrest attacked a Union base across the river at the former site of Johnsonville, at the mouth of Trace Creek, on November 4, 1864. Forrest's men captured several Union gunboats, transports, barges, twenty-six artillery pieces, several million dollars' worth of property, and 150 prisoners.

"Faith is the Duty of the Hour" is an apt summary of the action. Consequences and victory are not mentioned. At this stage of the war, Forrest could harass and distract the Union Army, but he could not affect their progress.

Henry County

5.2.1 Subject: Paris, Courthouse Common Soldier Statue, Confederate
Location: 213 West Washington Street, 38242   N 36 18 09 18 / W 88 19 32 16
Unveiled: September 20, 1899; dedicated: October 13, 1900
Medium: Marble
Monument is a statue of a Confederate soldier standing at parade rest, surmounting a base.

Pilot Knob, General Nathan B. Forrest, Obelisk

Inscription

[Relief of crossed flags]
HENRY CO. / CONFEDERATE SOLDIERS

NO COUNTRY EVER HAD TRUER SONS, / NO CAUSE NOBLER CHAMPIONS, / NO PEOPLE BOLDER DEFENDERS. / 1861–1865.

Paris: Henry County Courthouse Common Soldier Statue, Confederate

This is a prototypical soldier's monument on a courthouse lawn. It was erected by the Paris Chapter of the UDC and the Fitzgerald Bivouac, UCV, Henry County Memorial Association. Sculpted in marble, the figure stands with arms crossed and surmounts a limestone base. The sculpture of the soldier stands six feet tall; the base is three by ten by ten feet. The sculptor is unknown. However, the soldier's pensive countenance is reminiscent of a period painting of a Confederate soldier by John A. Elder titled "Appomattox."

At the monument's dedication on October 13, 1900, ex-governor James D. Porter, who served on the staff of Maj. Gen. Benjamin F. Cheatham during the war, observed that the soldiers of Henry County were reluctant warriors:

The war between the States was not promoted by the men of Henry County. They were conservative and peaceful. War to them was terrible to contemplate, but they were not afraid of it or of its sacrifices. They loved peace as they abhorred pusillanimity, but not peace at any price. There is a peace more destructive of the manhood of living men than war is destructive of his material body. Chains are worse than bayonets. . . . The men of Henry stood by the flag to the last; they participated in every battle of the Southwest. From Belmont to Bentonville they fell 'on the red sand of the battlefield with bloody corpses strewn,' and hundreds of them sleep in unmarked graves, but they are not forgotten.

The figure faces north. The figure's nose, hands, and eyes are marred, and the strap of the knapsack on his back is severed. The Paris 2521 Chapter of the UDC reports that the state undertook a restoration and cleaning of this and other courthouse monuments and reported that the marble is defective. At one time the figure held a rifle, but this has gone missing. The surrounding fence was installed circa 1989.

Several military units, including the 5th Tennessee Infantry, organized on the courthouse lawn during the war. Henry County contributed over twenty-five hundred men to military service for the Confederacy and is referred to as the "Volunteer County of the Volunteer State." Confederate veterans initiated the monument project, but their fund-raising efforts fell short, and the UDC succeeded them.

Weakley County

5.3.1 Subject: Dresden, Courthouse Common Soldier Statue, Confederate
Location: 116 West Main Street, 38225   N 36 17 30 80 / W 80 42 31 50
Dedicated: June 7, 1915; relocated: 1961
Medium: Marble
Monument is a statue of a Confederate soldier standing at parade rest, surmounting a base.

Inscription
CSA / 1865
[Relief of crossed swords and bugle]
IN HONOR OF THE / CONFEDERATE SOLDIERS / OF WEAKLEY COUNTY, / TENNESSEE / 1861–1865

1861 / WEAKLEY COUNTY FURNISHED / THREE COMPANIES OF THE 31ST / AND ONE COMPANY EACH OF THE / 9TH, 15TH, 27TH, 33RD, AND 51ST / TENN. CON. INFANTRY REGIMENTS / FOUR COMPANIES OF CAVALRY / AND NUMBERS OF SOLDIERS TO / OTHER COMMANDS IN THE / CONFEDERATE SERVICE.

CSA / 1865 / FURL THAT BANNER; / TRUE, 'TIS GORY, / YET 'TIS WREATHED / AROUND WITH GLORY, / AND 'TWILL LIVE IN / SONG AND STORY, / THOUGH ITS FOLDS ARE IN THE DUST.

Dresden: Weakley County Courthouse Common Soldier Statue, Confederate

CSA / 1861 / WEAKLEY COUNTY CONFEDERATE / SOLDIERS PARTICIPATED IN ALL / THE WESTERN BATTLES, / AMONG WHICH ARE: BELMONT, / DONALDSON [SIC], SHILOH, PERRYVILLE, / MURFREESBORO, CHICKAMAUGA, / MISSIONARY RIDGE, RESACA, / KENESAW MOUNTAIN, ATLANTA, / OKALONA, GUNTOWN, HARRISBURG, / FRANKLIN, NASHVILLE, / AND BENTONVILLE.

The surmounting figure of the Dresden courthouse monument faces south-west, in the direction of Shiloh. The sculpture is Italian marble; the base is

Georgia marble. The sculptor is unknown, but the soldier looks young; he stands at parade rest, with a countenance that is neither warlike nor bitter. The countenance is wistful, thoughtful, as if his youth had caused him to miss a destiny he might have fulfilled.

The excerpt beginning "Furl That Banner" is taken from "The Conquered Banner," the poetry of Father Abram Ryan (1838–86), a Roman Catholic priest known as the "Poet Priest of the Lost Cause," as well as a parish priest in Knoxville.

Weakley County soldiers were Confederates, and, as noted in the inscription, the units served in the western theater of war.

Obion County

Union City

5.4.1 Subject: Courthouse Common Soldier Statue, Confederate
Location: Kiwanis Park, corner of East Church Street and Depot, 38261
N 36 25 27 28 / W 89 03 22 50
Installed or dedicated: 1909
Media: Granite, marble
Monument is a statue of a Confederate soldier standing at parade rest, surmounting a base.

Inscription
[Front]
1861
[Crossed swords with bugle draped between them]
TO THE / CONFEDERATE / SOLDIERS OF / OBION COUNTY.

[CS national flag with broken staff]
TO THE CONFEDERATE SOLDIER / OF OBION COUNTY / WHO WAS KILLED IN BATTLE, / WHO STARVED IN FEDERAL PRISON AND WHO / HAS PRESERVED ANGLO-SAXON CIVILIZATION / IN THE SOUTH

[CSA national flag with broken staff]
ERECTED BY THE / LEONIDUS / POLK CHAPTER / U.D.C. / 1909

1861

1865

The monument was erected beside the courthouse in 1909, but when the former courthouse was torn down and replaced in the 1930s, it was moved here, circa 1940, beside the railroad tracks, formerly Railroad Park, present-day Kiwanis Park.

The figure of the common soldier is carved marble; the shaft is granite. The bitter tone and rebuke of the inscription is unusual for the time; monuments at the turn of the twentieth century tended to be more sentimental and celebratory.

Union City: City View Cemetery, Obelisk, Confederate

- The name Union City is apolitical—a description, really—derived from the crossing point of two railroads.

5.4.2 Subject: City View Cemetery, Obelisk, Confederate
Location: Edwards and Summer Streets, 38261   N 36 25 15 74 / W 89 02 50 34
Dedicated: October 21, 1869
Media: Fieldstone, plaster
Monument is a tiered shaft surmounting a four-tiered base.

Inscription
[Relief of sword, snapped in two]
UNKNOWN / CONFEDERATE / DEAD
[Erected through the efforts of Union City and Obion County citizens. / Dedicated October 21, 1869]

The Tennessee Historical Commission declares that this is the "First Monument to Unknown Confederate Dead." The monument stands thirty-four feet high: a tiered shaft, painted, made of stone, covered with plaster. The sculptor is unknown, but the obelisk is quintessentially funereal. The monument is on the National Registry of Historical Places.

- The Sons of Confederate Veterans (SCV) Camp No. 176 reports the dedication ceremonies with the following extract from a period account:

    At last, after incessant and persevering labor, the noble work of
    fitting up a cemetery, erecting a monument, and reinterring the re-
    mains of those who fell on the field of honor in defense of Southern
    rights was accomplished, and the morning of October 21, 1869, fixed
    for the funeral ceremony and final dedication of the holy place. As by
    special providence, the morning broke in perfect harmony with the
    solemn occasion, the heavy clouds hung dark and drifting over the
    face of the sky, the sun itself scarcely visible, seemed to participate

in the pervading gloom, and every individual appeared impressed with the dignity and grandeur belonging to the day.

Hornbeak City

5.4.3 Subject: SCV Cemetery Stele
Location: Cemetery Road, east of intersection of TR 21 and 183, off Main Street, 38232   N 36 19 52 02 / W 89 17 24 20
Dedicated: June 25, 2011
Medium: Granite
Monument is a granite slab.

Inscription

[CS battle flag]
IN HONOR OF / THE / CONFEDERATE SOLDIERS / BURIED HERE
DEDICATED 2010 CAMP 2111 SCV

This small-town hilltop cemetery displays a modest monument erected by the local SCV camp. By their account they did so with "one common goal. Heritage! We have the great honor of being descendants of Confederate soldiers who died for what they believed."

Dyer County

Dyersburg

5.5.1 Subject: Dyersburg, Courthouse Common Soldier Statue, Confederate
Location: 101 West Court Street, 38024   N 36 01 57 62 / W 86 23 08 90
Installed or dedicated: June 11, 1915
Medium: Granite
Monument is a private soldier standing at parade rest surmounting a shaft and base.

Inscription

[Front]
SHILOH
[Relief of laurel leaf, three crossed flags, two draped, one furled, twelve cannonballs]
TO THE MEMORY OF THE FAITHFUL / CONFEDERATE SOLDIERS OF DYER COUNTY, / NUMBER OF BATTLES FOUGHT BY THEM. / CONFEDERATE

PERRYVILLE / CHICKAMAUGA—MISSIONARY RIDGE
[Relief of national flag on shaft, partially furled sword, and scabbard]
/ BELMONT—RICHMOND / PEACHTREE CREEK—BENTONVILLE.

[Relief of three rifles stacked, one pack, one canteen]
HARRISBURG / JONESBORO—FRANKLIN / NASHVILLE—FORT PILLOW / MURFREESBORO.

[Relief of one cannon, ten cannonballs]
KENNESAW / PARKERS CROSS ROADS.–SELMA. / DIBRELS CROSS ROADS.–ATLANTA. / BRICE'S CROSSROADS.–RASACA [SIC].

Dyersburg: Dyer County Courthouse Common Soldier Statue, Confederate

The figure of a Confederate soldier standing at parade rest, facing north, was placed in front of the 1911 courthouse. The Morriss Bros. Company served as contractor. The sculptor is unknown. Local resident Jane Skeffington unveiled the monument at dedication ceremonies on the anniversary of the Battle of Shiloh in 1905.

Among the Confederate companies formed in Dyer County was Capt. Otho F. Strahl's Company K, 4th Tennessee Infantry, and Capt. Tyree H. Bell's Company B, 12th Tennessee Infantry. Both men rose to the rank of brigadier general. Strahl, killed at the battle of Franklin, is buried in Dyersburg's Old City Cemetery. Bell served under General Nathan B. Forrest, survived the war, and lived until 1902.

No major engagements took place in Dyer County, but foraging by the armies and partisan activity was extensive. Arson, apparently the act of a lone Confederate soldier, led to the burning of the courthouse in 1864. It was rebuilt in 1867 and was replaced by the present classical revival structure in 1911.

· Two bronze tablets are emplaced on adjoining sides of the north doors to the courthouse. Dedicated January 1, 1928, they were erected by the Dawson Bivouac, United Confederate Veterans, at a time when few veterans remained to offer living memory of the war. The first tablet reads:

[Crossed CSA battle flags]
"THE SUN NE'ER SHONE ON A BRAVER BAND / NOR BRAVER FOUGHT FOR A
FAIRER LAND."
[Unit roster]
PRESENTED TO THE FUTURE CITIZENS OF DYER COUNTY
UNITED CONFEDERATE VETERANS

· The second tablet reads:

[Crossed US flags]
"FOR OUR TOMORROW THEY GAVE THEIR TODAY"
KILLED IN ACTION [29 names] / DIED IN SERVICE [38 names] / DIED OF INJURIES
RECEIVED IN SERVICE [13 names]
1896—DAWSON BIVOUAC—1928
COMMANDERS [8 names]
PRESENTED TO THE FUTURE CITIZENS OF DYER COUNTY / UNITED
CONFEDERATE VETERANS

5.5.2 Subject: Old City Cemetery, Stele
Location: Corner of East Court Street and Liberty Avenue   N 36 01 53 44 /
W 89 22 45 56
Installed or dedicated: n.a.
Medium: Granite

Inscription

TO HONOR THE / CONFEDERATE COMPATRIOTS / WHO SLEEP ETERNALLY IN /
THIS HALLOWED GROUND / ERECTED AND DEDICATED / NOVEMBER 30, 2004, THE
140TH / ANNIVERSARY OF THE BATTLE OF / FRANKLIN AND DEATH OF BRIG. GEN
OTHO FRENCH STRAHL. BY THE / WILLIAM DAWSON CAMP #1821 OF / THE SONS OF
CONFEDERATE VETERANS
[Roster of 58 names in 2 columns]

At least nineteen Confederate soldiers are believed to be buried here in unmarked graves, but the graves of at least thirty-five Confederate veterans are
marked. The SCV camp gave this tribute to their "compatriots" in 2004 at a site
adjacent to the grave of Brig. Gen. Otho French Strahl. Strahl also has a monument to his memory at Winstead Hill on the Franklin battlefield (4.14.20).

· Adjacent tombstone, granite stele reads as follows:

OTHO FRENCH STRAHL / CONFEDERATE BRIGADIER GENERAL / WAR BETWEEN
THE STATES, 1861–1865 / BORN: 1832 HOMER TOWNSHIP / REACHED MATURITY
IN MALTA TOWNSHIP / MORGAN COUNTY / K.I.A. NOVEMBER 30, 1864 / BATTLE
OF FRANKLIN, TENNESSEE

This is Strahl's third and—presumably—final resting place. After his death
at the battle of Franklin, his body was interred in a potter's field section of Rose
Hill Cemetery near the Franklin battlefield. It was then moved to Ashwood
Cemetery at St. John's Episcopal Church near Columbia. Strahl was reinterred
here in 1901.

In 2001, the SCV marked Strahl's grave with a granite base surmounted by a cannon barrel. The cannon was originally used as a deck gun on the USS *Independence* during the Mexican War. It was also used at Fort Pillow during the Civil War.

Parks Cemetery Ridge Confederate Memorial Plaza, Dyer County

MONTICELLO GARDEN PAVILION

5.5.3 Subject: Southern Battle Flag, Stele
Location: 211 Ollie Pierce Lane   N 36 12 04 11 / W 89 12 10 38
Dedicated: August 2, 2008
Media: Bronze, granite
Monument is a granite stele.

Inscription

SOUTHERN BATTLE FLAG
ST. ANDREWS CROSS EMBLAZONS BLUE / ACROSS A BLOOD-RED FIELD. / ADORNED BY STARS OF PUREST WHITE; / ONE SOUTHERN BATTLE SHIELD. / FLY, DEAR FLAG, O'ER HEROES BRAVE / BOTH LIVING AND DEPARTED; / STAND FAST FOR THE SOUTHERN CAUSE / OUR ANCESTORS IMPARTED! / THEY GAVE THEIR ALL, SO MANY DIED / TO KEEP THAT BANNER FLYING.
FROM "DIXIE'S HEARTBEAT" BY BETTY ZEITZ.
PARKS CEMETERY RIDGE CONFEDERATE MEMORIAL PLAZA / ERECTED BY THE GEN. OTHO FRENCH STRAHL, / CAMP 176, UNION CITY, TN / SONS OF CONFEDERATE VETERANS, TENNESSEE DIVISION / DEDICATED AUGUST 2, 2008

[SCV seal]
THE CHARGE
COMMISSION TO THE SONS OF CONFEDERATE VETERANS
TO YOU, SONS OF CONFEDERATE VETERANS, WE WILL COMMIT THE VINDICATION OF THE CAUSE FOR WHICH WE FOUGHT. TO YOUR STRENGTH WILL BE GIVEN THE DEFENSE OF THE CONFEDERATE SOLDIER'S GOOD NAME, THE GUARDIANSHIP OF HIS HISTORY, THE EMULATION OF HIS VIRTUES, THE PERPETUATION OF THOSE PRIN-CIPLES WHICH HE LOVED AND WHICH YOU LOVE ALSO, AND THOSE IDEALS WHICH MADE HIM GLORIOUS AND WHICH YOU ALSO CHERISH. ARE YOU ALSO READY TO DIE FOR YOUR COUNTRY? IS YOUR LIFE WORTHY TO BE REMEMBERED ALONG WITH THEIRS? DO YOU CHOOSE FOR YOURSELF THE GREATNESS OF SOUL? / NOT IN THE CLAMOR OF THE CROWDED STREET, / NOT IN THE SHOUTS AND PLAUDITS OF THE THRONG, / BUT IN OURSELVES ARE TRIUMPH AND DEFEAT. / LT. GENERAL STEPHEN DILL LEE / NEW ORLEANS APRIL 25, 1906

"NOTHING FILLS ME WITH DEEPER SADNESS THAN TO SEE A SOUTHERN MAN APOL-OGIZING FOR THE DEFENSE WE MADE OF OUR INHERITANCE."
—JEFFERSON DAVIS 1808–1885

The dedication of the Parks Cemetery Ridge Confederate Memorial Plaza took place on April 17, 2010. This hilltop location with a large, prominent Confederate battle flag waving over a plaza is clearly visible to passersby on US 51, which at this writing is projected to be redesignated Interstate 69. SCV member William H. Parks II donated the cannon, the land, and funding for

Confederate Memorial Plaza,
Common Soldier Statue

DEDICATED TO THE MEMORY
OF CONFEDERATE SOLDIERS
WHO SERVED IN THE
WAR FOR SOUTHERN
INDEPENDENCE
1861–1865
ERECTED BY
SONS OF
CONFEDERATE VETERANS
GEN. OTHO FRENCH STRAHL
CAMP NO. 176 UNION CITY, TN
2012

the plaza. The remains of ten Confederate soldiers are buried in the Pierce Cemetery adjacent to the plaza. Seven headstones have been erected; the location of three remains unknown.

- Also on the grounds is a replica of an M1841, six-pound, smoothbore cannon dedicated June 25, 2011. The cannon was built on a scale 125 percent larger than the original model. Twelve state flags are displayed, left to right: South Carolina, Mississippi, Alabama, Georgia, Louisiana, Texas, Virginia, Arkansas, North Carolina, Tennessee, Kentucky, and Missouri—largely in order of their secession from the Union, though Florida is not present. Kentucky and Missouri were included on the flag of the Confederacy but did not secede from the Union.

- The "Charge to the Sons of Confederate Veterans" is excerpted from an address given by Lt. Gen. Stephen D. Lee at the United Confederate Veteran Reunion in New Orleans.

- The poem "Southern Battle Flag" is found in *Dixie's Heartbeat: Southern Poetry*, by Betty Zeitz, published in 2007.

5.5.4 Subject: Common Soldier Statue, Confederate
Installed or dedicated: April 28, 2012
Media: Concrete, granite
Monument is a statue of a Confederate soldier surmounting a base.

Inscription

[Front]
DEDICATED TO THE MEMORY / OF CONFEDERATE SOLDIERS, / WHO SERVED IN THE / WAR FOR SOUTHERN / INDEPENDENCE / 1861–1865 / ERECTED BY / SONS OF / CONFEDERATE VETERANS / GEN. OTHO FRENCH STRAHL / CAMP 176, UNION CITY, TN / 2012

CSA

[Blank]

SCV

The figure of this common soldier was cast in concrete from a mold taken from the Trenton, Tennessee, courthouse monument. The dedication was hosted by the SCV's Gen. Otho French Strahl Camp No. 176 of Union City.

Gibson County

Trenton

5.6.1 Subject: Courthouse Common Soldier Statue, Confederate
Location: 295 North College Street, 38382   N 35 58 51 21 / W 88 56 29 20
Dedicated: May 31, 1907; relocated: 1916
Media: Bronze, limestone, silicon bronze, white bronze
Monument is a Confederate soldier surmounting a shaft and base.

Inscription

[Front]
[Relief of Gen. R. E. Lee]
ERECTED TO THE MEMORY / OF OUR CONFEDERATE SOLDIERS / BY THE / RUSSELL-HILL CHAPTER, / U.D.C. / LEST WE FORGET.

1861–1865
[Relief of stacked muskets]

1861–1865
[Relief of General N. B. Forrest]

1861–1865
[Relief of anchor]

The monument, originally a statue made of white bronze surmounting a limestone base, stands twenty-five feet high, facing west, in front of the Gibson County courthouse completed July 1901. Edward Ward Carmack, a prominent newspaper editor and US senator, was the principal orator at the dedication

Trenton: Gibson County
Courthouse Common
Soldier Statue, Confederate

ceremonies. When first erected, it stood in the center of the street but was moved in 1916. The original statue was damaged in a storm in 2006, and its replacement was cast from the original in silicon bronze. The original medium, white bronze, otherwise known as zinc, was a specialty of the Monumental Bronze Company and has not been used as a medium since about 1917. Repairs were effected at a cost of $23,000.

- The battle of Trenton was fought at various locations in the city on December 20, 1862, as Union forces under the overall command of Maj. Gen. U. S. Grant moved toward Vicksburg. In an effort to harass or impede their progress, Confederate forces commanded by Brig. Gen. N. B. Forrest moved upon the Trenton depot of the Mobile and Ohio

Railroad. The Union soldiers on site surrendered after a short engagement. Confederate troops vandalized and ransacked the courthouse, destroyed supplies, then withdrew.

5.6.2 Subject: Oakland Cemetery, Confederate, Shaft and Urn
Location: 800 Brownsville Street, north of Armory (TR 54), 38382
N 35 58 19 56 / W 88 56 47 00
Installed: circa 1895
Media: Granite, limestone
Monument is a shaft and urn surmounting a granite base.

Inscription
[Front]
OUR BOYS

1861

THE [ILLEGIBLE] BANNER / ITS FLIGHT / TO GREAT [ILLEGIBLE]

1865

The remains of 141 Confederate soldiers are interred in this cemetery, most of them veterans. Oakland Cemetery was a battlefield for several hours during the war, however, when Maj. Gen. Nathan B. Forrest placed his artillery here during the battle of Trenton, and the Confederate soldiers killed in the battle were originally buried here. Six known Confederate soldiers are interred near this site along with at least three unknown Confederate dead.

This monument, of modest size, is unusually weathered. The urn is a replacement, and much of the inscription on the shaft is illegible. Still, a dominant sentiment is clear—"Our Boys"—and the site displays a Confederate battle flag.

5.6.3 Subject: Oakland Cemetery, Confederate Dead, Tablet
Location: N 35 58 15 19 / W 88 56 44 72
Installed or dedicated: 1910
Medium: Marble

Inscription
CONFEDERATE DEAD BURIED IN OAKLAND CEMETERY, TRENTON, TENN. / [Roster]

This marble slab, which faces up, is much weathered, and its inscription is practically illegible. However, ninety-three names are listed on a nearby tablet titled "Confederate dead buried in Confederate cemetery." In addition, granite stelae nearby list veterans of all wars, including the "Civil War." The flag of the United States presides over the site.

5.6.4 Subject: Bailey Park, Common Soldier Statue, Confederate
Location: 22nd Avenue (US 45W, TR 54), two blocks north of Main Street,
38343   N 35 49 20 98 / W 88 54 25 90
Installed or dedicated: September 24, 1914
Media: Concrete, granite, marble
Monument is a statue of a Confederate soldier standing at parade rest, sur-
mounting a base of four columns surrounding a central block.

Inscription

1861–1865
ERECTED BY / NATHAN BEDFORD / FORREST / CHAPTER NO. 926 / U.D.C. / IN
MEMORY OF / OUR SOUTHERN HEROES / OF GIBSON CO., TENN.

This visually impressive monument stands in a prominent place facing a busy
street near the parking lot of a very active and popular city park.

The sculptor is believed to be J. J. Snyder of Eclipse Marble Works in
Humboldt. The sponsoring United Daughters of the Confederacy (UDC) chapter is no longer extant. One source indicates that the statue was originally
located on Main Street in Humboldt. There is also uncertainty about when the
statue was erected—one source indicates 1912. However, Smithsonian records
indicate that September 24, 1914, is the date on the manuscript of a speech
delivered at the monument's unveiling. The base is twelve feet by six feet, ten
inches by six feet ten inches. The concrete base is nine feet by nine feet.

Bailey Park, Common Soldier Statue, Confederate

Lake County

Tiptonville

5.7.1 Subject: Jones Chapel Cemetery, Confederate
Location: Cronanville Cemetery, Jones Chapel, north of Tiptonville off TR 22
N 36 25 59 99 / W 89 28 41 20
Installed or dedicated: 1996
Medium: Granite
Monument is a stele surmounting a base.

Inscription
IN MEMORY OF THE BOYS IN GRAY WHO GAVE / THEIR ALL FOR THE CONFEDERATE
CAUSE / AT THE BATTLE OF ISLAND NUMBER 10 / IN / APRIL 1862
ERECTED BY LAKE COUNTY "TENN 200" COMMITTEE 1996

Jones Chapel Church of Christ dates from the establishment of the community of Cronanville in the nineteenth century. Approximately seventy-five Confederate dead are interred here, taken from the site of the siege and capture of Madrid Bend and Island No. 10. The Confederate defeat at Island No. 10 opened the Mississippi River to Union forces and the prospect of occupying Memphis, which Union naval and amphibious forces seized in June 1862.

5.7.2 Subject: Island No. 10, Battlefield Stele
Location: TR 22 and Cates Landing Road, approximately 0.5 mile north of
Jones Chapel   N 36 25 57 54 / W 89 28 46 56
Installed or dedicated: 1956
Media: Bronze, concrete, sandstone brick
Monument is a bronze plaque surmounting a concrete and sandstone brick base.

Inscription
[Extensive narrative in raised relief of the engagement at Island No. 10]
This monument commemorates the battle of Island No. 10, fought on April 8, 1862. The monument was erected in 1956 at a cost of $2,200 by the Lake County Civil War Centennial committee in cooperation with the Tennessee Historical Commission and displays a map and an extensive and detailed narrative of the battle. A wooden access ramp leads up to the monument. An American flag is displayed over the site.

The battlefield, approximately one mile north of the monument, is no longer above water; the monument is therefore particularly appropriate as a remembrance and commemoration.

Tipton County
Covington

5.9.1 Subject: Courthouse Common Soldier Statue, Confederate
Location: Tipton County Courthouse, 1 Liberty Avenue, 38019   N 35 33 50 11 /
W 89 38 47 98
Installed: 1894; dedicated: May 29, 1895
Media: Bronze, copper, granite
Monument is a Confederate cavalryman surmounting a base.

Inscription

[Front]
SHILOH
[Relief of three flags: two unfurled CSA battle flags, one furled CS national flag, twelve stacked cannonballs]
1894 / TO THE CONFEDERATE SOLDIERS / OF TIPTON COUNTY, WHOSE COURAGE / IN WAR, AND VIRTUES IN PEACE, HAVE / ILLUSTRATED THE HIGHEST TYPE OF / AMERICAN MANHOOD. / "NOR BRAVER BLED FOR A BRIGHTER LAND, / NOR BRIGHTER LAND HAD A CAUSE SO GRAND." / CONFEDERATE

PERRYVILLE / CHICKAMAUGA
[Relief of unfurled CSA national flag, two sheathed swords, crossed]

HARRISBURG / TISHOMINGO
[Relief of three stacked muskets, with canteen, blanket roll and knapsack]

KENNESAW / FRANKLIN
[Relief of field artillery piece]

Richard H. Munford conceived the idea for this courthouse monument in the 1870s, according to historian Gaylon N. Beasley. Munford worked on the project until his death in 1884, when others took up the cause. Funds—a total of $2,000—were raised by the Tipton County Confederate Monument Association and from other sources. The W. H. Mullins Company executed the statue; the Peter-Burghard Stone Company executed the monument as a whole.

The inscription displays actions—all western battles—in which Tipton's Confederate soldiers participated. The monument faces east on Main Street. The statue, standing seven feet high, is made of sheet copper with an antique bronze finish, and surmounts a Westerly granite base. The monument weighs approximately fifty thousand pounds and surmounts a plinth twenty by twenty by five inches, and a base twelve by seven by seven feet.

During the ceremonies, the parade included a procession of dignitaries, veterans marching by companies, and the Brighton Band. At the morning's dedication of the monument, speeches were given, and a choir sang "America."

"Mrs. Boyd, as 'Confederacy,' Mrs. Black as Columbia and forty-five young ladies representing the States of the Union, sang '[The] Star Spangled Banner['].

Covington Courthouse Common Soldier Statue, Confederate

... Mrs. Henry Sherrod recited [the poem] the 'Conquered Banner.' Miss Sarah Hill then pulled the cord that unveiled the monument.... The band next struck up 'Dixie' and the monument stood in full view and was greeted with shouts from thousands of voices."

Dinners were served at tables on the courthouse square. "Green Williams of Company A Confederate Veterans of Memphis sang several songs of Stephen Foster." Three salutes were fired by the veteran company to close the events.

· A bronze plaque at the base of the monument reads as follows:

> IN THE LATE 1870'S, EFFORTS WERE MADE TO RAISE THE / FUNDS NECESSARY TO ERECT A TIPTON COUNTY CONFEDERATE
> MONUMENT. THIS PROJECT WAS COMPLETED ON MAY 29, 1895. / ON APRIL 29, 1995, A CENTENNIAL OBSERVANCE AND
> REDEDICATION CEREMONY WAS HELD CULMINATING A FOUR YEAR / REPAIR AND RESTORATION PROJECT OF THE STATUE.
> DEDICATED IN GRATEFUL REMEMBRANCE / OF THOSE WHO MADE CONTRIBU-TIONS TO PERPETUATE THE
> MEMORY OF THESE CONFEDERATE [SIC] SOLDIERS AND THEIR MEMORIAL.

· The inscription beginning "Nor Braver Bled For a Brighter Land" is taken from the poem "The Sword of Robert Lee," by the poet and Roman Catholic priest, Abram Joseph Ryan.

5.9.2 Subject: R. H. Munford Cemetery, Confederate, Stele
Location: US 51 in Covington   N 35 33 28 60 / W 89 39 16 56
Installed or dedicated: June 4, 1989
Medium: Granite
Monument is a granite stele.

Inscription

FLAG POLE / DEDICATED JUNE 4, 1989 / IN MEMORY OF / THE CONFEDERATE
VETERANS / BURIED IN THE / MUNFORD CEMETERY / BY THE MEMBERS OF /
SIMONTON-WILCOX CAMP NO. 257 / SONS OF CONFEDERTE VETERANS

The custom of decorating the graves of Confederate veterans at the R. H.
Munford Cemetery dates from at least 1869. Memorial ceremonies are still
observed on the grounds. Over one thousand "Tiptonians" are said to have
served in the Confederate Army.

5.9.3 Subject: General Nathan B. Forrest, Stele
Location: Veterans Memorial and Nature Center, 751 Bert Johnston Avenue,
38019   N 35 33 21 27 / W 89 39 39 70
Dedicated: September 20, 1998
Medium: Granite
Monument is a granite stele.

Inscription

LAST SPEECH OF GENERAL NATHAN BEDFORD FORREST / SEPTEMBER 22, 1876,
COVINGTON TENNESSEE
SOLDIERS OF THE SEVENTH TENNESSEE CAVALRY, LADIES AND GENTLEMEN: I NAME
THE SOLDIERS FIRST BECAUSE I LOVE THEM THE BEST. . . . COMRADES, THROUGH
THE YEARS OF BLOODSHED AND WEARY MARCHES YOU WERE TRIED AND TRUE
SOLDIERS. SO THROUGH THE YEARS OF PEACE YOU HAVE BEEN GOOD CITIZENS,
AND NOW THAT WE ARE AGAIN UNITED UNDER THE OLD FLAG, I LOVE IT AS I DID
IN THE DAYS OF MY YOUTH, AND I FEEL SURE THAT YOU LOVE IT ALSO. . . . IT HAS
BEEN THOUGHT BY SOME THAT OUR SOCIAL REUNIONS WERE WRONG, AND THAT
THEY WOULD BE HERALDED TO THE NORTH AS AN EVIDENCE THAT WE WERE AGAIN
READY TO BREAK OUT INTO CIVIL WAR. BUT I THINK THAT THEY ARE RIGHT AND
PROPER, AND WE WILL SHOW OUR COUNTRYMEN BY OUR CONDUCT AND DIGNITY
THAT BRAVE SOLDIERS ARE ALWAYS GOOD CITIZENS AND LAW-ABIDING AND LOYAL
PEOPLE.NATHAN BEDFORD FORREST

IN REMEMBRANCE / WE HAVE LIFTED UP THIS MEMORIAL TESTIMONY OF OUR /
ENDURING FIDELITY TO THE MEMORY OF GENERAL NATHAN / BEDFORD FORREST
AND THE MEN OF FORREST'S CAVALRY. WE / COMMEMORATE THEIR LEGACY OF
UNSURPASSED COURAGE AND / FORTITUDE. THIS MONUMENT IS HISTORY IN
GRANITE, AND IT / SYMBOLIZES THEIR RECORD OF VALOR, HEROIC SUFFERING AND
/ SACRIFICE. "THEY REST IN HONOR, MOURNED BY A BEREAVED / PEOPLE, HAVING
IN LIFE BEEN TRUE TO THEMSELVES, THEIR / PEOPLE, AND THEIR GOD." / LET THIS

MONUMENT INSPIRE PATRIOTISM, FAITH IN GOD / AND DEVOTION TO DUTY IN THE
COMING GENERATIONS OF OUR / PEOPLE. / ERECTED BY
[Roster of six contributing organizations] [2 names]
SEPTEMBER 20, 1998

Reunions of Tipton County Confederate soldiers were held from 1876 to 1941.
Forrest enlisted in the 7th as a private in June 1861. Forrest gave his last public
address to veterans of the 7th Tennessee Cavalry at Covington in 1876. He died
just over one year after giving this speech, at the age of fifty-one, on October
29, 1877.

- The monument, facing west, is on the grounds of the Tipton County
  Museum, Veterans Memorial and Nature Center, which opened in
  1998. Granite columns and benches display the names of Tipton County servicemen, including 236 Confederate soldiers.

Henderson County
Parker's Crossroads

5.10.1 Subject: Freeman's Battery, Confederate, Obelisk
Location: TR 22, off I-24, Exit 108; North Loop Trail   N 35 47 49 93 /
W 88 23 25 64
Dedicated: June 8, 2002
Medium: Granite
Monument is a shaft surmounting a base.

Inscription
[Relief of six cannonballs]
FREEMAN'S BATTERY / FORREST'S ARTILLERY
[SCV seal]
DEDICATED TO / FREEMAN'S BATTERY / FORREST'S ARTILLERY AND / SAMUEL L.
FREEMAN. / GEN. NATHAN BEDFORD / FORREST'S FIRST ARTILLERY / CAPTAIN
FREEMAN'S ARTILLERY / FOUGHT NEAR HERE / DURING THE BATTLE OF / PARKER'S
CROSSROADS / DEC. 31, 1862

[Inscribed image of cannon piece served by five artillerists]
GEN. N. B. FORREST OPENED THE BATTLE OF PARKER'S / CROSSROADS BY PLACING /
A 12-PDR. BRONZE FIELD HOWITZER UNDER THE COMMAND / OF SGT. NAT BAXTER
ON A KNOLL IN HICKS FIELD FOUR HUNDRED YARDS FROM THE ENEMY. . . .
ERECTED JUNE 8, 2002 BY FREEMAN'S BATTERY FORREST'S ARTILLERY / CAMP 1939.
SONS OF CONFEDERATE VETERANS.

At this site, two brigades of Union troops under the command of Brig. Gen.
Jeremiah C. Sullivan engaged Forrest's cavalry and artillery expedition during
the latter's withdrawal after a successful incursion into West Tennessee.
Forrest's troopers first engaged Col. Cyrus L. Dunham's brigade, pressed them
aggressively, and wrapped around their flanks, leading Forrest to call for their

Parker's Crossroads: Freeman's Battery, Obelisk, Confederate

surrender. However, the Confederates were compelled to suddenly reverse front and engage Col. John W. Fuller's brigade, then maneuver past Dunham's troops before withdrawing south to Lexington and across the Tennessee River. The battle was a close call for Forrest's command, but the Confederates fought off or eluded the converging forces and made their escape. Estimated casualties in the engagement: Union, 237; Confederate, 500.

5.10.2 Subject: Morton's Battery, Confederate, Obelisk
Location: North Loop Trail   N 35 47 46 64 / W 88 23 23 86
Installed or dedicated: December 27, 2007
Media: Bronze, granite
Monument is an obelisk surmounting a base.

Inscription

MORTON'S BATTERY / DECEMBER 27, 1862–MAY 9, 1865
MORTON'S BATTERY SERVED AT PARKER'S CROSSROADS ON DEC. 31, 1862. THE
ARTILLERY WAS PLACED AT CLOSE RANGE AND ORDERED BY FORREST TO "GIVE 'EM
HELL." . . . FREEMAN AND MORTON WERE CONSPICUOUS FOR THEIR . . . INTREPID
MANAGEMENT OF THEIR GUNS. . . . GEN. FORREST COMMENDED THE ACTION OF HIS
ARTILLERY, "CAPTAIN FREEMAN AND LIEUTENANT MORTON, OF OUR BATTERIES,
WITH ALL OF THEIR MEN, DESERVE ESPECIAL MENTION, KEEPING UP, AS THEY DID,
A CONSTANT FIRE FROM THEIR PIECES. . . ." AFTER CAPT. FREEMAN'S DEATH, APRIL
19, 1863, CAPT. MORTON LATER BECAME GEN. FORREST'S CHIEF OF ARTILLERY.
ERECTED DECEMBER 27, 2007 / BY / FREEMAN'S BATTERY FORREST'S ARTILLERY /
CAMP 1939 / SONS OF CONFEDERATE VETERANS

This is the other SCV tribute to Forrest's artillery, in this case Morton's Battery. The inscription notes Forrest's sagacity and the "coolness . . . intelligence" and courage of Freeman and Morton on the field here. The unit was first organized at Nashville, May 15, 1861, and organized as Freeman's Battery on July 20, 1862. Freeman was killed April 19, 1863, on the Lewisburg Pike near Franklin. The battery saw service throughout the war, was surrendered on April 26, 1865, and was paroled at Greensboro, North Carolina, May 1, 1865.

5.10.3 Subject: Union Burial Site, Stele
Location: Stop 7, Parker's Crossroads   N 35 47 18 77 / W 88 23 09 44
Installed or dedicated: 1994
Media: Granite, plastic
Monument is a granite stele.

Inscription
UNION / BURIAL / SITE

Period records indicate that thirty Union dead were interred at this site after the battle: seventeen from the 122nd Illinois VI, four from the 50th Illinois VI, three from the 39th Iowa VI, and one from the 7th Wisconsin, 7th Battery, Light Artillery. The dead were removed to the national cemetery at Corinth in 1867, but recent archaeological investigations revealed at least one soldier's remains or effects.

The Parker's Crossroads Battlefield Association erected this granite stele, standing thirty-six inches high, forty inches wide, with a plastic facing and inscription, in 1994.

Decatur County

5.11.1 Subject: Decaturville, Courthouse Stele, Confederate
Location: 22 West Main Street, 38329   N 35 35 04 54 / W 88 07 11 84
Dedicated: July 23, 1978
Medium: Granite
Monument is a granite triptych surmounting a base.

Inscription
[UDC seal]
THE CAPT. NATHANIEL A. WESSON / CHAPTER OF THE UNITED / DAUGHTERS OF THE CONFEDERACY / DEDICATES THIS MONUMENT TO THE MEMORY OF / OUR CONFEDERATE ANCESTORS WHO FOUGHT SO / VALIANTLY DURING THE WAR BETWEEN THE STATES / 1861–1865 / IN MEMORIAM / RUTH EVELYN DODSON TOWNSEND / 1938–1977 / OUR CHAPTER PRESIDENT / [34 names]

[51 names of UDC members]

Unveiled July 23, 1978, this is one of the few Civil War monuments erected anywhere during the 1970s, and the only bicentennial-era monument in Tennessee. However, the 1976 bicentennial had an influence on the monument movement: a revival of interest and consequent wave of monumentation began at about this time and continued into the twenty-first century.

The UDC's Captain Nathaniel A. Wesson Chapter No. 2396 was chartered on September 20, 1975, with fifty-one members in Marbury Hall of Parsons United Methodist Church. It remains active at this writing. The first meeting is described as a festive and solemn occasion: "Mrs. Ruth Dodson Townsend . . . opened the meeting with a greeting to those present. Rev. Willard Watson, Pastor, gave the invocation. Mrs. Doris Scott extended a cordial welcome to guests and members. Each member introduced their guest. . . . Entertainment was furnished by Mrs. Jessie Ruth Tiller, Mrs. Linda Watkins, Mrs. Joy Veazey and Mrs. Ruth Dodson Townsend. They sang three Civil War songs, 'Susanna', 'The Bonnie Blue Flag' and 'Dixie' with Mrs. Townsend at the piano."

Madison County

Jackson

5.12.1 Subject: Courthouse Common Soldier Statue, Confederate
Location: 100 East Main Street, 38301   N 35 36 51 07 / W 88 49 08 60
Installed or dedicated: 1888
Media: Limestone, marble
Monument is a figure of a Confederate soldier surmounting a shaft and base.

Inscription

[Front]
RESACA / BENTONVILLE / NASHVILLE / MURFREESBOROUGH [*SIC*] / MISSIONARY RIDGE / 6TH / REGT. / TO THE / CONFEDERATE DEAD / OF MADISON CO. ERECTED 1888. / J. T. WHITEHEAD / BUILDER.

NEW HOPE / FRANKLIN / JONESBOROUGH / CHICKAMAUGA / FORT DONALDSON [*SIC*] / FEDERAL RECORDS SHOW THEY HAD / FROM FIRST TO LAST TWO MILLION SIX HUN- / DRED THOUSAND MEN IN SERVICE; WHILE THE / CONFEDERATES ALL TOLD HAD BUT LITTLE / OVER SIX HUNDRED THOUSAND.

SHILOH / ATLANTA / KENNESAW / PERRYVILLE / BRICES CROSS ROADS HISTORY IS AN IMPARTIAL WITNESS / TO ITS PHILOSOPHIC JUDGEMENT WE / COMMIT THE MOTIVES AND DEEDS / OF OUR IMMORTAL DEAD.

SELMA / BELMONT / DIBRELL'S RIDGE / HARRISBURG / PARKERS CROSS ROADS MADISON COUNTY / FURNISHED THE SOUTH / MORE SOLDIERS THAN / SHE HAD VOTERS.

This monument, of much-weathered white marble on a limestone base, stands on the northeast corner of the courthouse grounds and faces north. It was erected by "popular subscription and the Musidora McGorry Chapter No. 5, UDC, which erected a commemorative urn adjacent to this monument."

The inscription offers the acknowledgement that the Federals—"They"—won the victory, but also invokes the postwar conviction that overwhelming numbers and resources defeated the Confederacy. The inscription beginning "History is an impartial witness" is unclear. "Commit" may have been intended as "commend," for example.

Jackson: Madison County Courthouse Common Soldier Statue, Confederate

The 6th Tennessee Infantry was organized at Camp Beauregard, Jackson, on May 23, 1861, and fought in the engagements of the western theater from Belmont to Bentonville, including Shiloh, Corinth, Stones River, Atlanta, Franklin, and Nashville.

The statue stands nine by two by two feet on a base thirty-five by nine by twelve feet. The sculptor is unknown. J. T. Whitehead was the contractor.

5.12.2 Subject: Courthouse UDC Stele
Location: N 35 36 51 25 / W 88 49 08 10
Installed or dedicated: July 1905
Medium: Cast iron
Monument is an urn, in black, with gold lettering.

Inscription

PRESENTED BY / MUSIDORA MCGORRY, CHAPTER / U.D.C. NO 5 / JULY 1905

The Musidora McGorry Chapter of the UDC is no longer active, but they left this urn and the courthouse monument nearby as legacies. The reference to voters on the third (rear) side of the courthouse monument was inscribed before women's suffrage, of course, and implies that the wartime generation is the role model for generations of "true" Confederates to come. It is certainly true that women were crucial to the work of the monument movement and the postwar recovery of the South.

5.12.3 Subject: Salem Battlefield Stele
Location: 379 White Fern Road, Beech Bluff, 38313   N 35 37 47 85 /
W 88 45 53 66
Installed or dedicated: n.a.
Media: Marble, plastic
Monument is a marble shaft in the shape of a tree trunk.

Inscription

1861 / CSA / 1865 / LARGE OAK TREE
IT WAS AT THIS POINT / ON DEC. 19, 1862, THAT / COL. ENGELMANN (US) /
AMBUSHED A COLUMN / OF FORREST'S CAV- / ALRY (US). THEY WERE / FORCED
TO RETREAT / OUT OF RIFLE RANGE / AFTER SUFFERING / A SUBSTANTIAL LOSS.
/ THEIR ARTILLERY / WAS BROUGHT UP / AND SHELLED THE / FEDERALS UNTIL /
THEY WITHDREW.

Apart from the paving of nearby Cotton Grove Road and the commemoration
sites, the landscape of the Salem battlefield remains essentially unchanged
from the time the battle occurred in 1862. Federal troops posted behind the
crest of the ridges on both sides of the road near this site ambushed Forrest's
cavalry as the latter moved west on Cotton Grove Road toward Jackson. The
initial volley killed or wounded several men and horses.

5.12.4 Subject: Battlefield Shaft, CSA
Installed or dedicated: circa 1994
Media: Marble, plastic
Monument is a four-sided shaft surmounting a base.

Inscription

1861 / CSA / 1865 / BATTLE OF / SALEM CEMETERY / DEC. 19, 1862
CONFEDERATE / GEN. NATHAN B. FORREST / COMMANDING COL. B. J. BIFFLE'S CA- /
VALRY BATTALION OF / ABOUT 400 MEN. COL. T. G. WOODWARD'S TWO / CO.'S OF
KY CAVALRY / CAPT. S. L. FREEMAN'S ARTILLERY. . . . THE FEDERALS WERE FORCED
BACK TOWARD / JACKSON. / THIS MEMORIAL STONE IS DEDICATED TO THE /
GALLANT MEN OF THE CONFEDERATE ARMY.
ERECTED BY / J. B. INGRAM CAMP / SONS OF CONFEDERATE VETERANS

Approximately fifteen hundred men were engaged in the four-hour battle at
Salem Cemetery on December 19, 1862. These monuments offer detail and a
tribute to both sides, an equality that is not found on any other Tennessee
Civil War battlefield. Neither side gained a decisive advantage in the fighting.
Forrest's command was deterred from entering Jackson but was not deterred
from moving west and continuing its mission. Confederate losses are estimated at sixty-five killed, wounded, or missing; Federal losses: two killed, six
wounded.

The John Ingram Camp, SCV, maintains these grounds. Restored facilities—entrance, battlefield map, and flagpole—were dedicated in December 1994, on the 130th anniversary of the battle.

5.12.5 Subject: Battlefield Shaft, Union
Installed or dedicated: December 19, 2000
Media: Marble, plastic
Monument is a four-sided shaft surmounting a base.

Inscription

USA
THIS MEMORIAL STONE IS DEDICATED / TO THE GALLANT MEN OF THE / FEDERAL ARMY / AND THOSE KILLED IN ACTION / HERE. / BATTLE OF SALEM CEMETERY / DECEMBER 19, 1862 PVT. ELISHA STOUT / CO. G. 61ST ILL. INFANTRY / CORP. ADAM KEHL / CO. A 11TH ILL CAVALRY
ERECTED BY / SULTANA CAMP NO. 1 / SONS OF UNION VETERANS / GERMANTOWN, TN. / & / SALEM CEMETERY BATTLEFIELD ASSOC. / JACKSON, TN. / DECEMBER 19, 2000

Part of a dual tribute with an adjacent Confederate counterpart, this is the only Union monument on a battlefield on private property in West Tennessee.

5.12.6 Subject: Denmark, Denmark Church, Cemetery Stele
Location: 2799 Denmark Jackson Road, 38391   N 35 31 58 03 / W 89 00 03 08
Installed or dedicated: 1994
Media: Granite, steel
Monument is a shaft surmounting a base.

Inscription

DENMARK DANES / 1861–1865
ON 15 MAY 1861, ONE HUNDRED / AND FORTY SIX MEN SWORE / ALLEGIANCE TO THE SOUTH. / THIS UNIT BECAME KNOWN AS / CO. K, 6TH TENN. INF. REG., C.S.A. / "THE DENMARK DANES."
ONLY FORTY OF THE ORIGINAL / COMPANY SURVIVED THE FOUR / LONG YEARS OF WAR. THESE / MEN RETURNED HOME TO FIND / THEIR COMMUNITY IN A STATE / OF TOTAL DESTRUCTION.
MAY THEY REST IN PEACE

The "Denmark Danes," organized by Dr. John B. Ingram Jr. on May 23, 1861, mustered in as Company K of the 6th Tennessee Infantry under the leadership of Ingram, commander of the Denmark Danes during the war. Ingram's grave is in the church cemetery, as are the bodies of at least two soldiers killed in the Battle of Britton's Lane.

The Denmark Presbyterian Church was built in 1854. The interior still has graffiti left by Union prisoners of war taken after the Battle of Britton's Lane. The church is on the Estonallie Trail, once the main stage route to Memphis.

Union and Confederate troops frequented the site, and the 20th and 30th Illinois Infantry camped near the church on the eve of the Battle of Britton's Lane.

5.12.7 Subject: Britton's Lane, Battlefield Obelisk
Location: Off TR 18, Marker Deon, TR and Collins Road   N 35 29 24 31 / W 89 57 28 42
Unveiled: September 1, 1897
Media: Granite, marble
Monument is a marble obelisk.

Inscription

C.S.A. / ERECTED BY / JOHN INGRAM / BIVOUAC, / SEPT. 1, 1897, / TO HONOR AN / UNKNOWN NUMBER OF / CONFEDERATE / SOLDIERS, / WHO FELL IN BATTLE / ON THIS FIELD, / SEPT. 1, 1862 / AND MANY OF WHOM / ARE BURIED HERE. / BRITTON LANE.

The Battle of Britton's Lane was fought on September 1, 1862, five miles east of Denmark. Here a Confederate cavalry brigade commanded by Col. Frank C. Armstrong (acting brigadier general) engaged Federal forces commanded by Col. S. Dennis—two regiments of infantry, two cavalry troops, and a battery of artillery.

A four-hour engagement ensued. Confederates made several unsuccessful charges across open fields against Federal troops entrenched on higher ground. Though pressed hard, the Federal forces ultimately held the field and buried the dead, as noted above, and Armstrong withdrew.

Historian James D. Brewer notes that the results were indecisive. Armstrong had harassed Federal troops and disrupted Federal supply lines but took heavy casualties on this field: at least one hundred men were killed in action compared to Federal casualties of eight killed, fifty wounded, and fifty captured.

5.12.8 Subject: Britton's Lane, 7th Tennessee Cavalry, CSA, Stele
Location: N 35 29 23 33 / W 89 57 29 44
Installed or dedicated: 1992
Media: Bronze, granite
Monument is a plaque emplaced on a granite stele, surmounting a base.

Inscription

CONFEDERATE STATES OF AMERICA
THIS MONUMENT IS DEDICATED TO THE MEMORY OF THE / GALLANT MEN OF THE 7TH TENNESSEE CAVALRY, C.S.A., / COMANDED BY COL. WILLIAM H. JACKSON, AND TO THESE / MEN OF THE 7TH WHO FELL SEPTEMBER 1, 1862, AT THE BATTLE / OF BRITTON LANE IN DEFENSE OF THE CONFEDERACY, THE STATE / OF TENNESSEE, THEIR HOMELAND, BELIEFS, AND PRINCIPLES.
[Roster of 12 names in 2 columns]

Brownsville: Haywood County Courthouse Common Soldier Statue, Confederate

The 7th Tennessee Cavalry, which still claims an existence as a memorial unit in this inscription, is praised for their "Defense of the Confederacy, the State of Tennessee, their Homeland, Beliefs, and Principles." Another monument to the 7th is at Covington (5.9.3), which commemorates Forrest's speech to a postwar reunion of the regiment.

Haywood County

5.13.1 Subject: Brownsville, Courthouse Common Soldier Statue, Confederate
Location: 111 North Washington Avenue, 38012   N 35 35 37 62 / W 89 15 44 00
Dedicated: January 19, 1909
Medium: Granite
Monument is a statue of a common soldier surmounting a shaft and base.

Inscription
[CS national flag wrapped around shaft]
[Rifle in relief, with canteen and bayonet]
C.S.A.
TO THE CONFEDERATE / DEAD OF HAYWOOD COUNTY

[Relief of crossed swords]
C.S.A.

BELMONT, SHILOH, PERRYVILLE. / MURFREESBORO, CHICKAMAUGA. / ATLANTA,
FRANKLIN, CORINTH. / BRICES CROSS ROADS, OKALONA. / HARRISBURG, UNION
CITY, FORT PILLOW. / JOHNSONVILLE, VICKSBURG.

[Relief of cannon barrel with crossed rammers]
C.S.A.

TO THE FAITHFUL / CONFEDERATE WOMEN / OF HAYWOOD COUNTY, / 1861–1865

[Relief of anchor set in capstan, with stacked cannonballs]
C.S.A.

CONFEDERATE SERVICE / SIX HUNDRED THOUSAND / MEN, / FEDERAL SERVICE /
TWO MILLION SIX HUNDRED / THOUSAND MEN

Erected at a cost of $2,500 by the Hiram A. Bradford Camp No. 426, UCV and
the N. B. Forrest Chapter, UDC, this monument stands in front of the 1928
courthouse. Like the Jackson courthouse monument, the inscription on the
Brownsville monument invokes the postwar "lost cause" conviction that overwhelming numbers and resources defeated the Confederacy. The tribute to
women—Confederate Women of Haywood County—is uncommon but not
unique. The relief of an anchor set in a capstan is an unusual nautical feature,
but it may be a reference to an anchor as a symbol of redemption and hope
cited in Hebrews 6:19 ("Which hope we have as an anchor of the soul, both
sure and steadfast").

Hardin County

5.14.1 Subject: Savannah, Courthouse Shaft, Confederate
Location: West Main and Adams Streets, 38372   N 35 13 30 06 / W 88 15 02 34
Installed or dedicated: 1995
Medium: Granite
Monument is a four-sided shaft with crown, surmounting a plinth and base.

Inscription

ERECTED 1995 BY THE / BATTLE OF SHILOH CAMP #1454 / SONS OF CONFEDERATE
VETERANS

THIS MONUMENT ERECTED IN HONOR OF / THE GALLANT CONFEDERATE SOLDIERS
OF / HARDIN COUNTY WHO FOUGHT, DIED / AND SUFFERED DURING THE WAR
BETWEEN / THE STATES 1861–1865 / SACRED IS THE MEMORY OF THE / MEN AND
WOMEN OF HARDIN / COUNTY FOR THE SACRIFICES / MADE IN DEFENDING THE
HOMELAND / NOR SHALL YOUR GLORY / BE FORGOT.

POOR IS A NATION THAT / HAS NO HEROES / SHAMEFUL IS A NATION THAT HAS
HEROES AND FORGETS THEM. / NO NATION CAN LONG SURVIVE / WITHOUT PRIDE
IN ITS TRADITIONS.

CSA / CONFEDERATE UNITS FORMED IN HARDIN COUNTY / *[Roster]*

Hardin County voted against Tennessee's referendum on secession in 1861, according to historian Vicki Betts, and at least some residents of Savannah welcomed Union troops when they entered the city on March 8, 1862, one month before the battle of Shiloh. The cavalry units cited served in partisan roles with Forrest's and Chalmers' commands; the 1st, 34th (a.k.a. 4th), and 23rd Tennessee Infantry served with the Army of Tennessee. However, the SCV offered this courthouse shaft as a strong, even fervent manifesto in honor of the "Gallant Confederate Soldiers . . . of Hardin County."

Hardeman County
Bolivar

5.15.1 Subject: Bolivar, Courthouse Shaft and Urn, Confederate
Location: 100 North Main Street, 38008   N 35 15 23 03 / W 88 59 14 76
Installed and dedicated: 1873
Media: Limestone, marble
Monument is an obelisk covered with drapery and surmounted by an urn, the whole set on a tiered base.

Inscription
[Front]
[Relief of six draped flags. Three muskets pointed up, one drum]
TO THE / CONFEDERATE DEAD OF / HARDEMAN COUNTY TENNESSEE.
[Bronze plaque addition:]
ERECTED JANUARY 1873 / [Founder's mark] L.H. & J.B. FULLER / ST. LOUIS, MO.

[Relief of two flags, unidentified, crossed sword and musket pointed down]
IN HOPE OF / A JOYFUL RESURRECTION

[Relief of six tents, one flag pole]
"THOUGH MEN DESERVE, / THEY MAY NOT WIN SUCCESS, / THE BRAVE WILL HONOR
THE BRAVE, / VANQUISHED NONE THE LESS."

[Relief of one cannon, four unfurled flags]
HARDEMAN COUNTY / ERECTS / THIS MONUMENT TO / THE MEMORY OF / HER
SONS, / FALLEN IN THE SERVICE OF / THE CONFEDERATE STATES.

This is almost certainly the oldest courthouse monument in Tennessee. A proposal for the monument was published in the Bolivar *Bulletin* on April 28, 1866. A monument committee formed shortly thereafter. The record of the preamble of the monument committee reads in part,

> In as much as we deem it a sacred duty of the living to pay all respect to
> the memory of those who fell in the late struggle, giving up their lives in a
> cause which was ours as well as their own; and as many of the purest and
> best citizens of Hardeman County perished at the post of duty and now
> rest in graves unknown and unmarked, we believe it due from us to each

Bolivar: Hardeman County Courthouse Shaft and Urn, Confederate

and every one of them to transmit to posterity some testimonial of our appreciation of their sacrifice.

Approval for a courthouse site was eventually granted, but fund-raising was difficult and uneven in the economic distress of the time, and it was not erected until January 1873, at a cost of $3,000. As with other monument projects, the women succeeded the men in the task. Albert T. McNeal, a Confederate veteran and postwar attorney who wrote a history of the monument, observed that "I must say, in again rendering tribute to the women, that . . . as much [or more money] was raised by the ladies and the young girls."

Today the marble is much weathered on this decorated obelisk, which stands on the south side of the courthouse erected in 1868. McNeal observes that "individual names were not put upon the monument. The omission was deliberate however, and not especially on account of the expense. It was thought best not to do so, as some might be omitted inadvertently and there would have been distinctions in position not desirable."

- The expression "In Hope of a Joyful Resurrection" is common to English poetic epitaphs and may derive from 2 Corinthians 4:11.

Davis Bridge

5.15.2 Subject: Battlefield Stele
Location: South of TR 57, trail clearing west of Hatchie River, near Pocahontas, 38061   N 35 01 40 62 / W 88 47 49 84
Installed or dedicated: October 5, 1991
Medium: Marble

Inscription
IN MEMORY OF / THE CONFEDERATE / SOLDIERS WHO / DIED AND WERE / BURIED ON OR / NEAR THIS SITE / OCT 5 1862

5.15.3 Subject: Battlefield Shaft
Location: N 35 01 41 10 / W 88 47 49 50
Installed or dedicated: October 5, 1991
Medium: Marble
Monument is a stele.

Inscription
[SCV seal]
IN MEMORY OF THE MEN / WHO FOUGHT HERE / OCTOBER 5, 1862 / BATTLE OF DAVIS BRIDGE / POOR IS THE NATION THAT / HAS NO HEROES / SHAMEFUL IS THE NATION / THAT HAS THEM AND FORGETS. / CONFEDERATE

CSA

DUTY IS THE / SUBLIMEST WORD / IN OUR LANGUAGE. / DO YOUR DUTY IN / ALL THINGS. YOU / CANNOT DO MORE. / YOU SHOULD NEVER / WISH TO DO LESS. ROBERT E. LEE

CSA

After its defeat in the battle of Corinth, Confederate troops of the Army of West Tennessee under Maj. Gen. Earl Van Dorn moved west and confronted Maj. Gen. Edward O. C. Ord's Union troops at Davis Bridge over the Hatchie River. A battle for the bridge ensued on October 5, 1862, and continued all day. The Federals turned aside the advance of the Confederates when they crossed the river; the Confederates in turn held off the attacking Union forces upon their advance. Eventually, the Confederates withdrew and crossed the Hatchie River at Crum's Mill, six miles south.

- The Davis Bridge Memorial Association purchased 4.5 acres on the west bank of the Hatchie River in 1987. Today 839 acres of the battlefield are administered by the State of Tennessee as Big Hill Pond State Park and as a division of the Shiloh National Military Park.

- Archives in the Washington and Lee University contest the attribution of the quotation to R. E. Lee, although they do not deny the truth of the claim or the consonance with Lee's ethos, and note that after Lee's death there was found among his effects a sheet of paper on which he had written these words: "There is a true glory, and a true honor; the glory of duty done, the honor of integrity of principle."

Shelby County, Including Memphis
Memphis

5.16.1 Subject: Jefferson Davis, Statue
Location: Mississippi River Park, formerly Confederate Park, west side of North Front Street, between Court Street and Jefferson Avenue, 38103
N 35 08 48 88 / W 90 03 14 26
Installed: 1963; dedicated: October 4, 1964; removed: December 2017
Media: Bronze, granite
Monument is a full-length sculpted figure of Jefferson Davis surmounting a base.

Inscription
[Front]
JEFFERSON DAVIS / PRESIDENT OF / THE CONFEDERATE STATES / OF AMERICA / 1861–1865 / BEFORE THE WAR BETWEEN THE STATES / HE SERVED WITH DISTINCTION / AS A UNITED STATES CONGRESSMAN / AND TWICE AS A UNITED STATES SENATOR. / HE ALSO SERVED AS SECRETARY OF WAR / OF THE UNITED STATES. / HE WAS A TRUE AMERICAN PATRIOT

ERECTED BY / THE JEFFERSON DAVIS / MEMORIAL ASSOCIATION / OFFICERS [4 names] / THE UNITED DAUGHTERS OF THE CONFEDERACY / THE SONS OF THE CONFEDERATE VETERANS / THE CHILDREN OF THE CONFEDERACY / FRIENDS AND PATRIOTIC CITIZENS

After the war and his imprisonment, Davis lived in Memphis from 1869 to 1871, while serving as president of the Carolina Life Insurance Company. The figure of Davis stands with his right foot forward and his right arm raised above his head, gesturing east, perhaps in the direction of his home at Court Avenue between Third and Fourth Streets, arguably toward the nation he served as president. He holds a document in his left hand, perhaps the US Constitution, not unlike the statue of Davis on Monument Avenue, Richmond.

Jefferson Davis, Statue

This centennial-era commemoration unabashedly declares that Davis was "A True American Patriot."

The sculpture stands eight feet, six inches high. The Crone Monument Company served as fabricator; George E. Crone was the designer. Aldo Pero, the sculptor, also sculpted a bust of Robert E. Lee that stands in Fort Myers, Florida.

- A Memphis City Council resolution changed the name of Confederate Park to Memphis Park; Jefferson Davis Park to Mississippi River Park; and Nathan Bedford Forrest Park to Health Sciences Park. The monument was removed—during the night—in December 2017.

- On the west side of the park is a granite bench dedicated to the 154th Tennessee Infantry of the Confederate army. A 1909 bronze stele with a Confederate history stands nearby (N 35 08 47 52 / W 90 03 15 92). This stele describes the fortification of Memphis and—obliquely—the fall of the city to Union forces. The fall of Memphis is not mentioned; neither is the defeat of Confederate forces.

CONFEDERATE HISTORY OF MEMPHIS
THIS BLUFF WAS FORTIFIED BY GEN. PILLOW IN MAY 1862. THIRTYSEVEN
[SIC] COMPANIES WERE EQUIPPED HERE FOR THE CONFEDERATE SERVICE.
THE CONFEDERATE RAM, ARKANSAS, ONE OF THE FIRST IRON CLAD
BATTLESHIPS IN THE NAVY, WAS BUILT AND PARTIALLY ARMORED HERE, . . .
[A] CONFEDERATE FLEET OF 8 BOATS PROTECTED ONLY BY COTTON BALES . . .
GALLANTLY RESISTED [AN] ATTACK OF [A FEDERAL FLEET OF] 6 ARMORED

GUN BOATS, 4 RAMS AND 20 MORTAR BOATS. . . . THE ENGAGEMENT . . . WAS
THE FIRST BATTLE BETWEEN STEAM RAMS IN HISTORY. / AT DAWN ON AUGUST
21, 1864, GENERAL N. B. FORREST MADE HIS GRAND STRATEGIC RAID INTO
MEMPHIS. . . . AFTER SPENDING 2 HOURS HERE, FORREST CUT THE WIRES AND
LEFT THE CITY TAKING 500 PRISONERS, AND LARGE QUANTITIES OF SUPPLIES.
. . . . PRESIDENT DAVIS WAS A RESIDENT OF THIS CITY FOR 9 YEARS AFTER HIS
RELEASE FROM PRISON.
PALMS FOR THE SOUTHERN SOLDIER; / CROWNS FOR THE VETERAN'S HEAD, /
AND LOYAL LOVE AND HONOR / FOR OUR CONFEDERATE DEAD
ERECTED BY / CONFEDERATE DAMES / TYLER CHAPTER 1909

5.16.2 Subject: Capt. J. Harvey Mathes, Bust
Location: Confederate Park   N 35 08 48 13 / W 90 03 15 00
Installed or dedicated: 1908; removed: December 2017
Media: Bronze, granite
Monument is a bust of a likeness of Mathes in a double-breasted military coat.

Inscription
CAPT / J. HARVEY / MATHES / 37TH TENN. / C.S.A.

J. Harvey Mathes (1841–1902) was born in East Tennessee. He was wounded
and lost a leg during the Atlanta campaign on July 22, 1864. He survived his
wounds to become a journalist, editor, state legislator, and author of a biography of Nathan B. Forrest. The monument was sponsored by the Harvey Mathes
Chapter of the UDC. In the 1911 book *Historic Southern Monuments*, they call
the monument "our tribute to his memory, bearing with it the love and devotion of faithful hearts. Many lofty shafts erected to fallen heroes bear testimony of no greater merit than should be accorded to our own Harvey Mathes,
a gallant soldier, a loyal friend, a Christian gentleman."

- Upon his death, Mathes was interred at Elmwood Cemetery. His body
  was later reinterred in a family plot at Forest Hill Cemetery.
- Frederick C. Hibbard was sculptor; the founder is unknown. The
  sculpture is three feet by two feet by fifteen inches; the base is four by
  two by two feet. The monument was removed—during the night—in
  December 2017.

5.16.3 Subject: General Nathan B. Forrest, Equestrian Statue
Location: Health Sciences Park, formerly known as Forrest Park, Madison at
Dunlap near the University of Tennessee Health Science Center
N 35 08 21 00 / W 90 02 05 32
Dedicated: May 16, 1905; removed: December 2017
Media: Bronze, granite, marble
Monument is an equestrian statue surmounting a base.

Equestrian Monument of Nathan Bedford Forrest in Memphis

Inscription

[Front]

NATHAN·BEDFORD·FORREST. / MDCCCXXI·MDCCCLXXVII

THOSE HOOF BEATS DIE NOT UPON FAME'S CRIMSONED SOD, / BUT WILL RING
THROUGH HER SONG AND HER STORY; / HE FOUGHT LIKE A TITAN AND STRUCK LIKE
A GOD, / AND HIS DUST IS OUR ASHES OF GLORY.
VIRGINIA FRAZER BOYLE

1904. / ERECTED BY HIS COUNTRYMEN IN HONOR / OF THE MILITARY GENIUS OF /
LIEUTENANT GENERAL NATHAN BEDFORD FORREST. / CONFEDERATE STATES ARMY.
/ 1861–1865.

The only equestrian statue of a Civil War soldier in Tennessee is to this soldier, planter, businessman, politician, and slave dealer who was, according to
General William T. Sherman, "the most remarkable man our Civil War produced on either side." Forrest—who stood six foot five—sits astride his horse.
He wears a military uniform. His right hand holds a hat and rests on his hip;
his left hand holds the reins. A saber hangs from the saddle on his left side.

Forrest transcended the times in which he lived. His is the only equestrian statue in Tennessee apart from that for President Andrew Jackson, in
Nashville. Forrest had a sixth grade education and entered the war as a private,
but he ended the war with the rank of lieutenant general. General Ulysses S.
Grant considered Nathan Bedford Forrest "about the ablest cavalry general in
the South." He had no formal military training, but he is said to have possessed
an instinctual feel for maneuvering and tactics, and he was an inspiring leader.

Forrest was the first Grand Wizard of the Ku Klux Klan, but by some reputable accounts it was more of an insurgent movement during the Reconstruction
era, not the hateful violent white supremacy group of the twentieth and

twenty-first centuries. There is no assurance that the postwar Nathan Bedford Forrest would have condoned the behavior of groups whose actions took place decades after his death. On the other hand, condemnations of Forrest are many and not uninformed, including one reputable contemporary historian who labels him as the "psychopathic villain of Fort Pillow, a near illiterate ante-bellum slave-trading millionaire, and the first head of the original Ku Klux Klan."

He is remembered for his military tactics and leadership as well as his association with the Ku Klux Klan. His courage and his genius for tactics and leadership were evident at many battlefields—Fort Donelson, Shiloh, Chickamauga, Brice's Cross Roads, Tupelo, Memphis, Murfreesboro, and Nashville. However, the massacre at Fort Pillow took place under his overall command and remains a controversial and provocative part of his legacy. In fact, his legacy is part of twenty-first century politics.

The monument is 12 by 10.5 by 3.5 feet; the upper base is 5 by 11 by 4 feet; the lower base is 2 by 13 by 6 feet. The sculpture is bronze; the base is Tennessee marble. The height of the equestrian statue is 22 feet. The height of the bronze figure is 5 feet, and it weighs almost five tons. The monument was removed—during the night—in December 2017.

- Forrest lived in Memphis and also fought here during the war. Cavalry under his command raided Union-held Memphis on August 21, 1864. Moving at dawn and under the cover of fog, Forrest took the garrison by surprise and caused a great stir, but he was obliged to withdraw after several hours.

- The project for the monument was first proposed in 1886. A monument association was organized in 1891, a design was accepted, and the order was given to the sculptor, Charles H. Niehaus. The Republic Marble Company served as the contractor. The Forrest Monument Association donated $20,000 of the total cost of the project of some $35,000.

- Elaborate ceremonies accompanied the unveiling of the monument. The parade included surviving officers and common soldiers who rode with him. Judge J. P. Young, "one of Forrest's old troopers," was master of ceremonies. In opening the proceedings he said in part: "No one who did not ride with Forrest can have so keen an appreciation of the personal qualities of the man as those who were actually under his direct command, and who, from daily, hourly observation, witnessed his fertility of resource, his vehemence in battle and his soulful tenderness toward the stricken soldier, whether friend or foe."

- Forrest and his wife are buried here. They were originally interred in Elmwood Cemetery nearby but were reinterred here on November

11, 1904. On the base in front are two granite headstones installed in 2002, which replaced the originals:

NATHAN BEDFORD / FORREST
JULY 13, 1821 / OCTOBER 29, 1877

· To the right of Forrest is the grave of his wife:

MARY A. / FORREST / OCTOBER 24, 1826

Elmwood Cemetery

5.16.4 Subject: Confederate, Obelisk
Location: 824 South Dudley Street, 38104   N 35 07 23 39 / W 90 01 36 26
Dedicated: June 5, 1878
Media: Granite, marble
Monument is a three-tiered column.

Inscription
[Front]
CONFEDERATE DEAD.

ILLIS VICTORIAM NON IMMORTALI- / TATEM FATA NEGAVERUNT.

The grounds of Elmwood Cemetery include "Confederate Soldiers Rest," which inters more than one thousand Confederate soldiers and veterans. Others are buried throughout Elmwood. The first burial took place on June 17, 1861, the last in 1940.

The 1911 book *Historic Southern Monuments* refers to the central obelisk as "simple, lofty and beautiful" and notes that it is under the care of the "Confederate Historical Association, assisted by the Ladies' Memorial

Elmwood Cemetery, Obelisk, Confederate

Association." The cemetery grounds were donated at the beginning of the war for the "purpose of burying, free of charge, all soldiers who may die honorably in defense of our liberties." Memphis remained under Confederate control only until June 1862, so many of the dead are veterans who survived the war.

Of the development of the presiding monument, *Historic Southern Monuments* observes that

> Soon after the war all over the wrecked and desolated South the women again took matters into their own hands, and began to agitate the question of raising suitable monuments to commemorate the dust of our heroes which they had gathered into hallowed spots. . . . What the noble women of Memphis, Tenn., have done in this respect, is but an example of what the women everywhere have done, or are doing. . . . . a splendid gray granite shaft rises to heaven bearing the significant inscription on its face "Illis Victoriam non Immortalitatem, Frater, negaverunt," and the simple dedication "To our Confederate dead." This granite shaft cost the sum of $9,000. All this work was accomplished and paid for through the ardent patriotism, business enterprise, and executive ability of the women of that city.

· One Union general, Tennessee Brig. Gen. William J. Smith, is buried at Elmwood. Among the Confederate generals buried here: Maj. Gen. James P. Anderson; Brig. Gen. William H. Carroll; Brig. Gen. James R. Chalmers; Brig. Gen. William M. Gardner; Brig. Gen. George W. Gordon; Brig. Gen. Elkanah B. Greer; Brig. Gen. William Y. C. Humes; Brig. Gen. Gideon J. Pillow; Brig. Gen. Robert V. Richardson; Brig. Gen. Preston Smith; Brig. Gen. Alfred J. Vaughan, Jr.; Brig. Gen. Lucius M. Walker. Also buried here is wartime CS governor Isham G. Harris. Union soldiers buried at Elmwood during the war were moved to Memphis National Cemetery in 1868.

Memphis National Cemetery

5.16.5 Subject: State of Minnesota, Common Soldier Statue, Union
Location: 3568 Townes Avenue, 38122   N 35 10 29 35 / W 88 56 20 22
Dedicated: September 23, 1916
Media: Bronze, granite
Monument is a statue of a Union soldier surmounting a granite base.

Inscription

[Relief of crossed laurel leaves]
ERECTED A.D. 1916 BY THE / STATE OF MINNESOTA / IN MEMORY OF HER SOLDIERS / HERE BURIED WHO LOST THEIR LIVES / IN THE SERVICE OF THE UNITED STATES / IN THE WAR FOR THE / PRESERVATION OF THE UNION. / A.D. 1861–1865

State of Minnesota, Common Soldier Statue, Union, Memphis National Cemetery

The monument recognizes the service and mortal sacrifice of Minnesota soldiers "In the War for the Preservation of the Union." The 189 soldiers interred here are from the 3rd, 4th, 5th, 6th, 7th, 9th, and 10th Minnesota Infantry.

The monument was erected by the Minnesota Monument Commission. Native Minnesotan John K. Daniels was the sculptor. The bronze sculpture, standing sixteen feet high, depicts a Union soldier, head bowed, with his cap held against his heart and a hand resting atop his rifle, barrel pointing downward in a funereal position. The committee asked for a "Statue of a young Union soldier of moderate heroic size in U.S. standard bronze." Minnesota granite was stipulated as a medium, but the monument committee report noted that "a harsh winter and an unusual quantity of snow, led to the use Vermont granite instead." At the dedication, prayers were offered, speeches were given, and "veterans on both sides in the Civil War took part in a patriotic spirit." A highlight of the ceremonies was the singing of "Danny Boy" by Miss Elsa A. Gerber.

- Several military hospitals were established in Memphis after its fall to Union forces. A thirty-two-acre site was established as a cemetery northeast of the city. After the war, Memphis was selected as a central location for reinterments from battlefield, camp, and hospital cemeteries in West Tennessee. Memphis has the second-largest group of unknown dead interred in any national cemetery. It also inters many of the victims of the explosion of the SS *Sultana*.

- An identical monument by Daniels stands in Andersonville National Cemetery. Civil War monuments by Daniels also stand at Nashville National Cemetery (4.22.13) and Jefferson Barracks National Cemetery, St. Louis, Missouri.

State of Illinois, Common Soldier Statue, Union, Memphis National Cemetery

5.16.6 Subject: State of Illinois, Common Soldier Statue, Union
Location: N 35 10 22 44 / W 88 56 17 74
Dedicated: October 15, 1929
Media: Bronze, granite
Monument is figure of a Union soldier, surmounting a sarcophagus and base.

Inscription

THIS MONUMENT ERECTED BY / THE STATE OF ILLINOIS IN 1928 / TO THE GLORIOUS
MEMORY OF / THE SOLDIERS OF ILLINOIS WHO / FOUGHT IN THE CIVIL WAR /
1861–1865 / TO THE HEROES OF ILLINOIS /
[Bronze medallion: state seal of Illinois]
[A bronze tablet reads:]

Inscription

WHEN PRESIDENT LINCOLN CALLED FOR VOLUNTEERS TO DEFEND THE LIFE OF
OUR IMPERILED NATION, THESE VALIANT SONS OF ILLINOIS, TOGETHER, WITH
OTHER HEROES, OFFERED THEIR LIVES WITH PATRIOTISM UNSURPASSED. WITH
UNFLINCHING BRAVERY THEY FOUGHT THE BLOODY BATTLES OF THE GREAT
CIVIL WAR FOR UNION AND LIBERTY. UPON THEM THEREFORE A GRATEFUL STATE
BESTOWS THE CROWN OF UNDYING AFFECTION AND THE LAUREL OF VICTORY.
[Bronze medallion of the seal of the United States]

This sarcophagus by sculptor Leon Hermant of Chicago is in Section B of the
cemetery and consists of a pink-and-black granite base and a sarcophagus,
surmounted by the bronze figure of a deceased Union soldier lying atop a bier.
The figure reclines, appearing healthy and full bodied, as if he is merely resting.

He is young but not callow. His open right hand is at his side; a kepi is at his feet; he is in uniform, with a blanket roll and—apparently—a burial shroud; his left hand rests upon the chest with the fingers upon the shroud.

- Funded by the State of Illinois at a cost of $25,000. The architects were Schmidt, Garden and Erikson, Chicago; the contractors, Charles G. Blake Company, Chicago.

- Records indicate that the initiative for the monument came from "William R. Manierre, a member of Ulysses S. Grant Post, GAR, Chicago, [who] expressed himself to Dr. Charles O. Brown, commander of the post, as 'deeply grieved to see that the great State of Illinois had built no monument to the honor of his comrades whom the State had sent forth to battle and to die, of whom more than two thousand' were buried in the National Cemetery at Memphis. Brown later gave the dedication address for the monument and wrote the inscription beginning 'When President Abraham Lincoln called.'"

McNairy County

5.17.1 Subject: Selmer, Courthouse Shaft
Location: Court Avenue, 38375   N 35 10 15 19 / W 88 35 37 18
Installed or dedicated: 1994
Media: Granite, concrete
Monument is a granite shaft surmounting a concrete base.

Inscription
[Front]
[SCV seal]
ERECTED 1994 BY THE / BATTLE OF SHILOH CAMP #1454 / SONS OF CONFEDERATE VETERANS

THIS MONUMENT ERECTED IN HONOR / OF THE GALLANT CONFEDERATE / SOLDIERS OF MCNAIRY COUNTY WHO / FOUGHT, DIED AND SUFFERED / DURING THE WAR BETWEEN THE / STATES 1861–1865 / SACRED IS THE MEMORY OF THE / MEN AND WOMEN OF MCNAIRY / COUNTY FOR THE SACRIFICES THEY / MADE IN DEFENDING THEIR / HOMELAND

POOR IS A NATION THAT / HAS NO HEROES. / SHAMEFUL IS A NATION THAT HAS / HEROES AND FORGETS THEM. / NO NATION CAN LONG SURVIVE / WITHOUT PRIDE IN ITS TRADITIONS.

CSA / CONFEDERATE UNITS FORMED / IN MCNAIRY COUNTY:
[Roster]

McNairy County, from which Chester County was formed, voted against secession, 915 to 811 in February 1861, then voted for it 1,318 to 580 in June 1861, according to the Tennessee Historical Quarterly. Divisions of sentiment continued throughout the war. The SCV obelisk displays a detailed roster of Confederate units from this rural county, but five companies of Union troops were raised in the county.

- The exhortation beginning "Poor is a Nation" is anonymous; the expression is also invoked at Davis Bridge (5.15.3) and Hardin County (5.14.4).

Chester County

5.18.1 Subject: Henderson, Courthouse Shaft
Location: 133 East Main Street, 38340   N 35 26 23 95 / W 88 38 25 70
Installed or dedicated: 1996
Medium: Granite
Monument is a granite shaft surmounting a base.

Inscription
[Crossed US and Confederate battle flags]
MAY GOD BLESS THE SOLDIERS / OF BOTH SIDES WHO GAVE / THEIR LIVES IN THIS TERRIBLE / STRUGGLE AND HELP US TO / PRESERVE IN AN ACCURATE / MANNER THE MEMORY OF THEIR / GALLANT DEEDS FOR OUR / CHILDREN AND OUR / CHILDREN'S [*SIC*]
CHESTER COUNTY / BICENTENNIAL COMMITTEE / ROWLAND MONUMENTS / BETHEL STRINGS, TENN.

Sentiments were divided in the area where Chester County was formed in 1875. It was the last county formed in Tennessee and had no formal affiliation with secession. The Civil War is not mentioned by name on this monument. The granite shaft is a bipartisan bicentennial-era tribute to the "gallant deeds" of "both sides" in a conflict that is defined or alluded to by dint of the US flag and the Confederate battle flag.

- Scattered military activity took place in what is now Chester County during the Civil War, most notably an engagement involving a Union expedition from Corinth and cavalry commanded by General Nathan B. Forrest that took place at Jacks Creek on December 23, 1863.

6

CONCLUSION

T ENNESSEE'S CIVIL WAR monumentation is a significant and distinctive genre on its own account. However, a host of public wayside counter-narratives or parallel narratives in the form of plaques and tablets have been erected since the 1890s, and many of them address the subjects that Civil War monuments also address. Indeed, many of them stand in the same vicinity as the monuments considered here.

To omit them is, arguably, to leave an acoustic shadow over another dimension of public commemorations of the war. To include them on a comprehensive basis, however, would require a multivolume version of this book. For example, the War Department erected some 600 cast-iron tablets on the Shiloh battlefield and 600 cast-iron tablets at Chickamauga and Chattanooga at the turn of the twentieth century. Between 1952 and 1965, some 287 Civil War–related cast-iron roadside narratives were erected by the Tennessee Historical Commission. Between 2009 and 2016, some 400 markers and kiosks were erected by dint of a joint initiative of the Tennessee Department of Transportation, the Tennessee Department of Tourist Development, the Tennessee Civil War Sesquicentennial Commission, and the federally supported Tennessee Civil War National Heritage Area. In addition, the Tennessee Department of Environment and Conservation has oversight responsibility for such historical and war-related sites as Fort Pillow, today Fort Pillow State Park. Further, the Civil War Trust has worked to preserve significant Civil War battlefield acreage and erect accompanying tablature at such places as Chattanooga, Davis Bridge, Fort Donelson, Franklin, Parker's Crossroads, Shiloh, Spring Hill, and Stones River.

These wayside markers are not monuments: they offer flat, two-dimensional platforms to display narratives, summaries, and illustrations. Their makers eschew distinction: their architectural form is simple, uniform, relatively inexpensive—contemporary versions usually employ fiberglass or polyurethane—and decidedly understated. They are, by dint of their design, evidently designed for close interaction, at close proximity, at ground level, by a small number of persons standing over them.

To judge by their mission statements, these organizations have a broad mandate. The mission of the Tennessee Historical Commission, for example, is "to protect, preserve, interpret, maintain, and administer historic places; to encourage the inclusive diverse study of Tennessee's history for the benefit of future generations." The agency claims the discretion "to mark important locations, persons, and events in Tennessee history; to assist in worthy publication projects; to review, comment on and identify projects that will potentially impact historic properties." Of similar ambition is the Tennessee Civil War National Heritage Area declaration that its offices are charged with "tell[ing] the Whole Story of America's Greatest challenge, 1860–1875 . . . the powerful stories of vicious warfare, the demands of the homefront and occupation, the freedom of emancipation, and the enduring legacies of Reconstruction." Finally, in working with the Tennessee Department of Tourist Development, the tablature is reconciled with an organization whose mission "is to motivate travel to and within Tennessee by inspiring enjoyment, creating memories, producing a desire to return, and establishing key long-term relationships that result in visitors becoming residents."

On the one hand, wayside tablets creditably inform visitors/readers about their subject matter. The War Department's turn-of-the-century cast-iron tablets on the Shiloh and Chattanooga battlefields are assiduously focused on dispassionate descriptions of troop movements, leadership responsibility, and tactical military outcomes. The obligation of the War Department to be nonpartisan is preeminent. David W. Reed, the Shiloh Park Commission's first historian, insisted that small-unit monument inscriptions, such as regiments or batteries, be factual and historically accurate. Reed also mandated that inscriptions be without praise or criticism.

They are present in the hundreds; they display copious narrative detail, anecdotes, maps, and illustrations. Each of them serves to mediate and interpret the landscape, but there is a constraint in public institutional memory as depicted in wayside tablets, particularly if the narration is shaped to encourage harmony, that is to "encourage . . . people to return, or to live or work or visit here," as the Tennessee Department of Tourist Development would have it. Arguably, the tablets are consistent with what historian Drew Gilpin Faust calls "that most American of phrases: the pursuit of happiness." The Tennessee Encyclopedia entry for "Civil War monument," for example, concludes that "Civil War monuments remain in place as silent reminders of a tragic era in the state's history." The distinction between the past and the present in this appraisal is notable: the war is described as an unfortunate abstraction. It is not "our history"; it is not "Tennessee's history"; it is a detached concept—"a tragic era in the state's history." This disjunction is hard to square with the tangible facts of the war—2,900 engagements fought on the Tennessee landscape, and 122,000 graves of Confederate and Union soldiers at rest in Tennessee soil. War is not readily reconciled with the pursuit of happiness, of course, but the war is an inalienable part of the Tennessee landscape. Lincoln justly cautioned

USCT burial grounds, Maplewood Cemetery, Pulaski

his listeners during the Gettysburg Address that "in a larger sense, we can not dedicate—we can not consecrate—we can not hallow—this ground." Wayside tablets can be candid in describing the events of a landscape where they stand, but for all the effort made to place them in prominent place—doing so by the thousands in Tennessee—they cannot broach the depths of tragedy or irony or juxtaposition or paradox that the landscape continues to bear.

This not to say that the waysides serve no purpose or offer no lesson. They make their contribution: the past is acknowledged in the waysides; passersby are informed. However, for every marker commemorating the service of United States Colored Troops (USCT) soldiers at Maplewood Cemetery in Pulaski, for example, there is a Confederate cemetery monument nearby, mourning the dead. John Keegan, in his one-volume history of the war, observes that the topographical challenge of the war was an "element of resistance that had to be overcome and which never relented. . . . In a real sense, the North was fighting the country itself in its struggle to overcome the South." Keegan justly speaks in terms of geography: the rivers, the mountains, and the climate. I think it right to say that the South was fighting the same landscape, and, in a real sense, the various state and federal commissions and agencies are also fighting the landscape in their mission. There is a public history imperative or incentive to avoid, neglect, subvert, or understate the inalienable truths of the landscape: the waysides cannot come to terms with the nature of the landscape—the landscape does not comport well with mere anecdotes, images, or illustrations.

For example, state descriptions of West Tennessee's Fort Pillow State Park make no mention of the apparent massacre that took place on April 12, 1864. It was here that a force of some fifteen hundred Confederate soldiers led by

Maj. Gen. Nathan B. Forrest engaged a mixed force of about three hundred inexperienced white Tennessee Union soldiers and approximately three hundred USCT (African American) soldiers. After a tense struggle, the Federal defenses were breached and thereafter discipline among the Confederates broke down. Deaths totaled 64 percent of the black troops and at least 31 percent of the white Tennessee Union soldiers—a rate that far exceeded what occurred in the normal course of Civil War combat. Forrest claimed that the Federals refused to surrender until most had died, but testimony by Union and Confederate soldiers makes it seem evident that a massacre took place, regardless of the extent of Forrest's culpability, which continues to be debated to this day.

The site was abandoned after the battle and reverted to a kind of backwoods over the course of the next century, until 1971, when the grounds reopened in their present incarnation as a state park. Hiking and other recreational opportunities are described in the state park's literature, as are the fort's earthworks, but the events of April 12, 1864, are not broached. The official state literature informs readers that "the 1,642 acre Fort Pillow is known for it[s] well-preserved breastworks and reconstructed inner fort. The [Park] is designated as a Wildlife Observation Area by the Tennessee Wildlife Resources Agency and is frequented by bird watchers."

Similarly, there is no public acknowledgment of the combat service of the USCT at the battle of Nashville. The site of the charge of the 13th USCT at Peach Orchard Hill near present-day I-65 remains unmarked, for example, over 150 years after the two-day battle of December 15–16, 1864. Today the site is managed by the Tennessee Department of Transportation; a centennial-era marker stands on the grounds, but it makes no mention of the United States Colored Troops.

Of course, most of the sites of the Nashville battlefield remain unmarked. The largest monument—the so-called "Peace Monument" on the Granny White Pike at Battlefield Drive—is, arguably, a compromise, a monument to both sides, with a tribute to American soldiers of World War I as well, not "just" the battle of Nashville. Furthermore, Fort Negley has been preserved and developed as a municipal park in recent decades. The Tennessee Historical Commission erected twenty-five wayside cast tablets in the area.

It was southeast of Nashville that elements of the Union Fourth Corps and Major General James B. Steedman's Provisional Division, some twelve thousand white and black troops, waged a series of assaults against Confederate lines on the morning of December 16, 1864. The assaults were intended as a diversion from the main Union assault to the west. In this, the assaults were successful, although the losses were staggering: there were some twelve hundred Union casualties. The 12th, 13th, and 100th USCT attacked Peach Orchard Hill, near present-day I-65. The assault was repulsed; however, USCT soldiers

Orchard Hill, Nashville

were so effective that Confederate General John B. Hood came to believe that Peach Orchard Hill was the main point of the Union attack. The only Union regiment to reach the Confederate line was the 13th USCT. Of the 556 USCT troops engaged, 229 were wounded or killed—CSA Brig. Gen. James Holtzclaw cited their courage in his official report of the action, concluding that the USCT men "came only to die."

Today nothing marks the grounds where the 13th USCT fought. In itself, the absence is not a cause for condemnation, and a wayside marker does stand in the area. However, the significance of these multifarious inclusions and omissions scattered across the landscape merits appraisal. The tablets in their hundreds are, as an aggregate, a testimony to an endless qualification, redefining, or reductionism that, by definition, is ultimately dismissive or inconclusive. They testify to the impossibility of coming to a final word on the war. There is something vexing about the war that the wayside anecdote, image, or narrative cannot do justice to. The landscape demands a preacher, a priestly mediator: the monument is an inarticulate, three-dimensional fixture on the landscape. In his book *After the War: A Tour of the Southern States, 1865–1866*, the nineteenth-century writer, editor, and teacher W. T. Trowbridge describes his experience of touring the former states of the Confederacy shortly after the war. His travels took him to the Manassas battlefield, where he described the monument there—still standing—as "a silent preacher, with its breast of stone, and its austere face of stone, preaching inaudible lessons."

Several decades after embarking on the examination of the monument on the American landscape in a serious way, I can find no simpler or more cogent a description of the way the Civil War monument conforms to the landscape. There is, if you will, an epistemological and aesthetic discomfort or mystery associated with the prototypical monument of the war, the obelisk. In this regard, the coincident use of Egyptian revival motifs in commemorating the

Civil War is striking. Art historian Brian Curran observes that in "ancient Egypt, the obelisk was called a *Tekhen*—plural *tekhenu*—from a verb meaning 'to pierce,' evoking the obelisks' needle-like shape—both a symbolic and literal attempt to pierce the sky." An obelisk is cryptic—at once earthly, aloof, and transcendent. The form binds word, image, and medium—marble, granite, and the rest—to the soil. But they do not quite synthesize with either earth or sky, and it is peculiarly appropriate, as Curran notes, that the obelisk has no practical function, "[that] there is nothing practical about them, and for much of history their inscriptions, in Egyptian hieroglyphs, were completely inscrutable." By definition, the Civil War obelisk or statue or stele is analogical: it is a testimony to the inexpressible. At their best, the monuments are a homiletical stake in the ground, cryptically reminding residents and visitors of the virtues, flaws, and affections of the wartime generation—the "heart-ache[s] and thousand natural shocks" they were heir to. The war left unspeakable sorrows and unfathomable tragedies. It left a record of cruelty, avarice, mercy, and endurance. John Keegan observes that war brings out all the contradictions of human behavior: enormous courage, enormous folly, foolishness, responsibility in the service of foolishness, cowardice in the face of responsibility, genius, murder, and sublime self-sacrifice. Historian Alan Clark writes in turn that, as a student of war, one learns that incompetence, corruption, brutality, and waste are inseparable and take their toll.

This inclination to corruption, brutality, and waste is not just American; it is not ethnic, regional, racial, or institutional: it is a radical iniquity or immorality that every generation bears. "All we like sheep have gone astray" is the way the prophet Isaiah describes humanity. To truly walk the grounds of the Civil War battlefield, one must, at some level, contend with the same frustration that Lady Macbeth confronted by straining to discern and remove a guilt about deeds done or not done that will not be removed, that is too deep. "Out, damned spot!" she said. "Out, I say!" As a student of the American landscape, I prefer the image presented by American novelist and poet Herman Melville, who lived through the war, who wrote of storms behind storms in his poem "Misgivings," more specifically, "storms [that] are formed behind the storm we feel." Melville's poem and Lady Macbeth and the Civil War monument allude to something that is both ordinary and repugnant, something deeper: a base, inner corruption of the soul of humanity that was destined to give way to the war and its aftermath. The Civil War monument represents an insufficient sacrifice, a perpetual disequilibrium: life, breath, word, sacrament, and landscape.

Selected Sources

Ashdown, Paul, and Edward Caudill. *The Myth of Nathan Bedford Forrest*. Lanham, MD: Rowman & Littlefield, 2005.

Beagle, Donald Robert, and Bryan Albin Giemza. *Poet of the Lost Cause: A Life of Father Ryan*. Knoxville: University of Tennessee Press, 2008.

Bishop, Randy. *Tennessee's Civil War Battlefields: A Guide to their History and Preservation*. Gretna, LA: Pelican, 2010.

Blair, William. *Cities of the Dead: Contesting the Memory of the Civil War in the South, 1865–1914*. Chapel Hill: University of North Carolina Press, 2004.

Clark, Alan. *Barbarossa: The Russian-German Conflict, 1941–45*. New York: William Morrow, 1985.

Connelly, Thomas Lawrence. *Civil War Tennessee: Battles and Leaders*. Knoxville: University of Tennessee Press, 1979.

Cox, Karen L. *Dixie's Daughters: The United Daughters of the Confederacy and the Preservation of Confederate Culture*. Gainesville: University Press of Florida, 2003.

Cozzens, Peter. *No Better Place to Die: The Battle of Stones River*. Urbana: University of Illinois Press, 1990.

———. *The Shipwreck of Their Hopes: The Battles for Chattanooga*. Urbana: University of Illinois Press, 1994.

Cunningham, O. Edward. *Shiloh and the Western Campaign of 1862*. Edited by Gary D. Joiner and Timothy B. Smith. New York: Savas Beatie, 2007.

Curran, Brian. *Obelisk: A History*. Cambridge, MA: MIT Press, 2009.

Daniel, Larry J. *Shiloh: The Battle That Changed the Civil War*. New York: Simon & Schuster, 1997.

Directory of Civil War Monuments and Memorials in Tennessee. Nashville: Civil War Centennial Commission, 1963.

Elliott, Sam Davis. *Soldier of Tennessee: General Alexander P. Stewart and The Civil War in the West*. Baton Rouge: Louisiana State University Press, 1999.

Fahs, Alice, and Joan Waugh, eds. *The Memory of the Civil War in American Culture.* Chapel Hill: University of North Carolina Press, 2004.

Faust, Drew Gilpin. *Mothers of Invention: Women of the Slaveholding South in the American Civil War.* New York: Vintage, 1996.

———. *This Republic of Suffering: Death and the American Civil War.* New York: Alfred A. Knopf, 2008.

Foner, Eric. *Reconstruction, 1863–1877.* New York: Harper, 1988.

Foote, Shelby. *The Civil War: A Narrative.* 3 vols. New York: Random House, 1958–1974.

Foster, Gaines M. *Ghosts of the Confederacy: Defeat, the Lost Cause, and the Emergence of the New South, 1865–1913.* New York: Oxford University Press, 1987.

Fuller, Randall. *From Battlefields Rising: How the Civil War Transformed American Literature.* New York: Oxford University Press, 2011.

Gallagher, Gary, and Joan Waugh. *The American War: A History of the Civil War Era.* State College, PA: Flip Learning, 2015.

Garner, Stanton. *The Civil War World of Herman Melville.* Lawrence: University of Kansas Press, 1993.

Guelzo, Allen C. *Fateful Lightning: A New History of the Civil War & Reconstruction.* New York: Oxford University Press, 2012.

Hess, Earl J. *The Civil War in the West: Victory and Defeat from the Appalachians to the Mississippi.* Chapel Hill: University of North Carolina Press, 2012.

———. *The Knoxville Campaign: Burnside and Longstreet in East Tennessee.* Knoxville: University of Tennessee Press, 2012.

Hicken, Victor. *Illinois in the Civil War.* Urbana: University of Illinois, 1991.

Jacobson, Eric A. *The McGavock Confederate Cemetery: A Revised and Updated Compilation.* Nashville: n.p., 2007.

Janney, Carolyn E. *Burying the Dead But not the Past: Ladies' Memorial Association & the Lost Cause.* Chapel Hill: University of North Carolina Press, 2008.

Kammen, Michael. *Mystic Chords of Memory: The Transformation of Tradition in American Culture.* New York: Vintage, 1991.

Keegan, John. *The American Civil War: A Military History.* New York: Vintage, 2009.

———. *The Face of Battle.* 1976. New York: Penguin, 1978.

Linderman, Gerald E. *Embattled Courage: The Experience of Combat in the American Civil War.* New York: Simon & Schuster, 1987.

McDonough, James Lee. *Shiloh: In Hell Before Night.* Knoxville: University of Tennessee Press, 1977.

———. *Stones River—Bloody Winter in Tennessee.* Knoxville: University of Tennessee Press, 1980.

———. *War in Kentucky: From Shiloh to Perryville.* Knoxville: University of Tennessee Press, 1994.

———, and Thomas L. Connelly. *Five Tragic Hours: The Battle of Franklin.* Knoxville: University of Tennessee Press, 1983.

McMurry, Richard M. *Two Great Rebel Armies: An Essay in Confederate Military History.* Chapel Hill: University of North Carolina Press, 1989.

McWhiney, Grady, and Perry D. Jamieson. *Attack and Die: Civil War Military Tactics and the Southern Heritage.* Tuscaloosa: University of Alabama Press, 1982.

Neely, Jack. *The Marble City: A Photographic Tour of Knoxville's Graveyards*. Photographs by Aaron Jay. Knoxville: University of Tennessee Press, 1999.

Nemerov, Alexander. *Acting in the Night: Macbeth and the Places of the Civil War*. Berkeley: University of California Press, 2010.

Reaves, Stacy W. A. *History & Guide to the Monuments of Chickamauga National Park*. Charleston, SC: The History Press, 2013.

———. *History & Guide to the Monuments of Shiloh National Park*. Charleston, SC: The History Press, 2012.

Schantz, Mark S. *Awaiting the Heavenly Country: The Civil War and America's Culture of Death*. Ithaca, NY: Cornell University Press, 2008.

Scully, Vincent. *The Earth, the Temple, and the Gods: Greek Sacred Architecture*. San Antonio, TX: Trinity University Press, 2013.

Sedore, Timothy. *An Illustrated Guide to Virginia's Confederate Monuments*. Carbondale: Southern Illinois University Press, 2011.

Sifakis, Stewart. *Compendium of the Confederate Armies: Tennessee*. New York: Facts on File, 1992–1995.

Smith, Timothy B. *The Golden Age of Battlefield Preservation: The Decade of the 1890s and the Establishment of America's First Five Military Parks*. Knoxville: University of Tennessee Press, 2008.

———. *This Great Battlefield of Shiloh*. Knoxville: University of Tennessee Press, 2004.

———. *The Untold Story of Shiloh: The Battle and the Battlefield*. Knoxville: University of Tennessee Press, 2006.

Spruill, Matt. *Storming the Heights: A Guide to the Battle of Chattanooga*. Knoxville: University of Tennessee Press, 2003.

Stout, Harry S. *Upon the Altar of the Nation: A Moral History of the Civil War*. New York: Penguin, 2007.

Sword, Wiley. *Embrace an Angry Wind: The Confederacy's Last Hurrah: Spring Hill, Franklin, and Nashville*. New York: Harper Collins, 1992.

———. *Mountains Touched with Fire: Chattanooga Besieged, 1863*. New York: St. Martin's, 1995.

———. *Shiloh: Bloody April*. New York: Morrow, 1974.

Trowbridge, J. T. *The South: A Tour of It's Battlefields and Ruined Cities, A Journey Through the Desolated States, and Talks with the People*. CreateSpace Independent Publishing Platform, 2013.

Warner, Ezra J. *Generals in Grey: Lives of the Confederate Commanders*. Baton Rouge: Louisiana State University Press, 1959.

———. *Generals in Blue: Lives of the Union Commanders*. Baton Rouge: Louisiana State University Press, 1964.

West, Carroll Van, ed. *Tennessee History: The Land, the People, and the Culture*. Knoxville: University of Tennessee Press, 1998.

Wills, Brian S. *The Confederacy's Greatest Cavalryman: Nathan Bedford Forrest*. Lawrence: University Press of Kansas, 1992.

Wills, Garry. *Lincoln at Gettysburg: The Words that Remade America*. New York: Touchstone, 1992.

Wilson, Charles Reagan. *Baptized in Blood: The Religion of the Lost Cause*. Athens: University of Georgia Press, 1980.

Woodworth, Steven E. *Nothing but Victory: The Army of the Tennessee, 1861–1865*. New York: Albert A. Knopf, 2005.

————. *While God Is Marching On: The Religious World of Civil War Soldiers.* Lawrence: University Press of Kansas, 2001.

————. *Six Armies in Tennessee: The Chickamauga and Chattanooga Campaigns.* Lincoln: University of Nebraska Press, 1998.

Memorial Volumes

Confederated Southern Memorial Association. *History of the Confederated Memorial Associations of the South.* New Orleans, LA: Graham, 1904.

Emerson, Mrs. Bettie A. C. *Historic Southern Monuments. Representative Memorials of the Heroic Dead of the Southern Confederacy.* New York: Neale, 1911.

Maps

Kissel, Tim. "Shiloh Battlefield: A Unit of Shiloh National Military Park (Civil War battlefield series)." Aurora, CO: Trailhead Graphics, 2009.

Periodicals—selected, various

Confederate Veteran
Southern Historical Society Papers

Periodicals—Tours

Allen, Stacy D. "Shiloh: The Campaign and First Day's Battle." *Blue & Gray Magazine,* Winter 1997.

————. "Shiloh: Grant Strikes Back." *Blue & Gray Magazine,* Spring 1997.

Bearss, Ed. "Forrest's West Tennessee Campaign of 1862 and the Battle of Parker's Cross-Roads." *Blue & Gray Magazine,* Fall 2003.

Jacobson, Eric A. "Hood's Tennessee Campaign: From the Fall of Atlanta to the Battle of Franklin." *Blue & Gray Magazine,* Fall 2014.

Jobe, James. "The Battles for Fort Henry and Donelson." *Blue & Gray Magazine,* Spring 2012.

Lewis, Jim. "The Battle for Stones River: A Hard Earned Victory for Lincoln." *Blue & Gray Magazine,* Fall 2012.

Websites—selected

"Babcock-Smith House Museum," http://www.babcock-smithhouse.com/

The Civil War Trust, http://www.civilwar.org/

Frederick H. Dyer's Compendium "A Compendium of the War of the Rebellion" (Part 3), http://www.civilwararchive.com/regim.htm

Smithsonian Institution Research Information System, "Civil War Sculpture, Virginia" http://siris-collections.si.edu

Tennessee Historical Society, The University of Tennessee Press "Tennessee Encyclopedia of the Civil War." https://tennesseeencyclopedia.net/

Index

Page numbers in italics refer to illustrations.

Adams, John (Brig. Gen.), 6, 9, 312, 320, *327*, 330–331
African Americans, monuments/tributes, 27–28, 312, 367, *367*, 372, 430–431. *See also* US Colored Troops (USCT)
Afton, Lick Creek, TN, 242, *243*
Alabama, monuments/tributes, 132, *133*, 134, 150
Alabama troops: 160, 165, 187, 270, 284, 294, 295, 303, 324, *325*, 335–336, 341, 372, 392; 1st Infantry, 335; 2nd Infantry, 335; 4th Infantry, 335; 5th Infantry, 335; 6th Infantry, 335; 7th Cavalry, 335; 7th Infantry, 335; 8th Infantry, 335; 9th Infantry, 335; 13th Infantry, 335; 15th Infantry, 335; 19th Cavalry, 40; 19th Infantry, 335; 24th Infantry, 335; 25th Infantry, 335; 33rd Infantry, 268–269; Dent's Battery, 335; Eufaula Battery, 335; Garrity's Battery, 335; Goldwaite's Battery, 335; Kolb's Battery, 335; Lumsen's Battery, 335; Phelan's Battery, 335; Selden's Battery, 335
Albert Weiblen Marble & Granite Company, 121
Alexandria, TN, 19, 237, 281–282, 304
Altamont, TN, *ix*, 12, 19, 282–283, 304
American Revolution, 162–163, 311

Anderson, Samuel R. (Brig. Gen.), 364
Andrew Johnson National Cemetery, 241–242
Andrew Johnson National Historic Site, 239–240
Andrews' Raiders, 154
Antietam, 7, 18, 44, 159, 166, 172, 174, 210, *216*, 219, 222, 223, 256, 279
Appomattox, 13, 216, 280, 383
Architectural forms (summary), 33, 42, 428
Arkansas, monuments/tributes, 43, 106–107, 150, 252, 284, 294, 295, 303, 324, *325*, 335, 341, 372, 392
Arkansas troops: 1st Infantry, 106; 2nd Infantry, 106; 4th Infantry, 335; 5th Infantry, 335; 6th Infantry, 106, 335; 7th Infantry, 106, 335; 8th Infantry, 106, 335; 9th Infantry, 106, 335; 9th (14th Battalion) Infantry, 106; 13th Infantry, 106; 15th Infantry, 106; 19th Infantry, 335; 24th Infantry, 335; 25th Infantry, 335; Calvert's Battery (Shoup's Battalion), 106; Hubbard's Battery, 106; Roberts' Battery, 106; Trigg's Battery, 106
Arlington National Cemetery, 152, 258, 296
Army of Northern Virginia, 234, 249, 280, 348

Army of Tennessee, 134, 146, 153, 194, 209, 233, 234, 249, 250, 284, 293, 296, 297, 299, 303, 317, 319, 325, 326, 328, 330, 332, 345, 352, 362, 411
Army of the Cumberland, 7, 9, 18, 146, 149, 172, 192, 210, 223, 297, 339, 362
Army of the Ohio, 48, 54–130, 343
Army of the Potomac, 153, 155, 160, 162, 164, 174, 212, 253
Army of the Tennessee, 48, 50–227
Ashwood Cemetery, Columbia TN, 328
Atlanta, Georgia, 35n2, 147, 152, 154, 156, 329, 330, 416

Badger Brothers, 218, 221
Baltimore, 12, 28, 216
Baptist churches, 259
Bartow, Francis (Brig. Gen.), 35n10, 344
Bate, William B. (Brig. Gen.), 81, 297, 364
Battle Above the Clouds, 161
Beauregard, P. G. T. (Gen.), 43, 48,
Bedford County, 300–304, 301, 302
Benton County, 381–382, 382
Bentonville, NC, 329, 384, 385, 388, 404, 405
Bible verses, inscriptions, 2
    Corinthians 4:11, 413; Hebrews 6:19, 316, 410; Isaiah 53:6, 35n12, 88–89, 433; John 15:13, 310, 355; Matthew 28:19, 82; 1 Peter 2:4–6, 35n12
Bivouac of the Dead, 254, 258, 303, 305, 352
Bledsoe County, viii, ix, 270
Blountville, TN, ix, 230, 232, 233
Bolivar, TN, 17, 30, 378, 380, 411–412
Bradley County, ix, 228, 264, 266
Bragg, Braxton, (Lt. Gen.), 6, 9, 146, 194, 227, 296
Bragg Reservation, 8, 148, 193–202, 196, 199
Branson, Lloyd, 251
Bravery themes, inscriptions, 18, 52, 90, 102, 106, 180, 204, 224, 261, 283, 294, 295, 297, 299, 319, 331, 332, 333, 335, 346, 347, 363, 375, 390, 391, 398, 400, 411, 422. See also Courage themes, inscriptions
Breckinridge, John C. (Maj. Gen.), 345

Bristol, TN, ix, 4, 10, 33, 230, 231–232, 232, 245
Britton's Lane, 65, 70, 407–408
Bronx, xii, 290
Bronx Hall of Fame, xii
Brown, John C. (Maj. Gen.), 312
Brown, Kent Masterson, 345
Brownlow, Cayetta Ashland, 235
Brownlow, Walter Preston, 235
Buberl, Caspar, 214
Buell, Don Carlos (Maj. Gen.), 48. See also Army of the Ohio
Buford, Abraham (Brig. Gen.), 313
Burnside, Ambrose E. (Maj. Gen.), 253–258
Byron, George Gordon, 338

Calvary, 354
Campaigns summarized, 6–7, 35n2, 274
Cannon County, 304–307, 305
Carnton Plantation, 321
Carter, John C. (Brig. Gen.), 9, 327, 330
Carter, Samuel P. (Brig. Gen.), 313
Carter, Theodrick "Tod" (Capt.), 337
Carter House, 35n2, 320, 325, 337
Carthage, TN, ix, 272, 279
Celebration Era, 16–18
Chantilly, Virginia, 256
Chapel Hill, TN, ix, 299, 305–307, 306
Charlotte, TN, ix, 19, 30, 272, 377
Charlottesville, VA, 8, 12, 28
Chattanooga, campaign. See Campaigns summarized
Cheatham, Benjamin F. (Maj. Gen.), 364, 383
Cherokee National Forest, 231, 263
Chester County, 423, 424
Chickamauga campaign. See Campaigns summarized
citizen soldier, 32, 260, 291. See also Common soldiers
"Civil War" phrase, use of, 34n1
Claiborne County, 247, 247
Clarksville, TN, ix, 272, 274, 370–373, 371
Cleburne, Pat (Maj. Gen.), 8, 9, 12, 78, 81–82, 185, 283, 303–304, 320, 321, 325, 325, 334–335, 336
Cleveland, TN, ix, 12, 228, 230, 264–269
Cocke County, ix, 228, 246

Coffee County, *ix*, 272, 292

Columbia, TN, *ix*, 17, 272, 314–315, *314*, 328, 329, 330, 390

Company Aytch: Or, a Side Show of the Big Show (Watkins), 326

Comparison of States, 8–10

Common soldiers, 9–11, 11–20, 15, 16, 17, 21, *21*, 31, 34, 41, 68

Common soldiers, Confederate, monuments/tributes to, 81–82, *82*, 88–90, *88*, 106–107, *107*, 244–245, *245*, 260–261, *261*, 287–288, *288*, 302–302, *302*, 307–308, *308*, 309–311, *310*, 314–315, *314*, 318–320, 337–338, *338*, *354*, 356–359, *357*, 363–364, *363*, 368–369, 370–371, *370*, 373–375, *374*, 381–384, *383*, 388–390, *390*, 392, *392*, 393–395, *394*, 398–399, 404–405, *405*, 409, *409*

Common soldiers, Union, monuments/ tributes to, 102, 104–105, *105*, 112, 114–115, *114*, 119, *119*, 122, *122*, 141, 142, 155–157, *156*, 168–169, *169*, 170, 179–181, *181*, 189–190, *190*, 195, 207–209, *208*, 211–226, *212*, *215*, *217*, *219*, 238, *238*, 256–257, *256*, 366–367, *366*, 420–423, *421*, *422*

Confederate Dead, 4, 10, 17, 18, 30, 43–44, 78, 86, 87, 106, 137, 140, 150, 151, 247–249, *249*, 251–252, 264, 266, 269–270, *270*, 298, 302, 311, 313, 317, *317*, 320–324, *321*, 340–341, 350, 369, 374, 380, 387, 395, 397, 404, 411, 416, 419–420

Confederate Troops: 2nd Confederate Infantry, 89; 3rd Confederate Infantry, 89

Connecticut, monuments/tributes, 9, 146, 222–223

Connecticut troops: 5th Infantry, 222; 20th Infantry, 222–223

Courage themes, inscriptions, 18, 19, 27, 251, 279, 289, 294, 306, 307, 326, 332, 346, 348, 350, 370, 398, 400

Covington, TN, 299, 378, 398–401, 409

Cravens House, Chattanooga, 147, 164–173, *165*, *171*

Crescent Regiment, 38, 43, *120*

Crook, George (Brig. Gen.), 279, 300

Crosses, Christian, 14, 285, 286

Crossville, TN, 19, 274–275

Cumberland County, 274–276, *275*

Cunningham, S. A., 34, 329

Daniels, John K., 112, *368*, *421*

Davidson, Donald, 375

Davidson County, 353–370, *355*, *357*, *360*

Davis, Jefferson, xii, 8, 19, 31, 245, 304, 329, 359, 391, 414–415, *415*

Davis, Sam, 9, 11, 289, 309, 310–311, *310*, 313–314, *314*, 318, 347–348, 353–354, *354*, 357–358, *357*

Davis Bridge, Battle of, 380, 413–414

Death themes, inscriptions, xi–xiii, 10–11, 15, 18, 25, 32, 35n13, 40, 43, 101–103, 124, 283

Decatur County, 403–404

Decaturville, TN, *ix*, 19, *378*, 403–404

Defender, 232, 284

DeKalb County, 19, 279–283, *280*, *281*

Del Rio, TN, *ix*, 246, *246*

Denmark, Denmark Church Cemetery, 407–408

"Deo Vindice," 30, 297, 298, 318, 377, 380

Design, monuments, 20–27, *21–24*

Devotion theme, 18, 115, 121, 307, 308, 335, 352, 356, 363, 374, 375, 401, 416

Dickson County, *ix*, 30, 272, 377

"Dixie" (song), 20, 25, 245, 304, 399, 404

Dixie Highway, 246, *246*

Dodge, Grenville M. (Brig. Gen.), 100, 101, 137

Dresden, TN, *ix*, 19, *378*, 384–385

Duck River, 296, 301, 308

Duke, Basil (Brig. Gen.), 45, 82, 112, 115

Duty themes, inscriptions, 13, 25, 45, 90, 170, 218, 290, 298, 306, 309, 311, 313, 355, 358, 363, 381, 401, 411, 413, 414

Dyer County, *ix*, 19, 329, *378*, 375, 380, 388–389, *389*

Dyersburg, TN, *ix*, 329, *378*, 380, 388–389, *389*

Eastern Corinth Road, Shiloh NMP, *viii*, *38*, 106, 112

Eastern Flank Battlefield Park, Franklin, 8, 325–326

East Hill Cemetery, Bristol, TN, 231–232, *232*

East Tennessee State University, 234, 236

Egyptian revival, 17, 42, 343, 432, 433

Elder, John A., 383

"Elegy Written in a Country Churchyard" (Gray), 260

Eliot, T. S., 8, 89

Elliott, Sam Davis, 149

Emerson, Ralph Waldo, 362

Equestrian statue, 8, 28, 40, 103, 237, 380, 416–417

Erwin, TN, *ix*, 18, 33, 228, 230, 244–245, *245*

Ewell, Richard S. (Lt. Gen.), 364

Faith/faithfulness themes, inscriptions, 241, 290, 294, 312, 354, 358, 381, 388, 401, 410

Fayetteville, TN, *ix*, 25, *272*, 287–288, *288*

Florida, monuments/tributes, 43, 150, 252, 269, 284, 294, 295, 303, 321, 322, 341, 392, 415

Foote, Shelby, 334

Forrest, Mary A., 419

Forrest, Nathan Bedford (Lt. Gen.), xii, 8, 20, 28, 34, 66, 90, 93, 100, 114, 117, 127, 137, 274, 297–299, *297*, 305–307, *306*, 317–318, *317*, 332–333, 339, 351, 377, 380, 381–382, *382*, 389, 393, 394–395, 400–402, 406, 416–419, *417*, 424, 430–431

Fort Andrew Johnson, 356

Fort Donelson National Military Park, 18, 25, 373–376

Fort Negley, 364–365, 431

Fort Pillow, 7, 25, 46, 380, 388, 391, 410, 418, 428, 430–431

Fort Sanders, 7, 12, 18, 61, 79, 138, 230, 231, 251, 253, 259, 274

Franklin, TN, 274, 312, 316–337, *323*

Franklin County, 283–287, *284*

Freeman, Samuel L. (Capt.), 317–318, *325*, 332–333, 401–403, *402*, 406

Fry, Henry, 242

Fry, Jacob (Col.), 90

Gallatin, TN, *ix*, *272*, 366, 368–369

Garfield, James (Brig. Gen.), 54, 56, 58, 339–340

Gentsch, James, 41

Georgia, monuments/tributes, 28, 43, 103, 150, 152, 232, 248, 284, 294, 295, 252, 303, 324, 328, 341, 392

Georgia troops: 1st Cavalry, 248; 42nd Infantry, 260; 46th Infantry, 328; 65th Infantry, 328; 2nd Battalion Georgia Sharpshooters, 328

Gettysburg, PA, 6, 18, 25, 26, 35n2, 40–41, 44, 163, 164, 319, 325, 332, 342

Gettysburg Address, 29, 35n13, 42, 69, 236, 368, 430

Gibson County, 393–396, *394*

Giles County, 309–314, *310*, *314*

Gillem, Alvin C. (Maj. Gen.), 236, 237, 248

Gist, States Rights (Brig. Gen.), 327–328, *327*

"Gloria Victis," 11, 307

Govan, Daniel C. (Brig. Gen.), 334–335

Grand Army of the Republic, 238–239, *238*, 256, *256*, 266, 267

Grandbury, Hiram B. (Brig. Gen.), 8–9, 327, *327*, 328

Granger, Gordon (Maj. Gen.), 153, 333

Grant, Ulysses (Maj. Gen.), xiii, 6, 9, 10, 34, 36n1, 40, 43, 48, 50, 73, 91, 103, 146, 192, 374, 394, 417, 423. *See also* Army of the Tennessee

Grant's Last Line of Defense, 48, 49–59, *51*, *53*, *55*

Gray, Jim, 239, 311

Gray, Thomas, 248

Greene County, 22, 23, 236–243, *237*, *238*, *243*

Greeneville, TN, 22, 23, 236–242, *237*, *238*

Grundy County, *ix*, *272*, 282–283

Gulf wars, xiii

Hagerstown, MD, 44

Hale, Nathan, 311

Hallowed space, 88, 102, 120, 218, 248, 256, 316, 352, 390, 420, 430

Hamblen County, 248–250, *249*, *250*

Hamburg-Purdy Road, Review Field, Shiloh NMP, 90–94, *92*

Hamilton County, *viii*, 33, 144, 148, 227

Hardee, William J. (Lt. Gen.), 286, 335
Hardeman County, 411–414, *412*
Hardin County, 410–412, *412*
Harmon, Henry, 242–243, *243*
Harmon, Jacob, 242–243, *243*
Harris, Isham G., 230, 420
Haun, Christopher, 242–243, *243*
Haywood County, 409–411
Hazen, William B. (Col.), 343–344
Heath, Lyman, 309
"Hell's Half-Acre," 342, 344
Henderson County, 401–404, *402*
Henry County, 381–384, *383*
Hermant, Leon, 422
Heroes themes, inscriptions, 17, 26,
    132, 170, 251, 294, 299, 314, 319, 348,
    350, 354, 370, 391, 396, 410, 422, 423
Heroic themes, inscriptions, 151, 227,
    236, 287, 358
Hibbard, Frederick C., 102–103, 416
Hicken, Victor, 204, 320
Highbarger, Sam, 236
Hinshaw, Jacob, 242–243, *243*
Historic Southern Monuments, 354, 416,
    419, 420
Hodges Granite Company, 46
Hollywood Cemetery, Richmond,
    Virginia, 44
Holtzclaw, James (Brig. Gen.), 432
Hood, John B. (Lt. Gen.), 7, 9, 12, 284,
    315, 320, 325, 335, 338, 362, 376, 432
Horne, John Fletcher, 260–261, *261*
Horne, William Asbury, 260–261, *261*
Hornet's Nest, Shiloh NMP, 102, 106,
    112, 131
Howells, William Dean, 340
Hughes Granite and Marble
    Company, 46

Illinois, monuments/tributes, 9–10,
    15, 31, 40, 44–45, *44*, 49, 68–69, *69*,
    102–103, 146, 147, 194–195, *194*,
    216–218, *217*, 422–423, *423*
Illinois troops: 2nd Cavalry, 50–51,
    51; 2nd Infantry, 111; 2nd Regt.,
    Siege Artillery, 55; 4th Cavalry,
    50–51, *51*; 7th Infantry, 100; 8th
    Infantry, 96; 9th Infantry, 48–49,
    49, 125–126; 10th Infantry, 216–217;
11th Cavalry, 50–51, *51*, 407; 11th
    Infantry, 67, *67*; 12th Infantry,
    126; 13th Infantry, 173, 200; 14th
    Infantry, 76; 15th Cavalry, 216–217;
    15th Infantry, 95; 16th Infantry,
    216–217; 17th Infantry, 84; 18th
    Infantry, 96–97, *97*; 19th Infantry,
    194, 204; 20th Infantry, 70, 74,
    408; 21st Infantry, 216–217; 22nd
    Infantry, 193–194, *194*, 196; 24th
    Infantry, 216–217; 25th Infantry,
    188, 193–194, *194*; 26th Infantry,
    175; 27th Infantry, 193, 197; 28th
    Infantry, 111; 30th Infantry, 408;
    32nd Infantry, 111; 34th Infantry,
    216–217; 35th Infantry, 188,
    193–194; 36th Infantry, 193–194,
    198; 38th Infantry, 216–217;
    40th Infantry, 141, 179; 41st
    Infantry, 111, 113, 124–125, *125*;
    42nd Infantry, 93–194, *194*, 197;
    43rd Infantry, 66; 44th Infantry,
    93–194, *194*, 198; 45th Infantry,
    94, 212; 46th Infantry, 72; 48th
    Infantry, 93; 49th Infantry, 66;
    50th Infantry, 126–127, 403; 51st
    Infantry, 193–194, 196; 52nd
    Infantry, 137; 55th Infantry, 122,
    183; 56th Infantry, 178–179; 57th
    Infantry, 129; 58th Infantry, 44, *44*,
    100; 60th Infantry, 216–217; 61st
    Infantry, 90, 407; 63rd Infantry,
    147, 184; 65th Infantry, 330;
    66th Infantry, 59; 72nd Infantry,
    328; 73rd Infantry, 193–194, 198;
    74th Infantry, 193–194, 203; 75th
    Infantry, 166, 186, 193–194; 78th
    Infantry, 216–217; 79th Infantry, 12,
    194, 197, 254–256, *254*, 258, *258*; 80th
    Infantry, 216–217; 82nd Infantry,
    216–217; 84th Infantry, 167, 193–
    194; 85th Infantry, 216–217; 86th
    Infantry, 216–217; 88th Infantry,
    193, 202–203; 89th Infantry, 189,
    191, 193; 90th Infantry, 176; 92nd
    Infantry (Mounted), 216–217;
    93rd Infantry, 177–178, *178*; 96th
    Infantry, 216–217; 98th Infantry
    (Mounted), 216–217; 100th Infantry,

193; 101st Infantry, 216–217; 103rd Infantry, 182; 104th Infantry, 168, 193–194, 205, 351; 110th Infantry, 216–217, 343–344; 115th Infantry, 216–217; 122nd Infantry, 403; 123rd Infantry, 216–217; 125th Infantry, 216–217; 127th Infantry, 147, 184; Battery A, C, F, H, I, M, 216–217, *217*; Battery A, 1st Artillery, 125; Battery B, Illinois Artillery, 80, 216–217, *217*; Battery D, 1st Artillery, 95; Battery D, 2nd Artillery, 74, *75*; Battery E, 1st Artillery, 86; Battery E, 2nd Artillery, 60; Battery F, 2nd Artillery, 128, 216–217, *217*; Battery H, 1st Artillery, 50; Battery I, 1st Artillery, 61, 216–217, *217*; Chicago Board of Trade, 216–217; Illinois Cavalry, 44, 50–51, *51*

Indiana, monuments/tributes, 17, 28, 34, 40, 42, *42*, 45, 259–260, *260*

Indiana troops: 2nd Cavalry, 51, 344, 351; 6th Battery, 65; 6th Infantry, 97–98, *97*; 9th Battery, 60, *60*; 9th Infantry, 127, 312, 343–344; 11th Infantry, 45, 63–64; 15th Infantry, 90; 17th Infantry, 42, *42*, 54; 18th Battery, 297, 299–300; 23rd Infantry, 45, *45*, 61; 24th Infantry, 63; 25th Infantry, 94, 112; 29th Infantry, 77; 30th Infantry, 77; 31st Infantry, 109; 32nd Infantry, 73, 344; 36th Infantry, 129; 39th Infantry, 70; 40th Infantry, 91–92, *92*; 44th Infantry, 109–110; 51st Infantry, 42, *42*, 54; 57th Infantry, 91–92; 58th Infantry, 42, *42*, 54–55; 72nd Infantry, 300; 74th Infantry, 129

Inscriptions, 10, 11–16, *15*, *16*, 429, 433

Iowa, monuments/tributes, 9, 40, 41, 42, *42*, 47, *47*, 52–53, *53*, 68, 69, 114, 146, 166, 170, 179–181, *181*, 182, 207–210, *208*

Iowa troops: 1st Battery, 170; 2nd Infantry, 101, 110, 111, 113; 3rd Infantry, 95, 110, *110*; 4th Infantry, 170, 207–210, *208*; 5th Infantry, 179–180, *181*, 207–210, *208*; 6th Infantry, 140, 179–181, *181*; 7th Infantry, 113;

8th Infantry, 108, 207–210, *208*; 9th Infantry, 170, 207–210, *208*; 10th Infantry, 179–180, *181*, 207–210, *208*; 11th Infantry, 74–75, *75*; 12th Infantry, 41, 112–113; 13th Infantry, 95; 14th Infantry, 95, 107; 15th Infantry, 138–139; 16th Infantry, 138; 17th Infantry, 179, 170–180, *181*, 207–210, *208*; 25th Infantry, 170, 179–181, *181*, 207–210, *208*; 26th Infantry, 207–210, *208*; 30th Infantry, 170, 179–181, *181*, 207–210, *208*; 31st Infantry, 170, 179–181, *181*, 207–210, *208*; 39th Infantry, 403

Island Number Ten, 19, 397

Jackson, Thomas J. "Stonewall," xii, 8, 31

Jackson, TN, *ix*, *378*, 376, 404–405, *405*, 406

Jackson, William H. (Brig. Gen.), 364, 408

Johnson, Andrew (Pres.), 410

Johnson, Bushrod R. (Maj. Gen.), 297, 364

Johnston, Albert Sydney (Lt. Gen.), 6, 9, 46, 48, 101, 103, 121, 124

J. S. Culver Company, 69, 147, 195

Julin, Suzanne, 236

Kansas, monuments/tributes, 9, 146

Kansas troops: 7th Cavalry, 313; 8th Infantry, 189–190, *190*, 226; Kansas Bottom Tennessee Artillery, 260

Keegan, John, 430, 433

Kentucky, monuments/tributes, 43, 131, 134–135, *135*, 150, 392, 232, 237, 252, 258, 259–260, *260*, 284, 295, 298, 303, 304, 321, 322, 341, 352, 372

Kentucky troops, Confederate: 1st Cavalry, 298; 2nd Cavalry, 236, 304, 350; 3rd Cavalry, 298; 7th Cavalry, 312; Kentucky Brigade, 345

Kentucky troops, Union: 4th Infantry, 185; 6th Infantry, 312, 343; 10th Infantry, 185

Kilpatrick's Raid, 59

King, John H. (Maj.), 99

Kinney, Belle, 149, 356–358, *357*

Kipling, Rudyard, 301, 307

Knox County, 250–263, 257, 255, 258, 259, 261, 262

Knoxville, TN, 250–263, 257, 255, 258, 259, 261, 262

Knoxville National Cemetery, 12, 258–258, 258, 259

Korean War, xiii, 258

Ku Klux Klan, 28, 417, 418

Lafayette, TN, 353

Lake County, 397

Lebanon, TN, ix, 8, 34n, 348–351, 349

Lee, Robert E., xii, 26, 31, 234, 245, 246, 246, 415

"Lest We Forget" (Kipling), 292, 294, 300, 301, 307, 393

Lexington, KY, 236–237

Lilly, Eli (Capt.), 297–298, 300

Lincoln, Abraham, 29, 35n13, 99, 230, 242, 277, 329, 348, 423, 429

Lincoln County, 287–290, 288

Logan, John (Col.), 129

Longstreet, James A. (Lt. Gen.), 230, 231, 248–250, 250, 253–254, 253

Lookout Mountain, viii, 4, 12, 26, 147, 152, 155–160, 156, 158

Lost Cause, 14, 35–36n, 247, 252, 308, 386

Louisiana, monuments/tributes, 120–121, 120, 149–150, 284, 294, 295, 303, 322, 323, 341, 392

Louisiana troops: Crescent Regiment (19th Infantry) viii, 38, 43, 120–121, 120

Louisville, Kentucky, 45

Love/beloved themes, inscriptions, 18, 45, 151, 227, 244, 245, 251, 257, 258, 278, 287, 309–310, 313, 316, 329, 330, 338, 355, 375, 384, 391, 400, 416

Lowe, John R., 45

Lowe, William C., 180, 209

Lynchburg, TN, ix, 13, 272, 291–292

Macon County, 353

Madison County, ix, 378, 376, 404–405, 405, 406

Manchester, 292, 292

Marshall County, 307–309, 308

Maryland, monuments/tributes, 12, 46, 164, 215–216, 215

Maryland troops: 3rd Maryland Battery, (CS), 215–216, 215; 3rd Maryland Infantry (US), 215–216, 215

Massachusetts, monuments/tributes, 9, 146, 223

Massachusetts troops: 2nd Infantry, 223; 33rd Infantry, 223

Mathes, J. Harvey (Capt.), 416

Maury County, 314–318, 314, 315, 317

McConnelsville, Ohio, 329

McGavock, Caroline Winder "Carrie," 321

McGavock, John, 321

McGavock Confederate Cemetery, xv, 7, 320–324, 321

McKinley, William, 12, 155, 156

McLaws, Lafayette (Maj. Gen.), 249, 285

McMurry, Richard M., 6, 35

McNairy County, ix, 378, 423–424

Mecklin, Augustus H., 89

Melville, Herman, 433

Memphis, TN, viii, ix, xii, 2, 4, 8, 10, 12, 15, 17, 19, 20, 28, 32, 33, 34, 378, 380, 397, 399, 414–424, 415, 417, 421, 422

Mendenhall, John (Capt.), 127, 345, 345

Mercié, Marius Jean Antonin, 307

Merrill, Samuel P., 303

Methodist churches, 362, 404. See also Shiloh Church, Shiloh NMP

Michigan, monuments/tributes, 9, 19, 34, 40, 68, 104–105, 105, 205, 221, 223–224, 259–260, 260, 339, 346

Michigan troops: 1st Artillery, Company A, 346; 1st Engineers and Mechanics, 23–224, 346; 4th Cavalry, 346; 5th Battery, 346; 6th Battery, 346; 9th Infantry, 339; 10th Infantry, 221, 346; 11th Infantry, 205, 346; 12th Infantry, 104–105; 13th Infantry, 346; 15th Infantry, 104–105; 21st Infantry, 346; 25th Infantry, 346; Ross's Battery B, Light Artillery, 104–105

Middle Tennessee State University, 305

Mill Springs, KY, 187

Milroy, Robert (Brig. Gen.), 338

Minnesota, monuments/tributes, 9, 15, 15, 40, 68, 112, 368, *368*, 420–421, *421*

Minnesota troops: 1st Light Artillery, 15, *15*, 112; 2nd Infantry, 187, *187*; 3rd Infantry, 420–421, *421*; 4th Infantry, 420–421, *421*; 5th Infantry, 420–421, *421*; 6th Infantry, 420–421, *421*; 7th Infantry, 420–421, *421*; 9th Infantry, 420–421, *421*; 10th Infantry, 420–421, *421*

Minor Hill, 313, *313*

Missionary Ridge, 4, 35n2, 146–148, 149, 152, 159, 166, 174–209, *175, 178, 181, 186, 187, 190, 191, 192, 194, 196, 199, 203, 208*

Mississippi, monuments/tributes, 252, 284, 294, 295, 296, 303, 321, 322, 324, 325, 330–332, *331*, 341

Mississippi troops, 5th Infantry, 89; 6th Infantry, 330; 7th Infantry, 89; 9th Infantry, 89; 10th Infantry, 89; 14th Infantry, 330; 15th Infantry, 89, 330; 20th Infantry, 330; 22nd Infantry, 89; 23rd Infantry, 330; 43rd Infantry, 330; Adams' Cavalry Regiment, 89; Bains's (Vaiden) Battery, 89; Brewer's Battalion, 89; Byrne's Battery, 89; Harper's (Jefferson Light Artillery) Battery, 89; Lindsay's 1st Cavalry, 89; Stanford's Battery, 89; Swett's (Warren Light Artillery) Battery, 89

Missouri, monuments/tributes, 9, 19, 43, 131–132, *131*, 146, 259–260, *260*, 324, *324*, 333–334, 341, 392

Missouri troops, Confederate: 1st Infantry, 131–132, *131*; Barrett's Battery, 10th Light Artillery, 185, 216

Missouri troops, Union: 1st Light Artillery, Battery C, H, I, K, 131–132, *131*; 1st Light Artillery, Battery D, 178, 131–132, *131*; 1st Light Artillery, Mann's Battery; 2nd Infantry, 185, 199; 2nd Light Artillery, Battery F, 185, 199, *199*, 206; 3rd Infantry, 146, 206; 6th Infantry, 182, 185,

199; 8th Infantry, 131–132, *131*, 182–183, 185, 199, *199*; 9th Infantry, 173; 10th Infantry, 176, 185, 199, *199*; 12th Infantry, 146, 201, 206; 13th Infantry, 131–132, *131*, 141; 14th Infantry, 59, 131–132, *131*; 15th Infantry, 189, 185, 199, *199*; 17th Infantry, 146, 201, 206; 18th Infantry, 131–132, *131*; 21st Infantry, 131–132, *131*; 23rd Infantry, 131–132, *131*; 24th Missouri, 176; 25th Infantry, 131–132, *131*; 26th Infantry, 177, 185, 199, *199*; 27th Infantry, 210; 29th Infantry, 146, 201, 206; 31st Infantry, 146, 200, 206; 32nd Infantry, 146, 200, 206; Birge Sharpshooters, 131–132, *131*

Monroe County, 263

Montgomery County, 370–376, *371*

Monumental Bronze Company, 394. *See also* White bronze

Monument Avenue, Richmond, 380, 414

Moore, John Trotwood, 362

Moore County, 291–292, *292*

Moretti, Giuseppi, 361

Morgan, John H (Brig. Gen.), 22, *22*, 135, 230, 236–237, *237*, 274, 281–282, *281*, 351

Mulberry, TN, *viii, ix*, 9, 13, 15–16, *16*, 272, 290

Muldoon Granite Company, 45, 314, 375

Murfreesboro, TN, 274, 278, 337–346, *338, 342, 343, 345*

Nashville, TN, 27, 32, 33, 148, 244, 251, 274–276, 334, 353–368, *355, 357, 360, 362, 365, 367*

Nashville and Chattanooga Railroad, 296, 301, 304, 313, 344, 347

Nashville National Cemetery, 152, 366–369, *367, 368*

National Confederate Museum at Historic Elm Springs, 315

Navy, monuments/tributes, CS, 415–416

Neely, Jack, 260

New Jersey, monuments/tributes, 9, 26, 146, 218–219, *219*

New Jersey troops: 161, 16; 13th Infantry, 218; 33rd Infantry, 218

New York, monuments/tributes, 4, 9, 12, 26, 146, 155–157, *156*, 159, 160–167, *161*, *163*, *165*, 311

New York City, 10, 166, 223, 311

New York troops: 1st Light Artillery (Wiedrich's), 164–165, *165*; 8th Infantry, 160, *161*, 212–214, *213*; 15th Battery (Osburn's), 212–214, *213*; 45th Infantry, 160, *161*, 212–214, *213*; 58th Infantry, 160, *161*, 212–214, *213*; 60th Infantry, 164–166, *165*; 68th Infantry, 160, *161*, 212–214, *213*; 78th Infantry, 162, *163*; 79th Infantry, 12, 254–256, *255*, 258, *258*; 80th Infantry, 205–206; 102nd Infantry, 164–166, *165*, 205–206; 119th Infantry, 160, *161*, 212–214, *213*; 134th Infantry, 160, *161*, 212–214, *213*; 136th Infantry, 160, *161*, 212–214, *213*; 137th Infantry, 162, *163*, 164–166, *165*, 205–206; 141st Infantry, 160, *161*; 143rd Infantry, 160, *161*, 212–214, *213*; 149th Infantry, 162, *163*, 164–166, *165*, 205–206; 154th Infantry, 160, *161*, 212–214, *213*

Nicoli, Carlo, 364

Niehaus, Charles H., 418

North Carolina, monuments/tributes, 150, 232, 246, 252, 294, 295, 303, 321, 322, 341, 392

Obelisk, description, 20–21, *21*

Obion County, 13, 386–388, *387*

"Ode Sung at Magnolia Cemetery" (Timrod), 369

O'Hara, Theodore, 254, 258, 303, 305, 352

Ohio, monuments/tributes, *viii*, 9, 26, 40, 46, 48, 49, 144, 146, 154–155, *154*, 168–169, *169*, 191–192, *192*, 259–260, *260*, 329; 1st Cavalry, 191–192, *192*; 1st Infantry, 98–99, *99*; 1st Sharpshooters, 192; 2nd Infantry, 168–169, *169*; 3rd Cavalry, 191–192, *192*; 3rd Infantry, 191–192, *192*; 4th Cavalry, 191–192, *192*; 5th Battery, Artillery, 108–109; 5th Cavalry, 57; 5th Infantry, 168–169, *169*; 6th Infantry, 130; 7th Infantry, 168–169, *169*; 8th Battery, Artillery, 136; 10th Cavalry, 191–192, *192*; 10th Infantry, 216–217; 13th Infantry, 116, *116*; 14th Battery, Artillery, 71; 15th Infantry, 72–73, *73*; 16th Infantry, 216–217; 18th Cavalry, 191–192, *192*; 20th Infantry, 62; 21st Cavalry, 191–192, *192*; 22nd Infantry VI (ex–13th Missouri), 141; 23rd Infantry, 155–156, *156*; 24th Infantry, 130, 168–169, *169*, 216–217; 33rd Infantry, 168–169, *169*; 38th Infantry, 185–186, *186*; 40th Infantry, 168–169, *169*; 41st Infantry, 128, 343–344, *343*; 46th Infantry, 46, 139; 48th Infantry, 47, *47*, 83; 49th Infantry, 71; 51st Infantry, 168–169, *169*; 52nd Infantry, 191–192, *192*; 53rd Infantry, 87; 54th Infantry, 122–123, *123*; 56th Infantry, 57; 57th Infantry, 85; 59th Infantry, 117–118, *118*; 60th Infantry, 216–217; 64th Infantry, 58; 65th Infantry, 56; 66th Infantry, 168–169, *169*; 68th Infantry, 68; 70th Infantry, 81; 71st Infantry, 113; 76th Infantry, 64, 168–169, *169*; 77th Infantry, 85; 78th Infantry, 21, 62; 81st Infantry, 142–143, *143*; 94th Infantry, 168–169, *169*; 97th Infantry, 195; 98th Infantry, 191–192, *192*, 216–217; 99th Infantry, 169; 104th Infantry, 351; 106th Infantry, 351; 108th Infantry, 191–192, *192*, 347; 111th Infantry, 328; 113th Infantry, 191–192, *192*; 115th Infantry, 343–344, *343*; 121st Infantry, 191–192, *192*; 180th Infantry, 341; Aleshire's Light Artillery, 168–169, *169*; Battery A, 1st Light Artillery, 56; Battery G, 1st Light Artillery, 117

Ohio River, 282

Opdycke, Emerson (Col.), 320

Orchard Knob Reservation, *viii*, 144, 210–226, *211*, *215*, *217*, *219*, *225*

Overton, John William B. (Col.), 364

Paris, TN, *ix*, 381–383, *383*
Parker's Crossroads, *ix*, 7, 378, 380, 401–404, *402*, 428
Patriotism, 19, 52, 102, 279, 304, 307, 319, 335, 350, 369, 401, 420, 422
Payne, General E. A., 289
Peace themes, inscriptions, xii, xiii, 12, 18, 26, 32, 37, 155–157, *156*, 169, 195, 244, 246, 254, 320, 359–362, *360*, 384, 398, 400, 407, 431
Peay, Austin, 314
Pennsylvania, monuments/tributes, *viii*, 40, *144*, 146, 147, 332
Pennsylvania Reservation, Chattanooga, 174–176, *175*
Pennsylvania troops: 27th Infantry, 220–221; 27th Light Artillery, 148; 28th Infantry, 171–172, *171*, 173; 29th Infantry, 159, 206; 46th Infantry, 210–211, *211*; 73rd Infantry, 174–175, *175*; 75th Infantry, 212; 77th Infantry, 92–93; 109th Infantry, 220; 111th Infantry, 157–158, *158*, 206; 147th Infantry, 172–173; Battery E, Light Artillery, 222
Pennypacker, Samuel W., 93
Perry, Hinton, 156
Perryville, Battle of, 6
Petersburg, VA, 216, 256
Philadelphia Centennial Exposition, 290
Pickett's Charge, 319, 325
Pilot Knob, TN, 380, 381–382, *382*
Pittsburgh, PA, 222
Pittsburg Landing, TN, *8*, *38*, 48, 49, 51, 59, 76
Polk, Leonidas (Lt. Gen.), 296
Polk County, 231, 263–264, *264*
Pope, John (Capt.), 173
Powell, John Wesley (Capt.), 129
Presbyterian churches, 25, 248, 261, 359, 407
Putman, Holden (Col.), 178–179, *179*

Queen Victoria, 307
Quincy Granite, 147, 218

Railroads, 46, 162, 226, 231–231, 242, 249, 266, 341, 366, 377, 386, 395. *See*

also Nashville and Chattanooga Railroad
Rice, DeLong, 103, 105
Riverview Cemetery, Clarksville, 372
Robertson County, 370
Roman Catholicism. *See* Ryan, Abram Joseph (Fr.)
Rosecrans, William S. (Maj. Gen.), 6–7, 146, 192, 209–210
Rossville Gap. *See* Missionary Ridge
Rousseau, Lovell H. (Maj. Gen.), 338
Rutherford County, 337–348, *338, 342, 343, 345*
Ryan, Abram Joseph (Fr.), 252, 303, 320, 386, 417

Sacrifice theme, inscriptions, 12, 18, 102, 207, 257, 307, 332, 350, 356, 363, 400
Sailors. *See* Navy, monuments/tributes, CS
Salem Cemetery, Battle of, 406–408
Sanders, William P. (Col.), 274
Savage, Kirk, 27
Scripture. *See* Bible verses, inscriptions
Sessums, J. Kim, 8, 20, 88–90, *88*
Seven Pines, Battle of, 279
Sewanee. *See* University of the South, Sewanee
shaft or column, description, 20
Shelby County, 414–423, *415, 417, 421*
Shepherd, Oliver L. (Col.), 342
Sherman, William T. (Maj. Gen.), 9, 146, 417
Shiloh Church, Shiloh NMP, 80–90, *79, 88*
Shy, William (Col.), 299
slavery, 11, 27, 29, 31, 32, 36n, 36, 230, 241, 380
Smith, Thomas B. (Brig. Gen.), 299, 364
Smith County, 279
Smyrna, 9, 34, 309, 311–312
Sons of Confederate Veterans (SCV), xiii, 89, 231, 266, 271, 276, 279, 280, 281, 282, 283–284, *284*, 291, 298, 307, 317–318, 325–336, *325, 327, 331*, 340–341, 353, 359, 367, 372–373, 377, 378, 383, 390–393, 401, 402, 407, 409, 411, 413, 423–424

South Carolina, monuments/tributes, 150, 232, 295, 303, 322, 323, 328, 341, 369, 392

South Carolina troops: 5th Infantry, 328; 16th Infantry, 328; 24th Infantry, 328

South Mountain, MD, 256

Spanish-American War, 258

Sparta, TN, 59

Spotsylvania, VA, 216, 279

Spring Hill, TN, *ix*, 316–317, *317*, 333, 428

Spring Hill Cemetery, 316–317, *317*

SS *Sultana*, 231, 259, *259–260*, 421

States' rights, 27, 336

Statue, description, 20, 23, *23*

Stele, description, 20, 22, *22*

Stewart County, 373–376

St. John's Episcopal Church, Columbia, 329, 334, 408

Stone Mountain, GA, 28, 380

Stones River, Battle of, 337–346, *338, 342, 343, 345. See also* Murfreesboro, TN

Strahl, Otto (Brig. Gen.), 9, 329

Stumbaugh, Frederick M. (Col.), 93

Sullivan County, 231–233, *232*

Suman, Isaac C. B. (Col.), 344

Sumner County, 368–369

Sunken Road, Shiloh NMP, *viii*, 38, 106–119, *107, 110, 115, 116, 118, 119*

Sword, Wiley, 328, 335

Tennessee, monuments/tributes, 150–151, *151*, 231–232, *232*, 232–233, *233*, 250–53, *250, 253*, 256–258, *257*, 261, 281, 284, *284*, 292, 293, *293*, 295, 299, 302–304, *302*, 305–307, *306*, 325, *325*, 326, 332, 340–341, 346–347, 353–354, 356, 357–358, *357*, 360–361, 363–364, 372, 392

Tennessee Department of Tourist Development, 428, 429

Tennessee Historical Commission, 311, 320, 356, 367, 387, 415, 428, 431

Tennessee regions, *viii*, 2. *See also specific cities and counties*

Tennessee River, vii, 6, 38, 49, 106, 148, 150, 184, 195, 213, 276–278, *277, 278*, 356, 381, 402

Tennessee State Museum, 356

Tennessee troops, Confederate: 1st Cavalry, 232–233, *233*; 1st Infantry, 78, 289, 292, 326, 330, 354, 411; 1st Provisional, 330; 2nd Infantry, 43, 78, 81–82, *82*, 261; 3rd Cavalry ("Forrest's Escort"), 301; 3rd Infantry, 261, 281, 329; 4th Cavalry Battalion, 261, 281; 4th Infantry, 78, 292, 329, 330, 384, 411; 4th Provisional, 330; 5th Infantry, 78, 329, 384; 6th Infantry, 78, 330, 405, 407; 7th Cavalry, 400–401, 408–409, *409*; 7th Infantry, 280, 348; 8th Infantry, 292, 330; 9th Infantry, 78, 330, 384; 10th Cavalry, 377; 10th Infantry, 377; 11th Cavalry, 277; 11th Infantry, 377; 12th Infantry, 78, 384; 13th Infantry, 78; 15th Infantry, 78, 384; 16th Infantry, 276–278, *277, 278*, 330; 17th Infantry, 301; 19th Infantry, 78, 232–233, *233*, 329; 20th Infantry, 78, 299, 337; 22nd Infantry, 78; 23rd Infantry, 78, 411; 24th Infantry, 78, 329, 377; 24th Tennessee Sharpshooters, 377; 27th Infantry, 78, 330, 384; 28th Infantry, 78, 330; 31st Infantry, 329, 384; 33rd Infantry, 78, 329; 34th Infantry (a.k.a., 4th), 411; 38th Infantry, 78, 329, 330; 39th Infantry, 261, 281; 41st Infantry, 292, 329; 44th Infantry, 78; 45th Infantry, 78; 47th Infantry, 78; 49th Infantry, 377; 50th Infantry, 330, 377; 51st Infantry, 78, 384; 52nd Infantry, 78; 55th Infantry, 78; 59th Infantry, 261, 281; 62nd Infantry, 261, 281; 84th Infantry, 277; 154th Senior Infantry, 277, 415; Baxter's Artillery, 377; Crew's Battalion, 78; Freeman's Battery, 317–318, *318*, 333, 401–403, *402*; McClung's (Caswell Artillery) Battery, 78; Miller's (Pillow Flying Artillery) Battery, 78; Morton's Battery, 402–403; Polk's Battery, 78; Ross's Cavalry, 377; Rutledge's Battery, 78; Shelbyville Rebels, 301

Tennessee troops, Union: 1st Cavalry, 260; 2nd Cavalry, 260; 2nd Mounted Infantry, 259–260, *260*; 3rd Cavalry, 259–260, *260*; 3rd Infantry, 259–260, *260*; 3rd Mounted Infantry, 281; 4th Cavalry, 259–260, *260*; 4th Mounted Infantry, 301; 5th Mounted Infantry, 264, 301; 7th Cavalry, 259–260, *260*; 8th Cavalry, 259–260, *260*; 9th Cavalry, 259–260, *260*; 10th Mounted Infantry, 301; 11th Cavalry, 259–260, *260*, 281; 12th Cavalry, 259–260, *260*, 281

Texas, monuments/tributes, 43, 121, 150, 252, 294, 295, 305, 325, 328, 341, 375, 392

Texas troops: 2nd Infantry, 121; 7th Infantry, 375; 8th Cavalry (Terry's Texas Rangers), 121, 375–376, *376*; 9th Infantry, 121

Thermopylae, 82

Thompson's Station, TN, 316

Tiffany & Co., 149

Tilghman, Lloyd (Brig. Gen.), 330

Timrod, Henry, 369, 375

Tipton County, 398–399

Tishomingo Creek, Battle of, 65, 86, 398

Trajan's Column, 194–195, *194*

Trenches interring Confederate dead, Shiloh NMP, 78, 86, 87, 137, *137*

Trenton, TN, *ix*, 17, 378, 380, 393–395, *394*

Triebel, Frederick, 52

Triebel, Santina, 52

Trousdale County, 351

Trousdale House, 368–369

Troutt, Joseph Henry, 259–260, *260*

Tullahoma, TN, *ix*, 7, 20, 274, 284, 293–300, *293*, *297*

Unicoi County, 18, 244–245, *245*

Union common soldiers, monuments/tributes to. *See* Common soldiers, Union

United States Military Academy West Point, 148, 192, 237, 284, 286, 330

University of Tennessee, Chattanooga, 150, 152

University of Tennessee, Knoxville, 7, 256

University of Tennessee Health Science Center, 416

University of the South, Sewanee, 8, 9, 34, 272, 285–287, *286*

Unknown Confederate Dead, 17, 247, 248–249, *249*, 266, 270, *270*, 298, 349, 387, 395. *See also* Trenches interring Confederate dead, Shiloh NMP

Unknown dead, 248, 249, 421

US Army, Regulars: 46, 99, 342, *342*; 2nd Cavalry, 59; 4th Cavalry, 59, 318; 4th Infantry, 333; 5th Artillery, 342; 15th Infantry, 99, 342; 16th Infantry, 99, 342; 18th Infantry, 342; 19th Infantry, 99, 342; Terrill's Battery, 130

US Colored Troops (USCT): 27, 239, 312, *312*, 367, 431–432; 12th USCT, 431; 13th USCT, 367, 431–432; 100th USCT, 431; 111th USCT, 341

Valor, 18, 115, 121, 151, 214, 227, 256, 304, 307, 319, 335, 337, 352, 363, 369, 373, 374, 375, 400

Van Amringe Granite Company, 170, 180, 189, 192, 209, 216, 226

Van Buren County, 274, 276–278, *276*, *277*

Van Dorn, Earl (Maj. Gen.), 333, 413

Vermont Barre Granite, 46, 52, 82, 104, 107, 195, 364, 370

Vicksburg Campaign, 18, 41, 103, 394

Vietnam War, xiii, 19, 258, 316, 356

Virginia, monuments/tributes, Confederate, xii, 8, 28, 231–232, 252, 340–341, 371–372, 391–392

Virginia, monuments/tributes, Union, 259–260, *260*

Virginia troops, Confederate: 2nd Cavalry, 296; 22nd Infantry, 232

Walker, James, 161

War Between the States phrase, 18, 34n, 251, 292, 352, 356, 384, 414

War Department, 31, 40, 46, 103, 105, 146, 209, 242, 428, 429

Warren County, 276–278, *277*, *278*

Wartrace, TN, *ix*, 8, 19, 296, 303–304
Washington and Lee University, 414
Washington Confederate Cemetery,
    Hagerstown, 44
Washington County, 233–236, *234, 235*
Watkins, Sam, 326
Wauhatchie Pike, 162
Wayne County, 291
Waynesboro, TN, *ix*, 291
Weakley County, 384–386, *385*
Westminster Abby, 218
West Point. *See* United States Military
    Academy West Point
White bronze, 20, 193–194, *194, 394*
Whitman, Walt, 32, 37
Wicker Field, Shiloh NMP, 62–64
Wilder, John T. (Col.), 54, 257, 297–
    298, 300
Williamson County, 318–336, *321, 323,
    325, 327, 331*
Willow Mount Cemetery, Shelbyville,
    34, 302–303, *303*
Wilson, Woodrow, 103, 244
Wilson County, 348–351, *349*
Wilson's Creek, Battle of, 59
Winstead Hill, 304, 325–336, *325, 327, 331*
Wisconsin, monuments/tributes, 9,
    114–116, *115*, 146, 148, 224–225, *225*
Wisconsin troops: 1st Cavalry, 224–225,
    225; 1st Heavy Artillery, 224–225,
    225; 1st Infantry, 224–225, *225*; 3rd
    Battery, 224–225, *225*; 5th Infantry,
    224–225, *225*; 6th Battery, 224–225,
    225; 7th Infantry, 403; 8th Battery,
    224–225, *225*; 10th Battery, 224–225,
    225; 10th Infantry, 224–225, *225*;
    14th Infantry, 40, 114–116, *115*, 119,
    119; 15th Infantry, 190–191, 224–225,
    225; 16th Infantry, 114–116, *115*;
    18th Infantry, 114–116, *115*, 224–225,
    225; 21st Infantry, 224–225, *225*;
    24th Infantry, 202–203, *203*, 224–
    225, *225*; 26th Infantry, 224–225, *225*;
    43rd Infantry, 341, 347
Women, monuments/tributes to, 15,
    180, 244, *245*, 282–283, 289–290,
    292, 307, 348, 356–358, *357*, 362–363,
    362, 409–410, 412, 420, 423
Women's organizations, role in monu-
    ment movement, 10–11, 25, 29–30,
    43, 44, 78, 102, *102*, 106, 132, 151,
    227, 234, 246, 249, 253, 261, 264, 279,
    286, 289, 292, 294–296, 304, 319, 333,
    335, 340, 349, 359, 369, 370, 373, 396,
    403, 414
Woodbury, TN, *ix*, 304–305
Woolf Field, Shiloh NMP, 65–80, *67, 69,
    73, 75, 79*
World War I, xi, xiii, 18, 33, 169, 244,
    245, 258, 361, 375, 431
World War II, xiii, 5, 18, 258, 276,
    283, 285
Works Progress Administration
    (WPA), 365

Zabriskie, A. J., 156, 161, 162
Zollicoffer, Felix K. (Brig. Gen.), 364
Zolnay, George Julian, 354, 359

TIMOTHY SEDORE is Professor of English at the City University of New York, Bronx Community College. He regularly teaches undergraduate courses in composition, literature, and religious rhetoric. He is also an ordained Baptist minister.

Rev. Dr. Sedore is the author of a trilogy on Civil War monumentation in the American South. His book *Mississippi Civil War Monuments: The Illustrated Field Guide* joins *Tennessee Civil War Monuments: The Illustrated Field Guide* (Indiana University Press, 2020) and *An Illustrated Guide to Virginia's Confederate Monuments* as a survey and analysis of the legacy of the war on the American landscape.